THE ABC'S OF RUNNING AN ELEMENTARY CLASSROOM

THE ABC'S OF RUNNING AN ELEMENTARY CLASSROOM

Peggy E. Wicker, M.S.
Public School Elementary Classroom Teacher

Harriet U. Schultz
Professor of Teacher Education, Retired
California State University, Fullerton

Delmar Publishers

1945 - 1995
50 years

I(T)P An International Thomson Publishing Company

Albany • Bonn • Boston • Cincinnati • Detroit • London • Madrid • Melbourne
Mexico City • New York • Pacific Grove • Paris • San Francisco • Singapore • Tokyo
Toronto • Washington

NOTICE TO THE READER

Cover Design: John McDonald

Delmar Staff

Publisher: David C. Gordon
Associate Editor: Erin J. O'Connor
Production Editor: Colleen A. Corrice

Production Coordinator: James Zayicek
Art/Design Coordinator: Timothy J. Conners

COPYRIGHT © 1995
By Delmar Publishers
a division of International Thomson Publishing Inc.
The ITP logo is a trademark under license
Printed in the United States of America
For more information, contact:

Delmar Publishers
3 Columbia Circle, Box 15015
Albany, New York 12212-5015

International Thomson Publishing Europe
Berkshire House 168-173
High Holborn
London WC1V 7AA
England

Thomas Nelson Australia
102 Dodds Street
South Melbourne, 3205
Victoria, Australia

Nelson Canada
1120 Birchmount Road
Scarborough, Ontario
Canada M1K 5G4

International Thomson Editores
Campos Eliseos 385, Piso 7
Col Polanco
11560 Mexico D F Mexico

International Thomson Publishing GmbH
Königswinterer Strasse 418
53227 Bonn
Germany

International Thomson Publishing Asia
221 Henderson Road
#05-10 Henderson Building
Singapore 0315

International Thomson Publishing Japan
Hirakawacho Kyowa Building, 3F
2-2-1 Hirakawacho
Chiyoda-ku, Tokyo 102
Japan

1 2 3 4 5 6 7 8 9 10   xxx   01 00 99 98 97 96 95

Library of Congress Cataloging-in-Publication Data
Wicker, Peggy E.
    The ABC's of running an elementary classroom / Peggy E. Wicker ;
instructor guide, Harriet U. Schultz.
        p.   cm/
Includes bibliographical references and index.
ISBN 0-8273-5659-5
1. Elementary school teaching—Handbooks, manuals, etc.
2. Classroom management—Handbooks, manuals, etc. 3. Elementary
school teachers—Handbooks, manuals, etc. I. Schultz, Harriet U.
II. Title.
LB1555.W69   1995   94-29614
372.11'02—dc20   CIP

DEDICATION

To Michael Scott Wicker, a great help, a great son!

Table of Contents

Acknowledgments

The author gratefully acknowledges Cheryl Thompson, for her help and hard work, and Virginia Sullivan, for her expertise in teaching kindergarten and all her helpful suggestions.

The author also thankfully acknowledges Harriet U. Schultz, Professor of Teacher Education (retired), California State University, Fullerton, for writing the Instructor Guide. Finally, the author would like to thank and acknowledge the following reviewers whose knowledge and insight made this a better book:

Eugenia Blake, Ph.D.,
Campbell University;

Tim K. Campbell, Ed.D.,
University of Central Oklahoma;

Dennis J. Kear, Ph.D.,
Wichita State University;

Violet E. Leathers, Ed.D.,
University of Akron; and

Betty Jo Simmons, Ed.D.
Longwood College.

The author wishes to thank the following organizations who graciously supplied permission to use their material.

Junior Craft Book, Indianapolis, IN: Benjamin Franklin Literary & Medical Society, Inc. Copyright 1974 by the Saturday Evening Post Company. Reprinted by permission of the Children's Better Health Institute.

"More Short Plays for the Classroom: Primary," *Educational Insights.* Copyright 1982 by *Educational Insights.* Reprinted by permission.

Let's Drill (Cursive) by E. Rudolph, Wilkinsburg, PA: Hayes School Publishing Co., Inc. Copyright 1976 by Hayes School Publishing Co., Inc. Reprinted by permission.

Holiday Crafts (p. 12, p. 13, p. 46, p. 53), Palo Alto, CA: Monday Morning Books, Inc. Copyright 1985 by Monday Morning Books, Inc. Reprinted by permission. Monday Morning Books are distributed by Evan-Moor, 18 Lower Ragsdale Drive, Monterey, CA, 1-800-777-4362.

Burned Out! A Teacher Speaks Out by J. Dewey, Shelburne, VT: The New England Press, Inc. Reprinted by permission.

The *1991/92 Premier Elementary Reminder,* Irvine, CA: Premier School Agendas. Copyright 1991 Premier School Agendas. All rights reserved. No part of this publication may be reproduced without the written permission of the publisher.

String Art, by A. Schmidt, Eden Prairie, MN: Judy/Instructo. Copyright 1981. Reprinted by permission.

Make Your Own Pictionary, (p. 22, p. 25, p. 26, p. 77, p. 113), New York, NY: Sniffen Court Books, 153 East Court Street, New York, NY 10016, Tel. 212/679-7950, FAX 212/684-6137.

Turman Publishing Co., 1319 Dexter Avenue North, Suite 30, Seattle, WA 98109, 206/282-6900.

PrintMaster Plus graphics, owned and copyrighted by Unison World Software. Used with permission. For further information, please contact: Unison World Software, 1321 Harbor Bay Parkway, Alameda, CA 94501, 800/444-7553.

Introduction

Do you want to be an excellent teacher? Do you want the respect of your fellow teachers, parents, principal, and students? Do you want to make a difference?

Future and beginning teachers, this book will show you a multitude of ways to become a great teacher and love it, too. And for more experienced teachers, this book will show you how to implement simple programs to get substantial results.

Follow the Blueprint for Teaching Effectiveness introduced in this book and your lessons are guaranteed to be successes. Throughout the book, as well as in the section on the teaching-learning process, many exciting teaching techniques are described, and noteworthy information about the "hows" of student learning in the elementary classroom is furnished.

This book gives you information on such topics as how to interestingly handle students who finish their work well ahead of the rest of the class, how to run a geography bee and a math facts contest, how to successfully and enjoyably get through the first day of the school year, and how to plan for exciting field trips. *The ABC's* will show you *in detail* how to provide your students with excellent, challenging, lively lessons in every area of the curriculum.

This book also explains the complexities of the teaching-learning process and includes considerable and important research on the brain and how it functions in relation to classroom learning and behavior.

Do you want to know how to effectively mainstream, how to produce an outstanding Open House program, and how to constructively communicate with parents in a partnership format? This book is here to inform you.

Do you have questions about inclement weather, classroom visitors, school reviews, disaster drills, Back-to-School Night, combination classes, and awards assemblies? *The ABC's* has all the answers.

Do you need information about using incentive programs, classroom contests, classroom helpers, and cross-age tutors in your classroom? You will find all you need to know about these and myriad other subjects in *The ABC's*.

Do you want to know how to get a teaching job? This book will tell you *that,* too!

The ABC's is an alphabet book. Alphabet books are noted for their format and organization. They are reader friendly. Topics of interest can be located quickly in a stimulating format. This book will help you all the way from *a*ssignment accountability, bulletin boards, and duties to grading, history, and math. It will show you how to handle paperwork and plan for substitutes as well as use open-ended questioning strategies and teach research skills. This book will take you through test study notes, vade mecum, and writing all the way to the answer key*z!*

The ABC's has careful step-by-step directions on how to use certain machines that will enhance your program, and it is loaded with many exciting ideas. For those students who have difficulty learning their multiplication facts in the traditional manner, an alternative kinesthetic approach called Finger Facts is explained. The Four Keys to Academic Success and the Four Keys to Personal Success are presented, as well as a novel manipulative device to help students increase awareness of their self-esteem needs on a totally individual basis.

The ABC's gives you all the instructions for an assignment accountability chart to keep track of students' assignments in an unusual, but very effective manner. This simple system can be used with students who have difficulty keeping track of their work. It can be used just as easily with the entire class, which provides all students an equal opportunity of time with the teacher. In addition, this system helps students stay self-directed and motivated.

The use of composition books keeps parents informed on a daily basis. This communication system lets the parents know what is assigned for homework, which assignments are not completed, when and what to study to prepare for a test, and what their children's behavior is like.

The ABC's contains a detailed classroom behavior system that works, as well as samples of ways to individualize for students who have severe behavior problems. This behavior chart system will help you successfully manage your classroom and pinpoint students' exact behavior problems so that attention can be focused in the right place.

In addition to numerous practical ideas to use in your classroom, this book has many sections devoted to the latest research. You can read absorbing studies on a variety of curriculum areas as well as studies on such topics as gender equity, full inclusion, transition programs from elementary to middle school, what parents want in their children's schools, mental rehearsal, and induction programs for new elementary teachers.

The appendix of this book contains a substantial and comprehensive set of reproducibles for the elementary classroom. You can use many of the activities with your class right away.

These reproducibles are coded *Pt* (think "*Primary time*") for materials that can be used in primary grades (K–3), and *§* (think "*Secondary Section*") for those which can be used in upper grades (4–6). Depending on the skill range in your class, though, you can use some of the primary materials with upper grades or vice versa. With the codes, the students will not know the difference.

There are reproducible materials for a science fair, a math facts contest, and world and U.S. geography. Many reproducible activities in research skills, including graphs, tables, maps, grids, and reports for countries, states, and animals are included. In addition to reproducibles for art, drama, reading, writing, math and history, there is a speaking evaluation form as well as a list of enjoyable and stimulating speaking topics.

The appendix also contains many reproducible forms for parent communication, including progress reports and behavior contracts. There are two sets of reproducibles to leave for substitute teachers. One is a list of your classroom rules and where materials can be located; the other is a set of emergency lesson plans, one for the primary grades and one for the upper grades. In the upper grades, these plans can even be reproduced for your class so that each student has his or her own set of plans for the day's activities.

If you want to customize any of the reproducibles in this book to suit your specific or special needs, this book gives you detailed explanations of just how to do that.

The ABC's will introduce you to an interesting object, 2 inches by 3 inches and quite inexpensive, which can help focus and organize your class. It can have a sizable impact on running a classroom smoothly and successfully.

In addition, each chapter of *The ABC's* has a section of challenging questions and activities followed by a chapter project. Each project will be directly useful in your classroom, so your preparation time will be well spent and rewarding. Chapter 9, The XYZ's, contains midcourse and final reviews, as well as their answer keys. Answers for student activity sheets shown in the appendix also appear in Chapter 9.

How you run an elementary classroom can make an enormous difference to your career success and enjoyment. This means knowing how to have a classroom where both the curriculum and the management programs are productive and effective. Excellent curriculum, exciting day-to-day and week-to-week activities, and sound classroom management all enter into applying *The ABC's* to *your* classroom.

1

THE
ABC'S

Setting up a classroom so that it will run efficiently and smoothly is a most important aspect in teaching elementary school. A teacher's good ideas can be lost in a classroom where follow-through and structure are weak. This chapter introduces organizational techniques to help you establish and maintain a well-run classroom with strong student accountability and recognition. At the same time, it discloses methods of injecting challenge and excitement into that classroom to whet your students' appetites for cooperation and competition. Presented are the following techniques and methods to guide you to success in the classroom:

- Assignment Accountability Charts
- Assignments Completed Charts
- Awards Assemblies
- Back-to-School Night
- Bees
- Bell
- Books
- Bulletin Boards
- Classroom Rules
- Combination Classes
- Composition Books
- Contest—Section Charts
- Customized Reproducibles

The first part of this chapter presents the first three techniques: assignment accountability charts, assignments completed charts, and awards assemblies.

ASSIGNMENT ACCOUNTABILITY CHARTS

Many procedures can be used to help your classroom run efficiently and productively. One of these is an **assignment accountability chart.** When managing a classroom, it is important to let the students know that when you give an assignment which you want to be turned in to you, that you have a system which will simply and accurately show a record of this. If this record is kept in a grade or record book, this information is easily available to you; however, when this information is kept on a classroom chart, it is available to you, the students, and the parents any time of the day.

How to Make the Chart

This chart can totally cover one bulletin board in the classroom and list the students' assignments for one grading period. This system reserves your grade book for registering grades for tests, projects, reports, and so on, instead of including a marking system for daily assignments.

The bulletin board can be approximately 90 inches long and 46 inches high or even larger. Decide on a convenient, highly visible location.

First, cover the bulletin board with manila **tag** or any similar backing to act as a cushion.

Second, purchase at a teachers' supply store a border that has blue, yellow, and orange in it, or make your own border. It should be about 2 inches wide.

Third, if you would like your accountability chart to hold information for six subjects, get six strips of white butcher paper. Have three of them measure 18 inches wide and 36 inches tall. Have the other three measure 10 inches wide and 36 inches high.

Fourth, decide on a size for your **assignment boxes.** These are boxes in which you will place a check mark or stamp a happy face when the students' assignments are completed. Boxes 1-inch high by $^{15}\!/_{16}$-inch wide work beautifully. With each piece of your butcher paper in the vertical position, begin drawing your boxes with a fine-point black marker. Fill each strip of butcher paper with the same-sized boxes. It is vitally important that the bottom and top lines of the boxes are able to meet each other when going from one strip of butcher paper across to the next. (Figure 1-1 is an example of what the completed chart will look like.)

With the strips of butcher paper in the vertical position, use a meter or yard stick and a thick-pointed black marker to make a thick, dark line over every third horizontal line. Do this on all strips of the butcher paper. This allows for easy tracking later. Laminate these strips in a **roll laminator.**

Pin—do not staple yet—these strips to the bulletin board before you make anything more for this chart. The rest of the chart needs to work from these **laminated** strips of butcher paper so that everything will line up properly.

Fifth, prepare your four student name strips. Use enough yellow construction paper to make two strips 6½ inches wide by 46 inches long. Make two other strips 5 inches wide by 46 inches long. Twelve inches from the top of each of your four long strips, use a thick black marker to draw a horizontal line. Then pin each of the name strips to the bulletin board. The two wider strips go at each end of the chart. Pin the two narrower strips toward the center. Strips extend from the top of the board to the bottom.

Use a ruler to draw lines for the students' names. Match the name lines to the horizontal lines of the boxes so that tracking

Figure 1-1.   This chart ensures assignment accountability for all students. It provides equal care and attention to everyone.

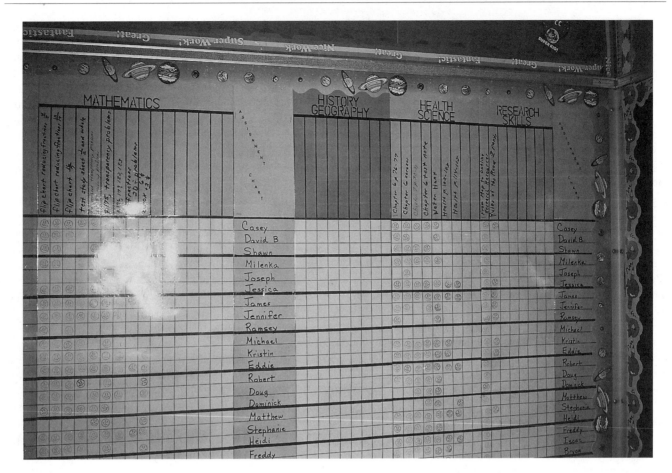

Figure 1-2. A close-up view of the last half of the assignment chart.

is easy. Darken every third line, just like you did for the assignment boxes. Be sure everything is lined up just right.

In the top 12 inches of each name strip, use a small stencil to letter *Assignment Chart* in black marker.

Sixth, get six pieces of 12-inch by 18-inch construction paper: two in orange, two in light blue, and two in light green. Place each piece of construction paper in the horizontal position. Four inches from the top, use a thick, black marker to draw a line across each. On top of each thick line, stencil the subject letters in black marker as follows: *reading* on orange, *writing* on light blue, *math* on light green, *history/geography* on orange, *science/health* on light blue, and *research skills* on light green. Do not make letters taller than 1 or 1¼ inches because the letters need to clear the border.

Pin the pieces of construction paper to the top of the bulletin board in the order listed in the preceding paragraph. Slide the excess paper under the name lists and overlap and underlay all other excess paper. Then use a black marker to draw medium-thick vertical lines to make assignment columns. Be sure the vertical lines match the vertical lines of the boxes on your butcher paper so that the assignment column flows right into the column of boxes below it. You can use the following: fifteen columns each for reading and writing, sixteen columns for math, nine columns each for history/geography and science/health, and eight columns for research skills. This chart will then provide you with fifteen spaces for reading assignments,

fifteen for writing, sixteen for math, and so on. (Physical education [PE], listening, speaking, and fine arts are not listed because generally grades in these subjects are based on tests for listening; speeches for speaking; participation for PE; and music, dance, plays, and art for fine arts.)

Vary the chart to meet your individual needs. If you have a lower primary grade, you might want to make much larger boxes on the butcher paper, possibly 1½ inches by 1½ inches. You could then have just two wide name strips with half of your students on one side of the chart and half on the other. You might select reading, writing, spelling, and math for subjects. Then you could have one or two extra columns for special projects.

When everything is aligned just the way you want it, staple the pieces of boxed butcher paper in place as you remove their pins. Then detach the yellow name strips—no names are on them yet—and the orange, light blue, and light green subject papers with the assignment columns—no assignments are listed in the columns yet, either. These chart pieces are now laminated.

When laminated, place your chart pieces in the proper spots and staple them in place. If you have not already put up your border, do so now. Then use black *nonpermanent* overhead pen to write your students' names on the yellow strips. If you have a small ledge right above your bulletin board, you can store your nonpermanent overhead pens and stamper there. Otherwise, decide on a convenient storage slot.

Once your chart is assembled, you can write on it with non-permanent overhead pens and use a dark-inked stamp on it. The laminating allows you to wash off any assignment titles, marks, or names when you are finished with a grading period.

How to Use the Chart

When listing assignments in the columns and recording marks in the boxes, use the darker colors of nonpermanent overhead pens—blue, black, green—because they are easier to see from a distance. Make your recording marks, for example, checks, with this kind of pen only or with a dark-inked X-stamper. Then the chart will be easy to read and simple to clean.

Storage of different colored pens close to the chart also makes it convenient to alternate colors in assignment columns so that the assignments clearly stand out and are effortlessly read. When you have **combination classes** (see Combination Classes in this chapter), you can use just one assignment column for both grades. For example, write one grade's assignment in green and the other grade's assignment in blue inside the same column.

When you are ready to correct a homework assignment together as a class or collect an assignment from your students, write exactly what the assignment is under the appropriate subject on the chart. Why "exactly"? The students need to be able to go to the chart at a later date to copy any assignments they have not completed because of absence or some other reason. They need to know exactly what the assignment is to complete it and get it recorded on the chart.

If you are not going to be collecting the assignment, say the students' names aloud. If they have the assignment completed, ready to correct on their desktops, they say *yes* after their name is called. If not, they say *no.* For those who say *yes,* make a mark in the appropriate box with overhead pen or use your happy face or star X-stamper to indicate assignment completion. (You may, on occasion, have students who are not required to do a particular assignment. They may be doing work for an English as a Second Language [ESL] class or a Learning Disabled [LD] class instead. Use the overhead pen to mark an *X* in those students' boxes so that it is easy for them to see whether they are up-to-date or are missing any assignments.)

If the assignment is going to be collected first, students can say *yes* as their names are called and place their completed paper or project on a table near the chart.

Important: Arrange furniture so that the students cannot touch the chart. Locate the chart at the front of the room and have furniture in front of it to keep it out of the students' reach. No one, except you or someone appointed by you, should be allowed to mark on the chart. This is very important because you will rely on the accuracy of this chart. It frees you to record in your grade book only test scores or assignments that receive a letter or percent grade. But, you *will* want to know the number of missing assignments (if any) for each student in the different subject areas to prepare **progress reports** and report cards. You can get this number easily and quickly from your chart.

With this chart, students always know when their work is up-to-date or what assignments they are missing. When they return from an absence, they can copy missed assignments from the chart. Each Friday, students can have **chart time,** a part of class time when they go to the chart and copy any missed assignments. They then can work on them over the weekend. Periodically throughout the week, you can collect overdues. When a student brings up an assignment, record a check mark, or stamp a happy face inside the student's box. Continue in this manner throughout the class.

When a grading period comes to an end (four or five weeks works well), you can tell the class well in advance that any assignments for the chart need to be completed and turned in before the closing date. No more overdues will be accepted after grades close. Every day for the week before grades close, students write in their **composition books** (see Composition Books in this chapter) right along with their regular homework: "Grades close on Friday, January 25," or whenever the grading period ends. This way, students and their parents have plenty of notice. There is no excuse for not completing any assignment.

At the end of a grading period, the assignment titles and all the check marks, names, or stamped happy faces are wiped off the chart. If you are using only overhead pen, you can clean with a soft paper towel and water. If you use a stamper, clean with a soft paper towel and a dry-erase spray cleaner to give the chart a refreshingly new sparkle.

You will never have to spend *any* time outside of class with this chart. It gets incorporated into the day just as does time spent on attendance, lunch count, and the collecting of various forms.

This assignment accountability chart can be a tremendous help. You never have to bother flipping through your grade book looking for some student's overdues, and it is especially helpful to students who are absent or get behind in their work. It totally eliminates such statements as these: "I've never heard of that assignment before; I was absent and don't know what's going on; I never got that assignment; or I'm *sure* I turned it in already.

Students quickly become accustomed to this routine and realize that they are accountable for all assignments. Parents clearly understand, too, and have something specific to work on with their children at home. This is a truly interactive process.

The assignment accountability chart system works very well to keep the students on track, maintain their motivation, hold them accountable for their assignments, and give them a sense of accomplishment. It also allows them a feeling of a fresh start at the beginning of each new grading period.

ASSIGNMENTS COMPLETED CHARTS

At the end of each grading period, all the students who do not have missing assignments in any subject have their names written on a "Students Who Have All Assignments Completed" chart. This is another permanent display and looks nice and colorful.

How to Make the Chart

Take four full pieces of fluorescent tag—one each of green, orange, yellow, and pink. Each piece of tag can be standard size, 27½ inches high and 20½ inches wide. Each can represent a quarter grading period.

Label the top of each piece of tag with the name of the quarter of the school year—*1st Quarter, 2nd Quarter,* and so on. The letters can be done on a **leteron machine,** or you can make your own letters. In smaller letters from the same machine, press out the letters for the subtitle, *1st Half.* Place this on the left side of the tag at the top, and place *2nd Half* on the right half at the top. This is done for each of the four quarters of the year.

Then, using an **Ellison die machine,** punch out the *inside* of the Ellison **die** large flower pattern. Use different colors of construction paper—six orange and six yellow to be placed on the fluorescent green tag, six yellow and six purple for the fluorescent orange tag, six orange and six blue for the fluorescent yellow tag, and six green and six blue for the fluorescent pink tag.

Each small flower is glued to the top of an award ribbon also made out of construction paper. You can use a yellow flower with an orange construction-paper ribbon for the *1st Half* of the first quarter. Put six of them at different angles on the left-hand side of the fluorescent green tag. Then, use orange flowers glued to yellow construction-paper ribbon for the *2nd Half* of the first quarter. Put six of those on the right-hand side of the fluorescent green tag at various angles. Continue with this pattern for the three other pieces of tag.

Then comes the most important thing. Laminate each of the charts. Once they are laminated, find a permanent spot for them in your classroom.

How to Use the Chart

Write the names of the students who have completed all assignments at the end of each grading period on the award ribbons. Write using nonpermanent overhead pens only. Keep adding more names to your display as the year progresses. Keep the names up for the entire school year. Then wash off the names and the chart is ready and waiting for names from your next year's class. Figure 1-4 shows a sample of a chart for the first and second halves of third and fourth quarters; however, this chart can easily be adapted to whatever type of grading periods you have in your district.

Figure 1-3. This makes into a nice award ribbon for the "All Assignments Completed" chart.

The charts look nice even at the beginning of the year without names on them. When students start seeing their names up there, they glow with pride. *All* students, regardless of their academic ability, have the opportunity to have their name displayed for each grading period by completing and turning in all their work. If they fall short on one period, they can still have success during the next one.

AWARDS ASSEMBLIES

Many schools have a quarterly awards assembly. The primary students often have their assembly at a separate time from the upper grades. This assembly is a time to honor students for their achievements over the quarter. Trophies are awarded to the student winners in such contests as math facts, spelling bee, geography bee, and physical fitness skills. In addition, perfect attendance certificates are given.

Some schools have a three-tiered honor roll system to give all students the opportunity of getting on the honor roll. Awards are presented for academic effort, regardless of grades; for achievement based on traditional grades; and for academic effort and achievement.

This way, the honor roll is not merely associated with the "smart" students. Students who are trying their hardest, regardless of ability, native language, learning disability, and so on, can be recognized for all the effort they put forth, can feel proud, and can be cheered by their school. This system helps to change the students' attitudes about the honor roll by giving students a real incentive to work their hardest and a real sense of accomplishment when they make the honor roll.

First is the effort honor roll, composed of students who do not have a B average but try really hard, as evidenced by a certain number of O's on their report card in certain subjects (O = Outstanding). You or your school can establish the criteria. Maybe the upper grade students will need at least five O's out of the eight subjects. These subjects can be: reading, writing, listening, speaking, math, research skills, history/geography, and science/health. The primary grade students might need at least five O's out of their subjects of work and study habits, citizenship and social habits, reading, writing, listening, speaking, mathematics, history/social science, and science/health.

Second is the achievement honor roll—those students with a B average in the designated subjects. Last is the effort and achievement honor roll—those with a B average and the required number of O's in the designated subjects. These students could get a certificate with a gold seal on it.

If you do not have these assemblies at your school, you might want to get them started. If that does not work out for you, you can have a quarterly "assembly" in your own classroom and pass out various awards at that time. Your students will love it!

Awards assemblies are great for the students. They are a chance for students to feel proud and to be admired and cheered by their classmates. See Figure A1-1 in the appendix for a sample achievement certificate that you can use for your class.

Assignment charts, assignments completed charts, and awards assemblies can all help your classroom stay organized, focused, and running smoothly. Plus, these three organiza-

Figure 1-4. When this chart is nicely constructed and laminated, it looks beautiful year after year. Students are proud when their names appear each grading period. Write their names with a nonpermanent, overhead pen.

tional techniques give students a sense of purpose and accomplishment as well as provide consistent opportunities for building self-esteem.

The second part of this chapter introduces you to Back-to-School Night, bees, a golden bell, special kinds of books, and bulletin boards.

BACK-TO-SCHOOL NIGHT

Back-to-School Night is an opportunity to present yourself and your program to the parents of your students. Good preparation is essential. This is the time to go over your classroom policies with the parents early in the school year. Even though you send your academic policies home for a parent signature along with homework policies, classroom rules, and a class schedule, it is a big help if the parents can see and hear you talk about these things. In addition to these most important items, spend some time talking about some of the interesting things their children will be doing in your class. This allows the parents a good opportunity to see your enthusiasm.

Display the students' books and workbooks for parents to look through. Have on display a sample of their children's work. At this time of the year, an art project might be nice.

Have a sign-in sheet prominently displayed near the door the parents will be entering, so you will know which parents attended your presentation. Have a column after parent names for them to write what classroom activities they will be able to help out with. Post a list of examples of things they could help with to jog their memories. Include such things as field trips, class parties, classroom chores (such as copying), being a guest speaker in your classroom on a certain topic (such as their career or an interesting hobby, their travels, and so on), and helping with small groups or individual students in the classroom.

It is natural to get nervous about this night. Practically all teachers do. Take several deep breaths and let each out very slowly. To help you feel more confident, write your major topics on the chalkboard or on a large chart in the classroom. Then after you finish speaking about one topic, glance at the chalkboard or chart to see what the next topic is. That way, you do not have to worry about everything you are going to say, just the first topic. Let the parents know by the way you talk, your tone of voice, your body language and enthusiasm, that you want the best for their children.

Tell parents a good time to call you if they need to speak with you before scheduled conferences as well as a good day of the week to come in for a conference if they feel it is necessary before official conference time. Emphasize that you and the parents are partners in providing the best education possible for their children.

BEES

Bees are an entertaining way to make studying specific information fun. To make them a good learning experience, let the students know the type of information they will be asked and the particular mode of response. These bees can be conducted just with your classroom or with the whole school.

One particular bee that is a lot of fun is a geography bee. The National Geographic Society sponsors an annual geography bee for fourth grade through eight grade. Your school can participate by registering with the Society. You will receive study materials, sample bee questions, actual bee questions for your school, a finalist written exam, winner certificates and prizes, and a chance for a student from your school (if the student does extremely well in the written exam) to go on to state and national finals.

After early rounds, you might have twelve or even more finalists. Try to have as many as seating will logistically allow. These students will get a good workout in geography preparing for the final round. To directly and actively involve the other students, let them know before the final round that during the bee, they will be using a marker to write what they think each answer is on a piece of paper.

When setting up a geography bee, it is important to help the students feel as comfortable and confident as possible. Students often feel less pressured when they are sitting rather than standing, and it is nice for them to have a little privacy while they are thinking of an answer. **Study carrels** do an excellent job of providing this, plus they allow the students to sit close together without seeing what any other student is writing.

Use a large chart for keeping score. Print the finalists' names on it in black marker. Record all tallies on this chart in black marker, too, so they are easily seen by the audience during the bee.

During the bee, the students can listen to a question, then set their study carrels on their desktops, and write their answer on a card made out of construction paper or tag. Have a stack of these on each finalist's desk. If the students write with a black marker, it is easier for the audience to see later.

After students write their answers, they wait behind their study carrels for time to be called. When time is up, the contestants fold their study carrels and hold up their cards if they have the right answer. This way the students who have incorrect answers, do not even have to show their answer cards.

At this time, after recording student tallies, the students in the audience can hold up their papers if they got the right answer, too. You might want to have a few small prizes for the students in the audience who have the most right answers. Be sure to tell them ahead of time so they will study hard. This will create more excitement and better learning in the audience.

When the bee is over, you can provide award certificates for all the participants and trophies to the top finalists. These could be presented to the students at your school or class awards assembly. Figure 1-5 shows two delighted participants in a geography bee.

BELL

A nice gold bell on your desk can be a real delight. When the students are busy working in their groups and you need to redirect their attention or make an announcement, a short ring of the bell can be the call to attention. Practice with your class to condition them to stop, look, and listen when the bell is rung. This saves your voice, gets students' attention immediately, and helps your classroom run smoothly.

BOOKS

These are books the students and the teacher can order through book clubs. The students get to order the books and

Figure 1-5. These students are enjoying the competition of a geography bee. They listen to the question, put up their study carrels for privacy, and write the answer with a black marker on a piece of white tag. When time is called, they listen to the answer. If they have it right, they hold up their answer card.

posters they like, and the teacher can get books and electric pencil sharpeners for the classroom by accumulating points. Schedule time in your lesson plan book for this because it does take time; however, it is very worthwhile because students' leisure-time reading greatly increases.

BULLETIN BOARDS

Your classroom will look great if you have nice bulletin boards, wall displays, and classroom decorations. Some of the permanent displays of various charts are handmade, but once they are up, they stay put.

For example, you can make a bulletin board that lists the various helping chores for the students. On the same board, **section contest charts** (see Contest—Section Charts in this chapter) can be placed. If these are nicely and colorfully decorated, they make a fine display year-round. On this same bulletin board, display a sample of student award certificates. This board can stay up all year and will look sharp.

A calendar bulletin board that changes each month always looks good. You can buy all the decorations for the different month displays at a teachers' supply store. When these materials are not displayed, store them in plastic wrap so they remain usable for several years. If you are artistically talented and have the time, make your own bulletin boards. Be sure to laminate your materials so that they will last.

Bulletin boards can act as motivators. Students enjoy being recognized for their good work; it helps them to take pride in their accomplishments and work even harder. Figure 1-6 is an example of acknowledging good workers' efforts through the use of a bulletin board.

Interactive bulletin boards are stimulating and excellent for the students. Students love looking at photo displays of classroom events and projects. Ask the students to create clever captions. Photos can be mounted on construction paper and hung from the light fixtures with a partially elongated paper clip and a piece of string or mounted right to the front and back of a thick piece of yarn and then hung. Besides providing enjoyment and interest, these photos help reinforce learning from earlier in the school year.

Having world, nation, state, and city maps on display is beneficial to the students. They will often refer to them for information. Maps help give them a sense of perspective.

Time lines also afford a sense of perspective. Time lines for city, state, United States, or world history facilitate learning throughout the year. They assist students in orienting themselves to the period of time on which they are currently focusing. Students are still able to see their previous periods of study as well as a view of exciting times yet to be introduced.

Teaching bulletin board packets, purchased at your local teachers' supply store, can help you construct a time line easily. They contain pictures and captions for various periods of history. Landmark date cards can easily be constructed using white tag, black-stenciled numbers, and a bright red-colored border. Laminate your materials and mount them on the wall. You will have a year-round interactive bulletin board of great interest to the students, one that will help them to understand major concepts and that will be conducive to continual reinforcement of past and present studies.

Open-ended questions, for which the students provide answers, can be placed on bulletin boards. A general history or science title can be given to the board to reflect a **thematic unit** in which your class is involved. Students can contribute artifacts, information, and illustrations to the board as they progress in their studies. Mount student work pieces on colored construction paper first. Then they will look very polished

Figure 1-6.   Students have their names on these beautiful butterflies. They get stickers on their butterflies when they demonstrate that they are "good workers." Courtesy of Carroll Maietta.

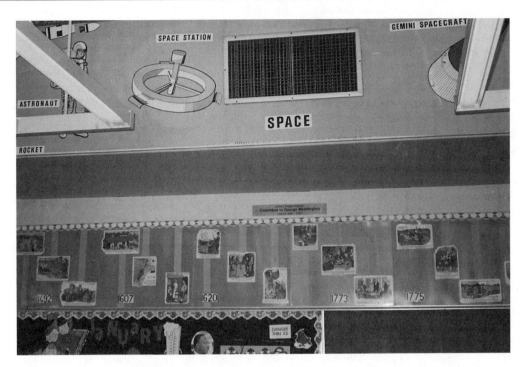

Figure 1-7.   A wall-mounted U.S. history time line with landmark dates makes an excellent learning presentation. It can be used as both an introduction to a new period of history and as a review prior to assessment.

when they are placed on the bulletin board. Be sure the bulletin board has plenty of space available for their work. If you do not have many bulletin boards built into your classroom, you can cover a voting booth with butcher paper, put an attractive border around it, and then mount the students' work. Figure 1-8 incorporates the use of a covered voting booth, a large table, and a clothesline to present a cross-curricular learning exhibit in a combination classroom.

Figure 1-8.   Corrugated paper that looks like brick makes a good lining for a voting booth. The Liberty Bells, a graphing of ordered pairs activity in math, look sharp on this background. The use of a clothesline and large display table makes it possible to show off T-shirt book reports, written history reports, and California mission projects.

Prominently display the classroom and school rules, the class schedule, the assignment accountability chart, and the assignments completed chart. If care is taken constructing these, if they are colorful and laminated, they will look nice all the time. Students will easily be able to refer to the school and class rules throughout the year whenever they need reminders. Students will use the assignment accountability chart on a daily basis. Students who do all their work can proudly see their name displayed for each grading period.

Wall displays that are used all year long as well as bulletin boards for the opening of school can be left up over the summer. This will allow you to devote more time to the critical area of planning your lessons in the first few days of the new school year.

The last part of this chapter ushers in a detailed discussion about classroom rules, combination classes, and composition books.

CLASSROOM RULES

One of the most important things in running an elementary classroom is to have a class that behaves well and knows the rules that lead to self-control. If behavior is good, everything else is enjoyable. It would be fabulous if all the students in the class behaved well, but that is unlikely; consequently, many types of classroom management plans are available. The most important thing is: Will yours work? The **behavior chart system** is one that does.

The first part of this system is making sure your students understand the rules. You can first guide the students in the development of appropriate rules for the classroom. It is definitely not too outlandish to "role-play" good behavior in relationship to the classroom rules. Your students will enjoy this too. You can role-play each rule, which makes each one very clear because the students can see the behavior you are describing. Help the students verbalize and understand the need for the rules and the reason why each rule is important. (Perhaps reading aloud Chapter 13, "The Schoolroom," in *Stuart Little,* by E. B. White, will help you illustrate this point.)

Following is a set of classroom rules that works well:

1. Line up quickly at the bell and enter the room quietly.
2. Stay in your seat when appropriate.
3. Stay quiet when appropriate.
4. Stay busy.
5. Follow directions quickly.
6. Act in a polite, respectful manner to all.
7. Never throw anything in the classroom.
8. Leave work areas neat and tidy.
9. Follow the rules of the school.

In the event of any severe disruption or unruly, rude, or belligerent behavior that does not respond to your correction, issue a **school citation** or **office referral** yourself. Explain on the form the nature of the problem. Let the students know that you will do this right from the beginning of the year.

With any kind of behavior system, it is prudent to copy any form or letter you send home with an individual student. Then you will have good documentation for that student. Record in your lesson plan book what it is you need back from whose parents, so you are sure the parents actually received the information. Sometimes it is easier and makes a bigger impact to use the U.S. mail. Have several envelopes in your desk with stamps and the school's return address already on them so that this will be easy to do.

With your classroom management program, if your students line up quickly and enter the room quietly, it will be a big help to you in getting **instructional time** started immediately. Increased time on-task increases achievement. Then students understand that when they enter the classroom, it is time to go to work.

There will be many, many times during the day when the students will be out of their seats going to another class, going to their group's **instructional lesson,** or going to work with other students on a particular project. During these times, you expect students to be out of their seats because they have directions to do so. For example, they may be rearranging furniture to move to their working groups, which gives all the students a nice, natural, energetic break.

But when students are supposed to be at a certain chair or spot on the floor working or listening or participating in a group discussion or project, that is where they should be, not wandering around visiting other groups or friends, getting paper, or sharpening pencils. Those things should be taken care of before school, at the beginning of class time, or at recess or lunch. It is disruptive and distracting to many students to have their classmates wandering around when they are supposed to be at work. When students are receiving instruction or working on a group or individual project, you want their attention focused on that and nothing else. Take into account the maturity level of your students when monitoring this behavior.

Students have plenty of opportunities to talk in the classroom. They will be answering questions, **brainstorming** with their learning groups, working together in small groups or with partners on a writing project, preparing for a play or puppet show, singing, and so on. But, when it is time to listen or work independently, those are the habits you want them to develop and practice. They learn to get right to work and to stay busy. This not only helps them complete their work and learn and understand new material and practice new skills, it allows the rest of the class that same opportunity, too, without distractions.

It is important for the students to be polite and respectful not only to all adults, which usually they are, but also to all the other students, which sometimes they are not. Some students get their feelings hurt very easily by unkind words or tones of voice. Make your students aware of this.

Make students aware of the danger of hitting, pushing, shoving, and so on. You do not want a student to break a tooth on the drinking fountain because he or she was shoved into it "accidentally" while getting a drink. The same kind of dangers apply to throwing things in the classroom. Let your students know that neither you nor they want an injured eye because of something thrown in the classroom. Prevention is best.

It is important that students learn to be responsible to keep their work areas neat and tidy. This includes picking up papers, books, pencils, markers, and so on from a table when they go there to work, cleaning up after an art project, pushing in chairs they have used at tables, and making sure their desks and the floor under them are nice and tidy before they leave each day.

In addition to ways to behave in the classroom, it is important for students to follow all the school rules. By having this as part of your classroom rules, it makes the students aware that their behavior needs to be appropriate not only in the classroom but also out on the playground, at the computer lab, in the library, and so on. This helps students learn to become good citizens everywhere at school, not just in their own classroom. If students receive office referrals, citations, or detentions outside of class, this too can be recorded on the behavior chart. It will help give you and the students a better overall picture of their behavior.

Then there are the matters of tissues for stuffy and runny noses, drinks during class time, and the use of the bathroom during class time. Find what works best for you. If the tissue box is left on the teacher's desk, when the students come up to get one or two pieces, they usually return to their seats and it is no problem whatsoever. Leaving it in a less conspicuous spot can cause problems. Students "visit" on the way to the tissues and on the way back.

The problem with getting drinks in the classroom and leaving the room to go to the bathroom is that one or two want drinks or the bathroom and pretty soon all the others are thinking about drinks and the bathroom for themselves, too. On some occasions, however, you may have a student who has a medical problem of some sort and needs to frequently get drinks or leave to go to the bathroom. For these one or two individuals, it usually is less disruptive if you let them know that they do not need to ask you first. For younger students, send them straight to the bathroom first and then out to play. For older students, it is more orderly and less disturbing when they get drinks and use the bathroom before school, at recess, at lunch, and after school. But, again, do what is comfortable and what works for you. Keep in mind, too, that you need to know where your students are at all times of the day.

If you have a primary grade, you can use this system, too, but you might want to simplify the rules. You could have just three rules:

1. Follow directions.
2. Keep hands and feet to self.
3. Be polite.

Explain each of these rules to your students. Guide them through a discussion to ensure that they understand the need for rules, the need for your specific classroom rules, and the behavior that shows the rule is being followed.

The second part of this behavior chart system is to post the rules on a classroom chart. Place it in a highly visible spot so that all the students can easily see it. They will need it.

Third, use a fresh behavior chart each week. See Figure A1-2 in the appendix for a sample behavior chart. This chart can be kept on a clipboard, which makes it easily accessible. If your classroom has "clippies" that slide across the two tracks above bulletin boards and chalkboards, one of these will make an excellent place to hang the clipboard.

How to Use a Behavior Chart

Before the first day of school, write each student's name in alphabetical order on the chart. Then copy a set for the next few weeks. Have a column for each day of the week with a column for totaling at the end of the week. This way a student who has a bad week one week gets to look at a fresh chart for the next week. However, keep all the previous weeks' charts at least until the quarter is over and you have had at least one parent conference. Better yet, keep them for the year.

Whenever a student breaks one of the classroom rules, record the rule number that was broken on the chart. If the student breaks several rules in one day, then record whatever are the appropriate numbers. Or ask the student to write her name on the board with the appropriate rule number after it. In the beginning of the year, students will glance over at the posted rules to get the number, but after a short period of time, upper-grade students, not surprisingly, never have to ask or check the chart for the rule number again. They always know.

Younger primary students may have to be told the rule number all year; however, if you are using the system with only three rules for primary, likely as not, by midyear, they too will probably know the rule number without being told. Either way, students will be absolutely clear about what is inappropriate, unacceptable behavior.

Then at a later, more convenient time, transfer any board names and numbers to the behavior chart on your clipboard.

When using this system with records that are accurately maintained, if you are going to be calling or sending information home about a student's behavior, you know exactly how the student is misbehaving and how frequently. Students will also know exactly what is going on with their behavior. Figure 1-9 shows sample boxes for two students for one week.

It is important to record on the chart when students are absent so that you do not look at some student who normally has poor behavior and think, "Wow! Great behavior on Tuesday!", when actually that student was absent on Tuesday.

When you implement this program, you may have many students who will have few or no marks on the behavior chart. Recognize these students for good behavior, both in the classroom with little awards or certificates and on report cards with good marks in behavior.

You can use this chart to fairly and accurately evaluate classroom behavior. Decide in advance how many numbers on the chart will cause a phone call or note sent home regarding behavior. Fifteen in a four- to five-week grading period might work well for you. Or, you may want fewer or more. Get what is comfortable and workable for you at your grade level. That way things will stay in control and students will function in a strong learning environment.

	M	T	W	TH	F
Melissa	8		5 3	2	
Matthew		5		4	1

Figure 1-9.

Decide in advance also the number of numbers for the students' behavior grades. Again, do what is comfortable for you. Do not be afraid of being too strict. It can be difficult to find that the class is frequently misbehaving and disruptive; however, if this happens to you, just begin anew by *consistently* enforcing the rules. The class will settle down as soon as the students understand that you mean business and you will follow through every time.

For behavior grades on progress reports and report cards, the following works quite well:

- Less than the number of weeks = O (Outstanding)
  In a four-week grading period, students who had their name down 0 times, 1 time, 2 times, and 3 times would get O's. You could fine-tune it by giving O+'s and O–'s.
- 1 times the number of weeks = S+ (Good)
  In a four-week grading period, students who had their names down 4, 5, 6, or 7 times would get an S+.
- 2 times the number of weeks = S (Satisfactory, Fair)
  Students with their names down 8, 9, 10 or 11 times would get an S.
- 3 times the number of weeks = N (Needs Improvement)
  Students with their names down 12, 13, 14, or 15 times would get an N.
- 4 times the number of weeks = U (Unsatisfactory)
  Students with their names down 16 or more times would get a U.

This system will help you give the same treatment to all your students. Otherwise, sometimes at report card time, you can be thinking that a particular student has not behaved well on a regular basis and deserves a low grade in behavior. When you check the chart, though, that may not be the case. Maybe the student has only had a few bad days recently, but generally does a pretty good job. Or if you are exceptionally fond of a student, you may think that this student is not all *that* bad, but when you check the chart, you see that, in fact, the grade will not be very good.

Many times, having a heart-to-heart talk with a student can make a big improvement in behavior. Also, incorporating the parent's assistance will help alleviate many problems. Consistent communication between the teacher, student, and parent is vitally important.

Commenting on a particular student's appropriate behavior loudly enough for the whole class to hear can be a real incentive to the other students. For example, you could say, "I like the way Jennifer is working." Then the other students will want to act like Jennifer. You could say, "Look at the way Joseph is sitting patiently and quietly for the assembly to begin." Then others will want to look like Joseph. If you do not overuse this technique, it can be very effective.

Dealing with Unusual Students in the Regular Classroom

At times you will have in your class one or two students, or maybe even more, who will be a real challenge to handle. They may not respond to your discipline plan or they may not be able to fit into your classroom with some degree of comfort.

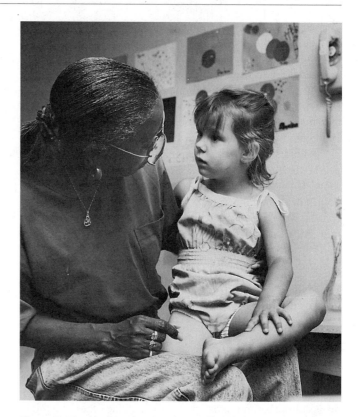

Figure 1-10. Having a heart-to-heart talk with an individual student can make a difference in improved behavior or achievement. Courtesy of Essa, *Introduction to Early Childhood Education,* © 1992 by Delmar Publishers, Inc.

It is important to put these students in perspective, so that they are one or two students in your room, not the focus of your day. You have an entire classroom to run. You do not want to get bogged down with one or two students to the point of lack of attention and energy for the other thirty; however, you do not want these few students not progressing in academic, physical and socialization skills, either. Informed planning is the key. You do not want to jeopardize your enthusiasm and optimism.

When confronted with the unusual student, try the following approaches:

1. Investigate the situation so that you can function and make decisions with as much background and knowledge as possible. Find out what your school's established discipline procedures are and follow those.
2. Develop two or three behavior plans.
3. Meet with involved adults.
4. Meet with student.
5. Implement the first plan, the second, if necessary, and the third, if needed. Persevere. Continue with what works.
6. Praise, reward, and punish consistently.

Investigating Behavior Problems

The first step, investigate, is extremely important. You need to have a good idea of what the problem is.

If your class includes a student who has some type of physical problem, disease, disability, or other special need, find out all you can about it. Many times, the literature will offer suggestions for a teacher. Talk with the student's doctors, parents, and other caretakers. Talk with former teachers. You want to feel as comfortable and as competent in dealing with the student as you possibly can. The student may already have another adult as an assistant. If not, ask the student if she would like a particular student to help out during the day and in what way. Do not assume that the student wants or needs help; she may be very self-sufficient.

Likewise, if your class includes a student who has emotional problems, first, investigate. Again, talk with parents, teachers, doctors, and former teachers. Become as familiar as you can with the emotional problems so you can have some idea of what the student is dealing with. These problems, just like physical disabilities and diseases, are trying for the student, too. Perhaps the child has no supervision or has been neglected. In other situations, the parents, older brothers and sisters, or even the student may be involved with drugs and alcohol. Parents or relatives may be in jail or in gangs. The child may not live with his parents at all. Maybe the parents have abandoned the child, or maybe the courts have taken the child away and placed your student in a group home. Or perhaps the student is a victim of abuse. Check with your school district and local laws about reporting abuse. If you are even suspicious of abuse, you are required by law to report it. Let the principal know, too, but you are the one responsible for reporting suspected abuse to Child Protective Services.

If your class includes a student who has some kind of a learning difficulty (either understanding material, retaining information, processing language, or attending), gather all the information you can about it. Speak with adults who are involved. Remember, the student is having a tough time, too.

This student may enter your classroom undiagnosed, may develop some sort of disease after the year starts, or may already be involved in counseling or a part-time special education program.

Whatever the situation, investigate and learn all you can. Sometimes problems are intertwined. A student may have just a physical disability. Another student may have both a physical and a learning disability. Or a student may have a learning disability and an emotional problem. Always check the student's **cum file** for information regarding grades, standardized test scores, psychological information, retentions, and so on. Check all school resources, including the principal.

Following is some general information about one type of problem you might find when you investigate. Be aware that research is ongoing in this area, so when presented with this type of challenge, check with doctors, counselors, and specialized school and district personnel for the latest information.

ADD and ADD/H.

Attention deficit disorder (ADD) is a problem that largely involves attending or focusing. **ADD/H** (or **ADHD**) is attention deficit disorder with **hypoactivity** or **hyperactivity** that can often lead to behavior problems. Students of any ability level, including very bright students, can have ADD.

ADD students are unable to focus or attend for any length of time. They are confronted by many environmental stimuli that need filtering so that the desired area receives their concentration; however, the filter-focus process is not working properly or as well as it should. ADD students with hypoactivity can sometimes fall through the cracks in the educational system. Although these students are calm, quiet, maybe even "spacey acting" in the classroom, the filter-focus problem is still there; consequently, they may be below average in academic performance and need to develop some coping devices to perform at a level comparable to their ability level.

ADD students with hyperactivity can be more noticeable in the classroom because of inability to attend as well as an over-abundance of activity—in and out of desk, fidgeting, constant talking, and so on. The inability to control behavior can be a major problem for these students and can interfere with academic performance.

ADD students can easily get off track. They often have a **low frustration tolerance** and a **low tolerance for failure.** Especially when faced with failure, these students can **shut down.** They can be impulsive and antsy, can have a wandering mind with only short spurts of focusing, and may take considerably longer than the other students to get started on a task. Sometimes ADD students may deliberately annoy other students and can be easily annoyed by others. With the inability to consistently pay attention, they may produce very little in relation to their ability. In frustration, these students may think they are stupid and cannot do a task, even though that is not the case.

Students with ADD/H need to be well rested to face the day successfully. Concepts must be continually repeated or they can be lost. These students need consistency in rewards and consequences. They may be academically behind the others in the class, but not necessarily. Just as these students will have to learn patience in dealing with their problems, you will need to have some patience, too.

It is very helpful if the parents or guardians have their child evaluated by a specialist who deals with learning disorders and who may be best able to determine if a trial on some medication would be beneficial. Students with ADD or ADD/H may learn to function in the regular classroom quite well and excel with some classroom or instructional modifications as provided under Section 504 of the Americans with Disabilities Act (ADA). Section 504 now includes students with impairments such as ADD/ADHD if this disability has a significant impact on major life experiences, such as learning. For 504-eligible students, accommodations and modifications must first be provided in the regular classroom. These students may be candidates for special education class, depending on what is decided at the meeting with the parents, school psychologist, special education teacher, principal, and you, all of whom are members of the **student study team (SST).**

You may encounter other students who do not have a specific learning disability, but may have emotional problems that greatly interfere in learning and in **socialization.** These students not only have trouble with academics but also have difficulty getting along with others.

These are serious problems that need to be addressed. Get all the help you can. As you gather information from the available sources, continue to keep a log and record the type and frequency of the undesirable behavior so you will have current information and documentation.

Speak with the parents and ask such questions as:

1. Is this a long-standing problem, or something more recent?
2. Is their child already on some kind of medication?
3. Is their child already in counseling or has it been tried or suggested?
4. Has this problem been discussed with the child's pediatrician?
5. Does their child eat a good breakfast?
6. Does their child need a snack at morning recess?
7. Does their child get a good night's sleep?
8. Is there a history of allergies?
9. What are things their child likes a great deal?

In your process of investigation, be sure you speak with everyone, including the principal and the **school psychologist,** and gather as much information from them as possible. If the student has not had a medical evaluation for the problem, suggest to the parents that it be done.

Your school psychologist might be willing to call the parents, too. She may be able to come into your classroom to observe the child and offer suggestions to you regarding the child's academic and socialization progress. Suggestions may be made for having the student and family go for some counseling.

A student may need several approaches. She may need medication, individual counseling, and family counseling. The earlier the treatment, the better. You want this student as well prepared as possible to be a productive member of society. You want this student to feel as comfortable and confident at school as possible.

Formulating Behavior Plans

As you approach the end of the investigation and have acquired information and suggestions from resource professionals, begin formulating three plans. If you only develop one, and it does not work, it can be very discouraging. But if you have some back-up plans, failure of the first will not be discouraging.

Use the information you gathered to help you develop your plans. By this time, you have had a chance to get to know your student. Do you know what her likes and dislikes are? Do you know what she would be willing to work for at school and at home? This is vital information to you and the success of your plans.

For example, if your student absolutely loves art and does not want to miss it ever, you have something for which she can work. Maybe its a period of free time in the class to work on the computer or play a board game. Your student might like to get a sticker each day and be able to save up for some prize.

At home, maybe she loves watching television or videos or playing some computer game or listening to a popular radio station or dirt bike riding or playing with model cars or a hundred other things and would be willing to work for them. What about going out with one of her parents for an ice cream cone, just the two of them?

As you develop your plan, keep in mind three things:

1. Motivation for the student;
2. Consistency in the rewards and consequences; and
3. Praise for the student to build self-esteem.

The planned intervention does not need to be complicated. Simple is best. Establish a time frame with specific dates for evaluation of progress.

Keep in mind that just developing a plan for you and the student can be a special thing for the student. Behavior can often improve just from the student's feeling of having a special, private little plan.

The following are some sample plans:

Plan 1. The student would like to earn a sticker each day along with an "improvement made" note (some cheery, attractive, notepaper with the word *improvement* on it) to his parents. That will be the consequence of improved behavior, along with television viewing for that afternoon and evening. The at-school consequence of poor behavior will be not receiving a sticker or note and sitting away from the other students for morning recess the following day. During that "sitting" recess, the student can do some busying task, such as writing a certain number of sentences. First-grade students may just be required to sit away from the other children during their morning recess. The at-home consequence of poor behavior will be no television for that afternoon and evening.

In plan 1, the student can start each day with the improvement made note taped to his desktop. When undesirable behavior occurs, tell the student what the undesirable behavior was and make a special, indelible mark on the bottom of the note. When desirable behavior occurs, tell the student what it was and stamp a happy face or star on the top part of the improvement made note.

At the end of the day, if the student has at least the agreed-to number of happy faces and not more than the agreed-to marks for poor behavior, simply cut off the bottom part of the note with the bad marks and throw that portion away. Then sign the improvement made note, give the student a sticker, and record N on your behavior chart if the student earned a note and sticker.

When the student arrives home, if he has earned a note, the student's parents see only the good part of the note. This allows the child to get positive praise with no negative mixed in with it.

Even if the student is having a bad day, keep alert for a display of good behavior. Go to the student's desk at least once in the morning and at least once in the afternoon when the student is exhibiting desirable behavior, and praise the student. Also, the first thing in the morning, look happy to see the student regardless of the kind of day yesterday was.

The standards are set. Enforce them consistently. Be sure to check that the student sits on the bench, if required, and completes any sentences, if given.

This may sound like a fairly lenient plan, but if the student's problems are severe, it is not. Be sure to look for *improvement,* not perfection. If this student were capable of perfection, you would not be developing this plan for him. In two to three weeks, be prepared to evaluate improvement made with this plan. Use your behavior chart to see how many *N*'s the student accumulated in the two to three weeks. Is this plan worthwhile? Should it continue or should another plan be tried?

Plan 2. This plan would be suitable for an upper-grade student only. Here, the student loves the following things: PE, playing Geo Safari® (an educational game) during class time, watching television, and listening to the radio. This student does not like isolation.

The student will begin the day sitting with the rest of the students. If it is a PE day, she will begin with the opportunity to participate in PE. If it is not a PE day, she will begin with the opportunity to play Geo Safari® the last twenty minutes of the day.

At the first undesirable behavior, the student will be given a study carrel to place on her desktop. At the second undesirable behavior of the day, the student will move her desk off into a corner of the classroom and leave her study carrel standing. At the third undesirable behavior of the day, the student will have a voting booth around her desk. Be sure the open part is facing you to ensure that she is as productively occupied as possible. At the fourth undesirable behavior of the day, the student loses PE/ Geo Safari®. At the fifth undesirable behavior of the day, the student will not receive an improvement note and the student loses the opportunity to watch television and listen to the radio. Record *N* on your behavior chart when you send an improvement note home so it is easier to evaluate at the close of the two-to-three week period.

To build self-esteem, even if the student is having a bad day, at least once in the morning and at least once in the afternoon, go to this student's desk when she is behaving appropriately and praise her for that behavior. Additionally, first thing in the morning, when your class is lining up to come into the classroom, go to this student's spot in line and say a warm, friendly hello.

Plan 3. The next student loves Nintendo®, more recognition at home, sitting with a partner during class time, and school special tickets. (In a school special ticket system, students collect special tickets given to them during the week by an adult for being especially good, helpful, and so on. Each Friday, there is a drawing and the winners are announced on the intercom system. Usually, the winner from each class goes down to the office and receives a prize. This is very popular with the students.)

In this plan, continue the regular use of your behavior chart. To begin the day, this student gets to sit with a helpful partner. Set a timer for one hour. When the beeper goes off, look on your behavior chart and on the board to see if this student has his name down. If not, place two school special tickets on the corner of his desk. Reset the timer for another hour. When the timer sounds, if the student does not have his name down, place two more school special tickets on his desk. Continue like this throughout the day. Be sure to use a timer or this sys-

tem will not work. Teachers are extremely busy during the day, and an hour can be over long before you realize it.

If the student collects at least four special tickets, a note is not sent home. Then, right before or right after dinner, the parents will put a sticker on a chart that is solely devoted to that child. The chart could be on the refrigerator or some other highly visible location. If the student does not collect at least four special tickets, a note goes home and the student will have no Nintendo® time that evening. Again, if you send notes home, write the student's name in your lesson plan book under the next day's first period subject so you are sure to collect it with a parent signature on it the next morning. If you do not get it back, telephone the parents at recess or lunch.

If sending the note home and back with the student becomes a trial, get a stack of envelopes and use your school address stamp to put on the return addresses. Stamp ten or fifteen envelopes. Then at the end of the day, if the student has a note to go home, drop it in the stamped envelope, put the parents' name and address on and drop it in a mailbox. If you do this— it is easy and effective—you must realize, however, that the down side is the parents will not get the note until the next afternoon; therefore, the program will have a little lag time of one day.

To help with self-esteem, compliment this student at least three times a day. First thing in the morning before the day begins, go to this student and compliment him on some part of his outfit. Before lunch, compliment the student on something he has said or done. Before dismissal, compliment this student again on something said or done, or on his nice haircut, and so on.

Meeting with the Student's Team

Your school's policy may be to try all the classroom modifications first. Then, if the interventions attempted have not met with success, a team meeting will take place. Bring your documentation with you so you are prepared for the meeting. If your school's policy is to meet first, then be prepared for the meeting with your ideas for plans.

The team meeting will probably include the principal, the school psychologist, a special education teacher, the speech therapist, the parents, and you. Parents are desperate to know what to do with their children. If they have something specific to do, they can be a big help. (If, for whatever reason, the parents are not able to follow through at home, at least continue with the school's part of the behavior plan so there is some success at school for the student.)

At the meeting, explain the plan. Discuss it. If this is a meeting after classroom modifications have been tried and they failed, be prepared to discuss what occurred. Elicit everyone's help in developing a new plan. Get it or a modification approved and begin the next day. Establish a specific date for evaluation of its success or failure. Be sure to keep records in case any patterns of poor or good behavior can be identified. This could be helpful in the development of later modifications.

After the adult meeting, meet with the student and explain the program to him. Let the student know you want him to be both academically and personally successful at school. You and the team want to promote self-control in the student. Make the student aware that people care about him and are willing to help in whatever way they can. The student needs to be assured that his cooperation is needed for success.

Throughout the plan, praise the student when appropriate, reward the student when a reward is earned, and punish the student (no TV, Nintendo®, and so on) when punishment is deserved. Do this consistently for success.

Again, in any of these plans, look for improvement, not perfection. These students need a lot of monitoring to reinforce desirable behaviors and to modify or eliminate undesirable behaviors. They need limits clearly set. Approach students and handle them with warmth, but let them know you mean business. Do the best you can. *Consistent rewards and consequences* are vital. (See also Chapter 5, The MNO's, under Mainstreaming and Full Inclusion.)

COMBINATION CLASSES

Combination classes can be two or three different grade levels, but usually two, in one classroom. These occur when the total number of students at a school does not divide evenly into the available number of classes.

Most preparation for these classes is in the area of history, geography, science, and health. Many math assignments will also be given out of two different grade-level books.

Three things can help you if and when you have a combination class. First is the students' good behavior. If you are working with one grade level while the other is busy at work, they need to be busy, not chatting or disrupting. If students need to be speaking to their partners or the members of their small group, whisper voices help the grade you are instructing to be less distracted.

Additionally, be sure you give clear directions to the grade you are not working with at that moment. Write the directions on the board or a chart, and ask several students to repeat the directions so that you can make any corrections if they are unclear.

Be sure the students understand how to do the work and what to do if they get stuck (for example, they could skip that part and go on to a part they do know how to do; they could have something prepared to work on in advance in case there were a problem with the assigned material; or they could work with one or two appointed students from that grade level who are available for brief tutoring). Be sure **early finishers** have something specific to do that they know about in advance. Well-occupied, well-behaved students will keep your combination class running smoothly.

The behavior chart also helps to maintain good behavior. Put a couple of names down and the students will settle down quickly and work productively. This allows you to devote pretty close to your full attention to whichever grade level you are meeting with at that time.

The second thing that is helpful in combination classes is to coordinate your history, geography, science, and health units time-wise so that both grade levels will be testing on the same day. This provides a quiet testing environment for all the students regardless of their grade.

The third thing that is helpful is having students who can take turns being the "reader" for homework answers for their grade level, even though many times you will be collecting the homework to check it yourself. Select a student who can read loudly, clearly, and slowly. Then one grade can be correcting math homework or spelling homework at the same time you are correcting homework with the other grade level. This saves a great deal of time and definitely helps things move along.

Be patient with the students in a combination class. The environment is more distracting to them than a traditional classroom. Also, be sure they get plenty of attention from you!

COMPOSITION BOOKS

Composition books can be used for recording students' daily homework assignments, dates of field trips and the need for permission slips, times of class parties and what students have volunteered to bring, when library books are due for the class library day, and reminders about school events such as dress-up day or Valentine card day. These books are a big help to both the students and their parents.

Depending on the size and sturdiness, one composition book may last the entire school year. Also available, and especially helpful to upper-grade students, are bound booklets with a calendar for the school year and a place to write homework assignments and other important information by each date. In addition, these booklets have lists of the U.S. presidents, the most commonly misspelled words, plus a place for the students to write other words that they misspell. There are also tips for better study habits as well as riddles, crossword puzzles, and other fun activities throughout.

Composition books really help students stay on-task and know exactly what they have each night for homework. Immediately after lunch each day, Monday through Thursday, have the students take out their composition books and copy that night's homework and any important class or school information from the chalkboard, chart, or transparency, whichever place you like to display it. Not only will students have this record, so will their parents.

Once in a while, you might have a reluctant student who takes out her composition book, but does not copy homework into it. If you run into this problem, it can be quickly solved by having another student check the reluctant student's composition book and stamp it when it is completely and correctly copied.

Using composition books does take some time each afternoon—about fifteen minutes—but it is well worth it. The students know what is going on at school and with their homework, and so do parents.

You probably will not assign homework on Friday. This is the day for chart time. Start early in the morning so everyone is ready after lunch with their composition books. Students go to the assignment accountability chart in twos or threes to copy the subject and titles of any assignments they are missing and the total number of assignments they are missing. If no assignments are missing, they write "Chart assignments missing = 0." Otherwise, they write "Chart assignments missing = 3," or "Chart assignments missing = 2," or whatever pertains to

Your Premier Elementary Reminder Can Help You:

Taking notes:
Clues to what is important
- whatever the teacher writes on the board.
- whenever the teacher says: "This is important. Remember it!"
- whatever the teacher says more than once.

Think . . . Act . . . Review . . .
T.A.R. applies to all your studies

THINK: What do you have to do?
ACT: Do it carefully.
REVIEW: Did you do the right thing?
      Is the result okay?

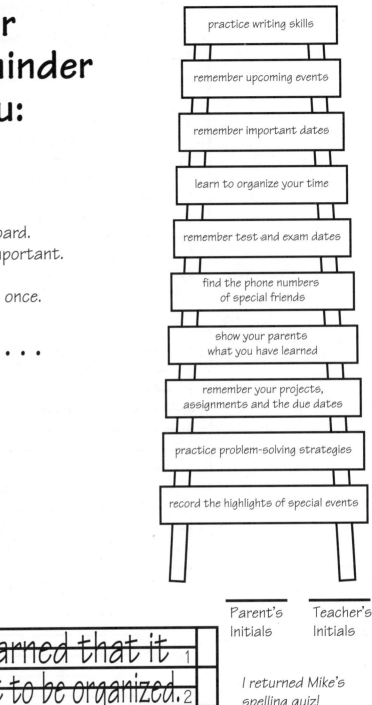

practice writing skills

remember upcoming events

remember important dates

learn to organize your time

remember test and exam dates

find the phone numbers of special friends

show your parents what you have learned

remember your projects, assignments and the due dates

practice problem-solving strategies

record the highlights of special events

TUESDAY   DAY ☐

October
22

Today I learned that it is important to be organized. 1 2

3

Our teachers showed us that organization involves order, neatness, planning and routine. 4

5

Now that my study skills are improving, I enjoy school much more! 6

Parent's Initials   Teacher's Initials

I returned Mike's spelling quiz! Please initial. R.H.

We'll work on it. Thanks! J.K.

Figure 1-11. Students may enjoy this type of composition book. Copyright © 1991 Premier School Agendas, 2081 Business Center Drive, Suite 180, Irvine, California, USA 92715-9945. All rights reserved. No part of this publication may be reproduced without the written permission of the publisher.

Parent's
Initials

Teacher's
Initials

DAY ☐   THURSDAY

November
21

1
2
3
4
5
6

Parent's
Initials

Teacher's
Initials

DAY ☐   FRIDAY

November
22

1
2
3
4
5
6

SATURDAY
November
23

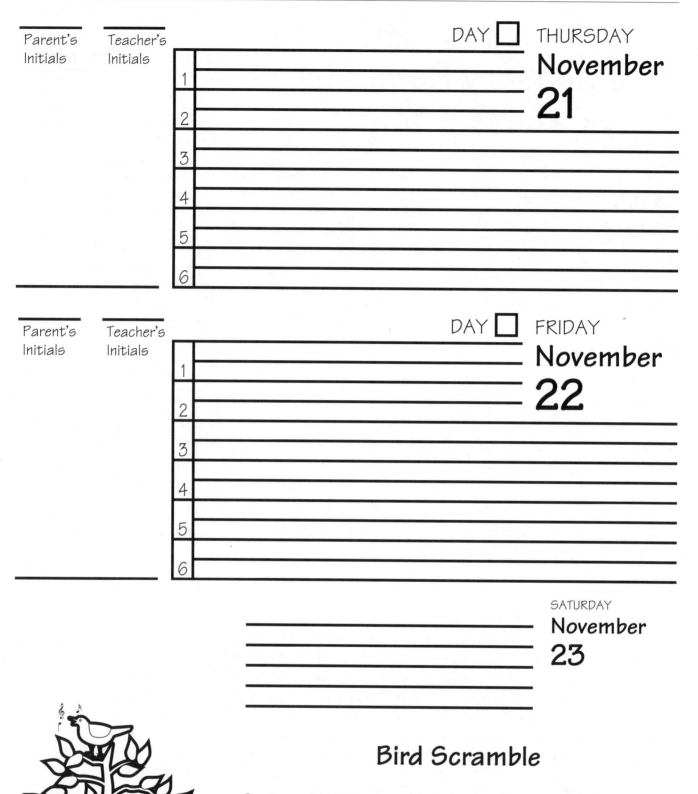

Bird Scramble

Contrary Mary keeps a birder's checklist on which she
records every bird she has identified. Below is part of her
list. Can you unscramble the names?

MBRINGHUMID   NEARC   KWOPRODECE   EHORN
SOUREG   LEELKRID   ONLO   KRLA
DALARML   VEDO   WNAS   LOW

them and have each missing assignment clearly listed in their composition books. Their missing assignments are any boxes from the assignment accountability chart that are not filled with a check, an X, or a stamp.

Establish some order for students to go to the chart: for example, they can go row by row, only two or three at a time; they can go in order of names on the chalkboard (students erase their names as they finish); or students who need more time at the chart because of absence can go first. Students can go up quietly according to the established schedule as long as they are not directly involved in an instructional lesson. Some students will not need to go to the chart at all, because they never have any overdues.

On Friday afternoon, during composition book time, get the class started on their afternoon work. Then call up each student to check his or her composition book and make sure any missing assignments are listed clearly. Then, using the behavior chart, record how many times that student's name was down that week. After that, sign the composition book and put a check by the student's name on the behavior chart to indicate you have seen that student. This also gives you a good opportunity to praise students for keeping up, to encourage those who are not to do better, or to work on a small reward system with a student to help him improve. Purchasing a signature stamp at your local stationery or office supplies store allows you to just stamp your signature and makes the whole process move very quickly.

With this system, students are keenly aware of any problems as are their parents. Opportunities for intervention abound. All students are treated fairly and in a consistent manner. All students will be conferring with the teacher on an individual basis for help and praise.

CONTEST—SECTION CHARTS

Having a section contest in your room is an excellent way to keep your class running well. And, it is fun, too! This contest will work at any grade level K–6.

First, decide on your **seating sections** for this contest. This can vary anywhere between three and six. Following are four different seating sections, any one of which you may use for the whole year or any combination of which you may use throughout the year.

The first example in Figure 1-12 has the students in partners in three seating sections. Similar to peer counseling, this arrangement is often helpful if you have several slow students. You can partner them with fast, independent workers who can keep them on-task.

This arrangement is also good if you have several **Limited-English-Proficient (LEP or LES, Limited-English-Speaking)** students you want to partner with students they feel comfortable with who can help them throughout the day. If you use this first seating section arrangement, you would make three section contest charts.

The next seating section arrangement, in Figure 1-13, works nicely for a class of students who get along well together. This

Teacher's Desk

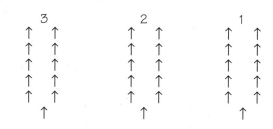

↑ = the direction the student is facing

Figure 1-12.   This seating arrangement helps if one or two students need tutoring. Students can sit next to students who are good study partners for them. At the back of the class, there could be three groups of three, or one group of three formed by the last student in each row.

arrangement allows them to work easily in pairs or groups of four with no movement of furniture. If you need a little more leeway for one or two students who need a little more space, place their desks either at the front of each row facing the teacher's desk or at the back of each row facing the teacher's desk. Make three charts if you use this seating pattern.

In the third seating section arrangement, as seen in Figure 1-14, the students are in larger groups. This pattern is excellent to enable students to see each other well and to hear with ease what is being said in the classroom. For this pattern, make three charts.

The last seating section arrangement, illustrated in Figure 1-15, is a good one for beginning teachers. In this arrangement, students do not have such close access to another student for unnecessary talking. If you have one or two talkative students, move their desks off to one side of the room or to the back of the room. Be sure to let them know their section number. This

Teacher's Desk

3	2	1
→ ←	→ ←	→ ←
→ ←	→ ←	→ ←
→ ←	→ ←	→ ←
→ ←	→ ←	→ ←
→ ←	→ ←	→ ←
→ ←	→ ←	→ ←

↑ = the direction the student is facing

Figure 1-13.   This arrangement makes nice work groups that can be changed as needed.

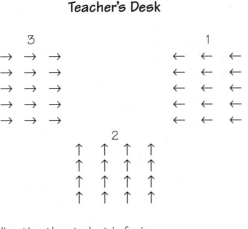

Teacher's Desk

↑ = the direction the student is facing

Figure 1-14. This arrangement enables *all* students to easily see and hear each other during class discussions.

type of arrangement allows the students ample opportunity to move around during the day to different locations in the classroom depending on where their group meets. It energizes the class to physically move chairs and themselves around the class to get into their various groups or to meet with their partner or tutor and provides a quick break, after which students are ready to work. If you use this pattern, make five section charts.

The size of your class may be a factor in how you seat students. If your class has only twenty-eight or twenty-nine students, then you will have plenty of room to spread out and any seating pattern would be fine. If, however, you have thirty-seven or thirty-eight students, you might want to select a pattern that takes up as little room as possible.

The most important thing is to select a seating arrangement that you are comfortable with and that works well for you. Start with a structured, conservative pattern; then, when classroom control is well established, you can get a little inventive.

Teacher's Desk

| 5 | 4 | 3 | 2 | 1 |

↑ = the direction the student is facing

Figure 1-15. This is a good arrangement for a beginning teacher who wants to have a conservative, orderly start of the school year. When paired learning or cooperative learning is done, the students simply move to their partner's or group's location. Since students are always moving to get into groups with this arrangement, the teacher can easily establish many different groupings to provide a diverse learning experience for the students.

After you have decided on your seating sections, make your charts, one for each section. Follow the directions on the border chart shown in Figure A1-3 in the appendix. If you are making five charts, copy five sets of borders, three for three charts, and so on. Ask the students, or if you have a primary class ask some upper-grade students, to color the borders for you in marker. The boxes could be in different colors or the box trim could be in a different color from the inside of the box.

Next, make three or five copies of the section contest chart (Figure A1-4). Keep the original section contest chart sheet for later copying. Cut out the colored borders and place them around the section contest chart, the two longer strips on the sides and the shorter strips on the top and bottom.

Mount each chart on construction paper or tag and laminate so that each will last.

Then, put the section charts on your bulletin board where all the students can easily see them. Copy a stack of section chart forms and place one over each laminated section chart. Now you are ready for some fun!

You can tell the students things like:

1. Any section that has all its progress report forms signed and returned tomorrow will get ten stamps on its section chart.
2. Any section that has no students' names down for the morning will earn seven stamps.
3. Any section that sits up nice and straight, listens attentively to this math (or history or geography or whatever) lesson, participates by answering questions and asking intelligent ones, and works quietly on the follow-up assignment will earn fifteen stamps. (You can use this one when the principal comes to observe a lesson. It's a winner!)
4. Any section that does not have any names down for causing any problems at the school assembly will earn eight stamps. The students absolutely love this.

You can buy little self-inked stamps at a stationery store. They come in happy faces, stars, Olympic rings, and many others. Then just stamp in the section contest chart boxes.

Whichever section gets its chart filled first wins the contest. For a prize, you could let each student pick out a pencil. Use school pencils, if you like. You also could purchase from a pencil company which sells pencils by the gross. There are solar system pencils, punctuation marks pencils, find the inventions pencils, African zoo animals pencils, and so forth. Or give something else for a prize.

After a section wins, remove each paper chart from the laminated chart. Ask how many students would like one of the colorfully stamped charts. Select three or five students to give the charts to. Then put up a new set of charts, and you are ready to go again.

If you have the same one or two sections winning all the time, move the students' desks around so all the sections have a chance at winning. Give all the winning sections prizes in the event of ties. If one section is only a stamp or two short of winning, you can consider it for prizes, too.

This contest does not need to be limited to things dealing with behavior or returning forms. "Five stamps for every section in which everyone has completed and returned their homework" works great, too.

CUSTOMIZED REPRODUCIBLES

If you want to customize any of the reproducibles in this book to suit your specific or special needs, here are a few ways to do just that. If you need to use correction fluid, use the kind that is "for copies."

If you do not particularly like some part of a reproducible and want it to say something else, then, on a separate piece of paper, outline in light pencil the shape or configuration of the part you do not need. Next, type what you want inside this configuration. Then, cut out the section you typed and glue-stick it over the original part you did not want. Presto! Now, make your master copy.

If the size of the shape or the configuration is quite large, and you want to replace it with only a few words or a short sentence, place a small graphic over part of the area. Then, outline in light pencil the shape that is left to fill. Type what you need in the shape or configuration in your outline, cut it out, and glue-stick it and the small graphic to the reproducible.

If you see something you would like to use in the middle of a reproducible page, just cut out that part and enlarge it. Glue-stick it to full-size paper, and make a master copy.

If you do not have access to a computer and printer for the graphic, just make your own. It is relatively easy, even if you are not a particularly great artist. Just follow these directions. First, make your rough sketch on white, unlined paper. Erase and redraw as necessary. Then, to darken the lines, go over the drawing in fine-point black marker. Next, go to a window. Place your drawing against the windowpane with the drawing facing you. Place a piece of white, unlined paper over it. With the outside light illuminating your drawing, trace it on to the fresh white paper. It will look very good and there will be no erasures or other messes. Cut your drawing out and glue-stick it to your original material. This way, the reproducibles look sharp and conform to your individual needs.

Let your students in on this technique, too. They can use paper clips to hold their scratch drawing to the fresh paper for their final masterpiece. They may need to take a couple of breaks, because arms tire quickly doing this.

For anything that you want enlarged or reduced, just visit your nearest copy center or local stationery store. Keep masters in a file by subject area. Keep answer keys with your masters.

Use what you like from the sample reproducible booklets in the appendix, too. You may want to use only a small section for a specific lesson, or you can utilize an entire booklet for an instructional unit.

You may want to make double-sided copies to conserve paper. Schedule one or two parent volunteers to do the copying, collating, and stapling at a time when the copier will not be in use. Then everything will be ready and waiting for you and

CHAPTER QUESTIONS

1. Explain how an assignment accountability chart could be helpful to a student who has been absent for the last two days.
2. How would an assignment accountability chart help a student who has been in the habit of not turning in assignments and then conveniently "forgetting" about them?
3. How could an assignment accountability chart reward a conscientious student?
4. Is there a point to having the students hand in all their assignments when some of the assignments will come in late? Explain your point of view.
5. What are your views on a schoolwide honor roll and awards assembly? What value do you think the students would place on it?
6. Describe an honor roll system in which each student at the school could get an award.
7. Describe a classroom seating arrangement appropriate for a first-year teacher to use when setting up the classroom at the beginning of the school year. Tell why you made your selection. Explain the advantages and the limitations.
8. Classroom control is extremely important for any teacher, but especially for a beginning teacher. What are the things you would do to establish and maintain control? Name and explain at least four things.
9. When you develop an individualized behavior plan, what are the three most important things to keep in mind?
10. Explain in detail how you would deal with a student who has unusually challenging behavior problems.
11. Name and explain three things you could do if you had a combination class. How would each be helpful to you?
12. Describe a plan for ensuring good behavior by your class at a school assembly.
13. Develop an individualized behavior plan of your own for a student who is continually rude to other students and can't get along with them.
14. How can the section chart contest act as a motivator? Name two ways you could use it.
15. The principal is coming to observe you teach a lesson in reading. How would you handle the classroom control part of the lesson?
16. Suppose you are going to have some kind of a bee at your school. What curriculum area would you find of interest? What would the procedures be before and during the bee? How would students qualify to be in the finals? What would the format be like?
17. Create an interactive bulletin board for your classroom in a subject of your choice. If you are more interested in upper grades, you might want to consider something in autobiographical diaries, geography, scientific process, or

mathematics application. If you are more interested in teaching primary grades, your board might be related to social skills, storytelling, classic tales, or vocabulary development.

18. Back-to-School Night is an important event. Assuming you have time for a thirty-minute presentation, how would you like to use the time? Be specific.

CHAPTER PROJECT

Interview an experienced teacher. Be sure to call first and set up an appointment. Ask the teacher to detail a plan that was used successfully with a chronically misbehaving student. Do not use the student's name, but ask the teacher to give you specific details about the student's family background and educational history. Take notes. Write this up as a case study.

BIBLIOGRAPHY

Workshop presentation: "Serious Disruptive Behavior Disorders in Childhood and Adolescence"; Steve Simpson, psychologist and consultant to the California Youth Authority, September 1992.

Workshop presentation: "Self-Esteem Issues and the LH/ADD Student (Depression, Anxiety in Children, Adolescents with Learning Disabilities—Symptoms, Diagnosis, Common Problems)"; Melissa Thomasson, Ph.D., clinical psychologist, adult dyslexic, and parent of an LD/ADD child.

2

THE DEF'S

Running an elementary classroom effectively is a complex process. Knowing a little additional information about the students and the first day of school, being aware of the importance of your extra responsibilities, and planning a fine, exciting curriculum that meets the needs of all the students and provides for students who finish assignments early are all part of this process. This chapter covers the following topics:

- Day Care
- Drills
- Duties
- Early Finishers
- Emergent Literacy
- Evaluations
- Expectations
- Facts
- Fair
- Field Trips
- Fine Arts
- First Day of School
- Flexibility

The first part of this chapter informs you of a way to find out a little additional information about some of your students and explains the importance of your role as teacher in the exercise of drills and duties.

DAY CARE

Many schools provide day care or child care for their students. These programs usually begin at 7:00 A.M. and close at 6:00 P.M. and offer a variety of activities for the students, including arts and crafts, games both inside and out, parties, and homework time.

If your school has such a program and you have students from your own class involved in it, it is worth your while to make periodic visits. It gives you the opportunity to see your students in a wider perspective and in a different setting. Your students will enjoy your visits, too.

DRILLS

Before the first day of school, find out what your school policies are on all the various drills. You will want to explain this to your students right away. Do some practice drills with them so they are prepared for an emergency.

A **take cover drill** can be called by you, the principal via the intercom, or by any adult out on the playground. This drill can be used during an earthquake, tornado, or the presence of some danger on campus, such as an armed intruder.

If the students are outside, have them lie facedown on the ground and cover their heads and eyes with their arms. When an adult lets them know it is safe, they can return to the buildings. Otherwise they can move on to the safe area they use for a **disaster drill**.

If the students are inside, have them get under a desk or table, cover their eyes with one arm, and use the other arm to cover their heads. Their heads should be under the desk or table itself, not out in the aisle where something could easily fall on them, causing head injury. Students should avoid putting their heads under a chair because it is not as strong as a desk or table. For the best head protection, it should be covered with both arms and under a desk or table. Have students stay in their safe area until given directions by an adult to move somewhere else.

A disaster drill usually involves an evacuation of the building to the assigned safe area. This can occur during a fire drill or after an earthquake or at any other time the building is considered unsafe.

Take all your disaster materials with you on all practice drills so that you are accustomed to doing that and will do it if there ever is a real disaster. At a minimum, your disaster pack should include a current roster of your students' names and an accountability form of some kind. The disaster team leaders will then know whether injured students who could not be moved are still in the building and in which rooms, whether students or adults are unaccounted for, and whether any injured people are with you. Be sure your pack is always ready with sharpened pencils and pens and fresh forms. You should know where disaster first-aid equipment is stored and how to get to it. In case of a real emergency, it would be extremely helpful to have stored some coloring and puzzle books for the students along with pencils and markers. If the students are on a wet grass area or a hot or wet blacktop for their assigned area, it would be a good idea to store some kind of tarps for comfort.

When you practice for any kind of drill, make it clear to your students that this is serious business and is not the time to do any talking, giggling, pushing, shoving, or running. Serious accidents can be caused by misbehavior during this time, especially running and pushing. If you have an upper grade, make the students aware that they are role models for the younger ones. They can set the tone. If they are well behaved, the

Figure 2-1. These students enjoy the before- and after-school activities of the day-care program provided on their campus from 7:00 A.M. to 6:00 P.M. Visiting these types of programs gives teachers additional insight and perspective into the lives of their students. Courtesy of Diane Way.

younger students will see this and follow suit. Let the students know that if a gap forms in their line during the exit process, no one should run to catch up to the next student. When they get to the assigned safe area, their line will fill in automatically.

You want your students calm and listening to all directions. If they are in the classroom for a take cover drill, go around and check each student's head to be sure it is properly covered. This will not take long and they will learn the proper position for safety. Plan under which furniture *you* will get for the drill. Be sure you are properly protected in an emergency so that you can help your students later.

For an evacuation drill, the last one to leave the classroom is you; however, if there is an injured student who cannot be moved, make him as comfortable as possible. Leave some kind of marker on your door so that your room is clearly identifiable as still containing an injured student. Then go to your students in the safe area and make sure they are all there. Write the names of any missing students; write the names of any injured students; and write the name and exact location of the injured student left in your classroom. Send this information to the person(s) in charge.

Be sure you do enough practices for evacuation drills so that the students feel very confident walking out of the classroom to the assigned safe area without you. Teach them where their second exit is, which they will use if their usual exit is blocked (and it might be). Then, if there is a real emergency with a blocked exit, students will not panic. They have already been taught to use a secondary exit.

When the students are out, turn off the lights and close the doors, if it is a fire drill. Be sure a door is unlocked so that emergency responders can get into your room if they need to. Always turn off the lights. In some drills, however, the doors are left open after the class exits. *Check to see what your school policies are regarding doors.*

You will also have assigned responsibilities during an evacuation drill. You may be assigned to first aid, supervising several groups of students, meeting parents at a predetermined gate for uniting them with their children, and so on. Find out what your responsibilities are and be sure you practice them so you feel confident in case of a real emergency.

DUTIES

> Learning is not attained by chance, it must be sought for with ardor and attended to with diligence.
>
> Letter to John Quincy Adams [May 8, 1780]
> From Abigail Adams (1744–1818)

Staying informed in the field of education is a major duty. In addition to reading education-related books, stay informed by reading professional magazines and newspapers. Be alert to changes due to needs in the workplace and new legislation that may require different emphases on curricular areas. New fields of study may be inaugurated or new assessment devices established.

It is important to make sure your training is updated. Go to district **in-services,** education-related college seminars, and professional workshops.

You may have many other duties as a teacher, which need to be handled in a serious, responsible manner. One of these is yard duty. This may be in the form of before-school playground or bus duty, recess playground duty, lunch emergency supervision, and after-school playground or bus duty. When you are assigned to one of these duties, it is imperative that you are there on time. If some kind of incident happens—a fight, an injury, an emergency illness, an intimidation or incidence of bullying, a threat, a campus intruder—you will be asked for information for the school report. This may occur during duty time before or after school. Be sure the office is informed about any such problems on the school grounds or on the way to and from school.

You are responsible if you are scheduled to be on duty. Be sure you are there. Move around, be observant, and correct situations that are potentially dangerous or harmful. You are responsible for the health and safety of the students. Be prompt so nothing happens before you get there. It is your duty to enforce your school discipline system to ensure schoolwide consistency and fairness.

While you are fulfilling your responsibility on the playground or at the bus you have another opportunity to learn more about your students and the students of your school. How do they interact on the playground? Do they play well in groups? Are they arguing frequently? Are they causing problems like throwing rocks or sand or getting into fights? Do they play by themselves? Who are their playground friends? Do they seem to enjoy themselves at recess? Do they sit with a good friend for the bus ride home?

Might there be some way you could be helpful to a student who does not seem to fit or seems unhappy? For example, you could talk to two or three students and encourage them to invite a lone student into their play, or you could try to get the student interested in handball or tetherball so he could play that at recess. Keep up with these students. Ask other yard supervisors to let you know if your particular student has continuing problems on the playground. Let your student know that you care. Talk with the student. Ask him what he would like to do. What would he like *you* to do?

It is also your duty to be alert in the classroom to individual problems, such as squinting, red eyes, or other signs of vision problems; repeatedly saying "What?" when someone speaks, or complaining about not hearing things; and symptoms of possible learning problems, such as extreme inattention, extreme fidgeting, and so on.

Some duties are associated with the law. You are required to report cases of suspected or actual child abuse to the proper authorities. Be alert for signs of child neglect, too: lack of supervision, dirty clothes, infrequent bathing, obviously poor medical and dental attention and improper diet, and obvious lack of rest.

Be sure to report any vandalism, including tagging or graffiti; physical or sexual assault; use of drugs/alcohol/tobacco; and any gang activity or wannabe activity, which can also be dangerous. (*Wannabes* are students who act and/or dress as if they "want to be" in a gang. If, in fact, students actually have nothing to do with gangs, it is dangerous for them to dress "as if.")

Learn and follow the specific procedures of your district's and school's reporting system. In all probability, you will make sure the office is informed. That includes the principal, assistant principal, and the school secretaries. These people need to know what is going on at the school. Inform the school nurse and psychologist, if problems are pertinent to them. District security may need to be notified and possibly the police, too. Community resources are available if problems occur on campus, but people need to be aware of the problem in order to help.

It is also your duty, as much as is possible, to be aware of changes in the family that affect your students. Divorce situations can be trying. Be aware of court rulings that dictate unusual child custody or access settlements for one of your students. Even though the responsibility of releasing a child to a parent or guardian is with the office, it is a good idea anyway to be informed when court rulings relate to one of your own students. Death of an extended family member or a family pet, severe illness in the family, or hospitalization of a family member can all have a strong impact on your students. They need extra support from you during these times of stress.

Among your duties as a teacher is attending meetings. Faculty meetings are usually held on a regular schedule. Arrive promptly. Pay attention, and take notes on everything that affects you. It is your duty to know every time schedule and program that pertains to you. Follow the programs and be sure everything is completed on time and you are where you belong on time. There also will be professional meetings, such as in-services and workshops, teacher association meetings, and school-based council meetings. You may be asked to participate in writing your school's educational plan. Help in any way you can.

Last among your duties is taking care of supplies and working on cum files. When you use school supplies, use them carefully and return unused materials to the store room. When you work on your cum files, work carefully and in black ink. Check your school's policy regarding removal of cum files from the administration building.

All these duties are part of your responsibilities as a professional. Be alert, be a good observer, and be aware of what happens on your campus as well as what happens in your classroom.

The second section of this chapter gives some insights into early finishers, emergent literacy, and the importance of teacher expectations and evaluations.

EARLY FINISHERS

What can you do with students who finish their assignments before the rest of the class to keep them well occupied and independent?

First and foremost, all early finishers must ask themselves if they have *any* missing assignments in any subject area. If the answer is *yes,* they should get started on that immediately.

But what if the student is all finished and has no overdues? No book reports, no math pages, no state or country reports are missing. The student is totally up-to-date. You may have many students like that in your class. These students may have good

test scores, too, so they do not need additional study. What can they do?

Some students are very self-motivated. They may enjoy writing poetry or songs, dabbling in original art projects, recording imaginative entries in their journals, or writing short stories. They may be deeply intrigued with their current blockbuster book.

Others enjoy working on class projects. They can be working toward completion of a large, complicated puzzle, or they can be compiling materials for a Big Book on creature projects.

Many students appreciate the extra time to get involved in a board game. When their free time is over, they can leave the pons in place, slide the board under a piece of furniture to keep it away from the flow of traffic, and continue the same game at their next opportunity.

Oftentimes, students enjoy the listening center when they finish their work early. If you get two or three copies of the same book, students can listen to the reading and follow along in their own copies.

Other students *love* working for extra credit. Copy assignments from duplicating books that have one whole page with about a ten- to twelve-paragraph story appropriate to different grade levels followed by a full page of comprehension questions. Lots of these types of books with high-interest articles are available at any teachers' supply store. These books have reading questions, language questions, and a variety of other activities. Students can learn a lot of interesting information while practicing their skills. When students are all up-to-date in their work, they can do one or more of these and hand them in for extra credit.

Students can correct these themselves with a provided answer key. Then they can use an **Easy Grader** to write the percentage. After that, they put their paper into the **To Be Recorded box.**

Early finishers could also read a chapter out of their health, science, or history book and answer all the chapter questions or do a chapter project. Pick chapters toward the end of the book that you are not likely to cover during class time. Have an assigned student corrector use the answer key and proceed as before. Record the extra credit numbers in your grade book under the "Extra Credit" column in health, science, or history.

Another extra credit project the students like is using an encyclopedia to write a report on a subject of their choice. Have them write a one-page report and draw a diagram or illustration to accompany it. Give it a letter grade and place it in the To Be Recorded box.

Some students like extra credit points in math. Have copies in the four basic operations plus pages of word problems available. Students could get involved in measurement problems and record the measurement data and write a summary of what they discovered. They can put their projects into the **To Be Corrected** box, and the process is put into action.

If you have these specific assignments for extra credit, you will know the time, energy, and learning that goes into these. That way the students have done a good amount of work and have received at least a satisfactory grade along with feedback on missed questions or problems.

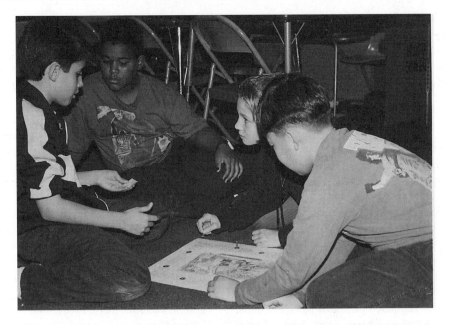

Figure 2-2.   These early finishers are playing a teacher-made geography game. Although making games is time-consuming, once they are done and laminated, they are enjoyed year after year. Activities like these keep students happily and productively busy.

Students enjoy working at the computer in their extra time, too. They can work on a continuing project, such as creative writing or poetry, and design a fancy border, font, and graphic to beautify it. Good computer software is available in many subject areas that students can use to strengthen and broaden their academic horizons.

Another activity that is excellent for learning and a great deal of fun and stimulation for the early finishers is the electronic game, Geo Safari®. Students happily learn by the hour playing this game. It has game cards that come in packets for science, history, geography, mental puzzles, and so on. Students can play at their desks by themselves or at a side area of

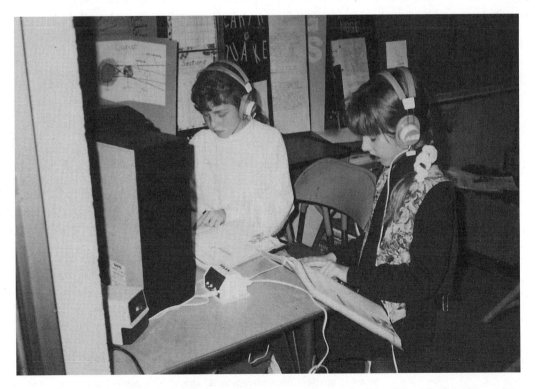

Figure 2-3.   Students who finish their assignments early can always enjoy an activity at the listening center.

the classroom with a partner or teams of partners. The buzzer included can be set for response time, which can be individualized. The students really learn this material and you will have early finishers who are well occupied and helping to keep your classroom running smoothly at the same time.

EMERGENT LITERACY

Emergent literacy refers to the beginnings or birth of both reading and writing. Such activities as holding and paging through books and scribbling are part of emergent literacy. Emergent literacy also includes dramatic play and puppetry. It involves creating narratives from the students' experiences. Telling stories, sending home easy books for the parents to read aloud to their children, and parents and teachers sharing with students wordless books and books with predictable text are all part of emergent literacy. It includes emphasizing **environmental print,** printed words or phrases that children are exposed to on a daily or regular basis, such as street signs, store names, cereal box titles, and so on. Environmental print can pertain to activities taking place within the classroom. Having class libraries in addition to a print-rich environment and a writing center and reading corner all help foster emergent literacy.

Research and Studies

Perlmutter and Laminack (1993) discuss the importance of teachers supporting all activities of emergent literacy. One example is the use of a dramatic play center. In this setting, students can use literacy-related props such as books, magazines, pencils, and so on that people might use in real-life situations. Neuman and Roskos (1993) reiterate the importance of the use of "office play," with adults acting as mediators. In addition to having notepads and pencils for scribbling and books to pretend to look up information in, labels can be placed in the "office" setting to act as environmental print. Young students can then begin to associate the written word with objects with which they are familiar. Even recognizing the initial letter of one of these words is an indicator of emergent literacy as is "child-meaningful" scribbling on a notepad and using books to "look up" information.

In a study by Aldridge and Rust (1987), at-risk first-graders were provided with an effective supplemental reading program of environmental print. They learned to read words on cereal boxes, candy wrappers, and newspaper ads. Even when identifying logos were removed, first-graders were still able to read the words.

Briggs and Richardson (1993) involved a group of second-graders in a study that emphasized environmental print as a means to literacy. Words that were in these students' environmental vocabulary were used in the classrooms and the students' teachers helped increase this list at school while the parents were encouraged to help develop and extend their children's environmental vocabulary at home.

Proudfoot (1992) points out opportunities for literacy in everyday situations. In a study done at a local laundromat, it was found that everyone there was literate while inside the laundromat. They were able to follow directions to properly operate the machines. In addition, they were able to "read" magazines or books to keep themselves entertained.

Vukelich (1993) emphasizes the importance of teachers having classrooms rich in the promotion of literacy. Kindergartners will then have many opportunities to include books, menus, pencils, crayons, and so on, even in their unstructured social interaction.

Otto's study with inner-city kindergartners (1993), also emphasized the necessity of exposing young students to the opportunity to interact with reading materials, even if they do not yet know how to read them. In her study, kindergartners used storybooks in the classroom and took several home each

Figure 2-4.   These two students have the regular assignments completed and have rushed to the excitement and challenge of Geo Safari®.

week for practice at home. The results of her study showed that all the students showed a stronger interaction with the books, and about one-third of the students even began tracking print by the end of the project.

Graves (1993) explained the emergent literacy strategy of teachers writing with their classes, explaining how they learned to write and allowing the classes to see the teachers correct mistakes in their own drafts. This provided the students with firsthand observation of the thought processes, rewriting, correcting, and proofreading that go into writing even by adults, their own teachers.

Computer use can be helpful in emergent literacy. *Hyper-Tales* is one example that can assist the emergent writer (Kelly & O'Kelly, 1993).

Use of **whole language,** including literature-based instruction, and writing instruction that uses **cooperative groups (learning groups)** for brainstorming, writing, revising, and proofing all provide a strong, supportive environment for the "emerg*ing*" writer. Study of specific vocabulary words as well as a program of formal instruction in spelling assist in the development of the writer (Allred, 1993).

Another study investigated children's awareness of how they were learning to read at home and at school (Stewart, 1992). Fifty-six kindergarten children were selected from two schools, one of which used instruction that was individualized and emphasized a whole language approach, but with language-experience activities, shared reading and writing, and phonics. In the other school, instruction was structured around a commercial phonics-based beginning program that emphasized whole-class instruction.

This study pointed out that kindergarten children can describe how they are learning to read. There are changes in how children talk about learning to read over time. There are differences in the children's awareness responses as a result of kindergarten instruction.

Home literacy is explained in part by parents' approach to literacy. Because schoolchildren have varying backgrounds and literate experiences at home, teachers should consider children's abilities and address the variation that exists in family environments within various ethnic groups. Asking children about how they are learning to read would help teachers refine instruction for young children.

The following study (Feitelson, Goldstein, Iraqui, & Share, 1993) examined the effects of reading stories in FusHa (literary or formal Arabic) to Arab kindergartners in Israel. The authors wanted to determine if the readings would have any effect on the kindergartners' understanding of FusHa (normally, an informal form of Arabic is spoken, called Aamiyya), and whether this would affect their emerging literacy skills.

Twelve kindergarten classes were randomly selected from a middle-sized Arab town in Israel. The town was selected for the study because of a low-income level and high crime rate, as well as a balanced distribution of children from different backgrounds in all the schools.

Because it was difficult to find suitable stories for the children written in FusHa, ten of the twelve stories used in this study for the treatment group were prepared especially for this study. In their final revisions, the language used in these stories was closest to Modern Standard Arabic, which is in between FusHa and Aamiyya and used in today's newspapers and other forms of media in the Arab world. However, since the teachers continued to refer to this language as FusHa, the authors used the same term.

The texts used in the control group were part of a series developed by the Early Childhood Language Development Program of the Curriculum Division of the Israeli Ministry of Education.

On listening comprehension tests, students in the experimental classes significantly outperformed those in the control classes. In the picture stories that the children in experimental classes told, they were better able to infer causal relationships from pictures and were better able to use causally connected episodes in telling their stories, as compared to the picture stories of the children in the control classes. Also, the stories told by the treatment group demonstrated they were more familiar with conventional endings to stories and were more apt to expect stories to have some sort of moral, whereas children in the control group were more inclined to describe each illustration separately, without combining them into a coherent story. Children in the treatment group also used a more varied vocabulary and proportionally more clauses.

Teachers were initially very reluctant to change their normal practices, but by the end of the study, they had changed their attitudes. Even after the study was over, teachers continued reading to their classes in FusHa and became more aware of their own vocabulary and tried to speak more correctly.

This study showed that it is possible to start the process of using a more prestigious standard language with children who grow up in **diglossic** situations before they enter school. Also, extensively exposing children to the more literary language, without demanding them to change the way they use their own oral language, resulted in the children using elements of the literary language in everyday conversation.

Another study by Otto (1991) examined emergent literacy through observations of assisted and independent storybook interactions. Two types of observations related to familiar storybooks were cited by Otto: observing students interacting with storybooks when they are able to do so independently, and observing students who need continual adult assistance with storybooks. Both groups were observed for their book handling behaviors. The students who interacted independently were also observed for their capabilities of retelling the story to a listening adult, not only for the completeness and accuracy of their retelling but also for their oral delivery. Those students who still needed continual adult assistance with storybook interaction were observed for the nature of the story segments they were able to reconstruct.

This study stated the importance of teachers carefully observing their students while this process of acquiring literacy is occurring over all the literacy-related behaviors of listening, speaking, reading, and writing, so that teachers are aware of their students' emergent literacy knowledge.

(More detailed information about the reading process is contained in Chapter 6, The PQR's. Detailed information about writing is included in Chapter 8, The V's & W's.)

EVALUATIONS

It is important to your own self-esteem and the success of your career that you get a good evaluation. If you experience any problems, get help immediately. Do not put it off thinking it will go away.

Where do you get help? Ask experienced teachers at your grade level for help. These can be teachers at your own school or from another. Ask your district mentor teachers or demonstration teachers who are at your grade level for their ideas. Ask your principal if you may take two or three personal in-service days to visit the classrooms of other excellent teachers in your district at your grade level. Take notes during your observations, and speak with the teachers after your visits. Explain your specific problems and ask for their suggestions.

Be prepared to make some changes if you want things to go differently in your classroom. You might need to be more explicit about the classroom rules and more consistent in classroom control. You might need to spend more time preparing your classes or more time detailing your lesson plans.

Being well prepared with your lessons will help your day run smoothly and will contribute to satisfactory evaluations. If you get bogged down with paperwork, and there is a lot of it, it can detract from your lesson preparation time. Get help. Have students self-correct their papers as much as is possible for your grade level. Ask a fifth- or sixth-grade student to help you with the correcting. Some of them are very accurate and competent with this and love doing it at their recess and lunch breaks. If you have a primary class, you can ask one or two upper-grade students to help in your room at their recess or lunch. Plan on a response of yes! Having tutors from another room in your classroom can be a big help, too.

Plan high-interest lessons well in advance of the day you will be teaching them. Ask experienced teachers at your grade level to critique them. Follow all good suggestions. Have all your materials ready before the day of your lessons, so everything will go well. Have a good follow-up activity planned so that the students are well occupied. Use consistent and fair discipline. Be well rested to have the energy it takes to do a good job.

Do whatever it takes to be successful, feel successful, have a good year, and receive a good evaluation.

EXPECTATIONS

High expectations are the order of every day. Expect the best from yourself. Expect the best from your students. And, a much more difficult task, teach your students to expect the best from themselves.

Help students learn to identify an area in which they would like to see improvement. Begin by focusing on one area only, but be very specific. Work in minute increments.

For example, consider the student who is interested in being neater with work, but turns in a paper that is messy. Habits are hard to break. Have this student recopy the assignment using neat printing or handwriting; then tell the student to select someone with whom to share both the original and recopied versions. If the student has done a considerably better job on the recopying, the response and reaction he'll get can be very rewarding and reinforcing.

Another example is to tell students that after fifteen minutes worth of work time, you are coming around to look at their papers to see their progress. At that time, hold up for the class to see any nice, neat papers. Encourage the students to model this type of paper. Then, quietly go to a student's desk who is not doing a neat job and encourage her to begin the assignment on a new paper.

You may have a student who expects more of himself in math. That student completes a math assignment, but when it is corrected in class, he misses quite a few problems. After explaining the problems, you could encourage the student to redo the assignment on a new piece of paper and hand it in again to you for correcting. Then the student would have the opportunity to correctly work the problems, receive some written, personal feedback from you, and maybe a stamp or sticker on his paper, too. This can be both encouraging and rewarding to the student.

Tell your students in advance that you will not be accepting assignments that are not neatly and completely done. If a problem says to explain something, tell the students you expect a full, written explanation, not a word or phrase. If they do not understand something, they are expected to get help rather than just make guesses.

Some students will arrive in your class with high expectations of themselves and excellent attitudes. But, unfortunately, others think they are "never any good at that" or "no good at anything." These are the students with low self-esteem who desperately need your guidance.

If they have papers with many errors, they may not have the attitude it takes to redo their work. Instead of an encouragement, redoing their assignment could be seen as another discouraging waste of time to them. With these students, you might want to start off by having them keep their papers and just "tell" you, on an individual basis, how they got their answers. Then you could quietly explain how the problems are done and observe them do two or three correctly. Offer praise and reassurance. Start small; work toward bigger and better.

If you start with your students and yourself at the beginning of the year continually working toward the better, after an entire school year, everyone will see that high expectations really do make a difference.

Research and Studies

In one study of 794 students in kindergarten through second grade in both public and parochial schools (Bennett, Gottesman, Rock, & Cerullo, 1993), it was determined that such subtleties as teachers' perceptions of students were linked to their judgments about student academic performance and expectation.

In a study done in Israel and New Zealand (Babad & Taylor, 1992), the same type of information was found. This study concluded that even when specific verbal information, cues, or other types of language were used, teachers being observed on videos still could be seen giving hidden messages regarding expectations through distinctive nonverbal styles.

A review of research (Ritts, Patterson, & Tubbs, 1992) found that different student expectations by teachers were based even on the physical attractiveness of the students. Physical attractiveness influenced higher and more favorable expectations not just in the social area, but also in the areas of academic ability and subject grading.

According to Hollins (1993), among the competencies for teaching today's students, especially those in diverse populations, is the necessity of identifying resources to help the teacher develop successful students so that high expectations for all students can be met. These resources might be at the school, at the district office, or in the community. High expectations for all students help promote student learning and progress.

Performance expectations (Good, 1993) provide a means of looking at the dynamics of classroom learning. Good believes that students may need to change their perceptions of teachers and even teachers may need to change their expectations of other teachers.

With performance-based assessment, it is more important than ever before that students understand that they are responsible for their learning. They come to school to get an education and they should not leave the classroom without it.

Marzano, et al. (1992) found six areas that are widely accepted and validated that deal with what students should expect to "get" at school, and what teachers and support personnel should be expected to provide. These areas include:

1. solid reasoning abilities;
2. demonstration of learning in different modes;
3. being able to get information from a number of different sources;
4. being able to communicate and work cooperatively;
5. being able to regulate self-learning; and
6. having good subject knowledge, including content, concepts, and learning strategies.

Area five is probably the most important: students having the ability to regulate their own learning. When students are in charge of their learning, they get busy on whatever their next project is after the regular classroom assignment is finished, or even in lieu of the regular assignment. All students see that a lot is expected of them. They can get interested in new areas of knowledge, become "experts" in particular areas, and act in the role of a teacher when they share their knowledge with other classmates.

Goal 3 of the National Education Goals adopted in 1990 includes the expectation that by the year 2000, students will be leaving grades 4, 8, and 12 by *demonstrating* competence in several areas, including English, geography, math, science, and history. Schools will provide an environment where students can learn to be responsible, productive citizens and ones who are interested in lifelong learning.

According to the National Assessment of Educational Progress report from 1991, however, schools need to improve student performance with higher expectations for all students. Nine-year-old students in 1991, according to the report, were not doing as well as nine-year-olds in the past. Recommendations to improve performance included more homework to extend the learning day and, specifically, more reading to replace television viewing.

It is most important to be aware of all of these types of research so that you can apply this information to yourself in your own classroom. In addition to overt expressions given to students about expectations, there are many subtle messages that can be sent of which the uninformed teacher may be unaware. Hidden messages, as well as verbal messages, also can be sent by the students to other students in regard to expectations. In this respect, the issue of expectations is much like the issue of gender equity (see Gender Equity in Chapter 3, The GHI's).

It is very important to have a supportive environment for your students, one in which they will thrive, one in which there are high expectations *for all, by all.* Work on reducing undesirable behaviors and introducing new, desirable ones that can be regularly reinforced. Emphasis can be on all students working to become better, in specific ways, than they are today.

Inform parents of the significance of reading and writing in the home. Reiterate the importance of their children completing homework assignments.

Provide a classroom atmosphere where hope is given to all students for success and acceptance.

The last section of this chapter presents some interesting curriculum programs: a facts contest, a fair, the use of field trips to enhance learning, and concrete ideas in fine arts. It discusses the importance of flexibility for a teacher and gives some helpful tips for the first day of school so that your class will run smoothly from Day One.

FACTS

Knowing math facts correctly and quickly is such a blessing. Armed with this knowledge, students can move faster through larger, more complex problems and a greater volume of work without getting discouraged. Also, once students learn the mathematical process necessary to solve a particular kind of problem, they can do these problems more quickly and with more poise when they know their facts.

In the primary grades, mastering the addition and subtraction facts is an important confidence builder. In the upper grades, keeping addition and subtraction facts polished while becoming proficient with multiplication and division facts allows students to approach the solving of mathematical problems with certainty and confidence.

Math Facts Contests

An annual math facts contest is an exciting activity that motivates students to master their facts. Students practice taking the facts tests every day in their regular classrooms for three weeks. Then, over a period of a week, they go to the school's media center or library to take their tests. If they pass there, they get a blue ribbon.

After the qualifying week goes by, next comes the race for the fastest student at each grade level. Each of these students is presented with a trophy at the school awards assembly.

If your school does not want to do this, but you do, you can always have the contest in your classroom. Ask the principal if she can take some money out of an account for you to buy award ribbons for each student who passes the test and one trophy (two, if you have a combination class) for the class winner. Or, if that is not feasible, award ribbons or certificates can be made on a computer.

The main idea is for *all* the students to pass and get a blue ribbon, so time allotments and the number of allowed errors are based on that goal.

K—Write the number one to ten in one minute with one or no errors.

K—Count out loud from one to twenty-five in one and a half minutes with two or fewer errors.

1st—Write answers for addition facts to ten in two and a half minutes with three or fewer errors.

1st—Write answers for subtraction facts to ten in two and a half minutes with three or fewer errors.

2nd—Write answers for all addition facts in two minutes with three or fewer errors.

2nd—Write answers for all subtraction facts in two minutes with three or fewer errors.

3rd—Write answers for multiplication facts to fives in one and three-fourths minutes with three or fewer errors.

4th, 5th, and 6th—Use a **T-sheet** for multiplication. Different T numbers can be given each time to keep students really on their toes, or you can use the same ones all the time. See Figure 2-5 for a sample T.

The teacher gives the T number; in the case of Figure 2-5, it is 7. The students write each T number on top of each T. When time begins, they write the answers.

4th—Write answers for all multiplication facts on a T-sheet in three minutes with three or fewer errors.

4th—Write answers for all division facts in two and a half minutes with three or fewer errors.

5th—Write answers for all multiplication facts on a T-sheet in two and a half minutes with three or fewer errors.

5th—Write answers for all division facts in two minutes with three or fewer errors.

Sample T

$$
\begin{array}{c|c}
 & 7 \\
\hline
5 & 35 \\
4 & 28 \\
9 & 63 \\
7 & 49 \\
etc. & etc. \\
\end{array}
$$

Figure 2-5.

6th—Write answers for all multiplication facts on a T- sheet in two minutes with three or fewer errors.

6th—Write answers for all division facts in one and three-fourths minutes with three or fewer errors.

In Figure A2-1 in the appendix, you will find addition, subtraction, multiplication, and division facts study sheets to use with grade levels first through sixth.

(*Note:* If you have not already read the introduction to this book, now would be a good time to do so. It explains the coding system used for all the elementary student activity sheets. With this system, only you will know if the material is suitable for primary grades or for upper grades. That way, if you wish to use some of the "primary" materials in "upper" grades, and you may very well want to with some or all of your class, the upper-grade students will not see what level the material is. At the top of all the activity pages in the appendix of each of the chapters, *Pt* stands for primary [think *Primary time*] and § stands for upper or intermediate [think *Secondary Section*]).

Finger Method for Multiplication

In addition to the facts study sheets, some **Finger Facts** study pages are included in the appendix. These are for students who have a difficult time learning their multiplication facts in the traditional manner. Usually, these are students who rely heavily on their fingers when computing addition and subtraction facts. This allows them the use of their fingers in computing for multiplication. This could be used with fifth- or sixth-grade students who still have trouble with multiplication facts.

Since the students will probably already know their twos and fives, these are good ones to begin with so that students get the idea of the finger method quickly. Students place their hands palms down on their desks, their fingers spread out, and their left pinky raised in the air. They have now nine fingers to work with. The right thumb is for "one," the right index finger for "two," and so on. The left thumb is for "six," the left index finger for "seven," and so on.

If, for example, the students are multiplying by 5, they "play" (like their desktop is a piano) their "one" thumb and say the answer, 5, aloud. (5 times 1 is 5.) Then they play their "two" finger and say the answer, 10, aloud. (5 times 2 is 10.) Then, as they play the appropriate finger, they continue to say aloud: 15, 20, 25, 30, 35, 40, 45 for the rest of the fives.

If they are practicing their sevens, they play their fingers in order and say aloud: 7, 14, 21, 28, 35, 42, 49, 56, 63. It is much easier for some students to memorize the answers for the facts in order than to try to master multiplication facts in the traditional way. If the fact is 7 times 6, they start reciting their sevens until their sixth finger is down and they will have the answer.

If the fact is 9 times 8, they start playing their fingers while reciting the nines aloud until they have played their eighth finger. Then they will have the answer. They would say: 9, 18, 27, 36, 45, 54, 63, 72. This also allows these students to easily see the number pattern of the difference of five between numbers in the series or the difference of nine between the numbers of the series.

If students are going to use this system, they should be sure they use the *same* fingers for addition and subtraction counting, assuming they count on their fingers, as they use for multiplication counting. In other words, if their left thumb is a six for them in addition and subtraction, it should be a six for them in multiplication, too.

It is, of course, preferable for students to compute without the use of their hands, but for some students, this actually holds them back because they have a retention problem.

Later, this system helps students select common denominators more easily because they see the number pattern for the answers to multiplication facts.

In addition to the facts study sheets, test papers are included in the appendix with the time allotments and number of errors allowed for a pass at each grade level. You will help the students get the facts job accomplished and feed a lot of excitement into your curriculum at the same time.

For information on other math areas, see Math in Chapter 5, The MNO's, and Research Skills in Chapter 6, The PQR's.

FAIR

Having a science fair in your classroom is something you might want to do in the spring. If you give specific directions to the students, it can turn out great.

The students can have a good time as well as be successful with their projects if they are willing to do two things:

1. Spend a good amount of time on their projects over a period of a few weeks. Some students will be so moti-

vated, they will spend hours doing their project. It will be terrific, too.

For other students, a suitable amount of time will be spent if you schedule a specified amount of homework time for their project over the period, provide a particular amount of classroom time with defined aspects of the project to be completed during that time, and send the general instructions for the science fair, with a due date, home for parent signatures.

2. Select a project that is realistic for their abilities and one that they find enticing.

Provide some broad parameters for the topics so students do not feel too constricted. If students need help deciding, furnish them with specific, grade-level-appropriate topics. Experiments right from their own science books can be great. Check at your school or in your district with other teachers at your grade level. Ask them for projects with which their students have had success.

Establish a date by which students will report to you their exact topics, what materials or resources they need, and from where they are getting them.

Copy into your lesson plan book who is doing which project so you do not have several students doing the same one.

The students can copy into their composition books the date the project is due and exactly what their project is going to be about.

Maybe it will be a collection of natural materials, like rocks, leaves, items that are recyclable, flowers, different types of soil, and so on. The collection can also be done with photos,

Figure 2-6. This student proudly displays his science fair project on earthquakes, complete with a model Richter scale.

Figure 2-7.   Assembling this truck's engine kept this student busy with his fair project.

magazine pictures, or hand-drawn pictures of things, such as different types of birds, pets, animals in the wild, or weather in different parts of the world.

Maybe it will be a model of some scientific thing, like a model of the solar system, or the layers of the Earth, or a model of a body organ such as the heart or ear. These models can be made out of clay or plaster of Paris and baked and painted.

Several students might want to do experiments. They might like to try an experiment which shows how salt is removed from water or an experiment that shows which foods contain starch or which materials are good conductors of electricity. Experiments are fun, but they are more difficult. Students will need to practice enough so that they will be able to confidently do and explain the experiment during the science fair.

Figure A2-2 in the appendix is a sample science fair form you can use in your classroom. Have the students write the date the project is due. Then they take the form home and have their parents sign it so that there are no surprises. Make the parent signature part of the students' regular homework to be recorded into the assignment accountability chart. Then let the students astonish you and their classmates with their completed projects!

More information on teaching science, apart from the fair, is in Chapter 7, The STU's, under Science.

FIELD TRIPS

What a way to learn!

Prepare your class for a field trip. Often, the place you are going to will send preparatory materials if you ask. These are usually quite good. For example, if you are going to a youth symphony at the performing arts center, you will get a work booklet for each student as well as a tape to play for your class. If you are going to an IMAX (Image Maximizing) theater, you will get some activity materials that can be copied for your class. Repertory companies who perform plays and musicals usually have some good materials. A variety of children's theater companies have some excellent theater productions. Arboretums and historical sites are other interesting places that usually have ready-made materials for field trips.

If prepared materials are not available, have students do research on one of the topics to be studied on the field trip. If there will be a question and answer period, have them prepare some questions in advance.

If you usually go on a particular field trip each year, you might want to make up your own materials. For example, if you take your class to Mission San Juan Capistrano in California, have questions for the students to answer or observations for them to write as they explore the mission grounds. You might want to have these types of activity pages for a trip to the zoo, a museum, or cities like San Francisco, New York, and Washington, D.C.

If students need to learn specific information on a trip or make particular observations, let them know ahead of time. Sometimes it is not possible to record information on paper while on the trip. It might be too windy at the tidepools or too dark at the planetarium. Students may be in kindergarten or first or second grade, and too young to proficiently record information. Encourage all these students to take their sharpened memories on the field trip.

If you take young students to a farm or small petting zoo, you may want them to be able to make or describe the sounds

Figure 2-8. Constellations that light up make a super fair project for this student. She is able to carefully and thoroughly explain her project to the other students.

the animals make. Students may have the opportunity to touch the animals so that they can later describe the texture of their skin or fur. What does the animal's tail look like? What about its ears and eyes? What does it eat? Remind the students, also, to listen carefully to the information the docent or guide provides. Later they may be drawing or coloring their favorite farm or petting zoo animal or taking part in a story dictation.

Thorough planning for a field trip helps ensure a successful and fun day. It is usually more fun to go with another class and less expensive, too. The cost of the bus can be shared by two classes. Schedule the bus well before the trip, especially for a trip toward the end of the year when district buses can be very busy.

Find out what bus charges and admission fees are. If you have school or Parent Teacher Association (PTA) funds to cover these expenses, that's great. Otherwise, send field trip permission slips home two to three weeks before the scheduled trip with the amount each child needs to pay. If a family has a financial problem, usually the PTA will take care of the fees for that child if you just ask nicely.

Collect all permission slips and take them with you on the trip. If an emergency occurs, you have parent phone numbers right there. No student goes on an off-campus trip without a permission slip.

It is always helpful to have a few parents along. (For some field trips, the place where you take the children may *require* the adult-to-student ratio to be one to ten.) Divide the students into compatible groups and have each group report to a parent. Have one group report to you. Give each parent a list of the students reporting to him or her. Let each parent know that any student causing trouble should be sent directly to you.

Prepare your class for appropriate behavior on a field trip, including exactly what is expected of them regarding the bus ride, behavior at the field trip location, use of the bathrooms, snacks, lunch, and responsibility for checking with parent supervisors. Do not allow a student to leave a parent group without a buddy and a verbal report to the parent in charge. Remind students to check with the parent upon returning. This is vitally important.

Have certain check times for parents: before lunch, after lunch, thirty minutes before bus boarding for use of the bathrooms, and twenty minutes before boarding. No student should leave the group during this last twenty minutes. Any problems should be immediately reported to the teacher at that twenty-minute check.

Count heads frequently throughout the field trip. Five minutes before the bus is to leave, board. Count heads again as a double check with the parents' count. Then you will be ready to depart on time. Bus drivers appreciate it if you leave when you say. One o'clock means 1:00, not 1:20 or 1:30. Leaving late causes bus drivers to be late for pickups at their assigned school.

When each and every student is carefully accounted for, when students know what is expected and are well behaved, the trip will be a pleasant experience for all.

After you return to school, have some follow-up activities planned for either that day or the next. The students will need to conclude their research with their firsthand observations. They could make an individual booklet with illustrations and informative captions, or a class booklet could be made including the students' drawings, research, and observations. Students could use clay or papier-mâché to make some of the items they observed. Or they could report to the class on one

Figure 2-9.   A field trip to a small petting zoo or a farm is an enjoyable learning experience, especially for young city students. Courtesy of Essa and Rogers, *An Early Childhood Curriculum: From Developmental Model to Application,* © 1992 by Delmar Publishers, Inc.

subtopic of what they learned: black holes, for example, or a particular star or constellation, or an animal.

Well-prepared field trips are a delight for all and a truly sound learning experience.

FINE ARTS

Fine arts can be a pleasure to teach, and most students find this area of the curriculum to be very enjoyable. The field of fine arts has four components: art, dance, drama, and music.

Art

Slow and steady wins the race.

> Aesop fl. c. 550 B.C.
> *The Hare and the Tortoise*

For excellent art projects, encourage your students to take their time to do a really nice job. Even simple art projects require a lot of time to look good. For example, a hand art project may sound simple. On a piece of construction paper, have students trace one of their hands a few times, overlapping it on the paper. Then they color in the many sections. Maybe one section will be stripes, another polka dots, another different-colored geometric figures, and so on. This takes a great deal of time to complete but looks fabulous when done.

Another example is outlining in pencil a relatively simple drawing on a piece of construction paper 4½ inches by 6

inches. Instead of coloring in what they drew, have students dot in the drawing with the tip of a fine-line marker. They should make no lines on the paper, only dots. This is a demanding art project, but the finished product looks beautiful.

Except for very young students, ask students to bring in sets of markers or colored pencils from home. Projects will look so much better than those done in crayon. For younger students, however, large crayons are easier to work with and, for kindergartners especially, use of paints at the easel is a very enjoyable experience.

When you are preparing for a project, think of all the different media you could use:

- papier mâché for maps or masks
- clay for pots or volcanoes
- construction paper—small, torn pieces to fill outlines or pieces in a variety of geometric figures
- markers
- colored pencils
- crayon
- paint—tempera and watercolor
- crepe paper
- tissue paper
- toothpicks
- beans
- wallpaper
- sunflower seeds

Figure 2-10. This kindergartner is enjoying herself at an easel using tempera paints. Her clothes are well protected, so she can paint with abandon. Courtesy of Essa, *Introduction to Early Childhood Education,* © 1992 by Delmar Publishers, Inc.

Figure 2-11. When kindergarten students have the assistance of a parent helper or volunteer right at their group's table, their artistic creativity can flow uninterrupted. Courtesy of Essa, *Introduction to Early Childhood Education,* © 1992 by Delmar Publishers, Inc.

- pretzels
- lifesavers

Some of these can be mixed together in the same project for a different look.

Especially in kindergarten, have all the needed art materials placed at various tables around the room. Volunteers or older elementary students can help you with this. Young students can then work in small groups with an aide or parent volunteers. This setting allows them to be creative, but at the same time have some assistance with the art media. If they have questions or problems, some knowledgeable person is right there to help.

You can think up your own art projects, visit your instructional media center/curriculum lab for many ideas, or purchase one of a variety of reproducible art project books from your teacher supply store. Some books have nice stand-up art projects. Some have special art projects to coordinate with history units on Lincoln and Washington, or to use in conjunction with Presidents' Day. Integrating art with your existing classroom themes makes learning interesting and gives it an enjoyable dimension.

You might want to select a weaving project, make a place mat or an ornament, decorate an invitation, or do a painting on an easel. You might want your project to be class participation in a poster contest or drawing contest. Maybe you will do a sewing project.

Whole series of art lessons are also available for the VCR. Students are taught by an artist and shown such things as shading, texturing, and perspective. Students do their art right along with the artist, following the directions and examples. Check to see if your school or district has a set of art videotapes.

After you have decided on a project, have all your materials and samples together before your class lesson. If certain mate-

rials need to be cut for the project, have that done before your lesson. It is a good idea to put the steps of the art project on the board so students do not get lost. Encourage the students to let their imaginations fly. However they want to do it will be fine. You will usually be pleasantly surprised.

The more organized you are, the better the lesson will be. Let the students know in advance that you expect a finished project from each one and that you will be marking it in some way in your grade book, either by giving it a grade or by just recording that the project was completed. Then keep one set of all materials for projects that worked well. Keep this set in your permanent art file.

Button art is a project that always turns out well. About a week before you schedule this project, ask the students to start bringing in any sized buttons in any color. Have them bring in their markers, too. You will need one piece of 9-inch by 12-inch yellow or pink construction paper for each student. Thermofax the master outline in Figure A2-3 in the appendix. Ditto it onto the pieces of construction paper. Also have a set of glue sticks.

On the day of the project, have the students take out their markers and buttons. Pass out the construction paper with the pattern on it. Have the students use their markers to outline and color in everything totally. No purple ditto line should show. Have them do their very best coloring. Then on top of the circles, have them glue on their buttons. Lay flat to dry. (See Figure 2-12.)

A string art project is another one that turns out well, but this is more difficult; however, students as early as beginning fourth grade can do a good job on it. Kindergartners and other primary students can do a good job if they are permitted to produce their own work and not follow a model.

For students using a pattern for their string art project, first, chop up enough pieces of 8-inch by 10-inch colored **railroad**

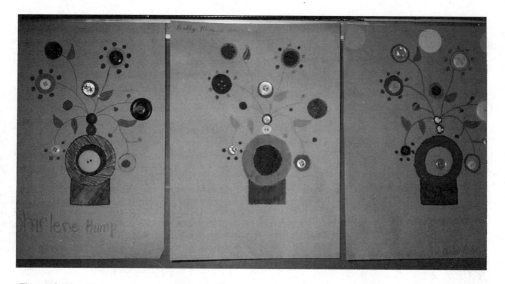

Figure 2-12.   Button art projects are beautiful.

board so that each student has one. Next, go to a yarn store and purchase different colors of thread (string) about the thickness of string. Buy a class set of blunt big-eyed needles. The needles can be used for years and the string can be used for several sewing projects. From your school's supply room or from other teachers' classrooms, get a class set of compasses. The sharp end of these will be used to poke holes later in the project.

Copy a class set of the master "Patriotic Stars" on white paper. ("Patriotic Stars" sheets are in the appendix. See Figure A2-4.) Use the chopper to trim the excess past the black-lined frame on the master. Copy a class set of "Patriotic Stars" instruction sheets. Get a class set of 9-inch by 12-inch construction paper. Select colors that will look nice as a border for your colored tag. Have a roll of masking tape, several pairs of scissors, and a set of glue sticks.

On the day of the project, have the thread and scissors out on a side table. Have students hang four pieces of masking tape about 2½ to 3 inches long on the edge of each student's desk. Let students select the color of tag they want. Pass out a "Patriotic Stars" pattern, instruction sheet, and a compass to each student. Write down each student's name as you give out a needle. (When the project is over, collect either the needle or money to replace a misplaced needle from each student.)

Roll up each piece of masking tape and place them on the four corners of the back of the "Patriotic Stars" pattern page. Affix this to the back of the colored tag.

Next, on the carpet or some relatively soft material, lay down the pattern and use the sharp point of the compass to poke through all the holes. Do not poke through too far or one hole could rip into another.

Now it is time to sew. Follow the instructions page. Whenever it is time to cut, the students cut the thread on the pattern side only, leaving about an extra inch or so of thread. Then they should use a piece of masking tape to tape aside that piece of string. If a student runs out of thread, even though it does not say "cut," that student should cut anyway and tape down the extra inch or so of yarn. Students should never cut on the good side of the tag because that side is their final project side.

Each star can be done in a different color of thread. Some students even do each section of each star in different colors. As each "Down-Up" is done, have the students cross it out so that they do not lose their places.

When all the sewing is done on the pattern, students often like to poke additional holes for their names to be sewn onto the project. They also enjoy sprinkling a little bit of glitter on their projects.

After this, each student will select a 9-inch by 12-inch piece of colored construction paper for the frame. Glue the pattern side to the good side of the construction paper. The project is finished and will look super.

You might want to schedule two or three art periods for this project, depending on the proficiency of your students. Be sure to demonstrate taping on the pattern page, threading a needle, cutting, and gluing on the backing or frame.

The students will get proficient at these string art projects and produce some excellent work. Once they get the idea, they can create their own sewing projects.

After these and other art projects are finished, hang them up. They can be put on a bulletin board, put up on the walls, put on a lined and bordered voting booth, taped to a chalkboard, or hung from the lights or ceiling. Your classroom will come alive and the students are pleased to see their projects displayed.

The last part of doing art projects is not always enjoyable, but it is a necessity. The classroom needs to be cleaned. All the art materials must be stored, glue bottles cleaned and put away, paints tidied and put in the cupboard, and any cups used to hold paint or water rinsed in the sink, dried, and shelved. Last, any scraps of paper or material left on the floor or out at the tables need to be trashed and the sink and counter areas need to be washed and dried.

Even beginning kindergarten students can help with classroom cleanup. Make it a game. Count out loud to "two" and each student picks up one piece of trash. While music is playing kindergartners throw the trash in the wastebasket. Then count aloud to "three" and they pick up another piece of trash. Play music and they throw it in the trash.

Figure 2-13. These fourth- and fifth-grade students are busy sewing a string art project like "Patriotic Stars." Students need to know how to thread a needle, and threaders help some students. They also need to know where to tie the knot on the string and how to use masking tape to secure their thread to the back of the project paper.

After demonstrating how it is done, permit kindergartners to take turns cleaning the sink and adjacent countertop, too. This helps them develop responsibility and pride in a well-done job that not only benefits them but the whole class.

Figure 2-14. Even at an early age, students can learn to help with cleaning up after an art project. Show them *what* to do and *how* to do it so that they will do a good job. Courtesy of Charlesworth, *Understanding Child Development,* 3e © 1992 by Delmar Publishers, Inc.

Dance

For the things we have to learn before we can do them, we learn by doing them.

Aristotle
Nicomachean Ethics Bk I

Dancing can be lots of fun for everyone. In addition to preparing the lesson, make sure to adequately explain to the students what you expect from them as far as behavior and participation are concerned. Involved students are productive ones.

Occasionally, though, you may have a handful of students who use this time as an opportunity to "act up," which can interfere with or spoil the experience for the others. A good way to handle this problem, should it arise, is to have your grade book with you. Under the fine arts section, write the name of your dance lesson. Then tell the students that right now, at the beginning of the lesson, everyone has an A. They will keep the A unless they do something specific to lose it.

The first time a student has a problem with behavior or participation, make a small mark in your grade book box by that student's name. If the same student has another problem, make another small mark in the box, and so on. Tell the students that those who have no marks at the end of the lesson will have an A recorded in their box; one mark, a B; two marks, a C; three marks, a D; and four or more marks, an F. Be sure you mark "absent" for any student not in the room for the dance lesson. Otherwise a student who was not even in the room would get an *A* because there would obviously be no marks in that box. This system works very well in the upper grades. It keeps students on track and productive while making the dance lesson a pleasure for *all* the students and the teacher.

The primary grades do well with simple dances, like "The Hokey Pokey" and the "Virginia Reel."

For folk and square dancing, be sure you are proficient at following the calls yourself before you begin teaching. You can pick up good folk and square dancing records either from your district or a local music store.

Move the furniture to the sides of the classroom or take your music system outside. It makes no difference if boys are partnered with boys or with girls and vice versa. Let the students select their own partners in the beginning. They will be more relaxed. Have the students watch as you teach a couple of steps to one square or group. Then play just that part of the record, tape, or CD until all the students are good at that part. Continue in segments like that until eventually the students get through the entire song. This will take a number of lessons. Do only a couple of steps at a time so that students do not get discouraged.

If you have upper-graders, who are more self-conscious, you can give the entire class an assignment. Then when everyone is busy working, call one small group over to the side of the classroom and work with that group on one or two steps. First teach without the music. Then let them practice to the music. Then have that group sit down and call another small group and so on. The students feel less self-conscious because they think their classmates are busy with an assignment, even though really they are all watching out of the corner of their eyes.

You can always choreograph your own dance to a musical piece you particularly like. It is easiest if you have a dance routine with some repetition in different parts of the song. The students will feel a lot of success and remember the dance more easily when they know that after they dance to a certain section of music, their routine will be repeated later in the song.

For an extra nice effect, you might let the students use rhythm sticks during the dance. They can shake them, click them, and cross them with their partner's sticks. This really emphasizes the beat of the music.

For a performance, when you want a little extra show and color, colored scarves could be used or various colors of crepe paper strips could be stapled to the ends of the rhythm sticks. Orange, yellow, pink, and sky blue look beautiful together. Save the tasseled sticks for a dress rehearsal because the tassels get ragged, ripped, and fall off after too many dances. It is worth the extra work, though, for a fabulous show.

Drama

For successful drama lessons, just follow the class management suggestions under Dance each time you meet for drama.

You might want to put on a play or puppet show for your students' parents, for another classroom, or just for your class's enjoyment.

Select plays appropriate to your grade level from your reading book or books on plays at your public library or from reproducible books at your local teachers' supply store.

Even more exciting than selecting plays is having your class write its own plays or role-play favorite stories. Divide your class into groups of seven to ten. Give your class a general topic such as winter excitement or holiday surprise. Have each group discuss what it would like to do for a play. Each group will list as many ideas as it can and vote on the favorite. Tell the groups right off that there must be at least as many characters as there are members of the group. Explain to the groups that you want from them the title of each play, a list of the characters, and a general idea of what the play is about.

A group recorder should write the information on a piece of paper and have it ready to give to you for your approval. In addition, after the groups have this much done, they should decide which two people in the group will actually write the play and give those names to you. Set a time limit for this group meeting—usually two different meeting times is best, about thirty to forty minutes each.

After you have explained script format, the playwrights can get together in their free time to write. You will probably need to assign some class time to them also.

When the first draft of the script is finished, the groups can meet again to make whatever changes they like and to select one student to type the first half and one to type the second half. Check the scripts at this time to be sure they are appropriate for the classroom.

Then a second draft can be written by the playwrights. After this has been carefully edited, give it to the two typists. These students can type it in the computer lab during class time or lunch time. Be sure they save it. After it is printed, look at it again. Make any necessary corrections. Then the typists can edit and print out a final copy. Make a copy for yourself and each member of the group. Do not forget to tell the playwrights and typists that you are giving them lots of extra credit in writing and drama.

The groups will need to meet to decide who will make scenery, exactly what they will make, and who will bring props. They can write a list of materials they will need. Some of the props they may need to get on their own. You can get the rest from the supply room.

If the students are doing a puppet show, they will need to make their puppets at home. Students can use styrofoam balls or sticks for the main frame of the puppet. Yarn can be used for hair, and felt pieces or other cloth can be used for clothing. Styrofoam balls can be decorated with paint, too.

Students will need plenty of time to practice so that they are very good. They need to be reminded to use extremely loud voices, enunciate clearly, and speak slowly so that they can be heard and understood. They need to practice "no talking" on stage except for their speaking parts. They also need to practice introducing their play and their characters and bowing.

A voting booth makes an excellent puppet stage. Three windows can be cut into the booth and each piece of excess cardboard can be folded down for a stage. The voting booth can be lined with colored butcher paper and then decorated. If your puppet show is going to take place in the winter time, it can be lined with brick corrugated paper and then decorated. This looks very sharp! String can be used to attach each end of the voting booth to stationary objects in the front of the classroom

Figure 2-15. The stage is a voting booth with three windows cut into it. Corrugated paper that looks like brick lines the stage and green velvet provides the backdrop. The students use stick puppets for this show.

above the chalkboard. One string can attach the center of the booth to an overhead lighting fixture so that the booth will not fall over when the play group is behind it. Lightweight material can be hung over the two side strings to hide the students behind the stage. Lightweight material can also be hung behind the windows of the voting booth to form a backdrop for the puppets.

If you follow these ideas, everyone will have a good time, including you, and the play or puppet show will be a great success. Videotape it and the students can enjoying seeing them-

selves and their classmates perform at a later date. (A sample classroom play about King Midas, which could be used at the primary grades, is included for enjoyment in your classroom. See Figure A2-5 in the appendix.)

Music

For enjoyment in this area of fine arts, use the same management system as that under Dance.

There are many different music lessons you can use and be successful and still have a good deal of variety:

Figure 2-16. These students, who use both cloth and stick puppets, are introducing their puppets to the audience.

- A lesson on staff, notes, and rests. Use any beginning piano music book to help you. When the students are competent, you can give them a short quiz and record their quiz grade under fine arts-music. Students can pretend they are playing the piano on their desks. This is very suitable for upper grades.
- Singing a song with the accompaniment of a record or CD. Use a music book (in the older grades) and record to get started or practice with the piano or guitar.
- Singing along with accompaniment—piano, guitar, record, auto harp, and so on. Sing certain types of songs, like those about U. S. history or patriotic songs. Be sure the music is loud so children feel uninhibited. They could have some laminated color pictures that illustrate parts of the song. When the appropriate part is sung, a student can hold up that picture. Students at all grade levels enjoy this.
- Singing rounds, like "Row, Row, Row Your Boat." This is more difficult but can be done at least at second grade and beyond.
- Singing descant. This requires quite a bit of practice, but when the students are good, they can sound very professional. Use a record for accompaniment. This is suitable for a performance and is probably best for upper grades.
- Listening to famous pieces and identifying title and composer. You can record parts of famous musical works on a tape, or play for the class different parts on a record or records. The students lose interest if the whole piece is played. Select about four different pieces. Have the titles written correctly on the board along with the composer's name after each title. When the students are proficient, give them a little quiz. Leave the information on the board, but keep mixing up the parts of the pieces and see if they can get them right. Then record their quiz grades. In the primary grades, the quiz can be simply telling their partners the name of the piece. In the upper grades, a pencil-paper test is fine.
- Listening to different types of music and identifying types, like classical, jazz, blues, rock, and so on. Again, you can use a tape or records. Follow the procedure for famous pieces. This is a more difficult skill and more appropriate for upper grades.
- Making instruments from cardboard or rubber bands, by poking holes, and so on. If the instruments are quite simple, they can be made with partners in a primary grade.
- Using rhythm instruments—tambourine, triangle, castanets, and bells—to accompany music. All age students like this, but the music needs to be extremely simple for the younger grades. More sophisticated rhythms are good for upper grades.
- Bringing instruments from home to school and playing a demonstration piece. The students can also identify their instruments and explain how they work. In an early primary grade, a parent could bring an instrument to class to show and play for the young students.
- Attending music assemblies. These are fun for any grade level, but at the primary assembly, it works well if the assembly time is quite short, like twenty minutes. Upper grades can be interested for forty-five minutes.
- Watching music programs on TV, especially for primary grades.
- Going on a field trip to a concert. As long as the concert has a program appropriate for your age-level students, this can be exciting from first grade up. It provides the students an opportunity to see a concert hall and hear professionals or youth professionals perform. School may be the only time some students have this experience.

FIRST DAY OF SCHOOL

A journey of a thousand miles must begin with a single step.

Lao-tzu (c. 604–531 B.C.)
from *The Way of Lao-tzu*

One of the most exhilarating days of the year is the first day of school. Students are anxious and eager to meet their new teacher, to see some of their classmates they have not seen since school was last in session, and to continue the exciting and stimulating learning process.

For you, the teacher, the most important thing is to be extremely well prepared or even overly prepared so that your day will move along smoothly and you can be of great help to your students.

Before this day ever begins, make sure you have attractive bulletin boards already up and all the students' textbooks, two sharpened pencils, crayons, a ruler, and three or four pieces of paper in each desk. Have all activity sheets run off, art paper out, and whatever is needed for your first-day lessons and home-school communications from the office. Your lesson plan book should be specific. Exactly what are you going to cover the first day? That will ensure that you will be ready for your students.

Next, have a name tag on each desk. Then students will know exactly where to sit. If you know in advance that a particular student needs to sit near the front of the class because of a vision, hearing, or learning problem, you can place that student where you think best. If you already know that certain students talk a lot or are in some way disruptive, place their name tags far away from each other. Surround them with model students. This will help them get started on the right track.

Place desks in an arrangement you are comfortable with and one that will not invite disruptions. You might want to put the desks in rows to get the year started. This allows for minimal interaction between individual students and is a good way to start out safely and confidently.

When students are involved in group learning, they can move chairs or desks to appropriate locations throughout the classroom. Have some tables set up with chairs at them so the students can use those locations for their groups, too. This movement provides the students with a nice energizer periodically throughout the day.

Later, after maybe four to five weeks, when things are moving along well, you may wish to rearrange the seats into different grouping patterns.

Before you begin class, introduce yourself, take roll, lunch count, and do the flag salute. Next, it is vitally important to slowly and carefully present the school rules (get a copy from your principal) to your class. Then you can direct the students, if you like, in developing a set of appropriate classroom rules. You may feel more comfortable starting out with a list of rules you think appropriate and revising them at a later date. Either way, be sure when they are ready that they are posted.

It is helpful to demonstrate the exact type of behavior you expect so that there is no uncertainty in the students' minds. Even though this can be tedious, it is necessary that your students know right from the beginning what you and the school expect from them. Begin enforcing these rules immediately, right on the first day of school. Enforce class and school rules equally and consistently so that the students know you mean business for everyone, without exception, all the time.

Now take the students on a practice evacuation drill to show them exactly where and how to evacuate if there is an emergency requiring evacuation. Explain duck and cover. Have students get under desks using their arms to protect their eyes and head. Let students know there is no talking or giggling during a drill. A drill and all practices are serious matters.

Next, especially if you teach kindergarten or first grade, show students where things they will need in the classroom are: paper drawer, glue cabinet, drinking fountain, and so on. Explain and show where your class plays at recess and lunch, where the bathrooms are, where lunch is eaten, and how to enter and exit the school grounds.

If you teach kindergarten or first grade, or you have a lot of non-English-speaking students, you might want to have labels around the classroom to help your students with the printed word. For example, at the drinking fountain, you could have printed clearly in lowercase on a piece of white tag "drinking fountain" or "I can get a drink here at the drinking fountain." Make sure you print it so it will match what the students will be seeing in their reading books. On the paper drawer, your sign could say "paper" or "This drawer has paper," and so on, and have an illustration to go with the wording.

You may have important papers to discuss with the students. There may be emergency cards for them to take home for their parents to complete. There may be first-day bulletins from the office that need to be discussed. You may have a parent letter to read and send home with your students.

Find out whether your class has any new students if you teach first through sixth grade. Appoint a buddy for each so that they get to know their way around and feel comfortable and accepted.

Finally, you will have time before recess to begin your first instructional lesson. Use the Blueprint for Effective Teaching in Chapter 7, The STU's, so it will be a good lesson. You might decide to have the students draw a picture of one thing they did during their vacation. Then they could tell the class about it while they show their picture. Or students could write a couple of sentences or a paragraph to go with their pictures and read this while they show their pictures to the class. Kindergarten students can draw the picture and you can write a dictated story.

If you have an early primary class or one with many students new to the school, you might ask the students to introduce themselves before they begin speaking about their drawings. This will make a nice lesson incorporating art, writing,

and speaking and will give the students a chance to get to know a little about their classmates.

Collect the papers after the students have their names on them. Be sure to collect a finished product from every student. When they do a good job, let them know.

While the students are working on this activity you can begin recording the students' textbook numbers in your grade book; students are accountable for these books being returned in a similar condition at the end of the year. Some schools have textbook accountability sheets from the office to send home with students.

Next, you could teach a handwriting or printing lesson. Model at the board or on the overhead what you would like the students to do.

A math lesson could follow. Make it easy enough so that all the students can be successful. You can tell the more advanced students to make up some harder problems for themselves or you can give them a challenging math-art activity sheet.

When the students are finished with their math assignment, read the answers to them in class. Let them correct their own papers. Encourage questions if they do not understand why an answer is wrong. Check to be sure all students have finished the assignment. If not, write their names down and check to be sure you collect their papers later that day or the next day and record them on the assignment accountability chart.

Now you could introduce to the class a book you enjoy very much. Tell them a little bit about it. Begin reading it to the class. Have them listen attentively. Ask questions as you read along so that you know your students are involved. Walk around the class to show the pictures so that everyone can see them clearly.

You might like to begin a social studies lesson. Introduce the new material thoroughly. Go over all new vocabulary. It is best to plan an activity that requires little reading until you are knowledgeable about your students' reading abilities. A map activity might be appropriate. Correct it together in class and let the students fix any errors. Then collect the assignment. Get a paper from each student.

If you have maps or vacation activities that the students did that look nice, you can mount them on colored construction paper and decorate your classroom with them.

Whatever other lessons or activities you want to fill your first day with, be sure it is *filled*.

Let the students go back individually or in pairs to select a book from your classroom library. Then students who finish an assignment early will have something to do at their desks.

Toward the end of the day, stop early enough to have the students gather together all the papers and forms they need to take home. Then summarize with your students before they go home. What did they learn today? What forms do they need to return the next day? How was the students' behavior? Their attitude? Their work habits? When they get lined up and ready to go, walk to the door and talk to your students as they leave. "Good-bye!" "See you tomorrow!" "Good job today," and so on.

What a day you have had! You are off to a great start.

Especially for the next few days, review at the beginning of each day where things are, what the daily schedule is (post it), what the class and school rules are, and what your expectations for the students are.

Collect all emergency card information. You might want to make copies of these cards for your personal file to have easy access to student addresses, phone numbers, and parent work numbers. You can also note with whom each of your students lives. Be sure to copy the parent signature, too, for future reference.

Collect any other forms sent home, such as library book and textbook responsibility forms and classroom management forms.

Then review at the end of each day how things went. Are your expectations being met? Are *all* the students turning in their assignments? Is classroom behavior excellent? Are students' work habits excellent? If there are problems, begin to work on them right away. Do not delay and let them get worse. Maybe some student needs a tutor. Communicate any major problems to the principal. Explain what you are doing in the classroom to help resolve the matter.

Make whatever adjustments are necessary to run your classroom smoothly and efficiently. Put forth the extra effort to stay on top of things. You will be glad you did. You will be happy in your classroom and love teaching.

FLEXIBILITY

Flexibility is a necessity for your own peace of mind and happiness.

Sometimes certain things come up during the day or week that are not planned. For example, someone pulls the fire alarm; there goes your class right in the middle of your excellent social studies lesson. Getting annoyed or upset will not help this situation. If your lesson plans are written in pencil or on the computer, check for the next free time slot and draw an arrow from today's social studies to your new time slot or move social studies to the new slot on your computer. Then continue on and do not worry about it.

Sometimes other unplanned things come up during the day or week. For example, you are notified on Wednesday that a primary grade assembly will be held at 9:10 that morning. And though the school may have known about it a week ago, this is the first you have heard about it. And though you know it will begin at 9:10, you have no information as to how long it will last.

For that day, after your thiry-five-minute assembly, draw your arrows or enter your commands and do not worry about it for today. Then have a talk with the other teachers and see if they would like to meet with the principal to develop a monthly calendar of events, times, locations, and length of presentations. This can be copied and given to each teacher. Then they can transfer all this information into their lesson plan books. This really helps your classroom and the entire school run smoothly. It also helps you to be more flexible when truly unavoidably unplanned events occur.

Sometimes you are teaching a lesson and for whatever reason, it is not going well. Be flexible. Shift gears. Go to another area within that subject or another subject altogether. When you have a few minutes, try to determine what the problem was with the flow of the lesson. Was it very late on an incredibly hot day? Were the students not sufficiently prepared ahead of time for this material? Was there some distraction? Do you need to present the material in a different way? Do you need to present the material later in the year? Decide. Then make appropriate adjustments.

Be flexible with other teachers, too. If most of the teachers at your school want to do something a certain way, ask yourself, "Will the school run more smoothly if we all are doing this certain something in a particular way?" If so, go with the majority. It is important for the management of your classroom to be flexible and to get along with the other teachers, the principal, the secretaries, and the custodians, because they are all part of your team.

CHAPTER QUESTIONS

1. How would you apply Lao-tzu's quote to a teacher's first day of school each school year?
2. What are things of importance for the teacher on the first day of the school year?
3. What two words describe how class and school rules should be enforced?
4. If you teach first through sixth grades and you have students new to the school (especially non-English speakers), how can you help them feel more comfortable and accepted? (In kindergarten, all of your students will undoubtedly be new to the school.)
5. For the first couple of weeks of school, it is important to review at the beginning of the day and summarize at the end of the day. What would you review and summarize?

6. You are taking your class on a field trip to an IMAX theater and a museum of life science and history. The bus ride will take forty minutes each way. You will see two shows at the theater, one at 10:00 and the other at 11:00. A brief intermission occurs between shows and your students can stay right in the theater. The second show ends at 11:40. You may enter the museum at any time. It is self-guiding. There is a nearby area of many picnic tables, trash cans, and rest rooms. Another class will accompany you on the trip.
   a. What things would you do to prepare your class academically for the trip?
   b. How would you prepare for the day from a management point of view?
   c. What would you do for a follow-up activity?

7. You teach the first grade. It is a Thursday afternoon and your students are in the middle of a painting lesson using watercolors. No one is finished yet. An unannounced disaster drill begins. First, it is duck and cover in the classroom. Then it is evacuate the classroom and go to your class's emergency area. Next, it is time to take roll and hand in your accountability form. The sweep and rescue team goes out. All students who are "pretend injured" are taken to the first aid station. Finally, the "all clear" bell is sounded and students return to the class. Your students leave for the day in fifteen minutes.
   a. How would you feel?
   b. What would you do?

8. Name the four components of fine arts.

9. You teach sixth grade. You know next to nothing about music. You feel uncertain and lack confidence.
   a. Plan a lesson you *could* teach and feel good about.
   b. Name two ways you could ensure the sixth-graders' willingness to participate.

10. Your fourth-grade class is sitting in groups of six or seven. You have already told them they will be writing their own Thanksgiving Day puppet shows. Write two specific directions you could give the groups.

11. When the students are presenting their play or puppet show, what three things should they concentrate on when speaking?

12. You teach second grade. You are about to begin teaching a square dance to your class. You will teach one square. What can you do to ensure the square listens and follows directions and the rest of the class pays attention to the square so when it is their turn, they are already somewhat prepared?

13. Your first-graders are going to paint tomorrow morning.
   a. What instructions will you give them?
   b. What materials will you have all ready before school begins?
   c. If you will need helpers, who will they be?

14. What are finger facts?

15. What are your county, state, and federal laws and procedures regarding child abuse? What are signs of child abuse? What are the legal responsibilities of a teacher in the reporting of child abuse? If you were to report a case of child abuse or suspected child abuse, specifically what would you do? Who would you report to? What is that person's telephone number? Who else would you tell? Who are you *required* to tell?

16. How could you get to better know a student of yours who goes to day care?

17. Plan two good assignments that could be available for early finishers in your classroom. Exactly what would the assignments be? How might they be corrected?

18. In what ways can you communicate to students in your classroom that you have high expectations for all?

19. Why is it important to report to your playground duty on time?

20. What do you personally need to work on to be more flexible? List two specific incidents that might occur during the day that would give you the opportunity to practice flexibility. What would you like to do in response to these two incidents?

21. What is emergent literacy? Explain it in the context of both reading and writing. How does whole language relate to emergent literacy?

22. What are some extraneous things that can inadvertently affect teacher judgment of students' potential and achievement?

23. In Marzano's study of the six areas dealing with expectations, select one area and explain how you will apply it to your classroom.

24. How can the district office or the community help teachers meet expectations for students?

25. Explain how students will be responsible for getting their own education in your classroom.

26. According to Goal 3 of the National Education Goals, by the year 2000, students will be leaving grades 4, 8, and 12 by *demonstrating* competence in several areas. Select one area and describe how students in your class will demonstrate competence.

27. Describe a minimum of five strategies for emergent literacy. Be sure to include whole language and environmental print.

CHAPTER PROJECT

Plan one dance appropriate for your grade level. Gather the materials you will need for the lesson. Write a set of detailed lesson plans on how you would teach the entire dance to your class. In addition to including the teaching of the material, write in your lesson plans how you will handle the behavior of the students.

REFERENCES

Aldridge, J. T., & Rust, D. (1987). A beginning reading strategy. *Academic Therapy, 22*(3), 323–326.

Allred, R. A. (1993). Integrating proven spelling content and methods with emerging literacy programs. *Reading Psychology, 14*(1), 15–31.

Babad, E. & Taylor, P. J. (1992). Transparency of teacher expectancies across language, cultural boundaries. *Journal of Educational Research, 86*(2), 120–125.

Bennett, R. E., Gottesman, R. L., Rock, D. A., & Cerullo, F. (1993). Influence of behavior perceptions and gender on teachers' judgments of students' academic skill. *Journal of Educational Psychology, 85*(2), 347–356.

Briggs, L. D., & Richardson, W. D. (1993). Children's knowledge of environmental print. *Reading Horizons, 33*(3), 224–235.

Feitelson, D., Goldstein, Z., Iraqi, J., and Share, D. L. (1993). Effects of listening to story reading on aspects of literacy acquisition in a diglossic situation. *Reading Research Quarterly, 28*(1), 71–79.

Good, T. L. (1993). New direction in research on teacher and student expectations. *Midwestern Educational Researcher, 6*(1), 7–10, 17, 33.

Graves, D. H. (1993). Let's rethink children's entry points into literacy. *Dimensions of Early Childhood, 21*(3), 8–10, 39.

Hollins, E. R. (1993). Assessing teacher competence for diverse populations. *Theory into practice, 32*(2), 93–99.

Kelly, A. E., & O'Kelly, J. B. (1993). Emergent literacy: Implications for the design of computer writing applications for children. *Journal of Computing in Childhood Education, 4*(1), 3–14.

Marzano, R. L., Kendall, J. S., Calamera, B., Fanning, J. M., Grady, J. B., Pickering, D., Sutton, J. T., Whisler, J. S., & Young, T. A. (1992). *Toward a comprehensive model of assessment.* Aurora, CO. Mid-Continent Regional Educational Lab.

National Assessment of Educational Progress. (1991). *Meeting Goal 3: How well are we doing? Education research report.* Washington, DC: Office of Educational Research and Improvement.

Neuman, S. B., & Roskos, K. (1993). Access to print for children of poverty: Differential effects of adult mediation and literacy-enriched play settings on environmental and functional print tasks. *American Educational Research Journal, 30*(1), 95–122.

Otto, B. (1991, May). *Informal assessment of emergent reading behaviors through observations of assisted and independent storybook interactions.* Paper presented at the 36th Annual International Reading Conference, Las Vegas, NV.

Otto, B. (1993). Signs of emergent literacy among inner-city kindergartners in a storybook reading program. *Reading and Writing Quarterly: Overcoming Learning Difficulties, 9*(2), 151–162.

Perlmutter, J. C., & Laminack, L. L. (1993). Sociodramatic play: A stage for practicing literacy. *Dimensions of Early Childhood, 21*(4), 13–16, 31.

Proudfoot, G. (1992). Pssst! There is literacy at the laundromat. *English Quarterly, 24*(1), 10–11.

Ritts, V., Patterson, M. L., & Tubbs, M. E. (1992). Expectations, impressions, and judgments of physically attractive students: A review. *Review of Educational Research, 62*(4), 413–426.

Stewart, J. (1992). Kindergarten students' awareness of reading at home and in school. *Journal of Educational Research, 86*(2), 95–104.

Vukelich, C. (1993). Play: A context for exploring the functions, features, and meaning of writing with peers. *Language Arts, 70*(5), 386–392.

BIBLIOGRAPHY

Harris, T. L., & Hodges, R. E. (1981). *A dictionary of reading and related terms.* Newark, DE: International Reading Association.

3

THE GHI'S

This chapter contains a number of ways to assist you in running your classroom efficiently, intelligently, and enthusiastically. Covered in this chapter are the following:

- Gender Equity
- Geography
- Grading: Traditional and Alternative Assessment
- Helpers
- History
- Holiday Parties
- Incentives
- Instructional Assistants
- Instructional Media Center

The first part of the chapter introduces you to the thought-provoking topic of gender equity and the exciting subject of geography. In addition, it provides insight to the "how's" of grade-keeping for report cards.

GENDER EQUITY

A great deal of stereotyping and treating of genders inequitably exists, some at an almost unconscious level. Gender-biased communications can be both verbal and nonverbal. There can be hidden messages in even everyday communication. Both boys and girls, men and women, are harmed by **gender inequity.** Hence, it is very important, at the beginning of your teaching career, to be aware of **gender bias** and to practice intentionally avoiding it. The more cognizant you are of this situation, the more easily you can correct yourself, your students, and printed or videotaped matter presented to them.

Research and Studies

In a study done by Milanovich (1988) at the Desegregation Assistance Center of the Intercultural Development Research Association in Texas, **image words** were displayed to show how inherent gender bias really is. Samples of image words included the following: secretary, Jew, fireman, plumber, and Mexican.

Since this study was a training module, subtle gender bias was identified to help the participant be alert to it. Gender inequities can be based on sex roles (the disciplinarian father), on occupation (she's just a secretary), on personality (stoic men), on physical characteristics and activities (boys are better at math, girls at writing; girls are better at sewing, boys at football), and on expectations (boys will have the high-paying jobs; girls, lesser-paying ones or none at all).

Consider the implications of the following, which were displayed for discussion in the study:

- Men are the "stronger sex," but they have "less stamina and endurance" than women.
- Continual use of he, his, him in both verbal and written communication when the reference really is to either sex.
- Girls and women "cry easily" and are "concerned with their appearance."
- Boys and men are "in control," "aggressive," "mathematical."
- Men spend "too much time at work" for a family life.
- Mothers are "nurturing."
- The *male* nurse just arrived at the hospital.
- The *lady* welder will handle that job.
- Look at that "chick"!
- Please see "the doctor and *his* secretary."
- I'll ask "my girl" to type this.

It is freeing when students are not exposed to this.

A number of body language and expression communicators were also highlighted during this study. Attention was called to the amount of physical space given an individual, whether standing or sitting. Beyond twelve feet, according to this study, was labeled *public;* beyond four feet, *social;* up to four feet, *personal;* and within eighteen inches, *intimate.* A wink, a nod of approval, a frown, narrowing the eyes, lowering the eyes (although this can be cultural), frowning, a look of surprise, shaking the head no, pointing and shaking the finger, hands on hips, and hands raised in the air as a gesture of helplessness can all have gender implications and innuendos about them.

Another article by Janet Bertolucci Castanos (1994) refers to commonplace, *seemingly* innocuous gender-related comments heard, especially in sports; teachers need to be alert to this type of language on the campus, too:

A father upset with his ten-year-old son's performance in a sports game—"You're such a woman. You play like a little girl."

A male coach annoyed with his boys' performance—"You're playing like a bunch of stupid girls."

Other comments are frequently heard that are gender-related but are not gender-equitable. For example, you hear sayings such as "tomboy" and "She's got balls," which usually have *positive* connotations; but you do not hear expressions such as, "You read like a dumb boy." "Stop whining and be a man," "Act like the man of the house," and "Don't be a sissy" are other frequent comments.

What can be done about this? According to Castanos (1994), "Intelligent, self-confident, and nonthreatened adults need to confront others when degrading terms are used. Coaches and others who work with children should not be allowed to berate any group of people due to race, religion, or sex" (p. 47).

In dealing with gender equity, it is important for you to be knowledgeable, but it is more important to actually *use* **inclusionary** terms and body language in communicating with your students, their parents, and your colleagues. Regardless of the type of communication, include everyone. Give messages that either sex is worthy; descriptors need be applied only to individuals.

GEOGRAPHY

Geography is a delightful subject to teach, because so many things can be done with it.

Figure A3-1 in the appendix is a short, simple booklet that can be used as a brief introduction to world geography in late third or fourth grade. As the world becomes smaller because of increased technology, it is important for even young children to have some exposure to continents and oceans and a simple understanding of ways in which some countries are unique.

Across-the-curriculum teaching and this geography booklet will help you with that. It contains pages that can be used as separate lessons in math, art, science, and history. You can use individual pages or groups of pages as separate lessons. You can also copy the condensed booklet and pass it out to your students as a geography unit. Many students feel a real sense of accomplishment when they have completed the booklet.

(*Note:* If you have not already read the introduction to this book, now would be a good time to do so. It explains the coding system used for all the elementary student activity sheets. With this system, only *you* will know if the material is suitable for primary grades or for upper grades. That way, if you wish to use some of the "primary" materials in "upper" grades, and you may very well want to with some or all of your class, the upper-grade students will not see what level the material is. At the top of all the activity pages in the appendix of each of the chapters, *Pt* stands for primary [think *Primary time*] and § stands for upper or intermediate [think *Secondary Section*]).

The first part of this booklet mixes geometry and geography. It presents the students with the opportunity to learn some geometric shapes that will later be superimposed on continents as a way of identifying them. Students will then be able to see relatively easily what land goes with which continent. All of this is done while they are enjoying coloring in their booklets.

Next, two countries in the world are presented for study: Mexico and Australia. A section on the special animals of Australia could be used as a separate science lesson. (An answer key is available in Chapter 9, The XYZ's.)

Last is a special award certificate your students receive upon the successful completion of their geography booklets. If you do not have a high-quality copier at your school, you might want to go to a local copy store where you can do your certificates in a nice color, high-quality bond. Then your students will receive a certificate that looks sharp.

Figure A3-2 in the appendix is a booklet covering U.S. geography. It is suitable for any upper grade four through six. If you are going to use it as a booklet, rather than an individual assignment, it is a good idea to get a parent signature on the cover of the booklet to let parents know well in advance what is required of their children and what they need to do to prepare for and do a good job on the test. You might consider asking the students to sign their own names to the covers of their booklets by the due date. This can help them feel a sense of responsibility for overseeing their own work. (Ask a parent volunteer to copy the booklet for you.)

In this booklet, as in world geography, students will be exposed to a number of different response modes, including short answer, matching, true-false, discovering messages inside circles, unscrambling, and so on.

This U.S. geography booklet contains a variety of map activities on the continent of North America and on the country of the United States, which is divided into those states west of the Mississippi and those states east of it. An alphabetical list of the states and their capitals and postal abbreviations is presented for the students' information.

Read and discuss the material together as a class, or have the students meet with partners and/or small groups for a **read around.** Then they can work on the activities and come together as a class to discuss and correct the activities.

The next section presents interesting information and challenging activities for the students for the following notable places in the United States: Honolulu, Hawaii; San Francisco, California; The Grand Canyon in Arizona; Niagara Falls in New York (and Canada); New York City, New York; and the capital of the United States, Washington, D.C. Have the students color the pictures in their booklets as they go along to focus their attention on each drawing and remember the material better.

Also included is a project for the students to do on one of the preceding places. The project incorporates writing a short report, doing an illustration, and making a map of the appropriate area.

After the students have completed their booklets, they prepare for a test. Map and information **study sheets** are provided, which present the most important information for the students to remember. Basically, if students spend plenty of time studying their maps and study sheets, they will do fine on the test. Nothing appears on the test that is not on the study sheet; the material is just presented in a slightly different way. If they concentrate on their map and study sheets, they will get the main concepts. Study sheets and test notes, which will be discussed later in Chapter 7, The STU's, are the tickets to success on tests.

For grading purposes, you can use a grade on the completed booklet, a project grade and a test grade.

When the students are finished with their booklets and have taken their tests and done a good job on both, they are geography winners and can be presented certificates that say so.

Figure A3-3 is a booklet that covers world geography and is suitable for a sixth-grade or an advanced fifth-grade class. Again, get a parent signature if you are using it as a booklet.

This booklet begins with map activities and introductory information about the world. Then the world is divided into the Western Hemisphere and the Eastern Hemisphere for study purposes.

In addition to map activities for the Western Hemisphere, there is a concentration on the continent of North America with special emphasis on Canada, Greenland, and the United States. Along with the map activities for the Eastern Hemisphere, there is a focus on the continent of Europe with special highlights on Russia, England, and Italy.

Next is a hemisphere project involving writing, drawing, and map making for the two hemispheres.

The study sheets follow this project. Again, nothing is on the test that is not on the study sheet in some form. If the students really put in the time it takes to learn their map and study sheets, they will learn the main concepts and do great on the test. The students can quiz each other in small groups. Soon, they will become very quick at locating a particular place on their maps.

Be sure to give students an adequate amount of time to take this test. Remember that some students work slowly and need more time to do the excellent work of which they are capable. Have activities planned for early finishers.

After students complete their booklets and tests and do a fine job on both, they really are "Number One in World Geography," just as the certificate proclaims.

If you do one of these booklets with your class, in addition to a geography bee, you will have quite a program. With your group of eager, involved students, you will have a solidly run classroom as well.

GRADING: TRADITIONAL AND ALTERNATIVE ASSESSMENT

You will need some sort of grading system for your students. Depending on your school and district, grades might be in the form of traditional letter grades (A–F), effort grades (O, S, U), a combination of both, or neither. Your district may be using, in the main, **traditional assessment,** primarily using more of the objective-type tests. Your district may be using one of a number of **alternative assessment** (also called **authentic**

assessment) methods, which are more performance based. Students may be given a short **prompt** and asked to respond orally or in writing, explaining what they know. Students may be given a selection to read, and using **marginalia,** show how they interact with the printed word. Students may be asked to demonstrate their knowledge by writing a friendly letter explaining the Declaration of Independence to a relative. Students may keep their work in **portfolios** and each month or quarter select their best piece and tell what is good about it. They might also write or tell in what ways they have improved and what they would like to focus on for the following quarter. Your district may use this type of **portfolio-based assessment.** (See a sample portfolio evaluation, including a **rubric,** for the student to complete in Figure A8-12 in the appendix at the end of the writing section.)

Your district's grading system may be based on whether or not certain objectives are met by the student; it may be structured around where the student is in relation to "grade level"; or it may simply be comments about the student's progress. In any case, you will need to keep samples or scores of the students' work to substantiate their grades.

Find out first thing what the grading policies are for your school and district, because you need to conform to these. Furthermore, find out what kind of regional testing your district administers and at what grade levels. Even if these tests are not given at your grade level, you need to begin preparing your students for the next one they will encounter. They need to be familiar with the material covered on these and the particular type of testing mode. For an explanation of the various types of test items, see How to Get Started in the Teaching-Learning Process section in Chapter 7, The STU's. Provide your students plenty of practice with these varieties of questions.

If you use a grade or record book, besides recording grades or checking if objectives have been met, establish some columns in your book for comments in certain areas. For example, under "handwriting," in addition to grades, write any letters the student is misforming. Then you can use this information to form a small skills group for instruction and practice in those letters.

Under "reading," make a column for oral reading and, in addition to recording an S (satisfactory), an N (needs improvement), and so on, write a comment about specific problems, such as: poor sight vocabulary, stumbling at first word in every sentence, misreading words, frequently skipping words, frequently saying words that are not there, is not able to retell what is read, is not able to draw conclusions based on what is read, and so on. Then you can have lessons applicable to those particular students.

In math, indicate whether a student is "weak" in multiplication facts, two-digit multipliers, borrowing, measurement, one-step story problems, and so on.

Write positive comments, too, such as: reads with expression, fast and accurate in division facts, excellent in writing story problems, very imaginative story writing, does excellent oral reports, beautiful scientific drawings, and so on.

After the students' grades are recorded, at the mid–grading period, complete progress reports. Send these home and get a return parent signature to ensure that the parents are informed about their children's progress in your class. When the official grading period ends, average grades from the second half of the period with those from the progress report and you will have your report card grades. (Progress reports, one for primary grades and one for upper grades, are included in Figures A6-3 and A6-4 in the appendix to give you some ideas.)

Included in the appendix are some sample grade-book forms for each subject for one entire grading period. These grading periods were based on a quarter system. The progress report grades would be calculated at the midquarter, after about four or five weeks. The report card grades would be calculated after another four or five weeks. (See Figure A3-4 in the appendix.) These will give you a good idea of the grade-keeping process. Because of available space, columns devoted to skill notes are not included. In your own grade book, however, you will have plenty of room for these notes, which are a very helpful teaching aid.

Let the students know, in advance, that if assignments are not turned in by them for recording on the classroom assignment accountability chart, their grade will be lowered. Students quickly learn that they need to consistently complete their work, pay close attention to lessons, and study material carefully to progress and succeed.

At the end of approximately a month, assignments, projects, tests, and so on have been given, completed, and recorded. Grades are closed, averaged, and sent home either in the form of progress reports or report cards. The assignment accountability chart is wiped clean and your classroom is ready for another refreshing start. Using these types of short grading periods is a real plus to keeping the pace of your classroom moving briskly and giving students a pleasurable sense of closure and energetic renewal.

Research and Studies

One school district of 12,000 highly diverse students K–12 in Indianapolis, Indiana, needed and wanted to make a change to improve student achievement (Thacker & McInerney, 1992). The entire district became focused on one thing: District students would pass the Indiana Statewide Test of Educational Progress (ISTEP). Staff development was provided in instructional strategies, curriculum development, and affective discipline. Parents were involved through informative newsletters and meetings. They learned at what grade levels their children would be tested; how they, at home, could help their children pass the test; and different test-taking strategies their children could use to enhance their achievement on the ISTEP. Everyone, including teachers, students, parents, principals, school employees, administrators, school board members, and state residents provided input. Everyone knew about the ISTEP, when it was taken and what it measured. If students did not pass the ISTEP, they were either required to go to summer school or repeat the grade. This became an **outcome-based** district.

The results were excellent. This school district scored higher than any other district in its county. In first, second, and third grades, the failure rate greatly decreased from 1990 to 1991: 11.0 percent down to 1.01 percent for first grade, 7.0

percent down to 1.54 percent for second grade, and 2.0 percent down to .10 percent for third (Thacker & McInerney, p. 22).

At the **cognitive level,** students need to question their new learning, find ways to link it to their own experiences, and relate it to prior knowledge. This involves their use of appropriate vocabulary for the learning, a comprehension of the learning, and some problem-solving strategies to use to apply the learning.

Teachers need to construct and/or use assessment devices that give the students the opportunity to apply their learning, rather than just recite it back. In addition to traditional-type tests, alternative assessment—also known as authentic, appropriate, performance, and direct assessment (FairTest, 1992)—uses such evaluative tools as classroom observations or documentations, journals, student demonstrations, and portfolios. For example, a student can read aloud and the teacher can record miscues and listen to the student retell the story. The student may be asked to conduct an experiment and explain what happened and how that can be applied to a general concept.

In traditional-type tests, usually a specific time is set aside for test completion. Students may have a mix of multiple-choice, true-false, fill-in-the-blank, matching and short-answer questions. These tests can be corrected fairly and relatively quickly and easily provide students with knowledge of results. Oftentimes, these tests are, in the main, at the recall level. When students perform at higher levels of the **taxonomy,** they will usually be required to do more writing. The more writing the students do, however, the more difficult tests are to correct with consistent fairness, especially from one time period to another, and the more time consuming.

When both traditional and alternative assessment are used, the teacher needs to be committed to the use of alternative assessment for at least part of every day or for certain subjects or for cross-curriculum projects, as can be seen from the findings in the upcoming study. Alternative assessment provides teachers with good insight into their students' thinking processes, comprehension of the material, ability to use and manipulate the learning, and personalities and interests. It allows a rewarding interaction between teacher and student, with individually customized comments provided for the students. When results are shared with the class, it allows for some of this appreciation to permeate the entire classroom of students.

Aschbacher (1992) conducted a study on alternative assessment. The participating teachers used either of two types, journals or portfolios. The main findings were: teachers needed to be very committed to alternative assessment for them to really use it over any length of time; extensive teacher training was needed for success; and teachers may need to become more focused on student outcomes than on providing interesting classroom activities.

Teachers who used journals used them in math class. They had their students write something related to math in their journals one day a week. Teachers attempted to go through the journals for content analysis for measurement, but they found this very difficult and were reluctant to use it as a grading device.

Teachers who used portfolios experienced similar problems. Even though the teachers were expected to give a course grade, many were reluctant to give the portfolio, which reflected work over a period of time, a grade. Some teachers mentioned their reluctance to show portfolios that were not done well, because they saw this as a reflection on their own ability to perform.

Other teachers remarked that they liked to grade low the first grading period to set high standards and use of portfolio assessment did not reflect that system, whereas others said that they liked to grade high first period to boost the students' confidence. Again, the portfolio system would not support that, since work in the second period might be higher quality but get a lower grade than work of lesser quality from the first grading period.

Many teachers found that the alternative assessment devices generated more paperwork, were not well-supported by parents, and were not worthwhile as a grading device unless their district offices were going to provide major support and commitment for this type of assessment on a long-term basis.

According to researchers Bryk (1988), and Stern and Keislar (1977), teachers are motivated by students engaged productively in interesting activities in the classroom, such as using math manipulatives, and by measurable performance on traditional tests. If teachers do not feel their students are productive and achieving and that they, as teachers, are reaching them, then teachers tend to experience burnout. Teachers seem more enthralled with the classroom teaching and activities than with the student outcomes. Student outcomes need to be clearly defined and listed. Only after that should an assessment device that will measure the outcomes be selected or created and used. Teachers may then be able to gear their motivation into the satisfaction of student outcomes and the activities that lead directly to that end.

Portfolios in Aschbacher's study (1992) were set up to include the following: a table of contents, two end-of-unit exams, one work that the student considered his or her best work, a special cross-curriculum project, something related to a field trip, two student self-evaluations written in March and June, and one paper on what the student thought about the class.

In Aschbacher's study, the teachers who were committed to alternative assessment noted that it was important for them to be part of a group of teachers implementing this program, rather than trying to do it alone. It gave them the chance to better know their students and to decide if activities the students were engaged in were really directed toward what they wanted to measure. Portfolios were the focal point of their instructional program, rather than a tangent as they were for the less-committed teachers. Three-fourths of the teachers who returned study surveys mentioned that they noticed a slight increase in student self-esteem and motivation. In one of the classrooms involved in the study, all the students wanted to take their portfolios home at the end of the year.

Performance assessment (authentic/alternative assessment) is not anything really new. It used to be used in education all the time before standardized tests replaced it. Performance assessment is still used today in some fields like law and medicine. It is a truer measure of performance (Perrone, 1991).

There are three criteria for performance assessment: "First, students must apply knowledge they have acquired. Second, students must complete a clearly specified task within the context of either a real or simulated exercise. Third, the task or completed product must be observed and rated with respect to specified criteria in accordance with specified procedures, requiring students to actually demonstrate proficiency" (Pierson & Beck, 1993, p. 30). Since performance assessments are more difficult to construct, involve more student time, and considerably more teacher time in evaluating, the benefits of performance assessment need to clearly outweigh the burdens. Valid, reliable measures need to be employed in the assessment so that the results are accepted as a true measure of student performance. For example, in portfolio assessment, it is important to use some kind of a checklist or rubric to show the assessment has a high degree of **validity** and **reliability.** Criteria can be established at each school, but they need to be clearly delineated for success on a long-term basis. If students will be taking some kind of schoolwide standardized or state test or a test such as the SAT for college-bound students, will the authentic assessment used at the school be a predictor of performance on that test? Are the tasks and tests related to real life, that is, do they have " '**ecological validity**'? For example, reading assessment tasks that involve narrative text may not be related to technical types of reading demanded in the workplace" (Pierson & Beck, 1993, p. 32). It is most important to have performance activities that are transferable to the workplace and are assessed using precise, tough criteria.

According to Lockledge and Hayn (1993), activities for alternative or authentic assessment should be directly "relevant to life outside of school" (p. 3) and require some sort of rubric for grading. The rubric sets the "standards a teacher could reasonably expect . . . from a prepared student" (p. 5). Alternative assessment is a direct measurement of students' depth of understanding. It can involve all levels of the taxonomy.

Tierney (1992) asked teachers to ask themselves if their methods of assessment "empower students" (p. 62). Portfolio assessment can do this. Students have the opportunity to explain what they have been learning, what they would like to learn or improve on, and what they think their best work is and why. This creates focus and ownership of the learning and a strong commitment to learning and the awareness that it is a lifelong process.

Scott G. Paris and his colleagues (1992) studied the need for alternative assessment of literacy to be customized to the needs of schools and districts. They studied the Kamehameha Elementary Education Program (KEEP) used in Hawaii in kindergarten through third grades, which was recently extended to sixth grade. This program fosters literacy among native Hawaiian students. Third-graders at Kamehameha Elementary were tested and their scores were compared with third-graders in other Island schools. The problem, however, was that the Stanford Achievement Test (SAT) was the measuring device, and it did not relate much to the KEEP program. Teachers in the KEEP schools spent approximately three months a year prepping their students for the Stanford so that they would do well. After the test was over, the "**canyon effect**" took place in the schools (Paris et al., 1992, p. 90). This was low motivation for the last month of school because learning and literacy were tied to the Stanford test, rather than envisioned as an ongoing process.

Therefore, a framework for alternative assessment was developed that would closely align with the main components of literacy: interacting with text in both reading and writing in everyday situations; understanding what literacy is and being motivated to develop it; developing reading and writing skills such that they can and are used on an independent basis for lifelong learning; understanding that reading and writing involves interaction with others to share and solve problems; and realizing that reading and writing link all areas of the curriculum and are directly connected to listening and speaking.

Each of these valued areas was codified so that it could be carefully and accurately measured. A scale for each area was developed that ranged from a low category comprising specific descriptors to a high category with specific descriptors. For example, the area of literacy knowledge had, among other descriptors: "low knowledge: unaware of text structures and genres; high knowledge: can identify and use several specific text structures and genres" (Paris et al., 1992, p. 93). For constructive reading, descriptors included: "low engagement: focus is on isolated facts; does not connect text elements" and "high engagement: identifies and elaborates plots, themes, or concepts" (Paris et al., 1992, p. 93).

The KEEP teachers then decided what they really valued in the curriculum, how they would collect and evaluate data regarding the achievement of their students, and had this directly connected to their everyday curriculum. In this way, assessment was a natural part of the teaching-learning process, it involved "real-life" problems on which the students were knowledgeable, and the assessment results were available immediately and could be used to plan interventions.

The frequency of assessment and its impact on learning have been heavily researched (Bangert-Drowns, Kulik, & Kulik, 1991). This particular study examined the effects of different uses of **adjunct questions** on test performance.

Adjunct questions accompany textbook chapters or sections to enhance learning. They can be in many forms and at all levels of the taxonomy. Sometimes adjunct questions precede a chapter, and sometimes they follow a chapter. At other times, they may be interspersed throughout the chapter. All adjunct questions may be identical to the chapter posttest; some may be identical, others not; or none of them may be identical and may not even be directly related to the posttest. Students, however, do best when the questions are repeated (Bangert-Drowns et al., 1991).

What effect do adjunct questions have on a criterion test containing related and unrelated questions? Questions at the lower end of the taxonomy have a positive correlation to related questions on a criterion test. Questions of higher-level thinking, have an even stronger positive effect on related questions on a criterion test. There is basically no correlation between either type of adjunct question with criterion test questions of an unrelated nature.

During the Bangert-Drowns, Kulik, and Kulik study, it was found that teachers who gave only a final at the end of the grading period could increase test scores by a standard deviation of 0.34 by adding just one more test. But continually increased testing resulted in a diminishing-return phenomenon; that is, there was little difference when the number of tests was doubled or tripled. However, when identical test items were spread among several tests instead of all on one test, scores were better on the series of smaller tests.

In addition, one of the testing groups was involved in a **mastery testing** situation. Mastery testing is a system where specific tests are used frequently during the teaching-learning cycle and students are not allowed to move on to new material until they have mastered the course material as evidenced by passing a test.

Classroom learning improves with mastery testing. It may be related to **corrective feedback,** in which students receive feedback on each item of their tests and remediation for those areas where skills or knowledge are deficient. In other words, just increasing the number of tests in a classroom will not nec-

essarily increase classroom learning, but when the frequent tests are part of a mastery testing system with corrective feedback and movement to new material based on mastery of old, this holds true.

For additional information on grading and assessment, see Research and Studies under the Expectations section in Chapter 2, The DEF's.

The second part of this chapter covers classroom helpers, who will make your classroom run well; history ideas for a fast-paced curriculum; and holiday parties.

HELPERS

The students are your helpers, and you can make a bulletin board built around what these helpers do (see Figure 3-1). When you make this wheel chart, if you have a class of about

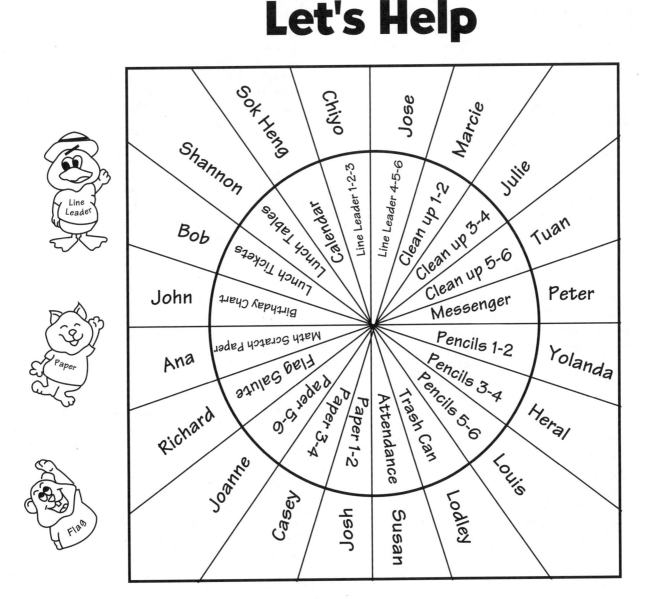

Let's Help

Figure 3-1. With this wheel chart, jobs are easy to handle and rotate.

thirty or so students, simply write some of the helping activities twice. Then students can work in pairs to complete the task. That way, you will always have students assigned to an activity year-round. If you leave some places blank on the wheel, then some students will not have a job for that two-week period and maybe the next, too.

After you make your helpers' wheel chart, you will have another bulletin board that looks nice and can be left up all year. Turn the wheel every two weeks or so to rotate the tasks.

It is important to explain each activity slowly and carefully so that the helpers will know exactly what to do and how you want it done. Students want to please, and many of them will take their roles as classroom helpers very seriously.

The following is a list of some activities you might like your helpers to assist you with:

Attendance   One student takes the attendance folder and lunch count down to the office each day and hurries back to class.

Paper   Divide your class into three to six sections. One or two students pass out the day's paper to one section while another one or two students take care of the next section, and so on. Students let the paper people know if they want paper by raising their hand with one, two, three, four, or five fingers up in the air to indicate how many they want.

There is no reason for any exchange of words with this system. That way, you can continue on with roll, lunch count, collecting miscellaneous forms, and so forth. Students who are out of their seats doing various jobs leave a note on top of their desks saying how much paper they want. Then students do not need to get paper any other time of the day.

Pencils   Put students in charge of sharpening pencils, one or two for each section. If you can get several electric pencil sharpeners into your classroom and plug them in at different locations around the classroom, this procedure works smoothly and quickly. Assign a pencil sharpener to each section. In some book clubs, you can save points from ordering students' books. Then, after you collect a certain number of points, you can order an electric pencil sharpener, and many other things too, including a stopwatch. Once you get one electric sharpener, start saving for the next one.

Students may leave up to five pencils on the top corner of their desk for sharpening. The student sharpeners collect these, sharpen them, and return them to each section with sharpened pencils held in open hands. Students take their pencils back, and no words are exchanged. Again, you continue with your everyday business.

Students are responsible for having at least three sharpened pencils for the day. Classroom pencil sharpeners are not used after the students have returned the pencils. Some students enjoy having their own hand-held, small pencil sharpeners in addition to having their pencils sharpened in the morning.

Transparencies   A couple of students can be in charge of washing transparencies. Have them use a squirt bottle filled with water and soft paper towels to wipe off non-permanent overhead pen marks; students should wear disposable gloves when they do this because it gets quite messy.

Classroom Clean Up   Have one student take the wastebasket and clean up paper, scraps, and so on on the floor in sections one and two, another student handles sections three and four, and a third can handle five and six. Students may throw away any trash from their desks at this time. Then they do not have to dispose of any trash during the day.

Scratch Paper   Almost daily, in the upper grades, the students will use scratch paper for math. Scratch paper is kept together in a stack. One student handles sections one and two, another handles three and four, and so forth.

Flag   After roll, lunch count, collecting of forms, and so on, the class stands for the flag salute. One student looks to make sure everyone is standing appropriately, then says, "Ready . . . Begin."

Line Leader   You can have students line up by sections. For example, sections one and two could be in one line and sections three and four in another, or sections one, two, three in one line and sections four, five, and six in the other. A leader is at the head of each of the two lines. This helps make a smooth transition from the playground to the classroom and also helps with meeting the gender equity requirements of Title IX at the same time, since sections are composed of boys and girls. Students enjoy their turn as head of the line.

Collecting Papers   This can be a wheel-chart assignment, or you can pick different people to do this as the need arises. Students love collecting papers, and if some student is having a low day, you just might want to choose her several different times during the same day to try to perk her up. Also, sometimes there is the need for papers to be collected by the grade the students are in rather than one mass collection. Then someone can collect from one grade while someone else collects from the other.

Messenger   This is everyone's favorite, especially if you have lots of messages and errands to run. The same one or two students take care of this until it is time to rotate job assignments.

HISTORY

History is sometimes its own subject and sometimes part of a larger subject called social studies or social science, which includes history, geography, and research skills. All three areas are discussed separately in this book, geography and history here in this chapter and research skills in Chapter 6, The PQR's; however, you can separate and group these materials as you like. If you do not have a separate subject of research skills, the appendix contains state and country reports and a variety of map, table, and graph-reading pages along with activities on latitude and longitude and climate types in the United States.

When teaching history, it is important for the students to have a sense of where the period of time they are studying fits into a time line. Displaying a time line in your classroom helps keep historical information more organized and memorable for your students.

When preparing your lessons for history, it works well to first write your assessment device. Then it will be clear to you just what you want your students to know.

Construct one or two open-ended questions on the topic. Use **scaffolding** to provide assistance to the students as to material you want included. The following is an example of an assessment device for the Boston Tea Party.

(Present a picture of the Boston Tea Party and a short caption at the top of the test or on an **overhead projector** transparency.)

The Boston Tea Party was one of the most famous events in U. S. history. Write a letter to a friend who does not know much about the tea party. Tell your friend:

1.   What led up to the tea party.
2.   What the reaction of the British was.
3.   How the tea party helped the colonies.

Be sure to include in your answer the following:

• Parliament's taxation policies
• England's military presence
• The three divisions of the colonies
• Loyalists and patriots

This test is suitable for fifth grade. It provides students the opportunity to write in their own words what they know and understand about the tea party. It provides enough structure for the less-able students and allows the advanced students to write to their heart's content. (See Figure A8-20 in the appendix for a graphic organizer that will help students prepare for this type of test.)

Although this type of test does take some time to correct, it provides a clear picture of student achievement in both history and writing. Do they know the Boston Tea Party? Do they know friendly letter format? Do they know how to write in a clear, readable style? Use this opportunity to record a grade for them in history, writing, and handwriting.

History is a good subject in which to incorporate listening and speaking. Have the students select small sections of the material in their text they are currently studying, or even a supplementary book on the same material, and give a report to the class. For a visual, they could print in large letters the title of their speech and use bulleting to key three or four important details. They could have a picture to accompany one of the concepts or one of the target vocabulary words.

When students give their speeches, they can use a pointer to direct their classmates' attention to each bullet as they explain it. Then they can show and explain their picture. Classmates can practice their listening skills and be prepared to answer two questions posed by each speaker.

Continually presenting the same information in a variety of modes like this really helps students develop a broader and deeper understanding of the material. They also become more familiar with the target vocabulary by seeing and hearing the words more frequently and by having pictures to associate with the words. They can more easily use these new words in their history work as well as in other areas of the curriculum.

Figures A3-5 and A3-6 in the appendix are sample activities to give you some ideas as to how student activities can be constructed. When you make your own activities or tests, use a word processor, if possible, so that the paper looks nice and can be used for a few years. Keep originals and transparencies in a binder so that they are not lost or misplaced.

Figure A3-5 is the first history activity. This is a general history exercise that can be used any day, any time during the year. It provides an opportunity for the students to really get a lot out of their material and express what they learned in three different forms: thoroughly explaining ten things they learned from their material; searching through their material to complete the title word or words; and writing a short play. When students work on this activity, they can work in groups of two or more. This will especially help them with brainstorming for play ideas. Primary students can do these activities orally in their groups. A group recorder could write down the first name or initials of each group member as they contributed.

Figure A3-6 in the appendix is on Christopher Columbus. This type of activity allows the students to place themselves in a period of history and pretend they are a particular historical person. It also makes them ponder about the thoughts and feelings of a famous person in history. After they finish this activity, they can meet with a partner or small group and share their information.

Another delightful thing to do in history is to have a feast for Thanksgiving. The students can dress as Indians or Pilgrims and bring to school some of the kinds of food the real

Figure 3-2.   Dressing up for a commemoration of the first Thanksgiving feast is an enjoyable experience for any student.

participants at the first Thanksgiving ate. This helps students to learn by doing.

As part of understanding some group in history, it is helpful to the students to make their own person. These types of cutout and glue-together figures, as well as cutouts of the Statue of Liberty, Lincoln's log cabin, and so on, are available in reproducible books at your local teachers' supply store. These are good history activities that can be used year-round. The students can gather information for their subject, write it up, and then build their person or cabin or whatever it might be. Students at any grade level enjoy this, and it makes a big imprint on their minds.

History class is a great opportunity to have a play or skit to explain some historical incident. Divide your class into four or five groups and have each group present a different period of history or a different event inside one period. This is fun for everyone, especially when the students dress for the part and have good props and scenery. Make sure each student has a part in the play and contributes to the total product. Be explicit about what you want from each group during the information-gathering process, during the practices, and during the play itself.

Projects are another exciting thing to do in history and give the students the opportunity to use their writing skills, arts and crafts skills, and their speaking skills when they present their projects to the class or a small group or even to another class. These generate a lot of class interest.

History can come alive through the use of high-interest videos, which can be used either as a culminating or an introductory activity. Leave enough light on in the classroom during the video so that the students can take notes. Afterward, they can share their thoughts with a partner and possibly add to their notes after the discussion. That learning can be incorporated into a writing activity or an art project or a combination of both. Students can even make their own history videos by dressing up as a particular historical character and using their earlier play ideas to present important concepts.

Research and Studies

History can be taught by means of a **graphic organizer.** For example, Armstrong (1991) used a graphic organizer, the frame, to work with reading at the fourth-grade level in the content area of social studies. A frame was constructed for the subject material. The frame was then carefully checked with the textbook material to be sure it covered concepts correctly and included the most important content. Using a "linked concept pair," the concepts in the text were able to be described and placed into frames. Fourth-grade students were successfully taught a **frame-based approach,** or text-based approach, to social studies.

In Brophy, Van Sledright, and Bredin's (1992) study on fifth-graders' knowledge about a history topic before and after a unit, a "KWL" sheet was used for assessment. The **KWL technique** is based on a reading comprehension strategy where students retrieve knowledge about a certain subject and then learn more about it with both a purpose for learning and the sense of accomplishment of having learned well. In KWL, *K* stands for what the students already *K*now or think they know. For preunit data, students are asked, during individual, taped interviews of fifteen to thirty minutes in length, to tell what they already know or think they know about a particular subject. *W* is next in KWL. Students being interviewed are asked what they *W*ant to learn about the topic. After the unit is presented, the students are given a paper-pencil test for *L*, what they *L*earned and a postunit interview. Generally, the preunit questions are used for the postunit test.

For this study, a small, select group of students in a fifth-grade classroom were to use the KWL technique for a unit on

Figure 3-3.   These students are bringing their own Pilgrims to a Thanksgiving feast.

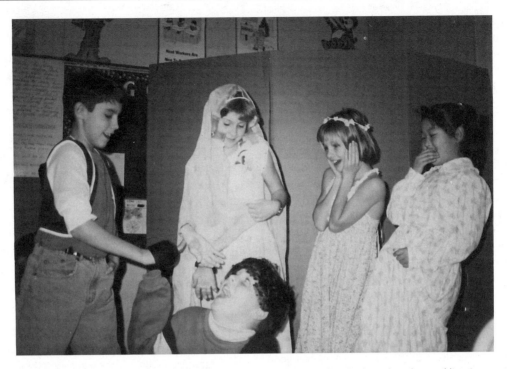

Figure 3-4. A good way of presenting a historical incident to the class is through a play or skit put on by a small group of students. The students can use artwork or props or they can dress up to intensify the reality of it.

European Explorations of America. They were asked the following questions:

1. When did the first Europeans discover America?
2. America was there the whole time. Why did it take so long to discover it?
3. What do explorers do?
4. How did New York Harbor look to the first European explorers? (This question was not asked in the postunit interview because all respondents got it right.)
5. What people were already here? (This question was not asked in the postunit interview either because all responded correctly.)
6. What was it like to be an explorer and why?
7. How did the explorers explore?
8. Where were they going and why?
9. Who paid for the explorations and why?
10. What did the explorers do when they got to America?
11. How were the Europeans and the Native Americans similar?
12. How were they different?
13. What did the Europeans learn from the Native Americans?
14. What did the Native Americans learn from the Europeans?
15. Who were the first Europeans to discover America?
16. Why did Columbus get credit for discovering America?
17. Might the Native Americans have discovered Europe around A.D. 1500?
18. How did America get its name?
19. Why were Native Americans called Indians?

20. What does this map tell you? (Students were shown a map illustrating the explorers' sailing routes from Europe to North America.)

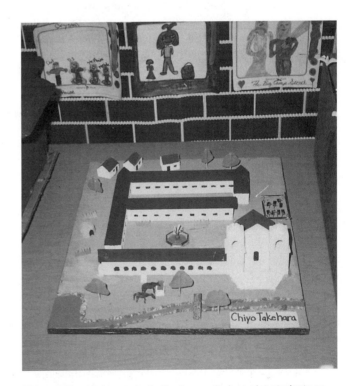

Figure 3-5. History projects like these missions give students an opportunity to use their creative talents as well as to see history come to life in miniature form.

21. After the explorers publicized their findings, what happened next in America?
22. Why is English spoken in the United States, Spanish in Mexico, and French in part of Canada?
23. What is the difference between an explorer and a colonist?
24. What would have happened if the Spanish had started by exploring the New England area?

These and other questions were all open-ended questions that gave students opportunities to show their **prior knowledge,** including any **misconceptions.** It also provided a general framework for their study of the information and helped them see, in addition to their own personal areas of interest, the focus areas of the posttest.

The researchers stated they could not rely too heavily on the *L* (Learned), because students took the posttest in their classroom with a social studies bulletin board displayed with exploration information, pictures, maps, and so on, and key words were posted around the classroom. The researchers noted that many students used the board and classroom environment as a prompt; however, the results showed that students got a good "feel" for the explorations, even though they still had some misconceptions.

It is important during the teaching of the unit that learning be built on correct knowledge and that misconceptions be identified and corrected. Historical misconceptions mentioned by the researchers in this study were such beliefs as Native Americans had to stay on reservations and descriptors for the Plains Indians stereotyped to all Indians. (It was also mentioned in the study that younger students at the kindergarten level had misconceptions about Native Americans and referred to them as always wearing animal skin and feathers, being mean, and killing.) Other fifth-grade misconceptions were that the Pilgrims discovered America, and, when words in a foreign language were identified, students assumed the language to be French (Brophy et al., 1992, pp. 16–17).

From all counts, the fifth-grade teacher, Nancy Bredin, did an outstanding job in teaching her class about the explorations. She created a bulletin board to emphasize important concepts in the explorations, she used maps, and she posted key words in one of three categories: people, places, or events. She used storytelling and biographical/historical selections from children's literature as well as articles from the magazine *Cobblestone* to teach the content. Students wrote compositions, did outlines, wrote profiles of the historical characters, and completed an "explorer's contract" for which they used their textbooks, encyclopedias, and their dictionaries for reference materials. She also used the KWL sheets as the pretest and posttest. An important finding: Many of the students were most *Want*ing to *L*earn if their answers on the pretest were correct. This type of approach keeps students interested, focused, and motivated.

If your history lessons are interesting, varied, and exciting; if the students know specifically what is expected of them academically; and if the behavior standards are clearly set and enforced, your classroom will be a place of pleasure and satisfaction for every history period.

HOLIDAY PARTIES

These days are normally specific days scheduled by your school. They may be to celebrate winter holidays, Valentine's Day, end of the school year, and so on. The PTA may provide some things to eat or drink, and the students bring in the rest. Room mothers call and ask the parents to bring or send with their children specific items for the parties.

Ask the students to help rearrange the room so that it is more conducive to a party atmosphere and the avoidance of spills. Detail good manners during a holiday party and ask the students to verbalize these and the reasons for them.

If you have a primary grade, enlist the help of a few parents or some responsible upper-grade students on a holiday party day. They can help pass out food and drink and clean up any spills; however, primary students can often be helpful in planning the party and helping with distributing the food. Primary students also will need plenty of time to eat.

If you have an upper grade, the students themselves can take care of everything. Appoint students to pass out plates, napkins, forks or spoons, and cups first. The students who bring in things for the party usually are the ones who want to pass out those items. If they want something other than punch, they can bring two-liter bottles of their favorite soft drinks to share. It is also nice to have a small ice chest in the classroom to hold ice cubes for soft drinks.

After whatever established amount of time for the holiday party has elapsed (approximately forty minutes), it is time to begin cleaning the classroom. Have some large trash bags from the custodian and ask two students to go around the class with a bag to collect trash. Unfinished drinks should be poured down the sink first, then trashed. If some desks are sticky, use a little cleaner and some paper towels to take care of this during the cleanup time. Ask all the students to lend a hand in cleanup and in return of furniture to its original place.

Holiday parties can be a fun time for all. Students always look forward eagerly to these days.

The last part of this chapter deals with the fun of incentives; the pleasure of an instructional assistant; and the wonderful world of the instructional media center. Use all this information for a beautifully run classroom!

INCENTIVES

Nothing great was ever achieved without enthusiasm.

Ralph Waldo Emerson
American essayist, poet, orator,
philosopher (1803–1882)

Incentives or prizes for accomplishments and assistance lend excitement to a classroom and a school. These are good self-esteem builders, too!

Following are incentive ideas and a brief description of each.

Good Luncher Recess

This is always popular. Good luncher recess is an extra ten-minute recess at a given time on a given day once a week. For example, it could be every Monday at 10:00. It is supervised by the principal, so the teachers get a break, too.

How do the students earn it? If the students from a particular classroom demonstrate each day at lunch during one week that they can eat lunch showing good manners, such as talking quietly, not throwing food, cleaning up all the trash, and not leaving the tables until they are dismissed, they get one point. Classes with a point for each day of the week get a good luncher recess the following Monday. If no class earned a point for each and every day, the classes with four points can earn a good luncher recess. No good luncher recess is awarded for anything less than three points. Points are given by the noon duty supervisors.

Students are thrilled when the qualifying classes are announced on the intercom once a week and they find out *their* class is a winner.

Class Special Tickets

Another favorite, these tickets can be given to students for many different reasons, including cleaning the classroom, demonstrating extra hard studying for a test, winning some class contest, winning at some board game, getting unusually difficult math problems correct, working well together on a group writing project or history research project, or demonstrating excellent behavior for a particular period of time or for a particular project. Just walking around the classroom and leaving a class special ticket on the corner of the desk of students' who are working particularly well can excite the classroom.

Ask one of your students to stamp your name or some other stamp identification on a batch of class special tickets. Then, after the students receive a ticket from you, they fill out *their* names, and drop them in the special ticket box.

A drawing can be held once a week or once every other week. The students love taking turns pulling a name out of the box. You can have two or three winners or even more, whatever you like. Prizes can be special pencils, posters, certificates, erasers, a certain amount of free time for a game, or a classroom privilege like being dismissed first for recess or first at the end of the school day.

After the drawing, discard the leftover special tickets. Then start all over again. A sheet of tickets is included for you. See Figure A3-7 in the appendix.

Positive Referrals

These are referrals to the office for *good* reasons. **Positive referrals** can be given for good behavior, a good grade on a test, a good speech, a good project, all homework completed, a special kindness to another student, a good attitude, and so on. A student can get a positive referral for something done during the week. Only one or two positive referrals can be given out each week, so they are very special.

You fill out the certificates, which are usually printed at the school's district office, and sign them. Give the certificates to the students. They take them down to the principal who signs them and gives them a little prize. If the principal is not available at that time, the school secretary can put the positive referrals on the principal's desk and send the students back to class.

When the principal has the opportunity, he can get on that classroom's intercom and ask these two students to please report to the office to get their positive referrals. These students will have pleased smiles on their faces as they leave the classroom.

Academic Prizes

These can be small certificates or little prizes given to the student who has the highest class average in each subject at the end of each grading period. Announce at the beginning of each grading period that this recognition will be given. Watch for some surprise students emerging bright and shining from the woodwork!

Standardized Test Prizes

Students love to hear the top **national percentiles** or **grade equivalencies** of students in their class. Announce at the beginning of the entire testing period that top scorers will be recognized. Let students know that all students you observe during the testing period who appear to be trying their hardest and actively engaged in the testing process will get a special, extra recess, a night or two of no homework, or special free time in the classroom.

Special Readers

This again involves your students and the principal. Select a small group of students (3–4) and have them prepare to read aloud a small part of the same story. Be sure they know what in the story led up to the part they are going to read aloud and what happened after.

At a scheduled time, have the students take their books plus one for the principal down to the principal's office. Then they can introduce the story to the principal, read aloud their parts while the principal follows along in the book they brought. Then the students can tell what happened in the rest of the story. If the principal likes, she can give the students a special reader certificate or an "I read to my principal" button.

Special Writers

This is basically the same as special readers except you select three or four students' writing projects—the final copies—and take them to the principal. She will read them and write a few comments back to the students. Then the papers are returned to the teacher. The students *love* reading the principal's comments.

Reading Incentive Programs

Several different companies sponsor these. The businesses will provide classroom charts, certificates, buttons, prizes, and so on. These programs usually involve the students on an individual basis, the classroom as a whole, and the parents.

Reader of the Month

If you participate in a reading incentive program, it is easy to pick the reader of the month. Just pick the student who reads the most books. If you cannot participate in an organized reading incentive program, select a student who has shown a good deal of progress in reading or who has completed a book that was challenging for them.

Student of the Month

You can select one student who has done an exceptionally good job for the month. You can give the student a certificate and maybe a special seal. Publish the student's name in one of your school's weekly bulletins. That student will glow.

You can make any of these certificates on a computer. Print out each master on white, high-quality bond. Then find a copier that produces good, clean, dark copies. Go to a stationery store or print shop if need be. Copy on to high-quality bond in gold, blue, or whatever color you wish. The extra care is well worth it. The certificates will look professional and you will be proud to give them to the students.

INSTRUCTIONAL ASSISTANTS

They go by a variety of other names, including teacher's aide, teacher's assistant, and so on. You might be lucky enough to have one.

Instructional assistants can help with small-group follow-up, small-group monitoring, one-to-one tutoring, correcting papers, creating bulletin boards, copying instructional materials, and so on.

It is your responsibility to have assistants' time planned for them. Have clear directions so that they will understand what you want done and how you would like it done. Written directions are usually best. Have available for them any materials they will need.

If you are in charge of evaluating your instructional assistant (sometimes just the principal does), make sure you look at the evaluation form early in the year. If there are any problems, let your assistant know. Give him suggestions for improvement. Do not have any surprises at evaluation time. Let your

Figure 3-6. This instructional assistant gives a listening test to a student who was absent the day the class took the test. Courtesy of Cheryl Thompson.

assistant know when he is doing a good job. Instructional assistants can be a real asset to any classroom.

INSTRUCTIONAL MEDIA CENTER

Also known as your district's curriculum lab, the media center is usually located at the district office. Go on a tour of this lab, and ask the person in charge to please explain the machines and their capabilities and the check-out process for materials.

This place is a gold mine. There are instructional materials for every subject. You will see nice art projects, book reports, classroom decoration ideas, and so on. Tag and railroad board are available in many beautiful colors, as well as butcher paper and construction paper.

The machines in the media center will fascinate you.

Leteron

This machine presses letters, question marks, commas, and so on on to a tape. Tape comes in black, brown, white, red, and royal blue. Letters come in uppercase, lowercase, and italics, as well as in various sizes. Leteron works perfectly for chart titles.

Follow these steps to operate the machine:

1. Plug in the cord and remove the cover.
2. Put in the Letertape cartridge, which contains the tape. Place the tape between the rollers.
3. As you guide the tape through the narrow tape slot on the top of the machine, replace the cover.
4. Set the spacing knob located on the left side of the machine. This will determine how close together your letters will be.
5. Immediately in front of the tape slot is another slot called the die slot. Take one of the metal die plates with the size and kind of letter you want and insert it into the die plate slot.
6. Press the actuator bar, a 4½-inch long bar directly in front of the die slot. The cover must be down or the machine will not work.
7. Use the scissor die plate to cut off the tape when you are finished with your letters.

Ellison Die Machine

This machine is excellent for bulletin board letters and decorations, calendar dates, placemats, bookmarks, and art projects. Besides rubber dies with uppercase and lowercase letters in a variety of sizes, there are dies with many, many designs that come in both small and large sizes. Just a few examples are: apple, rocking horse, USA, bunny, happy face, flower, tyrannosaurus, Halloween cat, bell, butterfly, leaves, holly, hearts, pioneers, pumpkin, shamrock, tepee, teddy bear, duck, and witch.

You can press dies onto construction paper, laminated construction paper, tag, and railroad board. Do not use **chipboard,** because it is too thick for the machine.

After you have punched out your design, if you like, you can place the design paper on the overhead projector. Tape a piece of large paper to your chalkboard. Then move the overhead the distance away from the chalkboard for the size object you would like. Trace the outline on the chalkboard paper. That way you can have a much larger picture of your snowman or turkey or brontosaurus or pterodactyl or frog for your art project or science project.

Follow these directions to operate the Ellison die machine:

1. Chop strips of paper about 5 inches wide.
2. Take the rubber die. The wooden side faces you. The rubber side faces down.
3. Place your strip of paper under the rubber die.
4. Slip the rubber die with the strip of paper under it into the machine.
5. Pull the long handle toward you and press down firmly. The die must press through all the paper if you have more than one strip.
6. Take out the die and paper. Replace the die. Punch out your final product.

Laminating Machine

Laminating a paper puts a thin coat of plastic on both sides of it. This can be done for preservation purposes. Without laminating, a paper will easily curl up, get a worn look to it, and fade. Charts that look beautiful can rapidly deteriorate if not laminated. A paper can also be laminated if you want instructions of some sort to be permanent—put them on before you laminate—but you want to be able to write on the paper and erase what you write. After the paper is laminated, use nonpermanent overhead pens to write on it. Clean using water and a soft paper towel.

For example, you could write the Preamble to the Constitution on a piece of 28-inch by 22-inch tag and decorate it with some American flags. Leave space for students' names. Then laminate the tag. When the students recite the Preamble, they can use blue and red overhead pens to sign their names. When you are ready for your next year's class, just wipe off the names of your current students. Your chart eagerly awaits its new names.

Writing paper, construction paper, tag, railroad board, and chipboard can all be laminated. There are press laminators and roll laminators. Chipboard must be used in the **press laminator.** It is too thick to pass through the rollers of the roll laminator.

Follow these instructions to operate the laminator:

1. Turn the heat switch on. Depending on the size of the laminator, the temperature needed varies. For the 25-inch roll laminator, a temperature of at least 250 degrees or more is needed. You will need to wait about fifteen minutes if no one has been using the laminator before you and it is cold.
2. If you are using a press laminator, take your laminating film and use the tacking iron to tack the laminating film in several places to your item to be laminated.
3. Check the temperature gauge on the top of the machine to be sure it is hot enough.
4. Then slip your item into the press, pull down the handle, and let it stay in the press for about four minutes.
5. If you are using a roll laminator, check the temperature gauge on the left-hand side of the machine to see if it is the right temperature for your size machine.
6. *Do not* start laminating until you have checked the back of the roll laminating machine to be positive the excess lamination is not about to feed back into the machine. It should move away from the machine.
7. Guide your item into the rollers as you push down on the front pedal.
8. Keep checking the back of the machine so that the lamination does not try to feed back into the rollers.
9. When your item is totally through so that you will be able to cut it off and still leave a little laminating material hanging out, take your foot off the pedal and then press it down quickly. The laminator will stop. You will have your final product.

At the instructional media center, the beginning of each month is the beginning of a million new ideas. Do not miss out on them!

CHAPTER QUESTIONS

1. What is gender equity?
2. Are you aware of any gender-biased comments you make? If so, how can you successfully eliminate this habit?
3. If you hear gender-biased statements from your students, how will you correct them? What if you hear them from your colleagues?
4. What are image words? Why are they a problem?
5. What is physical space? Can you write about it from a cultural point of view?
6. Devise a rubric for assessing expository writing for a grade level of your choosing.
7. What can you do in your classroom to prevent the canyon effect?
8. Explain validity and reliability for tests. What is ecological validity?
9. What are corrective feedback and mastery testing? How would you feel about using a system of mastery testing in math?
10. Write an open-ended question for a history test. Provide scaffolding with it.
11. Create an incentive program for a classroom. Describe it in detail.

12. Explain why incentive programs create enthusiasm and build self-esteem.
13. Write three days of specific plans for an instructional aide who works one hour a day in the classroom.
14. Name several things you will find to be helpful to you in an instructional media center's curriculum lab. Explain how you could use each.
15. Write a set of open-ended questions about Martin Luther King, Jr., appropriate for second-grade students.
16. What other materials could you present to your class when you have them do one of the geography booklets?
17. Explain the KWL technique.
18. What are the differences between traditional assessment and alternative assessment? Explain the advantages and disadvantages of each.
19. Construct a traditional and an alternative (authentic) assessment device to cover the same material for a unit in science or a selection in reading.
20. What did you learn from the ISTEP study?

CHAPTER PROJECT

Develop lesson plans for a history project on the first Thanksgiving, George Washington, or Abraham Lincoln. These plans can be for any grade level of your choice.

First, gather the written information you want for the lesson. Using specific pages from a grade-level history text is fine. Or you could select a number of books on the subject from the library and have the students share these or work in partners or groups. As part of your plans for this activity, have a group of open-ended questions and a group of set-response questions for the students to answer. If you would like the students to write a short report, detail the type of information and format you would like used. As the last part of this project, provide an accompanying art project. All the students can do the same project or there can be different projects for different groups.

You may also have various art projects and let the students select individually. The art project could be a large cutout and glue-together figure of Washington, Lincoln, Abe's log cabin, a Pilgrim or Indian at the first Thanksgiving, all of which are available at your local teachers' supply store in reproducible books. You might want the students to have a scene from the Revolutionary War, Civil War, or something related to the Emancipation Proclamation. When students are finished with their projects, you could then schedule time for oral presentations, maybe having each student plan one or two interesting things to say about their subject.

Have all your materials and lesson plans together in a folder. Include references to texts with page numbers and/or library books to be used by the students.

REFERENCES

Armstrong, J O. (1991). *Teacher-constructed frames for instruction with content area text* (Tech. Rep. No. 537, p. 73). Urbana, IL: University of Illinois at Urbana-Champaign. Center for the Study of Reading.

Aschbacher, P. R. (1992). *Issues in innovative assessment for classroom practice: Barriers and facilitators* (p. 76). Washington, DC: Office of Educational Research and Improvement.

Bangert-Drowns, R. L., Kulik, J. A., & Kulik, C-L. C. (1991). Effects of frequent classroom testing. *Journal of Educational Research, 85,*(2), 89–98.

Brophy, J., Van Sledright, B. A., & Bredin, N. (1992). *Fifth-graders' ideas about European exploration of the new world expressed before and after studying this topic within a U. S. history course.* East Lansing, MI: Michigan State University, The Center for the Learning and Teaching of Elementary Subjects, Institute for Research on Teaching.

Bryk, A. (1988). Musings on the moral life of schools. *American Journal of Education, 96,* 256–290.

Castanos, J. B. (1994). Watch what you say. *Santa Clara Magazine, 36*(2), 47.

Lockledge, A., & Hayn, J. A. (1993). *Preparing teachers for open response testing.* School of Education, University of North Carolina at Wilmington, U. S. Department of Education, Educational Resources Information Center (ERIC).

Milanovich, N. J. (1988). *Modeling equitable behavior in the classroom, training module V.* San Antonio, TX: Desegregation Assistance Center, Intercultural Development Research Association.

Paris, S. G., Calfee, R. C., Filby, N., Hiebert, E. H., Pearson, P. D., Valencia, S. W., & Wolf, K. P. (1992). A framework for authentic literacy assessment. *The Reading Teacher, 46*(2), 88–98.

Perrone, V. (1991). *Expanding student assessment.* Alexandria, VA: Association for Supervision and Curriculum Development.

Pierson, C. A. & Beck, S. S. (1993). Performance assessment: The realities that will influence the rewards. *Childhood Education, 62,* 29–32.

Stern, C., & Keislar, E. (1977). Teacher attitudes and attitude change: A research review. *Journal of Research and Development in Education, 10,* 63–76.

Stiggins, R. J., & Bridgeford, N. J. (1986). *Performance Assessment.* Baltimore, MD: The Johns Hopkins University Press.

Thacker, J. L., & McInerney, W. D. (1992). Changing academic culture to improve student achievement in the elementary schools. *ERS Spectrum, 10*(4), 18–23.

Tierney, R. J. (1992). Setting a new agenda for assessment. *Learning 92, 21*(3), 62–64.

What is authentic assessment? National Center for Fair and Open Testing (FairTest), Cambridge, MA, 1992.

4

THE JKL'S

This chapter covers some diverse, and interesting topics. It gives some practical information about an absolute necessity to running a classroom well; some solid, useful procedures for your students to use to guarantee academic success; four tough areas to deal with for personal success; a fascinating personal, private device to get your students started on increasing their self-concepts/self-esteem; and techniques for teaching one of the four component areas of integrated language arts. This chapter's topics are:

- Jobs and Interviews
- Keys to Academic Success
- Keys to Personal Success
- Key to Self-Concept/Self-Esteem
- Listening

The first part of this chapter deals with the basic necessity for running an elementary classroom well. First and foremost, you need the *opportunity* to do so. That opportunity is a job teaching elementary school.

JOBS AND INTERVIEWS

Preparing for a career in teaching elementary school can be an exciting time, but it is nothing compared to the thrill of your first job.

Researching Where to Apply

Research different school districts before you decide to which you will apply. Following are some of the questions to which you should find answers before applying.

1. Is the district a total growth district, a district that has growth in one geographical area but declining enrollment in another; a district that has growth at one level, for example, secondary, but declining enrollment at elementary; or a district of overall declining enrollment? What about transiency? What about political discord?

The answers to these questions relate directly to job security and satisfaction. Your best choice for a district, if you can find one in your area, is a district that has increasing enrollment at all levels, especially at the beginning grades—K, 1, and 2. Then you will know that if you do a good job, you will be back the next year. If you go on board with a district with declining enrollment, the usual policy is last on, first out, in which case you may get involved in an emotionally trying time. However, you may not really have much of a choice in your area, so just do the best you can.

Many districts offer newly certificated employees a temporary contract only. This contract automatically expires at the end of the school year, sometimes at the end of the semester. Then it may be the following September, after school starts and the district is sure of its enrollment, before it calls back the temporary contract holders. In most districts, once you have spent one year on a temporary contract, you will be on a first-year probationary contract when you start the new year. Be sure you check each district, though. Procedures vary dramatically even in neighboring areas.

Another problem can arise if you are hired at a school that is projected to have declining enrollment the following year. Then that school will undoubtedly lose a teacher. As mentioned, even if you are on a probationary contract, you will probably be the one to go. But if the district has growth at other elementary schools, you can go on involuntary transfer to one of them. This means you will have to start at a new school and probably a new grade, too, but at least you have some job protection.

Therefore, try to avoid, if you can, hiring on with a district of overall declining enrollment. They may need a few teachers the year you are looking for a job, but the following year, not only may they not need any of those new hires, they may have additional layoffs as well. Then you have to begin the job-seeking process all over again.

School transiency is another thing to give some consideration to before interviewing. Some schools have many students who are there for a few months, then gone. The class in June may be wholly different from what it was in September. If you are going to be interviewing at a school with a high turnover rate, will you still be satisfied with your year's work? If the answer is yes, you will have a good time. If no, look for a more stable school enrollment.

Some districts are in the midst of political turmoil, which can have a negative effect on employee morale. There may be turbulence on the school board or dissension between the district and the certificated and classified employees. Be aware of this first so that you are prepared for any skepticism or pessimism after you start teaching.

How can you find out about all these matters? Call or write each district office and request its enrollment for the elementary and secondary levels for the last few years and its projected enrollment for the next few years, especially in the early primary grades. The district office or the teachers' association will have information regarding projected new hires, the number of teachers on leave (all of whom are guaranteed a job when they return), and the number of teachers on temporary contracts who get rehired the next year. The district office would be able to inform you of the transiency rate at various schools. You can get information regarding political discord from the teachers' association or the local newspapers.

2. What is the district's financial state? It seems a dichotomy for districts to be making program and personnel cuts and be hiring, too, but it is very common. If a district is in poor financial condition and has a history of financial troubles compared with the surrounding districts, give this some serious consideration before applying. This information is obtainable from the county schools' office.

3. What is the district's salary schedule? Get a copy of it from the district office. How does it compare with those of districts in the surrounding thirty- to forty-mile range? Is there a **master's degree barrier?** How many steps does it have? Are there restrictions regarding the types of classes you can take to move over to another column?

When you are comparing salary schedules, for a realistic, solid picture, compare the beginning teachers' salaries with those of other districts, the salaries after about ten years of experience with those of the other districts, and the top pay and how many years this requires with those of others.

Check to see if there is a master's degree barrier. This means that you cannot enter the last salary-level column unless you have a master's, regardless of the number of units you have. Some districts do not have a master's barrier; instead, they pay a bonus for a master's. If you have either of these situations, it is advantageous to enroll in a master's degree program fairly early so that the courses you take to fulfill credential obligations and professional continuing education responsibilities are ones that can be applied toward your degree. Be aware that most, if not all, master's degree programs have a time limit of only a few years. After that, if you don't have your degree, your classes start becoming obsolete. You will have to begin replacing expired units.

Most districts present their salary schedules on a table of steps and columns. Steps are for the years of contract service and columns are for the total number of units you have acquired beyond your bachelor's. Districts with fewer steps are usually more advantageous because you can get to the higher salaries more quickly. Consider this when comparing salary schedules. Some districts have restrictions on the types of classes you can take for salary placement, so always check with your district before enrolling in *any* classes.

It is not uncommon for teachers with the identical amounts of education and contract service experience to be making vastly different salaries, although they are teaching within five or ten miles of each other. "Vastly different" can mean five to ten thousand dollars a year. If you can, go to the higher-paid districts.

4. What is the district's benefit package? Get a copy of it from the district office. Will money be deducted from your monthly check to help pay for the premium? Is there a large deductible? Are HMO's as well as an indemnity plan offered? Is there coverage in all areas of health, including physical and psychological therapy, vision care, and dental care as well as prescription costs? What is the situation regarding coverage of spouses or dependents? How does the district handle disability benefits?

If money is deducted from your check to pay for all or part of health insurance premiums or for dependent coverage, consider this factor when comparing salary schedules. A lower salary schedule *might* compare more favorably with a higher one if the latter had deductions for health care coverage.

Another consideration is the scope of the benefit package. If the district has poor dental coverage, it will not do you much good if you are in generally good health except for massive dental problems. Some prescription drugs can run as high as eighty to a hundred dollars. See if your district has good coverage for prescriptions.

If you have a preference for an indemnity plan over an HMO or vice versa, be sure the district offers what you want. If you want the HMO, check to see that the facility is in a convenient location for you.

Usually a district will have a built-in disability program. For example, if you are disabled, first you use your sick days, then you go to a system of your per diem minus the cost of the substitute teacher. Even if the district offers this or a similar plan, it is a good idea to purchase a group disability policy that can coordinate with the district's, especially if you or dependents rely on your teaching salary. Ask the district or teachers' association for pertinent information. Insurance companies often have a group rate for disability to fill the gap between what the district offers and a certain percentage of your total salary.

Take a look at each district's life insurance policy. Are they very similar, or do one or two districts have significantly better policies than the others? If you have a family that depends on your income, this can be an important item.

Applying for a Job

After you have closely researched the districts, make your application. This can be done by mail or in person. Consider the factor of being in the right place at the right time and go get the application in person if at all possible.

Interviewing for a Job

Now you are ready to prepare for the all-important interview.

You may be in an area where plenty of jobs are available for new teachers, or you may be in an area where the job market is extremely competitive. In either case, the interview is extremely important and will strongly determine whether you get a job offer from that district.

There are different types of interviews that you might face. Many districts do an initial screening interview at the district office prior to sending you to an interview at an individual school site. Frequently, you will be interviewed by a board of representatives from the district, probably including an elementary principal, rather than an individual. (It is not necessarily considered better to be interviewed by a board versus an individual; it mainly relates to district policy and size.)

Find out the names of the people interviewing you and the names of their positions. Copy this information in a notebook along with the district's name so you will have access to it later. If you are interviewed by just one person, get this person's name and position. Study the individual's face so that if you come across him or her in the future, you will be able to call the person by name. You can then reintroduce yourself and help the person recall that you interviewed around such and such a time. Tell the person you are still very interested in that district and definitely in pursuit of a job.

Somewhere along the interview line, you most likely will be interviewed by the principal of the school where the opening(s) exist. The principal may have a small team of teachers present during the interview or may have the teachers interview you at a later time. Follow the same procedures for a district interview. Be at your absolute best that day.

Figure A4-1 in the appendix contains information about interviews and some specific questions to prepare answers for *in advance* of the actual interview. You, just like all others, are going to be nervous prior to an interview, so the more prepared you are, the more confident you will feel. If you do not know an exact answer, speak to the part you do know. You are just beginning and are not expected to know everything.

It is important to convey to the principal and/or the interview team that you are flexible and a team player. Much policy decision is done at the local school site by the teachers. You must be able to work cooperatively and be accommodating in order to compromise.

An interview is considered a formal experience. Come professionally dressed and impeccably groomed. Sit up straight, act alert, and show an eagerness for the job. If it is offered to you and you do not want it, you can always say you need two days to make your decision. Then you can decline later. But if you do not act enthusiastic and effervescent, you are not going to get many job offers.

After you have had a fabulous interview, do some extensive follow up, especially if you are in a highly competitive area. This is where your notebook of names comes in handy. Write letters thanking the people who provided the opportunity for you to interview. You might write something like this:

I enjoyed meeting and interviewing with you on (whatever date). Thank you for affording me this worthwhile opportunity.

Your district presents itself as dynamic and innovative. I hope to be a part of your team. I'm looking forward to hearing from you soon.

Sincerely, etc.

Make sure you have your complete name typed so that it is easy to read. If you go by a nickname and you used it during the interview, include it in the letter, too.

Include your phone number and area code so that people can easily call you without having to search through records.

Call the individual principals with whom you have interviewed and tell them of your continued interest to keep your name fresh in their minds. Otherwise, your name is only one of many instead of one of the few who have done a good job following up their interviews.

Instead of calling certificated personnel at the district office, go there in person to see what progress is being made in getting you hired. Do not go just once, either. Go many times. Do what it takes. That way, you make yourself highly visible and instead of being one of the many, you will be one of the few—the few that get hired!

Research and Studies

Garman (1990) discovered that the two most highly associated qualities with employment of beginning teachers in Ohio were vitality and enthusiasm. Kowalski and colleagues (1992) found the top four characteristics were respect for students, honesty, ability to work with peers, and verbal communication. Unfortunately, these are characteristics that are not easily measured. Interestingly, quantity of experience, which rates the highest pay for teachers in most districts, was ranked fourth to the last in importance, and involvement in activities in high school and college, which has shown a statistical significance with experienced teachers who are identified as outstanding in their field (Kowalski & Weaver, 1988), was ranked third to the last.

A study by Walters (1992) reviewed a program at the College of Saint Elizabeth in New Jersey that incorporates computers throughout the teacher education program. By doing this, it is hoped that teachers will make computers and other forms of technology a normal part of the teaching/learning process. In turn, preservice teachers will be attractive as certified teachers to school districts that have invested in computers and other technology to be used in the classroom.

Every course taught in the education department at this college uses hands-on assignments and projects that integrate the computer into the content of the class. The assignments in the courses require the students to develop skills in four areas: awareness, adaptation, analysis, and application.

The awareness stage involves preservice teachers visiting schools where they observe the use of computers. Future teachers have the opportunity to recognize the computer as a normal tool for education and to become computer literate.

Adaptation entails applying learning theories to computerized analysis of student behaviors. Preservice teachers gain hands-on experience with computer-assisted teaching methods and learn how to interpret standardized tests and other teacher-developed instruments. They develop an understanding of the implications of technology for individual and group learning, and they use the computer to increase student interest and motivation.

The analysis step involves evaluating computer techniques and materials for instruction in reading and language arts. Preservice teachers increase their diagnostic skills by analyzing reading deficiencies with the computer. They become adept at evaluating software content for use in the elementary curriculum and relating computer games to increasing learning, student interest, motivation, and social skills. They acquire techniques to use computers with students with special needs and to use word processors to develop students' writing skills.

Finally, the application stage consists of using management and record keeping systems on the computer. Preservice teachers learn to develop and use alternate assessment methods. They are taught to use computer programs to create a database for research projects.

In addition to computer skills, preservice teachers must learn how to use a camcorder, overhead projector, film, slides, and copying systems.

Preservice teachers leave this program with competence in many technological areas. They will then apply this technology to the classroom.

The second part of this chapter introduces you to nine keys for your students—four for their academic success, four for their personal success, and one for their self-concept/self-esteem awareness.

KEYS TO ACADEMIC SUCCESS

Here are the four keys to academic success:

Key 1.   Completely finish and turn in all assignments in every subject area.

Key 2.   Study thoroughly and carefully at home for all tests.

Key 3.   Know well and with speed the basic addition, subtraction, multiplication, and division facts.

Key 4.   Proofread papers carefully for any problems in the following areas: missing words, complete sentences, capitals at the beginning of sentences, ending punctuation, correct spelling, correct computation in math, and the neatness of each paper, including the appropriate heading.

If you wish to pass out a copy of the Four Keys to Academic Success to your parents, see Figure A4-2.

The Four Keys to Academic Success can also be made into an eye-catching display in your classroom. A classroom wall above the chalkboards is a good place. Make the display 110 inches long and 32 inches high. Get enough pieces of royal blue railroad board to cover that area. Laminate the railroad board; otherwise, it will fade quickly. Staple it to the wall, and put a fancy bulletin-board border around the perimeter. Use *large* red and yellow bulletin-board letters for the title, *The Four Keys to Academic Success.* Place the title in the center. Then have each success statement with the key and number in front of the statement neatly written on a large piece of tagboard. Place it on the left-hand side of the display.

On yellow butcher paper, make a large sun. Use red and dark-blue markers to make the sun's eyes, nose, smile, and rays. Place this on the right-hand side of the display.

Your classroom assignment accountability chart (see Chapter 1) will be an immense help to your students in working with Key 1, completely finishing and turning in every assignment. Students can see at a glance if they are up-to-date with their work. If they are not, they can quickly and easily determine the exact assignment(s) they need to complete. It might be a math homework assignment, or a creative writing assignment; on the other hand, it might be a major report or project that will take a large amount of time. They need to schedule an adequate amount of time immediately, so the activity is not only completely finished, but also beautifully done.

Students need to learn at an early age that collected assignments need to be turned in by them as well as by their classmates. These are the specific assignments for which they will be held accountable. These assignments must be totally completed, every problem done well, every paragraph done well, and every page of a report properly included and completely finished. Both their achievement and effort grades will be affected by this. Completing and turning in all these assignments gives the students the practice time they need to develop and maintain their new skills. Otherwise, what is learned can be quickly forgotten.

The habit of completing and turning in all assignments is something that will be of great benefit to students not only all the way through school, but also in the workplace for which they are preparing. This helps make students reliable. People can count on them to complete tasks and deliver them to the necessary place or person. This is the kind of lifelong skill you want all your students to develop.

Key 2, studying at home for tests, is essential to learning material thoroughly and feeling confident with it. Time spent in the classroom learning and practicing is very important. Be sure to help students with all the important learning strategies so that they will do well on tests. Show them how to think out loud, check their prior knowledge, take notes, make up questions, make predictions, use graphic organizers, and relate new material to their own personal lives and experiences.

But time spent solely in the classroom is not enough. Additional time needs to be scheduled after school hours for good success. If a math test is scheduled on Thursday, students need to spend whatever time at home it takes them to have a good understanding of the skills and concepts. This will vary from student to student. One student may need twenty minutes, another may need thirty-five minutes, and a third may need an hour. It does not take students too long to determine their individual needs. Their goal is to be able to do the best they are capable of on the test.

This key will be important to your students throughout their lives. Just as they prepare for tests in their classrooms, so will they prepare for presentations and reports in the workplace. They want to give the best they can. It may take one worker two hours to prepare a good report, while it takes another worker three to prepare a similar report. The worker who needs three hours for a good report should schedule three and the two-hour worker should schedule two. That way, both will be pleased about the quality of their reports and feel successful and satisfied.

Key 3, knowing math facts with speed, is another area where students need confidence to be academically successful. Knowing all their math facts helps them move quickly through complicated problems and prevents discouragement. The knowledge and quickness gives them the eagerness to explore further in both concepts and skill complexities.

Obviously, students who use their fingers for math facts are not going to be as fast as those who have instant recall. But some elementary students do not have that type of recall, for any of a variety of reasons. They may *need* to use their fingers to provide themselves a kinesthetic approach to facts. That is why multiplication "finger facts" can be helpful to this kind of student. These students can get quite fast on their fingers. If this is what they need to move on and be successful, this is what they should do.

Not enough can be said about Key 4. Proofreading is another essential for academic success. Many students quickly complete an assignment and that's it. They do not want to be bothered looking it over, nor do they want to take the time to check for beginning capitals, correct computation, neat-looking papers or projects, or the appropriate heading, which includes a vital statistic: their name!

Oftentimes, you can help your students develop this desire and skill by providing class time for proofreading before you collect their papers. Have them point to each word of their paper, each sentence, each problem, and so on, beginning with their names at the top of their papers. Lead students through this process. Tell the class:

1. Check to see that your name is on your paper.
2. Check for beginning capitals for all your sentences.
3. Look for ending punctuation marks.
4. Now read your sentences to yourself to be sure they are complete sentences, make sense, and are interesting.
5. Check your spelling. Use a dictionary, an electronic speller, your spelling word list, or ask a classmate, who is a good speller, to give you a hand.
6. Last, check to be sure your paper is neat. Do not have any crossouts. Be sure indentions are neat and correct. Double-check that letters are neat and correctly formed.

Figure 4-1. This student is checking the assignment accountability chart to see whether she has any assignments to complete. She stays on top of her work in every subject area. (Key 1)

Figure 4-2.   This boy is studying at home for a history test, using his textbook and study sheet to prepare. (Key 2)

Then, collect their papers.

Another method that works well and fosters more independence of checking is to have the students write you a little note at the end of a particular assignment. Tell them what to write; for example, "I proofread my paper *X* number of times." Or you can be more specific in your directions; for example, "I proofread my paper for beginning capitals"; "I proofread for complete sentences"; "I proofread for a correct heading"; or "I proofread for neatness, especially for neat, correct indentions."

You can also have the students write you this kind of a note at the end of a test. This helps them look these papers over more carefully, as does having them write a note at the end of a project or report. Not only that, the students enjoy these little notes. Some write pretty outrageously large numbers for their proofreading times!

Proofreading is another skill that teachers hope their students will be using for the rest of their lives. Impress upon them the importance of reviewing their work before having it

Figure 4-3.   Two students are helping each other get better and faster at their math facts. (Key 3)

Figure 4-4. This student is busy completing a writing test. He has his personal list of spelling words and his dictionary to help him do a good job of proofreading. (Key 4)

collected, so that they will get in the habit of proofreading reports before they submit them to their bosses, proofing their material prior to a sales presentation, and checking their charts for typos and accuracy, and so on. Explain to them the transference of this skill to the work world.

Notice that nowhere in these four keys does it state that the student must be really smart. Why? It is not that important. There are plenty of smart students in elementary classrooms who do only a fair job because they do not use these keys, and there are lots of students of average ability who do a fine job because they do use them.

If students use these keys, they will be successful in *any* elementary classroom. Teach your students to use them and your classroom will be running beautifully.

In addition to the academic keys to success, you may also wish to have an academic mission for your class to help students and you, stay focused and goal-oriented.

Following is an academic mission statement that would be suitable for an upper grade. It will give you an idea of possible items to include. Decide what will be appropriate for your particular class and grade level. You might want to have a class brainstorming session to devise a list.

KEYS TO PERSONAL SUCCESS

Here are the four keys to personal success:

Key 1.   Always do your best.
Key 2.   Be polite and kind to others.
Key 3.   Follow laws and rules.
Key 4.   Be honest.

A copy of the personal success keys that you can give to your parents is contained in Figure A4-3 in the appendix.

Students need to struggle, reach and strive to discover what their best is. A large part of always doing your best is *wanting* to do your best and being willing to put in the time and effort it takes to do your best. Some students want good grades, but, unfortunately, they do not want to take the time to thoroughly study; or they want a beautiful, well-written report, but they do not want to actually spend the amount of necessary time and

ACADEMIC MISSION

Students will identify their work by writing their first and last names on their papers, the assigned subject and the specific assignment.

Students will submit assignments that are neatly and completely done.

Students will be able to correctly form and connect letters for upper- and lowercase in both printing and handwriting.

Students will be able to write a friendly letter containing a minimum of one paragraph using correct friendly letter format, appropriate paragraph structure, paragraph format, writing mechanics, and spelling. The paragraphs may describe a science experiment, a health issue, a history event or decision, a character in a story, or an interesting happening in a story. The paragraphs may be a retelling of a story, a reporting on a current event in the news, a school activity, a hobby, or an area of individual interest. Paragraphs may be of the creative, imaginative, original, or persuasive nature. They also may introduce an original piece of poetry, diary entries, or dialogue contained in the letter.

Students will be able to read aloud within one and a half years of their grade level and correctly retell what they have read.

Students will be able to read independently within one and a half years of their grade level and correctly locate and provide answers to comprehension questions.

Students will be able to locate words in the dictionary and locate subjects and topics in the encyclopedia.

Students will know their addition, subtraction, multiplication, and division facts.

Students will be able to add, subtract, multiply, and divide whole numbers.

Students will be able to solve and construct word problems that incorporate addition, subtraction, multiplication, and division of whole numbers.

Students will be able to conduct simple science experiments, record data, draw conclusions, and write an experiment summary followed by a personal response.

Students will have experiences working in learning groups as well as working independently.

effort to do a good job on it. They learn the hard way that these things do not just materialize to their satisfaction. They take time and hard work.

Other students want something but they do not do anything about it, or they do not do *enough* about it to get it accomplished or to bring it to fruition. Problems with self-concept or self-esteem can be behind this behavior. It is important to have positive feelings about yourself to do the things you want, and in some cases, to even *want* things that are for your betterment.

Constant encouragement and praise is beneficial to most students. Let them know that you are pleased with their work and effort. Help the students to learn to encourage each other in their achievements. Explain to your students that you hope they will be wanting to do their best in the workplace, and habits learned now will carry over to the rest of their life. Cite some of their sports, rock, movie, and TV idols as examples of people who are doing their best at work. Always doing your best is a big order of business for anyone.

The second key to personal success is being polite and kind to others. Students need to learn and practice respecting individual differences and managing conflicts in a calm, mutually agreeable way. Multicultural awareness is paramount so that students are not saying things they think are funny that actually are family, racial, ethnic, or cultural slurs.

Some students need a lot of encouragement, and others may need direct instruction. Many need to practice. Give students the words to use when they interact with their classmates: Please; thank you; excuse me; I'm sorry; you did a great job on your report; I loved your speech this morning; your outfit is sharp; your haircut is cute; may I help you with that problem?; and so on. Show them how it is done through your own behavior.

If someone is in the habit of being rude or unkind, it takes effort and practice to undo this bad habit. The support, encouragement, and praise of others is vitally important because it might be the only motivator for that student in the beginning.

Make the students aware that they will need this skill to get along well in their years in school as well as in their career years. Everyone—classmates, relatives, neighborhood children, teachers, doctors, police officers, bus drivers, sales clerks—*everyone* appreciates people who are polite and kind to others.

The third key to personal success is follow laws and rules. Just as there are rules in every family, there are rules for the classroom and for the school. In the larger society, these rules still exist but many of them are then called laws.

Students need to know from the outset that rules and laws need to be followed so that the classroom can be enjoyed by *all* students, so that the school is a safe place for all students, and so that society can be a desirable place for all law-abiding citizens. If rules are not obeyed, there are negative consequences. Likewise, if they are obeyed, there are positive consequences.

Point out some negative consequences to your students and help them understand that things are much more pleasant for them and for others if they abide by the rules. For example, it is much nicer to enjoy lunch period recess playing basketball, four square, and so on, than sitting inside writing sentences for misbehavior. It is much more enjoyable to stay on campus with

classmates than getting suspended for abusive language to the principal. It is a lot safer to be involved productively in a game on the playground at recess than to be throwing rocks. It is much more relaxing to drive a reasonable speed on the freeway than to get pulled over for a ticket.

Also indicate positive consequences to following rules and laws. These are not emphasized enough, because they are usually not as obvious as negative consequences. But students need to know that when they are following rules and laws, they are making life easier not just for themselves, but for everyone around them—parents, residents of the neighborhood, classmates, school personnel, and workers and customers at the local mall, grocery store, and so on. Students who are following rules and laws need to be keenly aware of this.

Other positive consequences are awards, recognition, and special privileges. For example, students can be called up at an assembly for citizen of the month awards. They can get award certificates in their classroom for following class and school rules. If their parents have a driving record that is free of moving violations, they can, in some states, renew their license by mail and save themselves a trip to the Department of Motor Vehicles.

Ensure that the students clearly understand rules and laws that pertain directly to them. Enlighten them on the reasoning behind these laws, and let them know lawful, intelligent, productive ways to handle laws that they think are wrong or unfair.

The fourth key is being honest. This is so simply said, but some people find this very difficult to do. One lie leads to another or one dishonest act leads to another, then another to cover that one, and so forth.

Give plenty of examples to your students of honesty so that you are sure they understand. For example, cheating on a test is dishonest, doing others' homework and having them say it is theirs is dishonest, intimidating school acquaintances into giving away their lunch money is dishonest, talking someone into doing something you know is wrong is dishonest, and telling lies is dishonest.

Of course, some lies are also against the law and people get into big trouble. If children get accustomed to being dishonest, little dishonest things can eventually lead to big dishonest things. The next thing they know, they are awaiting a criminal trial—theirs!

KEY TO SELF-CONCEPT/SELF-ESTEEM

A big part of being personally successful is having a good self-concept (self-image) and high self-esteem, which is connected to a person's self-concept. This is where wanting to do something right and actually doing it come into play.

The interrelatedness of self-concept and self-esteem with behavior, attitudes, and achievement has long been considered a fundamental premise in psychology. However, some controversy exists over which is influencing which in this relationship, especially in the area of achievement. Some feel that it is first necessary to have a good self-concept, with accompanying high self-esteem, before good achievement will exist. Some feel that the achievement is first, then comes positive feeling about the self in this area. Regardless of this horse-cart issue, it is an accepted assumption that self-concept/image and self-esteem can be worked on for improvement in the area of achievement.

In self-concept, the *concept* part is the product of learning and represents a remembering and organizing of past experiences. The *self* part is the distinct, essential identity of each individual that differentiates that person from all others. The self is defined in terms of others and includes a person's social habits, attitudes, and values.

Self-concept is people's "person" as known to themselves. It is their idea or mental image of what kind of a person or self they are, that is, how they envision themselves regardless of what their real behavior is like. *Self-esteem* is the degree to which people are confident about or satisfied with themselves; that is, how they feel about themselves.

Self-concept includes five areas: well-being (what students believe about their health, security and happiness); self-control/self-reliance (what students believe about their responsibility for their own decisions, emotions and behavior); competency (what students believe about their success in an activity or in interaction with others); acceptance by others (what students believe about their being well-liked by other people of both sexes); and acceptance of self (what students believe about their being OK people and consequently liking themselves and telling others about themselves).

Self-concept, then, when combined with self-esteem, is a very complex entity. It is a totality of what students feel or believe about themselves and other people in relation to themselves. It is important to recognize from the outset that students' self-concepts, at least as they are reported by them, may not necessarily coincide with their real selves. They may think or believe certain things about themselves that may not be borne out in their actions. For example, a student may believe that she always tries to do her best, when, in fact, her behavior does not verify this. Conversely, a student may believe that he does not really do well at anything, yet his behavior does not verify this either.

Self-concept is learned, a social product. Students think of themselves as they *think* others think of them. They usually act in accordance with their self-concepts, that is, they act in terms of what they think they are, what they think they can do, and what they think others expect them to do, all defined by their experiences in life and input from their significant others. So the way others treat children is very important. If people start treating them differently, their self-concepts and behaviors can begin to change.

Self-concept can be more important than the real self in affecting students' behavior, and self-esteem, their estimate of themselves, is also important because students feel it and experience it constantly. If they have low self-esteem, they can feel compelled to "fake it," to cover up for themselves. If they have high self-esteem, they usually feel competent and worthy of living and have self-respect.

Students with high self-esteem and positive self-concepts set high levels of aspirations and make every effort to achieve these levels. Students who conceive of themselves as "incompetent" set low levels or no levels at all and are *still* constantly frustrated or floundering around; consequently, these students may seem to give up or drop out.

When thinking about students' self-concepts and self-esteem, it is important to think of all their **references.** References include: their physical being; groups and persons with whom they identify (family, clubs, friends, school, church, city, state, nation); their possessions (clothes, money, house, etc.); and their reputations, honor, and accomplishments. If these references prosper and grow, the students feel good; if they dwindle or are attacked, they feel bad and defensive.

Another thing to consider, not to dishearten you about attempts at boosting self-esteem and nurturing self-concepts but to inform you about what you are dealing with, is that once students' self-concepts are developed and established, they remain relatively stable and are resistant to attempts to change them. But societal values and group values can change, and these can influence self-concept change.

Time and major disruptive events can cause changes in the "self." When going through a lot of changes, students can feel at odds with themselves until the self is reorganized. This can then be internalized into a changed self-concept.

The self-concept produces certain wants and goals that the students pursue, such as popularity, importance, grades, and so

Figure 4-5. Teachers can build feelings of self esteem and opportunities for personal success in their students by providing them opportunities to share interesting, school-appropriate information about their families. This boy is happy to show off the newest member of his family. Courtesy of Essa and Rogers, *An Early Childhood Curriculum: From Developmental Model to Application,* ©1992 by Delmar Publishers, Inc.

on. Students' motivation is to enhance the self-concept and to avoid any threats to it.

In the relationship between self-concept and learning, students will pursue what they think is appropriate, desirable, and possible for them to learn. This is important to remember when you are teaching any kind of lesson, but especially ones involving social skills.

In the relationship between self-concept and ability, how students think "significant others" see their abilities has a great influence on what levels of learning they will set for themselves and the degree to which they will motivate themselves to pursue these levels.

In addition, students with high self-esteem and positive self-concepts tend to associate and get cues from motivated people and set high aspiration levels for themselves, whereas students with low self-esteem and negative self-concepts tend to get cues from others similar to themselves and thus remain at a low level. Give consideration to this when pairing students for classroom work or outside activities.

Working with students on their self-concepts takes time and effort on everyone's part. Self-concept/self-esteem is a difficult thing to deal with, but progress can be made. The more you understand about self-concept/self-esteem, the more patience you will allow yourself and the more opportunities you will see to make some effective moves.

The Self-Image Q-Sort

A way to help your students in the area of self-concept/self-esteem awareness is the *Self-Image Q-Sort*. In the **Q-sort method,** the evaluator (the student) is given a set of items or statements. The items are placed in some kind of order to represent or characterize the evaluator.

Q-items are printed on separate cards so that the evaluator can arrange and rearrange the cards until she gets the desired representation. Normally in a Q-sort, the evaluator must place the items into a designated number of categories. The number of items and the number of categories are equal. Because of this, it can also be called a **forced item placement.** In this Q-sort, however, some modifications exist. There are twenty-six cards, and thirty boxes instead of twenty-six boxes. This gives the evaluator a little leeway with responses.

This enjoyable, yet informative, device includes twenty-six cards with statements about self-concept on them. There is a chart for the placement of the cards into the following categories according to how the evaluators (the students) think and feel each statement applies to them:

Most True
Very True
Somewhat True
Somewhat False
Very False
Most False

For simplicity, even though the self-concept areas have a great deal of overlap, each of the twenty-six cards in the *Self-Image Q-Sort* is listed in the self-concept area that is most descriptive of it.

Well-Being
1. I feel safe and secure with my teachers.
2. I have a poor attitude about many things.
3. I know I'm wanted by my family.
4. I am scared to do some things I'd like to do.

Figure 4-6. An activity like this helps build feelings of personal success and makes an excellent display. These second-grade students had their pictures taken while "at work." Then they wrote several interesting things about themselves. Courtesy of Carroll Maietta.

Figure 4-7. What a great builder of personal success. This lucky student is the focus of the class for one week. Courtesy of Wanda Grace.

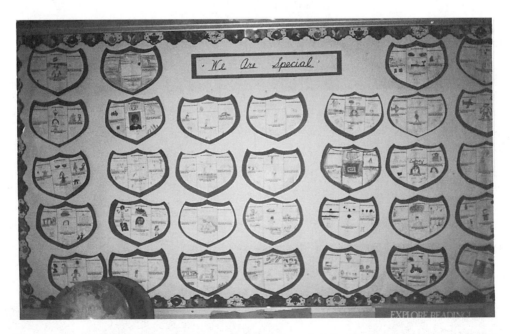

Figure 4-8. This activity gives students an opportunity to explore their family histories. Knowing more about themselves can help students appreciate how unique and special they are. Courtesy of Wanda Grace.

Self-Control/Self-Reliance
1. I can stand up for myself.
2. I get into trouble quite a lot.
3. I can usually solve my own problems.
4. I keep my temper in control.
5. I am often late in getting my work finished.
6. I always try to do my best.

Competency
1. I don't like to do new things.
2. I do well in my school work.
3. I think people expect too much of me.
4. I don't know how to get someone to like me.
5. I don't do really well at anything.

Acceptance by Others
1. I am well liked by other people.
2. I don't seem to fit in with others.
3. I am popular with members of the opposite sex.
4. I have an interest or hobby that my friend enjoys.

Acceptance of Self
1. I can tell other people what I feel.
2. I feel funny or strange about the way I act.
3. I like my name.
4. I don't like the way I look.
5. I feel very important.
6. I do not like myself very well.
7. I think I am an interesting person.

Students examine each card and place it in a box in whichever of the six rows they think best describes themselves for that statement. They continue until they are satisfied that all twenty-six cards are placed in an arrangement that represents them.

Next, the students are going to move some cards to correspond with their **ideal self,** which is a concept of what a person ought to be and how a person ought to act; the ideal self provides a standard for measurement of an individual's real behavior. The goal is to achieve an actual self that is close to the ideal self. They are never going to match perfectly and they certainly do not need to.

Students move those cards that are true for them now, but that they wish were false for them, into the dotted line area of the true boxes. Likewise, they move those cards that are basically false for them but that they wish were true for them, into the dotted line areas of the false boxes.

This activity helps students see their strengths and weaknesses in peace and quiet all by themselves. No paper or pencil is ever used. There are no right or wrong answers. In addition, no one is going to know what each student did with each card, because the students work privately, one at a time.

After students are finished with their card arrangement on the chart, they can pick *one* card statement that they slid down to the dotted box on which they would like to work. You are never going to know what card item they selected, however, or even *if* they selected a card item. You are just providing them the opportunity to work to improve this special and fragile

Figure 4-9.   This student can have lots of privacy with a study carrel while he works the *Self-Image Q-Sort.*

area. See Figure A4-4 in the appendix for materials to construct the *Self-Image Q-Sort*.

Many times, when students get to do something in the classroom off on their own in a special way, they will select something. If they select it themselves, they are more apt to at least be aware of this area. This alone can help them. They could begin work in this area, which would be a great benefit to them. Increasing self-esteem takes time and effort.

Remember, you are the one providing your students with the opportunity to become more aware and to begin to make changes. You are the one who can encourage them to respond to certain other students in new ways to help increase their self-esteem. You are the one who can provide short social skills lessons and include some of the card item information. You are the one who could make a difference!

Constructing The Self-Image Q-Sort

First, get a very thin, colored piece of tag 17 inches long and 11 inches high. Fold it in half. Glue-stick the front cover of the Q-sort to the front cover of your tag booklet. Then glue-stick page 1, the directions page, on the inside back of the front cover. Next, glue-stick page 3 to the inside of the back cover of the tag booklet. Then laminate everything, including page 2 with the card items. Finally, cut out each Q-card and you are ready to begin.

If you like, and do not mind a less sturdy version, you can just use a copier and make copies onto colored paper. Bright yellow or pink is nice. Be sure to laminate.

RESEARCH AND STUDIES

Proller's 1988 Adopt-a-Grandparent Program showed significant growth in positive attitudes toward the elderly by **at risk students** and increases in self-esteem by both at-risk and typical students. In this program, residents at a nursing home who were interested in being adopted made a videotape of themselves. Students watched these tapes and selected a "grandparent" whom they found enjoyable. At the peak of the program, 1,440 students and 925 nursing home residents were involved. Students visited their adopted grandparents bimonthly, although Proller pointed out that this became an unmanageable expense with buses for some schools.

One of the activities in which some of the students participated was exchanging letters with their new grandparents. This eliminated the expense problem and provided students an excellent way to sharpen their letter-writing skills and have a rewarding purpose for writing, too.

Motivation, another area to boost self-esteem, can be used as a means of increasing test scores, any test scores, and it can be done in an amazingly easy way. Brown and Walberg (1993) conducted a study in which K through 8 public school students were randomly assigned to a control group taking a standardized test and to an experimental group taking the same test. But the experimental group received a motivation factor, a set of special instructions to be read by the teacher from the following script: "It is really important that you do as well as you can on this test. [The test was Form 7 of the Mathematics Concepts subtest of the Iowa Test of Basic Skills

(ITBS)]. The test score you receive will let others see just how well I am doing in teaching you math this year. Your scores will be compared to students in other grades here at this school, as well as to those in other schools in Chicago. That is why it is extremely important to do the very best that you can. Do it for yourself, your parents, and me" (Brown & Walberg, 1993, p. 134).

The results: Across grade levels and across genders, the experimental group did remarkably better. The typical student's score in the experimental group rose from the 50th to the 62nd percentile (Brown & Walberg, 1993).

Bainbridge (1991) analyzed data from 5,352 questionnaires completed by parents in 1990 indicating their preferences regarding a number of different characteristics of schools or school systems.

SchoolMatch is a consulting firm that was used in this study. SchoolMatch provided information about schools and school systems to corporations selecting industrial sites and business locations. It also provided information to families relocating into specific geographic areas. SchoolMatch has given questionnaires to thousands of parents since 1986.

When parents are selecting schools for their kids, they do not necessarily conform to conventional wisdom on what is "best" or "most important." In this study, preferences regarding factors such as academic rigor, school system expenditures, school size, class size, and community characteristics varied from family to family.

School officials often send out literature equating biggest with best, such as stating their district is the largest in the area. Responses from parents and corporations, however, indicate that most of them are looking for neither very large nor very small school systems.

Few parents want their children in the most academically rigorous school, contrary to the assumptions of school officials. Instead, parents want their kids in an environment that allows them to *thrive* and *be happy*.

An article by Combs (1993) further explains the need for attention to students so that they are happy and comfortable, and discusses the importance of developing a plan to ease the transition from elementary to middle school. It then goes on to review a transition program used at Mt. Anthony Middle School, a seventh- and eighth-grade middle school.

Each year this school has more than 300 incoming seventh-graders from nine elementary schools in five districts, as well as a parochial school. The union school district has been recently established, so many members of the community were having trouble accepting the change from their own district schools to a large union one, making the transition of elementary school students to middle school especially important.

Two teams in the middle school coordinated planning for the transition program. The first team, the Coordinating Council (CC), consists of the principal, assistant principal, a seventh- to twelfth-grade guidance director, and an instructional supervisor. The other team, the Student Guidance Team (SGT), is staffed by the principal, assistant principal, guidance counselors, a school psychologist, a student assistance counselor, and a nurse.

Early in November, every elementary school principal receives a letter outlining the orientation program for the coming year. In late January, another letter providing a more detailed time line of the orientation process is sent to the principals, as well as to the central office administration and the six school board chairpersons.

Letters are also mailed in early November to inform and update teachers as to the chronology of upcoming events. In March, the sixth-grade teachers attend a conference with the administration, guidance staff, and seventh-grade teachers of the middle school. At that conference, the sixth-grade teachers' questions are answered about any changes in the program, registration procedures, or anything else.

Actual registration for seventh grade is done by the sixth-grade teachers when they meet with their students' parents in parent conferences held in April.

In early February, parents of sixth-grade students receive a letter inviting them to a parent orientation program in March. Each parent (about 80–85 percent attend) is given a booklet to help them work with their child, as well as to cope with and understand the changes their child will undergo in the next few years.

The program consists of a general introduction to the school, a further description of the student orientation program, and an explanation of some of the programs that students will be involved in once they start middle school. Then the parents are given a tour of the building, with current eighth-graders as their guides.

In mid-January, teachers begin the process of selecting seventh-graders to assist with the sixth-grade orientation program. These students, when they are eighth-graders, will be able to serve as tour guides for the parent tour mentioned above.

In mid-May, the principal, accompanied by some seventh-graders, begins visiting each elementary classroom. The sixth-graders are asked to submit questions they have about seventh grade, which the seventh-graders will be answering. The presentation by the principal and the seventh-graders consists of a review of the daily schedule, during which the seventh-graders tell about the type of work assigned in each class and offer suggestions that are helpful for the sixth-graders. Then they answer the questions the sixth-graders have prepared, as well as any new ones that may have arisen.

The schedules for incoming students are mailed out in early August, along with a letter inviting parents to accompany their children to school before the first day to walk through their schedule. The school is open for two weeks before the first day of class, including three evenings. Teachers are requested to leave a list of items required for their class posted on their door. Floor plans of the school, showing room numbers and teacher names, are also available. The mailing also includes some general information, such as the cost of lunch, gym clothes requirements, what to bring on the first day, safety information, and extracurricular activities. For the incoming students, there is a list of common questions about middle school that sixth-graders want to know.

During the first week of school, eighth-grade students—the same ones that accompanied the principal to the elementary schools the previous year—serve as guides in the hall during the periods between classes. Also, at the end of the day, the new seventh-graders are released five minutes early to find their lockers and their bus, if they take one.

At the end of the first week of school, students are given a copy of the Parent-Student Handbook to take home and have their parents review with them. The handbook contains the school rules and regulations, a calendar showing when report cards and notices are given out, as well as vacations and holidays, and some information on what the parents can expect from the school and what the school expects from the parents. It also includes a page asking parents to list the kinds of activities that they would be willing to help with and any special interests they would be willing to share with the students. Each student is asked to return this sheet to the school, where a database of this information is developed.

During the second week of school, each grade has an open house, where the parents attend a general meeting in the gym, after which they split up to meet with their children's teachers and then walk through the buildings to see some of the classrooms.

This orientation program has dramatically reduced the fears that both parents and children have about attending a new school. Surveys showed that this program has had a positive influence on both parents and students, and that parents of students who attended the school before the new orientation program was implemented are happy with the new format.

Another study related to self-esteem indicated that even though there are factors *not* under a school's control that are important predictors of behavior, some factors that *are* under the school's control are also associated with behavior. For example, a student's family background is not under the school's control. However, it has been found that schools with high-achieving and interested students, a drug-free environment, discipline and structure, a positive climate, and parent involvement have fewer behavioral problems (Weishew & Peng, 1993). These are factors over which the school has control. Given this, the article proposes ideas for school practices and policies to help improve student behavior.

This article analyzed data from the 1988 National Education Longitudinal Study. Although this study was conducted on a national sample of 1,051 schools with eighth-graders, it provides information worth the reflection of elementary teachers.

The most important factor in predicting misbehavior, as well as violent behavior, was the prevalence of substance abuse at the school. Other important variables associated with good behavior included a positive school climate and the student's attitude toward the school being positive. Factors such as less-severe punishment for repeated serious misconduct and not assigning students by ethnicity contributed to less-violent behavior.

The strongest predictor of substance abuse was grade span at the school: Schools with higher grade levels showed more drug abuse. Other important factors in low rates of substance of abuse included whether or not students could leave school grounds, a disciplined and structured environment, more severe action for first-time offenses, and a more flexible school environment.

Student boredom was the strongest predictor of preparedness for class. Schools where students report less boredom and a more positive perception of the school, small schools, and schools with teachers who often keep track of and correct homework showed more student preparedness for class.

Lower achievement was the strongest factor in predicting classroom misbehavior. Other factors in predicting classroom misbehavior included student boredom, negative school climate, and large schools.

The results of the study suggest that schools try to reduce misbehavior by eliminating substance abuse, improving school climate and student perceptions of their school, and administering discipline fairly. Additionally, programs to help students overcome disadvantaged backgrounds would be helpful, as well as dividing the school into smaller units.

To reduce substance abuse, the study proposes creating an environment at school that is disciplined and structured, but not inflexible. To improve students' preparedness for class, the study suggests reducing student boredom by perhaps tailoring the curriculum to student interests or needs. To increase students' self-esteem and sense of control, expand student input or responsibility in the function of the school or through counseling or activities. Limit the time students spend on extracurricular activities and encourage teachers to give feedback to the students as to how they are doing in the classroom.

Schools can improve classroom behavior by improving the relationship between the teacher and the students. This could be accomplished by having school counselors serve as mediators to help settle disputes between students and teachers, or by providing training to teachers on how to improve their relationship with the students.

This study does not by any means ignore the relationship between behavior and factors such as family life, environment, or parent involvement; it simply focuses on the factors that the school can control and suggests methods schools can use to improve student behavior by affecting those factors over which the schools have some control.

Mental rehearsal is another strategy related to self esteem and accomplishment. Although mental rehearsal is usually associated with second language acquisition, it is not just an activity of rehearsing out loud, but involves silent rehearsal, too (Guerrero, 1991). It can be a very elaborative process.

Guerrero learned that in addition to **din,** the involuntary playback of language in the mind of a learner of a foreign language or a second language, learners also voluntarily and silently rehearsed what they would say and do in various real-life situations in which they would be using the language and customs they were studying. This helped them to feel more self-confident and competent.

According to Guerrero, mental rehearsal is considered a successful tool in the field of psychology. Mental rehearsal can happen spontaneously in one's mind or can be consciously practiced. Spontaneously, it seemed to happen most often when a student was in a reflective mood or doing some dull chore. Voluntarily, students used it in a variety of areas besides speech and language. Math was one of them. This inner talking and playing through the motions boosted their self-esteem.

The last part of this chapter addresses one of the areas of integrated language arts: listening. It presents several ways to make your listening program educational and fascinating to your students.

LISTENING

Listening is one of the four components of **integrated language arts;** the other three are reading, writing, and speaking.

Children who have good listening skills will become better readers. Students who are good listeners in kindergarten and first grade are most likely to read with success by third grade. In addition, fifth-graders with good listening skills are most likely to be successful with high school aptitude and achievement tests.

Students have many opportunities in the classroom to listen. Encourage them to listen attentively. Give them a specific purpose for listening. Example: "After Rachel has finished her sharing about our field trip to the petting zoo, she will ask the class what her favorite part of the zoo trip was and why she liked that part so much. Listen carefully to what she says." Example: "After I give directions on the procedure for a duck and cover drill and show you how, I will repeat the directions two more times. Then I will call on five students to repeat the directions. Listen attentively." Example: "Listen carefully to today's chapter from *The Great Brain at the Academy.* Then be prepared to talk about your favorite part or retell the part where the Great Brain drives the train on the way to Salt Lake City."

You may also give listening tests. Short, high-interest articles with accompanying questions are good to use. These are found in many reproducible reading booklets at your local teachers' supply store. These materials will have a grade level on them, but since your students will not be reading them independently, you can select material that you find interesting without being overly concerned about the grade level. For some of the very short selections, you might want to select two or three to read instead of just one. Several selections are included for you in the appendix in the Figures A4-5 through A4-11. You may also want to use them as reading activities or as background information for a writing project.

(**Note:** If you have not already read the "Introduction" to this book, now would be a good time to do so. It explains the coding system used for all the elementary student activity sheets. With this system, only you will know if the material is suitable for primary grades or for upper grades. That way, if you wish to use some of the "primary" materials in "upper" grades, and you may very well want to with some or all of your class, the upper-grade students will not see what level the material is. At the top of all the activity pages in the appendix of each of the chapters, *Pt* stands for primary [think *Primary time*] and *§* stands for upper or intermediate [think *Secondary Section*]).

If you teach kindergarten, first grade, or second grade, begin a listening activity by asking the students to put away all their materials except one piece of paper and a pencil or crayon. Assign them a partner or have them get their own partners. Tell them that after you have read the story, you will ask the class a question. One partner will tell the other the answer. After a reasonable amount of time, you will tell the class the answer. If the first partner got it right, the second partner will put a tally mark under the first partner's name. Then you will ask another question and so on.

If you teach third, fourth, fifth, or sixth grade, have the students work independently. On the back of their papers or on another paper, they can take notes while you read the article. Help them understand what to write for their notes, so they are not trying to write every word. Students can write the answers to the questions on the front of the paper, but they may refer to their notes at any time. You can collect their papers to grade them later or you can correct as a class. Do not get overly concerned with spelling. If you can tell what the answer is, give them credit.

After your class is all set and they understand their responsibility during the question and answer part, introduce the article. Read the title, give any background information students might need, and explain any unusual words they may not have heard before.

Next, go around the class slowly, so that students can have a good, close-up look at any pictures that go with the article. The students love this. Then read each of the test questions twice to your class. If the question is the multiple-choice type, read the different selections to the class. If it is a fill-in-the-blank kind of question, be sure to let the students know so that when they hear the answer while you are reading, they can jot it down. This gives them a specific purpose for listening. Sometimes there will be questions that are fine for a reading test, but do not fit for a listening test. Just skip those questions.

Now you are ready to begin reading the article to your students. They will be able to tell by the enthusiastic tone of your voice that you enjoy this type of listening lesson. If you are reading to a class that is taking notes, adjust your reading speed to accommodate this. You might want to reread certain sections.

Then proceed to the question-answer section. Give the students a good amount of time to say or write their answers. Collect their answer sheets or "tally papers" if you are reading one selection only. Otherwise, introduce the next article and start the process over again. Your students will find this type of experience enjoyable as well educational.

In addition to these recommendations, a variety of listening tapes are available, which you can play for the whole class or station at a listening post. Tapes such as these teach a particular skill such as inference, following directions, or identifying sounds. Many tapes include interesting material with excellent stories and sound effects. Follow-up and follow-along materials can be reproduced for your class. There are tapes appropriate for primary classes and ones appropriate for upper grades. These tapes present an enjoyable change of pace for a listening experience.

RESEARCH AND STUDIES

A study by Brent and Anderson (1993) describes the indirect and direct teaching of listening strategies and shows how the practice of these strategies can be incorporated into ongoing activities in the whole language classroom.

Two second-grade classes were involved in this study. One was taught by a teacher who spent little time helping her students develop effective listening strategies. The other was taught by a teacher who incorporated listening instructions into her classroom in a natural way consistent with whole language philosophy (Brown & Mathie, 1990; Goodman, 1986).

Since listening will be one of the students' primary tools for learning new information for the rest of their lives, it should be integrated into all the language arts and skills. Teachers can help students become effective listeners by modeling good listening, teaching specific skill lessons, and encouraging application in meaningful settings.

Get yourself a good job, one you will love. Work with your students on two vital areas of the curriculum: academic success and personal success. Provide opportunities for your students to become aware of and increase their self-esteem. Present students with high-interest lessons in listening to increase their exposure to new, diverse material. Help them cultivate the life-long learning skill of listening. Do these things and your classroom will set sail and successfully face all challenges.

CHAPTER QUESTIONS

1. Name four major areas to consider before interviewing for a job teaching elementary school. Describe one task under each category.
2. What is a master's degree barrier?
3. How does high transiency affect an individual classroom?
4. The year following your hire, a new elementary school is opened in your district. In the five years prior to its opening, your district had not experienced any declining enrollment. What does this mean for your job security?
5. Describe what you think will be a typical interview at the district office. What might some of the questions be?

How will you act? How will you dress? What do you want to convey to the interview team?
6. Name three important things to do as a follow up to an interview.
7. What are the four keys to academic success?
8. How does the assignment accountability chart relate to Key 1?
9. What are the four keys to personal success?
10. Take one key and explain how it leads to personal success both in the classroom and in the work place.
11. What is a Q-Sort?
12. What do you know about self-concept and self-esteem?

13. What is the ideal self?

14. In relation to self-concept and self-esteem, what are references?

15. Why is it so difficult to change self-concept or increase self-esteem? Have you had any period of time when you have experienced low self-esteem? If so, how did you change your thinking to get through it and out of it?

16. There will probably be some students in your class with low self-esteem. They might think that people do not like them, that they cannot possibly do the work, that they are no good at things, and so on. Describe one specific activity you would like to do with either your whole class or with just one or two students to increase their self-esteem.

17. How can you get your class to listen more intently to a student's report?

18. In a listening test, why are the article's questions read to the class before reading the article to the class?

19. What is something you could do like Adopt-a-Grandparent to build self-esteem in your class?

20. What's your opinion about the script read to the students for the ITBS motivation study? Would you want to reword it in any way? If so, how? If not, why not?

21. In relation to the SchoolMatch study, ask five parents of students in elementary school or ones who have children about to enter what they would like for their children at school. Write a summary of the information you collect.

22. How can teachers of the last elementary grades help in the transition experience of their students to middle school? How can the elementary school help?

23. If your school had a parent-student handbook, what would you like to see in it?

24. How can you help your students with high achievement?

25. How can you help administer discipline fairly in your class and at your school so that students see they are being treated equitably and impartially?

26. Do you use mental rehearsal? How would you help your students with this strategy?

27. How have you stayed motivated throughout school? What strategies have worked for you that you would like to share with your students?

CHAPTER PROJECT

Develop a set of listening tests appropriate for a listening lesson. Have one set for primary grades, one set for upper grades. Include two tests in the set for primary, two for upper grade. Find high-interest articles of a rather short length. Be sure all your selections have some good-sized interesting pictures. If the tests that go with the articles have some questions inappropriate for a listening test, draw an *X* to cross out those numbers. Write one lesson plan for the primary grades including such things as a pause after a short amount of the article is read so the primary students can discuss with their partner what they have learned so far and a suitable method for scoring. For the upper-grade plan, include instructions on note taking and a good tool for evaluation.

MIDCOURSE REVIEW

A practice midcourse review test is included in Chapter 9, The XYZ's. It covers material in Chapter 1, The ABC's, Chapter 2, The DEF's, Chapter 3, The GHI's, and Chapter 4 the JKL's.

REFERENCES

Bainbridge, W. L., & Sundre, S. M. (1991). Factors that parents want in their children's schools. *ERS Spectrum, 9*(2), 3–6.

Brent, R., & Anderson, P. (1993). Developing children's classroom listening strategies. *The Reading Teacher, 47*(2), 122–126; 134–135.

Brown, H., & Mathie, V. (1990). *Inside whole language: A classroom view.* Portsmouth, NH: Heinemann.

Brown, S. M., & Walberg, H. J. (1993). Motivational effects on test scores of elementary students. *Journal of Educational Research, 86*(3), 133–136.

Combs, H. J. (1993). A middle school transition program: Addressing the social side of schooling. *ERS Spectrum, 11*(1), 12–21.

Garman, D. M. (1990). A study of the criteria employed in the selection of beginning teachers in Ohio during 1989–1990. *Dissertation Abstracts International, 51/11A,* 3573.

Goodman, K. (1986). *What's whole in Whole Language?* Portsmouth, NH: Heinemann.

Guerrero, M. C. M. de. (1991, March). *Mental rehearsal as a second language learning strategy.* Paper presented at the Annual Meeting of the Teachers of English to Speakers of Other Languages, New York, NY.

Kowalski, T. J., McDaniel, P., Place, A. W., & Reitzug, U. C. (1992). Factors that principals consider most important in selecting new teachers. *ERS Spectrum, 10*(3), 34–38.

Kowalski, T. J., & Weaver, R. (1988). Characteristics of outstanding teachers: An academic and social profile. *Action in Teacher Education, 10*(2), 93–100.

Proller, N. L. (1988). Adopt-a-Grandparent program, Dade County Public Schools. *ERS Spectrum, 6*(2), 30–34.

Reading comprehension and listening. Urbana, IL: University of Illinois at Urbana-Champaign, Center for the Study of Reading, 1983.

Walters, J. T. (1992, March). *Technology in the curriculum: The inclusion solution.* Paper presented at the 5th National Forum of the Association of Independent Liberal Arts Colleges for Teacher Education, Louisville, KY.

Weishew, N. L., & Peng, S. S. (1993). Variables predicting students' problem behaviors. *Journal of Educational Research, 87*(1), 5–7.

BIBLIOGRAPHY

Wade, T. C., Baker, T. B., & Morton, E. L. (1978). The status of psychological testing in clinical psychology: Relationships between test use and professional activities and orientations. *Journal of Personality Assessment, 42*(42), 3–11.

5

THE MNO'S

This chapter introduces you to people, equipment, and ideas that can be a tremendous benefit in running your classroom. It gives you some out-of-the-ordinary ideas in a vital curricular area, ideas that will help you provide an exciting, global program for your students. An important area related to spending is discussed as well as a topic of law that may now or in the future pertain directly to you. The topics for this chapter are:

- Machines
- Mainstreaming and Full Inclusion
- Master Teachers
- Math
- Mentor Teachers
- Money
- New Students
- Novel Monthly Events
- Open House

The first part of this chapter explains how machines, master teachers, and mentor teachers are all helpful resources. Money, mainstreaming, and full inclusion are all issues you well may need to know about; they are included here also.

MACHINES

A variety of machines are available to make your job easier. First on the list is the copier. It is great if you have one that staples and collates. If you are not blessed with a good copier, go to a copy store or stationery store that has a first-rate copying machine to copy special things that you want to look beautiful, like certificates for your students or important parent communications.

It is a big help in running your class smoothly if you copy sets of test note forms, speaking evaluation forms, class behavior lists, reading incentive forms, progress reports, and so on, for the entire school year. Store them in your cabinet.

Another machine you may use is the Ellison die machine. It cuts out different types of letters and designs, like bunnies, snowmen, and so on. The video camera can be used to tape class speeches, puppet shows, dances, and so on. The students love watching themselves on the screen later. A stereo system (turntable, dual tapes with a listening post hookup, and CD player) and a VCR are great machines in any classroom.

The overhead projector can be used in many classes. Place an overhead transparency on it and use any of various colored overhead pens to teach a lesson in writing, math, and so on. The different colors will show on the screen. These are temporary transparencies and can be wiped clean with water and a soft cloth or paper towel. Placing an already prepared transparency on the overhead can project its material on the screen to assist with a lesson. Professionally prepared transparencies come with some reading and math series. Ones in history, geography and science booklets can be purchased at a teachers' supply store. Some of these transparencies come with overlays, too. A permanent transparency can be made by sending a copy of the desired material attached to a blank overhead transparency through a thermofax machine. The overhead can also be used to enlarge the outline of a figure. Tape a piece of large construction paper to the chalkboard. Place the figure on the overhead. For example, a small bunny could be used. Move the overhead projector the necessary distance from the construction paper to produce the desired size. Then trace the outline on the construction paper. This can become a pattern for an art project. For example, the larger bunny can be traced on to pieces of tagboard. Lines can be penciled on the tag bunny to split it into eight or ten various-shaped sections. Different selections of wallpaper can be glued onto each section. Each section can then be outlined with X's in black marker to look like quilt stitching. Give the bunny eyes, eyelashes, and a mouth.

You also will be using several other machines on occasion: the thermofax, the ditto machine, the film projector, and the slide projector. Sometimes people are intimidated by machines that they do not feel confident running. Be sure to get in-serviced on these machines so that you can use them rather than avoid them.

Do not forget a simple machine like your camera. The students love having their pictures taken and displayed in the classroom.

Many schools have their own laminating machines. If you laminate materials, the plasticlike coating protects them not just from wear and tear but also from fading. A beautiful dark royal blue piece of tag can turn light blue in a year or so if it is not laminated.

If you want to teach an exciting history lesson, try the videodisc player. Each side of a videodisc holds regular video material, like news reports and presidents making speeches today and in the past. The discs also have thousands of still

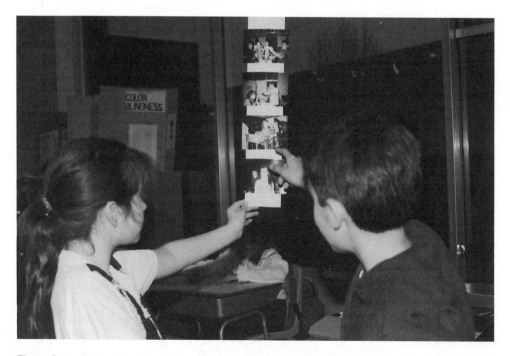

Figure 5-1.   A simple machine like a camera can provide students with hours of pleasure as they relive enjoyable learning experiences. Well-worded captions can reinforce previously taught skills and concepts.

frames on each side. You can show the new vocabulary words that the students will meet in the chapter lesson.

To access the discs, you can use a remote control device, a bar code reader, or computer software. When you access the disc, bingo! What you want appears immediately. The disc can be listened to in stereo in one language. Or it can be listened to in two languages at the same time, English and Spanish, when the students have on their headphones. You will have a great and different lesson.

Another interesting, ongoing activity involving a machine that you could introduce to your class is the **Electronic Bulletin Board,** the latest in telecommunications. You do need a modem and a cable hookup to your school. Then your students can send ads or write letters to students at another school. They could communicate with residents of a retirement home.

The computer lab is loaded with machines. There the students learn keyboarding skills, word processing, and how to make graphics, fonts, and borders. The Minnesota Educational Computing Consortium (MECC), as well as many other software developers, produces a good amount of software with math drills, reading skills, and so on. There are many educational games for the computer. A continual favorite is the *Carmen Sandiego* series, in which students learn about other countries' flags, money systems, monuments, and so on, all while trying to catch a thief who has stolen some national treasure.

MAINSTREAMING AND FULL INCLUSION

According to Public Law 94–142, the Education for All Handicapped Children Act, students must be provided an appropriate education in the least restrictive environment. All students need to be first thought of as regular education students. The burden of proof that a student cannot receive a satisfactory education in a regular classroom is on the school district.

Students with special needs should be thought of and spoken of as "students with special needs" or "students with disabilities" rather than "special-needs students" or "disabled students." The former emphasizes the "individual" first and the disability only as a secondary descriptor.

This law means that you might have students with special academic, behavioral, physical, or social needs, who once were placed and stayed full time in special day classes (**SDC**'s), in your class. If these students are able to function for a period or partial day or even full time (**full inclusion**) in your classroom, accommodations will need to be made to place them and to meet their needs in the regular classroom.

If you have a child in your classroom that you *think* has special needs, talk with teachers on your campus or in your district who have special education classes. They will have many good ideas that you can use to help your student. Instigate classroom modifications. Begin with one and try it for a while to see if it is helpful. If it doesn't work, begin another.

Document what you do. For example: "Beginning September 25, Student A was moved to the front of the class, the left-hand side. This area is not bordering other classrooms and is a quiet area of the room. This move was made to help this student stay on-task." Try this for a couple of weeks. Document any changes. If this does not work, move on to something else,

such as assigning the student a role-model buddy to help keep this student on-task or moving the student's desk right next to yours. Document when you begin and what effect the modification had.

Student B may have special academic needs; for example, that student can understand the work but is extremely slow. This pace causes the student to fall behind. You might begin by modifying this student's assignments. Perhaps this student could complete class work for homework instead of the regular homework assignments. Document when you begin and what progress is made.

Sometimes students with special needs do well if tests are read aloud to them by the teacher or another student. They may work better at the computer. They may need to be frequently called upon to keep their attention or they may need to repeat the directions for a particular activity so that you are sure they understand what to do. In addition, it often helps to have a time set aside each week to clean and organize their desks so they do not still have September's papers in their desks in February.

(Throughout this book under each curriculum area and in Chapter 7, The STU's, under the section Teaching-Learning Process, you will see many different ways of teaching to address the diverse needs and styles of learning of the students in your class, including those with special needs. In Chapter 1, The ABC's, under Classroom Rules, you will see modifications for classroom management for students with special needs.)

If your student is not meeting success with the modifications you have implemented, the student needs additional help. A student study team (SST) meeting needs to be scheduled. Begin this process early in the year because there can be a backlog of cases. You want the best for your student as soon as possible.

An SST will involve the parents, the principal, the school psychologist, a special education teacher, the speech therapist, and you. This is the time to bring your documentation of your classroom modifications as well as samples of the student's work and the cum file.

At the SST, the team will decide whether further assessment needs to be done, possibly in the area of language processing or achievement and IQ. The team may decide modifications need to be implemented in the home or that further classroom or school modifications are necessary. It is very reassuring to be part of a team when dealing with a student with special needs.

If you presently have at your school site any SDC classes, you may be asked to include one or two students in part of your program. Maintain close contact with those students' primary (homeroom) teacher, especially if students are mainstreamed for academic subjects. Sometimes, not always, these students need much more monitoring for their follow-up assignments. They may need more help in class with the directions and the assignments, and they may need to be checked closely to be sure each assignment is completed and turned in for recording. The SDC teacher can help you immensely with this by providing time and monitoring in the SDC class for *your* assignment to be finished.

Sometimes, though, SDC students may be placed in your class for such subjects as art and PE. This gives these students more opportunities to interact with a larger number of students of their same age group.

In providing for students with special needs, it is important to remember that they may not have high self-esteem and good social skills. You want to maintain an environment that is structured and supporting. If these students have some fairly serious disabilities, it is a good idea to have a discussion with your class prior to their arrival. This will be a perfect occasion for a few lessons on similarities and differences among people, focused especially on your students' age group. Let your students know that not everyone is the same, and tell them why. Some people have any of a variety of physical challenges. Explain some so the students will understand; for example, such disorders as epilepsy and cerebral palsy can be discussed. If you have students coming to your class with physical challenges, focus on their specific disabilities so that students will be more knowledgeable and accepting. Other students with special needs may have different types of learning disorders. Explain whatever is applicable, such as **dyslexia,** ADD/H, or **aphasia,** and so on. Try to give your students an idea of how it feels to face each school day with these challenges.

The students coming to your class may have some kind of emotional or psychological problem. They may act "weird" or "strange." Explain to your students that these behaviors are often the product of biochemical disorders or the by-product of medications they take for health problems. These students are not necessarily intentionally trying to be weird, strange, or difficult; that's just how they are right now and everyone is working with them to help them. "Everyone" is now going to include you and your students.

Students with special needs require your students' support and acceptance. Let your students know that making fun of these students will not be tolerated and is totally out of place. If this happens, go through your acceptance and understanding lessons with your class again. Make them aware that everyone deserves a fair chance. Everyone deserves to be treated in a polite manner and with respect. Tell your class that having these students in the room for part or all of the day will give your own students a great opportunity to prepare themselves as future adult citizens of a diverse society by learning and practicing tolerance, understanding, and acceptance.

When students are mainstreamed into your classroom, ask some of your students to be partners to these students. That way, if a student with special needs has any questions about what is going on, he can ask his partner. The partner can also keep him on-task.

When students come in, make sure you or one of your students have thoroughly explained the classroom rules to them, along with positive and negative consequences. When directions are given for a lesson, double-check that mainstreamed students understand what is expected of them. If they do not have an instructional assistant accompanying them, you could walk by their desk and whisper in their ear, "Do you know what to do?" If not, tell them you will get the class started and then be back to help them get started. Soon they will adapt to the routine.

A wonderful time to practice some social skills is with students mainstreamed or included for PE. (See PE in Chapter 6, The PQR's.) For example, along with the physical activity skill, the students could practice saying only nice and encouraging things to their classmates. Negative behavior can be ignored by the students, positive behavior recognized. When you praise caring behavior and your students praise their classmates who are kind and helpful to the mainstreamed students, then the other students will want to do things to earn your praise, too. Pretty soon, helpfulness and acceptance become the norm.

Research and Studies

The Freunds' 1989 study points out that teacher behaviors that are associated with teacher effectiveness of mildly disabled students can be taught to teachers in regular education who will be exposed to mildly disabled students in their classroom either through permanent placement or through mainstreaming. Ten specific teaching behaviors for effectiveness were listed:

1. Communicating teaching goals, objectives, and rationale clearly to the students so that they will attend and perform better.
2. Taking the responsibility for teaching, rather than blaming lack of learning on children, parents, home, and so on.
3. Having an efficient, well-run classroom with a maximum amount of time devoted to teaching.
4. Teaching for success; assessing, instructing, and reassessing to meet the needs of the class.
5. Modeling, demonstrating, explaining in different ways, especially during new learning.
6. Allowing the students a large amount of time to respond to questions, cues, and prompts; actively engaging them in the lesson.
7. Taking the students to **mastery level;** providing a solid foundation in all prerequisite skills; affording opportunities for overlearning.
8. Monitoring students during and after instruction; constantly checking for understanding.
9. Regularly providing corrective feedback, both basic and elaborated. (According to researchers Collins, Carnine, and Gersten [1987], with mildly disabled students, elaborated feedback resulted in higher learning.)
10. Recognizing the importance of a good emotional tone in the classroom; being encouraging and positive rather than criticizing or humiliating.

The Freunds linked this information to Madeline Hunter's "Hunter Instructional Skills Model" with her four basics of an instructional lesson: appropriate learning objective, teaching directed to the objective, students monitored with reteaching done as necessary, and knowledge of results or corrective feedback given promptly. In giving corrective feedback, demonstrating or repeating each student error helps the students see exactly what they are doing. Then students watch the modeling of the correct behavior so that they can see exactly what they need to change to be correct.

This study reports that this type of lesson structure format clearly provides an excellent guide and is not meant to interfere with teacher creativity, especially creativity in the selection of the learning activity. It is important however, not to be overly focused on interesting activities and to be very focused on student outcomes to get excellent results (Aschbacher, 1992).

Another inclusionary study (Davis, 1992) examined the extent to which children with mental retardation are being educated in inclusive settings. The 14th Annual Report to Congress on the implementation of the Individuals with Disabilities Education Act (**IDEA**) (Davis, 1992) summarized data for the 1989–90 school year reported by all states to the federal government regarding children receiving special education and related services. States get this information from their local education agencies annually. Data used for this study were for retarded students, ages sixteen to twenty-one, placed in different educational environments.

More than 93 percent of children with mental retardation were educated in 1989-90 in settings other than the regular classroom, and various government agencies had not fulfilled their responsibilities (per IDEA).

In 1989–90, the most common setting for education students with mental retardation was in separate classrooms (61%). Seventy-three percent of retarded children were educated in segregated settings. 31.5 percent of all children with disabilities were in regular classes, whereas 6.7 percent of children with mental retardation were in regular classes. 5.2 percent of all children with disabilities were in separate schools, and 12 percent of children with mental retardation were in such a setting.

Only two states educated more than 50 percent of students with mental retardation in regular classes: Massachusetts (59%) and Vermont (54%).

Eight states—New York, New Jersey, Georgia, Indiana, Illinois, Iowa, Florida, Mississippi, and the District of Columbia—placed less than 1 percent of students with mental retardation in regular classes.

Three states had more than 50 percent of their students with mental retardation in resource rooms: Iowa (64%), South Dakota (63%), and Kentucky (55%). Six states used resource rooms for less than 5 percent of students with mental retardation: California, New Jersey, Rhode Island, Illinois, New York, and Florida.

Another study (Zentall, Harper, & Stormont-Spurgin, 1993), on the organizational abilities of children with hyperactivity, sought to determine if deficits in organization could be documented in kids with ADHD across sources (that is, teachers, parents, and children) using a measure of both time and object organization.

Thirty-eight children (6–14 years old), initially identified and referred by psychologists and teachers and subsequently referred by parents, participated in this study.

Ten boys and three girls were enrolled in a summer skills program for children with attention, learning, and/or behavioral problems. Twenty-one boys and four girls were referred from a support group for parents of children with hyperactivity.

The Routh, Schroeder, and O'Tauma (1974) criteria of the Werry-Weiss-Peters inappropriate activity scale were used. Children two standard deviations above the mean for their age group were classified as hyperactive. Children falling below this criterion cutoff were included in the comparison group.

Children with hyperactivity, compared to the control group, reported that they did their homework but couldn't find it when it was done. They recognized that they acted or said things before thinking or planning. They also recognized they had trouble finding school supplies when they were needed and they lost things at school. They were only somewhat more likely to note that their clothes were crumpled and messy, and they thought their family put things where they could not find them. They marginally recognized that they did not put their own books in the same place when they came home.

Mothers of youths with hyperactivity, compared to those of children without hyperactivity, reported that they were more likely to get upset if their children were late for a planned meeting or activity, rated their children as less likely to organize time well, and rated themselves as less likely to teach their child to establish object placement routines or to retrace steps in the original placement of lost objects.

Fathers of children with hyperactivity were less likely to feel that their children organized toys, clothes, and homework papers well, but were more likely to feel their children did not organize time well. Fathers, in contrast to mothers, were more likely to offer ways to help their children become more organized by suggesting the creation of lists for multiple jobs or tasks.

Children with hyperactivity were relatively aware that they lacked the ability to organize various activities of their lives, recognized they had few established routines for placing objects in consistent locations, and reported greater situational reactivity in not completing projects and not delaying verbal and motor responses.

MASTER TEACHERS

Master teachers are primarily role models for student teachers and act as facilitators in the development of student teachers' management and teaching skills. Master teachers demonstrate different techniques for teaching a new lesson or a review lesson and provide the student teacher with the opportunity to see them teaching all the subjects and showing different grouping methods. They show a type of classroom control with which they feel comfortable and that has worked for them. They design their lesson plans in such a way that the student teacher can see how the day and week are managed.

Master teachers take the student teacher to faculty meetings and playground supervision. They have the student teacher sit in on parent-teacher conferences. They describe the different students in the classroom so the student teacher can better interact with the elementary students.

The master teachers can make arrangements for their student teacher to visit and observe in other classes on campus, such as speech therapy, ESL, LD, SDC, and the computer lab. They can also provide individualized in-services for all the audiovisual equipment and office machines.

Master teachers do their best to make student teachers feel comfortable at the school. They check lesson plans and make suggestions to ensure that good preparation has taken place. They critique lessons, jotting down comments and notes while the lesson is progressing, and then conferencing with the student teacher about it later that day. This is a time the master teacher can point out strengths and weaknesses of the lesson as well as offer tips and techniques for improvement. Did the student teacher follow the guidelines of the Blueprint for Effective Teaching (see Chapter 7)? Did the classroom students learn what they were supposed to learn? A copy of these notes and comments as well as any general suggestions or helpful hints is then given to the student teacher for future reference.

Master teachers are trained to know what to look for in a student teacher's lessons. They want to be able to help the student teacher evaluate her own lessons fairly soon. They will ask the student teacher how she felt about the lesson and about classroom control. What were the classroom students doing? Were they motivated? Was her follow-up activity appropriate? Did the student teacher's rationale for any grouping work out? What kind of questions did the classroom students ask? Were these anticipated or was the student teacher caught off guard by them?

Master teachers are responsible for giving student teachers at least one informal written evaluation about midterm and one formal evaluation at the end of that particular student teaching period. Master teachers do their best to be encouraging and make their expectations clear from the beginning. They work at building rapport between themselves and the student teacher and between the student teacher and the class. They help the student teacher plan ahead, allow her as much freedom as possible, and facilitate the process of her taking over the class for the required period of time.

There is also constant communication between the college or university supervisor, the master teacher, and the student teacher. Both the supervisor and the master teacher are doing whatever it takes to make student teaching a rewarding and successful experience.

Research and Studies

In working with your master teacher, it is helpful to observe the behaviors associated with a master teacher as well as to strive toward these yourself (Allen, 1987). According to Allen, master teachers have a superior knowledge of the curriculum and keep their knowledge up-to-date. In addition, they are able to maintain their enthusiasm for teaching.

Master teachers are good planners with both short-term and long-term goals. They use excellent teaching strategies; material is presented clearly, concisely, and addresses the different learning styles; the learning is relevant to their students; and they frequently check for understanding. Master teachers question, probe, and motivate students to achieve higher levels of learning. Good, prompt feedback is provided. Students are kept on-task and transition time is minimal.

Master teachers have well-organized classes, high student expectations, and creativity. They reinforce positive student behavior and work enterprisingly to eliminate negative, disruptive behavior. Master teachers have good working relationships with others, are well respected, and provide leadership in curriculum development and the improvement of school and district policies. Master teachers are self-motivated and willing to pursue excellence in other areas beyond the classroom.

MATH

Teaching math is an exciting experience. Because math lessons are fast paced, this period of the day seems very energizing. You can use the student text for part of the week, use manipulatives part of the time, do investigations and experiments, such as those in the **AIMS** program, and provide students ample opportunity to use their math knowledge with open-ended questions and demonstrations. A program such as this will allow you to teach all the strands of math: functions, measurement, logic and language, algebra, **discrete mathematics,** number, geometry, and statistics and probability.

Use the overhead projector at least part of the time when you teach math. That way you can use different colors of overhead pens to more exactly show the students the subskills. (Keep to the dark colors of overhead pens, which are more easily seen.)

Face the class when you use the overhead projector. Then you will not have to turn to write on the board or on a chart. After the students have completed each of their practice problems or activities, you can ask for all their eyes on the screen. Then work out the problem or have a student come to the overhead to work the problem. Then the students can check what they have done.

It is much easier to spot students who are having trouble when you use the overhead. Then you can provide assistance by going to their desk or table. Have them sit on the floor closer to the overhead and closer to you.

When you see some students struggling with something new, tell class members to raise their hands if they know what they are doing. Then tell the students who would like some help to go visit a student with his or her hand raised. Students will zoom to those desks. They love this. They can move back and forth a number of times during one lesson, and they can visit different students.

Other times, you might want a particular student to stay with another student for the entire math lesson. Perhaps you will permanently assign a math tutor to someone. Then, each time the class gets into math activities, the tutor automatically takes a chair to that student's desk and stays there for the math venture. The tutor points and shows and models for the student being tutored. When they need to talk, they whisper to maintain quiet in the classroom so that others can concentrate.

Encourage the students to say the problem-solving process "out loud" to themselves. For example, in the problem in Figure 5-4, the students would learn to say: 9 from 5, cannot do. Borrow or regroup. Cross out the 6, and so on. If they learn in the mathematical operation of addition to begin the process with the bottom number, they can **transfer** that learning to subtraction and right on to multiplication.

It is a real help when students understand such math concepts as number periods, place value applied to two-digit multiplier problems, or that three sixes is the same as $6 + 6 + 6$ is the same as 3×6.

Even when you have slowly and carefully presented the concept of place value as it applies to multiplication and you have carefully taught the steps of division, some students will still benefit from the use of **lattices.** Slower math students find

Figure 5-2.   These enthusiastic students are having a math lesson on an overhead projector. One advantage of the overhead projector is that the teacher can always maintain eye contact with the students. Another is the opportunity to use various-colored overhead transparency pens to emphasize different ideas and subskills.

these a big help in keeping their problems neat and organized. That way they do not get lost in the middle of a math problem. Figures A5-1, A5-2, and A5-3 in the appendix show some sample lattices for multiplication and division. They are coded § for use in any upper grade. Other activities are coded **Pt** for use in a primary class.

Figure 5-3.   This tutor is a classmate. When math class begins, the tutor gets a chair and sits by his partner's desk. Then he can answer any questions the student might have, model the correct way of listening and practicing during an instructional lesson, and keep the student on-target during the follow-up activity.

65
−19

Figure 5-4.

Another technique to use when you are teaching multiplication and division is to have the students use a finger or a small scrap of paper to cover a number they are not using so that they are not distracted by too many numbers. In the first problem in Figure 5-5, the students would cover the 4 when multiplying by the 3. This helps reinforce the concept of place value. Encouraging students to make a "ballpark" estimate is another help in getting an answer that makes sense. Round 26 to 30 and 34 to 30. 30 × 30 = 900. The answer should be right around 900.

In 984 ÷ 6, which is the second problem in Figure 5-5, students would cover the 84 with a small scrap of paper. As they progress through the problem, they would bring down the 8 and cover just the 4. Finally, they would uncover the 4 to bring it down. These scraps of papers can be very handy for students who have a hard time focusing in math operations. Again, as in any of the math operations, a ballpark estimate helps assure students they are on the right path. Students can follow the rules of rounding, if they like, but often it is easier to select numbers that are close in value but also easily manipulated in their heads. For example, 984 can be considered 1,000 and 6 is close to 5; therefore, 5 into 1,000 is 200, a problem students can easily learn to do in their heads. With an estimated answer, students know they will be looking for an answer in the neighborhood of 200 as opposed to 2 or 20 or 2,000. Estimating helps students see the big picture, rather than getting lost in the minute figurings.

Division with *one*-digit divisors becomes easier when you teach the division family:

Daddy	÷	Divide
Mommy	×	Multiply
Sister	−	Subtract
Brother	↓	Bring down
Relatives	R	Remainder

Tell students if they bring down a number, go right back to Daddy. If there is no number to bring down, go visit the relatives.

When students get into two-digit divisors, they can use markers in their quotients. They start with the word *Does*. For example, if the problem were 40 into 938, they would say: Does 40 go into 9? No! 9 is smaller than 40. Then does 40 go into 93? Yes! 93 is not smaller than 40. Put up a marker over the 3 and over any numbers following it. This prevents a com-

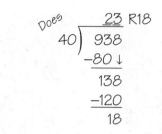

D	÷	< Does = markers / Cover to estimate
M	×	Carry by the divisor.
S	−	ONLY when the bottom number is not bigger
B	↓	
R		Always smaller than the divisor

Figure 5-6.

mon math problem of estimating 4 into 9 and putting the 2 over the 9.

The final division family is suitable for any *two*-digit divisor problem (see Figure 5-6).

For a ballpark estimation in the problem of 40 into 938, students can change the 40 to 50 and the 938 to 1,000. Then they can divide 50 into 1,000 in their heads and get 20. That way, they know they are looking for an answer around 20, not 2, not 200, and not 2,000.

It is always advisable for the students to check their math problems, but if they learn written checks for subtraction and division, this will clear up many difficulties (see Figure 5-7 for the two types of checks).

Introduce skills gradually so that students understand and get a good amount of practice. Schedule practice every night, about eight problems each night. Have students self-correct the next day in class. Do not grade. If students miss problems, they need to feel confident about saying so and getting help so that the misunderstanding is cleared up.

Example:

$$
\begin{array}{r}
708 \\
-\ 99 \\
+\ 609 \\
\hline
708
\end{array}
$$

708 matches 708.

Example:

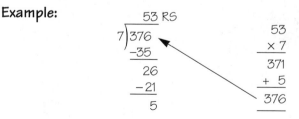

$$6\overline{)984}$$

$$
\begin{array}{r}
26 \\
\times\ 34 \\
\end{array}
$$

Figure 5-5.

Figure 5-7.

Write each student assignment in No. 2 pencil or black marker on white copy paper. Identify the assignment by the first problem only. Do not date the pages. Make up thirty assignments and, for assignment identification, be sure the first problem on each page is different. Then rotate throughout the year so that students do not lose skills they once had earlier in the year.

To keep these papers in good shape, use a three-hole punch and keep pages in a binder in sleeves. Students who are absent will always have access to the assignment.

When testing, be sure the students work totally independently so that you can determine exactly what they know. Do not let them select from a group of answers on a test unless they are required to show their work and the answer is validated by their work. Once-a-week testing in math is fine or, on the outside, once every two weeks.

Provide students with instruction and practice in reading, understanding, and solving word problems that require addition, subtraction, multiplication, and division of whole numbers. Teach one type of word problem at a time, addition, for example, and give the students plenty of practice. Work out loud together as a class or in teacher-directed groups so that students understand the process. Have them make up word problems of their own and solve them as a class. Teach students to look for key words in the word problems and clue words for the type of mathematical operation to be used. Teach them to identify the numbers with which they will be working. Alert them to number words. Teach students to do a ballpark estimation to put their answers in the right neighborhood.

When the problem is solved, have them reread the problem and see if their answers are reasonable and make sense. Students may need to draw little diagrams to help them better picture the problem. Check that all students are actively involved.

Preparing for Math Tests

One of the most important parts of teaching math is helping students to prepare for a test. Students need something *specific* to study. This is when a study sheet comes to the rescue. You make the study sheet for the students or, even better, have the whole class make one together as a one- or two-day math lesson. The study sheet has the same kind of problems the students will see on the test. For homework, students use their study sheet not only to study those problems, but to make up other sample problems and practice doing them, too. Students can then check with a calculator or ask an older brother or sister, Mom, or Dad to check.

Figures A5-4 through A5-7 in the appendix are sample study sheets for subtraction with borrowing, two-digit multipliers, two-digit divisors with zeros, and division of decimals. Use these as models for study sheets you make for different skills. When you develop a test to go with a study sheet, be sure it includes only the kinds of problems covered on the study sheet. This way the students have every opportunity to be well prepared for any and every math test.

One area of math that can cause difficulty on tests is word problems or story problems. Go through these step by step

with the students. Emphasize that there are four mathematical operations to choose from: addition, multiplication, subtraction, or division. This may seem self-evident, but it is not to the students. Make the students acutely aware that addition and multiplication will give an answer that is higher than those numbers given in the problem, whereas subtraction and division give lower answers. Students can be taught to ask themselves if they are looking for a higher or lower number. This helps set them on the right track.

Drawing pictures to illustrate the problem is a big help to some students. Also, all students need to be alert to the use of number words inside story problems. In one-step story problems, let the students know that *two* numbers will *always* be given to them; however, one or both of these numbers could be number words. They will then add or multiply these numbers or subtract or divide them. Then, when they get what they think might be the answer, teach them to ask themselves if their answer makes sense. If they follow this procedure with word problems, they will experience a good deal of success. Figure A5-8 in the appendix is a sample study sheet for one-step word problems. When you make the test, be sure it is limited to one-step word problems so the preparation matches the test.

When students are prepared for the test, they have a parent or other adult write on the study sheet how long they studied at home or after school for that particular test. The parent or adult supervisor then signs the study sheet. These can be regular homework assignments for math. Collect the study sheets and record them on the assignment accountability chart just like any other assignment. This system helps the students focus on the math concepts, skills, or activities being tested and lets the parents know what their children are learning in math at school.

Teaching Patterns and Spatial Relationships in Math

For a full understanding of math, it is important that the students learn the many patterns that exist in both numbers and figures. For example, $375 \times 561 \times 78 = 561 \times 78 \times \_\_\_\_$ can appear to be a rather difficult problem for a young elementary student. As soon as students see the pattern, though, this problem becomes a snap. (The answer is 375.) If they are not knowledgeable about patterns, they can begin trying to solve this problem by multiplying 375 times 561, which is not wrong but is a waste of time and demonstrates a lack of pattern awareness.

It is important to be aware of patterns with geometric figures, too. Teaching lines of symmetry and similar and congruent figures is a great help. Having younger students cut out different shapes helps them understand patterns.

Tangrams

It is advantageous in the development of your students' mathematical minds for them to be able to see spatial relationships. The use of **tangrams** is an excellent way to develop this ability, and the students can have fun at the same time. See Figure A5-9 in the appendix for the outline for a tangram set. This type of activity is suitable for primary or upper grade.

Figure 5-8. The teacher is helping this group be alert to mathematical concepts and patterns, such as 785 × 96 × 23 = 96 × 785 × ____ or 62121816 ÷ 2. The students learn how simple these problems are. Courtesy of Walt Lazar.

Before your students begin this activity, tell them these facts:

1. The seven pieces form a four-inch square.
2. The two small triangles, when put together, form a square.
3. The two large triangles, when put together, form a square.
4. Any piece can be used facing any direction and can be flipped over, too.

Figure 5-9. These young students are cutting out shapes to help them see patterns in math. Courtesy of Essa and Rogers, *An Early Childhood Curriculum: From Developmental Model to Application,* © 1992 by Delmar Publishers, Inc.

5. All seven pieces *must* be used, and no piece can be on the outside of the pattern outline.

Not only tell them this information, but also *demonstrate* so that they are successful with this activity. You can find lots of tangram outlines at your district's instructional media center in the curriculum lab. There are outlines of boats, trucks, zebras, and so on. Included for you in the appendix is Figure A5-10, a sample activity called Tangram Delight.

The Adams Cube

Another device like tangrams that the students enjoy month after month is the **Adams Cube.** A different outline appears on each face of the cube. There are five colorful plastic pieces that must fit *exactly* into each design. This is an activity students can work on individually or with a partner right at their desk.

Geoboards

Your students will love **geoboard problems.** Geoboards can be purchased, made by woodshop students in middle school or high school, or elementary students can construct (draw) their own from wood and nails. Then rubber bands are used for the various shapes. But if students have a marker, they can quickly draw a geoboard by touching their marker to their paper to make the array. They can then use pencils for their shapes and their work is clearly seen by them and their teacher.

When you begin, if you have a primary grade, start with a 3 equidistant points by 3 equidistant points; fourth grade and higher can easily use larger boards, 4 by 4's and 5 by 5's. See Figures A5-11 and A5-12 in the appendix for a sample of each.

Geoboards are simple once the students master the technique of counting the number of squares and the number of half squares or the total number of different-sized triangles inside the shape on the given geoboard. Then they need to be able to draw geoboards of their own and construct shapes of the *same area* as the given shape, but their shapes must be different looking.

It is easiest to use lined paper to make the geoboards, so that the points can be approximately equidistant from each other. This eliminates the need of a ruler. Boards need to be neat and horizontally and vertically straight. Have the students use markers to draw the points. They can touch the end of the marker to the paper and there will be a nice, easy-to-see point. Then have them draw the shapes in pencil. If they use pencil for the points, it can be too difficult to properly see the shapes when drawn.

Next, construct the figure. If the given shape is made of two squares and one triangle, which also means the exact same thing as five triangles, then the students will construct a different figure on their own geoboards but it will still contain two squares and one triangle or five triangles.

Once students see and are able to draw one-by-two triangles (one point at the vertex of the right angle, two end points on the hypotenuse), one-by-threes (one point at the vertex of the right angle, three points on the hypotenuse,) and so on, they will fly with this skill. Be sure they can use the appropriate oral and written language to thoroughly explain what they are doing.

Graphing

Graphing of ordered pairs of numbers is another skill that helps students see spatial arrangements. See Figure 5-10 for two examples of the beautiful products you can get from teaching this skill. These two are from a book called *Graphing Fun.* The projects have such titles as "Old Hose Nose" (an elephant) and "Rover Takes Over" (a dog). This book has all sorts of

other excellent activities with catchy titles like "Steady Eddie" (a turtle), "A Horse, Of Course," "Cheerful Earful" (another dog with long ears), "R-R-Ribbet" (a frog), and "A Philly Swinger" (the Liberty Bell).

These types of activities can be done with fourth, fifth, and sixth grades, but do not be afraid to try some of the easier ones in third. Your students will do a beautiful job as long as the explanation and directions are *very* clear.

Explain the following carefully, using the chalkboard or the overhead so that the students can easily see what you are doing:

1. Explain that sometimes their graph paper should be in the horizontal position and at other times, in the vertical. The directions sheet will always give this information.
2. Explain the numbering meticulously. There will always be one zero on the bottom left-hand corner. The students should number on the *lines,* not on the spaces. This is very important for the correct plotting of the points.
3. For ordered pairs, the first number is always on the horizontal axis and the second number is on the vertical axis.
4. (2,3) The numbers inside the parentheses tell what *point* to plot. To plot this point, first go *across* to line 2 on the horizontal axis. Then go *up* to line 3 on the vertical axis. Put a point at the intersection of the lines. (4,5)To plot this point, go across to line 4 on the horizontal axis. Then go up to line 5 on the vertical axis. Put a point at the intersection of the lines. Be sure the students make a *clearly visible* point so they do not get lost. Students should practice to themselves: across, then up; across, up; across, up; until they have the pattern.

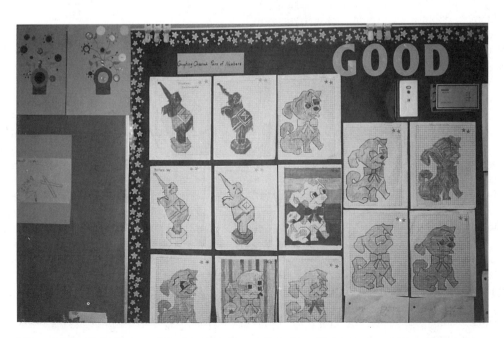

Figure 5-10. These dogs and elephants are the product of a math lesson on graphing of ordered pairs of numbers. Fourth-, fifth-, and sixth-graders, and sometimes even younger students, can be very successful with these projects. These are just like "Bounce That Ball" in the appendix.

5. Then connect the first point to the second.
6. Continue plotting points and connecting them to the previous points.
7. Stop means do not connect the next point to the last. Instead, start all over again connecting until you come to the word stop again. Then start all over again. The first point under stop is like the first point of the entire paper.
8. After each point is plotted, tell the students to cross out the ordered pair so they will always know where they are.
9. Explain to the students that they may go to the same point many times while they are graphing and that this is perfectly correct.
10. Sometimes the word *shade* will appear after a certain number of points have been plotted. Students *may* shade that particular part. If you are having your students color the entire picture when they are finished, do not have them do any shading.

If the students do a good job on the coloring, the math pictures look beautiful. Have the students color with colored pencils or markers for a splendid finished product. Then record and evaluate their pictures. Mount them on colored construction paper and put them on a bulletin board for a superb display. Have the students tell or write an explanation of what they did. Figure A5-13 in the appendix is a sample entitled, "Bounce That Ball."

Open-ended and Word Problems in Math

In teaching math, you will also want to be sure to train your students to competently deal with open-ended math problems. Students will need to have the skills to create a problem from given information, draw a conclusion from the comparison of two sets of data, and thoroughly explain how and why they came to that conclusion. They may need to determine the validity of a statement about a set of numbers or figures or problems and completely demonstrate how they determined whether or not the statement was valid. In addition to being able to talk about their figuring, they are going to need to be able to write about it. To help them do these things, give them lots of instruction and plenty of opportunities for practice.

For example, supposing one student has these numbers to work with: 7, 9, 11, 13, and 15. He adds $7 + 9$ and gets 16. Then He adds $9 + 11$ and gets 18. Next, he adds $11 + 13$ and gets 24. Last, he adds $13 + 15$ and gets 28. Another students points out that whenever you add odd numbers, the answer will be an even number. What about this? Is it true or false? How do you know? Give a thorough demonstration in writing of how you reached your answer.

Maybe your students are working on area. They may be given instruction to measure some objects and compute the area. They will need to be able to construct a table in which to record their data.

These types of problems are not easy for an elementary student. With practice, though, students will learn to begin manipulating the numbers to see what the facts are. It seems that an odd plus an odd is even. What about an odd plus an even? What about an even plus an even? What about an odd

plus an odd plus another odd? These are the kinds of manipulations and thinking students will have to do to become successful with these kinds of problems. They cannot just guess. They have to substantiate what they conclude with written evidence. These kinds of problems are both fun and challenging and are of the same type of thinking level as geoboards.

Your students will also be called upon to write word or story problems. Again, this is a very challenging area of the math curriculum. If students are to write a one-step story problem, for example, they need to have a clear understanding of the makeup of this type of problem. Be sure they have already learned to determine answers for story problems that are already written for them. This is a lower-level thinking skill than that used to devise their own problem and needs to be addressed first. (Go back to the previously presented Figure A5-8 in the appendix for the skill of solving already written word problems.)

Figure A5-14 in the appendix describes each step that leads to the eventual skill of writing a story problem from scratch. There is a big progression from

$$\begin{array}{r} \$\,32.95 \\ +\ 16.85 \\ \hline \$\,49.80 \end{array}$$

to

Cynthia deposited $12.50 in her savings account one week and $15.50 the following week. How much did she deposit altogether?

to

Write a one-step word problem to go with the following numbers and mathematical operation.

$$\begin{array}{r} \$\,1.48 \\ +\ 19.36 \\ \hline \$\,20.84 \end{array}$$

to

Write your very own story problem.

Grading Math

There are many ways of grading mathematics. A test on one skill can be graded, or a test reviewing several skills at one time can be evaluated. A composite grade can be given to an open-ended math test based on how well students explained their answers. Multiple-choice question tests can be given as well as fill-in-the-blank and true-false question tests.

A portfolio of math projects and tests can be kept for each student. In addition to teacher evaluation, the students can then evaluate themselves. They can note an area of improvement already made and an area where improvement could be made and how they will do it. They and you can make a comment on their overall performance.

When you take the time and care to prepare your students for the challenges of mathematics, when you implement all the math teaching techniques just discussed, you will have a superb program.

Two additional areas of mathematics are addressed in other parts of this book: math facts, under Facts in Chapter 2, The DEF's, and graphs and tables in Chapter 6, The PQR's, under Research Skills.

Research and Studies

Open-ended questions in math help students think. There is no single way to find a "right answer." Instead, these types of questions provide the learner with the opportunity to show thinking and problem-solving abilities.

Louise Burrell is a primary grade teacher in North Carolina. Investigations are the main method used in her math classes (Perlmutter, Bloom, & Burrell, 1993). Students construct their own investigations to solve problems in the various strands of math. In a large-group lesson, Burrell introduces a concept and then gives examples of some appropriate investigations; instructions, however, are general so that the young students can branch out on their own and do investigations that are appealing to them. This is in keeping with research that reveals that the only real learning that occurs is that which individuals construct and determine to have meaning for themselves (Baroody, 1987; Elkind, 1989).

Ownership of the learning is a significant factor. Students are empowered to develop critical thinking skills in a meaningful environment that is related to real life.

Burrell's students meet in small groups to determine the work that needs to be done each day. They set some standards for the work and plan to finish within the time framework. In their plan book, students write what they are trying to discover. Then they are off to their working center.

During the Perlmutter et al. study, students did an experiment in volume using water, sand, and blocks to measure. They practiced different ways to measure time, including how many jumping jacks it took for a particular student to tie his shoes. Students made pendulums using scissors and crayons. Other students did experiments with magnets, determining what materials they attracted and repelled. Some located items in the classroom that matched a particular geometric figure. Some measured the height of students using various objects. Students used flash cards, computers, and dice to help them develop and solve problems. They were very interested in math and found the activities challenging and enjoyable.

Students gathered information by way of surveys and graphed the answers. They played store and negotiated bargains. Sometimes in the midst of an investigation, students would get other ideas and go beyond the original investigation they had established for themselves.

After the manipulations were completed, students wrote what the investigation was about and what they learned. They wrote as best they could. (Remember, Burrell's students were only five to seven years old.) Then they spent some time sharing their investigations and even scheduled times when they would present their projects.

Students need to know how to solve everyday problems in math. Conceptual knowledge is vital for this to occur. Four dimensions are included: thinking and reasoning, such as hypothesizing, gathering data, and so on; settings, such as small group or individuals; tools, such as manipulatives, graphs, and so on; and attitudes and dispositions, such as participation and persistence (Pandey, 1990).

In California, mathematics assessment programs involve open-ended questions to allow students to construct their own answers rather than circling one of a given number of answers. They encourage students to solve problems in their own ways and in different ways and to be aware of diversity of responses. They allow students to show their depth of knowledge.

In Connecticut, students work in curriculum-assessment modules, which involve problems that may take a student or groups of students a week to solve, using all the available resources.

A study done on passivity in **cooperative learning** groups during math class showed that low-achieving students tended to be less active and involved in groups than were high achievers, but that they were more actively involved in cooperative groups than they were in the whole-group lessons (Mulryan, 1992).

In Mulryan's study, students had wide ranges of expectations in group settings. Some bright students viewed one of their roles as a helper to low-achieving students, whereas other bright students were not interested in this. Some thought the most important aspect of the math groups was to get the tasks done in as timely a manner as possible. Some groups considered the speed in which they completed the project to be as important as the outcome of the project itself. Some low achievers felt that they were not held individually accountable. Since it would be difficult for the teacher to tell in a group how much they contributed, they took a back seat and let the more able students proceed. This tends to be a repeat of the pattern that exists for low and high achievers in the large class setting. Low-achieving girls, especially, are at risk.

When setting up learning groups, it is important to require some sort of evidence of individual accountability, so the group will work as a whole and see that their job is not done until each and every member understands the material.

In the project or theme approach, students and teachers meet to discuss what they have learned, what they will do next, and how they will do it (Trepanier-Street, 1993). The projects are general; movement, for example. The big difference is that the project approach is child-centered; the students are the ones who decide what they will investigate within the topic and with whom they will do the project. Projects may also be started by the teacher when a need for a particular skill or concept is observed.

These projects can interweave math, science, language arts, and fine arts. Math strategies can be used to solve such problems as how high and wide the stage needs to be for a puppet show. With this approach, students see similarities, differences, and relationships between objects and concepts. They have the opportunity to continually examine a particular object, thereby developing deep and diversified knowledge.

The project/theme approach also helps develop continuity. Piaget stressed this need especially with young children. They become aware of what they already know and can see how new material is both alike and different to what they know. This is how students build learning and see a continuous flow from one area into another.

Kindergartners' abilities to classify, seriate, and conserve objects are significant predictors of their future achievement in first through fourth grades (Dudek, Strobel, & Thomas, 1987; Silliphant, 1983). Thus, trying to improve students' abilities in these areas would seem to be most beneficial. One study (Pasnak, Holt, Campbell, & McCutcheon, 1991) sought to see if this is true by separating kindergartners into two groups—one group to be taught classification, seriation, and conservation, the other group to be taught conventional mathematics.

The authors of this study asked the teachers of seventeen kindergarten classes at neighboring schools in northern Virginia to select the five students in their classrooms with the lowest ability, excepting language difficulties or other special situations. Of those students who completed the study, in the control group, fifteen were white and fourteen were minority, with ten blacks; in the experimental group, seventeen were white and eleven were minority, with seven blacks. No socioeconomic measures were available for the students.

The results of the study showed that for the low-achieving kindergartners, the Piacceleration program (developed from the learning set technique used to teach concrete operations necessary for success in the Piagetian operations of classification, seriation, and conservation) was significantly better than the current curriculum. The subjects of the study were at an age when they are transitioning from the late preoperational stage of cognitive development to the early concrete operational stage. Piacceleration instruction teaches all three operations necessary to make this transition. This study also concluded that command of the three concrete operations of classification, seriation, and conservation resulted in increased ability with both mathematical concepts as well as verbal comprehension.

MENTOR TEACHERS

Mentor teachers are those who have gone through a certain process to get this title. Usually, they need to have a minimum of five successful teaching years in the district. They write proposals for their projects and include their résumés. Someone from the instructional media center comes to their classroom to videotape a lesson. The tape, the proposal, and the résumé are sent to the mentor teacher selection committee for review and evaluation. Last, these teachers are interviewed by the committee, which then makes its selections for the upcoming year.

These teachers can be a big help to you. There will be mentors in writing, reading, math, geography, physical education, and fine arts. Other mentors teach classes on different methods of grouping, different uses of technology in the classroom, AIMS, and almost any other area you can imagine.

These mentors will present their classes for certain grade levels. For some great ideas, go to as many of these seminars as you can and/or get their materials to use in your classroom.

If you happen to have these kinds of mentor teachers— mentor teachers whose projects are devoted solely to helping *beginning* teachers—in your district, be sure to take advantage of them.

MONEY

This section discusses the kind of money you will need for your classroom for extra art supplies, award certificates, prizes, extra books, and field trips. You might want to buy photo booklets of places you have visited. These booklets have large, beautiful pictures with good, informative captions. The students thoroughly delight in these.

Your PTA may give you some money for classroom supplies and field trips, but you may not have enough school money to go on all the field trips you would like. Usually, if you put the admission fee and bus fee for a field trip right on the permission slip, the parents will pay because they want their children going on these trips, too. If you have a student who is not going on the trip because of financial reasons, take that student aside and let her know not to worry. You can find money in a school fund to take care of it. You want all your students to go on a trip regardless of the pressing financial responsibilities of their parents.

Maybe you would like your class to raise some extra money. You could have an annual jog-a-thon, which helps each class earn a surprising amount of money. Recycling cans is another good way for your classroom to get some extra money. If everyone contributes cans, you can collect quite a bit of money. If you are very ambitious, you could have a car wash or a cake and cookie sale. Whatever you decide, if the whole class participates, you will be very successful.

The second part of this chapter discusses the importance of welcoming new students and the exhilaration of a novel idea each month.

NEW STUDENTS

The most important thing to do with new students is to make them feel welcome. Introduce them to your class and your instructional assistant, if you have one. Ask one or two responsible, friendly, well-liked students to spend the day with these new students showing them the campus and where places of importance are located: bathrooms, drinking fountains, lunch tables, library, computer lab, and the office. Ask the assigned students to explain the class rules and procedures to them.

Give new students the appropriate texts, pencils, paper, and composition books. That day, add their names to the assignment accountability chart, the behavior chart, the helpers' wheel or chart, and to the list of names in your grade book for each subject. Provide a name tag. All this will help them feel like a part of the class much sooner.

The first day, especially, call on new students when you are reasonably sure they have the correct answer or can give an opinion on some subject your class is discussing. This helps them feel more accepted and a regular part of your classroom, even though they just arrived that day.

At the end of the first day, check with them that everything went all right, that they know where things are at the school, that they have had a chance to play with some classmates at recess or lunch, and so on. If a problem exists in any of these areas, begin work on it right away. Be sure they understand the homework assignment. Then give them a copy of your class schedule and the parent information letter to take home. Ask them to have their parents sign the letter and return it with their children the next school day. Then you know the parents have received some concrete information about what goes on in your classroom.

If you follow these practices for new students, their day will run smoothly and so will yours.

NOVEL MONTHLY EVENTS

Try to plan for at least one really exciting thing each month in your classroom so that the students will have something to look forward to eagerly. This helps the school year move along at a rapid pace.

You could do many things; and the following are merely examples.

September.   Have students create fabulous art projects to have out for Back-to-School Night and beautiful invitations for their parents to come for this special night.

October.   A schoolwide dress up for Halloween with classes teamed with other classes at the school to develop closer friendship ties. Upper grades could be partnered with primary grades. Friendship activities might involve writing and decorating a special friendship letter to the student, the older student teaching the younger one some academic skill, and both classrooms having a party together where the older student and his new friend, the younger student, sit together while they eat the goodies.

This is often the month for drug awareness and there are always many activities associated with that. It is vitally important students get correct information about drugs/alcohol at an early age and learn coping skills to deal with peer and societal pressure. There are good speakers you can get through the police or sheriff's department. They will come to your class to speak to the students and provide them with informative, interesting booklets. The students enjoy this very much.

November.   A Thanksgiving feast is always fun. Students can either dress themselves as Indians or Pilgrims, bring Indian or Pilgrim dolls, or bring beautifully colored large cutout figures. Students can sign up in advance for the kind of food and drink they will bring.

This might be a nice month for your geography bee, too.

December.   This is an excellent opportunity for a winter holiday program, which can involve puppet shows, plays, and singing. Decorate the classroom and help the students prepare for the program. Invite the parents to come to see your students' performance. This creates a very exciting atmosphere in your classroom.

January.   This can be a good month to take a field trip to the performing arts center or to a theater to see a children's play. Use the ready-made activities provided by the center or the theater to create interest and provide background for the students. If students are going to the performing arts for a concert, you can ask the students who have musical instruments at home to bring them to school and you can have your own little concert. These types of field trips and preparatory and follow-up activities are great fun and generate a lot of enthusiasm for the fine arts.

February.   Students always love Valentine's Day. Have them make mailboxes for their valentines to keep on their desks until the special day arrives. Make the students aware that they do not have to bring valentines, but, if they do, they should bring them for every student. It is a good idea to make a copy of the students' names and pass these out a few days before Valentine's Day so the students can properly address their cards.

Schedule a period of time before your party to let the students pass out their valentines and open them. Then they can sit down and eat.

February is also a good month for your math facts contest.

March.   A science fair is perfect for this month. This takes quite a bit of time, but when students do a good job, their projects look great and so will your classroom. The students love looking at each others' undertakings.

April.   An Open House program can be put on during this month. This is a chance for the students to demonstrate the dances they have learned. It is nice to have different students do historical readings that give information about the period in history during which these dances were popular. A performance of three or four dances works well. The students absolutely love this. Some do not want to do anything else in school except practice their dances.

May.   Poster, art, or writing contests are often held at this time of the year. These are a lot of fun to participate in and the students love the special attention of receiving participation certificates or winning some prize.

This is a good month too for a special speech. It could be a hobby speech where students bring their hobby to school to explain it to their classmates. The students could also give a speech on a historical character; they could dress up as the character and pretend they are that character during the speech.

This could be your month for a special history project, something that the students have constructed and bring to school to share and present to the others. These projects fascinate the students.

June.   This is the perfect month for a really thrilling field trip. If you are relatively near an IMAX or OMNIMAX theater, this is a great time to go see a couple of these shows. They are fabulous as well as very educational. Or this could be your month for a trip to the zoo or a wild animal park. Register in advance for a docent; the students find these people interesting and usually have lots of questions for them. Maybe you live close enough to a city that has historical tourist attractions. Many times students have not been to see them even though they live in nearby towns.

Something exciting at least once a month fills the bill.

The last part of this chapter covers an annual event that is always an exhilarating evening. This is a special, scheduled

Figure 5-11.   Hanging tinsel or narrow streamers from objects affixed to the ceiling or lights adds an eye-catching touch.

time for all the parents to come to school and visit their children's classrooms, see their work on display, and watch their special program.

OPEN HOUSE

Preparing for Open House is a busy, exciting time of the year.

If you have art or history projects hanging from the ceiling or light fixtures, you might want to consider hanging tinsel or narrow streamers to them to give a little added flare.

Plan way ahead for Open House by saving students' activities and projects over the entire school year. Mount them on colored construction paper and place them in various displays. If your bulletin boards are full, use masking tape and put them on the walls or chalkboards. Consider the following two things, though, if you use masking tape:

1. Masking tape will not support much weight.
2. A change in weather can affect the adhesiveness of the tape.

To avoid problems, place relatively heavy art projects on bulletin boards where you can use staples and straight pins, and place lightweight projects on chalkboards and walls.

Figure 5-12.   For Open House, your room will look nice if you decorate the chalkboards with students' work. Here the stereo system and megaphone are all ready for the students' performances.

Figure 5-13. Taping shoe writing projects or other student work to the wall under the chalkboards can dress up the classroom and give it a more "finished" look.

Remember the walls under the chalkboards; for a nice, dressy look, put up assignments there, too. Do not "masking tape" projects up more than a day or so ahead of Open House. Otherwise, you will be continually replacing the tape to rehang a fallen assignment. Even considering these problems, it is well worth the inconvenience for the sharp look your classroom will have. You might want to consider using Velcro® instead of masking tapes. It works well; *but* place a small piece on an out-of-the-way part of the wall first to ensure that a mark will not be left when the Velcro® is removed.

Another way to enhance the attractiveness of your room is to line a voting booth, border it, and set it up in the back of the

Figure 5-14. Voting booths can be fully extended, lined, set behind a table, and used as a background for students' work. This voting booth was lined in white. Red, white, and blue stars and stripes were used for a bright and colorful border. Students' poetry and art were mounted on colored paper. T-shirt book reports were hung on a clothesline and the tabletop was used to show California mission projects.

Figure 5-15. When decorating your class, remember what an effect hanging students' projects from the light fixtures can have. Open up a large paper clip, attach the project, and hang it up using a yardstick to hook the bent end of the paper clip to the light tray. Your room will look sharp for Open House. Courtesy of Carroll Maietta.

classroom with the students' work pinned to it. With a nice white, yellow, or pink butcher paper for the lining and a colorful border, this display will be a real eye-catcher.

You can make your classroom come alive for this special time of the year by hanging students' projects from the ceiling or light fixtures. Partially straighten a large paper clip, attach a piece of string to it, attach the project to the string, and loop the end of the paper clip over the edge of the light fixture using a thin yard or meter stick. This will make your classroom look fabulous for Open House.

Have your students work on state, country, animal, and so on, reports and set the due date a couple of weeks before Open

Figure 5-16. Parents enjoy looking through their children's work. Here, that work is placed in nice, neat booklets on top of each student's desk. This helps give the classroom a colorful atmosphere for Open House. Courtesy of Wanda Grace.

House; it looks nice to have these displayed on the students' desks.

In addition to turning your classroom into a showpiece, it is lots of fun to put on a program for parents. Plan on a huge turnout of parents and students. Spring, the time when Open House usually occurs, is a great time for the students to work on one of their fine arts components: dance.

You can teach the students several dances and form groups for who will perform which dance(s). While practicing is going on some students can be researching information about the dance's origin or the historical period during which it was popular. They can write the information in a short report. Then a student can introduce each dance by reading this information to the audience.

Many different types of dances are appropriate for different grade levels. Folk dances, square dances, Charleston dances, and disco dances are just some of the popular ones. Many square dance records will have one track with an explanation of the calls and the following track will have the song for the dance. Folk dances are relatively easy to teach and you can always choreograph any music you like. Create three or four separate routines for a song and then have the students repeat these once or twice throughout the dance.

For an Open House performance, you could have a student speak through a megaphone held by another student. This student could then read a historical report, or, for first and second grades, say a few introductory words to the audience before the first dance. Then the first dance could be some kind of folk dance. If you have early primary grades, one dance may be sufficient, depending on the level of difficulty and the readiness of your students.

Another student could read a report or say a few words on a different period in history, the Western period of U.S. history, for example, prior to a square dance. A third student could read about the Roaring Twenties, after which the students could do a version of the Charleston. A fourth student could read about historical events during the period of "disco fever" and the students could do a disco dance. Both the parents and the students enjoy these types of presentations and the students love practicing for them.

Have your classroom look sharp, have yourself organized and enthusiastic, have your students well prepared, and not only will your Open House be great, your year will be great, too—well run from beginning to end.

CHAPTER QUESTIONS

1. Pretend you are teaching second grade. You are ready to give a test covering simple addition and subtraction of whole numbers. Make up a sample study sheet or describe what you would have the students put on their student-made study sheet. How would you construct the test?

2. How would you explain graphing of ordered pairs to a fourth-grader?

3. How would you explain the use of tangrams to a third-grader? What would you say to explain its importance?

4. Explain how you could use an overhead projector to help teach a mathematical concept.

5. Develop one of your own novel ideas for a particular school month. What will it be? How will you implement it? What do you expect the student reaction to be?

6. Describe a telecommunications project in which you would like to involve your class.

7. You have been assigned to a 3-4 combination class for one of your student teaching experiences. You have just finished teaching a history lesson to the fourth-graders who are part of this 3-4 combination class. Specifically, what feedback would you expect to hear from your master teacher? Give examples of positive things he might say and write. Give examples of weaknesses that might be mentioned. How would you handle any negative criticism of your lesson or of classroom control?

8. Select a grade level. Then describe what you would do for an evening Open House.

9. You have a sixth-grade class. A student from an SDC class who is overly aggressive is mainstreamed into your classroom for PE. How would you make this a successful experience for all?

10. You have a second-grade class. A student who is a little "strange" acting from an SDC class on campus is being mainstreamed to your class for art. Your students already know who this student is and think he's "weird." What could you tell your students to help this be a positive experience for everyone?

11. How could your class earn extra money for field trips?

12. Describe ways you could help a new student feel more comfortable and confident.

13. What are two examples of classroom modifications that might be used to accommodate a student with ADHD who is fully included?

14. What can you do if you are implementing classroom modifications, but they are not successful?

15. Select three of the ten teacher behaviors associated with teacher effectiveness according to the Freunds. Comment on what you consider the value of each.

16. What are the four basics of Hunter's instructional lesson?

17. How can a master teacher best help you?

18. In what way is information from the Burrell study interesting and applicable to you?

19. How could you apply the study on passivity in cooperative learning groups during math to your role as a teacher?

20. In what way does Piaget's philosophy relate to project/theme units?

21. How could a mentor teacher be of help to you in your first few years of teaching?

CHAPTER PROJECT

Devise a graphing of ordered pairs project suitable to a grade level of your choice. If you use first grade, use a large, well-spaced graph with numbering maybe only to eight. First-graders might just plot the points and not connect them, since connecting is a much more difficult skill. Their plotted points could form a simple pattern, maybe some different-sized squares. Second-graders could have the same assignment, but they could connect the points. For third and up, you can get into a more sophisticated project.

First, make your graph-paper page nice and neat and copy a set for your students. Next, write your directions page containing the numbered pairs. Be sure to indicate in your directions the use of the words *across* and *up*. Then, make for yourself a sample pattern that you can use for an answer key. Last, plan for your students to color their projects using colored pencils or markers. If you schedule the project before Open House, you can have these for a beautiful display for the parents.

REFERENCES

Allen, T. (1987). Identifying behaviors of the master teacher. *ERS Spectrum, 5*(2), 42–47.

Aschbacher, P. R. (1992). *Issues in innovative assessment for classroom practice: Barriers and facilitators.* Washington, DC: Office of Educational Research and Improvement.

Baroody, A. J. (1987). *Children's mathematical thinking.* New York: Teachers College Press.

Collins, M., Carnine, D., & Gersten, R. (1987). Elaborated corrective feedback and the acquisition of reasoning skills: A study of computer assisted instruction. *Exceptional Children, 54,* 254–262.

Davis, S. (1992). Report card to the nation on inclusion in education of students with mental retardation. *The Arc,* 1–6, 24, 95.

Dudek, S. E., Strobel, M., & Thomas, A. D. (1987). Chronic learning problems and maturation. *Perceptual and Motor Skills,* 407–429.

Elkind, D. (1989). Developmentally appropriate practice: Philosophical and practical implications. *Phi Delta Kappan, 70*(2), 113–117.

Freund, L. A., & Freund, S. A. (1989). Effective instruction: Application of the Hunter Instructional Skills Model to staff development for mainstreaming. *ERS Spectrum, 7*(2), 28–32.

Mulryan, C. M. (1992). Student passivity during small groups in mathematics. *Journal of Educational Research, 85*(5), 261–273.

Pandey, T. (1990). *Authentic Mathematics Assessment,* California Department of Education, ERIC Clearinghouse on Tests, Measurement and Evaluation.

Pasnak, R., Holt, R., Campbell, J. W., & McCutcheon, L. (1991). Cognitive and achievement gains for kindergartners instructed in Piagetian operations. *Journal of Educational Research, 85*(1), 5–13.

Perlmutter, J. C., Bloom, L. & Burrell, L. (1993). Whole math through investigations. *Childhood Education, 70*(1), 20–24.

Routh, D. K., Schroeder, C. S., & O'Tauma, L. (1974). Development of activity level in children. *Developmental Psychology, 10,* 163–168.

Silliphant, V. M. (1983). Kindergarten reasoning and achievement in grades K–3. *Psychology in the Schools, 20*(3), 289–294.

Trepanier-Street, M. (1993). What's so new about the project approach? *Childhood Education, 70*(1), 25–29.

Zentall, S. S., Harper, G. W., & Stormont-Spurgin, M. (1993). Children with hyperactivity and their organizational abilities. *Journal of Educational Research, 87*(2), 112–117.

BIBLIOGRAPHY

Fankhauser, S. (1994). *Hands-on math: 5th grade activities that work every time.* A presentation through California Elementary Education Association.

6

THE PQR'S

This chapter presents some exceptional ideas for three areas of the curriculum—physical education, reading, and research skills. Being commendably prepared in these subjects will help your classroom run at a quick, exciting pace. In addition, this chapter gives you a recommendation about instituting a special time in your classroom. It also offers a multitude of suggestions for managing both the everyday, as well as the special, responsibilities of the elementary classroom teacher. Detailed in this chapter are the following topics:

- Paperwork
- Parent-Teacher Communication
- Physical Education
- Planning Time for Substitutes
- Questioning Strategies
- Quiet Time
- Reading
- Reports
- Research Skills

The first part of this chapter offers valuable information about paperwork, parent-teacher communication, teaching the subject of physical education, and planning time for a substitute teacher.

PAPERWORK

Perhaps the most valuable result of all education is the ability to make yourself do the thing you have to do, when it ought to be done, whether you like it or not; it is the first lesson that ought to be learned; and however early a man's training begins, it is probably the last lesson that he learns thoroughly.

Thomas Henry Huxley
1825–1895
Technical Education (1877)

Paperwork is never ending. There are forms to fill out, evaluations to write, and papers to correct. Report cards, progress reports, and cum files, the students' permanent records, also must be completed.

The *fastest* way to get paperwork done in a hurry is to complete it immediately when you first get it or learn about it. Do not bury the paper and think you will get to it at a later time.

Do the work correctly the *first* time. Follow all directions to ensure that you do not have to do it all over again. If you need some part explained, get help *then* so that you can record the information correctly. Then it is done and you do not end up losing papers and wasting time locating new ones. Turn in the completed forms without delay to the *right* person.

Do not let paperwork build up. Forms not turned into the office generate even more paperwork, such as notices that state: "Your student-of-the-month form was due last Thursday. Please get it in ASAP"; "Where is your evaluation for the inservice two weeks ago? We need it immediately"; or "Physical fitness reports were due last Friday. Please turn yours in promptly."

You do not want to look at this kind of communication in your mailbox, nor does the office staff or principal appreciate it when you do not have these items in on time. Take time then, at your first recess, or at lunch period to complete it *that day.*

Occasionally, it is not possible to do the paperwork immediately or there could be a certain type of paperwork that presents itself on a periodic basis. Then you need to move to the *surest* way to get paperwork done: Schedule it into your lesson plan book in bright colors of ink. You will be looking at this book every day anyway; now, you will see reminders for anything you need. Then you can take a few minutes from recess and/or lunch, and get the work done right then and there. Put a check after it in your lesson plan book once it is done. Then it is finished and off your mind.

Scheduling things into your lesson plan book will help prevent you from feeling totally overburdened. It allows you to get everything done, not forget a thing, and have it done on time, too.

Correct students' papers as quickly as you can, record them, and pass them back so that you and the students can see how they are doing. Feedback is very important to the students to help them make adjustments in the amount of time allocated to study. In addition, it is important to you to see what, if any, reteaching needs to be done.

A huge stack of uncorrected papers can be overwhelming. Have the students self-correct as much as they are able to competently do based on their grade level.

Usually by fourth grade, individual students in the classroom can help with correcting a class set of papers and do a fine job of it. If you have a lower primary class, a first or second grade, ask the teachers of the fourth-, fifth- and sixth-grade students whether one or two of their good correctors, collators, staplers, and so on would volunteer to lend you a hand. There are older students who will happily give up their recess or lunch period or both to help with the paperwork in a primary classroom. Take advantage of these students' generosity. They will love to help you.

Enlist the assistance of parents to help with your paper load. Some parents, who might feel reluctant to come into the classroom, are perfectly content typing parent letters at home, correcting spelling tests at home, or coming into the office workroom to prepare supplies for art and make reproducibles for your students. Do not think you are imposing on these people. Even though they are doing you a favor, you are doing them a favor, too, by giving them the opportunity to help in a way that they enjoy.

Schedule enough time to get *all* paperwork done. There are lots of time slots that could be put to good use if you just plan ahead. For example, suppose you have a dentist or doctor appointment and you will be sitting in the waiting room for a period of time. Take school forms to complete or papers to correct. On the bus, train, or plane are excellent places to get correcting done or various forms finished. Waiting at the airport for your flight or the flight of a friend or relative is a prime opportunity; just think ahead and have your paperwork with you. Suppose you are going to be waiting for two hours while your car is serviced—another perfect opportunity. When you complete paperwork in this manner, it feels like it is such a lesser burden. Instead of feeling bad and frustrated and moaning about all the time you wasted sitting at the airport, sitting in a waiting room, sitting on the train or bus, and so on, you can think of all the paperwork you accomplished and feel satisfied and rewarded.

Follow this system and you will always have the right handle on paperwork:

1. Complete paperwork correctly and thoroughly, and return it to the right person immediately. Take a few minutes from recess or lunch period to get this done.
2. Use "waiting time" and "transportation time" to correct papers and complete forms.
3. Enlist student and parent help.
4. Use a bright-colored pen to write reminders of what is due and when it is due directly in your lesson plan book. Check off the item when it is completed.

PARENT-TEACHER COMMUNICATION

Getting together is beginning.
Staying together is progress.
Working together is success.

Henry Ford

Teacher Suggestions for Parents

Think of parents as your partners in the education of your students, their children. Parents are the children's first teacher and can do a great deal to ensure their academic success. According to research, what parents do for their children as far as learning is more important than the family's socioeconomic status (Walberg, 1984; Hirsch, 1985).

Some parents are very effective teachers of their children, others less so. These others are the ones to whom you can be helpful. Gently and kindly giving them practical suggestions, research says, will bring about improvement and higher achievement in the classroom (Becker & Epstein, 1982; Hirsch, 1985; Walberg, 1984).

You may want to modify some of the following suggestions according to your grade level, but all children can benefit from their parents doing many of these suggested activities:

- Get records/tapes/CDs with counting songs for your child.
- Get records/tapes/CDs with math facts set to musical rhythm for your upper-grade child.
- Have a calculator available for your child to use.
- Read aloud to your child. Allow him to see the printed words. Discuss what you read. Ask tough questions. Talk about the meaning of some of the words. Try to relate the story to everyday life.
- Call your child's attention to letters and words on various boxes, jars, and cans around the house, and signs and billboards around town and on the highways. Being aware of environmental print is a great vocabulary builder.
- Let your child see you reading books or magazines for enjoyment purposes.
- Discuss the day's news and various TV programs.
- Ask to see your child's completed homework assignments.
- Listen to your child read to you.
- Get your child a public library card and take her on a regular basis.
- Quiz your child after he has prepared for a test.
- Ask your child how the school day went. Ask specific questions like: Who did you play with at recess? What did you do in math? What can you tell me about your last art project? What is making this a good year for you?
- Encourage your child to draw, scribble, or write stories of interest to her. When the story is finished, ask your child what it says or means. Make pleasant, accepting comments.
- Ask your child to retell a story you have read or one that has been read in the classroom or one that has been read independently.
- Ask your child questions about his world. Do not ask yes or no questions. Ask why, how, and what questions.
- Listen when your child speaks. Do not interrupt. Ask your child to listen when you speak and not to interrupt you.
- Tell your child, "I love you." Show that you care and are concerned about your child's happiness, well-being, and productivity.

These are just a few ideas. It is important to realize that parents are hungry for ways to help their children. You are someone who can provide many helpful suggestions.

Parents Volunteering for a Teacher

Some parents are able to help out in the classroom, some on a regular basis. They could help with an art project, especially holiday art projects. They could read a story to a small group of children. They might listen to a group of students read and discuss a story, or they might listen and discuss a story with students one at a time. Perhaps they will help a group with math. They might come to the class as a guest speaker and share special information they have that would be interesting to the students. Sometimes parents are able to bring in supplementary materials for a particular lesson.

Some parents might help with the "work" in a classroom: correcting papers or getting materials for an art project. Others might be able to accompany the class on a field trip. Parents who work all day and are not available to come to the classroom may be able to help at home by making learning games.

Figure 6-1. Watching educational programs on television as a family and discussing them during and/or afterward can be a profitable experience for all. Courtesy of Charlesworth, *Understanding Child Development,* 3e, © 1992 by Delmar Publishers, Inc.

Figure 6-2.   A parent volunteer is helping a student with her hand-writing. Courtesy of Cheryl Thompson.

Whatever you have your parent volunteers doing, be sure to have written plans for them so that they know exactly what to do. Help them feel comfortable in the classroom and let them know they are appreciated. They are a valuable resource.

Before you get involved with the upcoming three types of parent-teacher communications, it is important to be alert to possible problems the family may be dealing with: stress; drug abuse; alcohol abuse; violence; vulgarity; emotional problems; mental illness; lying; stealing; gangs; vandalism; some type of sexual, psychological, or physical abuse; poverty; overcrowding; divorce; and both parents or a single parent working two jobs. Any one of these can cause a lot of emotional upset to the family, both the parents and the children. You may not know that these things are occurring, but keep them in mind to be alert to any underlying problem that is affecting the student's behavior or achievement.

Be aware that some parents think in a different way from you. Although the following are amusing incidents, they are true. They are recorded by Anne C. Walde and Keith Baker in an article entitled "When Parents Don't Care If Their Children Learn" in *The Education Digest,* April 1991.

- A teacher told a parent his son was not doing his home-work. The parent said, "I know he isn't. He watches TV all the time and doesn't do his homework. I just don't know what to do." The teacher kindly suggested to turn off the TV. The parent replied, "Oh, he'd never let me do that!"
- A mother calls to explain why her son's homework is not done. "It forces him to think, and that just wore out his brain, so I had to let him watch TV."
- An annoyed parent calls the child's teacher. "Please stop bothering me with school stuff. I have to go to class, I have a business to run, and we are trying to sell our house. I don't have time for that child."

Try to help. Remind parents that, as parents, *they* are in charge of their children. Even if they are very busy and frustrated, they are still in charge and responsible.

Although you may have conflicts when you communicate with a parent, do the best you can. Do not take criticism personally or get into heated arguments. Stay calm. Be professional. Avoid sarcasm and be courteous. However, under no circumstances should you accept verbal abuse. Should this happen, inform the principal and have the principal present at all future meetings or on the extension during phone conversations.

The three types of parent-teacher communication discussed next are phone conversations, written communications, and conferences.

Teacher Phone Conversation with Parents

If you are initiating the call, be prepared with what you want to say and what you would like done. If the parent initiates the call, listen carefully. Be sure each party understands what will be done.

You might want to call parents to let them know that their child did a great job on a report. You might want to call parents to let them know their child is very sleepy and having difficulty paying attention. Determine why the child is sleepy and what can be done. Is the student watching the late, late show, or does she have some type of sleep disturbance? You might want to call other parents about their child not turning in a science project. Together decide what can be done to resolve this. Note the time and date of the call for your records.

On the phone, do your best to be both informative and understanding. You and the parents want to work together to do what is best for the child.

Teacher Written Communication with Parents

This type of communication may be a form letter, written behavior contract, or a handwritten note. Again, emphasize that you want to work with the parents for the benefit of the child. Be sure the forms are clear, well written, make sense, and communicate to the parents appropriate, relevant information about their child.

Figures A6-1 through A6-8 in the appendix are forms you might wish to use to communicate with your parents. A class schedule is always helpful to the parents as is information about your homework policies and grading periods.

There is a two-page form that details specific academic problems students might have and how parents can help. Included also are progress report forms, one suitable for primary grades and one appropriate for upper grades. These list all the subjects and have a box by each for grades. Furthermore, there is a list of skills in which some students may need to improve. Areas needing improvement can be so indicated with a check. These progress reports or something similar should be sent home midway through each grading period.

A classroom management form is next. This is helpful to send home early in the year, because it lists classroom rules with their positive and negative consequences. If you have a primary class, you can use the three classroom rules of "follow directions, keep hands and feet to self, and be polite" discussed in Chapter 1, The ABC's, instead of the longer set of rules.

If students are having problems with behavior, the forms in Figures A6-6, A6-7, and A6-8 in the appendix will be very useful. One form gives parents specific information about their children's misbehavior by stating the classroom rules and listing a number of subcategories that describe specific actions. This helps the parents and their children focus on exact behaviors, rather than generalities.

If this does not handle the misbehavior, a **behavior contract** can be sent home. The form has a place where students can write precisely what they will do to improve. The last form, a school citation, is one for drastic action. The students do not like these nor do their parents. This type of form generates office paperwork on the student along with office referrals and suspensions. Even though this form's primary purpose is for problems out on the playground, it can be used as effectively in the classroom by checking "Other" and writing the particular classroom problem.

These forms can be mailed to the parents. Since students are often reluctant to take these home, mailing is usually the fastest way of getting them into the parents' hands; mailing usually gets a stronger response, too. You can also have the students hand carry them, but be sure to write the students' names in your lesson plan book to ensure you get these back with parent signatures.

When you send home forms, such as classroom management or progress reports, for a parent signature, have the last section in your grade book set aside to mark these forms in when the students return them. Save all of these signed forms for the entire school year, because you might want to refer to them later in the year. Keep them together in a file folder for easy access.

If you would like the parents to take some kind of action, write in such a way that it is very clear to the parents exactly what you would like them to do. For example, if a student frequently leaves books at home, you might want the parents to check that the child leaves his fully loaded backpack leaning against the front door each evening before going to bed. When he opens the front door to leave for school, he will pick up the backpack.

Maybe a student is spending two and a half hours a night on fifty minutes worth of homework. You might want to suggest to the student's parents that the child set the timer on the oven or microwave for ten minutes. Then the child sees how much she can get done before the timer goes off. When the timer sounds, she shows someone her work. That person initials under the completed work. Then the timer is set again, and so forth. This can continue for maybe a week, after which the student can set the timer and check just with herself. The timer can then be set for longer periods of time. The student will find this surprisingly helpful.

Sometimes in written or phone communication, you might want to involve another person such as the district nurse, school psychologist, **speech therapist,** or school principal. For example, it might be obvious that a certain student is not receiving adequate medical or dental care. The parents may need assistance in locating affordable care. You might write that you have spoken with the nurse who states that appropri-

ate care can be found at several places. Have a list with names, addresses, and phone numbers ready for the parents. Another student might be frequently coming to school unbathed and with body odor. Again, it is helpful for both you and the nurse to communicate with this student and the parents. Another student might not have supervision after school. In a case like this, you may want to involve the district psychologist and your principal so that an appropriate means of child care can be established quickly.

Parent-Teacher Conferences

Sometimes there is one specific day and a series of **minimum days** set aside each year for conferences. You may need to schedule more for some cases. If there are unresolved problems, it is often very helpful for students as young as six and seven, as well as older students, to sit in on the conference. This can help clear the air and make communication direct and open to all.

It is important to be prepared for all conferences, but especially for the first conference dealing with a report card. In addition to having the report card ready, it helps to have samples of the student's work and any available test scores. If you are doing a home conference, have all the materials together in a folder. If you are having a conference at school, have the materials out on a table in the classroom, rather than on your desk. A table is usually less formal and less intimidating. It can convey more of a feeling of warmth, caring, and partnership.

Greet the parents and invite them to sit down at the table. Plan some positive things about the child that you can to communicate to the parents first. Then, you might want to make some general, but important, statements. Emphasize how important it is for the parents to check their child's composi-

Figure 6-3. It is very helpful when the teacher and parent meet for a conference to discuss, as a team, the child's strengths and weaknesses and establish some mutually agreed-upon goals. Courtesy of Essa, *Introduction to Early Childhood Education,* © 1992 by Delmar Publishers, Inc.

tion book, to be alert for any behavior contracts, to see that their child has a good breakfast before coming to school, to ensure a place and specific time to study and complete all homework, and to make every effort to see that their child gets to listen to someone read aloud to him in the evenings or on the weekend.

Then go over their child's report card, test scores, and sample papers. Use the positive first. Explain the student's strengths. Tell the parents about their child's attitude, work habits, achievement, and how he gets along with other students in class and on the playground. If things are going well with the child, let the parents know they are doing a good job. If some areas need improvement, a written plan is usually most helpful so that you, the parents, and their child will know exactly what to do.

Suppose, for example, certain students are weak in reading vocabulary and comprehension. Maybe their parents could take them to various places on short trips to increase their exposure to the world, consequently increasing their general knowledge. Maybe their grandparents could quiz them on vocabulary words, if the grandchildren would be interested in this. It could be made into a fun game.

Other students may not have mastered their math facts yet. Perhaps both parents work long hours, but you know these students have older brothers and sisters who still live at home. Could these siblings help with this situation? Would the child cooperate with the older sibling so that the helping situation would be one of pleasure?

Some students may have self-image or self-esteem problems. Could their parents ask their children about their school day when they get home? Could they take their children a few places, just the three of them, and leave other brothers and sisters with a baby sitter?

Be sure to ask parents if there are special things about their children that would be helpful for you to know. Often parents can tell you some positive things about their child that you may not already know. They can also provide a good deal of insight into any problem areas. You can usually decide together on an appropriate reward for their children when improvement and success are achieved.

Remember, too, that most parents are very eager to hear your suggestions about how they can help their children. Gentleness and kindness on your part go a long way. Strive to work well together to make a better partnership.

The best part of parent-teacher communication has been saved for last. This type of communication involves the opportunities to pleasantly surprise the parents once in a while via *mail*. Figures A6-9 and A6-10 in the appendix contain a citizenship award and a special note that can be mailed to the parents. Even when students know they are receiving these awards, there is just something extra about their parents getting the awards in the mail that makes it a special treat for everyone.

PHYSICAL EDUCATION

When you are organized and have success-oriented activities based on physical, social, and mental (self-esteem) development, physical education can be an energizing subject to teach, a real pleasure.

Focus your students on one or two skills for the lesson. Consider both physical and social skills. First, be sure you teach the skills by explaining and demonstrating so that no doubt remains in anyone's mind about what you expect. Younger primary children may need to just "experience" the jungle gym and "experience" giving and receiving rides in the wagon, riding trikes, playing in the sand, and so forth.

Figure 6-4. These young students are having PE in a loosely structured setting. They are having time just to "experience" the jungle gym.

Later on, though, students will have opportunities for learning gross motor skills to be applied in group games such as dodge ball and four square. Select age-appropriate activities so that your students have the gross motor coordination to be successful with the activities.

While students are practicing a particular physical skill they can practice the social skill of telling their classmates what a good job they are doing when they see classmates trying their best. This encourages students to recognize that, just as in other subjects in the curriculum, there will be a wide variety of abilities in PE. Those students who try, and are praised by their classmates for this on a regular basis, will make fine progress.

If you have an upper grade, you may be teaching ball-handling skills in preparation for basketball. You will see that some of the students are quite good at these skills, dribbling, for example, while others are not adept at all. You can appoint some of the more skilled students to work with the less skilled.

Now is the perfect time to have the students learn and practice a social skill during the lesson: Make only encouraging, supportive statements to those who are just learning. Give the students specific examples at the beginning of their lesson. For example, tell them they could say, "Good job, Jeremy!" or "Great try, Melissa!" Model this yourself for them so that they get the idea and are not reluctant to praise and encourage their classmates.

If some of the students do exceptionally well, be sure to take notice of this and call the class's attention to these students and their achievements. For some students, PE is their best subject and a chance to get some strong positive recognition.

Remind all students, too, that just as they help each other learn various skills in physical education, when they are on teams for basketball or volleyball they need to work cooperatively for the good of the team. This is an important time for students to practice saying encouraging, positive comments to *all* their classmates.

You will also want to prepare your students for individual physical fitness skills. Students can make good progress if they practice such skills as pull-ups, sit-ups, **sit and reach,** and the mile jog during the entire school year in the upper grades and running, jumping, skipping, and arm circles during the entire school year for lower grades.

Some good hamstring stretches are vital prior to the sit and reach. Be sure to teach your students to hold a stretch for at least twenty seconds to allow the entire muscle, not just the outside of it, to stretch. They should not do any bouncing during a stretch, and the stretch should not hurt.

When you work on physical fitness skills, have your class in small groups or with partners. You can have some students practicing sit ups while some are practicing sit-and reach. You can move from group to group or have each group rotate to you. You can then evaluate and record their progress.

Aerobic exercises in the classroom are very invigorating. Jogging in place, hopping, **half jacks,** and free, creative dancing all work well with a full class. It is especially fun to have some fast-paced music playing. In a situation like this, one of the skills could be: Try your hardest to keep up with the pace or gear your dance to the beat of the music.

A classroom exercise that is fun and more anaerobic than aerobic is done with groups of about eight students. Move desks to the center of the classroom to provide more room for the groups around the perimeter of the classroom.

Give each group an object, such as a small chair, a stapler, a stack of books, a stuffed animal, and so on. Make the objects quite different from one another. Then have a lively record ready to play. When the music starts, whoever is holding the object jumps up and down, turns around, and passes the object to the student to the right. The next student repeats the activity of the first, and so on until you take the needle off the record. Then whoever has the object walks with it, in a clockwise manner, to the next group.

For the next round, the student with the object could hop five times on the right foot, five times on the left, turn around twice, and pass the object to the next student. This continues until you stop the music, the students with the objects go to the next group, and you tell the class what the next activity will be.

One skill that students could practice during this exercise would be to stay quiet and listen when the activity direction is given. A social skill could be having the students *very politely* help those who are not as able to settle down right away for the direction. They could do this by gently tapping the student to get her attention and then putting their index finger to their lips to indicate quiet. Tell the students not to say *Shhh!* This just creates more noise, and the object is to eliminate noise so that everyone can hear the directions.

An activity that is similar to this, but allows for easy teacher movement throughout the class to observe and assist, is the establishment of stations to which students go for a specific activity for a specified amount of time. On a large piece of paper, write the name of a particular activity and draw a

Figure 6-5. Teaching age-appropriate ball-handling skills is part of the physical education program. Learning how to dribble the ball, pass it back and forth, bounce it to a classmate, shoot, and rebound are all important for the students to know.

Figure 6-6. These students are practicing sit ups in preparation for annual physical fitness assessment.

descriptive picture or diagram of the activity. For example, make a station sign for jogging in place, sit-ups, arm circles, jumping jacks, hopping, and so on. Make these large station signs colorful and laminate them for preservation.

Next, select some different speeds of music. Make sure all of it is easy to exercise to, enjoyable, and energizing. Make a tape. Record about twenty to forty-five seconds (or even longer, depending on your group and age level) of a vocal or instrumental song. Then record a blank space for about five to seven seconds. Select another musical piece and record twenty to forty-five seconds of it. Then record another five to seven seconds of blank space. Continue in this manner until you have a good selection for a PE class.

If you are not interested in pace variety for a lesson, record consecutive segments of the same song with the five to seven seconds of blank space in between the segments. If you like

Figure 6-7. Students can do many physical fitness activities in the classroom. Sit and reach, jogging in place, hopping, jumping jacks, and creative dancing, especially to music, can help develop lifelong fitness skills and habits.

variety, select a classical piece that has drastic pace and mood changes; record consecutive segments of it with five to seven seconds of blank space after each segment.

During the twenty to forty-five seconds of the music part of the tape, students will be at their activity stations doing whatever the station cards say. During the five to seven seconds of blank space, students go clockwise to the next station. If you have stations that are very taxing, you might want to put in one or two stations that give directions to sit and rest. If you mix the more able students with the less, a social skill could be for the more able to act as good models and give success tips to the less able.

Organized games are popular for PE, too. Do not assume the students know how to play, though. Maybe a handful will, not many more. If students are going to be playing **nationball,** the focus skills could be these two:

1. When you get out, run as fast as you can to the goal line and throw the ball. This keeps the game moving quickly.
2. Concentrate on saying nice, encouraging things to your classmates, like "Good, Angela, you threw the ball quickly" and "Great aim, Maude!" and "Way to hustle to the goal line, Dominick!"

For a greater variety of activity during the PE period for upper grades, you could divide the class into four groups with each group assigned a different activity. The activities could be handball, volleyball, four square, and kickball, with a specifically marked small court for kickball. Then the first group goes to handball, the second to volleyball, and so on. At the end of ten minutes, the groups rotate clockwise.

In this activity, one skill could be to leave the equipment in the court when the whistle blows and go to the next court as soon as it is vacated. The other skill could be to tell students who are struggling with the game skills such things as: "Keep trying, Jim!" and "You're doing a lot better, Maria!"

For a PE period for primary grades, you could divide the class into five groups. Start one group at the jungle gym, another group at the swings, a third group bouncing balls, a fourth throwing the ball in the air and trying to catch it, and a fifth rolling a ball to a partner.

After four or five minutes, blow a whistle for students to move to the next activity. It helps to have a number written in black in gigantic size on a piece of tag placed near the activity. Then the students at "three" go to "four" when the whistle blows, and so on.

Whether you are teaching PE in the classroom or outdoors, remember that PE is a class. It is not "free play." It is a time to teach and help your students acquire specific physical and social skills.

Check your school district's policy regarding the grading of physical education. Many districts have an effort-based grade. If this is the case in your district, jot a few comments to yourself about effort after you return to the class from a PE lesson. Then you can accurately evaluate. Students who are not physically talented can earn a high grade if they try their hardest.

If you teach primary grades, observe your students carefully to monitor their progress. If you are teaching PE in the upper grades, have your grade book or a clipboard with you; it is handy for your memory and helps to provide a little more structure for your program. At the top of your grade book column, write the date and skill for the lesson. Note all students who are absent, are not participating for a health reason that day, or for any other reason are not present for the lesson. Then record information about who needs extra help with a particular skill, who is doing a good job, who demonstrates team cooperation, and who is less physically talented but puts forth 100 percent effort for every class.

You may want to just use a plus and minus system. When you observe particular students demonstrating unusually good effort, record a + in their boxes. One student might have two or three pluses in her box during one lesson. When you observe students demonstrating poor effort, particularly if they are "goofing around" and not staying on-task, record a − in their boxes. Students might possibly have more than one minus, although it is unlikely, since they see you record information during the lesson. Later, you could convert these marks to conform to whatever grading system your district has. All the other students who were present for each lesson, but have no marks, could receive an *S* for satisfactory.

After a time, students really put forth the effort for that day's skills. They consider PE a subject in which to work and make progress, not just another play time. They not only get better with the physical activity skills, they greatly improve their social skills, too. During PE, it can be a real pleasure to teach them, observe their progress with physical skills, and see their awareness and success with social skills.

Students flourish in this kind of setting. They make progress and can feel it. They learn to interact with classmates in a supporting environment. They listen to and accept compliments from their classmates. With this kind of success, all students eagerly look forward to PE class.

PLANNING TIME FOR SUBSTITUTES

Although teachers do not like to miss school days, it is sometimes unavoidable. Therefore, it will help your classroom run smoothly in your absence if you leave a *substitute teacher form* detailing your classroom rules, how your classroom behavior system works, where materials can be found, and the location of seat work the substitute can use if he has any problems following your lesson plans. Even though you have your classroom rules posted in the room, it helps the substitute to see the rules early in the morning to understand how your system works.

Figure A6-11 in the appendix is a substitute teacher form you can use for your classroom. Keep a copy of it in the office, too, with the school's substitute information booklets.

You will know in advance when you must miss class because of an in-service or workshop; thus, you can leave detailed plans for the substitute. Leave lesson plans on an easily visible spot on your desk at all times. These plans should explain clearly to someone else (not you) what to do during the day. Many teachers plan their lessons a week in advance; others plan for only two or three days ahead. Either style is perfectly acceptable and, especially in some grade levels, it is difficult to plan far ahead. Do your lesson plans in pencil so that they are easy to change.

Sometimes, though, it may happen that you are going to be absent at a time when you have already been sick and have been dragging yourself to work. At times like these during the school year, you may not have good lesson plans because it is all you can do just to get yourself to work each day. This is especially true for cold and flu season. Your lesson plans may be adequate for you, but maybe not for a substitute.

You want your classroom to run smoothly, so plan ahead for a situation like this, even though it may never happen. Use a set of lesson plans that are general, cover all the subjects, and can be used at any time during the year. Then your students will be able to spend their time in a good learning environment for the day. They will tackle all the subjects and use many of their skills, and the substitute will appreciate a well-run day. Leave these **emergency lesson plans** right with your regular lesson plan book or folder. Figures A6-12 and A6-13 in the appendix are sample emergency lesson plans. Note the codes. One set is for primary grades (Pt), the other for upper grades (§). These can be modified in any way you like, but both will provide a highly productive day for your students in your absence.

The next part of this chapter informs you about the importance of questioning strategies. It also tells you about a special time you can develop for the classroom.

QUESTIONING STRATEGIES

Questioning strategies are especially important in a demonstration-based curriculum. Students need to be able to tell and write what they know, how they figured it out, what it means, what conclusions they draw, and what personal reactions or responses they have. To have your students do this, minimize the types of questions that can be answered with yes or no or one word.

Instead, use the strategy of open-ended, guided questioning, which allows you to play the role of facilitator in your students' learning. For example, you could ask students how they would run the school lunch program on campus or what changes they would make and why. If students say, "I don't know," guide them in thinking about issues by careful questioning. Considering how the food tastes, what do they think? Thinking about the food choices, what suggestions can they make? Reflecting upon the packaging, what ideas do they have?

Besides answers of yes or no, one word, or I don't know, be alert to "It's okay"; in other words, the student is telling you that she does not have particular thoughts on the subject, so it is "okay" the way it is. When confronted with this, use further questioning to help these students think harder and open their minds to endless possibilities. Suggest some lunch situations to them and ask them to predict what might happen. Have other students make suggestions and ask the reluctant ones what conclusions they would draw or why they think these things would happen. This will usually draw out even the most hesitant student.

Open-ended questioning allows the teacher to understand the students' thinking processes and more easily clarify any misconceptions. It also makes the student a much more active participant in the classroom. Guided questioning checks the students' prior knowledge and helps them to discover. It is a strategy on the order of the Socratic method. In preparation for a history test or science test or after reading a story, the students themselves can make up the questions and ask them to each other or to the class.

Think about the differences in the following pairs of questions:

Who is credited with discovering America?

How would Christopher Columbus's being a tailor rather than an explorer affect history?

What is the ending to the story?

What is a new ending to the story and why would you select it?

When did the Revolutionary War begin?

What was life like during the Revolutionary War for the colonists, thinking about their jobs, clothing, houses, education, and so on?

Was that story interesting?

What made that story interesting and what could be added to make it more so?

How much is 235 times 5?

What are some different things that can be done with the numbers 235 and 5?

What is the population of our city?

What are some things that might happen if the population of our city doubled?

Can you read the information for drinking water from the data chart?

Can you construct your own data chart and carry out an experiment?

Questions like the second one on the Revolutionary War can provide scaffolding for students and helps them, especially the reluctant or less-able ones, to do a lot more thinking (for example, in that question, they think about jobs, clothing, housing, education) and include a good deal more information.

Open-ended questioning strategies go hand in hand with eliciting and guiding the kind of thinking students will need to do in order to be successful in all areas of a demonstration-based curriculum.

Research and Studies

A study by Carlsen (1991) reexamined the research on teacher questioning from a sociolinguistic perspective. Most of the research in this field has been process-product research, in which student results are seen as an outcome of teacher behaviors. *Sociolinguistics* is concerned with the role of social context in interpreting spoken language, as well as how language and a given situation are interdependent.

The three criteria used to evaluate questioning in this study were: context; content; and responses and reactions of both teachers and students. For sociolinguistics, the context of the question means how the question fits in with the previous questions, with the people involved, and with their expectations of each other. Content is not just the words of the question, but one's knowledge of the subject and is concerned with the interactivity of questioning. What about responses and reactions to questions? Wait time, both between question and answer and between the answer and the next question, is seen as part of the questioning process.

Another study (Mevarech & Susak, 1993) showed that students can improve their questioning abilities by combining a cooperative learning method with a mastery learning method. In the *cooperative method,* students ask teachers questions as well as asking each other questions in groups. In the *mastery learning method,* students give feedback on how they are doing. It requires teaching and practicing the necessary skills and allows for time and help for those who do not master the skill on the first try. It has been shown that combining these two methods is more effective than using either one alone.

The participants in the study were 137 third-graders and 134 fourth-graders in Israel. There were no statistically significant differences between the experimental groups for sex, size, socioeconomic status, or reading comprehension.

The study measured ability in three areas: questioning skills, creativity, and achievement. The subjects were divided into four groups: a control group, a cooperative learning (CL) group, a mastery learning (ML) group, and a cooperative-mastery learning (CML) group. As far as questioning skills, after the treatment, the CML group almost tripled the amount of higher-cognitive questions they asked, and the CL group almost doubled their amount of higher-cognitive questions. Both groups asked significantly more of this kind of question than the other groups. The control group slightly decreased their amount of higher-cognitive questions, whereas the CL group increased their amount.

Creativity was measured in three areas: fluency, flexibility, and originality. For fluency and flexibility, the ML group improved more than the CML group, which improved more than either the CL or control groups. For originality, the CML group had higher scores than did the CL group, which scored higher than the ML group; the control group showed a slight decrease in this measure. As far as achievement, the study found no significant differences between any of the groups.

Before the study began, students asked mainly lower-cognitive questions. Once exposed to mastery questioning methods, however, students asked more higher-cognitive questions. The study also shows that improving students' use of higher-cogni-tive questions does not adversely affect their achievement. Thus, this study shows that incorporating basic skills and knowledge with higher age-appropriate cognitive skills can be promising.

QUIET TIME

Sometimes you need a little peace and quiet during the school day for a variety of reasons. You may have to collect money for field trips or from a **jog-a-thon.** You may need to collect field trip permission slips, emergency cards or progress report slips. All of this takes time to do, because you will need to keep accurate records of who turned in what and how much was it. Sometimes you just need some extra time to work with one or two students in some academic skill that pertains only to them.

Besides assigned seat work, there are many **sponge activities** that are easy to use, yet stimulating to the students. Announce that you will give some little prize to each of the students with the most items on their lists, provided that they work *quietly* and *independently* (see following examples of lists students can compile). When you are working with your one or two students or collecting field trip permissions, jog-a-thon money, and so on, if you talk in a whisper, so will the students with whom you are meeting. This creates an atmosphere of great productivity and little distraction for all.

At a specified time, when you have finished working with your one or two students or recording your field trip permission slips and accounting for the correct amount of money, tell the students, "Raise your hand if you have five items or more [start low so you will have an enthusiastic response!], seven items or more, ten items or more . . ." and so on. Then have a few students read their lists. If you tell the students that they can use a helping book, such as their history book, science book, dictionary, and so on, when they need to, they will get right to work and stay on-task. This creates a good learning experience for everyone.

The following quiet time activities work well for primary:

Print the first letter or the first two letters of as many _____ as you can.

classmates' names
games
things that move
colors
pieces of furniture
letters of the alphabet
things to eat
things you can see
things that make noise
toys
things in your house
things in your classroom

As an alternative to writing the letter(s), students can draw pictures or take turns whispering the information to a partner.

The following quiet time activities work well for upper grades:

Write as many _____ as you can.

state capitals
cities
countries
rivers
states
mountains
lakes
volcanoes
natural wonders
oceans and seas
football teams
basketball teams
baseball teams
flowers
names of schools (including colleges)
names of sports
names of cars
names of TV shows
names of movies
names of celebrities
names of adults on campus

These are great, and they are lots of fun, too. Do not forget to say *quietly* and *independently,* though, so you have quiet time.

The last part of this chapter explains how to have a broad-based reading program and how to make research skills a solid part of the curriculum. If you want your classroom to be well run, it is essential to be well prepared in these subjects and provide interesting, exciting lessons for the students as well as challenging follow-up activities.

READING

When the student is ready, the teacher appears.

Author unknown

Reading is one of the four components of integrated language arts along with writing, listening, and speaking. Integrated language arts occur much of the day in a thinking, meaning-centered curriculum. Students will interact and connect with curriculum content. They will read, write and speak about it, and listen to it. They will generate meaning from it and go beyond it to connect it to their personal experiences. They can participate in a literature-based curriculum with a whole language approach, which is a holistic approach to literacy. Students mix reading with writing in all curriculum areas. They can learn in large groups and small groups in an interactive manner by talking, writing, and doing. They will be in charge of their learning and be aware that integrated language arts is not something just for the classroom, but for life.

Storytelling is a good example of the total integration of language arts. This can be a fascinating topic to explore. "Popcorn" can be used as a strategy in storytelling. In this strategy,

one student begins a story, either one that is made up, one out of the literature book, or one about the current unit in social studies or science. The others listen. When the student speaking says "Popcorn" and a student's name, that student continues with the story until she says "Popcorn" and another student's name, who then continues the story. This can be a lot of fun and certainly reveals students' understanding of character traits and the story setting, problem, sequence, and solution.

As students approach a story or a unit in history or science, they will continually be using the integrated language arts. The stories or units students meet will be thematically organized. Students will need to develop a word bank and share prior knowledge and experiences with their classmates to get "into" the story or unit.

This is a time during **whole class instruction** to provide extra support for the students with lesser abilities or background disadvantages and for the Limited-English-Proficient (LEP) students. This is also a time when students who are more advanced can provide many interesting insights to the class.

The **target vocabulary** can be organized by word maps. A **word map** is a graphic organizer in which a word is written in the center of a chart or chalkboard. Students decide on a definition for the word, decide how the object looks, tastes, sounds, feels, and smells, and list some examples of the object as well as other word forms it has. Circles, boxes, or ovals can be placed around the descriptors in the separate categories with lines connecting them to the target vocabulary word. Target vocabulary can also be presented on large cards with accompanying illustrations. This method is especially helpful to the less-able readers.

Major concepts and ideas can be organized into a **cluster.** Write the concept or idea in the center of a large page or on the chalkboard. Draw a circle around it. In circles or ovals around it, have the students tell or write their related ideas. **Semantic webs,** which are similar to clusters but more elaborate and more structured, can be used to show categories, such as cause-effect or sequence. Once a category of the main idea is selected, students can then tell or write their ideas, but they must stick to the category. (See Figure A8-20 in the appendix for a graphic organizer that can be used to outline a story or book. Figure A8-14, also in the appendix, is an umbrella graphic organizer and can be used as a map, a cluster, or a web.)

As they go "through" the literature, students will make predictions, get clarification, and retell segments of the story. They will understand the elements of the story or unit: setting (place and time), mood, main characters, major problem, events leading to solution, solution to the problem, and personal reaction. Students can go through the literature as a whole class reading aloud or independently, or meet in groups for reading and retelling or meet with the teacher for **guided reading.** Guided reading is a strategy where *segments* of a story are focused on, with students making predictions about what they think will happen, checking their predictions as they progress through the story, and reading to find specific information and answers to questions that will provide good story understanding for them. Frequent checking for understanding is very important. Guided reading is a support from which the students with lesser abilities or other disadvantages can benefit.

When students go "beyond" the literature, in some way they will link the content to their lives and demonstrate the meaning the story had for them. Essentially, they make a response to the literature. This, again, is a time for extra support for the less able from both the teacher and the more advanced students.

Going beyond the literature can be done in a variety of ways, including interactive group activities such as a short skit or a group poster. Students can meet in learning groups or work independently, or a combination of both can occur during which students write a poem, a diary or journal entry, a letter to a classmate or relative, a description of a character, or a new ending to the story. They may decide to do a drawing and write a caption. They may use a **T-Graph.** On the left-hand side of the *T*, various selections of information from the story or unit can be written. On the right-hand side of the *T*, students can write or tell their personal reactions and understanding of each selection.

The following segments of this section on reading concentrate more directly on reading itself. The many aspects of reading are presented as well as a wide variety of activities and approaches to use with your class.

For studies, information, and strategies on emergent literacy, see Chapter 2, The DEF's.

Teacher Reads to Class

Part of teaching reading is the teacher reading a story aloud to the class. Reading at the same time each day helps your memory.

Before you begin reading, ask the students to clear their desks. As you read, explain or ask the students to explain any words, expressions, or situations with which the entire class may not be familiar. Be sure every student can clearly see all the pictures as you read along in the story. Always select a book you enjoy reading aloud and one that the students will appreciate, too.

The following are a few suggestions of books you might like to read to your class:

Primary Grades
Chicka Chicka Boom Boom, Bill Martin
Very Quiet Cricket, Eric Carle
Animalia, Graeme Base
Where the Sidewalk Ends, Shel Silverstein
The Boxcar Children, Gertrude Chandler Warner
If You Give a Mouse a Cookie, Laura Joffe Numeroff
Black and White, David Macaulay
Charlotte's Web, E. B. White
The Trumpet of the Swan, E. B. White
Charlie and the Chocolate Factory, Roald Dahl
Animal Homes, A National Geographic Action Book
The Mouse and the Motorcycle, Beverly Cleary
Runaway Ralph, Beverly Cleary
The Chocolate Touch, Patrick Skene Catling

Upper Grades
The Twits, Roald Dahl
Superfudge, Judy Blume
Tales of a Fourth Grade Nothing, Judy Blume
The Indian in the Cupboard, Lynne Reid Banks
The Great Brain at the Academy, John D. Fitzgerald
Nothing's Fair in Fifth Grade, Barthe DeClements
The Silver Crown, Robert C. O'Brien
The White Mountains, John Christopher
Tuck Everlasting, Natalie Babbit
Call It Courage, Armstrong Sperry
Call of the Wild, Jack London

Provide your students with the treasured experience of listening to their teacher read to them.

The Library

According to research, when students read a lot, their reading ability is improved. When they do a lot of reading both inside school and outside, their achievement level rises (Anderson et al., 1985; Hirsch, 1985). When they see the teacher read, the impact of reading is even more powerful.

Have a classroom library so that students can help themselves to a variety of books. Encourage parents to get their children library cards and make regular trips to the library. Sign your class up for a time to go to your school library on a regular basis. Ask the librarian to read a short story to your class before it is time to check out books.

After listening to a library story, the students could write the librarian a friendly letter retelling the story, telling about their favorite part, comparing one story to another, recommending whether that book should be read to other students, describing one of the characters, writing a new ending to the story, or explaining what age student would like to check it out and why.

Students enjoy the opportunity to buy books through classroom book programs. Each month a new selection of story books, activity books, and posters becomes available. In addition to popular selections for all grade levels, there are the *Guiness Book of World Records,* almanacs, pocket dictionaries, stamp collecting books, and baseball cards for upper-grade students. You can order once a month or once a quarter, whatever you like.

Reading Incentive Programs

Participating in a **reading incentive program** is a great way to boost independent reading. Many different programs are available with all the materials beautifully prepared for your class. Many of them have student certificates for each student who reads a certain number of books each month.

A visit to a local, independent book store and a pleasant talk with the manager might get your classroom an award certificate and a gift certificate for the student who reads the most books each month.

Book Reports

Creative book reports are another way to keep students motivated in independent reading. Reproducible booklets are available at your local teachers' supply store that have excellent, fun ideas for simple reports at the primary level and more sophisticated ones for the upper grades.

Figure 6-8. Being read to is part of any good reading program. During this class's time at the library, the students enjoy listening to the school librarian read *The Quiet Cricket,* by Eric Carle. Courtesy of Carolyn Pierce.

Book Report Big Top (see the publisher's index under The Learning Works in Chapter 9, The XYZ's for details) has several different kinds of book reports for late primary grades and any upper grade. There are such activities as fill-in reports, pencil reports, talking reports, hands-on reports, and so on. This book is full of reports that are relatively simple. If the reports are colored very nicely with markers and cut out when finished, they look beautiful around the classroom and the students are intrigued by each other's work.

One such report from *Big Top* is called "T-Shirt Tale." On the page to be reproduced, a T-shirt is printed with a line at the top to write the title of the book, a line at the bottom of the shirt to write the author's name, and a place in the middle of the shirt to draw a picture about the book. When the picture and shirt are beautifully colored, the shirt can be hung up on a clothesline in your classroom. (Arts and crafts stores have small clothespins that can be used to hang up the shirts.) The students enjoy examining each other's work and asking questions about the books.

Another report from *Big Top* is called "Color a Book." Once this is completed, the title and author of the book will be displayed plus five new words the student learned from the story. "Color a Book" makes another nice exhibit. Students get exposure to new words and can ask the student who completed the report what a word means.

Many other unique reports are included in *Book Report Big Top,* including "Tell a Tale," "Story Wheel," "Pretzel People," and "Stretch a Face." These are fun and turn out great.

In addition to these unusual formats, there are more traditional types of book reports such as dioramas, bookmarks, and book posters, and the students are also challenged by *Electronic Bookshelf.* This program can begin in first and second grades and continue up through the grades. The students select an *Electronic Bookshelf* book. Display a list, or the librarian can place a marker on the book's spine. After one of these books is read, the students go to the computer and load the software for *Electronic Bookshelf.* Print the sequence for loading on a piece of poster board.

Next, a set of questions will appear for the particular book. If students pass the quiz, their names will be recorded automatically with a "Pass." There are several sets of questions for each book. If the students do not pass the test the first time, they return to the computer at a later date after doing some rereading and face a different set of questions. Students feel a real sense of accomplishment when they look at their data disk and see the list of books they have read and for which they have passed tests.

Book reports are something that can be planned at least a semester in advance, if not for the whole year. Maybe you would like to have a book report due every two weeks. The students could be assigned to read a part of their book report book each night. For the last two or three days of the two-week period, they could work on the book report itself. Younger students could use journals with plain paper to record their responses and reactions to books using simple drawings, phrases, or sentences.

Phonics and Decoding

According to research, most students do better with a phonics program taught in the very early grades (Anderson et al., 1985). If students are not taught **phonics**, they can learn by the **"look-say" method.** Basically, students memorize words that will be used in their reading stories. Confidence with a list of basic sight vocabulary is helpful.

For an upper-grade student who has weak phonics skills, the look-say method may be more suitable; however, the look-say

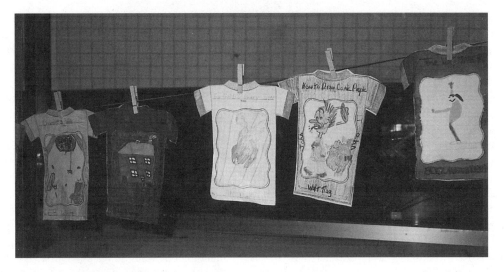

Figure 6-9. These T-shirt book reports make a novel classroom display. Students always enjoy these types of reports.

method may be appropriate for some students at all levels. Check first to see whether their phonics skills are poor because of frequent absence, or whether a learning problem is preventing them from mastering phonics.

Students can also learn how to decode by recognizing **base or root words** and learning to recognize prefixes and suffixes. Instruction and practice in the meanings of prefixes and suffixes is very beneficial.

Oral Reading Fluency

It takes fluent models to listen to and plenty of practice to develop fluency when reading aloud. Students must know how to pronounce individual words, read in small thought groups, and then read in larger thought groups—whole sentences or large parts of sentences.

Expression is another part of oral reading fluency. When reading expressively, students show they understand what they are reading. Expressive reading is also much easier and more enjoyable to listen to, especially over a period of time.

Students can practice shared reading by reading to a partner in the classroom, reading to a brother, sister, or parent, or even reading into the tape recorder and playing it back. Students can ask for assessment and help as they need them. Students can also follow along in a book as a fluent reader reads aloud. This provides a model for the learner.

Vocabulary Development

When students are ready to begin a new story, introduce them to the new words for that story. Put the words on the chalkboard or overhead. Ask whether any students can already say the words. Pronounce each word yourself twice. Then have the class altogether, out loud, pronounce each word twice. Continue with this until you assess the class's fluency with these words. You may even want to call on various individual students who have volunteered. You can ask small groups sitting close to one another to say the words aloud together to be positive they can all pronounce the words easily and correctly. Be patient with your students, and take an adequate amount of

time so that they feel comfortable pronouncing these new words.

If the vocabulary words have prefixes or suffixes, and you have an upper grade, calling your class's attention to that will help students with increasing their understanding of other root words with similar prefixes or suffixes. Divide the words into syllables to help pronunciation. If the students struggle on a particular part of the word, tell them it sounds just like _____ (some other word they already know). Place the accent marks on the word and help the students with the correct voice **inflection.**

Next, select a method to teach the meaning of the word. Vary your method every few stories to give students good exposure to the different methods.

Students can be told the meaning of each word outright by a student in the room who already knows the meaning or by the teacher. The teacher might give a series of clues as to what the word means and let the class guess. Each clue could be closer and closer to the meaning of the word.

Students can learn to use **context clues** to determine the meaning of each word. Younger students can use text pictures to give them clues.

To teach students how to **scan,** tell the students to open their books to a particular page and scan that page for the first vocabulary word. When students are in lower grades, they can scan by running their index finger quickly under each printed line from left to right. Students in the upper grades can scan by spreading four fingers (not their thumb) across the center of the page. They move their four fingers together down the center of the page under each line of print. With the help of peripheral vision, they locate the word, and then read the sentence that contains the vocabulary word. They may have to read the sentences before and after. Occasionally, they will need to read the entire paragraph.

In upper grades, draw students' attention to the use of a comma as a device to further explain a word. This technique is common and will be used frequently in their social studies and science texts. Example: The student will study the table of contents, which lists all parts, sections, chapters, and unit titles of the book, as well as the glossary and the index. Notice the comma after *contents* and after *book*. The words inside describe *table of contents*. Another example: As you come to boldfaced words, those in dark black type, be sure you thoroughly understand them, because they are the key terms of the chapter. Notice again that by use of commas, the term *boldfaced* is explained right in the sentence. Sometimes the comma technique is used with the word *or*. Example: The boy's kin, or family, were ready to visit him in Chicago. Notice again how the word *kin* is defined right in the text. Point this out to students as they learn to use context clues to determine the meaning of their new vocabulary words.

Students can also, as a class, use their glossary to find the meaning of the new words. Then discuss these as a class.

Have students use a dictionary to locate their new words and determine their meanings. Be sure to call students' attention to sample sentences in the glossary or dictionary, which provide additional help in explaining the meaning of the word. Sometimes there is a sketch or picture to further explain the new word. The part of speech will also be listed and, oftentimes, several synonyms are given. These are all helpful tools for the students to use, but they need to be *taught* all these skills. They will not just automatically know them. Teach these skills in conjunction with an activity that will require the use of each so that students clearly see the purpose.

You might want to present the class with a crossword puzzle for the new vocabulary words with some other words they already know included to help them. Students could use their dictionary or glossary in conjunction with this activity.

Whatever method you select to present new vocabulary words, be sure the students can use the words in sentences to show they really understand the meaning and use of the word.

It is also helpful with vocabulary development to have a class **word of the week.** The students can learn how to pronounce the word, what it means, what part of speech it is, how to spell it, and how to use it in a sentence. The word can be colorfully displayed for the week.

Students can make their own dictionary of words that are important to them. They can write short definitions after them or use small pictures to refresh their memories.

Comprehension

Research shows that students comprehend a story better when the teacher provides both introductory and follow-up activities. All ages of students are usually taught as a whole class out of the same book. Sometimes students may be in some kind of groups and might be reading from different books at their own levels. The approach to introducing the story and providing follow-up activities is basically the same for either method.

Teachers can introduce a story in a number of ways. The teacher can tell the students what type of literature they will be reading—fiction, historical fiction, fantasy, fairy tale, nonfiction, scientific or historical information, biography, and so on—and explain why the story is classified as it is.

The students will almost always need some background information on the story. What are the characters like? Are some things special or unusual about them? Do events happen in the story with which the students will not be familiar? Maybe they need some help understanding a particular disability, a special need, an unusual celebration, or a specific historical period.

Introduce events or characters in the story to whom the students will be able to relate. Ask the students to tell personal experiences they have had that are like the situations presented during this introduction to the story. They can also make predictions about what may be happening in the story and tell what they already know about the topic.

Some stories adapt themselves well to the **SQRRR** method (*S*urvey, *Q*uestion, *R*ead, *R*eview, *R*eread). This is a particularly helpful technique if you are teaching upper grades. You can lead students through surveying and questioning by asking them to do several things as a class. Have someone read aloud the title of the story. Look through the story for any pictures, graphs, or tables. Call on students to tell the page number and read the picture caption. If there is no caption, ask the students to guess what might be taking place. Study each graph or table. Read the title and information on the axes of the graph or the rows and columns of the table. What information does the graph or table give? Then look for and discuss special words in boldface or italics. Next, read through all the subtitles. Last, discuss what this story or article *might* be about and what kind of questions it might answer. Have the students make a list of these questions with enough space to write the answers in later.

Another way to prepare the students for the story is to have them read the entire first paragraph, then the first sentence (frequently the topic sentence) of each of the subsequent paragraphs, and finally, the entire last paragraph. This technique gives them an excellent overview and is effective in reading social studies and science textbooks; it also works extremely well for stories in the literature books. Younger students can read the first sentence of each paragraph in a particular *section* of the story. They will be amazed what a helpful frame it makes.

Next, the students need a purpose for reading this story. It may be pure enjoyment. It may be to discover the answers to certain questions, either their class-made questions, or questions at the end of the story or some accompanying resource book. The students need to know these questions in advance so that they can look for the answers as they read. The purpose may be to decide on a favorite part that the students will later draw. It may be to act this story out in a class play or to retell this story to their partners.

The purpose is often related to what is being read. Is it a story in a reader? Is it a chapter or section in a history or science book? Is it an article from a reading kit, a weekly student newspaper, or an encyclopedia?

Now that the students have their background information and purpose, it is time for them to get the words and thoughts of the story into their heads. Encourage the students to really experience the story by putting themselves into the story. Have them try to identify with one of the characters in the story or even pretend they are one of the inanimate objects. Tell them to use their five senses to make the story come alive: feel the warmth of the early afternoon sun as they touch the soft fur of the timid animal; taste the cold, thick, frothy chocolate milk shake; see the exciting details of the recovered fossils; listen to the excited voices and lively music of the square dance in the old McDaniels' barn; and smell the thick, pitch black, putrid fumes from the tire factory fire. Remind them to think about the problems in the story and how they might be solved. The more the student is into a story, the easier it is to understand.

The most difficult way for students to get information from text is having them read the entire story all the way through silently and independently, with no break for discussion. If they are doing this, having their list of questions will help provide them with some framework in which to operate.

This would also be an excellent time for the students to do marginalia for the first couple of pages of the story. In this technique, students are presented with part of a story typed on the left-hand side of a paper only, and the right-hand side is available for them to write in the *margin;* hence, its name. As they read along, they can write their comments, questions about the understanding of some part or questions to the author of the story, drawings about what they think is going on in the story, feelings they have as they are reading, or even a statement about the author's choice of a particular word. This strategy can be used even with beginning readers, since pictures are perfectly acceptable.

The purpose of marginalia is for the students to show in what way and to what degree they interact with the story; consequently, it works perfectly well to have the students use their readers, fold a piece of paper in half lengthwise and do marginalia for the left-hand page of their reader on that paper. Fold another paper in half and use it for marginalia for the right-hand page of the story. You could also cut half-piece strips for students' use as their right-hand and left-hand margins. Marginalia can make the challenge of reading independently more meaningful and easier.

For good success with this, let the students share their marginalia with the class. The less creative students will get the idea in a hurry when they hear interesting questions and comments and see thoughtful drawings in their classmates' marginalia. This skill will really show you the sharp thinkers of the class.

Right after marginalia, students can do **personal connection.** In this strategy, students write about the ways they can connect this story part to their own lives. Does something about one of the characters remind them of something when they were younger? Then they can tell or write about it. Even though the story may be about something that never happened in *their* lives, did they have a similar feeling to one a character had? Then they can describe the similar feeling and under what circumstances it took place in their lives. Maybe students have a friend about which a character in the story reminds them. Then they can tell about their friend and connect this to the story. Personal connection creates a deeper understanding of the story part and helps make it directly relevant to the students' lives.

Besides reading independently, there are several easier ways to get information from a particular story. It can be read aloud by the teacher while the students follow along in their books. As a change of pace, the story can be on a tape. Every page or so (or with slower readers, every paragraph), the teacher can ask questions. The class can answer these and have any discussion needed to clarify the meaning of the story.

The entire class can all read out loud together with the teacher's voice leading. This is great for expressive reading. After reading a page or when coming to some especially interesting part, the class can discuss it. Or after reading a page, the students can talk to their partners about what they read.

The teacher can call student by student to read aloud while the rest of the class follows along in their books. This is an excellent opportunity for the teacher to evaluate oral reading. Another approach is to have the students take turns reading aloud in small groups; the teachers meets with each group to evaluate.

A grade is not really helpful, but you can write comments in your grade book, like "repeats many words," "weak sight vocabulary," "smooth and expressive," or "runs sentences together." Then when you meet with each of your students, you have something very specific to discuss with them. Students who need to improve know exactly on what they need to work.

"Popcorn," which was discussed earlier, is another popular method that the students enjoy. One student begins reading in a loud voice while the rest of the students follow along in their books. After the first student reads for a while, he or she says, "Popcorn!" and calls out another student's name. The student called begins reading where the first student left off, and so on, until the story is finished. You can always interrupt if certain parts of the story need clarifying.

Besides whole class methods, many grouping strategies are effective. Students can read aloud with their partners or take turns reading aloud in small groups. You might instruct the groups to pause at the end of each page to make predictions about what they think will happen next. Are their predictions reasonable, based on the story's information? Which of their predictions came true?

Groups such as these are especially helpful to non- or Limited-English-Speaking students. If they have questions or misunderstandings, they can ask for immediate help from their group. Students can explain or act out parts with which these students have difficulty.

Furthermore, students can read using the **"mouth to ear" method.** Two chairs are placed side by side, each facing the opposite direction. When the students sit down, one's ear will be right next to the other's mouth. One student reads in a whisper while the other listens. Then they switch roles. This works well, because students pay closer attention than when reading is done aloud. Additionally, this strategy eliminates general classroom noise, which some learners find distracting, and gives the teacher a nice opportunity to visit each set of partners to discuss the story with them in a whisper, too.

Students can meet in partners or small groups with pencil and paper in addition to their reading material. They can read the story first together and stay right in their group to reread and answer all the questions together. Or they can read until they find an answer, write it down right then, and continue reading until they find the next answer. An alternative strategy is to meet in partners or small groups and make a group chart with the answers to the questions.

The students might meet in their groups, read the story together, and begin preparations for a skit or a newscast. Or the students might meet in groups for a teacher-led activity. For example, with fourth-graders, you could have a list prepared ahead of time of various important events and characters' feelings or responses that occur in the story. Then tell the students, **"Skim** to find out how Mr. Twit felt when Mrs. Twit pulled her eyeball trick on him." (Be sure you have taught the skill of skimming first.) Students in the group can watch each other skim and if a student needs help locating the information, the others are right there to help.

Since there are so many ways for the students to read a story, presenting a variety of ways in your classroom makes for more fun and interest. Sometimes it is helpful to use the same technique for two or three stories in a row so that the students get good at it.

Perhaps, as a class, students will identify the words that begin paragraph one, three, or five on a particular page. They might distinguish between significant and insignificant details in the story. They might practice making inferences and drawing conclusions. They might use their story to answer the five *W* questions and the *H* question: *who, what, where, when, why, and how.* Or perhaps they are going to make a class outline of the story. They may be reviewing the **elements of a story:** setting, characters, problem(s), personal reaction, and solution(s) to the problem(s). Perhaps they will focus on only one or two elements.

Sometimes the students will do the actual reading in their groups but return to the whole class for class follow-up activities. Possibly the students will, as a class, complete a **story frame** or make a **story map** or **character map.**

A story frame is a short type of outline of the story. Usually, there are blanks that need a word or phrase to complete the sentence. A story frame is a minute composite of the story.

Similar to a story frame is a story map. This is another type of outline of the story, but it is much more general in that the students are required to do significantly more writing with few clues. A story map usually includes the characters, the setting, the major events, the story ending and a personal reaction, all of which are also considered elements of the story. Figure A6-14 and the first part of Figure A6-17 in the appendix are sample story maps you can use with your class.

A character map is like an outline of the character. It includes such things as where the character lives, what family the character has, what hobbies the character has, what work the character does, what personality traits does the character shows, and so on.

The students may also read in their groups but return to the whole class for independent follow-up activities. Maybe they will write their responses to different sections of the story in a **journal.** They will identify the page and paragraph number to which they are responding. Perhaps they will write several diary entries about the story. Maybe they will write a friendly letter to one of the characters or write a business letter to one of the companies. Possibly each student will do a cartoon strip of a different assigned part of the story. When the strips are finished, they can be linked together to make the story one again.

The students might do a **quote.** In this technique, the students copy word for word a small part of the story that caught their interest, maybe a sentence or two, maybe less. After it is copied, they then write what is happening in that part of the story and why they chose it to quote. Figure A6-15 and the middle section of A6-17, both in the appendix, are sample pages for quotes. This skill helps students analyze very small segments of a story, article or poem.

Double entry journal is a technique where students directly relate something in the story to something they have experienced. For example, they may select a certain event in the story and write three things about it on the left half of their paper. Then, they select something in their lives that this event reminds them of and write three things about it on the right half of their paper. This is another way of helping students analyze the story and relate it to their own experiences. Figure A6-16 in the appendix is a sample page you can use for double entry journal.

Another procedure students can use to help them see similarities and differences is the **Venn diagram.** If simplified, this can be done with primary and upper grades. Inside two lengthwise ovals that overlap in the center, students list everything they can to describe one character (or setting or story ending, and so on) in the oval on the left. Then they list everything they can to describe another character (or setting, story ending, and so on) in the oval on the right. Each description that fits *both* characters goes in the center overlapping. When you teach this skill, though, do not have students concentrate on similarities. They should just list *everything* they can for one, then everything they can for the other. *Then,* they can look through their lists and cross out similarities in ovals and rewrite those in the center overlapping. The middle of Figure A6-17 in the appendix has a sample Venn diagram you can use with your class.

Another technique that helps demonstrate comprehension is **picture explanation.** The students draw a picture about something that happened in their story or article. After the picture is drawn, they tell or write about it. It is much easier to do a good and thorough writing job if students select a part of the story where something unusual, interesting, or exciting happens. See the end of Figure A6-17 for a sample of this activity. The sample includes scaffolding to assist the students in doing a thorough job.

Be sure all the skills are thoroughly taught to the students *first* so that they will have a clear understanding of how to complete their assigned tasks. Go through these skills step by step with you **modeling** everything as you go along. After you do this a number of times with each skill, the students will be able to work on their own, not before.

Provide continual teacher-directed, student-active reading experiences for the students. Present them with material of a readability level and interest appropriate to them and build from there.

Meet with students and teach them and model for them the reading skills of studying the title and any pictures, making predictions, reading the entire first paragraph, the first sentences of each of the following paragraphs and the entire last paragraph. Call on students to do this aloud so that you can check on their expression and understanding. Have the students tell what they know so far and what they might learn. Have students read aloud the set of comprehension questions so that they have a specific purpose when they read the whole story or article. Make sure the students understand what the questions are asking.

Then read the entire story or article, rereading the first paragraph, all the subsequent paragraphs, and the last paragraph. Discuss the story as students take turns reading to clear up misconceptions. Ask the students to retell each paragraph in their own words, state the main idea of the paragraph in their own words, or tell about an important detail in their own words.

If this story or article reminds them about something in their own lives or that of their family or friends, ask them to share. They may already have information on this article or story from outside the classroom activities or experiences that they can share to enrich everyone's understanding.

Teach students how to highlight the important parts of an article or story, if the article or story is on consumable material. As they are reading along, ask them if they have heard one of the comprehension questions answered yet. They can underline in marker or use a highlighter to call attention to these answers. Remind them of this frequently so that they are tuned in to the article as they read.

After the reading and discussion is over, have the students read the first question and write the answer. Then correct that before going on to the next. If some students had the wrong answer, together as a group, locate the paragraph that contains the answer. Reread it for those who misunderstood. Make sure they understand before going to the second question.

This entire process is done together in a group or total class, step by step and aloud, so that all the students can understand and participate in the process. Whatever you use for material for the practicing, use that same type and level of material for the tests.

A test is appropriate to check students' knowledge of new vocabulary words, after several are learned. A combination test covering both matching of words with their meanings and using the vocabulary words to fill in blanks in sentences is a good idea. If you want to make the test really difficult and your job of correcting Herculean, ask the students to write their own sentences for each vocabulary word. Their sentences must show they know the meaning of each word.

Do not let the list of vocabulary words get very long. Remember, although *you* already know all these words, the students do not. Help them with clues about how to remember the words' meanings.

For tests, to see how well the students read and comprehend *independently,* a story in the reader, one not yet assigned for this school year, can be used with a set of comprehension questions to answer. Pages with reading selections and follow-up questions from reproducible books, of which there are many by grade level and some even by semester, can be copied and distributed to the class.

Some of these books' follow-up questions or activities are not all comprehension related. Be sure you count only those questions directly related to comprehension for the students' comprehension grades. That way you will have an accurate picture of what and how much your students understand by themselves. If you comment on subskills, such as noting details, understanding main ideas, using context clues, draw-

ing conclusions, and so on, you can again provide your students with specific, helpful information about their independent reading.

When students are taking a reading comprehension test, they read silently using the same process they have practiced, they perform totally independently, and they answer the questions totally independently. After the tests are corrected, go over them with the group or class so that any misinformation or problems are cleared up right then. Practicing is continual, and testing can be done once every two or three weeks.

For reteaching and remediation, you can meet with students on a one-to-one basis, or you can form a skill group for those weak in noting details, another for those weak in main ideas, and so on. Sometimes just going over the test slowly and carefully in a skill group and locating the exact answers will show certain students that their problem is they are not taking the time to read carefully and thoroughly to get the exact answer. They are getting a close answer, but they are not hitting the nail on the head. In other situations, the students have to repeatedly go through the thinking process that is involved to have better success with a skill like drawing conclusions.

Figure A6-18 in the appendix is a sample comprehension test that you can use with your classroom if you have a sixth grade or a very advanced fifth. In addition to having the students answer the questions on the article on Julius Caesar, you could ask them to write and draw what they learned from the article or use an encyclopedia to discover more information about Caesar and this period in history.

Figure A6-19, in the appendix also, is a portfolio evaluation form for reading. This can be completed by the students. It gives them the opportunity to note what they have improved in, name one thing they would like to do better in, describe how they will approach this area to improve, and explain what they think their overall work is like in reading. Meeting with students in one-to-one situations to discuss these portfolio evaluations is *very* enlightening.

In this type of reading program, students will often finish their work at different times. In addition to opportunities for leisure reading, provide challenging activities such as Geo Safari®, Go to the Head of the Class®, Scrabble®, On Assignment, or puzzles for those students who complete their work early.

In summation, in your role as facilitator in the development of student awareness and appreciation of the varieties of excellent literature, read to your class books you know they will enjoy. Provide a regular time for your class to visit the school library. Let them check out books of interest to them and hear the librarian read stories. Furnish a classroom library and encourage your students' parents to take them to the public library on a regular basis. All this will help expose your students to the wonderful world of reading.

In your role as facilitator in the development of the academic skills needed to create thoughtful readers, introduce activities that provide vocabulary enrichment. Help students develop a solid background for their stories or articles and a clear purpose for reading. Assist them with understanding fact, opinion, and bias. Provide diverse opportunities for student interaction with the written word via marginalia, picture explanation, sequencing, story analysis, and character mapping. Give students lots of time to draw pictures of their favorite part of the story, article, or poem. Have them tell or write why they liked this part. Have them tell, write, or dramatize what they learned. Inspire them to tell or write a new ending to the story, create an additional character, or retell the story in the form of a cartoon. These academic skills are extremely important and will increase your students' confidence in their abilities to experience the many forms of literature in the amazing world of reading.

As facilitator, provide different approaches—such as whole class reading, partner reading, mouth-to-ear whisper reading, popcorn reading, and so on—to the actual reading of stories, articles, and poetry. Evaluate individual achievement in the areas of oral reading, vocabulary development, and comprehension so that you can strongly support your students with instruction and practice in their weak areas and help them polish their strong ones.

The excitement of this world of reading offers its own motivation and rewards. Help your eager students into this world to instill a lifelong desire to read.

Research and Studies

An article by Chaney (1993) shows that alphabet books are not just for very young children. Older children, ages eight to eleven, can also benefit from this type of book. Alphabet books have many features that make them useful as an educational tool. They are organized in a sequence and are concise, they contain pictures or illustrations, and many of them are organized around a particular theme. Also, the text of these books may be a narrative or even a poem. Most thematically organized alphabet books can thus provide twenty-six passages of related textual material.

The article reviewed four different uses for alphabet books. The first use is as an introduction to a new topic. Alphabet books organized around a theme can give students an overview of a topic, such as dinosaurs, geology, history, and so on, before presenting an in-depth look at the subject. The second use is as a stimulus for research. Students can look at thematically related alphabet books and get ideas to do reports or projects from the pictures, text, or overall theme of the book. The third use is promoting the development of oral and written language. Some alphabet books have illustrations containing many objects beginning with the same letter or list many words that begin with the same letter or even contain projects to create and illustrate other words that contain words beginning with a certain letter (such as *care* and *scary* from *car*). The fourth use examined in this article is to increase multicultural awareness. Certain alphabet books may focus on a particular race of people or include many different ethnicities. These books can also focus on different foods people eat or word origins, for example.

Alphabet books have been traditionally relegated to use by younger children. As this article demonstrates, however, alphabet books can benefit readers of all ages and abilities.

Levin's 1992 study intended to open prospective teachers' minds about using whole language in K–3 classrooms as opposed to using traditional basal texts or a skills-oriented approach. This study, which allowed teachers to experiment with different instructional strategies within the whole language approach, helped them develop more enthusiasm for this approach and use more holistic strategies when confronting the needs of beginning readers.

Jane Hansen has conducted a great deal of classroom-based research in the area of the development of reading and writing, especially in K–5. In one of her recent studies (Hansen, 1992), she discovered that children felt they learned how to read by reading books and they learned how to write by writing. When establishing their writing goals, they announced they would pursue these in class, because they had many opportunities to write about things they do every day. But a problem arose when establishing their reading goals; students said they would have to pursue these at home, because there were no assigned times in the classroom to read books of their own choosing. In writing, they were in control and they would practice and further their writing skills at school. In reading, they were not in control, so they would pursue and practice their skills at home.

"Hallmarks of the new reading program were lots of time for children to read from books of their choice, opportunities for children to talk about books with their classmates, no ability groups, and sessions within which children could plan their growth as readers" (Hansen, 1992, p. 102). In this new program, teachers first rewrote the section of the report card dealing with reading and, second, they involved the students in the evaluation of reading, including direct input for their report card reading grade. Teachers of older students had them write what they wanted to learn in reading. Teachers of younger students (grade 1) interviewed each student in reading and writing. Students said what they had already learned and what they wanted to learn and how they would go about it while the teacher copied this information into the students' reading and writing folders. This information was shared with parents at the first scheduled conference at the end of October. There was a very positive response as the parents either read their children's own words about learning or the teacher read the words and ideas to them.

In this program, students were taught where and how to get help. Cross-age tutors were invaluable. Teacher time was spent on helping students discover the learning in areas of the students' own choosing. Students looked to each other as untapped sources of information. Evaluation was ongoing. ". . . [W]hen a child had just shared dialogue, another child would say, 'Oh! I want to learn quotation marks! That's the next thing I'm gonna learn'" (Hansen, 1992, p. 103).

According to researchers Allington and McGill-Franzen (1990), students with reading difficulties need larger amounts of high-quality instruction in the regular classroom rather than in pull-out programs such as Chapter I for the economically disadvantaged or in resource rooms for the mildly disabled. They also emphasize that rarely is the school's reading program considered in what is wrong with students not being competent readers. It is usually the child's hyperactivity or poor home environment. If students are not learning to read well, early intervention strategies need to be employed to attack the problem as early as possible in the regular classroom.

Allington and McGill-Franzen (1990) designed their study to measure the numbers of opportunities provided students to read and write and the number of minutes actively engaged in this activity over the entire day, during their special program time as well as their regular classroom time. Their findings indicated that very little time was well spent in these two types of pull-out programs. Time was spent on getting to and from the program, greeting time, waiting time, and completing activity sheets with the teacher monitoring. Little time was spent in teacher-directed reading of materials with practice on comprehension, even though research indicates that is how reading improvement occurs (Leinhardt, Bickel, & Pallay, 1982; Leinhardt, Zigmond, & Cooley, 1981). According to Allington and McGill-Franzen (1990), time and expense used to classify and label students and place them in Chapter I or resource room programs was not justified. Extensive **teacher-directed time** reading text materials and being involved in comprehension activities, either in a small group or total class, is what counts for students.

Holistic Reading Assessment (HRA), (Beaver, Carter, & Sonedicker, 1992) is a program for elementary teachers to assess the reading of their students in a ten-minute individual reading conference. Teachers attend an in-service in this assessment technique and practice scoring using videotapes of student readers. Teachers have had a 90 percent agreement rate within one point on scoring these tests (Beaver et al., 1992). Based on this information, teachers set up an intervention plan for each student.

The student is informed two weeks in advance that there will be an HRA conference and the student should select and begin to read the book for the conference. The observation form for the conference consists of six parts:

1. The book that will be used for the HRA conference, one that the student has not read before, heard read aloud before, or seen on a movie. (It might be very helpful if teachers at each grade level had a list of books, chapters, or articles on their grade level, below their grade level, and above their grade level, all of which they were familiar with and from which their students would select for the HRA conference. Then teachers would be able to carefully evaluate when the student retells the story, gives the author's purpose in writing and evaluates the book, article or chapter for recommendation to others.)

2. **Wide reading** of the student as verified by a student-kept reading log to determine if the student is or is not a reader.

3. The ability of the student to "construct meaning" from reading as demonstrated by retelling the story, giving information about why the author wrote the story and whether or not they would recommend it.

4. The ability of the student to "read aloud" fluently, with few **miscues,** and to retell what was just read aloud.

5. What the student thinks about his or her own abilities as a reader, both strengths and weaknesses; "attitude" about reading.

6. The intervention that is planned, such as getting the student to finish each book started and to be exposed to a wide variety of books; or, if the student selected a book for the conference that was at his or her frustration level, rather than instructional or independent level, that the student will be guided in a new selection and scheduled for a new conference; or SQRRR, book discussion groups, and written retellings of stories for those with low comprehension will be emphasized; and **echo reading** and **Readers' Theater** for those with fluency problems will be introduced.

Attitude and literacy promotion through interest centers and book publishing and work displays will take place for all students.

The preceding areas 2 through 5 are listed on the HRA Scoring Guide. A student can score from 1 to 6 in each of the four areas, 1 being the lowest ("inability to retell with prompting," for example, in area 3, "constructing meaning") and 6 being the highest ("effectively structures and organizes retelling; includes all components: story idea, major events, characters and story ending; interprets, analyzes or summarizes story; may critique author or literary purpose," for example, also in area 3, "constructing meaning"). The student's number from 1 to 6 that best describes overall reading proficiency in the four areas is the student's final HRA score.

With this program, conferences can be held throughout the year. Instructional strategies can be used in the classroom to remediate those with low scores and to help develop behaviors and attitudes associated with strong readers. Library reading selections can be monitored to ensure appropriate reading level and exposure to different genres. Teachers can define and evaluate specific criteria for reading on a districtwide basis.

According to Nagy and Herman (1987), the best predictor of reading achievement is word knowledge. A strong and enriched vocabulary is important not only in reading but also to make writing come alive. This word knowledge is especially important in the lower grades. In understanding words, young students begin to formulate new concepts. Students need a curriculum that is experienced-based to imprint these words and concepts into their brains.

When working with students in reading and writing, it is important to check their prior knowledge carefully, for it is on this that they will build. According to Reiber and Carton (1987), students need to develop two types of concepts: spontaneous concepts, which they get from their environment and are able to translate into words, and "scientific" concepts, which they learn in the classroom from specialized vocabulary and experience-based curriculum.

A study on word-concept development was done with adolescents having various learning and language disorders, most of whom were at about the fifth-grade thinking level (Wiig, Freedman, & Secord, 1992). All the teachers and specialists involved with the students worked as equal members of a team for word-concept development with these students. Targeted vocabulary was taught using a thematic approach, so the curriculum would have direct meaning for these students. **Holistic evaluations** were used. For example, one of the themes focused on time concepts and included such word concepts as "points in time (for example, time of day, week . . .), onset/duration (for example, . . . throughout, meanwhile), relative points (for example, early, late, recently) . . . [and] concepts were later expanded to historical time . . ." (Wiig et al., 1992, p. 280).

When units were introduced, teachers probed carefully checking for prior knowledge and any misconceptions. They used **guided questioning** and scaffolding. Both of these have the teacher in the role of facilitator rather than controller. Students are guided, as in the deductive reasoning process, to the discovery of new concepts and as they become more grounded in their learning and confidence with the support structure of the teacher and classmates, the teacher becomes less and less controlling as students grasp the concepts. A building has a lot of help when it is first constructed or has extensive remodeling. The scaffolding stays as long as it is necessary. When the building is able to stand by itself, it does.

Students in this study were led in the process of **semantic word webbing.** Students were encouraged to carefully and thoroughly examine the meanings of words, study words for their similarities and differences, and then group them and classify them. They studied pictures or artifacts and had discussions. If they were talking about animals, they would see and discuss what a particular animal looks like and sounds like as compared to another; that is what were their similarities and differences. They generated "meaninged-words," one after another, leading toward labels for abstract concepts, devising a complicated network that spins and connects words and concepts.

Words and concepts can be learned in a variety of ways, including imparting direct knowledge. Since the students in this study were not progressing, this particular approach was not used. Instead, teachers were trained in providing experiential learning (models, hands on, and so on).

Teachers used the inductive method with students. Students were asked to identify objects that could be wide or narrow. Guided questioning and scaffolding were used to develop the concept of *size*—its relative width versus its relative length.

A study of the effects of repeated reading and assisted nonrepetitive strategies, such as echo reading, cloze reading, and unison reading, on reading and error rate, as well as comprehension was undertaken with sixth-grade Chapter I students (Homan, Klesius, & Hite, 1993). This study investigated the transfer effects of these strategies on comprehension and fluency with sixth-grade Chapter I students. The study specifically addressed the following questions:

1. Do the instructional methods of repeated reading and assisted nonrepetitive reading have any effect on the reading performance of sixth-grade Chapter I students?
2. Is the effect of repeated reading instruction significantly greater than that of assisted nonrepetitive reading methods on their reading performance?

Twenty-six below-grade-level readers in a Chapter I program in two sixth-grade centers in a large metropolitan area participated. The schools were located in inner-city areas, but to obtain racial balance, 80 percent of the students were bussed in from the suburbs.

Students in this study qualified for Chapter I by scoring in the bottom 30 percent on the combined vocabulary and comprehension scores on the Comprehensive Test of Basic Skills (CTBS).

Participants were reading at a high fourth- or beginning fifth-grade level and were reading from a fifth-grade reading series.

Students in three teachers' classes were randomly assigned to one of the two treatments: Thirteen were assigned to repeated readings and thirteen to nonrepetitive oral reading strategies.

The two treatments were each implemented by three teachers three times a week, twenty minutes each session, for seven weeks during the one and a half hours of reading/language arts instruction. Teacher 1 worked with a group of four students in each treatment. Teacher 2 had five students in the repeated reading group and four in the assisted nonrepetitive strategies group. Teacher 3 had four students in the repeated reading group and five in the other. During the hour-and-a-half time block for reading/language arts, each teacher spent twenty minutes with one treatment group and twenty minutes with the other group.

The strategies used in the assisted nonrepetitive reading treatment were echo reading, unison reading, and cloze reading. The students read stories ranging from one to twelve pages, as well as one-page poetry selections. They read for twenty minutes, completing as much of a story or stories as they could. The instruction methods were rotated, with echo reading the first day, cloze the second, and unison the third.

Repeated reading was done by students pairing off and repeatedly reading a selection with close teacher supervision. The first student read the first page of the story, or the page following the one he had finished reading in the previous session. Each reader was directed to repeatedly read the same page four times. (This number was arrived at by the researchers' previous experience with this strategy and Stoddard's [1988] finding that three readings resulted in recall equivalent to seven readings.) Peers were told not to give assistance when the reader could not pronounce a word. The reader was encouraged to attempt a pronunciation and, if necessary, skip the word. Students were informed that with rereadings they would probably be able to figure out the word themselves.

There were no significant differences between groups at pretest for reading rate, error rate, or comprehension; however, a significant gain in comprehension occurred in the repeated readings and assisted nonrepetitive reading methods. This may have been because the students focused on connected reading three times a week, twenty minutes a session. The specific type of instructional reading method used appears to be of secondary importance.

This finding stresses the value of allocating time for students to engage in connected reading. When the same amount of practice was allowed, repeated reading was not necessarily a more effective means for increasing reading speed than nonrepetitive reading.

Although repeated reading appears to facilitate growth in fluency and comprehension that is transferable to new material, it has a number of drawbacks, including that some students find repetition of the same passage boring, and limitation of student exposure to a breadth of vocabulary, content topics, and genre.

Alternatives to repeated reading, such as assisted nonrepetitive reading, enable beginning readers to have successful early experiences with reading. They facilitate the development of both accurate and automatic recognition of sight vocabulary.

For older, at-risk readers, repeated reading of a selection may be met with resistance from individuals who view the activity as punishment for not reading a selection well enough the first time. The teacher may need to give a relevant purpose for the repeated reading, such as reading to younger children, using a chart to show improving reading rates, reading with expression to other class members, making an audiotape for the listening center or for teacher listening, or engaging in a dramatic reading of the selection for an audience.

This study demonstrated the equivalent benefits of using assisted nonrepetitive instructional strategies that do not have some of the repeated reading drawbacks.

Additional time spent on connected reading apparently improves comprehension scores for remedial students, even over a short time period. Therefore, instructional methods that encourage more student reading should be a primary instructional goal.

Repeated readings of expository material may cause objection in older readers, but repeated readings of poetry will likely have some of the same appeal that predictable pattern books have for younger children. However, reading of expository material is beneficial for recall and the redundancy of rereading may help students derive word meanings from the context.

When used wisely, repeated readings have a legitimate place in the reading program in all grade levels. The strategy complements assisted nonrepetitive reading strategies, which have the advantage of exposing students to a wider range of vocabulary, content topics, and literary genre.

The purpose of the Elementary and Secondary Education Act Chapter I Literacy Summer School program was to provide intervention to underachieving first-grade students whose reading ability was below average (Pollock, 1992). The first desired result was to have at least 50 percent of the first-grade students in the treatment group reach an appropriate text reading level for promotion to second grade. The other desired outcome was to have parents of at least 75 percent of Chapter I students in the treatment group participate by visiting the classroom, volunteering in the classroom, assisting with homework, reading to or being read to by their children, or attending parent-teacher conferences during the summer school program.

First-grade students in five schools throughout the Columbus, Ohio, public school district, each consisting of two classes of fifteen to eighteen students, were taught by either a trained Reading Recovery teacher or a regular classroom teacher familiar with Reading Recovery techniques.

The parents or guardians of each student in the program were asked to attend three in-service sessions at the site where their child would attend the program. These in-services were conducted by two trained Reading Recovery teachers and focused on ways the parents or guardians could support their child's literacy acquisition at home.

To be eligible for the program, students had to have met the following criteria: The student's classroom teacher had rated the pupil as below average in reading ability; the student had scored below the thirty-seventh percentile in total reading on the Spring 1992 MAT6 standardized test; parents had agreed to arrange for daily transportation to and from one of the program sites; and parents had agreed to attend three parent meetings.

Of the 162 students served, 108 of them attended the program the required 80 percent of the instructional period and were included in the treatment group. Of the 108 pupils in the treatment group, 85 reached the appropriate level, meeting the first desired outcome. Parents of all 108 students in the treatment group participated in the program, meeting the second desired outcome.

Teachers judged that of all pupils served, 137 (84.6%) showed improvement, including 54 (33.3%) who showed much improvement. Of the 108 treatment group pupils, 106 (98.1%) were judged as showing improvement, with 46 (42.6%) showing much improvement.

Another study (Denner & McGinley, 1992) examined a prereading method called *story impressions* (McGinley & Denner, 1987), which uses writing as one of its prereading activities. The authors wanted to see whether the actual process of writing, instead of just prediction testing, which is used in many prereading methods, was a key to the story-impressions prereading method's effectiveness. Even though the participants were seventh- and eighth-graders, the treatments and results are worthy of consideration and application at the elementary level.

The participants in the study were ninety-six seventh- and eighth-grade volunteers from two junior high schools in a city in southeastern Idaho. The students were grouped by reading ability and grade level. Then they were randomly assigned to one of three treatments: a read-only control group; a group using story impressions with composing a story guess; and a group using story impressions with listening predictions. Thirty-two students were assigned to each treatment, with sixteen above-average and sixteen below-average readers.

The group using story impressions with a story guess was told to look over the story impressions and come up with a story guess and to focus on the content instead of grammar, spelling, and so on. Then, individually, students were given the story impressions to look over and each one made an independent story guess.

The group using story impressions with listening predictions were given the same set of story impressions as the previous group and asked to list their predictions about the story's plot. The students wrote their predictions independent of the group. The control group did nothing until the second phase of the study.

All of the students in the study were assembled into a large common area for the second phase of the study. Each of them was given a copy of "Never Trust a Lady," which they then read for the first time. After they had all finished reading the story, they were asked to take the same completion test.

The results of this study demonstrated that using the story impressions method with a written story guess was effective for readers of *all ability levels*. Also, it was not necessary for the students to guess the detail of the story for this method to be effective.

Students usually read textbooks, stories, and articles, but fail to make connections between them. One article (Hartman & Hartman, 1993) discusses ways to encourage students to read beyond a single text. The article deals with the following four questions: What types of texts can be used? What are ways to arrange texts? In what activities can students engage? How can outcomes be represented?

Many different types of texts can be used, and a text does not necessarily have to be printed language. It can also be art, music, drama, personal experience, or anything that signifies meaning. The advantages to using this expanded definition of text are that the students can use a greater number and variety of texts when investigating a topic, and that students can relearn how to move between linguistic and nonlinguistic texts of all types, a skill that they unlearn as they go through school.

The overall goal of arranging texts is to arrange a set of texts that have many possible connections and that will meet your objectives and keep students interested. The article mentioned two basic ways of arranging texts, by type and by structure. Texts can be arranged by type, for example, by organizing a collection by theme, topic, or issue.

The article explained five different ways to arrange texts by structure. The first method is using companion texts, such as a trilogy of stories. Authors often make references to their other books or may bring characters from other books into another one. A second way to arrange texts by structure is to use complementary texts. This method entails organizing texts around a *particular* theme or topic, for example. Since a single text seldom tells the whole story or all sides of a story, reading many texts gives students a chance to see all sides of the story and make connections between the texts. A third method of organizing texts is by synoptic texts. To do this, choose a story or event and read several different accounts or versions of it. The article gave an example of using different versions of *Cinderella* from different countries to see how different cultures tell their own versions of the story. The fourth method mentioned in this article is to use disruptive texts, which present conflicting or nonstandard interpretations or perspectives on an event, theme, and so on. The example in the article was using different accounts of the death of a famous general from a history textbook, a children's book, in a painting, and a retelling by a historian. The final method discussed in the article for organizing texts by structure is to reread texts. Many different methods were presented, but the basic idea was to see how students' ideas and perceptions of the text change over time.

The types of activities in which students can engage range from closed-ended to open-ended activities. Closed-ended activities would be, for example, asking why a particular character in a particular book did some particular action. Open-ended activities, on the other hand, are almost unlimited in their scope. An example of an open-ended activity would be asking students to make their own connections between stories and to look at additional sources to broaden their perspectives.

The final question the article addressed is how outcomes representing students' understandings and responses from reading across texts can be represented. At one end of the possible range of outcomes is the unimedium response, such as singing, writing, or drawing the connections the students have made between texts. A more multimedia response would be writing a report and presenting it to the class, or maybe drawing pictures of connections made during group discussion. Students could also make and act out a play after reading several versions of a story. More extreme multimedia responses may require a redefinition of the classroom and the teacher's place in it.

Another article (Dole, Duffy, Roehler, & Pearson, 1991) reviewed the current research on reading comprehension and how it is taught. It attempted to answer the question: What should be used to teach comprehension and how should it be taught?

As it is taught today, reading comprehension is thought of as a set of skills to be mastered, which, when put together, result in comprehension. This article proposes teaching strategies instead of skills. Strategies have many advantages over traditional skills. Readers have control of strategies, how to use them, which ones to use, and the ability to adapt them to any situation, whereas skills are pretty much inflexible routines, applied to everything in the same way. Strategies concentrate on reasoning abilities; skills involve lower-order thinking. When readers use strategies, they are aware of their using them and can change or adapt if they do not understand what they are reading. On the other hand, when they use traditional skills, they just read the material and it is assumed that these skills will automatically be used, without a conscious effort made to apply them.

The article goes through five strategies that the authors believe should be taught. The first strategy is *determining importance.* Good readers are able to tell what the author considers important, and thus focus more on that, resulting in better comprehension. The second strategy the article mentions is *summarizing information.* This entails choosing some information to be included while ignoring other information. It means consolidating some parts while explaining others in depth so that others can understand. It means integrating all of the material into a coherent whole. The third strategy is *drawing inferences,* which is the crux of reading comprehension. Readers must draw inferences from text all the time to answer questions or better construct in their minds what the author is trying to get across. The fourth strategy is *generating questions.* Students who create their own questions better comprehend stories than those who just answer teacher questions. The final strategy the article discusses is *monitoring comprehension.* Good readers are able to monitor their level of comprehension and change or adapt reading strategies to fit the situation.

The article then reviews some teaching methods that assist students in learning comprehension. First, teachers adapt their methods to the situation, based on many factors, such as their purpose, the feedback or responses of students, and the demands of the material. Teachers provide support for students when learning new strategies by using examples, elaborating, or giving explicit instructions for the material being taught. Gradually, teachers have to provide less support as students learn and become more comfortable applying new strategies. Finally, to be effective, teachers must be aware of the complexities of the meanings of material created by the interaction of teachers and students.

Another article (Garner, 1990) explores why people sometimes do *not* use learning strategies, even though they improve reading comprehension. The article discusses five major reasons: poor monitoring of cognitive processes; using simple routines that accomplish the task; having an insufficient base of knowledge; having classroom barriers to use strategies; and not transferring strategies to new or related situations.

People are not likely to use learning strategies or change the ones they are using if they are unaware that they are not learning. Also, certain conditions or situations may cause people not to cognitively monitor their learning, such as if the job is not viewed as being important, if the person does not need to follow some instructions, or if the person is using a lot of memory resources at the time.

Sometimes people use routines that produce a result, but not necessarily the desired one, because it has become almost second nature to use them. This also restricts the learning process.

Another reason people do not use learning strategies is that they do not have enough knowledge to select a strategy to use. An example of this may be a student trying to study for an exam but not knowing what kind of test it will be—essay, multiple choice, and so on. This knowledge deficiency prevents that student from choosing an effective learning strategy.

The article also mentions classroom barriers to using learning strategies. For example, classrooms are very ability-oriented and competitive, and some students may appear indifferent toward learning. This may just be a shield they use to protect them from their feelings of failure (Covington, 1985). Another example is having goals that do not require the use of strategic activities. A classroom can either be mainly performance-goal oriented, where students are trying to outdo others and be successful with little effort, or mastery-goal oriented, where students are more concerned with the actual process of learning and acquiring new skills (Ames & Archer, 1988). Students in the mastery-goal oriented classrooms reported using more learning strategies than those in performance-goal classrooms, according to Ames and Archer.

A final reason put forth in the article as to why people may not use learning strategies is that they do not transfer strategies to new or related material or situations. For example, teachers usually teach a method for solving a problem and students only apply it to that problem or type of problem and do not transfer the way of thinking to other situations. Students can transfer new strategies; they just need to be shown how.

The article ends by stating that future research into this area must include the fact that different strategies are used in different settings.

Another article (Commeyras, Osborn, & Bruce, 1993) summarizes teachers' reactions to the *Framework for the 1992 National Assessment of Educational Progress (NAEP)*. The authors mailed out a thousand questionnaires in August 1991, to randomly selected teachers who were members of the International Reading Association (IRA) and received 312 responses. A large majority of those who responded were elementary school teachers (84%); the rest were either middle school, high school, special education, or Chapter I teachers.

The *Framework for the 1992 NAEP* in reading proposed using passages that were full-length and authentic, not made up to test specific things. A majority (65%) of the respondents agreed with this.

The *Framework* also proposed testing reading in three situations: reading for literary experience, reading to obtain information, and reading to perform a task. More than 80 percent of the teachers ranked assessing reading in these three areas as "very important" or "absolutely essential." Most support went to reading to perform a task, which was said to be "absolutely essential," followed by reading to get information, and, finally, reading for literary experience, which only 33 percent ranked as "absolutely essential."

The *Framework* proposed testing readers' abilities in four areas: forming an initial understanding of the material, developing an interpretation of it, generating a response and personal reflection, and illustrating a critical stance. Most of the teachers (85%) strongly agreed with evaluating these four cognitive abilities. Almost all of the teachers (97%) agreed with the inclusion of open-ended items called for in the *Framework*. The reason for including them was to test a student's ability to respond thoughtfully and in an organized manner to the reading passages. Only 15 percent of the teachers thought the inclusion of the oral reading section was necessary. This test was designed to assess students' fluency by analyzing and timing their oral reading. A little over half of the teachers thought the portfolio assessment study was very important. This assessment analyzed students' classroom work in reading, what they read in the classroom and what they read on their own time. A little over half of the teachers strongly supported the metacognitive study, which examined the students' use of reading strategies. The final question dealt with state-by-state reporting of the data for the NAEP. The response was mixed, with many fearing misuse of data reported in this manner.

In qualifying their conclusions, the authors point out that the teachers never saw any of the test passages or other questions, and that the respondents were more likely to be informed of current issues and thinking in reading because they all received a copy of *The Reading Teacher* with their membership to the IRA.

REPORTS

Reports can be given in any subject, but usually are a part of language arts, history, geography, science, or health. When you assign a report, it is important that you carefully explain all the skills the students will be using. They should receive specific information on the approximate length of the report, the format, examples of any complex material they need to know, and so on.

Figure A6-20 in the appendix is an example of a science report suitable for second or third grades. There are a series of specific questions the students need to be sure are addressed in their reports. Question 9 provides a beginning experience with the idea of a bibliography. The students are informed that artwork is required and that they need to be prepared to share their reports with the rest of the class. Younger primary students can draw pictures and dictate a story for their "report."

Figure A6-21, also in the appendix, is a sample state report suitable for any upper grade. It gives specific directions as to the written part of the report, the artwork and the graphs.

When you assign something of this nature, go through it slowly and carefully during class time so that the students are confident about knowing what is expected. Be sure students understand the basics of note taking. Make sure they understand the use of sources, such as encyclopedias, magazines, library books, and so on. Then have them write the due date on the last page of the directions booklet and take it home for a parent signature. Then parents know right at the beginning what is required and when it is due.

It works well to do the report's title page and the bibliography as a total class. Set aside a day when the students have on hand all materials used for information for their report. Then you also can use the overhead projector and do a sample title page and give the students time right then to do theirs. You also can do a sample bibliography and have the students do theirs right then. It will take a whole class period, but the students will get the idea and do a good job. Or, you may have students who wish to do their title pages and bibliographies on the computer when they do the rest of their report.

When you set aside a class period to work on the reports, specify what you want to be covered. For example: "Today is the time to take notes about your state's climate, population, location, lakes, mountains, national parks, and any other unusual geographic features." You might want to set your classroom timer in increments of fifteen minutes. When the timer sounds, ask the students to see what they have accomplished and tell their partner or neighbor about it. Continue on with this. It really helps the students to keep focused and

accomplish an amount of work they are pleased with. Reports such as these provide excellent projects for early finishers.

You could also have a two-night homework assignment of drawing their state map. The first night, students could write the title of their state at the top of a piece of white, unlined paper. Then they could draw the outline of their state with markings for the important lakes, rivers, mountains, bays, and so on. The second night, they could label the important cities and the state capital and color the map and the title.

Making a vertical bar graph, a line graph, and a table will be difficult for all the students. Figure A6-21 has a sample of these, which the students can use as models. Explain each carefully. Demonstration skills, such as these, require a higher level of thinking.

Impress upon your students the importance of having a neat report, one with careful art work; neat handwriting, printing, or word processing; a great cover; and fastened together in a sturdy manner.

Figure A6-22 in the appendix is a country report suitable for sixth grade or an advanced fifth. All the information is carefully presented to the students. Give them a due date and have them get a parent signature. Since students get little experience with bibliographies, it is a good idea, even with sixth grade, to do the bibliography as a class so students are practicing that skill correctly.

Students are asked in the country report to make a combination vertical bar and line graph to show the average precipitation and low temperatures of two cities or two areas (like lowlands and highlands). Then they will make a table about populations and a pie graph to show urban and rural areas. A sample of each one of these is given in the directions to the country report, but, again, making a graph is a difficult skill. Explain everything thoroughly.

Figure 6-10.   Here the students are doing an AIMS lesson that will help them with their graphing skills. Courtesy of Carroll Maietta.

When specific directions are given for reports, when well-structured class time is provided, and when suitable and specific homework is given, students can be very successful with these kind of reports and proud of their final products.

RESEARCH SKILLS

This area of the curriculum can be taught as a separate subject or incorporated into all areas of the curriculum. It is much easier to cover the skills thoroughly if it is taught separately. If the students do not have plenty of practice in this area, they will not find accessing information an easy task.

Research skills are very important for lifelong learning. Students and adults both are constantly being exposed to things about which they know little, if anything. Those who can confidently and easily locate and understand explanations about this new material will look it up and become informed.

Students need to be well versed in alphabetizing. They will need this skill for indexes, encyclopedias, glossaries, and dictionaries. Give them plenty of opportunities to practice and enough time to be accurate.

Students also need to be familiar with the parts of a book. Being proficient in the use of the table of contents, the glossary, the title page, and the index is important for good readers.

Students will need skills in map, table, graph, and chart reading, too, because they will see these kinds of graphics everywhere. Their texts, encyclopedias, newspapers, and almanacs contain many graphic representations.

When students are presented with easy-to-read graphs, tables, charts, and maps that have relatively simple questions, they can begin successfully getting information. Frequent participation in making total-class graphs, tables, maps, and charts helps students acquire these skills and concepts. Students will need to be able to make or construct their own maps, graphs, tables, and the like, too. In the upper grades, students will need to be able to draw maps "freehand" from memory.

Figures A6-23 through A6-34, all in the appendix, contain sample materials you can use in your classroom for both primary and upper grades. There are maps to read; horizontal and vertical bar graphs to decipher; pie graphs, line graphs, and pictographs to interpret; tables, time lines, and grids in latitude and longitude to understand, as well as legends, keys, and scales. These activity sheets are also useful for math. After students get enough practice, have them construct their own with either provided or invented data.

One exciting way for the students to practice their almanac and map skills is with the computer game series, *Where in the World Is Carmen Sandiego? Where in the US...? Where in Europe...?* and so on. With proper guidance, students as young as third grade can begin with the *Where in the World,* the easiest of the group.

Once students learn how to play these games, they are hooked. They will use intense thinking skills and learn a great deal about world geography, world history, and solving crimes.

Students can practice their dictionary skills in contests to see which section of the classroom can have all its members find the correct word the fastest. They can apply all their research skills when doing a report like the animal, state, or country reports. They can go back and forth from atlas to history book to encyclopedia to work on an activity like "Using Reference Materials" in Figure A6-35 in the appendix.

Figure 6-11. These students are using a variety of reference sources to pool their research on Washington, D.C. When students understand the time frame for their work, they are very eager and productive.

Figure 6-12. *Where in the World Is Carmen Sandiego?* has these students using their almanacs and world maps. They are racing against the clock to capture the criminal who stole one of the world's treasures.

It is very important for students to be able to look up entries in the indexes of their history and science books. An excellent assignment to give students is to list three very specific topics on the chalkboard or chart. Have the students look each topic up in the index, record the page number(s) the information is found on, and write a sentence (or a paragraph or more, depending on your group) about what they read. This way, they will get experience with locating topics as well as subtopics, and they will learn how their indexes show which pages have maps or pictures.

Another variation to this activity is to list several topics, maybe seven or eight, and have students use their indexes to look up each entry, record the appropriate page numbers, and, after reading, tell one unusual piece of information for each entry.

Students of all levels of capability find the computer program, *The Electronic Encyclopedia,* exciting and useful. Students learn how to do searches and can use the information for papers, reports, or just general interest.

With these types of activities, students will become well versed with accessing information and simultaneously quite knowledgeable about a variety of topics.

When you have your lessons ready to go, your students on target, and good communication with your parents, your classroom will hum!

CHAPTER QUESTIONS

1. Describe the relationship you would like to have with your students' parents.
2. Describe four suggestions you can make to parents who ask for ideas to help their children at home with reading and math.
3. A parent is coming to volunteer in your classroom tomorrow for two hours. Write a set of instructions for this person.
4. A single parent of one of your students works two jobs and is gone each day from 6:30 A.M. to 8:00 P.M. What effects might this have on your student's task of complet-

ing homework? If this parent were to ask for your help, what suggestions could you make?
5. Name and explain three things you would do to prepare for a substitute.
6. You have had conflicts with a particular parent in the past and you discover colleagues have, too. Now this parent has resorted to being verbally abusive. What should you do?
7. What are two things you should be alert to when dealing with parents?
8. Besides being polite, prepared, and listening carefully, what one major thing do you want the parents to know as

a result of your phone conversation, written communication, or conference? In what way is this important?

9. Who are other people you might want to involve in your communications with parents? What purpose could they serve?

10. What benefits, if any, do you see to a parent-teacher conference with the student present?

11. How can you be sure to remember to collect a note sent home to one student's parents?

12. How can you keep track of parent signatures on the total-class communications taken home by the students to be sure the information was received by the parents?

13. How are you planning to handle the paperwork load?

14. Describe the "personal connection" reading strategy. In what ways is it important?

15. Name one book you would like to read to a class. For which grade level would you read? List three reasons your book would be a good selection.

16. Describe the methods for introducing a new story to the class. Give one reason why each is important.

17. Describe a reading technique that can be used to glean the main content of a selection, especially in history or science.

18. Describe two methods students can use when reading a story. What are the benefits and/or challenges of each?

19. Describe three different follow-up activities to a story.

20. List all the components of a broad-based reading program.

21. What does the quote "When the student is ready, the teacher appears" mean to you?

22. In what ways are research skills needed for lifelong learning?

23. Select a grade level. Name two research skills that you think are most important at that level. How would you teach each?

24. What is a good sponge activity for some quiet time?

25. Describe the four different uses for alphabet books.

26. How can you help access prior knowledge with students, especially LEP's? In relation to prior knowledge, explain what misconceptions are.

27. What problem did the K–5 students have with reading in the Hansen study? How could you avoid this in your classroom?

28. According to Leinhardt's research, what is the number one way at school that reading improvement occurs?

29. Describe the six parts of the observation form for the student-teacher conference for HRA.

30. In the students with the "fifth-grade thinking level," how was word-concept development achieved?

31. Explain the strategy of assisted nonrepetitive reading used in the study with the Chapter I students.

32. How would you teach your first-graders to play four square?

33. Explain the strategy of guided questioning.

CHAPTER PROJECT

Develop a set of reading assignments for one specific story. Choose whichever grade level you would like. Name the story. Write the grade level for which it is appropriate. Include a *selection* of activities from the following: marginalia; personal connection; story map; quote; Venn diagram; picture explanation; writing about a favorite part of the story and drawing an accompanying picture; making up and writing five challenging questions for the story and their answers; writing five words from the story that are not seen much or maybe never seen and writing a definition for each; and making up a totally different ending to the story and drawing a picture that illustrates it.

REFERENCES

Allington, R. L., & McGill-Franzen, A. (1990). Children with reading problems: How we wrongfully classify them and fail to teach many to read. *ERS Spectrum, 8*(4), 3–9.

Ames, C., & Archer, J. (1988). Achievement goals in the classroom: Students' learning strategies and motivation processes. *Journal of Educational Psychology, 80,* 260–267.

Anderson, R. C., et al. (1985). *Becoming a nation of readers: The report of the Commission on Reading.* Urbana, IL: University of Illinois at Urbana-Champaign. Center for the Study of Reading.

Beaver, J., Carter, M., & Sonedicker, J. (1992). The holistic reading assessment: Providing specific feedback to guide instruction. *ERS Spectrum, 10*(3), 39–46.

Carlsen, W. S. (1991). Questioning in classrooms: A sociolinguistic perspective. *Review of Educational Research, 61*(2), 157–175.

Chaney, J. H. (1993). Alphabet books: Resources for learning. *The Reading Teacher, 47*(2), 96–104.

Commeyras, M., Osborn, J., & Bruce, B. C. (1993). *What do classroom teachers think about the 1992 NAEP in reading?* Urbana, IL: University of Illinois at Urbana-Champaign, College of Education. Center for the Study of Reading.

Covington, M. V. (1985). Strategic thinking and the fear of failure. In S. F. Chipman, J. W. Seagal and R. Glaser (Eds.). *Thinking and learning skills, Vol. 1* (pp. 389–416). Hillsdale, NJ: Lawrence Erlbaum Associates, Inc.

Denner, P. R., & McGinley, W. J. (1992). Effects of prereading activities on junior high students' recall. *Journal of Educational Research, 86*(1), 11–19.

Dole, J. A., Duffy, G. G., Roehler, L. R., & Pearson, D. P. (1991). Moving from the old to the new: Research on reading comprehension instruction. *Review of Educational Research, 61*(2), 239–257.

Garner, R. (1990). When children and adults do not use learning strategies: Toward a theory of settings. *Review of Educational Research, 60*(4), 517–527.

Hansen, J. (1992). Students' evaluations bring reading and writing together. *The Reading Teacher, 46*(2), 100–105.

Hartman, D. K., & Hartman, J. A. (1993). Reading across texts: Expanding the role of the reader. *The Reading Teacher, 47*(3), 202–211.

Hirsch, E. D., Jr. (1985). Cultural literacy and the schools. *American Educator, 9*(2).

Homan, S. P., Klesius, J. P., & Hite, C. (1993). Effects of repeated readings and nonrepetitive strategies on students' fluency and comprehension. *Journal of Educational Research, 87*(2), 94–99.

Leinhardt, G., Bickel, W., & Pallay, A. (1982). Unlabeled but still entitled: Toward more effective remediation. *Teachers College Record, 84*, 391–422.

Leinhardt, G., Zigmond, N., & Cooley, W. (1981). Reading instruction and its effects. *American Educational Research Journal, 18*, 343–361.

Levin, J. (1992). *Expanding prospective teachers' beliefs about the reading process to enable changes in classroom practice through the use of whole language.* Nova University.

McGinley, W. J., & Denner, P. R. (1987). Story impressions: A prereading/writing activity. *Journal of Reading, 31,* 248–253.

Mevarech, Z. R., & Susak, Z. (1993). Effects of learning with cooperative-mastery method on elementary students. *Journal of Educational Research, 86*(4), 197–205.

Nagy, W. E., & Herman, P. A. (1987). Breadth and depth of vocabulary knowledge: Implications for acquisition and instruction. In M. G. McKeown & M. E. Curtis (Eds.), *The Nature of Vocabulary Acquisition* (pp. 19–35). Hillsdale, NJ: Lawrence Erlbaum Associates, Inc.

Pollock, J. S. (1992). Professional Specialist, under the supervision of Williams, E. Jane, PhD. *Final evaluation report Chapter I early literacy summer school.* Columbus: Ohio. Public Schools Department of Program Evaluations.

Reiber, R. W., & Carton, A. S. (1987). *The collected works of L. S. Vygotsky, Volume 1.* New York: Plenum Press.

Stoddard, K. (1988). The effects of instructional methods on reading rate and comprehension. *Dissertation Abstracts International, DAI, 50*, Section A, 656.

Walberg, H. J. (1984). Families as partners in educational productivity. *Phi Delta Kappan, 65*(6), 397–400.

Wiig, E. H., Freedman, E., & Secord, W. A. (1992). Developing words and concepts in the classroom: A holistic-thematic approach. *Intervention in School and Clinic, 27*(5), 278–285.

BIBLIOGRAPHY

Becker, H. J., & Epstein, J. (1982). Parent involvement: A survey of teacher practices. *The Elementary School Journal, 83*(2), 85–102.

Black E. (1994). *Reading, thinking and writing about literature.* A workshop sponsored by CEEA (California Elementary Education Association), presented at Irvine, California.

Cruz, D. (1994). *Reviving your 5th grade PE program.* A workshop sponsored by CEEA, presented at Irvine, California.

Cunningham, C., & Morris, G. S. D. (1990). *Elementary physical education, a comprehensive program.* Encino, CA: 21st Century Education Enterprises.

Humphreys, L. G., & Davey, T. C. (1983). *Anticipation of gains in general information: A comparison of verbal aptitude, reading comprehension, and listening.* Urbana, IL: University of Illinois at Urbana-Champaign. Center for the Study of Reading.

Smith, R. M., Diercks, E., Molek, R., Rutherford, J., & Waldorf, J. (1988). Comprehensive use of technology leading to excellence in a school district. *ERS Spectrum, 6*(2), 23–29.

7

THE STU'S

To make your classroom run smoothly, it is important to have things in your room under control. In this vein, this chapter will help you with two additional curricular areas and give you valuable information about the entire domain of the teaching-learning process. It presents four easy things to do that can make a real difference in your class.

But it is not enough for a well-run classroom to just have things inside it carefully managed. Why not? Happenings on your campus will directly affect you and your classroom. Just as you prepare your subjects for teaching and your classroom control policies for good direction, you also need to prepare for and be informed about site activities such as school councils and school reviews.

This chapter also provides you with a few tips about student teaching to give you early practice in running a classroom successfully.

The topics for this chapter are:

- School-Based Councils
- School Reviews
- Science
- Speaking
- Student Responsibilities
- Student Teachers and Beginning Teachers
- Teaching-Learning Process
- Test Study Notes
- Tutors
- Using a Digital Timer

The first part of this chapter presents information on school councils and school reviews, and it introduces two additional areas of the curriculum: science and speaking. Student responsibilities that will help your classroom run smoothly are given in addition to some helpful hints about the student-teaching experience.

SCHOOL-BASED COUNCILS

Councils may be site-based, decision-making **school site councils** or school improvement plan councils. They may have many other names, but usually teachers, parents, and the principal are involved. The council helps formulate ideas and make decisions about school discipline, some curricular matters, procedures during school reviews, and so on. Learn what is being discussed in this group. Get active in this organization, and get heard. See if you can be instrumental in getting *one* positive change made at your school.

SCHOOL REVIEWS

These are reviews of each individual school in certain areas of the curriculum. Usually, the schools pick the area or areas for which they would like the review. The school plan covering those areas is the criterion for the review.

One year, schools may have only an in-house review. The review team would be composed of teachers and parents from the school. Another year, there may be a district review. Then the review team would be made up solely of teachers and principals from other schools in the district. Usually, about every fourth or fifth year, there will be a state review. This review team includes principals and teachers from other districts.

In preparation, the school personnel do a self-study. They look at what they said they would do in their school plan for, say math and fine arts, and see what evidence they have that they are, in fact, doing that schoolwide.

Evidence can be gathered by various means. Talking to students, teachers, instructional assistants, principals, playground supervisors, and parents is probably the most helpful way. Projects, reports, art work, and so on, displayed in the classroom is another good way. Evidence can also be gathered by observing lessons in the classrooms on the review days.

Before the review team comes to your class, it is important to know exactly what the members will be looking for so that you can have *evidence* of those things out and available and/or students' assignments or projects in those areas up on your bulletin boards. Appoint students in your class who can answer questions the team may have. This will help the **school review** team assess the total program.

On the days of the review, schedule your day so that the visiting team members get a chance to see lessons in the areas being evaluated. Also, try to take a few minutes from your lesson to speak with the team about exciting things going on in your room that they are not able to see that day. If the team gets either visible evidence or verbal information of relevant activities going on, your school will get a good review. Be aware, though, that for most reviews it is considered standard procedure to list areas where improvement could take place as well as areas that are strong.

SCIENCE

Francis Bacon (1561–1626) is famous in education for advocating the **inductive method** and the spirit of scientific investigation. The inductive method itself goes back to Aristotle, but Bacon explained exactly how it should operate:

1. Remove prejudice.
2. Observe thoroughly.
3. Carefully tabulate data.
4. Study *exceptions* as a check to accuracy.
5. Form your generalization.

Figure 7-1. Think about an aquarium for your kindergarten classroom. Notice this student's enjoyment of science in action. Courtesy of Essa and Rogers, *An Early Childhood Curriculum: From Developmental Model to Application,* © 1992 by Delmar Publishers, Inc.

Figure 7-2. Kindergarten students are very curious about displays such as this one. Courtesy of Essa, *Introduction to Early Childhood Education,* © 1992 by Delmar Publishers, Inc.

When teaching science, it is important to have your students observing, handling, examining, recording data, seeing similarities, and looking for differences. Provide students the opportunity, when they complete an observation or experiment, to write what took place in the science activity and what they learned from it. Then they can begin forming generalizations.

To help encourage and maintain scientific curiosity, have science displays in the classroom, like an aquarium or ant farm. Bring interesting animals to the class for observation and care.

Build your lessons around a **focus activity.** If you have a class of kindergartners, your focus activity could be having students watch and touch a live snake. Ask someone to bring one to your classroom. This fascinates students.

Students could then draw or paint their own versions of snakes. They could show how a snake's mouth opens with their hands and learn why snakes have this unusual feature. They could "dance" to snake music.

You could have a lesson with an experiment as its focus. Students love this. Or build a lesson around a classification exercise, like classification of rocks. Bring several microscopes to class and let the students examine different items, like bug parts or cheek cells. Have your students learn the parts of a microscope in conjunction with this exercise.

When you are beginning, it is best to set out all the science materials well before the lesson. If the lesson will be in the morning, put everything out before school starts. If it is going to be in the afternoon, put the materials out during lunch period. Then everything will be ready for you and your students.

After you get a good amount of practice, you can set up during the class time right before science. If, for example, you are doing an experiment on cheek cells and this is your first microscope activity of the year, while your students are busy finishing their math assignment take microscopes out of your cupboard one by one and set them up at four or five different stations around the room. This is an unbelievable motivator. The students cannot wait for their science lesson to begin. Let them know it will not begin until they are finished with their math. They will work harder than you have ever seen them work before!

Continue putting out paper towels, toothpicks, slides, and slide covers at each station; plug in each of the microscopes to be sure the lights are good. Then get out a container and put some water in it. Last, get out tincture of iodine (to be used only by you) and mix it into the water to create the staining solution for the slide specimens. Have a pipette ready.

When their math is finished, students are more than ready to hear about the microscope and its use, what the toothpicks are for (to scrape cheek cells from inside their mouths), and to hear that you will visit the stations to drop staining solution from the pipette on to their slides after they have placed a specimen of their cheek cells on them. Show them where to put the used toothpicks and slides when they are finished with their exami-

Figure 7-3.   A live snake is the focus activity for this science lesson. The students are excitedly observing, touching, and pointing. Courtesy of Essa, *Introduction to Early Childhood Education,* © 1992 by Delmar Publishers, Inc.

Figure 7-4.   This lesson's focus activity is an experiment. All the materials were organized and ready for these eager students.

nation to keep everything sanitary. Then have students write an **experiment summary** telling what they did in the experiment, how it turned out, and how they felt about it.

What about the students who are waiting to use the microscopes? They will have an enjoyable, educational assignment to do while they are waiting, one that helps them learn the scientific material well: They will do a **scientific drawing.** For this lesson, the drawing will be the parts of an animal cell and maybe even the parts of a microscope, too. At other times of the year, though, students can do scientific drawings on the parts of the ear, the eye, the skin, the brain, or the digestive system.

Students draw on white duplicating paper. Have them write a good title at the top, neatly done, possibly stenciled. Have them color all the parts of the drawing neatly with colored pencils or markers. Be sure they label all the parts with the correctly spelled words. This provides your students with the opportunity to become more familiar with pertinent scientific terms and to encapsulate the learning in color.

When students take their time and do a nice, neat job, these scientific drawings can turn out to be just beautiful. Mount them on a piece of construction paper and decorate your classroom with them.

Figure 7-5.   These students are in the midst of an AIMS lesson. Sometimes it is perplexing figuring out what will happen in a science experiment. Courtesy of Carroll Maietta.

This cheek cell lesson may take two to three days, especially if the students draw the microscope. Some students will go to the microscopes and do their experiment summaries the first day while the others work on their scientific drawings. Then they switch the next day. They will enjoy the entire lesson, you can be sure!

When you get ready to assess, do it over small amounts of material. You can, if you like, use the scientific drawings as a test or combine students' drawings and their experiment summaries for a grade. For a chapter test, though, be sure students have or make a study sheet so that they focus on the most important concepts and skills. Make the assessment demonstration-based. Students can write, tell, or draw about what they learned. They can apply what they learned to a similar experiment, set it up, conduct it, and then write their experiment summary. This can be done individually over a period of time or it can be done in groups simultaneously.

Science is an excellent opportunity for the application level of a skill like classifying. It is also an opportunity for the students to work in small groups around microscopes, rock collections, and **estimation jars**.

A field trip coordinates with science perfectly and with pre-trip activities as well as posttrip follow-ups, this makes a powerful lesson. Take the students to such places as a zoo, a wild animal park, or a planetarium.

After the students have been studying a scientific concept, a video about this subject is captivating. For example, if your students are studying the ear, they could see a short video on the parts of the ear and some ear surgery. Then they could study a model of the ear, take it apart, and examine each piece. They could learn about decibels and otoscopes. They could draw pictures of the inner or middle ear or a picture of the brain with the auditory center highlighted and labeled.

You could give your students a science lesson or series of lessons using the AIMS materials. These materials and lessons are suitable for about any grade level.

The appendix contains some science materials for use with your class. (Remember, *Pt* is for primary and *§* is for upper grade; however, make any modifications you like.) In addition to doing the activity on latitude and climate in Figure A7-1 with an upper grade, show the class a video on climate in different areas of the world and relate it to latitude. Students may decide on some major city in the world, find out about its climate, and see how its climate relates to latitude. Maybe one of your students will select a city close to the low latitudes which she expected to be quite hot. Then she discovers that elevation can have an effect, too. This is an opportunity for her to share and explain this information to the rest of the class.

You could add to the volcano activity in Figure A7-2 in the appendix by having some or all of the students make volcanoes. This would be a good activity for upper-grade students to do with partners. Students could label all the parts of the volcano or get really sophisticated and make a volcano that erupts. If students have any difficulty, work together as a class. Present the vocabulary on cards with accompanying pictures so that the students remember them. Before students start the volcano writing activity, they can first *tell* their partners what happens. This helps students more clearly understand as well as stay focused.

The generic activities in Figure A7-3 in the appendix can be done with any science or health lesson anytime during the year. Shorten or simplify these activities for primary grades.

Figures A7-4, A7-5, and A7-6 in the appendix are science experiments that you can demonstrate for your class, or have the students use the material themselves. These experiments directly focus on classification, prediction, estimation, and hypothesizing in the scientific method.

If you decide to do the fingerprint classification, an ordinary ink pad works fine for the students to use on their fingers. Have them roll their print onto the paper so the print does not smudge. Either an encyclopedia or a book on fingerprinting will have pictures of the basic classifications.

If you decide to do the experiment in Figure A7-6 with your class, be sure only *you* are handling the chemicals needed and perform the experiment *outside*. If you have an area of your school grounds with a slope, you can place your experiment table at the bottom and students can sit on the slope. Then they will all have a good view.

You can get a Hardness Test Kit from HACH, Box 389, Loveland, CO 80538 (Phone: 303-669-3050) or from your local soft water or water conditioning business office. Then have the students collect the different types of water needed for the experiment. Do not feel limited to just those listed in Figure A7-6. Ocean water, if available, or water with dishwasher detergent added, fabric softener added, bleach added, and so on can make interesting samples.

Before you take your class outside, distribute the Figure A7-6 handout. Discuss what could make water hard or soft. Explain to them that, for this experiment, very soft water is considered a *1* and very hard water would be around a *15*. Let them predict using numbers from *less than 1* for extremely soft to *25* for extremely hard. Have them write their predictions on the Figure A7-6 handout. Have them decide on a hypothesis and write it. Then, have the students take outside with them a pencil, a book to write on, and their copy of Figure A7-6.

Place all materials on the table outside and begin the test. Fill the small test tube full of the water you are going to test first. Then pour it into the mixing bottle. Add one level measuring "spoonful" of the Hardness reagent. Use the dropper provided in the kit and begin slowly adding the titrant solution to the mixing bottle *one drop* at a time while swirling the mixing bottle. Have the students count each drop as you add it.

When you begin, the solution in the mixing bottle will be pink. Keep adding the titrant solution one drop at a time until the solution turns blue. The total hardness of the water in grains per gallon is equal to the number of drops of the titrant solution used. As each sample is tested, students should write down on their handouts the actual number of grains of hardness for that sample.

Back in the classroom, students can compare their predictions with the actual grains of hardness and write their experiment summary and their feelings about the experiment on the backs of their papers. This experiment generates a good deal of interest, especially since students have to collect their water samples before the experiment day. (See Figure A8-15 in the appendix for an experiment/activity synopsis suitable for the scientific process.)

To summarize, be knowledgeable and prepared for your science lessons. Present scientific skills, concepts, and information in many different, exciting forms. Guide the students in the art of discovery. Have them write what took place in their activity and what they learned. Plan one or two science field trips. Evaluate relatively small segments, and keep assessments demonstration based.

If you want to hold a science fair during the year, go back to Chapter 2, The DEF's, for all the information and forms. This can create real excitement in any classroom.

RESEARCH AND STUDIES

Willerman and MacHarg (1991) designed an interesting study on using a **concept map** as an **advance organizer** or graphic organizer for science projects. Instead of having the students make their own concept maps, science students in the experimental group copied the teacher-constructed concept map from overhead transparencies while the teacher explained it. Students thus had very detailed maps. Each student's map was checked for accuracy. The map was done in a *hierarchical* manner (that is, subconcepts were listed under more general concepts) at the beginning of the unit.

The control group received an introductory lesson, a discussion of objectives of the unit, and several questions to act as motivators. Scores on the teacher-made achievement tests, which were multiple-choice, fill-in-the-blank, and true-false type questions, were significantly higher for the experimental group. This study was done with eighth-grade science students; however, it appears to show the importance of using a teacher-directed graphic organizer with material that is hierarchical. This pertains to science units at the elementary as well as at the middle-school level.

It is important to keep abreast of the latest studies to incorporate interesting and varied techniques into your science curriculum.

SPEAKING

Thou art a scholar; speak to it, Horatio.

Hamlet
William Shakespeare (1564–1616)

Speaking is another area of integrated language arts. Good speaking skills help students progress in reading, writing, and listening. Students need to be able to talk about what they know and what they are learning.

Informal Speaking

Students have many opportunities during the school day to practice informal speaking. They may be discussing with a partner something they both just finished reading. They may be in a group brainstorming for ideas on what to put into a play about a little lost bunny. Or they may be conversing with their friends on the playground during lunch period.

Even during times of informal speech, it helps students to practice speaking grammatically correctly. If they are consistently corrected by teachers and peers, pretty soon they begin to correct themselves. Eventually, the mistakes disappear:

No more double negatives: "I don't have no field trip permission slip today."
No more incorrect personal pronouns: "Me and my family went to the library on Saturday."
No more incorrect irregular verb forms: "I brung/brang my puppet to school on Tuesday."

When students speak correctly, it is easier for them to write correctly.

Storytelling is an art that allows students to motivate their classmates to work harder and more successfully in the areas of reading, writing and listening. If a student is telling the story *Three Billy Goats Gruff*, he will have to spend time practicing at home. The student could be expressive and dramatic and use different voices. Maybe he will have a little stuffed billy goat to hold while making the presentation.

Other students will then be motivated to read or reread that book. They might want to write a different ending to the story or draw a picture and write a caption to go with their favorite part of the story or with their new ending.

Storytelling can be used informally, too. The reading strategy of "popcorn" can be applied. In this technique, one student begins by making up a story. When she says popcorn and a classmate's name, that student continues making up the story until he says popcorn and another student's name. As an alternative to making up a story, popcorn storytelling could be used for the retelling of a story read in class.

Storytelling can be used with history or science just as easily. One student begins telling about a period of time or an event being studied in history. After popcorn and name, the called-upon student tells something else about that period or elaborates upon the commentary of the first student. In science, one student can begin telling about the materials needed for a science experiment or activity. Then popcorn, name, and the called-upon student continues to describe the materials or begins to describe the actual experiment, and so on.

Formal Speaking

Besides the many informal experiences, students need opportunities in the classroom for formal speaking. The more opportunities they have and the more they understand about good preparation, the easier it becomes for them to speak to the class.

If students are being evaluated during their speech, they must understand the evaluation criteria. What is meant by posture and poise? Explain this thoroughly and give a demonstration. Tell your students about eye contact and show them what it looks like. Explain why their voices need to be loud and clear. Give demonstrations of weak, soft voices so that students can easily understand the problem.

Students who give speeches, need to speak for an adequate amount of time. Be sure the students know the time frame for each speech they give. Last, the students must be well prepared. This requires time spent at home. Explain carefully the topic of each speech. Give suggestions as to subtopics to be covered. If students need to complete interviews, do research, or get materials to prepare for the speech, be sure they are given an adequate amount of time. Figure A7-7 in the appendix is a sample **speaking evaluation form** you may use with your class.

Giving Speeches

Sometimes students give reports to the class, like student council reports, reports on what was accomplished in their group discussion, and so on. Other times, though, students will give presentations that require outside preparation.

Students are much more at ease and confident when giving a report if they are holding something—not notes, but some object related to their report or something to be used in their report. Even pictures help, but be sure to explain to the students that any picture used must be large enough to be easily seen by the whole class or one that can be passed around the class. Give a few demonstrations to the students on how to show a picture to the whole class so that they clearly understand how it is done. Often, it is a good idea to have some of the students sit on the floor and some at their desks to enable everyone to see comfortably.

You might decide to borrow the megaphone from the office on the day of speeches. A student helper can hold the megaphone while the student giving the report holds the mike. Teach the helpers not to point the megaphone toward the student speaker and teach the speakers how to correctly speak into a mike to prevent feedback. The use of a megaphone ensures an enjoyable experience for all.

If you select high-interest topics for speeches, the students will be excited to give their speeches and will be interested in listening to all the others, too. A two-minute time allotment (except for demonstration speeches, which take longer) moves the speaking period along nicely and maintains student interest.

The following selections make good, interesting speeches:

- Have students hold mystery objects behind their backs. After they describe the object to the class, they ask the other students to raise their hands if they know what it is. If they call on three students and no one guesses correctly, they tell the class what their mystery object is. Students should not show their objects to any students out on the playground before school. Otherwise, some students in the class might already know what the mystery object is before the report.
- Have students demonstrate to the class how to do something. Examples: how to cook something (bring a small playhouse cooking oven), how to do origami, how to take care of a rabbit, how to make a model of something, and so on.
- Have students dress up as historical characters. They should tell the class three interesting things about the character's childhood and several interesting things about the character's adult life. For what is the character famous? Have students use the first person for their reports.
- Have students draw full-length pictures of a character in a book they have read on body-sized pieces of butcher paper. Then they cut a hole for their head to stick through. While standing behind the butcher paper and putting their head through the hole, students tell the class the title and author of their book. They then tell what their character does in the story. Have them use first person for this report.
- Have students bring items related to their hobbies to class and tell about them.

Figure 7-6. This student has drawn a character from a book she has read. Now she is putting her own face through the head hole in the butcher paper and reporting to the class on her character. She uses first person for her report.

- Have students show and tell the class about a report they did on a city, state, country, animal, and so on. They should tell a minimum of five interesting things, and show and explain any pictures and graphs.
- Have students show and explain their science fair projects to the class.
- Have students draw a favorite sports hero on the overhead projector. They should bring an item that has something to do with that person or sport, then tell who the person is, three interesting things about the person, and why that person is famous in sports.
- Have students describe someone at your school. They should say three things about that person's physical appearance and at least five things about what the person likes and does. Remind them to say nothing derogatory about the person. The class has three chances to guess correctly.
- Have students use their history or science books or the encyclopedia to find some information they think will be of interest to the class. They should have visuals to go with their speeches. (If students speak on a science or history topic currently being studied, these speaking activities can add a good deal of depth to the study and provide students with the opportunity of hearing and seeing this material over and over again.)
- Have students draw something on the overhead projector that is simple to draw but that will be hard for the class to guess. They should use two or three different colored overhead pens. Stick to dark-colored inks: blues, greens, blacks. They then say ten things about their drawing, and the class has three guesses to get it right. It is helpful to give seven or eight students their transparencies in advance so that

they can draw their pictures. Then that group of speeches will run through quickly and smoothly. Have two students assigned to wash the transparencies. Then give another group their transparencies. Let them do their drawings, and so on.

All of these assignments give the students excellent formal speaking opportunities and make for an interesting, exciting day.

STUDENT RESPONSIBILITIES

Students who are assigned various helping chores in the classroom can develop a good sense of responsibility. In addition to regular chores, having a classroom animal for the students to take turns caring for is a real responsibility builder. You might decide, for example, besides the students' other chores, to have a rabbit in your classroom. Besides learning about this animal and seeing it in action, students can begin to appreciate the care it needs on a daily basis. Each weekend or school holiday, students can take turns being responsible for having their parents take the rabbit home for them so it can receive proper care.

Assign the following responsibilities to students at any elementary level to help your classroom run very efficiently. Tell your students:

1. Have markers, colored pencils, or crayons for art projects and for science, health, reading, and history drawings.
2. Keep two or three pencils in your desk. They can be sharpened first thing in the morning. This eliminates distractions with pencil sharpening during the rest of the

day. If a pencil breaks or gets dull, just use one of your other ones.
3. Have a binder or folder for organization so that your papers are not lost.
4. Be sure the correct mark is made by your name on the assignment chart when you turn in any assignment.
5. Copy homework and behavior information into your composition book correctly and completely. Bring your composition book home each night so your parents can see it. When notices are sent home, place them inside your composition book, get a parent signature if necessary, and return everything to school the next day.
6. Try your hardest—study hard for all tests and quizzes; complete all assignments, activities, and projects; and have no marks on the behavior chart during the week.

Above all else, the foremost student responsibility is to get an education and not leave school without it. Some students think school is something forced on them, so they resist getting educated and do not want to work. Therefore, take whatever time it requires to help students see that an education is something they have to "get." They need to want it, to see value in it, to go after it. Nobody is going to hold their pencil for them or get into their minds and make them listen. It is something they do for themselves with the help of others. When students understand this, they become more involved, more interested, more productive. They see school as their opportunity to learn academic and social skills that they will need and use for the rest of their lives.

STUDENT TEACHERS AND BEGINNING TEACHERS

This section discusses the challenges and responsibilities of student teachers and first-year teachers. Strategies are given to make both of these experiences productive and successful.

Student Teachers

What are a student teacher's responsibilities?

First, be prompt in arriving at your assigned classroom. Come well dressed and nicely groomed. Speak in a clearly heard voice and check that your printing or handwriting on the chalkboard, overhead, or chart is neat and easily seen. Come with a will-learn, can-do, can't-wait-to-get-at-it attitude!

Learn how the master teacher's classroom control plan operates so that you can continue with it when you are in the classroom.

Study the class routine. Learn the class schedule so that you can follow it as much as possible. Also learn the homework policies, since you will need to follow these, too. Observe the master teacher doing the opening exercises, recess preparation, lunch preparation, and dismissal activities. How are the attendance sheet markings done? How is lunch count done? Is some part of the daily bulletin read to the students? How are miscellaneous announcements handled? Do some students go home for lunch and others stay on campus, or does everyone eat lunch at school? What about school buses? How many are there? Who rides them? What about safety drills? What are the

Figure 7-7.   Students are curious and fascinated by animals in the classroom. They learn to observe, love, and care for the animal, which helps increase self-esteem as well as develop student responsibility. Courtesy of Essa, *Introduction to Early Childhood Education,* © 1992 by Delmar Publishers, Inc.

procedures for a fire drill, a take cover drill, and an evacuation drill? What do you do during these drills? What are the policies for collecting, correcting, and recording assignments?

Study the master teacher's lesson plan book to visualize what the students have already studied this year and what special activities they have done. Study the lesson plan book for the first couple of weeks of the school year to see how the teacher got started. Question your master teacher about this so that you have some concrete ideas about what to do. Take notes to refer to later.

Next, study the students. Who goes to special classes, such as **speech therapy,** ESL, or LD, and what are they learning in those classes? Which students seem to struggle in certain areas? Which students seem especially bright? Which students are easily distracted? Which students seem to present a discipline problem? Who is friends with whom? In general, how do the students seem to get along with each other? Are there tutors in the class who go out to other classes? To which ones do they go and in what way do they help there? When do the students go to the library and the computer lab? What kind of activities do the students enjoy at recess and lunch period? Are there after-school activities on the campus? What are they and who goes to them? Do some of the students go to day care? What do they do there?

Study the campus. Where is the library, the computer lab, the speech therapy room, and the LD rooms? Are there any SDC classes on the campus? If so, what are these classes for and who goes to them? Ask your master teacher whether you may visit these rooms to experience first hand what their operation is like. Is there a day-care center. If so, where is it and what are its hours?

Attend faculty meetings with your master teacher and go to yard duty, too. It will give you some good perspective to go to a teachers' association meeting as well as a school board meeting.

All of this will help you with this student-teaching assignment as well as give you broad, valuable information about the field of education.

Student teaching is very hard, but exciting work. A lot of planning, discussing, and evaluating needs to be done with your master teacher. Many papers need correcting. Lessons must be taught, and discipline problems need to be dealt with effectively. Helping the students individually, in small groups, and as a total class is on your "to do" list. Assisting students with both academic and social skills is necessary. Students will have personal problems, too, and you can be a good listener for them.

Blueprint for Effective Teaching

Figure A7-8 in the appendix is a **Blueprint for Effective Teaching** that student teachers and beginning teachers can use for any and every lesson. Follow it and your lessons are *guaranteed* to be successful! Study it very carefully. Notice that each step begins with an *action* word: ready, set, teach, listen and watch, assign, monitor, check, review, evaluate, and record. Do all of these for a lesson, and you are in business.

When you are ready to begin preparing for your first lesson, follow the steps on the Blueprint. Have all your materials *ready*. Plan to move around the classroom and encourage stu-

dent participation. Ask your master teacher to critique your lesson plan; then, incorporate any suggestions.

When you are ready to begin teaching your first lesson, be sure you *set* the students. This is so important. You can have great ideas and material, but if the students are not set in good behavior with a frame of reference from which to operate, focused on why the learning is important and what they will be expected to do, when you get ready to *teach,* the lesson will not go anywhere near as well as you would like. You could end up feeling frustrated and discouraged instead of thrilled and speechless!

Do a self-evaluation when you are completely finished with the lesson. How did it go? What parts went extremely well? What were problem areas? How can they be resolved? Did the students understand the follow-up assignment, and were they able to complete it?

Next, meet with your master teacher to go over the lesson. Listen to all comments. Ask for any clarification you need to fully understand what to do.

Be sure that the assignment you gave the students is corrected, discussed, and returned. If individuals had problems, meet with them for reteaching.

Then begin planning your next lesson. Soon, besides individual lessons, you will begin long-term planning. Maybe you will have a three-day science lesson or a two-week history project. Always get your lesson plans critiqued by your master teacher well before the lesson and follow the Blueprint for Effective Teaching. Evaluate yourself after each lesson. Then ask your master teacher for an evaluation.

It can be very beneficial to you to ask a trusted friend or your master teacher to videotape you teaching a lesson. Have the focus be on you. Then critique it later. Check your voice, sayings, and expressions. How is the lesson's pace? How are the clarity and understandability? Ask your master teacher to help you with this.

It can also be helpful to do a videotape during your lesson that focuses on the students rather than you. When you critique the tape, ask your master teacher for help again. If there are problems, what suggestions does the master teacher have for improvement?

Beginning Teachers

What additional responsibilities does a beginning teacher have?

If you follow the instructions in this book for preparing and presenting lessons, meeting student needs, classroom management, duties, paperwork, and meetings, you will do fine. You should be aware, though, of some legal matters.

Conduct business in a professional, ethical manner. If you are suspicious of child abuse, it is your duty to report your suspicions to child protection services. If you are meeting with a student during recess, lunch, or before or after school, it is advisable to leave your classroom door open to protect yourself from any charges, false though they may be, and to protect your career.

Even when you conduct yourself in an impeccable manner, you still may find yourself charged with some offense. It happens.

In the event that you are charged with an offense, the single most important thing you can do is to *not* speak with *any* police officer or investigator, regardless of whether the charges are outrageous. What you say can later be used against you. You may be nervous, flabbergasted, or angry and say things that are harmful, things you may later regret.

What *should* you do in the face of any charges? Contact your teachers' association *immediately* and get an attorney. Liability insurance is provided for you through your state teachers' association. It is hoped that you will never need to do this, but it is always better to be knowledgeable about the justice system before any personal need.

Returning to a more joyous topic, know ahead of time that classes can *love* student teachers and beginning teachers. Be prepared. Be enthusiastic. You will be a winner.

RESEARCH AND STUDIES

McInnis (1990) found in her first year of contract teaching that student teaching and professional teaching were quite different from each other. Such areas as how many minutes were to be devoted to the various curriculum areas to fulfill state requirements, curriculum objectives to be addressed at each grade level to adhere to district policies, grading policies of the district, and so on had not been addressed during student teaching. McInnis's biggest problem was her fear of appearing weak, unprepared, unskilled, and not up to the job if she asked for help, which she desperately needed. In her college training she was infused with a lot of theory, but not much practicality. She finally convinced herself that asking for help was a sign of strength.

McInnis established folders for all of her students in which she kept student papers and parent communications. This provided good **documentation** for parent meetings or child studies. The need for documentation was another area that had not been addressed in her student-teacher training.

Beginning teachers need to know all of the following: how to order audiovisual materials for their district, the criteria for their observations and evaluation, a teacher on the same staff who can be approached for guidance and direction, the practices regarding parent-teacher conferences, and effective, practical discipline programs that work with real students. Beginning teachers should have as light a load as possible to enable them to make the transition from student teacher to professional teacher and to help them maintain their enthusiasm.

An article by Huling-Austin (1992) discusses implications of findings from research on learning to teach and how they might be applied to teacher induction practices and programs. This report urges a beginning of the process of bridging the two independent, yet closely related fields of inquiry (teacher induction and learning to teach) that have potential for improving teacher induction and mentoring programs.

In the fall of 1990, a teacher education faculty group at Southwest Texas State University reviewed more than eighty studies of learning to teach in order to integrate findings into the university's teacher education program. The article is based on the Huling-Austin's work in that program looking for applications to teacher induction and mentoring programs and practices.

This research supports induction practices that include assigning a mentor teacher and allowing the beginning teacher to observe as well as to be observed. Other approaches that the author suggested include: the use of cohort groups for beginning teachers, the use of a *differentiated evaluation system* (one for beginning teachers, another for advanced), and the inclusion of new content in mentor teacher programs, such as schema theory, how to use case studies, and conducting discussions about subject matter.

A number of practices that frequently are used with beginning teachers were called into question in this article, such as giving novice teachers assignments involving multiple teaching preparations, classes out of their areas of expertise, and demanding extracurricular responsibilities. It was suggested that these practices not only increase stress but also hinder the process of learning to teach.

Another study was done by the Teacher Evaluation Committee of the Association of Childhood Education International in 1992 and 1993. This group found that successful elementary school teachers need to have knowledge of the general elementary school curriculum, as well as a strong foundation in educational psychology and development, and opportunities to examine and implement good teaching/learning practices through professional and field experiences; consequently, teacher preparation programs should include the following subjects: general education, elementary education foundations, child development, the learning/teaching process, curriculum and methodology, and clinical/field experience.

To be able to optimally expand children's abilities to grow and develop in all areas, teacher preparation programs must have a broad foundation in many academic areas, with advanced study in at least one area of specialty. Preparation experiences, therefore, should develop in preservice elementary school teachers the abilities to comprehend, analyze, synthesize, and evaluate a wide range of published materials; the ability to communicate with people from diverse backgrounds, both orally and in writing; and the ability to teach with understanding, skill, and confidence a broad range of academic subjects.

Teacher preparation programs should design experiences that help preservice elementary teachers understand the historical, philosophical, psychological, cultural, and social foundations of elementary education.

Through experiences with children of different ages, cultural and linguistic backgrounds, and exceptionalities, preservice elementary teachers should learn how to provide optimal learning experiences that will help children grow intellectually, emotionally, socially, physically, and creatively.

Teachers should be familiar with and keep up with current research findings on the teaching-learning process and be able to apply these findings in the classroom.

Preservice elementary teachers must be generalists, with study and experiences in all areas of the curriculum, and they should be prepared to organize and implement a variety of proven methods of instruction. They should have gradually increased responsibilities in the classroom and be provided with opportunities to work with children at different grade levels with varying backgrounds, capabilities, and activities. Also, preservice teachers should be allowed to critically select and use appropriate materials, resources, and technology and to have experience with classroom management and a variety of evaluation techniques.

Hawkins (1991) describes an evaluation of two Montgomery County Public Schools' induction programs for newly hired elementary school teachers. The evaluation was conducted to see how well these two programs met their goals, which were to ease the entrance of new teachers into the profession, and to develop and retain quality teachers.

Teachers only participated in one of the two programs, so comparisons between the two programs are merely indirect.

In February 1990, a survey was mailed to every 1989–90 newly hired teacher, approximately 600 teachers. The survey was returned by 442 teachers. Seventy-two percent of respondents were in the Teacher Consultant Program (TCP), 5 percent in the Local School Support Team (LSST), and 23 percent were in neither induction program, but were more experienced than the others.

In June 1990, a second survey was mailed to all first- and second-year teachers participating in the Local School Support Team (LSST) program. The teachers in this program participated in induction activities for two years. Thirty-seven teachers returned the survey (88% response rate).

A survey was also mailed to all colleague and consultant teachers in June 1990. All 39 of the colleague teachers and 81 of the 87 consultant teachers returned the survey.

Personnel records were reviewed for those new teachers who left Montgomery County Public Schools during the 1989–90 school years to calculate retention rates.

LSST matches the new teacher with a colleague teacher in the same school building for a two-year period. TCP matches several first-year teachers with a teacher consultant in another school building. TCP operates in all non-LSST schools. Colleague teachers generally work with one new teacher; consultant teachers generally work with a team of between three and five new teachers.

Colleague teachers give direct assistance to new teachers, since they are right next door. Consultant teachers, on the other hand, give indirect assistance, because new teachers have to leave their school buildings for meetings or telephone the consultant teacher. Participants in the LSST program met more often than those in TCP.

More than 70 percent of the colleague teachers had observed their new teachers teach and conferred with them about their teaching, compared to less than 20 percent of the consultant teachers. Fifty-three percent of colleague teachers said their new teachers observed other teachers, compared to 29 percent of consultant teachers.

The number of teachers demonstrating their techniques and strategies to their new teachers was high in both programs (84% for consultants, 79% for colleagues).

New teachers in the LSST program relied on their mentors to a greater extent than those in TCP.

Sixty-seven percent of the new teachers in LSST responded that they "strongly agreed" that their colleague teacher was a valuable resource, compared to only 48 percent of new teachers in TCP. Assistance provided in curriculum issues, room arrangement, district policies, back-to-school night, and parent-teacher conferences were rated highest.

Benefits of an induction program for the school included improved teamwork, better instruction, and a well-organized curriculum, according to the mentor teachers. For the colleague and consultant teachers, benefits from participation in the induction program included an opportunity to get new ideas and to learn new techniques and approaches to instruction from teachers who just came out of college.

There was no difference between the two programs in the rate of teachers leaving. Teachers who did not participate in the program left at a slightly higher rate than those in the induction programs.

One study (Brookhart & Rusnak, 1993) was undertaken to identify the characteristics of a successful urban teacher in order to offer illustrations and specific examples to student teachers.

For this study, the Pittsburgh Public Schools English Division director recommended twelve secondary school English teachers from throughout the district. Eight of them were interviewed for the study; six were white, two were black, and six were female, two were male. The teachers were interviewed at their schools about one lesson they taught recently that they considered successful and then were asked several questions.

The following is a list of characteristic student reactions that signaled the teachers that their lessons were successful: participation in class, volunteering, good or improved performance on tests or projects, thinking of class as being fun, understanding, giving complete and specific answers, doing original work, remaining on task, realizing the importance of the material, changing their views or attitudes about learning, not wanting to leave when class ends, putting in time and effort, trying their best, asking for feedback from the teacher, showing initiative, giving information, questioning basic ideas, changing thinking, giving as well as taking criticism, and applying knowledge in future assignments.

Some of the lessons described by the teachers were related to the Pittsburgh Research-based Instructional Supervisory Model (PRISM), a model of instruction that the Pittsburgh Public Schools teach through staff development. Teachers characterized their classes with phrases such as student-centered lessons, explicit connections between students' lives and the material being taught, giving and receiving feedback, mutual respect between teacher and students, emphasizing modeling, enthusiasm from the teacher, academic goals that are both broad and stated explicitly, higher order thinking, and students having a sense that the material is important.

These teachers were more likely to plan more thoroughly before class, to use more modeling, to be less spontaneous about teaching as far as changing a lesson during class, and to allow the students' socioeconomic status to affect their treatment of the students less than expected by the researchers.

Metcalf and Cruickshank (1991) sought to show that there is a relationship between teacher clarity and the achievement of students, and that preservice teachers can be taught clarity.

Preservice teachers participated in the Clarity Training Program (CTP), which had three major goals: establishing specific training objectives, developing cognitive understanding of the

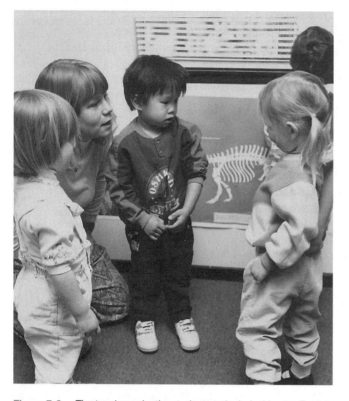

Figure 7-8. The teacher asks the students to include this non-English-speaking student in their play so that he will feel at home in the class and accepted by the others. The teacher also assigns this new student a partner to help him during the day. Courtesy of Essa, *Introduction to Early Childhood Education,* © 1992 by Delmar Publishers, Inc.

Figure 7-9. Young students enjoy reading aloud, and up close, to their teacher, aides, or volunteer. Courtesy of Essa, *Introduction to Early Childhood Education,* © 1992 by Delmar Publishers, Inc.

required skills, and developing skills performance. The study was carried out with juniors and seniors in education at Ohio State University.

Teachers were observed and rated on their use of low-inference behaviors, moderate-inference behaviors, and their overall level of clarity. Low-inference behaviors included: adequately answering students' questions, teaching lessons in a step-by-step fashion, giving enough examples of how to do the material, presenting material in a logical fashion, and sufficiently informing the students of the lesson's objectives and what they should be able to do by the end of the lesson. Moderate-inference behaviors included: stressing what parts of the lesson were important, explaining the content, assessing the students' understanding of material, allowing students to digest material, and explaining better or going more in-depth when a topic was not understood.

The results of the study showed that teachers can be trained to present material more clearly and when they do, they produce more student learning than do untrained teachers. On the other hand, clarity-trained teachers were not shown to increase student satisfaction.

Many schools today are increasing their standards for admission to their teacher education programs. One study (Heller & Clay, 1993) examined whether increasing standards produced better teachers. The criteria examined in this study were: years of experience; grade point average; Professional Knowledge, General Knowledge, Communication Skills, and

Specialty Area scores on the NTE; SAT English and Math scores; and high school class rank.

This study showed that these variables were not good predictors of teacher effectiveness, a result that agrees with other previous research in this area. As another study concluded, "We are essentially without any reliable predictors of who will or will not be good teachers" (Schalock, 1988, p. 8).

Heller and Clay's study offered a couple of explanations for this conclusion. First, using these standards made the group of teachers more homogeneous, and thus it is harder to distinguish among them by using the variables used in this study. Perhaps these variables are not the most important predictors of teacher effectiveness after all. Some researchers believe that personality, not cognitive ability is the best predictor of teacher success. That being said, low scores in areas such as reading, writing, and mathematics will almost surely lead to ineffective teaching (Conklin, 1985). So, although high scores in these areas are not the best predictors of teacher effectiveness, they are still helpful in determining whether a teacher will be successful.

Although the last study mentioned here concentrated on secondary education rather than elementary, it is still of interest. It compared the teaching efficacy of experienced teachers with that of preservice teachers to see whether their effectiveness was related to their beliefs about their ability to teach (Benz, Bradley, Alderman, & Flowers, 1992).

The subjects of this study were students just entering secondary teacher-education, students already in secondary education courses, secondary student teachers, practicing secondary school teachers, faculty of teacher education, and student-teaching supervisors who were not part of a college faculty.

The results of the study showed that the classroom teachers had a lower perceived efficacy than either preservice teachers or those on the college faculty. This was perhaps due to college teachers being more distant from the day-to-day classroom. Preservice teachers may have been more naive, with preconceived ideas about how children interact, motivation, and the like. Perhaps practicing teachers had not received any motivational training. In planning and evaluation, however, more experienced teachers were shown to be more effective. According to the researchers, an important goal of teacher education programs should be helping preservice teachers develop beliefs that will improve their classroom decision making.

It is important to remember that teaching and learning always occur across the curriculum. A large amount of information throughout this book has focused on various teaching strategies. The second section of this chapter will give you some additional details on the complexities of the teaching-learning process, with some special information about kindergarten and two concrete techniques to use for success.

TEACHING-LEARNING PROCESS

The ideal condition
Would be, I admit, that men should be right by instinct;
But since we are all likely to go astray,
The reasonable thing is to learn from those who can teach.

Sophocles, c. 495–406 B.C.
Antigone [c. 442 B.C.]

Teaching in Kindergarten

Kindergarten is like no other class. It is best to overplan and have lots of alternatives, especially in the beginning of the year when you are getting to know your class and its skills. You never know for sure just what you are going to see the first few days. Have lots of visuals and hands-on activities, like puppets, pictures, and nursery rhyme videos. You may have some **NEP (Non-English-Proficient)** students to deal with and these types of activities are very helpful and more familiar and comforting to them.

Alternate active times with quiet-time activities. Students can look at pictures in age-appropriate books. They can tell one another what they think is happening in the picture. Students can take turns sitting with the teacher, a volunteer, an aide, or an older student to page through a book and to tell what they see. It is a nice idea, too, in kindergarten, to have one special paper or project the students can take home each day to give to their parents.

It is important to teach safety rules to students in all grades but especially to the kindergartners. They need to learn to stay with an adult supervisor from the time they arrive each morning until they are picked up by their parents, safely aboard the bus, or dismissed to walk home.

In kindergarten, art is coordinated with stories and music. For example, you might read a *Winnie the Pooh* story, teach his song, and have your students make a cutout Pooh that can be fastened with brads so that it moves. Several days may be used in such a project. Students can be drawing their own pictures and dictating stories about Pooh and his friends. This may be your students' first experience of beginning to understand written communication.

Any hands-on materials allow young students to visualize and explore. For example, when they are finger painting or coloring, they can be learning the primary colors and which colors mix together to form another color. Measurement and cooking are great combination lessons, too.

Kindergartners will face these more advanced skills in later years:

1. Ordering: largest to smallest, beginning to end, and so on
2. Classifying: grouping items together according to similarities and giving the group a label or name, or being presented with labels and sorting through items and placing them appropriately
3. Challenging concepts: Would this figure still be a rectangle if we did such and such to it? or Would this character still be considered compassionate if she did such and such a thing?

Figure 7-10. Hands-on materials help young students explore, visualize, and share their discoveries. Courtesy of Charlesworth, *Understanding Child Development*, 3e, © 1992 by Delmar Publishers Inc.

4. Determining cause and effect: What happened first and is a reason for other occurrences? and What are the direct results?

5. Drawing conclusions and inferring: After reading three things that a story character does, telling how that character feels

6. Predicting: Based on what they have read so far, what do students think is going to happen next?

But, it all starts in kindergarten!

How to Start the Teaching-Learning Process

Ask yourself the following four questions to get started at the beginning of the year:

1. *Where* are your students in the development of their academic and social skills?
2. *How* do they learn?
3. *What* do you want your students to know?
4. *When* have they learned it?

Prepare and teach from these points of reference. Then you will have lessons appropriate to your students: challenging, but not impossible; **multimodal** oriented, not totally visual or auditory; focused toward an attainable goal, not sidetracked on many tangents; aware when appropriate learning has occurred, neither belaboring material nor moving on before understanding and confidence have been secured.

1. Where Are Your Students?

You do not have to give an elaborate pretest to your students to get a good idea of where they are. Put a few questions or problems on the board and walk around watching while the students attempt to solve them. Have the class read a story aloud. Call on students. Listen to them read. Ask each student one or two questions about the material she or he reads. Ask students to write one or two sentences or a paragraph and walk around to see what they can do. At other times you might want to assess learning in a one-on-one situation. Then start wherever your students are and begin to build from there.

2. How Do They Learn?

The basic three modalities of learning are **visual, auditory,** and **kinesthetic.** Some students have a strong preference for one; some students use two, off and on; and some students use all three most of the time. Visual clues could be such sayings as: I see. Get the picture? Auditory clues could be: Am I hearing you right? It doesn't sound right to me. Kinesthetic clues can be: It feels good. It tickles me. Get a hold of that. Get a grip on it. Latch on to it.

In your classroom, you will undoubtedly have students using all of these modalities, so be sure to incorporate them into your lessons. Watch for students who are learning primarily through *one* mode. You will have to devote some extra attention to them, especially if the mode is totally auditory. Make sure to repeat enough times aloud for these students to understand what to do. Spend a little extra time if you have students with learning disorders, as you probably will, either individually or as a small group, getting them started on the assign-

Figure 7-11.   This teacher assesses his student's entry-level knowledge during an individual conference. Courtesy of Charlesworth, *Understanding Child Development*, 3e, © 1992 by Delmar Publishers Inc.

ment. Double-check that they have the learning. Teach them to **compensate** by trying extra hard and having an assigned buddy to go to when they get stuck on something. This helps foster more independence for these students and helps with their self-confidence, too.

Students learn by being taught to think critically. How can they take new material, mix it with knowledge they already have, and come up with something slightly different?

Figure 7-12.   This student is a strong auditory learner. The teacher makes adjustments in her style to accommodate all the learning modalities. Courtesy of Essa, *Introduction to Early Childhood Education,* © 1992 by Delmar Publishers, Inc.

Figure 7-13. Although it may not look like it, this is a whole-class lesson. The students all face the teacher for the first set of instructions. Then they practice the learning with their partner and help teach each other. Then they face the teacher again for the next step in the learning and so on. This gives the teacher time to walk around and meet with students in pairs, too.

Make sure to teach at all the levels of the taxonomy, to mesh the higher-order thinking skills of analyzing, judging, drawing conclusions, and recommending with the lower-level thinking skills of recalling and listing. Ask the students what they notice, what they remember, in what way things are the same, and how they are different. Ask students to predict what might happen next in a story. Ask them how they figured out an answer. Asking these types of questions helps produce sharp thinkers.

Following is an example of Bloom's taxonomy (Bloom, 1968) with some sample questions so that you are sure you deal with all the levels.

Classification Name	*Example*
1. Knowledge (remembering or recall)	1. List the four . . . Who discovered . . .?
2. Comprehension (understanding)	2. Explain . . . Give evidence for . . .
3. Application (solving, making use of the known)	3. What might happen . . .? What other possibilities . . .?
4. Analysis (taking apart the unknown)	4. Which are facts, which are opinions? Which parts of the story might not have really happened?
5. Synthesis (creating, putting together the new)	5. What would you do if . . .? Make up . . .
6. Evaluations (judging the outcome)	6. Recommend . . . Criticize . . . Which of the books would you say has the greatest value and why?

In addition to using all levels of the taxonomy, students will pay close attention if you incorporate their names into your lesson, as if they are a character in the lesson or as if you are speaking solely to them. Walk around the classroom; that keeps them on their toes, too.

Students are often motivated by the use of **mnemonic devices** such as HOMES for the five Great Lakes. They can use some part of their name or a hobby for an acronym. Some students find these fascinating and will remember this material very well years later.

Students will be motivated in areas they find interesting and challenging. Relate the learning to them personally by calling on them to share their experiences of being in similar circumstances themselves, or maybe a relative who has had a similar experience. Students are further motivated by being provided with high-interest follow-up assignments and receiving from you the directions such as the following: Now you *get* to do this writing assignment.

Your timing and pacing of the lesson, your confidence, your subject knowledge, and your feeling of warmth and understanding all relate to motivating the students. A whole-class or small-group lesson with a lively pace, good time management, and an enthusiastic teacher who knows the material is a winner. Students are curious and ask lots of questions. Be prepared and organized and have good classroom control. Focus on one thing at a time.

Just because you have something written in your lesson plan book does not mean you *have* to do it. Adjust the level of difficulty during a lesson if you see that the students are squirmy or in over their heads. They may even need an alternate activity.

3. What Do You Want the Students to Know?

You must first be *exactly* sure in your own mind of the learning. Have your lesson well prepared and all the materials

Figure 7-14. This teacher knows what she wants her students to discover and learn. Showing and doing are part of the teaching-learning process. Courtesy of Carroll Maietta.

right at hand. Follow the Blueprint for Effective Teaching step by step. Tell what the learning is or help students discover it so that they have a frame of reference from which to operate. For example, if you are presenting a three-day lesson, say, "Today we're going to do (such and such), tomorrow (such and such), and the following day (such and such)." Then students have a little blueprint in their minds of what they are doing, just as you have *your* own written blueprint.

Teach them the appropriate language to use for the skills. Anticipate areas that might cause problems, and have alternative teaching methods planned for those *before* you teach the lesson. This will be very difficult when you first start out. Jot notes to yourself in your lesson plan book by any lesson that had a part that stumped the students. Then you will be doubly prepared the next time.

Ask students to review the learning. Be sure they have it straight. Then, make sure your directions are clear. Repeat them yourself at least twice and write them on the chalkboard, overhead, or classroom chart. Ask three to five students to explain what they are to do. Right then, clear up any misconceptions. When students thoroughly understand what they are to do, they get right to work. Otherwise, you will see a lot of frustration. If so, stop the activity and go over the lesson again slowly. Ask the students to tell you exactly what they do not understand or what they need to know in order to do the follow-up assignment. Do more, maybe all, of the assignment together as a class until they get the idea. Then give them additional opportunities for practice the following day.

Give students homework. This provides the opportunity to get in more practice time for their skills and more work time for their projects and activities. Practice makes experts.

4. When Have Your Students Learned the Material?

Students need to be able to demonstrate in some way what they know. They can take a written test of the multiple-choice/true-false/**sentence completion** variety. This might be a teacher-made test or a publisher's test for the students' text. Either way, be sure students have a study sheet so that they are well prepared both for the content and for this particular testing mode.

If students are to take a regional, standardized test, they might need additional practice to understand the particular type of test format and some basic test-taking strategies. Such things as eliminating outrageous answers and deciding between two choices is a learned strategy. Knowing whether the particular test penalizes guesses is a learned strategy. Using a piece of construction paper as a marker for their answer keys to avoid writing answer 21 in the space for 22 is a learned test-taking strategy. If students do not know the answer at all and cannot eliminate, and it is a test where they can guess, choosing one of the middle answer bubbles is something they can learn to do.

Students may take a more demonstration-based regional test. These tests can include open-ended questions where students must explain the thinking process they used to figure out the answer for a math problem, such as a geoboard problem. Besides solving math problems and explaining how they did them in writing, students may have "grid-in" problems for which they use a grid answer sheet. The grid may include columns with options for decimal points and fraction lines as well as numbers one through nine and zero through nine. When using a grid answer sheet, if students do not know how to solve the problem at all, they are not going to guess the answer correctly.

In science, students may be asked to conduct an experiment and write the results. They may take an open-ended test in reading where they are required to write their thoughts and feelings on different parts of a story or show comparisons and contrasts or justify a recommendation. They may take a writing test in which they connect a reading story to an experience in their own lives.

Students may take a test in history that requires them to draw a map of a particular area of the world freehand. Then, they may write to answer one or more open-ended questions. Scaffolding may be provided with the questions to help focus the students. The scaffolding will usually be bulleted and be similar to the following for a question about the Declaration of Independence:

Be sure to include in your answer:

- The reason it was written
- What's said about the King of England
- Meaning of "being created equal"
- Importance of each colony signing

You need to make it very clear to your students that whoever will be correcting their tests does not know what they are thinking. Students must write *everything* on the test to clearly explain their answers, their thinking processes, and their feelings.

Marginalia, double entry journal, clusters, personal connection, open mind, quote, journal writing in science and math, written explanations of math problems, written summaries of science experiments, practice with drawing maps freehand, and responding to open-ended history questions with scaffolding will all help you provide your students with the types of experiences needed for success.

Besides *fully open-ended* questions, these tests may have *justified multiple-choice* questions. These are multiple-choice questions in which students must write in their own words why they selected a particular answer. They must describe their reasoning process in written form right on the test.

Enhanced multiple-choice questions are another variety that students might encounter on a regional test. They provide choices of answers and, normally, students do not have to write about their reasoning process, *but* the answer choices are usually very detailed and complex. Generally, students must know what they are doing to select the correct answer.

Sentence completion is another type of "semi" open-ended item. Students must have the knowledge and skills to write an answer that completes the sentence. Sentence completion is similar to the (fill-in-the-blank) type of question.

Your students may encounter *corrected true-false* items. In these types of items, when students decide a statement is false, they must write a correction to the item. This could involve writing just a word or as much as a phrase. Students need practice with this type of item to be alert to errors as they read.

Your students will need you to provide them plenty of opportunities throughout the year for these different testing modes in their everyday classroom tests. Then the regional test, whatever kind it is, will be a familiar situation for them.

Students can demonstrate their skill and knowledge in other ways besides written tests. They can do a project, build something, or do a report. They can give an oral presentation to the class or a small group.

In addition, students may assess themselves on their student portfolio evaluation forms, or they may assess each other by grading or making comments of strengths and weaknesses or listing areas for improvement.

Another way to demonstrate knowledge is to have students draw the answer to questions. Small graphics are good. Charts and graphs work well as does a large picture. This type of assessment gives excellent information and the students enjoy it because of its difference.

Use all these various teaching and testing techniques. They work with learning disabled, low-average, average, above-average, and gifted students. These techniques run the gamut and will keep your students sharp and on target.

Teaching Strategies and Modalities
Creating Learning Groups

Groups often go by a variety of names. They may be called **committees,** cooperative groups, **collaborative groups, corporate groups,** and so on. Groups will usually be part of your day.

Moving furniture and going to a new location in the classroom is an excellent and exhilarating break in between subjects. This facilitates a variety of grouping types: **random grouping, self-selected groups,** and groups appointed by you to increase certain students' social skills, to expose students with lower skills in a particular area to students with brilliance there, to pair a shy student with a more outgoing one, or to pair a popular student with a less popular one.

When students are working in a learning group, it is important that *each* student is accountable for learning. When the group gets together to work on a project, the students need to help each other accomplish the task so that all the members of the group have learned whatever they are assigned. Groups should ask themselves the two famous questions: How does it look? How does it sound? If their heads are supposed to be together conferring with each other, then "heads together" is how it looks. If they are in a read around, then one voice at a time reading with praising afterward is how it sounds.

When having the class work in learning groups on an activity or when giving a class assignment, give an adequate amount of time. It is very frustrating to get an assignment, get into it, and then have time called. Giving appropriate time also helps individuals and groups get the job done.

Did each member of the group contribute? What is the group's product? Is the product finished? Each individual and the group as a whole need to ask and answer these questions.

For example, the group may be formed to brainstorm for ideas on a writing assignment. What is the product? The list of ideas. Did each person contribute? Yes! The **group recorder** wrote initials by all the ideas after the list was composed. When one of the members initially had no contribution, the group waited for that student's new and different ideas and praised the student for the contribution. Is the product finished? Yes! The group list has a good amount of ideas; some have been crossed out as not functional or less desirable, the rest will be used for the project.

Figure 7-15. These students are working in a partnership to prepare for a science test. This is a real motivator for many students. The teacher needs to give clear directions about how to prepare for a test with a partner and what material should be covered. A time frame should be given and monitoring should be done to be sure the students stay on task. A total class oral review is a profitable follow-up to this type of activity.

Make copies for the students and that group is all ready to go to the second phase of the project: writing a first draft.

The product may not always be so clear-cut. Suppose the students are getting into groups of two or three to study for a science test. Now the product is less tangible, but still defined. The product is stronger learning in science in preparation for the test. This will be shown by students asking and answering each others' questions in a **round robin.** One student asks a question of the next. That one answers and asks a question of the next. The person in charge of recording information could write the key word in each question that is asked in that group. That format will get everyone participating. When is it finished? It is finished when the students have a good number of key words on their group's list and the students *feel* that they have a stronger knowledge of the material.

When you use this teaching strategy of learning groups, be sure the social as well as the academic skills are clearly defined by you and monitored by you as well as by the group. Then students will get right to their groups and get busy. When they have questions that cannot be solved by the group, have them raise their hands and you go to them rather than having them come to you. This greatly helps the productivity level of the class, because students stay working at their assigned locations.

While students are in their groups have them ask each other for clarification in their thinking. Both words and actions may be needed so that all students understand fully. Groups need some time to evaluate their social and academic skills at the end of a group meeting, too. Did the group members listen when one student was speaking and did they look at the speaker? Did group members stick with the assignment, or did they wander off and start talking about last night's TV shows?

Did they compliment each other when good ideas were given? Did they all stay at the physical location assigned to the group? Did everyone in the group participate? Did everyone *thank* each other for their participation?

Since groups will finish their work at different times, have something specific planned for those students that will keep them away from where the other groups are located. An activity on the class computer is excellent for a primary grade or a round of Geo Safari® is perfect for an upper grade.

Transfer and Link

Always teach for the transfer of learning. Teach students to add by starting with the bottom number, because that learning transfers to both subtraction and multiplication where they will begin with the bottom number. When you are teaching paragraph indentions, make the students aware that they will use this in letter writing, invitations, thank-you's, reports, and so on. Then they will be prepared to transfer this skill to the new situation.

Students need to link their new learning to the old and to their personal experiences. It is much easier to understand and remember new material when linking is done as a regular practice.

Listening to Writing

A good way to let students experience different, interesting styles of writing is to let the students read their writing projects to the class. This can be done a number of ways. Students can get into small groups of five and take turns reading their papers to the group. Then the group can select one to present to the class. You can always ask for volunteers to read their papers to the class. And, of course, you can read selected papers yourself to the class. This gives you the opportunity to tell the class to listen to a specific technique or style as you read aloud in an expressive way.

Figure 7-16. This girl has finished her group work and is back at the computer busy with her project. Courtesy of Charlesworth, *Understanding Child Development,* 3e, ©1992 by Delmar Publishers, Inc.

Students as Teachers

The students can also be in the role of teacher either as individuals or as part of a group. When they do their presentations, encourage them to use some kind of medium. Make them aware of the different ways in which students learn. Good teaching incorporates methods to accommodate all the modalities.

A Wanting and Nurturing Environment

The key to having a highly productive classroom is to provide an environment where the students *want* to learn, *want* to do assignments, *want* to achieve. Certain skills are not as exciting to learn as others, but they still have to be mastered. When you feel some class reluctance or lack of enthusiasm, is is time to institute a little contest or have the students work in pairs and

Figure 7-17. These students are transferring and applying their learning to the computer. Courtesy of Fred Porter.

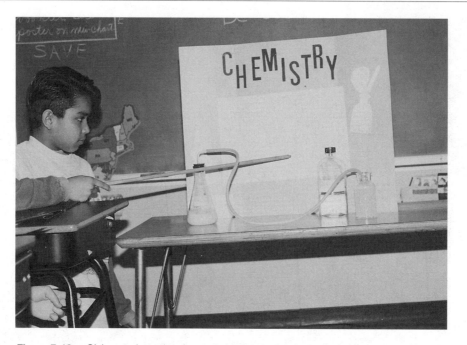

Figure 7-18.   Giving students the chance to be the teacher is a valuable experience for everyone. The rest of the students can practice their listening skills with their attention directed toward a classmate.

monitor each others' work. These are such simple things, but you will be amazed at the enthusiasm and energy they generate.

Prepare teaching units in history and science for your grade level. That way you will have good, high-interest lessons; specific skills, concepts, and knowledge for the students to attain; interesting and motivational assignments and projects; and appropriate, diverse assessments.

Summarize at end of each day. What did your students learn today? The major points of lessons can be reviewed at this time. Do not forget to recall learning of social skills, too.

How you feel about yourself and teaching has a major impact on running your classroom. Students learn best in a comfortable, positive environment. You are the one who sets the tone. If you feel any negativity or lethargy creeping around your room, make some quick, simple changes.

This would be a good time for a row or group contest. Get the class into six groups. Tell them the kind of math problem you are going to give, like division with one-digit divisors. Each group selects its representative to go to the chalkboard for the problem. The first person at the board who gets the

Figure 7-19.   This lesson captures students' interest. It makes them eager to participate and motivated to learn. Courtesy of Carroll Maietta.

Figure 7-20. Notice how this teacher has the students' interest and attention. A warm, caring approach is delightful to all. Courtesy of Walt Lazar.

answer correct gets her group checked to be sure everyone in the group at least worked on the problem. If so, give that section a tally. No student can go to the board more than two consecutive times. You could have a small prize for the top two sections. Run that in your class for a couple of days and your room will be energized!

When you think of your room, you want only positives to come to your mind: warmth, wonderful, well-behaved, and welcome. If you start feeling worn out or something other than wonderful, be willing to make whatever changes it takes to get back to feeling great again. Sometimes it is just more consistency in rule enforcement. Sometimes it is the introduction of a class puppet show, a play, a dance, or a song. Small changes can let you have a superb year.

Research and Studies

Hemisphericity is the term given to the functions of the different sides of the brain. The right hemisphere is oriented toward fine arts, creativity, fantasy, and the visual/spatial/musical processes. It deals with sensing and movement on the left side of the body. The left hemisphere is math, logic, speech, and language oriented. It deals with sensing and movement on the right side of the body. Even though the two cross over, some students are much more **right-brained** than their classmates; others are more **left-brained.**

From the *Wada test,* it is known that 95 percent of all right-handed people have speech/language in the left hemisphere, 5 percent in the right. In left-handers, 70 percent have speech/language in the left, 15 percent in the right, and 15 percent in both. But these **hemispheres** need to communicate back and forth through the **corpus callosum.** If there is early brain damage, the undamaged hemisphere will usually help.

Dendrites, along with soma, are receptors for messages so that the entire circuit link is made in the thinking process. A stimulating environment may be able to make up for some early damage here. A study was done by M. R. Rosenzweig

using rats to determine the effect of the environment on the brain (Bloom, 1985). The rats in the enriched environment had thicker **cerebral cortices** than the rats in isolation. This study was replicated sixteen times, every time with the same result. The enriched rats' dendrites had more spines, which serve as receivers in **synaptic contacts.** Neurons in the enriched rats' cerebral cortices grew in size and in the number of connections between them.

Myriad things, including environmental effects, affect the brain's **plasticity.** Take the word *lot.* Just think what the brain can do with this word, especially if it has had lots of enriching experiences. It can think of a play lot, a sand lot, a lot of something, one's lot in life, being chosen by lot, a plot of ground, someone's bad lot, "the lot," meaning the whole quantity, and Lot, Abraham's nephew who fled Sodom after being warned by two angels and whose wife looked back and was turned into a pillar of salt.

Karl Lashley did various experiments with **immediate memory,** the ability to recall a few items from passing scenery; **short-term memory,** the ability to store information for a few hours or days; and **long-term memory,** the ability to store information for a long period, including for life (Bloom, Lazerson, & Hofstadter, 1985).

Lashley tried to discover how memory is organized in the brain, but to no avail. His student, Donald Hebb, however, discovered that short-term memory left no permanent traces on the brain. By contrast, long-term memory left permanent traces, structural changes in the nervous system. Hebb thought these were caused by "*repeated* activation of a loop of neurons . . . [which] would cause the synapses between them to become functionally connected" (Bloom et al., 1985, p. 190).

The **hippocampus** is necessary to store long-term information. Remove a person's hippocampi and that person will have immediate and short-term memory only.

Chunking helps students remember more. In short-term memory, they can keep seven, plus or minus two, items. One item can be a letter or a number or a word. But if they chunk, one item can be an entire sentence or thought. For example, one chunk can be "*Every Good Boy Does Fine*/FACE." The italicized letters are the line names of a music staff and the letters in FACE are the space names in the staff.

In reading, first the reader **decodes** letter by letter, then word by word. Then one item eventually becomes a chunk of words at a time. Chunking facilitates good learning and memory.

A study by Engle, Carullo, and Collins (1991) sought to determine if the increased ability to follow complex directions with age is related to an increase in memory span. The study examined first-, third-, and sixth-graders by giving them word-span and reading-span assignments and then evaluating their reading comprehension (listening comprehension for first-graders) and their ability to follow directions given orally.

The results of the study showed that the word span of the students increased from first and third grades to sixth grade, but the sentence-span test showed all three groups were about equal in processing and recall levels. The researchers interpreted this finding by explaining that when processing (a component of working memory) is not varied, then working memory's functional storage capacity does not vary either, at least in the ages in this study. So, although students increase procedural proficiency, their *working memory* storage does not increase with age. The study further concluded that working memory is limited, probably to the activity of three or four knowledge structures at once. Chunking or grouping can increase the effective amount of information in working memory, especially if it is material with which students are familiar.

Teachers need be aware of this limitation on working memory and not give students directions with more than three or four propositions; nor should they use a lot of phonologically similar or confusing words. Finally, teachers should be aware that this capacity differs from individual to individual.

Placing students in learning groups is an area that needs a great deal of teacher attention. For some state testing, students are assigned randomly, which is something teachers cannot influence. But in your classroom, besides providing students with occasional opportunities with random grouping, it is important to establish learning groups where good, productive interaction will occur.

Battistich, Solomon, and Delucchi (1993) conducted a study that showed that students in learning groups with high-quality interaction helped each other, worked productively, and had positively correlated scores on standardized testing. Students in these groups liked school more, were more concerned for others, and had a good level of motivation.

In contrast, however, were students in groups with low-quality interaction. Outcomes were negatively associated with classroom environment, motivation, and standardized test scores. Their study showed that students with "low status" were often ignored or impugned, whereas those of "high status" were respected and admired regardless of positive or quality contributions to the group. Some learning groups bred resentment among members and some students felt that they did all the work while others engaged in **"social loafing"** (Battistich et al., 1993, p. 20). Success in group learning is related to the quality of the interpersonal interactions occurring within the group.

This study used 18 fourth- through sixth-grade classrooms in the San Francisco Bay Area in California. One district was suburban and middle and upper-middle class. The other was urban with a minority (primarily Hispanic) population of 50 to 70 percent, many Limited-English-Proficient students and many in a lower socioeconomic class.

The observers for this study spent some forty hours in training, using videotapes of classroom activities and practice visits to classrooms until they came to an 80 percent agreement rate for evaluation (Battistich et al., 1993). Observers entered the classrooms and critiqued interaction in groups when students were in groups (which varied from once a month to once a week to once a day) or in "pseudogroups." Pseudogroups were comprised of four to six students sitting in close proximity to one another, although they were not involved in a formal group activity.

Observers were looking for such evidence as friendliness, helpfulness, collaboration, and mutual concern. These qualities were further measured by use of a questionnaire. Student academic outcome was measured in the first district by means of an open-ended reading comprehension test and in the second district by means of the Comprehensive Test of Basic Skills (CTBS), a traditional standardized test.

The major finding of this study was that just having students work in cooperative groups without ensuring that the group has the skills and dynamics to work together productively can produce negative results both in social and in academic outcomes. To offset this, it is vital to specifically instruct your students each time they meet in a learning group to practice certain social skills, such as taking turns, respecting one another, having a helpful attitude toward one another, and focusing on the accomplishment of a product where everyone has the opportunity to contribute and their contributions are valued.

According to this study, the best teachers did not use cooperative groups more often than the others, but when they used learning groups, they set them up well and monitored them closely for high-quality interaction.

It is also important when teaching to be aware that teachers are teaching to multiple intelligences. According to studies on multiple intelligences (Gardner, 1983/1985; Lazear, 1991, 1992), there are seven different intelligences: verbal/linguistic; logical/mathematical; visual/spatial; body/kinesthetic; musical/rhythmic; interpersonal; and intrapersonal. When teaching to a diverse population with differing levels of "ability," it is important and rewarding to be able to use the word *intelligence* in a much broader way than previously used. Students who are excellent at dancing or sports have body/kinesthetic intelligence. Those who are skilled at painting, drawing, and pretending have visual/spatial intelligence. Students who cooperate in groups, divide the work, and understand others' feelings have interpersonal intelligence. Intrapersonal intelligence is the awareness of one's own thinking or acting, being extremely good at focusing, concentrating, and meditating. According to Gardner (1983), in order to have intrapersonal intelligence, the individual needs to be proficient with all the other intelligences.

In addition to being aware of multiple intelligences, another approach to teaching is by way of thematic units (Bilbe, Kornman, & Spann, 1992; Wepner, 1992; Wiig, Freedman, & Secord, 1992). These are general subjects appropriate to and of interest to a particular grade level. The students study the theme using key vocabulary terms and major concepts. These could be on cards with meaningful, colorful drawings and displayed around the room. Students also use some or all of the following in the thematic-unit approach: manipulatives and models; text and library reference books and magazines; printed material read aloud by the teacher; discussions and learning groups; displays and games; interactive bulletin boards (the title of the board might be a question, such as "What Is Sound?" or simply, "All About Crawly Creatures"; they also may involve graphs to which students contribute data or classifications under which students put samples); computers with appropriate software (*The Treehouse, The Whole Neighborhood, Muppet Math, Puppetmaker, Animal Rescue, Kidstime,* and so on), videos, filmstrips, videodiscs, and other technology; interviews; and primary source material.

Thematic units are a cross-curriculum experience. While involved in the thematic unit students utilize reading, writing, speaking, listening, social studies, science, math, fine arts, and research skills. Provide specific activities so that this occurs. For example, students can write a friendly letter to an assigned classmate or a parent explaining one exciting thing they learned and draw a picture to go with it. A small group could put on a puppet show or play to exemplify a major concept. Some students could make a clay model or a poster of what they are studying. A student may be able to bring a speaker on the subject to address the class.

Once students are involved in a particular subject, they may find topics that are of great interest to them, which they can explore in a way that meets their capabilities and needs. Besides the materials that you provide for them, students may want to go to their local library or travel agency or get information from home. When students decide they have something of interest to add to the classroom thematic bulletin board, they can ask to have it mounted.

When teaching your students in thematic units, be sure to make them responsible for specific skills, the **lexicon** (key vocabulary terms), and the major concepts. An open-ended pretest will give you information about what they already know and are very sure about, give you a chance to clear up any misconceptions or **pseudoconcepts** they may have, and let you find out what they would like to know. Provide opportunities for individual exploration, especially if you have one or two students who do a good job on the pretest.

The students need you teaching and guiding them through the unit activities. Check frequently to be sure appropriate skills are being learned, vocabulary is being clearly understood and students are confidently pronouncing the words, and that the concepts (the ones on the pretest) are actually being understood, manipulated, and extended. Students will undoubtedly need help individually and in small groups to fully comprehend this material. In addition to the many activities students will do throughout the unit, do not neglect to give the open-ended pretest as a posttest so that the students get the satisfaction of seeing the comparison and noting their improvement. You will, too!

Teacher expectations of student outcomes are also related to the teaching-learning process. See Expectations in Chapter 2, The DEF's, for more information on this crucial area.

TEST STUDY NOTES

Test study notes really encourage student studying and help keep test scores high. The students write their names at the top of the note. Then they tell their parents that they are going to be studying for a history test, math test, or whatever the case may be. After they have finished studying, their parents write on the note how long the students studied for whatever subject as well as the specific material that was studied. Specific material examples are: a study sheet for two-digit multipliers, vocabulary words for Chapter 3, first ten spelling words on the spelling words list, and so on.

With these notes, the parents know that their children are having a test the next day and the specific material the test covers. They know how long their children studied during time at home or after school. Frequently, parents will quiz their children about the material studied and send them back to study more if they do not know it well enough. Test study notes are extremely effective. Figure A7-9 in the appendix is a set of sample test study notes for your classroom.

TUTORS

Students love to tutor. They can tutor their own classmates or go to lower grades to help individual students. When students tutor in lower grades, it helps the organization of your classroom if they have a set time each day that they are to leave. In a combination class, a student in the higher grade can help a lower-grader. Or maybe a tutor will be assigned to help a Limited-English-Proficient student. Tutors are a big help to everyone—the students being tutored, the tutors themselves (with increased self-esteem and the acquisition of skills it takes to instruct), and you, the teacher.

The last part of this chapter may seem a little mundane right after a discussion of the teaching-learning process and the use of tutors and test study notes to support it. But this device is an inexpensive investment in class motivation and organization.

USING A DIGITAL TIMER

A digital timer has settings for hours and minutes. A repeating buzzer goes off when the time is up. After about twenty seconds, the buzzer will go off by itself if you have not already pressed "alarm stop." The timer can stand up on your desk or on a student's desk or, with its magnetic back strip, it can be attached to the overhead projector.

Do your students need some more time to complete their writing assignment? Do some of them need as much as twenty-five more minutes? Set the **timer.** Those few who need the twenty-five minutes will really work hard when that timer is on. Tell the students to work on their assignment quietly at their seats until the buzzer sounds.

If some students finish before the timer goes off, they can read their library books or involve themselves in an activity,

Figure 7-21. After completing their assignments, reading a library book is often a pleasure. If students get introduced to one book in a series, they will often read the entire series. This student is enjoying *The Indian in the Cupboard,* by Lynn Reid Banks.

Figure 7-22. The students in this class use their time very productively when their regular assignments are completed. The teacher has the opportunity to assist any students who are stumped by a section of their program. Courtesy of Fred Porter.

such as computer programming, at a spot located around the periphery of the classroom so as not to distract those involved in the writing assignment. You can then provide assistance to those individuals still writing or those groups who need it at the computer.

The digital timer can also be set on assembly days. Set it to sound five minutes before the assembly begins. Once it is set, everyone in the classroom, including you, can direct their full attention to the classroom activities and not worry about

the clock. When the timer sounds, line up and go to the assembly.

The digital timer can be used for a variety of other purposes, too, including physical fitness tests, math facts timing, and speeches. It makes a big difference, and the students love it!

Running an elementary classroom is a real challenge. You will meet this challenge successfully if you use the Blueprint for Effective Teaching, present exciting lessons, and provide an enthusiastic and caring environment for your students.

CHAPTER QUESTIONS

1. How was the teacher-constructed concept map used for science?
2. List criteria that you think are important for a good speech.
3. How can you provide an atmosphere that is a big confidence booster to a student giving a speech?
4. Make up two speaking assignments, one for a primary class and one for an upper grade.
5. What is the purpose of a test study note?
6. Describe at least two different ways to use tutors. Describe the kind of students you would appoint for cross-age tutoring in another classroom. Explain your reasoning.

7. How did McInnis address her biggest problem when she began her teaching career? In what way can you relate to this?
8. Explain what you think about the differentiated evaluation system for teachers.
9. You are going to teach a science lesson in fingerprint classification. What would you do for the *Ready* part of the Blueprint for Effective Teaching?
10. What four questions can you ask yourself to help get started with your students in the academic arena?
11. Your class has just finished reading and doing a variety of activities for the book, *From the Mixed-Up Files of*

Mrs. Basil E. Frankweiler. Make up five different test-mode questions to cover this information:

> Claudia selected her younger brother, Jamie, to take to New York City with her when she ran away from home. Jamie could keep a secret and not tell their parents and he had saved some money, which Claudia desperately needed.

> You could select a true-false, a multiple-choice, a fill-in-the-blank, or an open-ended question of some sort; instructions for some kind of graphic; and so on.

12. Name and describe at least two different kinds of groups. When and how could they be used?
13. How can chunking help your students?
14. Name one way that each student in a group could be held accountable.
15. How can you develop students who are responsible?
16. Describe two motivators to use during a lesson.
17. If a second-grade classroom gets into groups to discuss getting along with each other better out on the playground, what might the product be?
18. To *set* the students for a lesson, what are the three things to do?
19. What should you do during *listen and watch?*
20. What is the most important thing to remember when giving an assignment?
21. What does teaching for transfer mean? Describe a situation where you could use this strategy.
22. Explain Francis Bacon's inductive method. Write a lesson plan for a science lesson using the inductive method.
23. Create an activity sheet for a reading lesson that would reflect Bloom's taxonomy, level four.
24. In view of Rosenzweig's study, how can you make the classroom a stimulating place? Name three things you could do.
25. Applying the findings of Lashley's student, Donald Hebb, how would you get something into a student's long-term memory?
26. Prior to chunking, how many items can be kept in short-term memory?
27. What are thematic units? Prepare a brief outline for a thematic unit for the study of the family, community living, city life, or a state's admission to the Union. Be sure to incorporate all the areas of the curriculum.
28. If you had the opportunity to participate in the LSST or TCP program, which one would you choose and why?
29. According to Battistich, what is behind group work success? How can you apply that to your class?
30. In the San Francisco Bay Area study, what did the "best" teachers do?
31. What are multiple intelligences?

CHAPTER PROJECT

Choose one level, either primary or upper grade. Select a focus activity and build a science lesson around it. The focus activity could be a field trip, an experiment, a collection, a video, and so on. Approximately how many days will the lesson last? Follow the Blueprint for Effective Teaching. List all the materials you will need and all the activities the students will be doing. Prepare an assessment device.

REFERENCES

Association for Childhood Education International, Teacher Evaluation Committee. (1993). Preparation of elementary teachers. *Childhood Education, 70*(1), 34–35.

Battistich, V., Solomon, D., & Delucchi, K. (1993). Interaction processes and student outcomes in cooperative learning groups. *The Elementary School Journal, 94*(1), 19–32.

Benz, C. R., Bradley, L., Alderman, M. K., & Flowers, M. A. (1992). Personal teaching efficacy: Developmental relationships in education. *Journal of Educational Research, 85*(5), 274–285.

Bilbe, R. & Kornman, N. with Spann, M. B. (1992). Teaching with themes. *Instructor, 102*(2), 84–85.

Bloom, B. S. *Taxonomy of educational objectives; The classification of educational goals.* New York: David McKay, © 1956, 1968.

Bloom, F. E., Lazerson, A., & Hofstadter, L. (1985). *Brain, mind, and behavior.* New York: W. H. Freeman and Company.

Brookhart, S. M., & Rusnak, T. G. (1993). A pedagogy of enrichment, not poverty: Successful lessons of exemplary urban teachers. *Journal of Teacher Education, 44*(1), 17–26.

Conklin, R. C. (1985). Teacher competency testing: The present situation and some concerns on how some teachers are tested. *Education Canada, 25*(1), 12–15.

Engle, R. W., Carullo, J. J., & Collins, K. W. (1991). Individual differences in working memory for comprehension and following directions. *Journal of Educational Research, 84*(5), 253–262.

Gardner, H., *Frames of Mind.* New York: Basic Books, ©1983, 1985.

Hawkins, J. A., Jr. (1991). Induction programs for new elementary school teachers in Montgomery County public schools. *ERS Spectrum, 9*(3), 10–17.

Heller, H. W. & Clay, R. J. (1993). Predictors of teaching effectiveness: The efficacy of various standards to predict the success of graduates from a teacher education program. *ERS Spectrum, 11*(1), 7–11.

Huling-Austin, L. (1992). Research on learning to teach: Implications for teacher induction and mentoring programs. *Journal of Teacher Education, 43*(3), 173–179.

Lazear, D. (1991). *Seven ways of knowing*. Palatine, IL: Skylight Publishers.

Lazear, D. (1992). *Seven ways of teaching*. Palatine, IL: Skylight Publishers.

McInnis, B. J. (1990). What administrators should know about the needs of the beginning teacher: A personal perspective. *ERS Spectrum, 8*(4), 10–16.

Metcalf, K. K., & Cruickshank, D. R. (1991). Can teachers be trained to make clear presentations? *Journal of Educational Research, 85*(2), 107–115.

Schalock, H. D. (1988). Teacher selection: A problem of admission criteria, certification criteria, or prediction of job performance? In William J. Gephart & Jerry Ayers (Eds.), Teacher education evaluation (pp. 1–22). Boston: Kluver Academic Publishers.

Wepner, S. B. (1992). Technology and thematic units: A primary example. (International Reading Association). *The Reading Teacher, 46*(3), 260–263.

Wiig, E. H., Freedman, E., & Secord, W. A. (1992). Developing words and concepts in the classroom: A holistic-thematic approach. *Intervention in School and Clinic, 27*(5), 278–285.

Willerman, M. & MacHarg, R. A. (1991). The concept map as an advance organizer. *Journal of Research in Science Teaching, 28*(8), 705–711.

BIBLIOGRAPHY

Bellezza, F. (1981). Mnemonic devices: Classification, characteristics, and criteria. *Review of Educational Research, 51*(2), 247–275.

Berliner, D. C. (1984). The half-full glass: A review of research on teaching. In P. L. Hosford (Ed.), Using what we know about teaching (pp. 51–84). Alexandria, VA: Association for Supervision and Curriculum Development.

Hirsch, E. D., Jr. (1985). Cultural literacy and the schools. *American Educator, 9*(2).

Little, J. W. (1982). Norms of collegiality and experimentation: Workplace conditions of school success. *American Educational Research Journal, 19*(3), 325–346.

Rosenshine, B. (1983). Teaching functions in instructional programs. *Elementary School Journal, 83*(4), 335–351.

Segal, J., Chipman, S., & Glaser, R. (1985). *Thinking and learning skills, vol. 1: Relating instruction to research*. Hillsdale, NJ: Erlbaum Associates.

Sullivan, V. (1992). *Questionnaire responses on teaching kindergarten*.

Walberg, H. J. (1984). Improving the productivity of America's schools. *Educational Leadership, 41*(8), 19–27.

Walberg, H. J. (1985). Homework's powerful effects on learning. *Educational Leadership, 42*(7), 76–79.

8

THE V'S AND W'S

Managing an elementary classroom is a comprehensive task. It involves talent and know-how. It means flexibility and surprises. To help you deal with this awesome responsibility, you might need something of a personal organizer. You might also need some help preparing for the unknown—those little surprises—and the known of the everyday curriculum. This chapter enlightens you in the following areas:

- Vade Mecum
- Visitors
- Weather
- Writing
- Writing—Research and Studies

The first part of this chapter introduces you to an object that, though you may not have ever heard of it, will help you to run your classroom. With it, you can keep track of any papers, teacher manuals, and so on, that you cart back and forth from school to home. It will help keep you organized. This first part also gives you some tips about your conduct during classroom visitations.

VADE MECUM

(vä' dē mē' kəm)—something frequently carried about, as a handbook. Latin: literally, go with me.

The Random House Dictionary, Bantam Books, 1980.

A teacher's **vade mecum** can be a cart system, which is described next. Get a luggage carrier at any department store. Next, get a "Keep Box" at any discount store. Then, for total satisfaction, go to a welding shop and ask the workers there to make a hooking frame piece like the one shown in the diagram in Figure 8-1. Have them paint it black. This should be a sturdy, thick piece. It keeps the box from slipping off the luggage carrier when it gets pulled at a brisk pace or taken around a corner. Take the Keep Box and the luggage carrier with you to the welding shop so that they can make the frame piece properly. Inform them you might be carrying a heavy load, textbooks, for example. Then the piece will support properly.

The luggage carrier has a knob that adjusts the height for pulling or pushing. It also easily folds up to put in the trunk of your car. The hooking frame piece is separate and is removed prior to folding the carrier.

The box itself is sturdy plastic and opens on the top from the center. One half of the top opens toward you, the other half opens away from you. Two pieces overlap to seal it shut. The box can be left open or half open anytime. It also has two side ridges so that it is very easy to lift.

In the morning when you arrive at work, take the luggage carrier out of your trunk and unfold it. Then place the black frame on it. Last, take your box out of your trunk and put it on the black frame. Then you are ready for the entire day. You can store anything you want in the box: books, papers, grade book, professional literature, lunch, soft drinks or water, pens, pencils, purse, brief case, and so on. The entire cart goes anywhere: up over curbs, over gravel, up and down ramps, and in and out all doors. Even when it is overloaded with heavyweight materials, it is easy to pull. The students, naturally, will love to take it to the classroom for you.

If you have any kind of back problems, as long as you load and unload this properly from your car, this cart can be a major blessing because you do not have to carry anything around anymore. If your back is a problem to you, have a cardboard

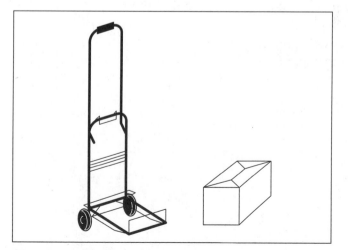

Figure 8-1.

carton or a milk case (from the local grocery store) in your trunk. When it is time to load your car, shift any heavy things from your Keep Box to the cardboard carton. Then, pick up your box with both hands and place it in the trunk. When you arrive at school, unload the carrier and box first. *Then,* shift the heavier materials in smaller lightweight loads into the box.

Besides helping to keep all your work and personal belongings organized, tidy, and easy to move, your vade mecum is a real back preserver.

VISITORS

Occasionally, you will have visitors to your classroom. Typical visitors are a district's superintendent, a member of the school board, or principals and teachers from another school or district on a school evaluation.

Sometimes visitors may just "pop in." You do not know they are coming, but here they are. Surprise!

In these cases, if you are in the middle of a lesson, it is usually best to continue on, unless the person indicates he wants to speak to you regarding some matter. In that case, give the students a task to keep them well occupied and go see the visitor.

This is not the time to start wishing you wore something more suitable to work today or thinking your grooming is not up to par. The time to think about personal appearance and grooming is when you are home getting ready for work. It is important to dress appropriately for your job.

Nor is this the time to start worrying about what a complete mess your classroom is, even though you know that having a nice, neat classroom is very important. The time for that worry was yesterday afternoon before you dismissed your students. Be sure the students do a good job of cleaning and tidying before they leave each day. Have yourself and your classroom looking their best every day so that you are not caught off guard. However, an unexpected visitor is normally a rare thing.

Most of the time, you will know about a visitor in advance. Then be sure to dress well and look your nicest. Be sure your classroom is picked up and looking sharp. Let your students know who is going to be visiting, because they are always curious.

Set up your lesson plans to allow some time for you to visit with your visitor, if you know the approximate time the person will be arriving. If you only know the visitor will be on campus a certain day, but you have no time slot, it is best just to go about your business. If the person comes in during a lesson, it is fine to go on with the lesson. Visitors often are interested to see at least part of the lesson you are teaching. Some, if not most, of the visitors who are teachers will not have had their own classrooms for many years. They well might be coming from personal everyday elementary classroom experience that is ten, fifteen, maybe twenty years old. It is a much more informative visit for them if they are able to see things in their usual routine.

If you are having visitors because of a school review, also known as a **PQR (Program Quality Review),** inform your students so that they will be expecting some questions from the reviewers. Appoint various students to be in charge of explaining to the visitors your math program or your language arts program, or whatever programs are being reviewed. Place a large name tag on these students' desks delineating on which curricular area they can expound. Display on your classroom bulletin boards student work that gives evidence of what you have been doing in specific curricular areas as well as evidence of what you teach **cross-curriculum.** Your school will undoubtedly have a certain routine it uses. Be sure to follow the policies of your school during a review.

No matter what is happening or when, plan ahead and have a neat classroom and student work displayed as a matter of course. Come well groomed and nicely dressed every day, not just special days or visitor days. Have expertly planned lessons every day, five days a week. Most important, relax and be yourself; you will do a great job!

The second part of this chapter provides information to help you deal with another possible unknown: inclement weather. It is, however, like a classroom visitor. Sometimes you know about it, sometimes you do not. Therefore, be prepared.

This part also explains many different ways to teach the essential subject of writing, which not only includes all types of writing, but also its subskills of spelling, printing, and handwriting.

WEATHER

Inclement weather for one or two days is not such a big problem, but it can be wearing if it drags on day after day. If there are big storms with lightning, thunder, and high winds, the students can get pretty hyper and anxious; some may need a little comforting and reassurance, younger students especially. In between class periods, it is a good idea to have the students do some aerobic activities, maybe to music; some "Simon Says"; or an activity record. Since they are not getting their usual amount of exercise, they can get quite restless.

Three things will help ease the strain of inclement weather on everyone during recess and lunch periods: plenty of activities available for the students, keen awareness on the part of the students of the need for extra good behavior during these times, and a buddy teacher for you, to give you a break, too.

Have activities for inclement weather stored in an easily accessible place for the students. Many different types of activities are available that can keep them well occupied. Board games, especially Monopoly®, Pay Day®, Go to the Head of the Class®, Game of the States®, Scrabble®, and so on, are popular. If there is a place to leave the games out during inclement weather, then the students can get started on a game at recess and continue where they left off at lunch. Blocks and table toys are fun as is the enjoyment and challenge of a puzzle. Simple art projects can be provided for the students as well as computer and/or electronic games.

Find out who wants to play what. Then write the name of the activity and list the students' names under it. Spread the activities around the perimeter of the room and place one or two activities in the center of the room. Let the students know that whatever they selected will be their activity for the day. There is no switching. They are to stay at that activity's location. If it turns out that they are not happy with that activity, even though they selected it themselves, they can change the next day. This way, students are spread around the room in small clusters and stay with one group. This makes it an easier situation to supervise for whomever is in charge at recess or lunch.

Appoint a student in each group to be the group leader. Then, if disagreements occur during the game about some rule, or whose turn it is, and so on, that student will call for a show of hands during the dispute. Majority rules. Explain this concept to your students and role-play, especially with the younger ones, until they get the idea. It does not work to have students ask the supervisor to settle these kinds of problems because the supervisor is usually in charge of two classrooms and has to move back and forth between the rooms.

When students need to leave the classroom to go to the bathroom during recess or lunch, they should go in groups of two to four only. You do not want a large group leaving at the same time, because it can cause problems in the bathrooms. As soon as they return, two more can leave, and so on. This method encourages students to leave, take care of business, and return quickly, because they know other students are waiting for them.

Have students eat their recess snacks and lunches sitting at their own desks and talking quietly with their neighbors. When the supervisor allows it, they can get up to throw out their trash in the lunch trash receptacle only. Do not have the students dispose of food remnants in the classroom wastebaskets or soon you will be having some unwanted visitors—ants.

All of these instructions should be given and thoroughly explained before you leave for your break so that the students know exactly what is expected of them. Then write on the board in big letters "Dictionary—10," or "Math Papers—2," or "Corner—10," or whatever might be suitable for your grade level. Let your class and the supervisor know that, if—for whatever reason—some student causes problems, the supervisor will write that student's name on the board under one of these areas. If students get their name written under Dictionary—10 by the supervisor, they are to immediately return to their desks, take out their dictionaries and write the full definition, pronunciation, and so on for ten words. Afterward, they can return to their game. If students get their names under Math Papers—2, they go to a designated area of the class, pick up the two math papers, return to their desk and complete them both, after which they can return to their game. Likewise, if students get their names under Corner—10, they must spend ten minutes in a designated corner or spot in the class, after which time they may return to their game. Select whatever is appropriate to your grade level.

Make it clear to the students that if they want to enjoy themselves, they need to be responsible for good behavior. Have the supervisor leave the name or names on the board until you return. Then collect the work or check to be sure the student sat in the designated spot. If you find a consistent problem with one or two students, confine them to activities alone at their desk until they decide they are willing to put forth the effort to improve their behavior.

After explaining all of this to the class, then you are ready to leave the classroom for your lunch. Be sure to tell your students in the presence of the supervisor that you support his or her decisions and the students are to help out by being on their best behavior and following all the rules. Make them aware of the difficulty of the supervisor's job.

Plan in advance with your next-door neighbor teacher a routine of who will take a quick break first and who will go second. Attend to all of these items and your classroom should run smoothly in your absence.

WRITING

The spoken word perishes; the written word remains.

Latin Proverb

The whole area of integrated language arts has four components: reading, writing, listening, and speaking. Even though teaching and learning occur across the curriculum, each of these components will be addressed separately.

For information on the beginnings of writing, see Emergent Literacy in Chapter 2, The DEF's.

The Writing Process

Learning to write well is a demanding process. Go slowly, carefully, gently, and patiently. Writing, according to research, is best learned using the writing process. Altogether there are five parts.

First is the **prewrite,** where students use some sort of brainstorming device. During this process, students write every idea as it comes to them. Then they select and organize the best of their ideas and eliminate the others. Prewrite is the single most important stage in the writing process and is vital to the success of the paper.

Fluency drills are a fun and quick way to prepare students for this all-important skill of brainstorming. Give the class a category, such as *fruit.* When you say go, they write as many fruits as they can think of in twenty seconds. When time is up, ask, How many students have more than three? more than six? more than ten? and so on. Your students will delight in this.

In the second stage of the writing process, students write their *first draft.*

Third, they *edit and revise.* During this stage, the students might ask others for their opinions about and suggestions for the revision of the first draft. What parts are especially good? What changes can be made? What format or mechanical changes need to be made?

Students should look for a variety of things during their edit: correct format for a friendly letter, a business letter, a paragraph, a multiparagraph project, a script, a diary entry, or a poem; a catchy title, if applicable; correct right and left margins; correct spelling; correct use of capitals and punctuation; and use of complete sentences with good grammar. Sometimes, you might want to have the students edit for only one or two things, such as ending punctuation and correct use of margins.

Fourth is the *final copy.*

Fifth is *proofreading* of the final copy. This fifth step is critical to the overall quality of the paper. It ensures correct format, mechanics, and grammar, as well as high-quality content on the final copy, which will be "published" in some way, graded, displayed, placed in a class booklet, or filed in the individual student's portfolio.

Figure 8-2. These students are in the first stage—brainstorming—of a group writing project. A timekeeper, leader, and recorder help this group stay focused and productive.

It helps students who are working on their final drafts to have on their desks or tables a dictionary appropriate to their grade level, from small primary dictionary booklets for first and second grades to intermediate or college dictionaries for upper grades. Other aids include: an alphabetical list of commonly misspelled words; students' own personal lists of words they have misspelled in earlier writings; a hand-held spelling computer; and, for upper-grade students, a thesaurus. These items will give students an excellent word bank for spelling and use of synonyms.

Spelling is often taught as a separate subject during the writing process. If it is, it is essential that high-utility word lists be incorporated into the program. These word lists can be developed by grade level at your school.

If spelling is not a separate subject but is incorporated into the writing program, students should have good dictionary skills to check the spelling of the words they use. They should have a list of frequently misspelled words, and, most importantly, their own personal list. This personal list is composed of words the students already have shown they do not know how to spell, which students should concentrate on because those are the words that they will be using again and again. Those are the words they need to learn to spell and then begin spelling them correctly whenever they write that word, no matter which area of the curriculum they happen to be in at the moment. All learning is across the curriculum. All application levels are across the curriculum.

This personal list can be added to as newly used words are misspelled. Students will need frequent pretests and posttests on their lists to become proficient. Self-correcting is an excellent helper.

In addition, it is very helpful to have repeated class lessons on the correct use and spelling of *there, their, they're; to, too,* and *two; it's* and *its;* and *your* and *you're.* These high-use words can be perennial problems. On their personal lists, students could add explanatory notes such as *they're = they are; their = possession,* and so on, to help them use these words correctly. Students could place these words on cards with the meanings on the back, quiz each other, reshuffle the cards, and "play" again. Frequent card games and quizzes can help keep the students focused on the importance of using these words correctly, as well as give them lots of practice.

The appendix contains spelling study sheets on *there, their,* and *they're; to, two,* and *too;* and a list of common problem words in spelling. See Figures A8-1, A8-2, and A8-3 in the appendix. (*Pt* is for primary and *§* is for upper grade; however, make any modifications you like.)

Students also enjoy bonus words from the *Morrison-McCall Spelling Scale* (for grades 2 to 8) by J. Cayce Morrison and William A. McCall (Morrison, 1923). There are many easy words on these lists, such as *run, book, go, up, time, street, spring, any,* and *suit,* but they also contain many harder words. These words are so much fun because the grade level of each word is listed along with a sentence in which the word is used. For example, *mortgage* is at the mark for 11.7 (eleventh grade, seventh month). *Lieutenant* is 13.0. The students love the words with high grade levels, especially the college level. Exposure to some of the tougher words for their grade level creates a desire in the students to expand their writing vocabularies.

Sentence dictation is an important way to see the use of spelling words at the application level. It also provides students the opportunity and practice of writing sentences with proper nouns in the middle, or words or phrases in a series, or using quotations correctly in titles and conversation. This will be a great help in their total writing program.

Many students enjoy doing their final copies on a computer, not only because their papers might look neater, but also because they can take advantage of the spell check and the variety of fonts. Students who can compose at the computer might want to use the computer's thesaurus as well.

Journal writing and some creative writing can often be accomplished in a relatively short period of time.

Writing assignments of any length, however, will not be accomplished during one writing period. One assignment may take as long as a week or two, especially if the students need to do research and take notes first, or if along with the writing, there will be some kind of illustrating or publishing in book format. Be sure to schedule enough classroom time and an appropriate amount of homework time so that the students' final projects are excellent.

Let students know exactly what they are to complete in any one writing period. Do not just give the assignment and schedule several periods of time. That is not specific enough for most students.

Teaching the Writing Process

The entire writing process must be taught step by step, skill by skill. The particular type of writing assignment (poem; friendly or business letter; diary or journal entry; power, descriptive, summary, time-order, or explanatory paragraph; multiparagraph writing project; persuasive article, essay, or autobiographical incident; or some type of research report) must also be taught thoroughly, carefully, step by step. This can be done in groups or with the total class.

Figure 8-3.   This student enjoys composing at the computer. Built-in helpers are a thesaurus and spell check. When he is ready for his final copy, this student can "dress up" his paper with a special font and border.

Also, be sure students have all the prerequisite skills for the assignment. For example, if they are doing a report in the latter part of fourth grade, do they have note-taking skills? Will they need to know how to write a table of contents or a bibliography? Do they know when to start a new paragraph? In fifth and sixth grades, do they know good paragraph transitions?

Encourage the students to write using their five senses as much as possible. Alert them to the different writing styles of their reading text, their social studies and science texts, and their library books. When students have completed their final copy, ask them to share their paragraph(s) with the class. That way the class is exposed to different writing styles, different approaches to the same material, different ways to incorporate humor, and so on. Then they can add to their own repertoire.

When you begin teaching the writing process and particular kind of writing you want the students to do for an upcoming assignment, it is often fun to work with the whole class. Use an overhead projector, the chalkboard, or large sheets of writing paper hanging on the board or attached to an easel.

Suppose you are going to teach your class how to prepare for the following writing assignment: Write two sentences telling about a zoo animal. First, prepare ahead of time by selecting four animals you are going to use yourself. Have one or two books on each animal. These books should be of a reading level appropriate to your grade level. Have everything ready for the chalkboard, large writing paper, or transparencies for the overhead.

Introduce your lesson. Then tell the students they will be brainstorming to develop a list of interesting things to say about an elephant. Write down everything the students say. Then give your books on elephants to a couple of students. Ask them to get partners. Have them look through the books to see if they can get any more ideas. Be sure students understand that when they are brainstorming they should write every idea they think of without making any judgments about good and bad. Model that for them.

Next, review your list. Ask the class to vote once for their favorite description. Select the top two items. You may have to have a runoff to get the top two, or you might want to lump two items together as one. Circle the most popular. This step in the writing process is extremely important to getting a high-interest paper.

Step two is to write the first draft. Do this on another transparency or a fresh piece of paper while your students watch.

Step three is to edit and revise. Ask your students: Could the sentences say more? Do they sound interesting? Do they start with capitals? What about ending periods? Make whatever changes the class likes.

Step four is to write the final copy. Do this while your class watches. And don't forget to do the fifth and final step—proofread your final copy.

Then begin this process all over again with your second animal. Depending on the grade level, this can be done on the same day or another day. But by the time you finish your fourth animal, the students will have the idea. Then they are ready for the writing assignment. Tell them they may not use one of the four demonstration animals. Have books out on other animals, which students may look through for ideas. Of course, if they

have been to the zoo, they will have lots of ideas right in their own heads. Have the students work independently on the writing assignment or in groups of two to four. Encourage the students to use their best printing or handwriting on their final copy.

Perhaps you will have a lesson on writing a **time-order paragraph,** the easiest kind of paragraph to write. This type of paragraph always turns out very well as early as third grade and can be easily expanded into a larger paragraph for later grades. It begins with a topic sentence followed by sentences starting with each time-order word: *first, next, then,* and *finally* or *at last.* It is effortless to extend this five-sentence paragraph to a seven-sentence paragraph by inserting *second* and *third* between *first* and *next,* or limit its length by using *first, next, at last.*

Do at least one paragraph together as a class so that the students understand what is expected before you give your assignment. It could be: Write a time-order paragraph on finding a friend lost on a camping trip in Yosemite National Park.

Suppose your total-class practice time-order paragraph will be on a day in the life of Michael Jordan. Begin with the brainstorming and/or clustering process. List as many ideas as your class can think of about things Michael Jordan might have done in a day. Do your vote. Decide the order in which Michael would have done these things during his day. Continue right through the writing process for the first draft, revisions and editing, final copy, and final proofreading.

Go through each step slowly to ensure students understand what is being done and how it is done. Leave up the final copy of the class paragraph so that students can refer to it as a model. Then give students their own time-order paragraph assignment.

Figure 8-4 is an example of a total-class time-order paragraph done during the teaching process. Notice the catchy, rhyming title and the use of a question sentence for a topic sentence.

A Busy Day for Michael J.!

Do you know how busy one of Michael Jordan's days was? First, he went to the gym to work out. Second, he signed autographs for his fan club. Next, he went down to the police station to pay a ticket for ramming a Rolls Royce with his Lamborghini. Then, he played against the Lakers at The Forum and slam-dunked with his tongue hanging out. At last, he sped to McDonald's for a delicious Big Mac and orange soda and then home for a deserved rest.

Time-Order Paragraph

Topic sentence—NEVER a time-order word
Time-order words:

5 sentence paragraph	First Next Then Finally	7 sentence paragraph	First Second Third Next Then At last

Figure 8-4.

Another type of paragraph with which students have great success is the **power paragraph** (also called a **powergraph**). In its beginning form, 1-2-2 (topic sentence and two details), it is very appropriate for primary grades. Its form gets more sophisticated as students show their readiness.

Suppose you are going to be giving your class an assignment to write a powergraph using the 1-2-3-2-3-4 format (topic sentence, first detail, explanation or description of the detail, second detail, explanation or description of that detail, and conclusion). The topic could be: cities to visit. Prepare the students in advance by going through the writing process step by step, as a total class (or in groups, if you like). Demonstrate the importance of brainstorming in achieving an interesting paper.

Maybe you are going to do your class practice powergraph on reasons for owning a dog. Have the students brainstorm for as many reasons as they can think of for owning a dog. Encourage them to be humorous and even outrageous.

After your students have selected the two best reasons for owning a dog, have them tell more about each reason and give some examples. Next, ask your students to select a favorite explanation for each reason. Then begin your first draft as the class watches. Most of the paragraph will already be written from your selections from all the brainstorming. Continue right through the writing process until the class has finished the final proofreading. Leave the final copy up as a model for your students.

Figure 8-5 is a sample total-class powergraph. Notice the use of a question in the title, the easy-to-write topic sentence, and the use of an exclamation sentence for a conclusion.

Many types of writing can be done as one paragraph or as a multiparagraph project—letters, summarizing, report writing, comparing and contrasting, persuasive writing, and so on, especially in the upper grades.

One format that students are successful with and thoroughly enjoy is the multiparagraph part of the **UCI (University of California at Irvine) Writing Project.** This is especially appropriate for any upper grade, and the format is easily adapted to many different topics.

Basically, five areas are covered: (1) person (whether the student will write in first, second, or third); (2) setting; (3) conflict (usually three obstacles, but can be more or fewer); (4) objective (usually survival); and (5) assignment (what the character has to accomplish).

In the introductory paragraph, students include who they are in the story, the setting, their assignment, and objective. Then a paragraph is devoted to each obstacle. This is where brainstorming for interesting and unique ideas is vital. Finally, a concluding sentence or paragraph is written.

After you do your class lesson (see Blueprint for Effective Teaching in Chapter 7, STU's), the students can work on these types of projects in groups of three or four, or independently. One student can write the introductory paragraph and concluding statement or paragraph, while each of the other students writes on an obstacle. (See Figure 8-6 for a sample obstacle paragraph.) This is great fun, especially when you can think of some interesting topics for your students. Be sure the students have a clear understanding of the person, setting, assignment, obstacles, and objective before meeting in their groups.

Project papers that you can use with your students about a newscaster, a police officer, and an Irish Setter are included in Figures A8-4, A8-5, and A8-6 in the appendix.

Students' writing can also be directly linked to a story in their reader. They can use a cluster to write information about a character in their story. In the center circle, they write the character's name. Inside the surrounding ovals, they can

---

Should You Own a Dog?

There are two reasons for owning a dog. One is that it offers a lot of protection. When a ferocious pit bull comes into your backyard, your dog can do a body slam on it and bite its legs off. Another reason for owning a dog is that it provides warmth and friendship. Your dog will always want to cuddle with you and give you lots of licks. If you have something to celebrate, your dog will celebrate with you. If you are sad, your dog will be there for you. How great it is to own a dog!

Power Paragraph

Powers:
1. Topic sentence
   There are two . . .
      2. One is . . .
         3. Tell about it.
      2. The other is . . .
         3. Tell about it
4. Conclusion

Powers:
1. Topic sentence
   There are three . . .
      2. The first is . . .
         3. Tell about it.
      2. The second is . . .
         3. Tell about it.
      2. The last is . . .
         3. Tell about it.
4. Conclusion

Figure 8-5.

Sample Obstacle Paragraph

I heard an eardrum-bursting roar. Huddling behind the bushes but staring straight at my eyes was a large, scraggly lion. I showed him all of my karate moves to scare him off, but he just stared. In vain, I tried to stare him down, so that totally intimidated, he'd crawl away. At last, I took my secret weapon out of my pocket and showed it to him. Slowly and meekly he came toward me, his tongue out. I gently placed a yummy green lifesaver in his mouth and he lay down contentedly.

UCI Writing Project—Obstacle Paragragh

*Person:	1st—I, me; my, mine; we, us, ours
	2nd—You; your, yours
	3rd—He/she, him/her; they, them; their, theirs
*Setting:	Where and when the story takes place
*Assignment:	What the character will be doing
*Obstacles:	Problems the character will encounter
*Objective:	Condition character will be in at end of the story

Figure 8-6.

Figure 8-7.   Students working on group writing projects can often get help from a thesaurus, a dictionary, or a hand-held speller.

answer each question as completely as possible. What does the character look like? Where does she live? What does she like to do? What family does she have? Then, using a new cluster, they can fill in the center circle with their own name and write in as much as they can think of about themselves to answer the questions for the ovals. As a final part of this writing activity, they can use the cluster with their own name in the center and write about themselves incorporating the cluster information. Figures A8-7 and A8-8 in the appendix are sample clusters with Figure A8-9 as a follow-up paragraph activity.

Clusters can be on any topic in reading, history, science, health, and so on. If the students are given this type of format repeatedly, they become expert in using these skills and can apply them in every subject.

Another writing technique, mentioned previously in Chapter 6, is the double entry journal. See the first page of Figure A8-10 in the appendix. This presents a good opportunity to compare two sets of information, one directly related to the story in the reader, one directly related to the student. One column of the double entry journal can be used for a certain event that happened in the story; the companion column can be used for a similar event that happened in the student's life. A double entry journal will help students to interact more with the story to determine how a story incident can relate to them personally.

For example, a story character might have been paralyzed. Even though your student is not paralyzed, maybe he was in the hospital and had to ride in a wheelchair. Then your student can link that personal experience with the character in the story. How did your student feel? What were all the happenings surrounding his incident? This writing approach can facilitate deep thinking on the part of the student and make for very interesting writing.

Figure A8-10 in the appendix is a four-page writing activity. It incorporates double entry journal and clusters as part of a preparation for writing about a time in the student's life. In addition, Figure A8-11 in the appendix can be used as a writing test.

It presents some different choices of writing tasks and it allows the students a wide arena to demonstrate their writing expertise.

All of these different types of writing make use of a format. This usually keeps students from rambling in their writing and provides them with a blueprint for pleasure and success.

Grading the Writing Process

There are various ways to grade these types of writing papers. Use an overall letter grade, or write one grade for mechanics, one grade for content. Grade just one area; for example, give a grade for use of strong topic sentences, catchy titles, well-written sentences, good transitions, or correct format. You can use some kind of rubric or paragraph evaluation form.

You do not have to give a writing assignment a grade at all; just comment about a strength and a comment about an area that needs improvement are very helpful. Try to show the students right on their papers *how* they could improve the area you selected.

Possibly the best feedback for students is a combination of a grade *and* a comment about strengths and weaknesses. Then, after the students have seen their papers, they might like to redo them before they are placed in the students' portfolios, displayed around the classroom, or read to the class by the students.

Other Writing Opportunities and Projects

Provide your students with lots of other writing opportunities, too. After a field trip, they can write a thank-you letter to the parents who accompanied the class. They can write and decorate invitations to Back-to-School Night and Open House. They can interview teachers, students, parents, or siblings on a particular topic and write up the interview or compare and contrast teachers' and students' opinions on a controversial subject. They even can write scripts for their plays.

Another adventure is writing a **pop-up book.** Students can make a part of each picture pop up and write the accompanying story part at the bottom of the page. The center of each page pops up with a large, hand-drawn picture glued to the pop-up center. Background drawing is done above the picture and the story sentence goes below the picture.

Use 9-inch by 12-inch white construction paper for the pages. Place the construction paper in the lengthwise vertical position. Fold the paper in half (top to bottom) so the book will open from the bottom. Make a light pencil mark at the outside center of the fold. Then beginning at the center of the fold, draw a light line 1½ inches to the left of the center. Extend the line down 2½ inches. Do the same on the right side of the center mark. Next, with the paper still folded, cut the paper right down each of the lines. Open the page. Pull the center of the fold toward you. Close the page and press it down so its flat. Now you have one page of a pop-up book.

The cover of the book can be bound using colorful material and colored binding tape or cereal boxes. Even though this is a huge amount of work, the finished product is very exciting. Watch out that the students do not make their books too long. Drawing the illustrations for each page, although fun, is also laborious.

You can make a class booklet out of one assignment. After the students are finished with their writing and decorating, laminate the papers. Have a student do a cover design. Use your district's book-binding machine to put it together.

Selecting a class in another part of the country to have as pen pals is always delightful. Besides practicing their letter-writing skills, students can send pencils, stickers, little stuffed animals, and photos to their pen pals. Sending and receiving class videos is a thrill, too.

Having your class practice writing excellent answers to the **five W's** (*who, what, where, when,* and *why*) and the one *H* question (*how*) will be a skill they will transfer into social studies and science. Go through this skill carefully with your class to teach them how to answer the questions in intelligent, well-worded sentences, rather than in weak phrases or dependent clauses. Help them see how to restate some of each question into their answer.

W question: *Why* did the two dogs get into a fight?

Weak, nonsentence answer: Because they were mad at each other.
Better answer: The two dogs got into a fight because one of the dogs stole the other's bone.
Another good answer: The two dogs got into a fight because Shadow bit Rover's tail.

Many of the beginning skills eventually lead to more advanced writing. Some are the more traditional approaches of tracing letters, connecting letters, fitting words into boxes, writing words, writing phrases, and writing one, two, and three-word sentences. These learnings totally interconnect with reading. For your use, Figures A8-12 through A8-16 in the appendix are samples of five beginning skills activities. These are coded *Pt* for primary and could be used in first grade.

There are other more holistic approaches to facilitate beginning literacy. Use of environmental print in your classroom can greatly help with literacy development. With this approach, students can become alert to looking for words and sayings in

their environment even when they are *not* in class, for example, when looking at a cereal box or a candy wrapper. Some students do well with invented spelling, too. This allows them the freedom to communicate their ideas in an uninhibited manner. Any of these strategies work well with students working to acquire written language.

For a change of pace in your class, though, you can play some writing tapes. Accompanying reproducible materials are distributed to the students. They follow along with the instructions and examples given on the tapes. The tapes are periodically turned off to let the students complete their sections. Tapes are available on writing business letters, summarizing, and correct use of capitals, just to name a few.

Another favorite activity is having a follow-up project to a film or video. Tell the students in advance that they will be drawing a picture of their favorite part and writing a one-sentence caption or a three-sentence caption.

Suppose you decide to show *The Rats of NIMH* in your fourth-grade classroom. Treat it like a reading story. Introduce vocabulary words used in the video whose meanings may be unclear or unknown to your students. Provide your students with some background as a frame for the story. Put on the board words or names they might want to use in their captions. Then show the video.

Perhaps you want to teach your fifth- or sixth-graders to compare and contrast and to evaluate. You could introduce the book *The Wind in the Willows,* or maybe only a section from it. Tell your students before they begin reading to pay attention to one character they would like to write about and draw. Tell them also they will be making a list of five or six incidents involving this character. In addition, they should pay attention to how they "experience" the book or selection as they read it. After the reading, have the students complete their activity.

Next, you might want to show the video *The Wind in the Willows* to the same class. Since the students will already have a good background for the story, ask them to concentrate on how they "experience" seeing the video. How is their selected character presented in the video? After the viewing, have them list five or six experiences they had watching the video that they did not have reading the book. They could also compare and contrast their characters as shown in the video with their characters described in the book.

Then, you might want to take this same class to a live production of *The Wind in the Willows.* Tell them to be prepared to observe their characters and to be alert to the experience of seeing a play. Then they can compare reading the book with seeing the video with seeing the play. They can make evaluations. Which medium did they enjoy most? Why? Which medium gave the most information about their characters? What do they see as the benefits of participating in all three media presentations of *The Wind in the Willows?*

Another area of writing where students can exercise their creativity is poetry. After the students have selected something in nature, have them write a haiku. They can write their final copy on a piece of white, unlined paper. Then, using markers or colored pencils, they can do a beautiful job decorating it. When mounted on colored construction paper, it makes a very nice display.

You could have your primary class read together a sample Thanksgiving poem or you could read one to your students. Then they could write their own "thanks" poem, maybe just two or three lines of free verse. They could do a turkey collage to complete this project. Included for you are a Thanksgiving poem and a turkey art project in Figure A8-17 in the appendix.

Maybe your class will read an Easter egg poem and then attempt their own about the Easter Bunny. Do not worry about length, format, or rhyming. Students could write *Easter Bunny:* or just *Bunny:* followed by a list of words that are thought of about the Easter Bunny. Have them capitalize each word and write each word on a separate line, all the words lined up, one below the other.

Have all the students copy their final drafts of their poem onto paper and make a bunny to go with it. Included for you are a sample Easter egg poem and a bunny art project in Figure A8-18 in the appendix. Your class might even want to make a poetry book or a picture album.

Of course, you will want the students to apply their manuscript or cursive skills while doing this writing. You are the one who will model these for your students. Provide them with plenty of opportunities to practice both at school and at home.

Writing Portfolios, Organizers, and Assessment Devices

Students may wish to select samples of their work to place in portfolios. Be sure the date is on them first to enable students to evaluate their progress. Explain to the students exactly what a portfolio is and how it will provide them the opportunity to reflect on their work and realize their progress.

At the end of each quarter, place one paper the student has done totally independently in the classroom, which has been evaluated by the teacher, in the student's portfolio. Tell the student in advance that this will go into the portfolio to be sure it will represent a best effort.

After students have had the chance to review their portfolios, to select the best piece and write what they like about it, to write what they have learned and made improvement on, and to set new goals, schedule a meeting with each student individually. Review the portfolio together and delineate ways to meet the established goals. This will take approximately fifteen minutes per student. Be sure the other students understand their work responsibilities so that your attention can be directed to your student and his or her portfolio.

Students can take portfolios home to share with their parents, ask for comments, and return to school. At the end of the year, after their final evaluation, students can take the portfolios home to keep.

When using portfolios, it is important that the system be manageable. Decide how often to collect samples: once a month, twice a quarter, after each unit, and so on. Have a place to store the portfolios.

Portfolio evaluations can be as simple as students periodically selecting a particular piece and telling why they liked it and on what they would like to improve. The original paper along with the student's comments can be filed in the individual folder. If you like, portfolio evaluations can be more complex and involve a rubric for the different areas of written language in addition to a student's reflection.

Sample portfolio evaluations are included for you in Figure A8-19 in the appendix. One is for the primary grades, although it could just as easily be used in the upper grades. The other version, which includes a rubric, is more suitable just for the upper grades. These portfolio evaluations can be used by the students or the teacher to evaluate any one, two, or more areas of writing: creativity, style, format, mechanics, and so on. They can also be used as an overall evaluation tool for writing in its broadest context.

Figures A8-20, A8-21 and A8-22 are organizers students can use to help them write successfully in any subject. Figure A8-20 is a graphic organizer for language arts or history. It helps students analyze the various parts of a story or an event in history. Once students complete the organizer, they will be very prepared to write their papers.

Figure A8-21 is another organizer called an umbrella. It is general and can be used as a story, character or concept map, a cluster, or a web. It can be used for any subject. Since the entire umbrella does not have to be filled out, this activity is suitable for any grade level. Adjust the level of difficulty for the grade and skills of your particular group.

Figure A8-22 is an experiment/activity synopsis suitable for science. It can be used as the actual writing activity or as a prewrite.

In writing, especially, it is very worthwhile to give a pretest of a somewhat general nature before any new teaching. This could be done by the students totally independently. Then you will know what your students really have mastered. After that, set outcomes and plan activities that will direct the students well beyond where they are.

When you give a pretest, some students may excel on it. Help them establish other goals that are challenging to them and toward which they are motivated. Monitor them and their work to make sure they are well occupied and progressing.

The following is an example of an assessment device you might use in fourth, fifth, or sixth grades to ensure individual accountability.

Directions to the students:

This test is to be done in the classroom totally independently. You may use a speller, a personal spelling list, and a thesaurus or the dictionary. You may *not* ask the teacher, classroom helper, tutor, or any student for help. You will need to have a partner to write to and that student will write to you.

Use **friendly letter format.** Tell all about each of these areas:

1. your family and pets
2. something interesting about the city or state in which you live
3. your favorite after-school, weekend or vacation activity

You could correct for the following:

Correct spelling for high-utility list words, correct spelling for address and city and state in heading, correct spelling for complimentary close

Correctness of friendly letter format, including all five parts: heading, with the student's address, city, state, and zip code, and the date written correctly; greeting written correctly with capitals and comma; body with indentions for paragraphs and correct use of margins; complimentary close written correctly and with a comma; and signature written in the correct place

Content of paper, including responsive, related content; adequate length for the assignment; interesting, commanding language and enriched vocabulary; good sentence structure; good transitions, and ease of understanding (Later in the year, you might want to ask if the product shows growth in written language for each student.)

Cursive or printing, including correct formation and usage of upper- and lowercase letters, correct connections between letters, and neatness

Using a friendly letter as a device to measure progress in student portfolios is an excellent idea for a variety of reasons. First, if you have each student select a partner to write to, their final or "published" product will always have eager eyes awaiting it. This also allows each student to be a *writer* and a *reader* of a letter. Students can be encouraged to praise the student whose letter they read and also offer some helpful suggestions.

Second, use of a friendly letter ensures that all students can correctly write their address, city, state and zip.

Third, the body of the friendly letter can easily be varied to go across the curriculum and use different writing modes. For example, a student could write a friendly letter to a classmate explaining some aspect of Colonial America that the classmate probably does not already know. History books, library books, encyclopedias, interviews of parents, and so on could be used to gather information for note taking. To explain the information in the letter, the student will have to carefully learn the material.

The body of the letter could be narrative, expository, or persuasive. It could include writing about exciting trips, experiments in science, solving problems in math, persuading a classmate to avoid drugs, retelling reading stories, writing about someone's life, or pretending a classmate is some important historical character or sports hero and writing to the classmate from that perspective. It could even include some original poetry or be autobiographical.

Fourth, this type of format allows students to use any and all levels of the taxonomy and really demonstrate their capabilities and talents in writing. You may have students who struggle to write one short paragraph and others who can write four of five good ones loaded with enriched vocabulary and original ideas.

Fifth, this allows direct measurement of the depth of knowledge and skills the students have, which is a major purpose of alternative assessment.

Last, good ability at using friendly letter format and writing paragraphs of varying content and style are skills directly related to real life.

Encourage your students to have all their writing projects—no matter how small, no matter which subject they are writing in—represent their best effort. Ask them to check all their papers for high-quality content and appearance. That way they will be proud of their work and so will you. Collect samples of their work throughout the year so that their progress is apparent to them, their parents, and you.

Research and Studies

Mavrogenes, Hagemann, and Wallace (1991) studied three methods used to promote literacy in kindergarten and Grade 1:

1. IBM's *Write to Read* (WTR) program, a multimedia approach where students write what they say and read what they write;
2. A **free writing** program to accompany recent research on emergent literacy where children write whatever they can and even scribbles are fine; and
3. Use of a handbook that defined writing objectives by grade level, K to 8.

The most interesting finding in this study dealt with kindergarten. Students in the group using the free writing method significantly outscored both of the other groups using the other methods in every area: writing samples, word analysis, comprehension, and spelling. However, the kindergarten classes participating in the free writing group were all-day kindergartens whereas students using the other methods were only half-day, and no first grade classes participated in free writing. The fact that kindergarten free writing students spent more time each day at school could be a strong factor in the results.

The *WTR* group outperformed the control group—the handbook group—at a significant level in three out of four areas in kindergarten: encoding, word attack, as measured by the CTBS (Comprehensive Test of Basic Skills), and spelling. The *WTR* group outperformed at a significant level in two out of five areas in first grade: word analysis, as measured by the ITBS (Iowa Test of Basic Skills), and invented spelling.

According to the study, *WTR* appears to do a better job at developing word analysis skills, but not an overall better job as compared with paper-pencil approaches. In addition, teachers using *WTR* and free writing had more in-servicing than did the control (handbook) group.

The Developmental Writing Program (Matthews & Turner, 1987) underscores the need for a systematic writing process to be used in the elementary grades. Although this program uses a writing process, its main strength is the continual in-servicing of the elementary teachers, during which time the teachers are given writing assignments they must complete. The theory is that if the teachers sit in the students' spots, they will experience similar fears and frustrations, motivating them to be keenly aware of the need for a process.

At the first in-service, teachers were provided a guide that included 163 lesson activities geared to the district's 63 learning objectives. They were also furnished with a student handbook that contained a writing process guide and a minithesaurus.

Teachers had a classroom observation checklist to keep them focused on the importance of writing: Is there evidence that students are being instructed in the writing process, that they are learning vocabulary and sentence, paragraph, and multiparagraph writing? Are dictionaries, thesauri, personal spelling lists, and high-utility word lists available to students? Do students have the opportunity to share their writing, and is it displayed?

Gettinger (1993) examined to what extent a procedure that had been shown to improve spelling in research could be implemented in the classroom. The procedure that was incorporated allowed enough time for students to master the material, provided feedback to students that allowed them to compare their spellings to correct versions, and used student-supervised practice.

Sixty-five third-grade students from three classrooms in a mostly white, middle-class suburban school district participated in this study. Entire classes were randomly assigned to treatments.

The results of this study demonstrated that higher test scores were achieved using the error imitation and correction procedure than either traditional methods or the modified traditional instruction. The treatment was successfully executed as part of the normal classroom routine. This demonstrated that the techniques supported in the research could be transferred to the classroom.

A study by Roberts and Samuels (1993) compared a computer-based program of teaching handwriting to more traditional methods. Three methods were examined. In the first method, students followed computer-based handwriting activities using the computer with a pen tablet to trace on-screen letters. The second method was the traditional pen-and-paper instruction, tracing letter forms. In the third method, used to control for the potential motivational effects of using a computer in the first treatment, students used a light pen to trace and copy letters on a Touch Window.

The subjects of this study were fourth- through sixth-graders who were selected by their teachers on the basis of poor handwriting skills. These students had no severe language difficulties, no serious attendance or behavioral problems, normal vision or corrected normal vision, no diagnosis of a neuromotor disability, and had previously received instruction in cursive writing. Students with learning disabilities as well as normal-achieving students were included.

The results of this study showed that the traditional pen-and-paper method was better than the computer-based program used in this study, developed by Lally and Macleod (Lally & Macleod, 1982). This is not to say, however, that all computer-based programs for teaching handwriting are less effective than traditional methods.

This study also showed that handwriting is a skill made up of many different parts, and when students are learning new elements of this skill, their writing slows down. The findings suggest that the different components of handwriting skill must be studied separately. In that way, perhaps the techniques that work best on each component can be incorporated into a new method of teaching handwriting that is either computer-based or traditional.

Moore and Caldwell (1993) compared the effects on the quality of narrative writing of three different planning activities: one using drawing; another using drama; and the third using a teacher-led discussion with a follow-up writing activity and then more traditional language arts follow-up activities. Two second-grade and two third-grade classes were divided into three groups, a drama group, a drawing group, and a control group that used discussion. The grade levels were randomly mixed, as was the gender of the subjects, throughout the three groups.

All three groups individually discussed facets of narrative literature for a fifteen-minute period at the beginning of each week. After that, the drama group spent forty-five minutes in a drama session, which began with a dramatic activity focusing and building on the theme of the discussion. After the warm-up, students worked on their ideas for their stories by discussing them, participating in role-playing activities, and improvising main scenes with a partner and then presenting them to the whole class.

The drawing group spent forty-five minutes drawing and thirty minutes writing after the group discussion. This group also participated in warm-up exercises, using different drawing activities to build on the theme discussed with the group. Then, seated around tables to discuss ideas with each other, students drew storyboards for their stories, showing the characters, setting, and major scenes from the plot.

The control group, after the discussion, spent thirty minutes writing their stories and then forty-five minutes on a traditional language-arts program.

The results of this study showed that the drama and drawing methods were more effective planning activities for writing than traditional discussion. Rehearsing a story in different media helped beginning writers develop their stories more fully. Also, this study demonstrated that prewriting methods were effective and that, perhaps, more time than is traditional should be allotted to them.

Mavrogenes and Bezruczko (1993) sought to identify the influences on the development of writing in children. The source for their data was the Longitudinal Study of Children at Risk, an ongoing study in the Chicago Public Schools that has followed more than a thousand low-income African American students from kindergarten through fourth grade. Questionnaires were also given to teachers, parents, and children at different stages throughout the Longitudinal Study.

The students' writing abilities were determined by reviewing their answers to two questions on the questionnaire they received in the fourth year of the study. The questions were "Tell us what you like about school" and "How do you think school could be made better?"

The results of the Longitudinal Study showed that, overall, writing scores were very low, with the highest 10 percent getting 88 percent of the total points on the test and the lowest 10 percent only getting 22 percent. One reason for this is that students did not like writing. Also, writing questions were rated lower than reading questions by all three groups (parents, teachers, and students). A possible explanation as to why the students did not like to write is that they did not do very much of it, and thus did not know how to do it. Other factors that were rated low by teachers included students' reading for pleasure; behavior; concentration; responsibility; motivation; and ease of learning. Parents ranked as low the rate that their children wrote stories or notes and read for pleasure, as well as doing things with the children, such as going on outings or going to the library.

Two items that did receive high rankings were teachers' ratings of parents' interest in their children's progress and parents' ranking of their reading to their children. Although these two were positive, the other low rankings were more related to success in school and in writing.

Factors such as teacher and student expectations, motivation, maturity, behavior, and self-confidence were all correlated with students' writing ability. On the other hand, students' and parents' ratings of how well the students liked reading and writing did not correlate with the scores on the writing ability tests. Other factors correlated with good writing ability were parents' participation in activities at school; students' cognitive readiness, level of concentration, and interest in school; and having either teachers or students read books to the students. Students liking to have stories read to them, however, was negatively correlated with writing ability. The article by Mavrogenes and Bezruczko offers explanations for this, ranging from students not enjoying the book to some students enjoy being read to instead of writing. Living with a single parent was also negatively correlated with writing ability.

Mavrogenes and Bezruczko's article ends with two recommendations. The first is to include more writing in the curriculum, taught by teachers who are familiar with and knowledgeable about writing. Teachers must realize that grammar, punctuation, and spelling are only a small part of the writing process. Children must learn that writing is done with a purpose in mind and for a certain audience. Writing must be organized to make sense to others. Editing is important. Mechanics such as grammar and punctuation are useful as tools to help clarify about what the student is writing.

The second suggestion is that schools should pay more attention to things like teacher expectations and student self-confidence. If factors such as student self-confidence could be improved, then other factors, such as behavior and motivation would be improved, leading to greater success in the classroom.

When your students are working on all the various projects, experiments, and activities across the curriculum that you have prepared for them, take class and individual photos of them. Take photos of the students having fun on different field trips, explaining their science projects, dancing in their performances, putting on their puppet shows and skits, working on group writing projects, and receiving awards. Display these around the room with their work. The students love to see themselves and their work on the chalkboards, walls, and bulletin boards.

As with all the student activity sheets, follow the directions in the introduction to this book to make whatever adjustments and modifications you need to suit your class. When you create your own activity sheets, be sure to use white paper and black ink for a good copy. Make them nice and neat. If you can, use a word processor. Then if you have a primary grade, you can use a good-sized font so that your students can read the material easily. Even if you feel rushed or pressured by time constraints, do not forget to preserve what you make either by carefully filing it or by laminating it.

Keep informed about all the research in the field of education. Read professional magazines and journals, and attend workshops and in-services. Be prepared to continually update your information and skills.

Use the various techniques presented in this book to create a powerful program. Be energetic, enthusiastic, and well prepared and your students will find you delightful. Your elementary classroom will be running as easily as you can say the ABC's!

CHAPTER QUESTIONS

1. Thirty students must remain in your classroom during lunch period because of inclement weather. A noon-duty supervisor will be going back and forth between your room and the room next door. Name a minimum of six specific activities your students could do. How many students will each activity involve?

2. During inclement weather when you are not able to be with your class, how will you help students learn to handle disagreements on their own? What will be your policy for a student who is misbehaving?

3. What does *vade mecum* mean to you? If you could create your own vade mecum, what would it be, how would it be used, and why would you like it?

4. How can students be helpful to classroom visitors?

5. Name the parts of the writing process. Select one to explain.

6. Name at least six different types of writing that students may be assigned. Describe an occasion when one of them might be used.

7. Spelling is part of the broad spectrum of writing. What does this mean for the teaching of spelling? What does this mean in beginning literacy?

8. Before giving a writing assignment, what prerequisite skills do you need to check to be sure the students have?

9. Name three things students can learn from having their classmates' writing assignments read to them?

10. Why are students successful with time-order paragraphs, power writing, UCI multiparagraph writing projects, writing clusters, and double entry journals?

11. Name one method of grading a writing assignment. What are its benefits and limitations?

12. How can a video be effectively used in a writing assignment?

13. What type of poetry do you like? Create a poem that you could share with an elementary classroom. What about it do you think the students would especially like?

14. What is your appraisal of each of the methods of the *Write to Read* program, free writing, and the use of a handbook to promote literacy in kindergarten and first grade?

15. In the Developmental Writing Program, what do teachers do at the in-services? What is your opinion about this?

16. What are some of the components of the classroom observation checklist in the Developmental Writing Program?

17. Why was the technique of error imitation and correction considered transferable to the classroom?

18. Why was the treatment of using a light pen for students to trace on a Touch Window used?

19. According to Roberts and Samuels, what is handwriting? What would this mean for your classroom?

20. Explain what the drawing group and the drama group did for their planning activities. Why were these methods effective?

21. In the Longitudinal Study of Children at Risk, how were the students' writing abilities determined?

22. Explain the two recommendations for writing improvement made by Mavrogenes and Bezruczko in their analysis of the study of children at risk.

CHAPTER PROJECTS

Develop a writing lesson on a topic you like and for a grade level of your choice. Use the Blueprint for Teaching Effectiveness as a guide.

Have a lesson that presents an item in two different forms. For example, an animal in two forms: a picture of an animal and a live animal; a car in two forms: a picture of a car and a remote-controlled car; a picture of a science experiment and the same experiment done in the classroom; reading a poem or short article about a butterfly while the students take notes, and showing a real butterfly; a scientific picture of the ear or eye and a take-apart model of the ear or eye; and so on.

If you prepare for a primary class, use the writing cluster. After the presentation, the students can, with a partner, write the name of the animal in their center circle and identify whether it was the picture or the live one. Then they can write one thing they learned inside each circle. In the other circle, they can write "Animal (live)" or whatever it was. Then have them write four *different* things they learned from touching the animal or taking apart the model of the ear or eye or whatever the case may be.

If you have an upper-grade class, teach the double entry journal. Proceed as for using the cluster method, but have the students list as many things as they can that they learned from the picture and as many things as they can that they learned from the live animal or model.

The same day or on another day, have your students do the second part of the lesson, either using their cluster or double entry journal. If you are planning for a primary grade, have the students put their three or four learnings from the first cluster into a set of sentences. Then have them put their three or four learnings from the second cluster into a set of sentences. As a class, decide on a good title for their activity. Have a ten- or fifteen-minute period where the students can help each other with proofreading. Have them make a final copy in their best printing. They could make a picture to go with their writing. Mount the work on construction paper and plan to put it up on a bulletin board after evaluation.

If you are planning for an upper grade, have the students use their double entry journals to compare and contrast information from the picture and the live animal or use their double entry journal to select the side that has more information. Have them write about this and explain why they think they were able to write more information in this category. Schedule a proofreading period. An accompanying drawing is always nice and, of course, the students like this. Then plan to collect, evaluate, and put up on the bulletin board.

FINAL REVIEW

A final review practice test is included in the following chapter, Chapter 9, The XYZ's. It primarily covers material in Chapter 5, The MNO's, Chapter 6, The PQR's, Chapter 7, The STU's, and Chapter 8, The V's & W's. In addition to this final review, it is important to do the following: restudy the midcourse review, reread the introduction to this text, review the chapter material and questions, and thoroughly study the glossary.

REFERENCES

Gettinger, M. (1993). Effects of error correction on third graders' spelling. *Journal of Educational Research, 87*(1), 39–45.

Lally, M. & Macleod, I. (1982). Development of skills through computers: Achieving an effective, enjoyable learning environment. *Impact of Science on Society, 32*(4), 449–460.

Matthews, J., & Turner, S. D. (1987). The developmental writing program. *ERS Spectrum, 5*(1), 11–16.

Mavrogenes, N. A., & Bezruczko, N. (1993). Influences on writing development. *Journal of Educational Research, 86*(4), 237–245.

Mavrogenes, N. A., Hagemann, M., & Wallace, T. (1991). A comparative study of three methods of promoting literacy in kindergarten and first grade. *ERS Spectrum, 9*(3), 3–9.

Moore, B. H., & Caldwell, H. (1993). Drama and drawing for narrative writing in primary grades. *Journal of Educational Research, 87*(2), 100–109.

Morrison, J. C. (1923). Morrison-McCall spelling scale for grades 2 to 8 by J. Cayce Morrison and William A. McCall. Yonkers-on-Hudson, NY: ook company.

Roberts, G. I., & Samuels, M. T. (1993). Handwriting remediation: A comparison of computer-based and traditional approaches. *Journal of Educational Research, 87*(2), 118–125.

BIBLIOGRAPHY

Teale, W. H., & Sulzby, E. (1986). *Emergent literacy: Writing and reading.* Norwood, NJ: Ablex, p. 23.

9

THE XYZ'S

ELEMENTARY STUDENT ACTIVITIES
ANSWER KEYS

The ABC's

No answer keys are needed.

The DEF's

FACTS

ADDITION

7	9	6	9	6	7
9	4	8	6	7	2
5	10	8	9	6	8
9	5	5	7	8	9
8	7	10	9	10	7
3	4	6	10	10	8
10	5	5	10	7	10
9	4	10	10	10	9

SUBTRACTION

0	1	5	5	1	0
0	3	1	3	2	2
7	6	3	2	1	3
6	4	4	5	3	0
4	0	8	2	1	1
2	6	3	5	9	5
5	4	4	1	6	0
2	1	2	2	4	3

ROBOMAN

```
Yellow
Green                    Yellow              Green
Brown    Yellow   Purple   Yellow            Brown
                  Green
         Black    Purple   Black
              Orange   Orange
              Blue     Blue
              Red      Red
              Black    Black
           Orange
                        Yellow
                 Red
                       Blue
```

ADVANCED SUBTRACTION

0	1	5	5	1	0
3	3	1	3	1	2
7	1	3	2	1	2
6	4	4	5	3	4
4	5	7	6	7	6
2	9	7	7	9	6
5	7	3	9	4	8
6	5	8	9	8	9

YUMMY SUNDAE

```
              Red
              White
Brown    Pink    Brown
         Pink
Brown             Black
         Pink
Black             Brown
         Pink
Brown    Pink    Black
Blue     Orange  Purple
```

MULTIPLICATION Pt

10	20	0	8	8	12
0	4	12	9	10	1
16	28	30	15	6	12
25	4	0	24	18	18
0	40	9	2	6	32
27	16	12	7	35	36
24	14	20	40	9	6
45	12	15	21	24	5

ADVANCED MULTIPLICATION T-SHEET

Answers will vary depending on the T number. If you want to practice using the same T numbers all the time, the following will work as an answer key:

2	*4*	*6*	*8*
10	8	30	40
8	16	6	56
18	24	24	8
6	32	0	0
14	0	42	16
16	4	48	24
12	12	36	48
4	20	18	64
2	36	54	72
0	28	12	32

3	*5*	*7*	*9*
6	5	63	45
18	45	49	36
24	10	35	63
0	40	21	54
3	15	7	9
9	35	0	18
12	20	56	81
15	30	42	72
27	25	28	0
21	0	14	27

DIVISION

9	3	5	9	3
1	8	9	8	9
4	4	5	5	8
3	1	4	6	7
7	8	6	8	8
5	5	7	6	5
2	3	4	3	9
2	0	9	8	5
6	7	2	4	8
2	7	7	6	6

Chapter 3 The GHI's

GEOGRAPHY
  MY GEOGRAPHY BOOKLET

FIRST, GEOMETRY (Geometry Activity)

Blue   Green
              Yellow
Brown   Red
              Purple
              Orange

SAME SHAPES, DIFFERENT POSITIONS
(Geometry Activity)

Blue	Purple	Green
Brown		Orange
Yellow	Red	

CONTINENTS AND OCEANS OF THE WORLD
(Geography Activity)

Blue	Yellow	Brown
Green	Red	Purple
	Orange	

CONTINENT SHAPES

1. Antarctica   2. Australia
3. Asia   4. North America
5. Africa   6. South America
        7. Europe

MEXICO: OUR NEIGHBOR TO THE SOUTH
(Activities)

1. Ten states: California, Nevada, Utah, Wyoming, Colorado, Arizona, New Mexico, Oklahoma, Kansas, and Texas
2. Chihuahua: on a warm plateau
   Mexico City: in the cool mountains
   Chichén Itzá: on the hot plains

AUSTRALIA ACTIVITY

1. Kangaroo: either gray or red
   Koala: Back is gray or brown
     Tummy is white
   Wombat: brown
   Dingo: yellow and brown OR white and black
   Tasmanian Devil: all black OR black and white
2.
special animal	koala
capital of Australia	Canberra
almost no one lives here	Never-Never Land
summer for our country	winter for their country

MY GEOGRAPHY BOOKLET
MAP ACTIVITIES

1. Alaska is part of the United States
2. Greenland is not part of the country of Canada. It's a province of Denmark.
3. North America
4. United States, USA, or US
5. Atlantic Ocean
6. Pacific Ocean
7. Mexico
8. Rio Grande
9. Mexico City

10. Washington, D. C.
11. Ottawa
12. Gulf of Mexico
13. Hawaii is not part of North America and this is a map for the continent of North America only. Hawaii is too far out in the ocean to be considered part of a continent; therefore, it is part of Oceania.
14. - - - - - - - - - - - - - - - - - (dotted line)
15. North America

CITY SCRAMBLE—WEST
1. Oahu
2. Pearl Harbor
3. luau
4. hula
5. aloha
6. tourism
7. San Francisco
8. suspension
9. subway
10. cable car
11. Silicon Valley

WONDERS SEARCH
1. Colorado River
2. helicopter
3. The Grand Canyon
4. flat
5. Niagara Falls
6. Horseshoe
7. water
8. erosion

WONDERS CIRCLES
Message:
Erosion reshapes
Niagara Falls each year.
Message:
Be brave.
Fly into the canyon.

Message:
Get your slicker.
See the falls.
Message:
The Grand Canyon—
A natural wonder

CITY SCRAMBLE—EAST
1. megalopolis
2. permanent
3. Potomac River
4. Hudson River
5. boroughs
6. scarce
7. New York City
8. Ellis Island
9. Manhattan

UNITED STATES GEOGRAPHY—STUDY SHEET
1. Because of severe erosion problems, the water is diverted to preserve the American Falls.
2. The Grand Canyon was formed from the force of the Colorado River cutting deeper and deeper into the land. It is located in Arizona.

3. New York City
4. High-rise apartments are built. Since parking space is very limited, people use public transportation: buses, subways, taxis, and so on. Manufacturing companies that don't take up much space, such as printing, publishing, and clothing, are found in this city.
5. The Statue of Liberty was given to our country as a symbol of friendship by France. It is located on Liberty Island in the New York Harbor.
6. Washington, D.C.
7. Potomac River
8. the Declaration of Independence, the Constitution, and the Bill of Rights
9. Oahu
10. Golden Gate Bridge
11. The USS *Arizona* Memorial is in Pearl Harbor, a little west of downtown Honolulu, Hawaii. It is dedicated to all the people who died in the Japanese surprise attack on Pearl Harbor on December 7, 1941. About 1,000 dead men are still on the sunken USS *Arizona*.
12. Washington, D.C.
13. Canada and the U.S.
14. Washington, D.C.
15. New York City

UNITED STATES GEOGRAPHY TEST
1. F
2. F
3. F
4. T
5. T
6. Hawaii (Pearl Harbor near Honolulu)
7. the peninsula that San Francisco is on and Marin County to the north
8. Hudson River
9. by the erosion of the Colorado River
10. Washington, D.C.
11. builds high-rises; OR has manufacturing companies that take up little space; OR has abundant public transportation because parking is very limited
12. France
13. B
14. D
15. E
16. A
17. C
18. b
19. a
20. d

WORLD GEOGRAPHY BOOKLET
INTRODUCTION ACTIVITY
1. Oceania
2. Asia
3. Pacific
4. approximately 4.7 billion
5. New countries are formed and others become larger as a result of independence movements and wars.

6. Russia, Canada, China, U.S., Brazil
7. China, India, U.S., Indonesia, Brazil
8. North America, South America, part of Antarctica
9. Europe, Asia, Africa, Australia, part of Antarctica
10. Usually a poor, developing nation; lack of skilled labor force; a population increasing too fast for the nation's ability to produce or trade for food; needing training for its farmers, money for modern transportation and machinery, water supplies and power sources for energy
11. developed = industrialized, has natural resources, skilled labor, a population size which can be supported; may have major pollution problems
    developing = lack of natural resources or ability to get to them, unskilled labor, farmers need training, money needed for modern machinery and transportation, population size too large to adequately support
12. Chinese and English
13. oil
14. UN (United Nations)

WESTERN HEMISPHERE
1–17. (coloring on map)
18. North America and South America
19. Central America, the West Indies, U.S., Canada, Mexico, and Greenland (a province of Denmark)
20. Tuesday
21. The three are: the Grand Canyon of the Colorado River, Paricutin, and the harbor at Rio de Janeiro (Students select one on which to write.)
22. The three are: the Golden Gate Bridge, the Empire State Building, and the Alaska Highway (Students select one on which to write.)

WESTERN HEMISPHERE MATCH AND FILL IN
1. midnight sun
2. tundra
3. island
4. provinces
5. Montreal
6. St. Lawrence River

Column A
e   Cape Canaveral
g   Alaska Highway
f   Rockies
h   Horseshoe Falls
i   over three times the size of all five Great Lakes
c   home of The Underground City
d   *Skate*
b   Aleutian Islands
a   els

MAP ACTIVITIES (Eastern Hemisphere)
1.–44. (coloring on map)
45. Europe, Africa, Asia, Australia
46. Select one of the following: the French and Spanish caves with prehistoric paintings in Europe, Victoria Falls in Africa, Mt. Everest in the Himalayan Mountains of

Asia, or the Great Barrier Reef of Australia. Tell why you selected it.
47. Select one of the following: the Ukraine's Dneproges Dam; Harwell, England's, Atomic Energy Research Establishment; or the Eiffel Tower of Paris, France. Tell why you selected it.
48. the Pyramids of Egypt in Africa

EASTERN HEMISPHERE MYSTERY QUESTION
1. popul A tion
2.   c E remonies
3.   Vol G a GREAT
4.   No R way
5.   fif T y
6.   A lps
7.   E N gland
8.   pe T rol
9.   R omance BRITAIN
10. Casp I an
11. Euras I a
12.   B alkan

WORLD GEOGRAPHY STUDY SHEET
1. Provinces
2. Oceania is made up of the many islands of the Pacific not considered close enough to a continent to be part of that continent. Hawaii is part of Oceania.
3. The United States ranks fourth.
4. The United States ranks third.
5. China and India
6. Chinese, English, Hindustani, and Spanish
7. Asia and the Pacific Ocean
8. about 4.7 billion
9. North America, South America, and part of Antarctica
10. Europe, Africa, Asia, Australia, and part of Antarctica
11. The International Date Line is in the Western Hemisphere. It mostly follows 180 degrees longitude. Those living on the east side are one day ahead of those living on the west. The date line zigzags around somewhat so that no country will have two different days at the same time.
12. three natural: the Grand Canyon, Paricutin, and the harbor at Rio de Janeiro
    three modern: the Golden Gate Bridge, the Empire State Building, and the Alaska Highway
13. "Midnight Sun" means areas of the polar regions that have sun continuously for at least twenty-four hours. Norway is called the "Land of the Midnight Sun." In northern Norway, there is continuous sunlight from May through July. The South Pole has midnight sun from mid-September to mid-March.
14. Denmark
15. French and English
16. The Underground City is a huge shopping area of over 200 shops and restaurants under Montreal's downtown streets. You can take an escalator from most of the major hotels to get down there. It is the largest underground

shopping center in the world. It is located in Montreal, Quebec, in Canada.

17. conterminous (also called contiguous)
18. 134°F in Death Valley, California, USA
19. −81°F at Snag in the Yukon Territory of Canada
20. Both are mass transits. Els are above ground and subways are below.
21. It is the area of the world where civilization began.
22. The Great Pyramids of Egypt in Africa
23. Since no body of water separates Europe and Asia, they are sometimes referred to as Eurasia.
24. Ural Mountains, Ural River, the Caspian Sea, and the Black Sea
25. the Caspian Sea
26. London, England
27. An ACV is an Air Cushion Vehicle, also called a hovercraft. It travels on a cushion of compressed air provided by two or more large fans blowing downward on air beneath the craft. The hovercraft, which travels just above water or land, can go backward, forward, or sideways. It can turn or hover.
28. The Leaning Tower of Pisa is in Italy.

WORLD GEOGRAPHY TEST

1. F
2. T
3. T
4. F
5. T
6. Norway — Land of the Midnight Sun
7. Denmark — country to which Greenland belongs
8. Asia — largest continent
9. Ural Mtns. — partial border between Europe and Asia
10. Eurasia — Europe and Asia considered together as one continent
11. Oceania is the many islands of the Pacific that are not close enough to a continent to be considered part of that continent. Hawaii is part of Oceania.
12. The International Date Line is in the Western Hemisphere. It mostly follows 180 degrees West longitude. Those living on the east side are one day ahead of those living on the west. The date line zigzags around somewhat so that no country will have two different days at the same time.
13. The Underground City is a large shopping area under the downtown streets of Montreal. It has over 200 stores and restaurants. Most downtown hotels have access via escalators. It is located in Montreal, Quebec, in Canada.
14. Death Valley, California, USA
15. An ACV is a hovercraft, also known as an air cushioned vehicle. It travels on a cushion of compressed air provided by two or more large fans blowing downward on air beneath the craft. The hovercraft, which travels just above water or land, can go backward, forward, or sideways. It can turn or hover.
16. China and India
17. Europe, Asia, Africa, and Australia
18. Any two: Alaska Highway, the Empire State Building, and the Golden Gate Bridge
19. French and English
20. Chinese, English, Hindustani, and Spanish (any order)

HISTORY
CHRISTOPHER COLUMBUS

1. 1492
2. Spain
3. King Ferdinand and Queen Isabella of Spain
4. Gold, spices, riches; establish a trade center for East to West trade
5. Some people thought the Earth was flat. If you sailed too far away from land, your ship would fall off the Earth. Others believed there were terrible sea monsters that would attack your ship if you sailed too far from land.
6. Answers will vary, but mixed feelings of hope and excitement with fear and worry about the crew, the supplies, the weather, etcetera.
7. Answers will vary, but Columbus probably didn't want to turn back. He was an explorer and loved adventure and loved the sea. He had visions of establishing a great trade center and being revered as a trader. However, he was under great pressure to turn back from some of the frightened crew members. They were concerned about sailing all the way back against the wind.
8. the island of San Salvador in the Bahamas in the West Indies and then on to the Bay of Bariay off Cuba
9. a. Natives of the islands, whom Columbus called Indians because he was sure he was in the East Indies
   b. Natives smoking cigars; the Europeans had not seen tobacco before this
   c. On Hispaniola, he saw trees like the ones in Spain, so he named the island "Spanish Island."
10. a. Some captured "Indians"
    b. Some of his crew; forty of his men he left in the New World to search for gold
11. Answers will vary, but could include something about a triumphant feeling after returning from his first voyage. He was named Admiral of the Ocean Sea and Viceroy of the Indies. But, after later voyages, Columbus fell into disfavor with Ferdinand and Isabella because he did not establish a world trade center or bring back riches for them, and the colonists at Hispaniola were unruly and dissatisfied.
12. On the first couple of voyages, Ferdinand and Isabella were very pleased, but on the fourth voyage, they sent him to the New World to get him out of Spain. They were very unhappy with him.
13. a. To check on all the men he left at Hispaniola
    b. Bring over from Europe all the new colonists for the New World; he had about 1,000 men on board
    c. To further his explorations for the spice cities of the East

Chapter 4 The JKL's

LISTENING

PLANTS HAVE FEELINGS, TOO
1. b
2. c
3. c
4. b

NILE CROCODILE
1. c
2. b
3. b
4. b

MARTIN LUTHER KING
1. a
2. c
3. b
4. b

THE TASMANIAN DEVIL
1. b
2. c
3. b
4. a

THE POLAR BEAR
1. c
2. a
3. b
4. a. T
   b. T
   c. F
5. a
6. a. 5
   b. 1
   c. 3
   d. 2
   e. 4
7. a
8. b
9. Answers will vary, but the polar bear at nine feet tall is taller than most bears and has a more powerful bite, too. It is the most dangerous hunter of the polar region.

ISIAH THOMAS
1. c
2. a
3. guard
4. F
   F
   T
5. c
6. a. T
   b. F
   c. T
   d. T

7. x demonstrated/showed
   x boasting/bragging
8. a
9. This is purely a matter of opinion, but a reason should be given for the answer.
   Example: I like college basketball because the players are closer to my age.
   Example: I like pro ball better because I have some cards of the pro players.

Chapter 5 The MNO's

MATH

GEOBOARD PROBLEMS 4x4's
1. Yes
2. Answers will vary, but should include something about determining the number of squares and triangles or the total number of triangles inside Geoboard *X* and comparing that with the number inside the figure in Geoboard *Y*. There are 2½ squares in each or five triangles in each.
3. Each figure needs to be made up of five triangles.

GEOBOARD PROBLEMS 5x5's
1. Yes
2. Answers will vary but should include the fact that each figure is made up of six squares or twelve triangles.
3. Each figure needs to be made up of twelve triangles.

BOUNCE THAT BALL
There is a picture of the final product on the page directly preceding the directions sheets with the ordered pairs of numbers.

WRITING A ONE-STEP STORY PROBLEM
A. Answers will vary. Example: Sam had $1.48. Jim gave him $19.36. How much money does Sam have now?
B. There are 736 students enrolled in Packard Elementary School. On Tuesday, 29 were absent. How many students were present on Tuesday?
C. There were 21 flowers in each row of Hector's garden. He had thirteen rows altogether. How many flower plants were in Hector's garden?
D. Marlene has been saving buttons for her three best friends. Marlene now has 636 buttons and is going to split them evenly among her three friends. How many buttons will each friend get?

Chapter 6 The PQR's

READING

JULIUS CAESAR
Vocabulary
1. orator
2. famous
3. translated
4. unbelievable
5. continent
6. opponents
7. skilled

Locating Details in the Story

1. I came, I saw, I conquered.
2. Egypt
3. 100 B.C. to 44 B.C.
4. Pompey, Brutus, and Cassius
5. Cleopatra
6. Italy
7. stabbed
8. murdered before Caesar got to him in Egypt
9. Rome

Main Ideas

1. Julius Caesar was a famous military leader and helped make Rome the center of the Roman Empire. He was also a famous orator.
2. Some people within the Roman Empire were afraid of Caesar's power.
3. He let the Senate know he had just conquered Turkey. His famous speech: *Veni, vidi, vici.*
4. His greatest accomplishment was his military prowess in building great strength into the Roman Empire.

Drawing Conclusions

1. Probably he was, since he took time out of his military work to fall in love with Cleopatra and make her head of Egypt.
2. No, *circa* would not be needed today because there are accurate records of births and deaths and historical events.

RESEARCH SKILLS

READING A MAP—IDAHO

1. 200 miles
2. Boise
3. Coeur d'Alene
4. Idaho Falls

AUSTRALIA—READING A MAP

1. Australia
2. Pacific Ocean
3. Indian Ocean
4. Tasmania

JOE'S BUDGET Pt

1. Joe's budget
2. food
3. 23%
4. Answers will vary, but might include cards, magazines, toys, amusement parks, and so on.

DAILY HIGH TEMPERATURES Pt

1. daily high temperatures during a heat wave
2. Friday
3. Monday
4. 95°

MOLLY AND HER JUMP ROPE Pt

1. the number of times in a row Molly jumps rope during the week
2. Wednesday
3. Friday
4. Tuesday and Saturday

POPULATION OF A RURAL AREA §

1. four cities in rural areas and their populations
2. Smallville
3. Ghost Town
4. countrylike
5. Trail Junction and Ghost Town

THE FAMILY CAR TRIP §

1. the distances between cities during a trip in the family car
2. City C to City D
3. 500 miles
4. about 2,150 miles

COOKIE SALE §

1. how many cookies certain children sold during a cookie sale
2. Martin
3. Mary
4. Bob

MOLLY AND HER JUMP ROPE §

1. the number of times Molly jumped rope during the days of the week
2. Wednesday
3. Friday
4. around 67
5. four

DAILY HIGH TEMPERATURES §

1. daily high temperatures during a heat wave
2. 95°
3. Friday
4. two
5. Monday and Sunday

JOE'S BUDGET §

1. Joe's budget
2. food
3. 15%
4. $7.50

HOW A PACKAGE GETS DELIVERED

1. how a package gets delivered across the nation overnight
2. by 10:00 A.M.
3. between 8:00 P.M. and 4:00 A.M.
4. between 5:00 P.M. and 8:00 P.M. to the airport; between 4:00 A.M. and 7:00 A.M. from the airport
5. seventeen hours

FIVE U.S. CITIES
1. 4,884 miles
2. $912
3. $1,368
4. 2,747 miles; $662
5. $724

READING A MAP AND A TABLE
1. 12,592 miles
2. 3,037 miles
3. $653
4. 8,875 miles
5. $2,167
6. $1,431
7. day coach
8. $736

LATITUDE AND LONGITUDE
Latitudes and longitudes are approximate.
1. 30° N, 90° W
2. 48° N, 122° W
3. 43° N, 115° W
4. 35° N, 90° W
5. 41° N, 80° W
6. 37° N, 100° W
7. 41° N, 112° W
8. 33° N, 80° W
9. 41° N, 74° W
10. 44° N, 87° W

TYPES OF CLIMATE IN THE UNITED STATES
1. one
2. very long, bitterly cold winter; little precipitation; short, chilly summer
3. polar
4. desert-like; long, hot summer; short, cool winter; little precipitation
5. southwestern
6. steppe
7. icecap
8. Tropical wet and dry (also called savanna)
9. Answers will vary. The state used must be named. The name of the climate classification(s) should be stated. Example: Louisiana—humid subtropical
10. marine: long, cool summer; short, mild winter; precipitation, especially in winter; frequent fogs and mists
11. humid subtropical
12. fogs and mists
13. This means a medium or good amount of rainfall. In fact, Louisiana averages 56 inches of rainfall a year and has had over 100 inches of rainfall in some years.
14. As air rises and expands, it cools. Also colder air cannot hold as much moisture as warm air. So different elevations in the highlands can have very different climates. If a particular highlands area is sloping to the south, it could be warmer than the same level land sloping to the colder north.
15. humid continental

SPECIALTIES OF THE UNITED STATES
1. special places in the U.S.
2. New York
3. Seattle
4. Mile High City
5. New Orleans
6. San Francisco
7. Chicago

USING A SCALE
1. Little Rock and Memphis = 135 miles
2. Atlanta and Charlotte = 270 miles
3. Memphis and Charlotte = 540 miles
4. Wichita and Washington, D.C. = 1,080 miles
5. Wichita and New Orleans = 675 miles

USING REFERENCE MATERIALS
Answer key is upside down on the bottom of the student activity page.

Chapter 7 The STU's

SCIENCE
LATITUDE AND CLIMATE
1–3. (coloring on map)
4. Antarctica
5. temperate or mild
6. tropical
7. temperate or mild
8. North America and Europe
9. summer
10. total sunlight

VOLCANOES
Wordsearch   crater
                volcano
                lava
                magma
                Lassen
                pumice
                ash

AN ERUPTING VOLCANO
The intense heat inside the Earth is so strong that it begins to melt rocks that are about 15 to 100 miles inside the Earth. When the melting begins, a lot of gas is produced. This mixes with the melted rock, also known as magma. This lighter-weight material starts rising toward the Earth's surface just because it IS lighter than the heavy rocks around it. All this pressure that's created causes the magma to keep pushing its way up to the surface of the Earth. The way out is through the top and sides of the volcano. Gas blasts out and magma flows down the sides of the volcano. This molten rock is now called lava.

VOLCANO CROSSWORD PUZZLE
Across
1. volcanoes

5. Pacific
6. erupted
7. islands
8. crops
9. Lassen Peak
Down
2. Oregon
3. conterminous
4. Cascades
10. Kea or Loa

Chapter 8 The V's and W's
TO, TWO, TOO

1. to
2. two
3. too
4. to, too
5. too
6. two, to, too

IN THE SWIM
A white duck paddling in the water

A SLED RIDE
ice
coat
boots
mittens
snowman

LIST OF PUBLISHERS

Children's Better Health Institute
Benjamin Franklin Literary & Medical Society, Inc.
1100 Waterway Blvd.
P.O. Box 567
Indianapolis, IN 46206
(317) 636-8881
(Many interesting materials including "Button Picture" from *Junior Craft Book;* various magazines: *Turtle* for preschool, *Humpty Dumpty* for kindergarten, *Children's Playmate* for first grade, *Jack and Jill* for second grade, *Child Life* for third grade, and *Children's Digest* for fourth grade)

Educational Insights
USA: 19650 S. Rancho Way
Dominguez Hills, CA 90220
Canada: P.O. Box 19033
Postal Station "A"
Toronto, Ontario M5W 2W8
Tel: (800) 933-3277
    (310) 637-2131
Fax: (310) 605-5048
(*More Short Plays for the Classroom,* including "King Midas" and others)

Frank Schaffer Publications, Inc.
1028 Via Mirabel
Palos Verdes Estates, CA 90274
(800) 421-5533
(Many excellent reproducibles in every subject area and grade level; good book report reproducibles; also puts out a magazine with many good ideas and reproducibles)

Hayes School Publishing Co., Inc.
321 Pennwood Avenue
Wilkinsburg, PA 15221
(412) 371-2374
(Many blackline masters, including many for handwriting; diplomas and certificates; workbooks and bulletin board aids)

Judy/Instructo
Simon & Schuster Education Group
6442 City West Parkway, Suite 300
Eden Prairie, MN 55344
Tel: (612) 946-0046
Fax: (612) 946-0050 (Editorial)
    (612) 946-0055 (Finance)
(*String Art*—many sewing projects, including "Patriotic Stars," "MOM," "DAD," "Hexagon," "Christmas Tree," "Jack-o-Lantern," and so on, for patient, dexterous third graders, and for fourth-graders on up)

The Learning Works, Inc.
5720 Thornwood
Goleta, CA 93117
(800) 235-5767
(Fine reproducibles such as *Book Report Big Top* and *Composition Capers* both third through sixth)

Monday Morning Books, Inc.
Distributed by Evan-Moor
18 Lower Ragsdale Drive
Monterey, CA 93940
(800) 777-4326
(Good poems and art projects from *Holiday Crafts*—could modify for children as young as first grade)

Premier School Agendas
A division of Premier Agendas, Inc.
2081 Business Center Drive, Suite 180
Irvine, CA 92715-9945
Tel: (714) 752-4025
    (800) 447-2034
Fax: (714) 786-1486
    (616) 285-3141
(Maker of *Premier Elementary Reminder,* an excellent book for recording homework assignments, second through sixth)

Sniffen Court Books
153 East 30 Street
New York, NY 10016
Tel: (212) 679-7950
Fax: (212) 684-6137
   (Publisher of *Make Your Own Pictionary* K–2)

Teacher Created Materials, Inc.
6421 Industry Way
Westminster, CA 92683
(714) 891-7895
(800) 662-4321
   (Many good materials, especially *Big and Easy Art for Patriotic Holidays* third through sixth)

Turman Publishing Co.
1319 Dexter Avenue North, Suite 30
Seattle, WA 98109
(206) 282-6900
   (Excellent, high-interest reading reproducibles, such as *Reading Success Stories,* third to fourth; *Amazing Animals,* third and sixth; *Fantastic Mystery Stories,* third; *Famous People Stories,* sixth; *Mexican Americans,* third and fourth; and so on.)

Unison World Software
1321 Harbor Bay Parkway
Alameda, CA 94501
(800) 444-7553
   (*PrintMaster Plus* graphics used in this book are owned and copyrighted by Unison World Software. Used with permission.)

MIDCOURSE REVIEW

* Listening can be evaluated informally or formally with a test. Get an individual assessment.
* Students need to be held accountable for their assignments. The assignment accountability chart is an easy way to do this.
* Gender equity means treating both sexes equally and respectfully in spoken words and body language.
* With the behavior chart system, the students and parents know exactly what areas need improvement and students with excellent behavior are continually recognized.
* Nonteaching duties are all important, but any duty directly dealing with supervision of students is very serious.
* Keep parents informed by sending progress reports home midway through the grading period.
* Allowing chart time at the end of each week for the students to copy any missing assignments helps keep them on target.
* The "All Assignments Completed" chart helps provide those students whose with a sense of pride and accomplishment.

* Back-to-School Night is an opportunity for you to present yourself and your program to the parents.
* Laminating charts helps to keep them looking good year-round.
* Portfolios contain students' work and can be used for student and teacher evaluation of progress.
* An easy grader is a cardboard sliding device very helpful for placing percentage on corrected papers.
* A rubric is a holistic scoring device that can be used by a student or teacher.
* Environmental print could be found on a cereal box.
* A test related to real life has ecological validity.
* Finger Facts might be used for children who are nontraditional learners.
* The Ellison die can be very helpful with bulletin board letters, calendars, and art projects.
* Instructional time is considered to be the school day exclusive of recesses and lunch.
* Grade equivalencies are often used as a measurement device for standardized tests.
* Diglossia is a term used when referring to languages that have one standard for formality but another for common use.
* Low frustration tolerance is a term used to describe students who exhibit extreme agitation and excessive crankiness when trying to learn.
* Interactive bulletin boards are ones that students both contribute to and receive information from.
* The Four Keys to Academic Success are:
   Key 1.   Completely finish and turn in all assignments in every subject area.
   Key 2.   Study thoroughly and carefully at home for all tests.
   Key 3.   Know well and with speed the basic addition, subtraction, multiplication, and division facts.
   Key 4.   Proofread papers carefully.
* The Four Keys to Personal Success are:
   Key 1.   Always do your best.
   Key 2.   Be polite and kind to others.
   Key 3.   Follow laws and rules.
   Key 4.   Be honest.
* Emergent literacy is an ongoing process during which students begin to be able to read, write, actively listen, and speak.
* The following are the five areas of self-esteem and one Q-item for each area. Q-items can be both positive and negative.
   1. Well-Being
      I feel save and secure with my teachers.
   2. Self-Control/Self-Reliance
      I get into trouble quite a lot.
   3. Competency
      I do well in my school work.
   4. Acceptance by Others
      I have an interest or hobby that my friend enjoys.
   5. Acceptance of Self
      I do not like myself very well.

- For a field trip, be sure you have secured the bus well in advance of the trip. Prepare your students both academically and behaviorally for the trip. Take student permission slips including emergency phone numbers with you on the trip. Take adult helpers and take admission fees if they have not been prepaid. Don't forget to provide good follow-up activities when the students return to class.
- In most traditional assessments, students are presented with closed items, such as true-false, multiple-choice, yes-no, and so on. In alternative assessment, students are presented with open-ended items, such as performing and summarizing an experiment, answering scaffolded questions, and completing enhanced or justified multiple-choice items.

Traditional Assessment
True or false The Anasazi were the ones who gathered water in ditches for their corn.
Multiple-choice The Indians followed the large animals from Asia into North America during the
   a. Paleo-Indian Epoch
   b. Beringian Epoch
   c. Post-Archaic Epoch
   d. Archaic Epoch

Alternative (Authentic) Assessment
Scaffolded question Write what you know about the Anasazi Indian tribe. Include an explanation of the following:
- Where they lived
- What the climate was like
- What important crop they grew
- How they watered this crop
- How their houses were special

Justified multiple-choice The large animals crossed from Asia into North America during the
   a. Paleo-Indian Epoch
   b. Beringian Epoch
   c. Post-Archaic Epoch
   d. Archaic Epoch

Explain what hidden word helped you with the answer.

_____
_____
_____

Explain how the Indians responded to this move.

_____
_____
_____

FINAL REVIEW

Directions: Since the following material covers only the second half of the text, to be totally prepared for the final, restudy all the chapter questions and the midcourse review. Then, thoroughly study the glossary.

- A study sheet has prepared questions that outline the most important concepts or skills of the learning.
- The most important thing to do with new students is to make them feel welcome. Ask one or two responsible, friendly, well-liked students to spend the day with them showing them around. Give the new students the appropriate texts and materials. Check with them to make sure everything is going well for them.
- Teaching for transfer is extremely important. You want the current learning organized in such a way that the students can transfer it to a new situation.
- If you are having state or regional testing in which group work is involved, the most likely type of grouping will be a form of random grouping established by the state testers and usually coded on student test booklets.
- A videodisc player is able to present a lesson simultaneously in two different languages.
- If you have students who are mainstreamed, maintain close contact with their homeroom or primary teacher.
- When contacting a parent, be prepared with what you want to say and what you would like done. Listen to the parent carefully.
- There are a variety of situations in which you might want to confer with other district or school employees, such as the nurse, school psychologist, or the district office special education program specialist. They are all part of your team.
- When you teach physical education, teach a physical activity skill as well as a social skill.
- For reading development, remind parents to ask their children to retell a story.
- The overhead projector is an excellent way to teach multiplication with two-digit multipliers. You can use different colors of pen to show the process and reinforce the concept of place value.
- Lattices make fine frames for teaching multiplication and division.
- Geoboards show areas in different figures or shapes.
- Mentor teachers are those who inservice other teachers and provide a variety of curriculum materials.
- Master teachers are those who act as role models for student teachers and guide their development into first-rate teachers.
- When dealing with paperwork, do it correctly, promptly, and turn it in to the right person.
- ADD is attention deficit disorder. ADD/H or ADHD is attention deficit hyperactivity disorder.
- Dyslexia is a disorder that impairs the ability to read.
- A beginning teacher should set up materials for a science lesson well in advance of the lesson.
- School site councils are usually composed of teachers, parents, and the principal.
- The three basic learning modalities are visual (seeing), auditory (hearing), the kinesthetic (touching, feeling, manipulating, moving, tightening of the muscles). Address all three when you are teaching.
- When students can correctly explain and/or use the material you have taught, then they have learned it.

- To determine your students' skills at the beginning of the year, a quick pretest or observation is appropriate.
- One way students can understand concepts is to do a scientific drawing.
- In kindergarten, it is especially important to alternate very active times with quiet-time activities.
- When students speak correctly, it is easier for them to write correctly. Correct their oral language errors.
- Teachers' timing and pacing of the lesson, their subject knowledge, their level of confidence, and their feelings of warmth and understanding all relate to motivating the students.
- A self-study is done by a school to prepare for a school review.
- Students who thoroughly practice their study sheets will be well prepared for a test.
- The functioning of the different sides of the brain is called hemisphericity.
- When giving students directions for an assignment, tell the students slowly and clearly what to do. Write the directions on the board. Ask several students to repeat the directions as *they* understand them. This is the time to clear up any misunderstanding.
- Memory devices such as HOMES are called mnemonic devices.
- When students work in learning groups, each individual group member is held accountable for the learning.
- A device that motivates students to work really hard and fast is a digital timer.
- When using learning groups, academic skills as well as social skills should be taught.
- When inclement weather strikes, it is important to have a buddy teacher, to make sure the students behave at their best, and to make sure there are plenty of activities for the students to keep them well occupied.
- Being able to link learnings into groups is called chunking.
- Being able to relate learnings to previous ones, future ones, and personal experience is called transfer.
- Students need the prerequisite skills in order for them to be successful with an assignment.
- Fluency drills help prepare students for brainstorming.
- Person, setting, conflict or obstacles, objective, and assignment are the five areas covered in one of the multiparagraph UCI Writing Project models.
- An important way for students to see spelling at the application level is sentence dictation.
- A good way to provide students with feedback on a writing assignment is a combination of a grade and a comment about strengths and weaknesses.
- When preparing a thematic unit, include various areas of the curriculum, student activities, grouping, teaching and learning strategies, the identified learnings, type of assessment device, and teacher expectations.
- Ovals that overlap in the center to show similarities and differences are called Venn diagrams.
- Quote is the activity in which students copy a small passage from a story, write what is happening in that part, and why they chose it.

- A story frame is an outline of a story in which blanks need completing with a word or phrase.
- A story map usually includes the characters, setting, story problem, major events, story ending or solution, and a personal reaction.
- Double-entry journal has one column for listing three items describing an event in the story and the other column for listing three items describing a related incident in the reader's life.
- A group of circles with supporting information surrounding a central circle containing the main idea or topic is called a cluster.
- A character map can include such things as personality traits, hobbies, and work.
- For the reading technique of marginalia, have the left half of a paper contain the text and the right half of the paper for students to write the author questions, to make comments about the passage, and/or to draw pictures to illustrate the meaning of the text.
- Picture explanation can be used in any curricular area, but it is usually associated with reading and history. Students draw a picture of some part of a selection of material they have read and explain their picture in detail. This strategy helps reinforce learning and concepts.
- Personal connection is another strategy that reinforces learning and concepts. Personal connection usually follows marginalia. Students connect what they have read or studied to their own personal life or experiences.
- Deciphering the written word to pronounce it correctly is called decoding.
- Reading and deriving meaning from the written word is called encoding.
- Make students aware of context clues, information given in a paragraph or a nearby paragraph that helps them define a word.
- An experiment around which a lesson is built is called a focus activity.
- *AIMS* is a program in math and science using manipulatives.
- A T-sheet can be used for multiplication facts tests that are timed.
- Adams Cube is a device like Tangrams.
- LEP stands for Limited-English Proficient.
- A taxonomy is a system of classification of levels of learning.
- A computer or board game using geography and research skills to travel to catch a thief is *Carmen Sandiego®*.
- Reading, writing, listening, and speaking are the four components of integrated language arts.
- Demonstrating the desired behavior, usually during the teaching of a new skill, is called modeling.
- When mainstreaming a student with special psycho-physiological needs into your PE class, explain to your class that this student needs support and acceptance. Making fun of this student is totally unacceptable and will not be tolerated. Tell your class that having this student in the room for PE will give them a great opportunity to prepare themselves to be future adult citizens of society by learning and practic-

ing tolerance, understanding, and acceptance. Praise the students who are kind and helpful to this student. Appoint a popular student as a buddy. Be sure the mainstreamed student understands the classroom rules and procedures. After giving the class directions for the physical activity and the social skill for the lesson, inconspicuously check with the mainstreamed student to be sure he or she understands the directions.

- Ask yourself these questions to get you started:
  1. *Where* are your students in the development of their academic and social skills?
  2. *How* do they learn?
  3. *What* do you want your students to know?
  4. *When* have they learned it?
- If you want to use the overhead projector to teach your class how to write two interesting sentences about a zoo animal, have *four* animals selected ahead of time. Have one or two books on each at the appropriate reading level. Tell the students they will be brainstorming to develop a list of interesting things to say about one of the animals. Write down everything the students say on your overhead transparencies. Then, continue through the writing process. Allow the students to vote for the two brainstorming items they like best. Write the first draft on a new transparency while your students watch. Edit and revise together as a class. Write the final copy on another transparency. Proofread that together as a class. Continue on with the other animals. When students see and participate in this process as a class, they learn to do a fine job of writing.
- In a writing portfolio, you could have students keep poetry, letters, sentence dictation, spelling tests, handwriting sam-

ples, creative writing, essays, narratives, persuasive paragraphs, plays, story writing, expository writing, and cross-curriculum writing in history, geography, science, or health.

- The ten steps of the Blueprint for Effective Teaching are: ready, set, teach, listen and watch, assign, monitor, check, review, evaluate, and record.
- When conferencing with parents at the end of a grading period, having samples of their child's work is very helpful. If a student is trying, but low achieving, ask the parents if they or a relative could take the child on short trips to increase the child's general knowledge. Maybe an older sibling could quiz their brother or sister on vocabulary words. Tutoring or a work-up for detection of possible learning disorders could be suggested. Ask the parents if there are special things about their child that would be helpful for you to know. Have a written plan.

If students are not completing work, emphasize how important it is for the parents to check their child's composition book each night. Make the parents aware that a special study place and time is often helpful. Maybe their child could have some small reward for completing work during the week. Have a written plan.

In both cases, proceed to explain the child's report card, test scores, and sample papers. Explain the child's strengths and weaknesses. Discuss the child's attitude, work habits, achievement, and social development.

End on a positive note. Work as a team.

GLOSSARY

A

Adams Cube   A device like tangrams. Five plastic pieces must be fitted into a different insert on each side of the cube. All five pieces must be used and must fit together to fill the insert. Cubes are about 4″ × 4″ × 4″.

ADD   *Attention Deficit Disorder,* a disorder in which students are unable to deal with the many stimuli in the environment. They are unable or less able than those unaffected with this disorder to screen out the irrelevant stimuli and focus on the task at hand; consequently, they are unable to concentrate well on the lesson and are continually and easily distracted. A variety of medications are available for this disorder.

ADD/H or ADHD   The same as ADD but with an additional diagnosis of either hyperactivity or hypoactivity. Hyperactivity is the inability to settle oneself physically so as to concentrate at the task at hand. Students with hyperactivity are moving around all the time, jittery, out of their seat, and so on. Students with hypoactivity are "spacey" and lethargic and unable to concentrate well. A variety of medications are available for this disorder.

Adjunct questions   Questions added to textbooks to enhance learning; for example, chapter questions. Questions can be at different cognitive levels, they can have a varied format and can be located at the beginning of a chapter or section, interspersed throughout, or at the end. They can be identical or related to the posttest.

Advance organizer   A way to gather ideas, concepts, comparisons, and so on, in visual, graphic form at the beginning of a chapter or unit. Examples of graphic organizers are concept map, story map, cluster, diagram, and so on.

AIMS   A program in math and science that uses a variety of manipulatives as the base of the lessons. Materials and lessons are available from first through sixth grades.

Alternative assessment   Use of journals, portfolios, classroom observations, and so on, as assessment devices, as opposed to the more traditional assessment devices of multiple-choice, true-false, short answer, and matching questions.

Aphasia   A brain disorder that involves the lack of usual ability in understanding spoken language or the lack of usual ability in using spoken words correctly and coherently. Sometimes, both situations exist.

Assessment   See **alternative assessment** and **traditional assessment.**

Assignment accountability chart   A large chart, approximately 90 inches long and 46 inches high minimum, displayed in the classroom, on which the subjects and the exact description of each assignment are listed. When assignments are ready to be corrected and/or collected, a mark is recorded in each student's box for that assignment: check = assignment accounted for; zero = assignment not accounted for; or square = absent from school or out of the classroom when the assignment was collected and/or corrected. With this chart, students always know what assignments, if any, they are missing. When stu-

dents return from an absence, they can copy missed assignments from the chart. (*See* Figure 1-1 in Chapter 1, The ABC's.)

Assignment boxes   The boxes under each assignment listed on the assignment accountability chart and to the right of each student's name for recording the status of each assignment: accounted for, unaccounted for, or student absent or out of the classroom.

At-risk students   Students, who for reasons such as low self-esteem, truancy, repeated tardies, low grades, minimal effort, gang affiliations, drug problems, and so on, are considered in danger of dropping out of school.

Attention deficit disorder   *See* **ADD.**

Auditory   A mode of learning primarily by hearing, rather than by seeing or sensing.

Authentic assessment   *See* **alternative assessment.**

B

Back-to-School Night   A night at the beginning of the year, usually within the first month of school, on which teachers present themselves and their program to the parents of their students.

Base or root words   The main parts of words, excluding prefixes and suffixes, that have meaning. For example, *invent* is the root word or base word for *invention.*

Bees   Gatherings of students, often from several grade levels, to compete in an academic subject, such as spelling or geography.

Behavior chart system   A system of recording rule numbers after a student's name when the student breaks that classroom rule. This is very helpful for students who need to improve, because they know exactly what they need to do. More guidance and help can be provided by the teacher. This system also has a set of rewards and consequences. (*See* Figure 1-9 in Chapter 1, The ABC's.)

Behavior contract   A contract, written and signed by the students and their parents, to establish and individualize a class behavior system. (*See* Figure A6-7 in the appendix for a sample.)

Blueprint for Effective Teaching   A blueprint for a lesson that guarantees success. It is composed of the following action words: ready, set, teach, listen and watch, assign, monitor, check, review, evaluate, and record. (*See* Figure A7-8 in the appendix.)

Brainstorming   The most important part of the writing process. This is where all the ideas are generated. Then a selection is made about which ideas to include in the paper.

C

Canyon effect   A motivational fall that occurs after a major testing experience if the test is considered the sole measure of proficiency. For example, the students correctly or incorrectly view a standardized test like CTBS or ITBS, as the measurement device of the year; it may be given in late April or early May and then the students "coast" for the rest of the year.

Carmen Sandiego   A computer game (also a board game) involving traveling around the world trying to catch the thief of some country's national treasure. Continual use is made of a world map and an almanac. Students get exposure to different money systems, places of interest in the country, and so on. This is an entire series, including *Where in the World Is Carmen Sandiego? Where in the USA Is Carmen Sandiego? Where in Europe Is Carmen Sandiego?* and *Where in Time Is Carmen Sandiego?*

Cerebral cortices (sing. cortex)   The outermost layer of the cerebrum. The cerebrum is in charge of voluntary actions and mental activity. Brain cells produce electrical signals by chemical means. Whether or not the brain functions properly depends on a large number of complex chemicals that the brain cells produce.

Character map   An outline of the character. It includes such things as where the character lives, what family the character has, what hobbies the character has, what work the character does, what personality traits are shown, and so on.

Chart time   The time given at the end of each week, usually Friday, for the students to go to the assignment accountability chart and copy any assignments they are missing into their composition books. They can then complete these over the weekend.

Chipboard   A piece of cardboard that is thicker than both tagboard and railroad board. It is too thick to go through a roll laminator.

Chunking   A technique to help people remember more. In short-term memory, a person can keep seven, plus or minus two, items. One item can be a letter or a number or a word. But if the person chunks, one item can be an entire sentence or thought.

Cluster   A group of circles, used for supporting information, surrounding a central circle that contains the main idea. This strategy can be used for organization of prior knowledge, review of information related to a main concept in history or science, or as a prewrite. (*See* Figures A8-7, A8-8, and the middle of Figure A8-10.)

Cognitive level   Level of knowing, understanding.

Collaborative groups   Another name for learning groups. *See* **learning groups.**

Combination classes   A self-contained class where there is more than one grade level, such as a 4–5, a fourth and fifth combination, or a 2–3, a second and third grade combination, and so on.

Committees   Another name for learning groups. *See* **learning groups.**

Compensate   A strategy used to make up for or counterbalance a learning disability by trying extra hard and having an assigned buddy to go to when stuck on a problem or activity. For example, to be successful in class, a student may have to study for an extra hour each night. Or the student will need history and science tests read aloud to do a good job. This is especially true for a student with poor reading skills.

Composition books   Regular composition books from the school supply (or purchased by students at a local supermarket or drugstore) in which students copy their homework each night and on Friday, copy any overdues they have from the assignment chart.

Concept map   A type of graphic organizer in which the main concepts are mapped, usually in hierarchical order.

Contest-section chart   *See* **section contest charts.**

Context clues   Information given in the paragraph or a nearby paragraph that helps the student determine the meaning of a word without looking it up in a glossary or dictionary. Students can be taught to recognize the use of a comma as a clue that the words following it will often define or further explain the word or words immediately preceding it. Students can also be taught that the use of a comma before or after a boldfaced word is a clue that the words preceding or following it will very likely explain the boldfaced word. The use of the word *or* in conjunction with a comma is another common device used to define words in context. Students can be taught to read the words around the word they don't know, read the sentence preceding the unknown word and the sentence following it, and last, to reread the entire paragraph.

Cooperative groups   *See* **learning groups.**

Cooperative learning   The learning that comes from a learning group. See **learning groups.** Learning can be a social skill, an academic skill, or both. The group is responsible for some kind of product, which can be written or just an exchange of ideas. Each student in the group is held accountable for the learning.

Corporate groups   Another name for learning groups. *See* **learning groups.**

Corpus callosum   The largest of the bundles of nerve fibers that connect the left and right hemispheres of the brain. Communication between the hemispheres takes place with the help of the corpus callosum. If there is early brain damage, the undamaged hemisphere will usually help the other.

Corrective feedback   Both basic and elaborated feedback; means approximately the same as "knowledge of results." Students are given corrective feedback as promptly as possible so that they will know where they are in the acquisition of a skill. Basic feedback can be as simple as *yes* or *no,* it can be some kind of a grade on an assignment or test, or it can be some short comment such as "Good work." Elaborated feedback can be detailed written comments on tests or assignments with time set aside for the students to read and study them and ask questions, if necessary.

Cross-curriculum   Teaching and learning that can be applied in all subject areas.

Cum file   A student's permanent records. They contain standardized test data, report cards, and health information as well as addresses and phone numbers. At the end of each year, the teacher completes the cums for the students. Since parents may see their children's cum files when they want, it is not a place to keep commentaries, especially negative ones, about the student.

D

Decodes   When beginning to read, the reader decodes or combines each of the letters in a word to formulate that word. Decoding does not imply understanding, but just that the beginning reader is able to say the words. *En*coding is determining meaning from phrases, sentences, and paragraphs.

Dendrites   Short, branching fibers that, along with soma, are receptors for messages so that an entire circuit link is made in the brain. They pick up impulses from the longest fiber in other neurons and send the message to the cell body through a linking point called a synapse. A stimulating environment may be able to make up for some early damage here.

Die   A rubber die for the Ellison machine. *See* **Ellison die machine.**

Diglossic   Possessing two types of a language: a formal, higher literary style and a more colloquial style; refers to both written and spoken word.

Din   Subconscious language playback that learners of new languages experience.

Disaster drill   A drill held for any kind of emergency in the classroom or outside. If building evacuation is necessary, each classroom should be supplied with a backpack or some such similar container to keep current attendance lists, pencils, pens, reporting forms, and so on. A system should be established so those in charge know if there are any students not accounted for; any students who are injured, but with the class outside the building; or any students who are seriously injured, could not be moved, and what their exact location is.

Discrete mathematics   A strand of math that takes information and makes sense of it. It involves ways of counting, pathways, and networks. Venn diagrams, graphs, charts, factorization, combinations, and permutations are all examples of discrete mathematics.

Documentation   Students' papers, parent-teacher communications, and classroom observations regarding students' performance academically or behaviorally. They are very useful when keeping track of student progress and can also be taken to a child study meeting or reviewed in a parent conference.

Double entry journal   A reading/writing technique in which students can directly relate something in a story to something they have experienced. This technique helps students analyze the story and relate it to their own experiences. (*See* Figures A6-16 and A8-10 in the appendix.)

Dyslexia   A brain disorder that impairs the ability to read. Incorrect letters and/or reversed letters are seen or the order of letters and/or numbers can be seen reversed from the way they really are. It is thought that people with dyslexia have unstable eye dominance, which could be reflective of unstable cerebral control.

Dyslexics   People with dyslexia.

E

Early finishers   Students, who when given a class assignment, finish it well before the rest of the class. These students need to have plenty of opportunities to select interesting, challenging activities after they have finished their regular work.

Easy Grader   A cardboard sliding device that makes it easy to determine grades for assignments. For example, if there were 33 questions on the test, you would slide the Easy Grader to 33 and it would tell you the percentage grades for students who missed one, two, three, and so on, items.

Echo reading   A technique in which the teacher (or other adult or advanced student) reads a short amount of material and the student rereads or echoes that same material. More is read and more is echoed. This is a prime opportunity for students to hear an expressive voice pronounce the words they are about to read.

Ecological validity   Performance assessment activities that are related to real life and the workplace.

Electronic Bookshelf   A computer program of sets of questions covering books identified as *Electronic Bookshelf* books. Students read one of these books, go to the computer, load the program and the data disk, and attempt to answer the questions for their book. If they pass, the computer records this information. If they do not pass, they can reread and take a test again. It will not be the same test, though, because each book has about five sets of tests.

Electronic Bulletin Board   A telecommunications program. The school needs a modem and cable hookup to participate. Students can send ads, write letters to students at another school, or communicate with residents of a retirement home.

Elements of a story   Setting (place and time), mood, main characters, major problem, events leading to solution, solution to the problem, and personal reaction.

Ellison die machine   A machine that is excellent for creating bulletin board letters and decorations, calendar dates, placemats, bookmarks, and art projects. Besides rubber dies with upper- and lowercase letters in a variety of sizes, there are dies with many designs, which come in both small and large sizes—apples, pumpkins, snowmen, flowers, and many more. This machine can be used with regular paper, construction paper, or tagboard.

Emergency lesson plans   Lesson plans that can be kept by or with your lesson plan book in case you have been sick, involved in a family emergency, or for whatever reason have not left appropriate plans for a sub. These can be used any day, year-round. (*See* Figures A6-12 and A6-13 in the appendix.)

Emergent literacy   The beginnings of students' activities to show that they are interrelating with the written and spoken word. Even young children's scribblings are considered part of emergent literacy.

Environmental print   Words in everyday environment to which young children as well as adults are continually exposed. Street signs, cereal box words, candy wrapper words, and so on, are all part of environmental print.

ESL   *E*nglish as a *S*econd *L*anguage. Students who are in regular classrooms may leave to go to a resource room for instruction in English for one period a day. Sometimes students who are non–English speaking may go to a school that is an English skills center for the district. When a proficiency level for success in a regular classroom is attained, the student then returns to the home school.

Estimation jars   Jars filled with items, the number of which students are going to estimate. When students are taught to visualize a small area of the jar and think how many items are in that part, they can learn to proceed from that part to the whole jar. Lots of practice gives them estimation skills, too.

Experiment summary   A written summary done after a scientific experiment is completed, data have been recorded, and the results determined. It includes not only an explanation of the entire experiment but also what feelings the person experienced in relation to the experiment.

F

Finger facts   A math technique for students who have a difficult time learning their multiplication facts in the traditional manner. Usually, these are students who rely heavily on their fingers when computing addition and subtraction facts. This system allows them the use of their fingers in computing for multiplication. (*See* Chapter 2, The DEF's, under Facts for a more detailed explanation.)

Five W's   Used for interviewing and writing an informative article: *who, what, where, when, why.*

Focus activity   The experiment, the classification, the microscope, and so on, in any subject, but especially in science, around which the teacher builds a particular lesson.

Forced item placement   In the Q-sort method, when the number of Q-item cards equals the number of categories; that is, the evaluator is forced to put a card in every category.

Frame-based approach   A strategy used in content areas of the curriculum. For example, a frame of a history unit is developed by the teacher. It is then carefully checked with the student text to be sure the concepts are clearly present and the important information from the text is included for the frame.

Free writing   A process where students write whatever they can, including scribbling.

Full inclusion   *See* **inclusionary.**

G

Gender bias   Communicating verbally or nonverbally in a way that excludes one sex or is demeaning to one sex.

Gender equity   Including both sexes in an equal, respectful way both in written and spoken words and in communications using body language; equality especially applies to roles, expectations, occupations, physical characteristics, abilities, interests, and personalities.

Geoboard problems   A math activity in which students use actual geoboards to form shapes with rubber bands (or they can draw their own geoboards with a marker). In a 5 by 5 geoboard, there are five points across and five points down for a total block of 25 points. Students learn to compare areas of one shape to another. They may be given one shape and asked to draw three more of the same area but of a different appearance.

Grade equivalencies   A measurement device for standardized tests. Instead of percentiles (see **national percentiles**), grade levels are used to show similarities of performance. For example, a student may score 38 on a certain reading compre-

hension test. The grade equivalency for that score might be 5.3 (fifth grade, third month). This means that the tester did as well as fifth-graders who are in their third month of school. The student being tested, though, may be in second grade or tenth grade.

Graphic organizer   One of many systems or models used to highlight certain information or the main concepts. Examples of graphic organizers are clusters, double entry journals, story maps, story frames, character maps, and so on.

Group recorder   The member of the cooperative group who writes the group members' ideas as they are given.

Guided questioning   *See* **Questioning.**

Guided reading   A reading strategy in which segments of a story are focused on, with students making predictions about what they think will happen, checking their predictions as they progress through the story, and reading to find specific information and answers to questions that will provide good story understanding for them.

H

Half jacks   Half of a jumping jack. This activity takes up less room than a regular jumping jack and can be worked into an aerobic program held in the classroom.

Hemisphericity   Refers to the functions of the different sides of the brain. *See* **hemispheres.**

Hemispheres   Refers to the two halves of the brain, the left hemisphere and the right hemisphere. These hemispheres communicate back and forth through the corpus callosum, a mass of fibers connecting the two hemispheres. From surgery on epileptics whose corpus callosum was cut producing a split brain situation, it has been learned that the right hemisphere of the brain usually deals with visual, spatial, musical processes, expressing emotions, and sensing and moving on the body's left side. The left hemisphere usually deals with speech, language, math, logic, and sensing and moving on the right side of the body.

Hippocampus   A ridge along each side of the cerebral cortex. It is believed that chemical and physical changes occur in the hippocampi when memory is being stored. Remove a person's hippocampi and that person will have immediate and short-term memory only.

Holistic evaluations   An assessment where the whole is evaluated rather than the parts. Often a rubric is used to keep the evaluations as reliable as possible. Students might have a grade of 4 on a scale of 1 to 6, rather than "so many" wrong equals a 92, an "A."

Holistic Reading Assessment (HRA)   Ten-minute individual student conferences for which the student selects a book, brings a "wide reading" log, and participates in an assessment of oral reading fluency and comprehension, after which the teacher plans needed interventions.

Hyperactivity   Abnormally active; excessively active; unable to sit still even for a short period of time; often in conjunction with ADD.

Hypoactivity   Abnormally inactive; excessively inactive; "spacey" and lethargic; often in conjunction with ADD.

Ideal self   A concept of what a person ought to be and how a person ought to act. It provides a standard for measurement of an individual's real behavior. The goal in working with self image is to get the actual self closer to the ideal self.

Image words   Words such as *secretary, Jew, plumber,* and so on, displayed at a gender equity training session to call awareness to words that produce images of *male* or *female.*

Immediate memory   The ability to recall a few items from passing scenery.

Inclusionary   Including, in a respectful and equal way, everyone appropriate to the situation: both genders; all abilities, including physically challenged, learning disabled, infirmed, and so on; all personalities. Full inclusion refers to the opportunity for all students to participate in the school's total program, including integration into a regular classroom full time.

IDEA   Individuals with Disabilities Education Act.

Inductive method   A scientific method for which Francis Bacon is famous in the field of education; it actually goes back to Aristotle. This is how Bacon explained the method should work: remove prejudice; observe thoroughly; carefully tabulate data; study exceptions as a check to accuracy; and form your generalization.

Inflection   The change in the pitch and tone of the voice. When students read out loud right along with their teacher, they will adopt the same inflections the teacher uses.

In-services   Workshops or seminars held during the school day, after school, or at a staff development day.

Instructional lesson   A review lesson or the presentation of a new learning that basically follows the steps of the Blueprint for Effective Teaching. (*See* Figure A7-8 in the appendix.)

Instructional time   The time of the day when students are not at recess or lunch. They may be engaged in any number of activities, including PE, going to the library, having a lesson in science, doing geoboards in math, studying in partners for a history test, working on a report, meeting with their group to prepare a puppet show, and so on.

Integrated language arts   The four components considered as a whole: reading, writing, listening, and speaking.

Interactive bulletin board   One in which students actively interrelate by contributing material in the form of pictures, maps, data for graphs, questions for the class, and/or by following directions from the board to complete various searches or activities.

J

Jog-a-thon   A school-sponsored event in which the students ask relatives, friends and teachers to pledge so much money per lap that they complete on a school course. The money is then used for classroom expenses, such as field trips, art supplies, special books or supplementary materials, classroom games, and so on.

Journal   A book to write responses to stories with the page number and paragraph number to which the response applies, a place to write a friendly letter to one of the characters or a business letter to a company mentioned in the story, a place to summarize a science experiment and give a personal reaction to it, and so on.

K

Kinesthetic   One of the modalities of learning. In the kinesthetic approach, students experience movement or strain or tightening in their muscles, joints, and/or tendons. This helps to impress the learning.

KWL technique   A technique (especially useful in social studies and science) that promotes learning by first asking students to delineate their knowledge of a particular topic and second to state what they want to learn about this topic. Then the learning builds from students' accurate knowledge and any misconceptions are identified and corrected. KWL means *K*nows, *W*ants, *L*earns.

L

Laminated   A thin coating of lamina, a plasticlike material, applied to paper or piece of tagboard in a press or roll laminator.

Lattices   Frames for multiplication problems with double-digit multipliers and for division problems with single-digit divisors, which help reinforce the concept of place value. They help keep students on track. (*See* Figures A5-1, A5-2, and A5-3 in the appendix.)

LD   Learning Disabled; those with learning disabilities. Part-time pull-out programs are available for students with identified learning disorders who have at least an average IQ and are considered to be able to benefit from the program. Usually, there needs to be a substantial discrepancy between ability and performance as verified by individual testing administered by a specialist such as a special education teacher or a school psychologist. As students progress in this program, the goal is to return them full time to the regular classroom. IEP's (*I*ndividual *E*ducation *P*lans) are completed for these students and regular evaluations are held.

Learning groups   One of a number of names given to small groups working together in the classroom. Each group can have a leader, a recorder to write the group's ideas, a timer to see that the group moves along so it can accomplish its task, and a motivator or encourager to help reluctant students and praise contributions of all the group members. Each student in the group is held accountable for the learning.

Left brained   Operating more from the left hemisphere than from the right. The left hemisphere is in charge of math and logic and is language oriented.

Leteron machine   A machine that presses letters, question marks, commas, and so on, on to a tape. Tape comes in black, brown, white, red, and royal blue. Letters come in uppercase, lowercase, italics, as well as various sizes. This machine can be used to make beautiful chart titles.

Lexicon   Special vocabulary; the key vocabulary terms needed for a lesson or unit so that the major concepts are clearly understood.

Limited-English-Proficient (LEP or LES, Limited-English-Speaking)   Students who have some degree of proficiency in the English language, but not enough to test out of an ESL program. When they pass the test, they are reclassified FEP, *Fluent English Proficient*.

Long-term memory   The ability to store information for a long period, including for life.

"Look-say" method   A method in which students learn to look at a word and say it. They repeat this process until they have learned the individual word. Then they go on to the next word. Little or no phonics is used.

Low frustration tolerance   Describes students who get extremely agitated when they do not get something rather quickly (new learning especially) and become cranky and unwilling to keep trying. Sometimes students, in addition to fussing, will simply **shut down** for a time.

Low tolerance for failure   Somewhat like low frustration tolerance, but more generalized. For example, if a student does not do well in math for a time, he will no longer try in that subject. The attitude is: I'm no good at that so why bother even trying. I won't ever get it. Forget it.

M

Marginalia   A reading technique which involves interaction between the reader and the author and/or characters in the story. Part of a story is reprinted on the left half of a paper. The right half is left blank for the writing of *margin*alia. This consists of questions the students might have for the author as they read the passage. They might remark about the use of words that strike their fancy. They may comment about something in their life of which the story reminds them. They may wish to draw pictures that represent parts of the selection. They might want to write how they feel about certain parts as they're reading. A completed page of marginalia looks like text from the story on the left half of the page and notes, phrases, sentences, drawings, comments, and so on, on the right half of the paper.

Master teachers   Those exemplary teachers who act as role models for student teachers; who provide guidance, critiquing, and evaluation of their lessons, their interaction with elementary students, their classroom control, and their other daily and weekly responsibilities; and who work closely with the student teachers' college or university supervisor to make the student teaching experience successful and rewarding.

Master's degree barrier   A condition that some school districts have as part of their salary schedule. This means a teacher without a master's degree cannot enter the last column on the salary schedule regardless of the number of educational units after the bachelor's degree the teacher has.

Mastery level   The time when students are able to consistently demonstrate competence with a skill over a long period of time. All prerequisite skills need to have been mastered first.

Mastery testing   Frequent testing with individualized corrective feedback; the student does not proceed to new material until the material under study is mastered as evidenced by passing a test.

Mental rehearsal   A process usually used in the acquisition of a second language; however, it can be used as a confidence builder in any area. Individuals plan in their mind what they are going to say or do before the situation actually occurs.

Mentor teacher   A teacher who has additional responsibilities in some special area of the curriculum or some other area of need of the classroom teachers. Mentor teachers may write curriculum, give in-services, or provide special assistance to teachers new to their district.

Minimum days   Shortened school days where the students attend the minimum number of minutes to qualify for ADA (average daily attendance)—usually approximately four hours of instructional time. Then students are dismissed to go home. For the rest of these days, teachers may be attending an in-service, writing their school plans, preparing for a school review, or holding parent-teacher conferences.

Misconceptions   Misunderstandings and errors in students' prior knowledge of a subject. It is important to be alert to these and correct them. A good way of doing this is pretest and posttest students using open-ended questions.

Miscues   Mistakes made in oral reading that may or may not influence the meaning of the text; those disrupting the meaning of the text need remediation.

Mnemonic devices   Memory devices, such as HOMES for the five Great Lakes: *H*uron, *O*ntario, *M*ichigan, *E*rie and *S*uperior.

Modeling   Demonstrating the desired behavior, usually during the teaching of a new skill.

"Mouth-to-ear" method   A method of reading the story "aloud." Each student takes a chair and gets a partner. Students put their chairs side by side, each facing the opposite direction. When the students sit down, one's ear will be right next to the other's mouth. One student reads in a whisper while the other listens and follows along in the reader. Then they switch roles after every paragraph or every page.

Multimodal   Multimodal oriented; describes the student who relies on more than one mode in learning. For example, the student may be a sometime visual and sometime auditory learner, or an auditory and kinesthetic learner, and so on.

N

National percentiles   In standardized testing based on nationwide sampling, the numbers that divide the individuals in the sampling into one hundred groups of equal frequency. For example, if a student took a certain standardized test and scored 38 in vocabulary, he might be in the 95th percentile. This means that the student did as well as 95 percent of the students who took the test.

Nationball   A game played on a volleyball court (no net). Five students from team A are goalies behind the far service line. The rest of team A stands in the near half-court. Five students from team B are goalies behind the near service line. The rest stand in the far half-court. As try to peg the Bs who are inside the court and vice versa. Players inside the court are out when hit by a ball that has not bounced and one they are unable to catch before it bounces. Goalies can throw the ball over the heads of opponents to their teammates inside the court and vice versa. This tires the opponents quickly and makes for easier pegging. When a student is out, he or she becomes a goalie. Every student can be *in* only one time, including the original five goalies. The opponents of the first empty half-court win.

NEP (non-English-Proficient or NES, Non-English-Speaking)   Students who have little or no proficiency with the English language.

O

Office referral   A consequence that can vary, depending on the school's behavior system. It can be a slip given to a student by an adult on campus to refer the student to the office for discipline. It can also be generated from the office. A student is *told* to go to the office for causing a problem and the principal issues a referral form that must be signed by the student's parent. This can be issued in conjunction with a suspension.

Open-ended   Questions that are not of the variety of true-false, multiple-choice, or matching questions. These types of questions require a higher level of thinking. For example, *how did Columbus feel after he returned to Spain from his first voyage? Describe an experience you have had during or after which you felt a similar feeling to Columbus's.*

Outcome-based   Programs, instruction directed toward specific, measurable end results.

Overhead projector   A machine that projects an image onto a screen.

P

Personal connection   A reading strategy in which students write or tell the way a story or story part connects to their own lives.

Phonics   A system assigning certain sounds to individual letters of the alphabet as well as to consonant blends (*thr*) and vowel digraphs (*oa*). This system is then applied to decode written material.

Picture explanation   An explanation that can be written for any subject, but is usually associated with reading and history. A picture about some part of the story or chapter is drawn and a detailed explanation of the picture is given.

Plasticity   The ability to be easily molded; the brain's plasticity is affected by many things, including environmental effects.

Pop-up book   A book written and illustrated by the students in which the center of each page pops up with a large, hand-drawn picture glued to the pop-up center. It also has background drawing above the picture and the story sentence below the picture.

Portfolio   A collection of a student's work that contains samplings in a particular area. A writing portfolio might contain samples from the beginning of the year of a student's handwriting, spelling, and narrative or expository writing. Teachers can meet with students individually and determine what area the student would be interested in improving. Sampling might be taken three or four more times during the year to note progress or add a new area of concentration. Some portfolios have a sample writing activity at the beginning of the year and a similar writing activity given at the end of the year for comparison.

Portfolio-based assessments and evaluations   Evaluations that can be done by the students, the teachers, or both. A comparison is made between samples from the beginning of the year with samples taken later in the year. Students and/or teachers can also just evaluate an assignment from the beginning of the year to determine specific areas on which the students wish to work. (*See* Figure A8-19 in the appendix.)

Positive referrals   Referrals to the office for good reasons, such as good behavior, a good test grade, a good speech or project, improvement made in some area, and so on. The student's name is written on the award slip along with the date and why the referral is given. The student takes this to the principal for congratulations and a small reward.

Power paragraph (or powergraph)   A type of paragraph writing that assigns powers to the different sentences. (*See* Figure 8-5.)

PQR (Program Quality Review)   *See* **school review.**

Press laminator   A machine that needs to be heated, with the lamina and the desired material put in the press for lamination. *See* **laminated.**

Prewrite   The first step of the writing process that involves the use of some type of brainstorming. Students list as fast as they can the ideas that come to mind on the given topic. No judgment is made as to the worth of the ideas. After all the ideas are generated, then students go through them, selecting the best to use in the writing activity. This is the most important step in the writing process, because it ensures lots of good ideas in the final product.

Prior knowledge   Background, ideas, and experiences about a particular or related subject. Before students begin a study of something new or before they begin a story, they should check their prior knowledge. Teachers need to be alert to prior knowledge containing any misinformation or pseudo-concepts and be ready to help the students come to a truer understanding.

Progress reports   Reports sent home at approximately the middle of each grading period. This lets the students and the parents know what is happening academically and behaviorally at school. (A sample progress report is in Figure A6-4 in the appendix.)

Prompt   A stimulus or starter to an activity or test, such as an introductory paragraph, picture, graph, and so on, about the topic. The student's response is addressed to the prompt.

Prompting   Providing students with hints, use of specific words, encouragement to do or tell more, and so on, to carefully assess their performance.

Pseudoconcepts   Misinterpretations of a fact or concept.

Q

Questioning   A technique used to elicit information. *Closed questioning* elicits yes-no, true-false, or one or two words for an answer. *Open-ended questioning* allows the teacher to see the students' thinking processes and more easily clarify any misconceptions. It also makes the student a much more active participant in the classroom. *Guided questioning* checks the students' prior knowledge and helps them to discover. It is a strategy on the order of the Socratic method. In preparation for a history test or science test or after reading a story, the students themselves can make up the questions and ask them to each other or to the class.

Q-Sort method   A method in which the evaluator is given a set of items or statements to place in some kind of order to represent or characterize the evaluator. Q-items are printed on separate cards so that the evaluator can arrange and rearrange the cards until he gets the desired representation.

Quote   A reading technique in which the students copy word for word a small part of the story that caught their interest, maybe a sentence or two, maybe less. After it is copied, they write what is happening in that part of the story and why they chose it to quote. This skill helps students analyze very small segments of a story, article, or poem.

R

Railroad board   A slightly thicker piece of cardboard than tagboard. It comes in a wide variety of colors. It makes an excellent base for string art projects.

Random grouping   Groups formed on the basis of counting off, drawing names from a box, and so on. In this type of grouping, some groups may really need to practice the social skills of being polite and respectful to each member of the group.

Read around   A system in which small groups of students are seated in circles to practice reading. Each student, in order, takes a turn to read aloud to the group either a paragraph or a page. It is often very helpful for the whole group if, after each student reads aloud, the student briefly retells the main idea of what was read.

Readers' Theater   An excellent reading comprehension technique. Any part of a narrative can be used for this. Students select characters whose parts they will read, and a narrator is chosen to read all the words not spoken by the characters (words not in quotations). Students then read a section exactly as it is written, taking a turn when their character speaks. The same section can be read several times, switching students so that all get the opportunity.

Reading incentive program   A strategy used to motivate students to read. A variety of these programs are sponsored by different businesses, or a school can run its own. Students who read a certain minimum number of books a month get a certain prize. Classrooms in which all the students read the minimum number each month get a class prize.

References   Related to self-concept; include students' physical being, persons, and groups with which they identify (family, friends, clubs, school, church, city, state, nation), their possessions (clothes, money, house, etc.), and their reputation, honor, and accomplishments. If these references prosper and grow, the students feel good; if they dwindle or are attacked, they feel bad and defensive.

Reliability   *Consistency* of test scores over items and over a period of time.

Right brained   Operating more from the right side of the brain than from the left. The right brain deals with fine arts, creativity, and fantasy.

Roll laminator   A laminator that comes in different widths; the material needing to be laminated is fed into a roller device in this machine. For good results, the laminating machine should be heated to 250° and some lead should be allowed by pressing the foot pedal for a little bit before beginning insertion of the instructional material. Chipboard is too thick to go through a roll laminator. Use a press laminator for it.

Round robin   Any situation such as one student asking a question to the next, that one answering and asking a question to the next, and so on. The group recorder could write the key word in each question.

Rubric   A scoring device that sets the standards for the student product and makes assessing more reliable.

S

Scaffolding   A strategy to provide support for students in their thinking and especially in their writing. Its purpose is to let the students be more independent. As they are able to do this, the teacher takes less control. Scaffolding can be provided in an open-ended question test or activity. Following the question, the scaffolding can be bulleted. For example, for a question on immigrants to the United States, this scaffolding could be provided: Be sure to include in your answer information about

* how racism and nativism affected the immigrants,
* their living conditions in the large cities, and
* job and education availability.

Scan   A reading technique in which students use four spread-out fingers of the right hand (or left) to move down a page quickly looking for some specific information. Students can be taught to be aware of dates, proper nouns, boldface, and italics to help them scan successfully.

School citation   A discipline form given to students by a school employee, such as a teacher, custodian, instructional assistant, or playground supervisor. This form generates paperwork on a student in the office. Students do not like to get these forms and neither do their parents. (See Figure A6-8 in the appendix.)

School site councils   Councils involving the teachers, parents, and principal that help to formulate ideas and to make decisions about school discipline, some curricular matters, procedures during school reviews, and so on.

School psychologist   The person, usually assigned several schools, who is in charge of the following: administering individual IQ tests; observing individual students in the classroom to get information as to how well they are able to pay attention and interact with their classmates; being present at child studies—along with the teacher, parents, principal, speech therapist, and special education teacher—to listen to the problems the student is having, what actions have already been taken, what progress has been made; and helping in the decision of what program would best meet the needs of the student.

School review Same as PQR (Program Quality Review); reviews of each individual school in certain areas of the curriculum. Usually, the schools pick the area or areas for which they would like the review. The school plan covering those curriculum areas is the criterion for the review.

Scientific drawing Drawings of the parts of the ear, eye, digestive system, brain, microscope, or whatever is being studied. Students draw the picture, label the parts with correctly spelled words, give the drawing a title, and color it carefully and neatly. Whatever is drawn is easily called to memory.

SDC *Special Day Class;* refers to any self-contained classroom of students identified as special education students. These can be students who have severe emotional disturbances, learning disorders, and/or physical disabilities such that they function better in a special day class than in the regular classroom.

Seating sections Any of a variety of arrangements of the students' desks so that they are in definable sections suitable for the section chart contest.

Section contest charts Charts on which the sections or rows accumulate stamps toward filling their chart and winning the contest. (*See* Figure A1-4 in the appendix.)

Self-selected groups Groups that the students choose for themselves. For some groups, this is great, and they will be very productive. Other times, students with discipline problems attract each other into a group. This group will need to be carefully monitored. Another problem is that all low students may end up in one group. This is another group that will need careful monitoring and help.

Semantic webs (Also called **semantic word webbing**); a technique similar to clusters but more *elaborate* and more *structured.* Webs can be used to show categories, such as cause-effect or sequence. Once a category of the main idea is selected, students can then tell or write their ideas, but they must stick to the category.

Semantic word webbing. *See* **semantic webs.**

Sentence completion A test item that is basically the same as "fill in the blank." It can require one or more words to complete the sentence correctly.

Short-term memory The ability to store information for a few hours or days.

Shut down The tuning out or turning off by a student who is overwhelmed, overly frustrated, or extremely emotionally upset.

Sit and reach A boxlike structure used as a measurement device for annual physical fitness testing. Two students sit on the floor facing each other with their feet pressed against the middle of the box; one leans forward to reach as far as possible without bending the knees. There is a tape for measuring the distance on the top of the sit and reach box.

Skim A reading technique used to get the main idea of a story or chapter. Students can use their index finger to move quickly down each page.

Socialization Relating well to others, getting along. Some students are highly socialized whereas others are not and need work in this area.

Social loafing Nonproductive behavior in group learning, primarily caused by group dynamics assigning insignificance to "low status" students' ideas, thereby resulting in these particular students doing nothing in the groups even though the group may have a final product.

Speaking evaluation form A form that allows the teacher to evaluate speaking in five different areas and give a letter grade to the speech. The five areas are: posture/poise, eye contact, loud and clear voice, adequate time speaking, and well prepared. (*See* Figure A7-7 in the appendix.)

Speech therapist The individual who tests students to determine their ability to process language and makes recommendations as to the best program for the student. The speech therapist also provides speech therapy for students who have identified difficulties in speaking and/or language processing.

Speech therapy The process of remediation of a student with a speech or language problem. *See* **speech therapist.**

Sponge activities Activities to keep students well occupied during a period of transition, such as roll and lunch count at the beginning of the day or an activity to work on in their spare time in the classroom. (*See* Chapter 6, The PQR's, under Quiet Time for a list of samples.)

SQRRR (*S*urvey, *Q*uestion, *R*ead, *R*eview, *R*eread); a reading strategy that will be helpful to students their entire lives. Students learn surveying techniques: reading the title and author; going through each page looking for and studying pictures and making predictions about what might be happening; reading all headings, boldfaced and italicized words; and studying any charts, tables and graphs. This gives an excellent overview of the story or chapter. Next, students form their own questions concerning what they'd like to know from the story. If the chapter or article has its own questions, they would then read those and be on the alert for the answers as they read. This sets a purpose for reading. Then the students read the article or chapter, tell or write (recite) what they learned, and check their answers to be sure they got correct information. If there were errors, students review the material and discover the correct information.

Stimulus See **prompt.**

Story frame A short type of outline of the story. Frequently, blanks need completing with a word or two or maybe a phrase. A story frame is a minute composite of the story.

Story map Another type of outline of the story that is much more general in that students are required to do significantly more writing with very few clues. A story map usually includes the characters, the setting, the problem of the story, the major events, the story ending or solution, and a personal reaction. (*See* Figures A6-14 and A6-17 in the appendix.)

Student study team (SST) A team, usually including the principal, special education teacher, school psychologist, speech therapist, classroom teacher, and parents, that meets to discuss special academic, emotional, social, or physical needs of a student.

Study carrel A piece of cardboard about 24 inches high, placed on the student's desk to help keep distractions to a minimum. The front should be approximately as wide as the desk.

The length of the sides should be approximately as long as the sides of the desk. Carrels are especially useful when students are taking a history or health test and the teacher reads the test questions aloud for a small group who would otherwise get bogged down with the reading portion even though they have a good grasp of the information. Study carrels can easily be made from tagboard and then laminated for preservation.

Study sheet   Teacher- and/or student-prepared questions that outline the most important concepts or skills of the learning. Study sheets should be prepared in such a way that even though the questions will be in a different format, the students will be thoroughly prepared for a test if they know everything on the study sheet.

Substitute teacher form   A form that introduces a substitute to the rules of the class and how its discipline policy works. It alerts the sub to any children who have special needs, who leave the classroom for LD, ESL, tutoring, and so on. (*See* Figure A6-11 in the appendix.)

Synaptic contacts   The points of contact in the brain where a branch of one neuron sends a message to a branch of another neuron. The messages go in only one direction. Each neuron, of which there are from ten billion to a hundred billion in the brain, is capable of forming synapses with thousands of other nerve cells.

T

Tag   Also called tagboard; a thin piece of cardboard that comes in wide-lined, narrow-lined, and unlined manila. It also comes in various colors, including fluorescents.

Take cover drill   A drill for students and teachers to practice protecting themselves from falling or flying objects.

Tangrams   Configurations used in math to help develop the students' perceptions of spatial relationships. Usually seven different geometric shapes must be placed inside an outline of some kind, such as a boat, house, zebra, and so on. Students must juggle these pieces around until every piece is used and they all fit inside the outline.

Target vocabulary   Words in the story, chapter, or unit that are considered "new" to students. These need to be explained very carefully, so students are able to comfortably and knowledgeably use them when writing and speaking on the topic.

Taxonomy   A system of classification of levels of learning and appropriate questions and activities to elicit the desired learning. Bloom's taxonomy has six classifications or levels listed in ascending order, least difficult to most sophisticated: knowledge, comprehension, application, analysis, synthesis, and evaluation.

Teacher-directed time   Time when the teacher is actively engaged with the students, either in whole group or small group instruction and practice. Correcting students' papers or monitoring their activity is not considered part of teacher-directed time.

Test study notes   Notes written by the students' parents confirming that their children spent an expressed amount of time studying a specifically stated assignment. These notes really help keep test scores high.

T-Graph   An organizer that can be used effectively at the end of a story or chapter. On the left-hand side of the *T,* various selections of information from the story, chapter or unit can be written. On the right-hand side of the *T,* students can write or tell their personal reactions and understanding of each selection.

Thematic units   Lessons in which learning is built around a central subject, such as sound, whales, dinosaurs, the American Revolution, and so on. Key vocabulary, major concepts, and relevant skills are taught in a cross-curriculum approach.

Time-order paragraph   The type of paragraph that begins with a topic sentence, followed by sentences beginning with time-order words: first, next, then, finally. It can be expanded by writing a topic sentence and using these time-order words: first, second, third, next, then, at last. (*See* Figure 8-4.)

Timer   A small digital device that will help your class run smoothly and stay targeted. It also helps students plan their work load more easily.

To be corrected box   A standard-sized box, approximately 9 inches by 12 inches and available through your school supplies, which is used to help keep students' work organized. When tests, projects, and writing assignments are collected, they are placed in this box until they are ready to be corrected.

To be recorded box   A standard-sized box, approximately 9 inches by 12 inches and available through your school supplies, which is used to help keep students' assignments organized. After tests, projects, and writing assignments have been *corrected,* they go to this box to wait for recording in the teacher's grade book. After recording, they are transferred to the "To be returned" box for delivery to the students.

Traditional assessment   Tests of a closed nature, expecting a minimal response, such as true-false, simple multiple-choice, yes-no, and so on.

Transfer   The ability to carry over one learning into a new learning. Teaching for transfer is extremely important. For example, teaching students to add starting with the bottom number transfers to subtraction and multiplication.

T-sheet   A sheet on which students take multiplication facts tests. There is a long "T" with numbers one through nine in various orders on the left side of the vertical stem of the T. When the students are ready to begin the test, they are given a T number, for example 4, which they place on top of the horizontal bar of the T. When time begins, the students start writing the correct products on the right-hand side of the vertical stem of the T. (*See* Figure 2-5 in Chapter 2 and Figure A2-18 in the appendix.)

U

UCI (University of California, Irvine) Writing Project   A variety of writing ideas, most notably the multiparagraph writing project. Five areas are addressed in the multiparagraph project: (1) what person the story will be written in; (2) what the setting will be; (3) what the conflict will be (usually includes three obstacles); (4) what the objective of the main character is; and (5) what that character's assignment is. (*See* Figures A8-4, A8-5, and A8-6 in the appendix.)

V

Vade mecum   Something frequently carried about, in this book's case, a cart.

Validity   Test items measuring exactly what is intended to be measured.

Venn diagram   A skill that helps students see similarities and differences. Inside two lengthwise ovals (there can be more) that overlap in the center, students list everything they can to describe one character (or setting or story ending, and so on) in the oval on the left. Then they list everything they can to describe another character in the oval on the right. The descriptions that fit both elements being compared go in the center overlap. (*See* Figure A6-17 in the appendix.)

Visual   The mode of learning by sight or vision.

W

Whole class instruction   A lesson presented to the class as a whole, rather than to subgroups.

Whole language   A holistic approach to literacy, in which students mix reading, writing, speaking, and listening throughout the curriculum. They can learn in whole class groups or smaller learning groups. They learn in an experiencing, interactive manner, and they demonstrate what they learn.

Wide reading   Student reading that reflects different levels of reading as well as different genres. This can be used to determine if the student is a reader or not; that is, whether the student reads beyond what is assigned, and if so, the amount and type of reading.

Word map   A graphic organizer in which a word is written in the center of a chart or chalkboard and students decide on a definition for it; decide how the object looks, tastes, sounds, feels, and smells; and list some examples of the object as well as other word forms it has. Circles, boxes, or ovals can be placed around the descriptors in the separate categories.

Word of the week   A system to help extend students' vocabulary and sharpen their spelling skills. On Monday, a card that has on it a word probably not known at the grade level is introduced to the class. The pronunciation of the word and a sample sentence are also on the front of the card. The meaning is on the back. The card is placed in a highly visible spot for the week. On Friday, the students see if they can pronounce the word correctly, spell it, tell or write what it means, and use it in a good sentence where its meaning is exhibited.

THE
APPENDICES

FACTS

Elementary forms are coded for easy use.

Pt   Think "primary time" for primary grades

§   Think "secondary section" for upper grades

Depending on the needs and readiness of your students, you can use a "primary" activity in an upper-grade class or with a small group of upper-grade students. You can use an "upper-grade" activity in a primary class or with a small group of primary students. In either case, because of the codes, you can comfortably use these materials without the concern that your students will be able to identify the grade level.

Certificate of Achievement

_____

has been selected as a member of
the schools's honor roll for this grading period .

_____   _____
Teacher   Principal

PT §

Behavior

Students' Names	M	T	W	Th	F	Total
	PT §					

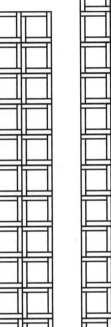

Directions for the frame of the section contest chart:

I. After copying one copy of the section contest chart , place the two long borders FIRST on to the SIDES of the chart.

2. Place the thin short border on the top of the chart under the chart title. Make it overlap the side borders.

3. Place the thick short border on the bottom of the chart.

4. Use the boxes in the border to help you line it up correctly. Glue-stick the border in place.

5. Then copy a stack of bordered charts so you'll have lots of extras.

6. Determine how many seating sections you want in your class. If you decide on four, get four pieces of 9 x 12 construction paper in yellow or pink or whatever you like.

7. Staple each of your four charts on to the four pieces of construction paper.

8. Staple the construction paper charts to your bulletin board.

9. Now you're ready!!

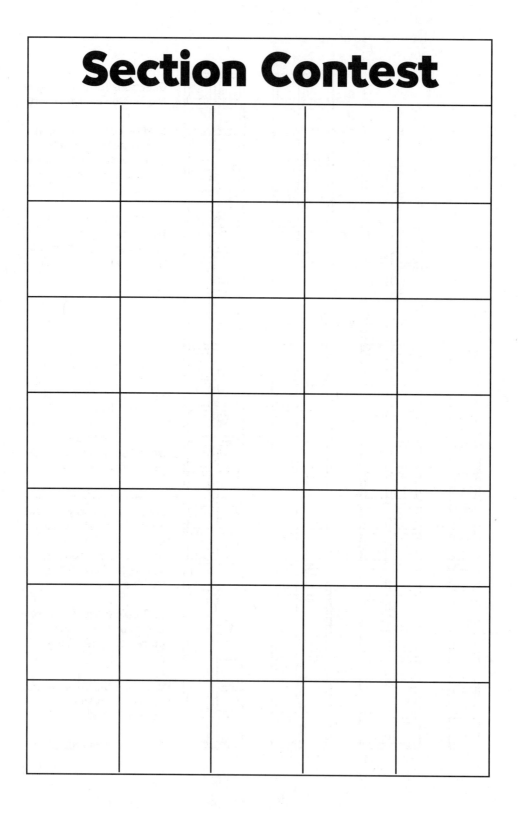

Section Contest

Addition Facts

1

1 + 0 = 1
1 + 1 = 2
1 + 2 = 3
1 + 3 = 4
1 + 4 = 5
1 + 5 = 6
1 + 6 = 7
1 + 7 = 8
1 + 8 = 9
1 + 9 = 10

2

2 + 0 = 2
2 + 1 = 3
2 + 2 = 4
2 + 3 = 5
2 + 4 = 6
2 + 5 = 7
2 + 6 = 8
2 + 7 = 9
2 + 8 = 10

3

3 + 0 = 3
3 + 1 = 4
3 + 2 = 5
3 + 3 = 6
3 + 4 = 7
3 + 5 = 8
3 + 6 = 9
3 + 7 = 10

4

4 + 0 = 4
4 + 1 = 5
4 + 2 = 6
4 + 3 = 7
4 + 4 = 8
4 + 5 = 9
4 + 6 = 10

5

5 + 0 = 5
5 + 1 = 6
5 + 2 = 7
5 + 3 = 8
5 + 4 = 9
5 + 5 = 10

6

6 + 0 = 6
6 + 1 = 7
6 + 2 = 8
6 + 3 = 9
6 + 4 = 10

7

7 + 0 = 7
7 + 1 = 8
7 + 2 = 9
7 + 3 = 10

8

8 + 0 = 8
8 + 1 = 9
8 + 2 = 10

9

9 + 0 = 9
9 + 1 = 10

Addition

Name _____

Time: 1-1/2 minutes **Errors:** 3 or fewer

2 5	5 4	0 6	8 1	4 2	4 3
9 0	2 2	4 4	3 3	5 2	1 1
2 3	9 1	5 3	2 7	1 5	2 6
3 6	4 1	3 2	7 0	0 8	6 3
3 5	0 7	1 9	2 7	6 4	6 1
1 2	3 1	1 5	2 8	7 3	1 7
5 5	1 4	3 2	4 6	0 7	3 7
4 5	2 2	9 1	7 3	6 4	1 8

Subtraction Facts

1

1 − 0 = 1
1 − 1 = 0

2

2 − 0 = 2
2 − 1 = 1
2 − 2 = 0

3

3 − 0 = 3
3 − 1 = 2
3 − 2 = 1
3 − 3 = 0

4

4 − 0 = 4
4 − 1 = 3
4 − 2 = 2
4 − 3 = 1
4 − 4 = 0

5

5 − 0 = 5
5 − 1 = 4
5 − 2 = 3
5 − 3 = 2
5 − 4 = 1
5 − 5 = 0

6

6 − 0 = 6
6 − 1 = 5
6 − 2 = 4
6 − 3 = 3
6 − 4 = 2
6 − 5 = 1
6 − 6 = 0

7

7 − 0 = 7
7 − 1 = 6
7 − 2 = 5
7 − 3 = 4
7 − 4 = 3
7 − 5 = 2
7 − 6 = 1
7 − 7 = 0

8

8 − 0 = 8
8 − 1 = 7
8 − 2 = 6
8 − 3 = 5
8 − 4 = 4
8 − 5 = 3
8 − 6 = 2
8 − 7 = 1
8 − 8 = 0

9

9 − 0 = 9
9 − 1 = 8
9 − 2 = 7
9 − 3 = 6
9 − 4 = 5
9 − 5 = 4
9 − 6 = 3
9 − 7 = 2
9 − 8 = 1
9 − 9 = 0

10

10 − 0 = 10
10 − 1 = 9
10 − 2 = 8
10 − 3 = 7
10 − 4 = 6
10 − 5 = 5
10 − 6 = 4
10 − 7 = 3
10 − 8 = 2
10 − 9 = 1
10 − 10 = 0

Subtraction

Time: 2-1/2 minutes **Errors: 3 or fewer**

9 −9	7 −6	8 −3	5 −0	3 −2	6 −6
8 −8	5 −2	4 −3	9 −6	2 −0	5 −3
9 −2	6 −0	4 −1	7 −5	2 −1	3 −0
8 −2	9 −5	8 −4	7 −2	7 −4	5 −5
7 −3	2 −2	9 −1	6 −4	9 −8	5 −4
9 −7	10 −4	8 −5	6 −1	10 −1	9 −4
10 −5	6 −2	5 −1	1 −0	7 −1	8 −8
4 −2	10 −9	8 −6	3 −1	4 −0	6 −3

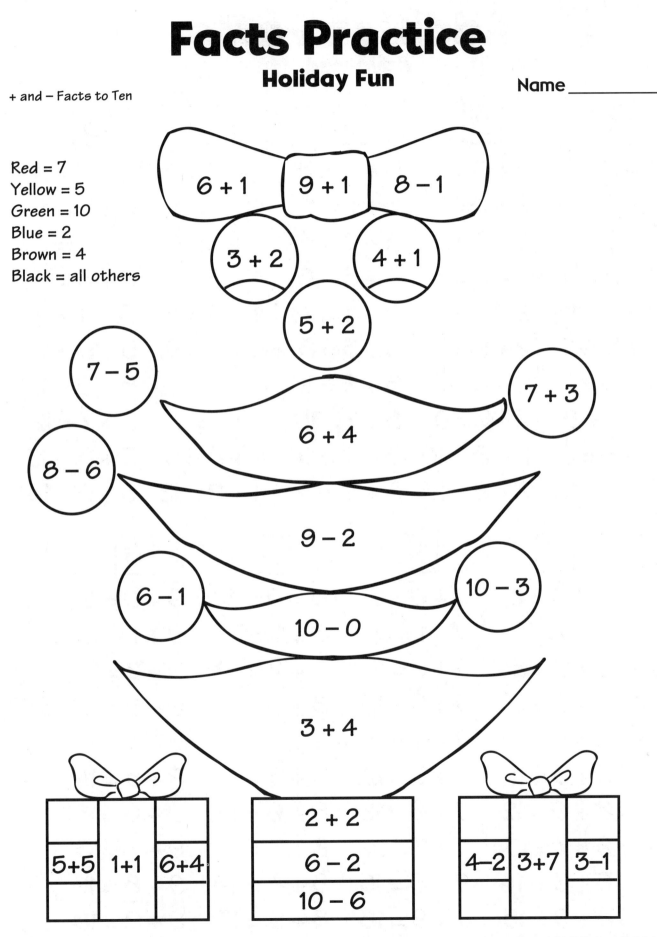

PT

Facts Practice
Holiday Fun

+ and – Facts to Ten

Name _____

Red = 7
Yellow = 5
Green = 10
Blue = 2
Brown = 4
Black = all others

6 + 1   9 + 1   8 – 1

3 + 2   4 + 1

5 + 2

7 – 5   6 + 4   7 + 3

8 – 6   9 – 2

6 – 1   10 – 0   10 – 3

3 + 4

5+5 1+1 6+4

2 + 2
6 – 2
10 – 6

4–2 3+7 3–1

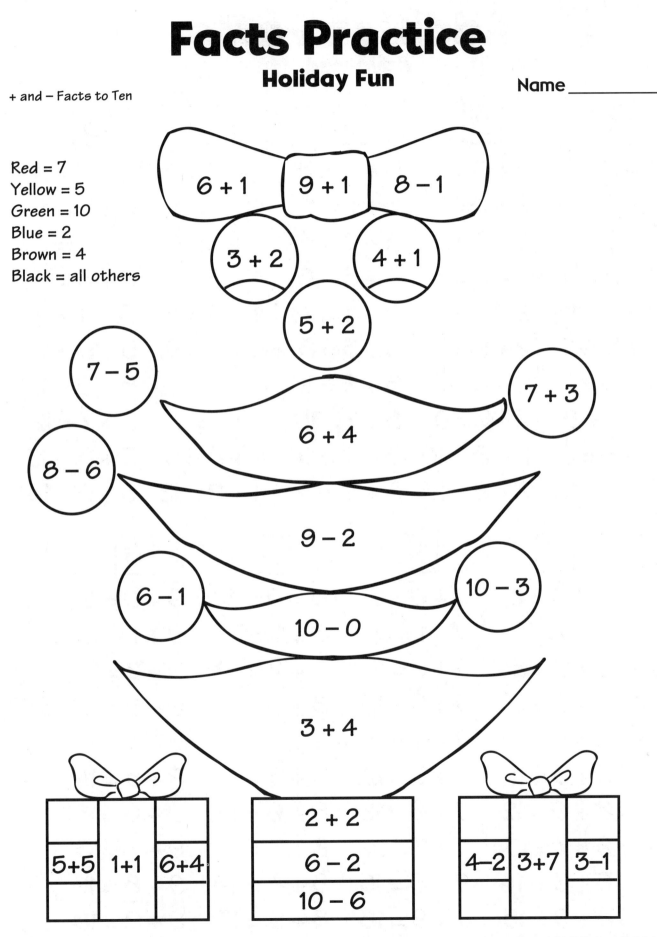

Addition Facts
Advanced

1

1 + 0 = 1
1 + 1 = 2
1 + 2 = 3
1 + 3 = 4
1 + 4 = 5
1 + 5 = 6
1 + 6 = 7
1 + 7 = 8
1 + 8 = 9
1 + 9 = 10

2

2 + 0 = 2
2 + 1 = 3
2 + 2 = 4
2 + 3 = 5
2 + 4 = 6
2 + 5 = 7
2 + 6 = 8
2 + 7 = 9
2 + 8 = 10
2 + 9 = 11

3

3 + 0 = 3
3 + 1 = 4
3 + 2 = 5
3 + 3 = 6
3 + 4 = 7
3 + 5 = 8
3 + 6 = 9
3 + 7 = 10
3 + 8 = 11
3 + 9 = 12

4

4 + 0 = 4
4 + 1 = 5
4 + 2 = 6
4 + 3 = 7
4 + 4 = 8
4 + 5 = 9
4 + 6 = 10
4 + 7 = 11
4 + 8 = 12
4 + 9 = 13

5

5 + 0 = 5
5 + 1 = 6
5 + 2 = 7
5 + 3 = 8
5 + 4 = 9
5 + 5 = 10
5 + 6 = 11
5 + 7 = 12
5 + 8 = 13
5 + 9 = 14

6

6 + 0 = 6
6 + 1 = 7
6 + 2 = 8
6 + 3 = 9
6 + 4 = 10
6 + 5 = 11
6 + 6 = 12
6 + 7 = 13
6 + 8 = 14
6 + 9 = 15

7

7 + 0 = 7
7 + 1 = 8
7 + 2 = 9
7 + 3 = 10
7 + 4 = 11
7 + 5 = 12
7 + 6 = 13
7 + 7 = 14
7 + 8 = 15
7 + 9 = 16

8

8 + 0 = 8
8 + 1 = 9
8 + 2 = 10
8 + 3 = 11
8 + 4 = 12
8 + 5 = 13
8 + 6 = 14
8 + 7 = 15
8 + 8 = 16
8 + 9 = 17

9

9 + 0 = 9
9 + 1 = 10
9 + 2 = 11
9 + 3 = 12
9 + 4 = 13
9 + 5 = 14
9 + 6 = 15
9 + 7 = 16
9 + 8 = 17
9 + 9 = 18

Addition
Advanced

Time: 2 minutes

Name _____

Errors: 3 or fewer

2	5	0	8	4	2
5	4	6	1	7	4
9	2	3	3	6	0
9	2	4	3	7	5
6	9	7	8	3	2
6	1	7	4	7	6
3	4	2	5	4	6
6	1	3	5	4	3
9	6	7	8	8	9
5	8	4	3	9	4
9	9	5	7	7	9
8	2	8	6	8	7
5	3	2	6	5	8
7	9	8	9	6	8
6	8	9	7	6	8
5	5	6	3	4	4

Subtraction Facts 1–10

$\boxed{1}$	$\boxed{2}$	$\boxed{3}$	$\boxed{4}$	$\boxed{5}$
$1-0=1$	$2-0=2$	$3-0=3$	$4-0=4$	$5-0=5$
$1-1=0$	$2-1=1$	$3-1=2$	$4-1=3$	$5-1=4$
	$2-2=0$	$3-2=1$	$4-2=2$	$5-2=3$
		$3-3=0$	$4-3=1$	$5-3=2$
			$4-4=0$	$5-4=1$
				$5-5=0$

$\boxed{6}$	$\boxed{7}$	$\boxed{8}$	$\boxed{9}$	$\boxed{10}$
$6-0=6$	$7-0=7$	$8-0=8$	$9-0=9$	$10-0=10$
$6-1=5$	$7-1=6$	$8-1=7$	$9-1=8$	$10-1=9$
$6-2=4$	$7-2=5$	$8-2=6$	$9-2=7$	$10-2=8$
$6-3=3$	$7-3=4$	$8-3=5$	$9-3=6$	$10-3=7$
$6-4=2$	$7-4=3$	$8-4=4$	$9-4=5$	$10-4=6$
$6-5=1$	$7-5=2$	$8-5=3$	$9-5=4$	$10-5=5$
$6-6=0$	$7-6=1$	$8-6=2$	$9-6=3$	$10-6=4$
	$7-7=0$	$8-7=1$	$9-7=2$	$10-7=3$
		$8-8=0$	$9-8=1$	$10-8=2$
			$9-9=0$	$10-9=1$
				$10-10=0$

Subtraction Facts 11-18

11

$11 - 9 = 2$
$11 - 8 = 3$
$11 - 7 = 4$
$11 - 6 = 5$
$11 - 5 = 6$
$11 - 4 = 7$
$11 - 3 = 8$
$11 - 2 = 9$

12

$12 - 9 = 3$
$12 - 8 = 4$
$12 - 7 = 5$
$12 - 6 = 6$
$12 - 5 = 7$
$12 - 4 = 8$
$12 - 3 = 9$

13

$13 - 9 = 4$
$13 - 8 = 5$
$13 - 7 = 6$
$13 - 6 = 7$
$13 - 5 = 8$
$13 - 4 = 9$

14

$14 - 9 = 5$
$14 - 8 = 6$
$14 - 7 = 7$
$14 - 6 = 8$
$14 - 5 = 9$

15

$15 - 9 = 6$
$15 - 8 = 7$
$15 - 7 = 8$
$15 - 6 = 9$

16

$16 - 9 = 7$
$16 - 8 = 8$
$16 - 7 = 9$

17

$17 - 9 = 8$
$17 - 8 = 9$

18

$18 - 9 = 9$

Name _____

Facts Practice
Roboman

+ and − Facts

Red = 15
Green = 8
Purple = 9
Yellow = 13
Blue = 14
Black = 11
Brown = 12
Orange = 7

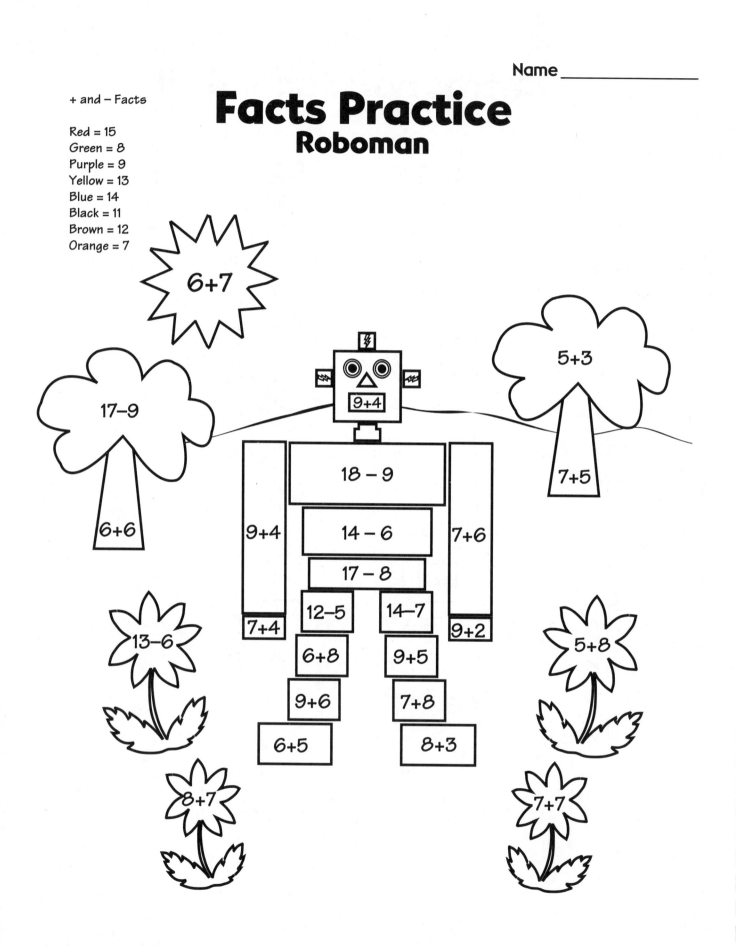

6+7

5+3

17−9

7+5

6+6

9+4

18 − 9

14 − 6

7+6

17 − 8

7+4

12−5

14−7

9+2

13−6

6+8

9+5

5+8

9+6

7+8

6+5

8+3

8+7

7+7

Name _____

Time: 2 minutes

Subtraction
Advanced

Errors: 3 or fewer

9 −9	7 −6	8 −3	5 −0	3 −2	6 −6
8 −5	5 −2	5 −4	9 −6	8 −7	5 −3
9 −2	9 −8	4 −1	7 −5	2 −1	4 −2
8 −2	9 −5	8 −4	7 −2	7 −4	6 −2
7 −3	13 −8	10 −3	12 −6	11 −4	14 −8
11 −9	17 −8	14 −7	15 −8	10 −1	13 −7
10 −5	13 −6	12 −9	15 −6	13 −9	11 −3
11 −5	14 −9	14 −6	18 −9	17 −9	16 −7

Multiplication Facts

1

1 x 1 = 1
1 x 2 = 2
1 x 3 = 3
1 x 4 = 4
1 x 5 = 5
1 x 6 = 6
1 x 7 = 7
1 x 8 = 8
1 x 9 = 9

2

2 x 1 = 2
2 x 2 = 4
2 x 3 = 6
2 x 4 = 8
2 x 5 = 10
2 x 6 = 12
2 x 7 = 14
2 x 8 = 16
2 x 9 = 18

3

3 x 1 = 3
3 x 2 = 6
3 x 3 = 9
3 x 4 = 12
3 x 5 = 15
3 x 6 = 18
3 x 7 = 21
3 x 8 = 24
3 x 9 = 27

4

4 x 1 = 4
4 x 2 = 8
4 x 3 = 12
4 x 4 = 16
4 x 5 = 20
4 x 6 = 24
4 x 7 = 28
4 x 8 = 32
4 x 9 = 36

5

5 x 1 = 5
5 x 2 = 10
5 x 3 = 15
5 x 4 = 20
5 x 5 = 25
5 x 6 = 30
5 x 7 = 35
5 x 8 = 40
5 x 9 = 45

Times Facts to Five

Pink = 12
Red = 15
Brown = 6
Black = 16
White = 18
Purple = 32
Orange = 45
Blue = 25

Name _____

Facts Practice
Yummy Sundae

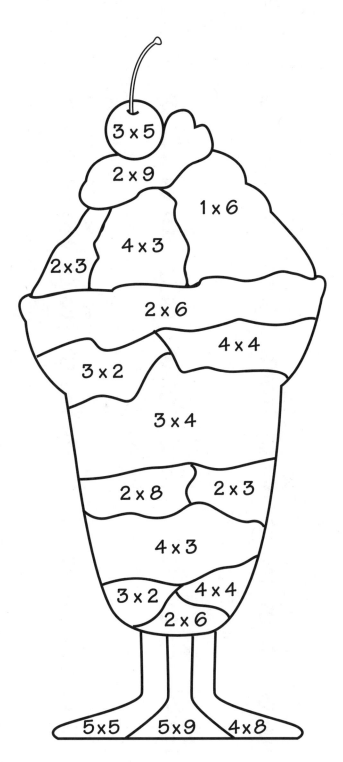

3 x 5

2 x 9

1 x 6

4 x 3

2 x 3

2 x 6

4 x 4

3 x 2

3 x 4

2 x 8   2 x 3

4 x 3

3 x 2   4 x 4

2 x 6

5 x 5   5 x 9   4 x 8

PT

Name _____

Time: 1-3/4 minutes **Multiplication** **Errors:** 3 or fewer

2 x5	5 x4	0 x5	8 x1	4 x2	4 x3
9 x0	2 x2	3 x4	3 x3	5 x2	1 x1
8 x2	7 x4	6 x5	5 x3	3 x2	6 x2
5 x5	4 x1	0 x2	8 x3	9 x2	6 x3
0 x4	8 x5	3 x3	1 x2	6 x1	8 x4
9 x3	4 x4	6 x2	7 x1	7 x5	9 x4
8 x3	7 x2	5 x4	8 x5	9 x1	2 x3
9 x5	3 x4	3 x5	7 x3	6 x4	1 x5

Multiplication Facts
Advanced

§

2	3	4	5
$2 \times 1 = 2$	$3 \times 1 = 3$	$4 \times 1 = 4$	$5 \times 1 = 5$
$2 \times 2 = 4$	$3 \times 2 = 6$	$4 \times 2 = 8$	$5 \times 2 = 10$
$2 \times 3 = 6$	$3 \times 3 = 9$	$4 \times 3 = 12$	$5 \times 3 = 15$
$2 \times 4 = 8$	$3 \times 4 = 12$	$4 \times 4 = 16$	$5 \times 4 = 20$
$2 \times 5 = 10$	$3 \times 5 = 15$	$4 \times 5 = 20$	$5 \times 5 = 25$
$2 \times 6 = 12$	$3 \times 6 = 18$	$4 \times 6 = 24$	$5 \times 6 = 30$
$2 \times 7 = 14$	$3 \times 7 = 21$	$4 \times 7 = 28$	$5 \times 7 = 35$
$2 \times 8 = 16$	$3 \times 8 = 24$	$4 \times 8 = 32$	$5 \times 8 = 40$
$2 \times 9 = 18$	$3 \times 9 = 27$	$4 \times 9 = 36$	$5 \times 9 = 45$

6	7	8	9
$6 \times 1 = 6$	$7 \times 1 = 7$	$8 \times 1 = 8$	$9 \times 1 = 9$
$6 \times 2 = 12$	$7 \times 2 = 14$	$8 \times 2 = 16$	$9 \times 2 = 18$
$6 \times 3 = 18$	$7 \times 3 = 21$	$8 \times 3 = 24$	$9 \times 3 = 27$
$6 \times 4 = 24$	$7 \times 4 = 28$	$8 \times 4 = 32$	$9 \times 4 = 36$
$6 \times 5 = 30$	$7 \times 5 = 35$	$8 \times 5 = 40$	$9 \times 5 = 45$
$6 \times 6 = 36$	$7 \times 6 = 42$	$8 \times 6 = 48$	$9 \times 6 = 54$
$6 \times 7 = 42$	$7 \times 7 = 49$	$8 \times 7 = 56$	$9 \times 7 = 63$
$6 \times 8 = 48$	$7 \times 8 = 56$	$8 \times 8 = 64$	$9 \times 8 = 72$
$6 \times 9 = 54$	$7 \times 9 = 63$	$8 \times 9 = 72$	$9 \times 9 = 81$

Finger Facts

	2's	3's	4's	5's	6's
(1)	2	3	4	5	6
(2)	4	6	8	10	12
(3)	6	9	12	15	18
(4)	8	12	16	20	24
(5)	10	15	20	25	30
(6)	12	18	24	30	36
(7)	14	21	28	35	42
(8)	16	24	32	40	48
(9)	18	27	36	45	54

	7's	8's	9's	commutative property
(1)	7	8	9	$4 \times 7 = 28$
(2)	14	16	18	$7 \times 4 = 28$
(3)	21	24	27	$9 \times 6 = 54$
(4)	28	32	36	$6 \times 9 = 54$
(5)	35	40	45	$7 \times 8 = 56$
(6)	42	48	54	$8 \times 7 = 56$
(7)	49	56	63	$7 \times 9 = 63$
(8)	56	64	72	$9 \times 7 = 63$
(9)	63	72	81	$8 \times 9 = 72$
				$9 \times 8 = 72$

Name _____

Facts
Practice Sheet

Time: 45 secs.

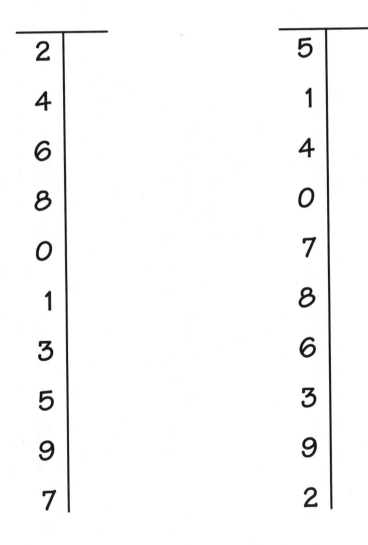

2	5
4	1
6	4
8	0
0	7
1	8
3	6
5	3
9	9
7	2

Multiplication
Advanced

Time: 2 1/2
minutes

Name _____

Errors:
3 or fewer

5	2	5	5
4	4	1	7
9	6	4	1
3	8	0	0
7	0	7	2
8	1	8	3
6	3	6	6
2	5	3	8
1	9	9	9
0	7	2	4

2	1	9	5
6	9	7	4
8	2	5	7
0	8	3	6
1	3	1	1
3	7	0	2
4	4	8	9
5	6	6	8
9	5	4	0
7	0	2	3

Division Facts

1 $1\overline{)1}\,^1$ $1\overline{)2}\,^2$ $1\overline{)4}\,^4$ $1\overline{)5}\,^5$ $1\overline{)6}\,^6$ $1\overline{)7}\,^7$ $1\overline{)8}\,^8$ $1\overline{)9}\,^9$

2 $2\overline{)2}\,^1$ $2\overline{)4}\,^2$ $2\overline{)6}\,^3$ $2\overline{)8}\,^4$ $2\overline{)10}\,^5$ $2\overline{)12}\,^6$ $2\overline{)14}\,^7$ $2\overline{)16}\,^8$ $2\overline{)18}\,^9$

3 $3\overline{)3}\,^1$ $3\overline{)6}\,^2$ $3\overline{)9}\,^3$ $3\overline{)12}\,^4$ $3\overline{)15}\,^5$ $3\overline{)18}\,^6$ $3\overline{)21}\,^7$ $3\overline{)24}\,^8$ $3\overline{)27}\,^9$

4 $4\overline{)4}\,^1$ $4\overline{)8}\,^2$ $4\overline{)12}\,^3$ $4\overline{)16}\,^4$ $4\overline{)20}\,^5$ $4\overline{)24}\,^6$ $4\overline{)28}\,^7$ $4\overline{)32}\,^8$ $4\overline{)36}\,^9$

5 $5\overline{)5}\,^1$ $5\overline{)10}\,^2$ $5\overline{)15}\,^3$ $5\overline{)20}\,^4$ $5\overline{)25}\,^5$ $5\overline{)30}\,^6$ $5\overline{)35}\,^7$ $5\overline{)40}\,^8$ $5\overline{)45}\,^9$

6 $6\overline{)6}\,^1$ $6\overline{)12}\,^2$ $6\overline{)18}\,^3$ $6\overline{)24}\,^4$ $6\overline{)30}\,^5$ $6\overline{)36}\,^6$ $6\overline{)42}\,^7$ $6\overline{)48}\,^8$ $6\overline{)54}\,^9$

7 $7\overline{)7}\,^1$ $7\overline{)14}\,^2$ $7\overline{)21}\,^3$ $7\overline{)28}\,^4$ $7\overline{)35}\,^5$ $7\overline{)42}\,^6$ $7\overline{)49}\,^7$ $7\overline{)56}\,^8$ $7\overline{)63}\,^9$

8 $8\overline{)8}\,^1$ $8\overline{)16}\,^2$ $8\overline{)24}\,^3$ $8\overline{)32}\,^4$ $8\overline{)40}\,^5$ $8\overline{)48}\,^6$ $8\overline{)56}\,^7$ $8\overline{)64}\,^8$ $8\overline{)72}\,^9$

9 $9\overline{)9}\,^1$ $9\overline{)18}\,^2$ $9\overline{)27}\,^3$ $9\overline{)36}\,^4$ $9\overline{)45}\,^5$ $9\overline{)54}\,^6$ $9\overline{)63}\,^7$ $9\overline{)72}\,^8$ $9\overline{)81}\,^9$

Division Facts may be written three different ways:

$$9\overline{)54}\,^6 \qquad 54 \div 9 = 6 \qquad \frac{54}{9} = 6$$

Division

Name _____

$9\overline{)81}$ $7\overline{)21}$ $8\overline{)40}$ $6\overline{)54}$ $5\overline{)15}$

$5\overline{)5}$ $6\overline{)48}$ $3\overline{)27}$ $9\overline{)72}$ $7\overline{)63}$

$5\overline{)20}$ $8\overline{)32}$ $2\overline{)10}$ $5\overline{)25}$ $2\overline{)16}$

$8\overline{)24}$ $9\overline{)9}$ $6\overline{)24}$ $4\overline{)24}$ $9\overline{)63}$

$2\overline{)14}$ $7\overline{)56}$ $5\overline{)30}$ $3\overline{)24}$ $8\overline{)64}$

$4\overline{)20}$ $9\overline{)45}$ $3\overline{)21}$ $2\overline{)12}$ $6\overline{)30}$

$8\overline{)16}$ $6\overline{)18}$ $4\overline{)16}$ $9\overline{)27}$ $5\overline{)45}$

$6\overline{)12}$ $9\overline{)0}$ $2\overline{)18}$ $4\overline{)32}$ $7\overline{)35}$

$8\overline{)48}$ $4\overline{)28}$ $7\overline{)14}$ $9\overline{)36}$ $5\overline{)40}$

$5\overline{)10}$ $6\overline{)42}$ $8\overline{)56}$ $3\overline{)18}$ $7\overline{)42}$

Science Fair

We will be having a science fair

in _____ on _____ .

You will be successful if you are willing to do these two things:

1. Spend a good amount of time on your project over a few weeks.
2. Select a project that is realistic for your abilities AND one that you find ENTICING!!!

These are the things for you to do.

1. Select a subject. Then pick a topic. Decide EXACTLY what you will do. You can select from the list of subjects.
   Example: subject = the heart
            topic = heart attacks
2. Use the scientific process.
   a. Make up a question or a list of questions you would like answers to. What are some things you'd like to know about your topic?
   b. Investigate. Read books, magazines, or encyclopedia articles about your topic.
   c. Record all information or observations about your topic.
   d. Write your report.
   e. Proofread so there are no errors.
3. Make a background out of tag or a similar material.
4. Glue-stick on ALL information—your topic, why you selected it, and the scientific process that you used.
5. If you have an experiment, have it set up right in front of your background. Be sure it works.
6. The background needs to look absolutely BEAUTIFUL with excellent drawings, good title lettering, and neat printing or handwriting. Be sure your NAME is on the front of your background.
7. Bring your project to school on _____ .

(Science Fair Continued)
List of subjects:

1. Different animals' teeth
2. The ocean's floor
3. Test for colorblindness
4. One of the planets or the Moon
5. One or all of the five senses
6. The effect of sunlight on plants
7. The layers of the Earth
8. The ear
9. The eye
10. The skin
11. The nose
12. The lungs
13. The digestive system
14. Earthquakes
15. Volcanoes
16. The tongue and its detection of different flavors
17. Different types of birds' beaks
18. Penguins
19. Salmon
20. Hibernation of animals
21. The Gulf Stream
22. Microbes
23. Types of rocks
24. An animal and how it lives
25. Insects
26. Trees
27. Plants
28. The heart
29. Wind vane
30. A SAFE chemistry, physics, or biology experiment
31. A collection of rocks, plants, grasses, bugs, bird nest materials, etc.
32. Herbivores, carnivores, or omnivores
33. Bones or muscles
34. A thermometer
35. Molecules
36. The volume of different objects
37. Wind
38. Storms
39. Pollution
40. Clouds
41. Microscope
42. Eclipses
43. Constellations
44. Tides
45. Land and water forms, for example: mountains, straits, plateaus, bays, peninsulas, etc.

Button Art Project

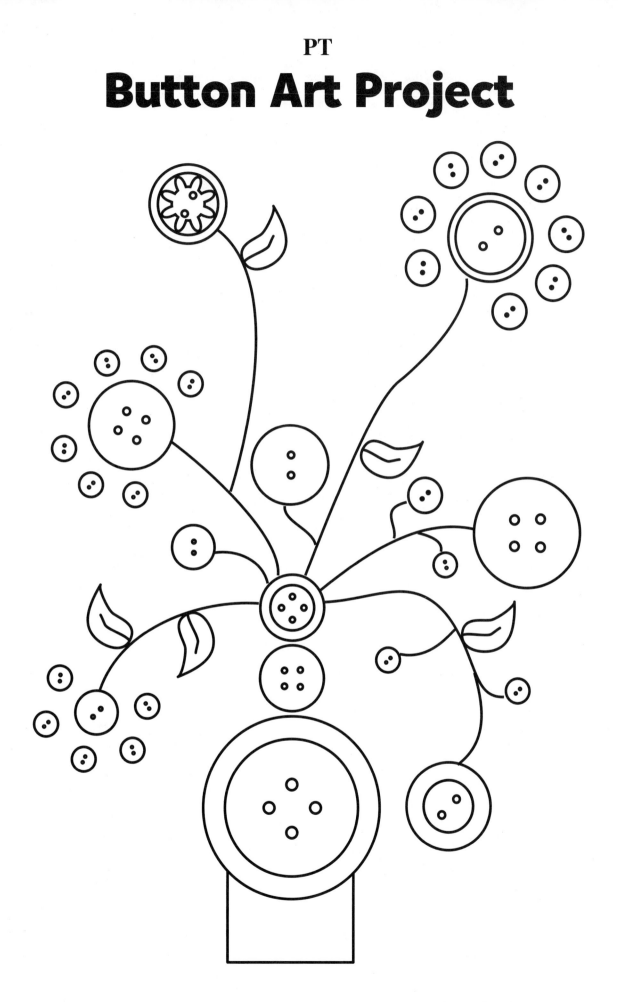

§

Patriotic Stars

STAR A

Down	Up	
*1	*7	
8	2	
3	9	
10	4	
5	11	cut
11	17	
18	12	
13	19	
20	14	
15	21	cut
21	27	
28	22	
23	29	
30	24	
25	31	cut
31	37	
38	32	
33	39	
40	34	
35	41	cut
41	47	
48	42	
43	49	
50	44	
45	1	
6	11	
16	11	
16	21	
26	21	
26	31	
36	31	
36	41	
46	41	
46	1	
6	1	cut

STAR B

Down	Up	
*1	*7	
8	2	
3	9	
10	4	
5	11	cut
11	17	
18	12	
13	19	
20	14	
15	21	cut
21	27	
28	22	
23	29	
30	24	
25	31	cut
31	37	
38	32	
33	39	
40	34	
35	41	cut
41	47	
48	42	
43	49	
50	44	
45	1	
6	11	
16	11	
16	21	
26	21	
26	31	
36	31	
36	41	
46	41	
46	1	
6	1	cut

Be sure to begin
at the correct place
Start
*1 Down *7 Up

STAR C

Down	Up		Down	Up
1	8		49	56
9	2		57	50
3	10		51	58
11	4		59	52
5	12		53	60
13	6	cut	1	54
13	20		55	1
21	14		7	1
15	22		7	13
23	16		19	13
17	24		19	25
25	18	cut	31	25
25	32		31	37
33	26		43	37
27	34		43	49
35	28		55	49
29	36			cut
37	30	cut		
37	44			
45	38			
39	46			
47	40			
41	48			
49	42	cut		

IN 8601 String Art © 1981 Author: Annette Schmidt, Editor: Carole Charters
Published by Judy/Instructo, 6442 City West Parkway, Eden Prairie, MN 55344

Geography

PT §

Prime Minister:	Your dinner has been waiting for you. Here is a steak and a baked potato.

(The Prime Minister hands King Midas a tray.)

King Midas:	(takes tray) Look! Look! The tray has turned to gold! The knife and fork have turned to gold!
Prime Minister:	The steak has turned to gold!
Treasurer:	Even the baked potato has turned to gold!
King Midas:	(tasting potato) Ouch! I burned myself on my hot gold potato. Quick! Give me water!

(The Prime Minister hands King Midas a glass.)

King Midas:	(tries to drink) Oh no! The water has turned to gold! I'm thirsty. What can I do? What can I do?

(Mimi, King Midas's daughter, runs in.)

Mimi:	Daddy, what is wrong? You look ill! Let me rub your head.

(As Mimi touches King Midas's head, she becomes as stiff as a statue.)

King Midas:	This is terrible! My little daughter Mimi has turned into gold! I'll never ask for more gold again as long as I live.

(The Wizard steps forward.)

Wizard:	Do you really mean it?
King Midas:	Yes.
Wizard:	Cross your heart?

(King Midas crosses his heart.)

Wizard:	Then I will take away your foolish wish.

(The Wizard snaps his fingers and Mimi moves.)

Mimi:	Daddy, what happened?
King Midas:	Mimi, I have learned a lesson. There are many, many things more important than gold!

(All actors hold hands, come to the front of the stage, and bow.)

THE END

King Midas

Getting Ready for Your Play

Characters: Prime Minister, King Midas, Treasurer, Wizard, Mimi (the King's daughter)

Props: throne, fork, drinking glass, steak, baked potato, crown for King Midas

Suggestions:
1. Make steak, baked potato, and King's crown from construction paper.
2. Use teacher's chair for the throne.

(The scene takes place at the palace. King Midas is sitting on his throne.)

Prime Minister:	Your Majesty, you seem to be sad.
King Midas:	*(sighs)* I am sad. I want more gold!
Prime Minister:	But Your Majesty, you already have more gold than any other king.
King Midas:	That doesn't matter. I'm not happy. Bring me the Treasurer.
Prime Minister:	*(yelling)* Send in the Treasurer!

(The Treasurer enters.)

Treasurer:	*(bowing)* I am the keeper of the gold. What do you wish, O King?
King Midas:	More gold!
Treasurer:	That is impossible, Your Majesty. All of the royal gold mines are empty. There is only coal left.
King Midas:	Coal? I don't want coal! I'm going to stamp my feet until I get gold! *(stamps feet up and down)*
Prime Minister:	Send for the Wizard!

(The Wizard enters.)

Wizard:	What is all this noise? Is there an earthquake?
King Midas:	*(stamping feet)* I want gold!
Wizard:	Stop that stamping, and I will give you your wish!
King Midas:	*(stopping and smiling)* My wish?
Wizard:	From this moment on, everything you touch will turn to gold!
King Midas:	That is wonderful! I'm hungry from all that stamping. Bring me something to eat!

§

Patriotic Stars

Pattern Sheet

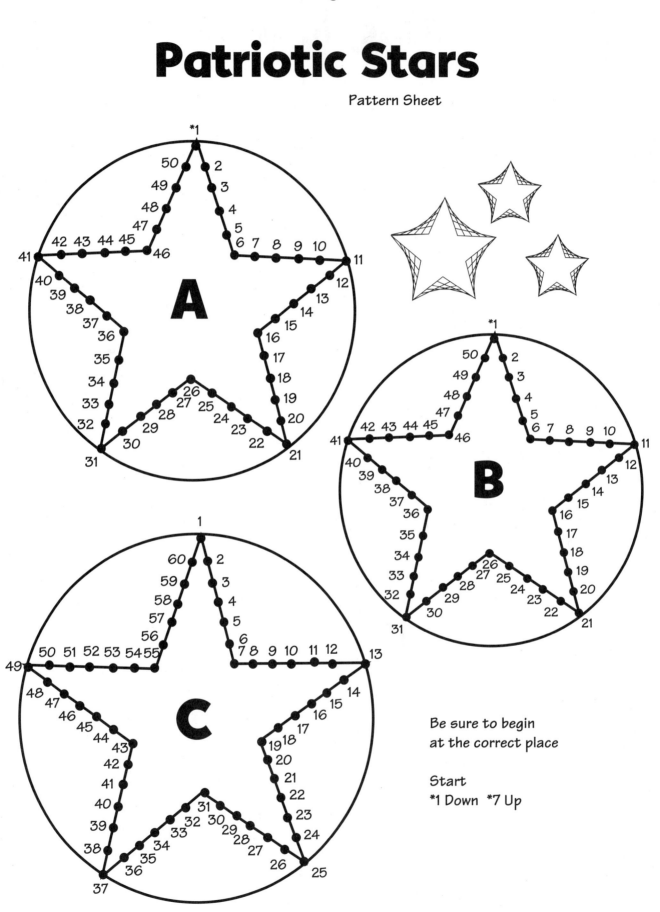

Be sure to begin
at the correct place

Start
*1 Down *7 Up

IN 8601 String Art © 1981 Author: Annette Schmidt, Editor: Carole Charters
Published by Judy/Instructo, 6442 City West Parkway, Eden Prairie, MN 55344

My Geography Booklet

Name _____

First, Geometry!

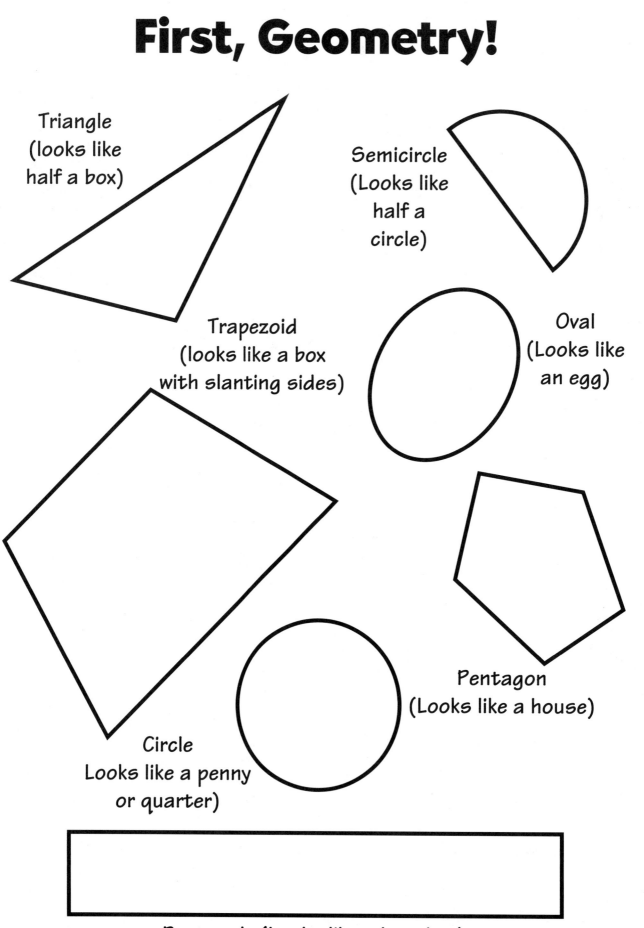

Triangle
(looks like
half a box)

Semicircle
(Looks like
half a
circle)

Trapezoid
(looks like a box
with slanting sides)

Oval
(Looks like
an egg)

Pentagon
(Looks like a house)

Circle
Looks like a penny
or quarter)

Rectangle (Looks like a long box)

Same Shapes, Different Positions

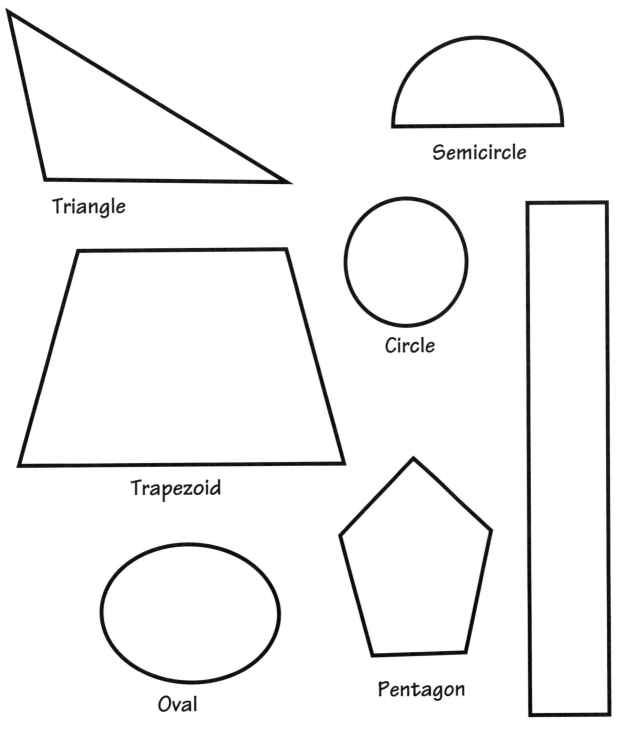

Triangle

Semicircle

Trapezoid

Circle

Oval

Pentagon

Rectangle

Geometry Activity

Directions: Use "First, Geometry!" and "Same Shapes, Different Positions" pages.

1. Color both <u>triangles</u> BLUE.

2. Color both <u>semicircles</u> GREEN.

3. Color both <u>ovals</u> YELLOW.

4. Color both <u>pentagons</u> RED.

5. Color both <u>trapezoids</u> BROWN.

6. Color both <u>circles</u> PURPLE.

7. Color both <u>rectangles</u> ORANGE.

Now, Geography!
Continents and Oceans of the World

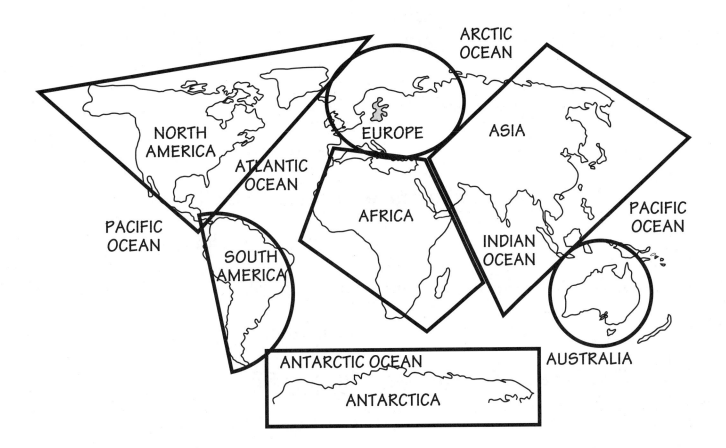

There are seven continents in the world. They are:

NORTH AMERICA

SOUTH AMERICA

EUROPE

ASIA

AUSTRALIA

AFRICA

ANTARCTICA

There are five oceans in the world. They are:

PACIFIC OCEAN

ATLANTIC OCEAN

INDIAN OCEAN

ARCTIC OCEAN

ANTARCTIC OCEAN

Geography Activity

Directions: Do the following on the map called CONTINENTS AND OCEANS OF THE WORLD:

Color the land inside the <u>triangle</u> BLUE.

It's North America.

Color the land inside the <u>semicircle</u> GREEN.

It's South America.

Color the land inside the <u>oval</u> YELLOW.

It's Europe.

Color the land inside the <u>pentagon</u> RED.

It's Africa.

Color the land inside the <u>trapezoid</u> BROWN.

It's Asia.

Color the land inside the <u>circle</u> PURPLE.

It's Australia.

Color the land inside the <u>rectangle</u> ORANGE.

It's Antarctica.

Continent Shapes

Name the continents, and color each a different color.

1. _____

2. _____

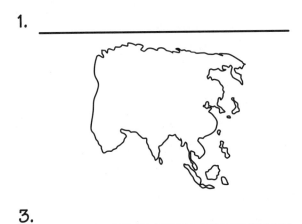

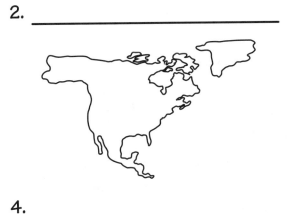

3. _____

4. _____

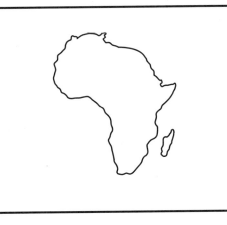

5. _____

6. _____

7. _____

Mexico
Our Neighbor to the South

New Words

  border: the edge of a country
  coast: the edge of land next to an
    ocean or sea
  plateau: a high, flat piece of land
  triangle: a shape with three sides

Mexico is a large country. It is just south of the United States. It shares a long border with the United States. The Pacific Ocean is on its west coast. The Gulf of Mexico and the Caribbean Sea are on its east coast.

Mexico is shaped like a large triangle. The northern edge of Mexico is wide. This is the part that is next to the United States. The narrow part of the country is to the south.

Land that is now part of the United States used to be part of Mexico. This land is now the states of California, Nevada, Utah, Arizona, New Mexico, Texas, and parts of Wyoming, Colorado, Kansas, and Oklahoma.

Most of Mexico is covered with mountains. There are also plains, plateaus, and jungles. The temperature in Mexico is based on how high up you are. This is measured in feet above sea level. If a mountain is 5,000 feet high, this means that the top of the mountain is 5,000 feet higher than the ocean. If you are high in the mountains, many feet above sea level, it is cool. If you are on a smaller mountain or a plateau, it is warmer. If you are on land that is not much higher than the ocean, it is very hot.

Activities

1. Look at the map of Mexico and the United States. Draw a line around the part of the United States that used to be part of Mexico. Follow the dotted line on the map for help. Draw another line around both Mexico and this part of the United States. How many states used to be partly or all in Mexico?

2. There are three places marked on the map. Each place has a temperature next to it. This temperature shows how hot it might be in the month of July. Tell whether you think each place is in the cool mountains, on a warm plateau, or on the hot plains. Write your answers next to the names of the places on the map.

Chihuahua–71°

Chichén Itzá–85°

Mexico City–64°

Australia

Indian
Ocean

Great Barrier Reef

Pacific
Ocean

Indian
Ocean

☆ Canberra

Australia is the only continent that is a country. It is sometimes called "the land down under" because it is below the Equator. When we have summer, it is winter down there.

The inland of Australia is very dry, sandy, and rocky. Almost no one lives there. It is called "Never-Never Land."

The big cities of Australia are by the ocean in the south and east. Canberra is the capital of Australia. Sydney is another big city.

Australia has some special animals. There are some MARSUPIALS. These are animals who give birth to babies. Right after the baby is born, it stays in a pouch in its mother's tummy. A pouch is like a bag or a sack. The baby grows more in the pouch. Some examples of marsupials in Australia are kangaroos, koalas, and wombats. Australia also has a special dog called the dingo and a very interesting animal called the Tasmanian devil.

Special Animals

KANGAROO

The kangaroo is the largest marsupial. The adult male can be 6 to 7 feet tall. It can weigh 100 to 150 pounds. Some kangaroos are gray. Some are red. The kangaroo can hop on its back legs as fast as 40 miles per hour. Its tail is three feet long. The tail is used for balance so the kangaroo doesn't fall over. The enemies of the kangaroo are humans and dingoes.

KOALA

The koala is not a bear. It only looks like a teddy bear. Its fur is gray or brown on its back. Its tummy has white fur. It is 25 to 30 inches tall. It weighs 15 to 30 pounds. It has no tail. It is a marsupial. The koala spends all its time in trees. It sleeps in the day. At night, it eats the leaves and bark of eucalyptus trees.

WOMBAT

The wombat is fat and has brown fur. It is 3 to 4 feet long. It weighs from 30 to 70 pounds. It has small ears. It is a marsupial. It eats grass.

DINGO

The dingo is a wild dog. It is medium size. It has yellow and brown fur. Some have white and black fur. Dingoes howl instead of bark. They kill sheep and wallabies, which are small kangaroos.

TASMANIAN DEVIL

It is 3 to 4 feet long. It is all black or some black with white. It is a night hunter. It snarls, growls, coughs, and barks. Its teeth can crush bones. Its stomach can digest feathers, fur, and bones. When it gets mad, its ears turn red.

Australia Activity

Directions:

1. Color each special animal its correct color.

2. Draw a line to match column A with column B.

A

special animal

capital of Australia

almost no one lives here

summer for our country

B

Canberra

winter for their country

koala

Never-Never Land

Geography
Winner

Name _____

My Geography Booklet

Name _____

Map Activities

For the Map of
the Continent of North America

Color the United States yellow. Color Mexico green. Color Canada red. All the islands between the main part of Canada and Greenland should be colored red, too. Color Central America brown. Color the West Indies orange. Color Greenland purple. Color all water blue. When you color the rivers, watch out NOT to color over their names.

Use the map to answer these questions. Reminder: the entire names of continents, countries, rivers, oceans, gulfs, and lakes are all proper nouns and must be capitalized. (Example: Colorado River)

1. You should have colored Alaska yellow. Why? _____

   _____

2. Why do you think Greenland is not the same color as Canada? _____

   _____

3. What is the name of our continent? _____

4. What is the name of our country? _____

5. What ocean borders our country on the east? _____

6. What ocean borders our country on the west? _____

7. What country is directly south of ours? _____

8. What is the name of the river that partially separates the U. S. and Mexico and acts as a natural boundary?

   _____

9. What is the capital of Mexico? _____

10. What is the capital of the U. S.? _____

11. What is the capital of Canada? _____

12. The longest river in the United States is the Mississippi. Into what gulf does it empty?

   _____

13. One of our states, which is famous as an island vacation spot, is not on this map. Why is it not on the map? (Hint: Look up the definition of "continent" in your dictionary.)

   _____

14. How is a national boundary represented on this map? _____

15. The West Indies and Central America are part of which continent? _____

The Continent of North America

Arctic Ocean

Greenland
(Denmark)

Bering
Sea

Yukon River

Alaska
(U.S.)

CANADA

Hudson
Bay

Pacific
Ocean

Great
Lakes

Ottawa

Great
Salt
Lake

Missouri River

Mississippi

UNITED STATES

Washington, D.C.

Colorado River

Arkansas

Red River

Ohio River

River

Rio Grande

Atlantic
Ocean

Gulf of
Mexico

MEXICO

Mexico
City

West Indies

Caribbean Sea

Central
America

KEY

National Boundaries ·····

National Capitals ✪

The U. S. West of the Mississippi

The U. S. East of the Mississippi

On the following pages is a two-page map of the United States with the Mississippi River as the divider. Inside each state is its postal abbreviation and a dot to represent the location of its capital. The page after the map pages has all the states listed in alphabetical order giving their postal abbreviation, state name, and state capital.

Practice learning the state names, abbreviations, and capitals. Notice the SHAPE of each state. Notice WHERE the state is. Is it in the southern United States, the northern, eastern or western United States? This will help you learn the states. Study the map thoroughly. Notice especially that New York State is in two areas and so are Virginia and Michigan. Notice the unusual shape of Maryland.

Things to do on the two large U. S. maps:

1. Color Hawaii pink.

2. Color California green.

3. Color all of New York red.

4. Color Arizona purple.

5. Color Washington, D. C. yellow.

6. Color the Great Lakes blue.

7. While you're coloring all the other states any color you like think of their shape and where they are.

The United States
West of the Mississippi River

KEY

⭐ State Capital

The United States
East of the Mississippi River

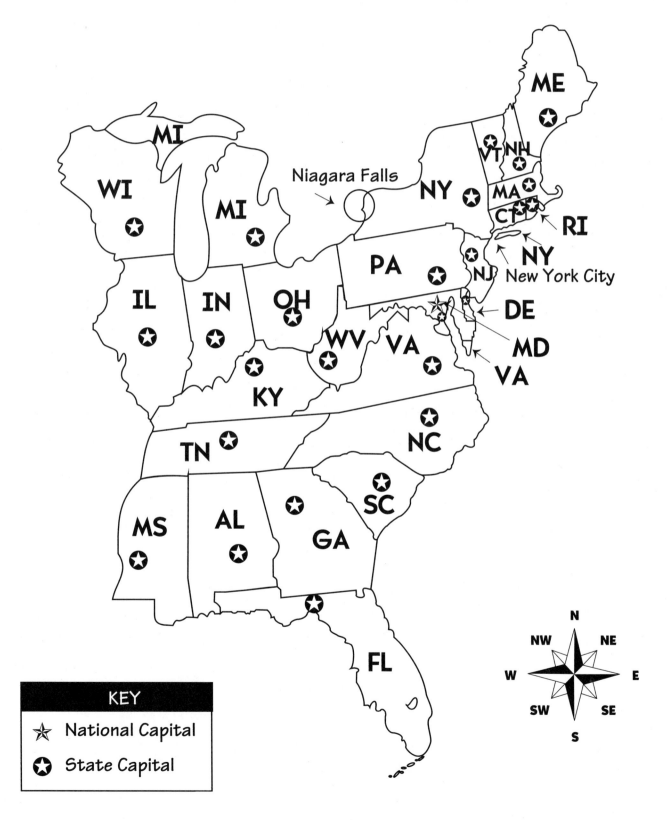

Niagara Falls

New York City

KEY

★ National Capital

✪ State Capital

States and Capitals

AL—Alabama	Montgomery	MT—Montana	Helena
AK—Alaska	Juneau	NE—Nebraska	Lincoln
AZ—Arizona	Phoenix	NV—Nevada	Carson City
AR—Arkansas	Little Rock	NH—New Hampshire	Concord
CA—California	Sacramento	NJ—New Jersey	Trenton
CO—Colorado	Denver	NM—New Mexico	Santa Fe
CT—Connecticut	Hartford	NY—New York	Albany
DE—Delaware	Dover	NC—North Carolina	Raleigh
FL—Florida	Tallahassee	ND—North Dakota	Bismarck
GA—Georgia	Atlanta	OH—Ohio	Columbus
HI—Hawaii	Honolulu	OK—Oklahoma	Oklahoma City
ID—Idaho	Boise	OR—Oregon	Salem
IL—Illinois	Springfield	PA—Pennsylvania	Harrisburg
IN—Indiana	Indianapolis	RI—Rhode Island	Providence
IA—Iowa	Des Moines	SC—South Carolina	Columbia
KS—Kansas	Topeka	SD—South Dakota	Pierre
KY—Kentucky	Frankfort	TN—Tennessee	Nashville
LA—Louisiana	Baton Rouge	TX—Texas	Austin
ME—Maine	Augusta	UT—Utah	Salt Lake City
MD—Maryland	Annapolis	VT—Vermont	Montpelier
MA—Massachusetts	Boston	VA—Virginia	Richmond
MI—Michigan	Lansing	WA—Washington	Olympia
MN—Minnesota	St. Paul	WV—West Virginia	Charleston
MS—Mississippi	Jackson	WI—Wisconsin	Madison
MO—Missouri	Jefferson City	WY—Wyoming	Cheyenne

Honolulu

Honolulu is a major sea and airport and is also the capital of the Hawaiian Islands, which were originally called the Sandwich Islands. Honolulu is located on the island of Oahu about 2,000 miles from the continental United States. Most Hawaiians live on the southeastern side of Oahu near Honolulu. Honolulu is a bustling city of approximately 365,000 people. Really, though, Honolulu covers the entire island of Oahu and has about 765,000 people, but most people refer only to the large urban area on the southeastern coast as Honolulu. When you walk around in Honolulu, you have to remember that you're walking on the top of a volcano.

Military defense used to be Honolulu's main industry. The important naval base of Pearl Harbor with the USS Arizona Memorial is nearby. Pearl Harbor was attacked by the Japanese on December 7, 1941. This drew the United States into World War II. The USS Arizona Memorial is dedicated to all the people who died on Oahu that Sunday morning. Today the United States uses Hawaii as a stopover point for refueling airplanes on long flights and also as a means of keeping a close watch on the Pacific.

Recently, however, tourism has become Honolulu's main industry. It is no wonder, since Honolulu has a year-round nice climate with warm temperatures and frequent, but short, spells of rain. A visitor can tan at Waikiki Beach in December. Honolulu is also famous for its luaus—feasts where a pig is roasted in an underground oven called an imu. Hula dancers, welcoming leis (wreaths of flowers to place around your neck when you land in Honolulu), and its most famous word ALOHA, which means both "hello" and "good-bye," help make Honolulu an exciting place to visit. Aloha!

San Francisco

A port city on San Francisco Bay, beautiful San Francisco is the center of air and sea transportation routes going to places all over the world. It is located on the northern end of a peninsula. San Francisco has a pleasant year-round climate, usually not too hot or cold. Port cities attract large populations because of the many job opportunities. San Francisco's population is about 680,000 making it one of the largest cities in California.

San Francisco is famous for its Chinatown, where many Chinese live and work. It is the largest Chinese community in the United States. San Francisco is also famous, unfortunately, for its earthquakes, the largest of which was in 1906. Connecting San Francisco with Marin County to the north is the world-famous Golden Gate Bridge. It is one of the longest suspension bridges in the world. There is also a double-decker bridge linking San Francisco with Oakland to the east. Outgoing traffic and incoming traffic travel on two different levels on this bridge. San Francisco's subway system, called BART (Bay Area Rapid Transit), travels under the city and travels underwater across to Oakland in the Trans-Bay Tube. Because San Francisco is so hilly, its cable cars are a fun means of transportation.

Included in San Francisco are several islands in the Pacific Ocean and in the San Francisco Bay. The most famous of these is Alcatraz, which used to be a prison for very dangerous criminals. It was called "the Rock." In the Russian Hill area of San Francisco is the crookedest street in the world. It's part of Lombard Street and it makes ten very sharp turns in only one city block. Finally, just south of the city is the Silicon Valley, home of computer technology.

City Scramble—West

Directions: Unscramble the word or words inside the brackets to find the answer. Write your answer on the line or lines at the end of each sentence.

1. Most Hawaiians live near Honolulu on the island of [UHAO]. _____
2. An important naval base near Honolulu is [LREAP ROBRAH]. _____ _____
3. A feast in Honolulu where a pig is roasted in an imu is called a [UUAL]. _____
4. A famous dance in Honolulu is the [AHUL]. _____
5. In Honolulu, this word means both "hello" and "good-bye." The word is [AAOHL]. _____
6. Honolulu's main industry is [MTRISUO]. _____
7. Located on the end of a peninsula is the famous city of [NSA CCRASFION]. _____
   _____
8. The Golden Gate Bridge in San Francisco is one of the longest [SSSNNPEUIO] bridges in the world.
   _____
9. BART is a [BYSAUW] system in San Francisco. _____
10. Because San Francisco is so hilly, one means of transportation is the [BECLA RAC]. _____
    _____
11. Just south of San Francisco is a major computer technology area called the [NLSOIIC LLVYAE].
    _____ _____

The Grand Canyon

Millions of years ago the land at the Grand Canyon was almost flat, but the Colorado River cut deeper and deeper into the land to form this great canyon—the largest canyon in the world. The Grand Canyon is one of the seven natural wonders of the world and the only one of these seven to be located in the United States. It's in the state of Arizona. The Grand Canyon is a national park run by the U.S. government.

The Grand Canyon is 217 miles long and one mile deep and varies from 4 to 18 miles wide. If you stand at a lookout point, even on a clear day, you can see only a small piece of the canyon. It is a 200-mile automobile trip rim to rim. Some of the deepest rock in the canyon is over two billion years old. Long ago, the Pueblo Indians lived here and today there are still ruins of Pueblo houses to be sighted. There are over 100 kinds of animals and over 200 kinds of birds in the canyon.

At the bottom of the canyon is the Havasupai (Hăv ə sōō' pī) Indian Village, considered the most beautiful Indian reservation in the United States. You can spend the night there at the 24-room Supai Lodge. Be prepared for a big temperature change. There is a big difference in temperature between the bottom of the canyon and the top. The bottom can be a sweltering 110 degrees and on the same day, the top, because of the high elevation, can be a pleasant 75 degrees.

There are several ways to go down into the canyon. If you like to rough it, you can hike down or go by mule. You can take a pleasant ride in a small, fifteen-seater airplane. Or if you're the adventuresome sort, you can go down in a helicopter. Until recently, small tourist planes and helicopters could go 1,500 feet down into the canyon; however, some went quite a bit deeper. The ride is breathtaking. But because of a crash and many complaints about the constant noise from the planes and helicopters, air flights are more limited now.

Not far from the Grand Canyon are the Grand Canyon Caverns. They were formed by the erosion of an inland sea and by volcanic and earthquake activity. You can get into a modern elevator and go 21 stories down into the earth to look at these caverns. The original "elevator" in 1927 consisted of the person being lowered into the earth with a rope around his waist and a flashlight in his hand. The ride cost 25 cents. Today there is one mile of lighted trail. When the lights are turned off, you can't see your own hand in front of your face because it is pitch black down there. Because of the depth of the caverns, the temperature is always around 57 degrees. One area of the caverns is a nuclear bomb shelter with supplies for an emergency. Another area of the caverns is being used by the University of New Mexico to study cosmic rays. The Grand Canyon Caverns are one of the largest, completely dry, well-preserved cave systems in the world.

Nearby the Grand Canyon and not far from the caverns is the village of Tusayan (Tōō sī͞ n). There is an IMAX theater there where you can see an awesome show of the history of the Grand Canyon on a six-story high movie screen with six-track stereophonic sound.

Niagara Falls

Niagara Falls is a natural wonder located on the Niagara River, which forms part of the boundary between the United States and Canada. The Niagara River flows northward from Lake Erie to Lake Ontario. About halfway, there is a steep cliff and when the water drops over the edge of the cliff, there it is— Niagara Falls!

Niagara Falls has two waterfalls side by side. The American Falls is in New York. It's 167 feet high and 1,000 feet wide. Only about 10 percent of the water from the Niagara River is allowed to go over the American Falls because of rapid erosion. If the water weren't controlled, pretty soon there would be no more American Falls.

Horseshoe Falls is in Ontario, Canada. It is 158 feet high and 2,600 feet wide. 90 percent of the water from the Niagara River flows over it. The force of the water changes the shape of this set of falls, too. About three feet from the top is lost each year to erosion.

Niagara Falls is an important natural resource. The tremendous water power that is generated is used for electricity.

In the cold months, the Niagara Falls area has snow and ice, but in the warm months, Niagara Falls is a tourist attraction. If you go there, you can see the falls from various lookout points. Or you can go down in an elevator toward the bottom of the American Falls, take off your shoes, and put on a pair of soft, cloth booties and a rain slicker with a hood. Then you can go out to the falls on a wooden stairway to get a close-up look. One of the landings is called Hurricane Point, where the wind and mist is so strong you can hardly see. You feel like you're going to be blown over. Even with the slicker on, you still get soaked.

You can also take a helicopter ride to see the falls, but that's not as exciting as the Maid of the Mist boat ride. You don a slicker again, get on an open boat, and go right out to the middle of the mighty Horseshoe Falls. It feels like the boat will overturn. Everyone gets soaked. It's a spectacular trip.

Wonders Search

```
T H E G R A N D Q A R F M
A E R S W R T C N M O C R
R E O H S X Z A M E P E S
N L M T E A D N Q R V R S
I A F A S W R Y S I X O T
C O L O R A D O R C B S A
S Q A B O T D N F A C I C
H S T C H E N O O N S O D
O R B D M R T V R Y Z N E
H E L I C O P T E R Y X U
```

Directions: Solve each clue. Write the answers on the lines—one letter to a line. Then find the answer in the word search. Letters for the words can go upward, downward, across, backward, forward, and diagonally.

1. This shaped the Grand Canyon.

   __ __ __ __ __ __ __ __   __ __ __ __ __

2. You can fly the canyon in one of these.

   __ __ __ __ __ __ __ __ __ __ __

3. This is one of the seven natural wonders of the world.

   __ __ __   __ __ __ __ __   __ __ __ __ __ __

4. Millions of years ago, the Grand Canyon area looked like this. __ __ __ __

5. These falls are in New York. __ __ __ __ __ __ __ __

6. These falls are in Ontario, Canada. __ __ __ __ __ __ __ __ __ __

7. The Horseshoe Falls gets 90 percent of this from the Niagara River.

   __ __ __ __ __

8. This force has a big effect upon the falls. __ __ __ __ __ __ __

Wonders Circles

Directions: Inside each circle, draw only THREE STRAIGHT lines to group the letters into six words. Each line must be straight. After you figure out where to draw the three lines, the six words will form a message. Words inside the circles are from the pages on the Grand Canyon and Niagara Falls. Use your ruler to help you figure out where lines might go. This is VERY CHALLENGING. Be patient. The first one is done for you. Good Luck!

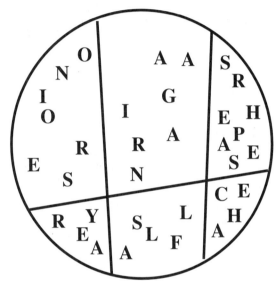

Message: Erosion reshapes Niagara Falls each year.

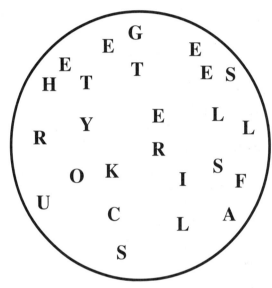

Message: _____
_____

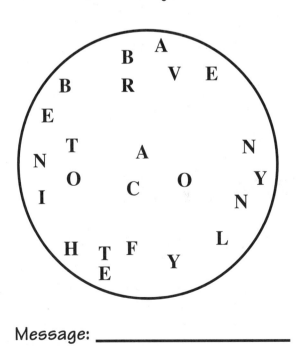

Message: _____
_____

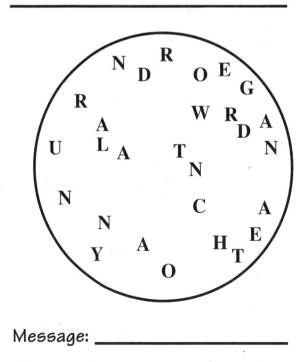

Message: _____
_____

New York City

Another great seaport, New York City, is in the southeastern part of New York State at the mouth of the Hudson River. It was the first capital of our country between 1785 and 1790. New York City is made up of five sections called boroughs. These are Manhattan, the smallest borough and on a long, narrow island; Queens, the largest and on the northwest corner of Long Island; Staten Island, an island southwest of Manhattan; the Bronx, the only borough not separated from New York State by water, although it is on the eastern side of the Hudson River; and Brooklyn, the most populous borough with about 2,225,000 people, located on the southwest tip of Long Island. Each one of these boroughs is a separate county of New York State. New York City, with a population of over 7 million, is the largest city in the United States. Transportation in and out of this city is continually going on by way of La Guardia and JFK airports and major ocean liners.

Land is scarce in New York City; consequently, high-rise apartments and co-ops are very expensive and difficult to get. Parking is extremely limited in the city. The land cannot be wasted on parking lots; therefore, people use public transportation methods of buses, taxis, and subways. Manufacturing companies specialize in fields where their buildings take up very little space, fields such as printing, publishing, and manufacturing of clothing.

Many of our largest banks, insurance companies, and the stock exchanges are located on or near the famous Wall Street in Manhattan. People go for operas, plays, and musicals to the Metropolitan Opera House, on- and off-Broadway theaters, and Carnegie Hall. Radio City Music Hall is located in this city along with the 102-story-high Empire State Building, at one time the tallest building in the world. The United Nations headquarters are in New York City. The UN is an organization started in 1945 that has over 150 countries working for world peace. At the UN, many different languages are spoken and interpreters are plentiful.

Very close to New York City are two famous islands located in the upper New York Harbor. Ellis Island is where the immigrants were processed and enemy aliens detained until 1954 when it closed. Liberty Island houses the Statue of Liberty, given to our country as a symbol of friendship by France. Both islands are a short ferry ride from Battery Park at the southwestern tip of Manhattan. Both islands are now part of the Statue of Liberty National Monument and are owned by the U.S. government.

People from all over the world come to see the Statue of Liberty. The statue represents a proud woman holding a torch in her right hand and a tablet with the date of the Declaration of Independence in her left hand. Her crown is like seven sun rays, representing the seven continents and seven seas of the world. A broken shackle is at her feet symbolizing freedom.

Washington, D.C.

Washington, D.C. is the only city in the United States that is not part of a state. It lies in the District of Columbia, federal land given by Maryland. D.C. as it is often called, lies between Maryland and Virginia. It is on the east bank of the Potomac River. It is part of a megalopolis (an urban area consisting of several large, adjoining cities) along with Boston, New York City, and Philadelphia. About 70 percent of Washington's residents are black. No other large U.S. city has such a big percentage.

Before 1790, our country had a number of temporary capitals, including New York City and Philadelphia. Then Congress decided the United States needed a permanent capital, centrally located for the colonies and located on the Potomac River for easy transportation. President Washington chose the site. Originally, the District of Columbia was 100 square miles and included the cities of Washington, Alexandria, and Georgetown. Alexandria was returned to Virginia, however, and Georgetown was annexed to Washington. Today Washington and the District of Columbia are one and the same with a land size of 67 square miles and a population of about 640,000.

There are many important buildings in D.C. The White House, where the president of our country lives and works, is at 1600 Pennsylvania Avenue. The U.S. Congress meets at the Capitol Building. This building is on an area of D.C. that is raised up 88 feet and is easily seen; consequently, it has the nickname of "The Hill." The Supreme Court Building is the most important court of law in the United States. It has nine judges called justices who make sure the Constitution is being followed. The National Archives Building houses three valuable documents—the Declaration of Independence, The Constitution, and the Bill of Rights. The Smithsonian Institution, the Lincoln Memorial, the Washington Monument, and the Kennedy Center for the Performing Arts are located in this busy, exciting city. Nearby, in Arlington, are the Pentagon, which houses the Department of Defense, and Arlington Cemetery with the Tomb of the Unknown Soldier.

Washington, D.C. is the center of our federal government and is a symbol of U.S. history and tradition. The Capitol houses the House of Representatives and the Senate Chambers. On the top of the Capitol Dome is the bronze Statue of Freedom. The White House has 107 rooms but only eleven are open to the public. All presidents except George Washington lived there. The Washington Monument is a 555-foot-tall marble obelisk, the tallest masonry construction in the world. You can take a 70-second elevator ride to the 500-foot level and look out. There is also a stairway of 898 steps. The Lincoln Memorial is on the eastern bank of the Potomac River. A huge statue of Lincoln sits behind the pillars. There are 36 columns, each representing a state when Lincoln died. The Pentagon is in Arlington, Virginia, across the Potomac River from Washington, D.C. The building houses the Department of Defense and is the largest office building in the world.

City Scramble—East

Directions: Unscramble the word or words inside the brackets to find the answer. Write your answer on the line or lines at the end of each sentence.

1. Washington, D.C. is part of a [SILOPOLAGEM] along the stretch with Boston, New York City, and

   Philadelphia. _____

2. Washington, D.C. became our country's first [RMEPNNTAE] capital. _____

3. D.C. is located on the [MPOCAOT VIERR]. _____ _____

4. Located at the mouth of the [DHSNUO RRVIE] is New York City. _____ _____

5. New York City has five [GHSROBOU]. _____

6. New York City has many high-rises because land there is [CCRESA]. _____

7. The United Nations is in [WNE KRYO YTIC]. _____ _____ _____

8. Many immigrants were processed and many enemy aliens were detained at [LLESI DSLIAN].

   _____ _____

9. One of the boroughs of New York City is [HTTNAAANM]. _____

U. S. Geography Project

WRITE one city or natural wonder of the U.S. List all the things about it you have learned. Using this list, write a rough draft in paragraph format covering what you've selected, what you know about it, and why it is of interest to you. Then revise your paper so it sounds good. Write your final copy and proofread thoroughly. Give your paper a title.

DRAW something to illustrate your city or wonder. Use unlined paper. Color your paper nicely. Write a short caption under your drawing so it's clear what your drawing is. Give your paper a title.

MAKE a map of the area where your city or wonder is located. (For example, if you're doing the Grand Canyon, you could make a map of Arizona and the states directly north of it.) Get a sturdy piece of chip board or poster board. Paint it black using poster paints or tempera. Use papîer mâché or some similar building material for your map. After everything is dry, paint it. Neatly stick labels on your map for the name of the state(s), bodies of water, city, or wonder, etc. Give your project a title. Proofread for correct spelling and correct use of capital letters. Make you map look neat, too!

Hemisphere Project

WRITE one thing of interest to you in the Western Hemisphere. List all the things about it that you have learned. Using this list, write a rough draft in paragraph format covering what you've selected, what you know about it, and why it is of interest to you. Do the same for the Eastern Hemisphere. Revise your paper so it sounds good. Write your final copy and proofread it thoroughly. Give your paper a title.

DRAW something to illustrate your selection from the Western Hemisphere and something to illustrate your selection from the Eastern Hemisphere. Use unlined paper. Label each drawing so it's clear what they are. Color nicely. Give your paper a title.

MAKE a map of either the Western Hemisphere or the Eastern Hemisphere. Get a sturdy piece of chip board or poster board. Paint it blue (for oceans and seas) using tempera or poster paints. Use papîer mâché or some similar building material for the continents. After they dry, paint them. Make a legend for your map listing your hemisphere's continents, oceans, major seas, Equator location, etc. Give your project a title. Proofread for correct spelling and correct use of capital letters. Make your map look neat, too!

Blank Practice Map

KEY

National Boundaries ------

National Capitals   ✪

United States Geography Study Sheet

Directions: Write the answers on the back of the paper or on a separate piece of paper.

1. Why is so much water from the Niagara River diverted from the American Falls to the Canadian (Horseshoe) Falls?

2. How was the Grand Canyon formed and where is it located?

3. What city was the first capital of the United States?

4. Land is scarce in New York City. What adjustments are made to handle the problem?

5. How did the United States get the Statue of Liberty and where is it located?

6. What is the only city in the United States that is not part of a state?

7. Washington, D.C. is on the east bank of which river?

8. Name three valuable documents housed in the National Archives Building.

9. On which island do most Hawaiians live?

10. What is the name of the world-famous suspension bridge linking San Francisco to Marin County?

11. Where is the USS Arizona Memorial and what does it commemorate?

12. What is the name of the city with the Smithsonian Institution and the Lincoln Memorial?

13. Which two countries share Niagara Falls?

14. Which city is located on the Potomac River?

15. Which city is located at the mouth of the Hudson River?

United States Geography Test

TRUE or FALSE
Print a T for true or an F for false.

1. _____ Most Hawaiians live on the island of Maui.
2. _____ The Statue of Liberty was a gift from England.
3. _____ Water from the Niagara River is diverted from the Canadian (Horseshoe) Falls to the American Falls.
4. _____ The Grand Canyon is located in Arizona.
5. _____ New York City was the first capital of the United States of America.

SHORT ANSWER

6. Where is the USS Arizona Memorial located?
_____

7. The Golden Gate Bridge connects what two places?
_____

8. New York City is located at the mouth of what river?
_____

9. How was the Grand Canyon formed?
_____

10. Name the only city in the United States that is not part of a state.
_____

11. Land is scarce in New York City. Name one thing New York does.
_____

12. What country gave the Statue of Liberty to the United States?
_____

MATCHING
Write the letter of the best match from the second column on the line in front of the first column.

13. _____ Countries that share Niagara Falls   A.   Arizona
14. _____ Cause of the Grand Canyon   B.   The U.S. and Canada
15. _____ City located on the Potomac River   C.   New York Harbor
16. _____ State where the Grand Canyon is located   D.   Erosion
17. _____ Location of the Statue of Liberty   E.   Washington, D.C.

§

MULTIPLE CHOICE
Circle the letter next to the one best answer.

18. The USS Arizona Memorial commemorates
    a. the completion of the Grand Canyon.
    b. the Japanese attack on Pearl Harbor.
    c. the U.S. entry into World War I.
    d. Arizona becoming a state.

19. Adjustments to handle the problem of land scarcity in New York City include
    a. high-rise buildings and mass transit.
    b. the Statue of Liberty and the U.N.
    c. Niagara Falls and the Hudson River.
    d. Queens, Manhattan, and Long Island.

20. Both the Smithsonian Institution and the Lincoln Memorial are located in which city?
    a. New York City, New York
    b. San Francisco, California
    c. Lincoln, Nebraska
    d. Washington, D.C.

FRIENDLY LETTER

Write a friendly letter to a classmate about a trip you'd like to make to one of the cities or wonders you've just studied. Select a city or wonder that you've never been to before. Include places you'd like to see there. Explain why you selected those places. Use friendly letter format.

DIRECTIONS: Write the following in the correct spots on the map of North America.

United States (U.S.)
Alaska (U.S.)
Mississippi River
Rio Grande
Great Lakes
U.S. capital: Washington, D.C.
Gulf of California

Gulf of Mexico
Pacific Ocean
Atlantic Ocean
Arctic Ocean
Mexico
Mexico capital: Mexico City
Canada

Canada capital: Ottawa
Central America
West Indies
Caribbean Sea
Bering Sea
Greenland
Where you live

KEY

National Boundaries ······

National Capitals ✪

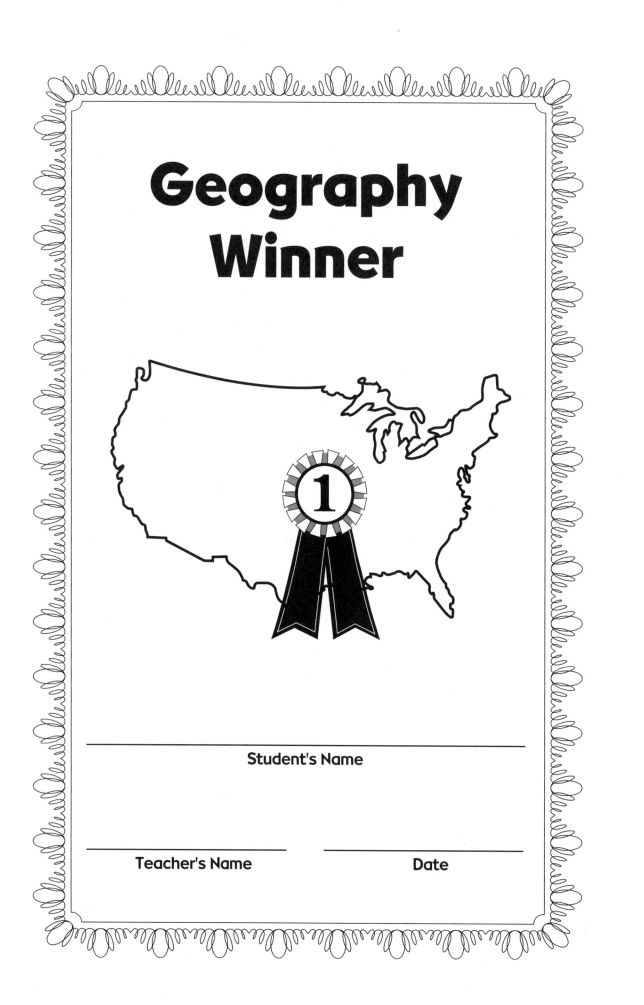

Geography Winner

Student's Name

Teacher's Name

Date

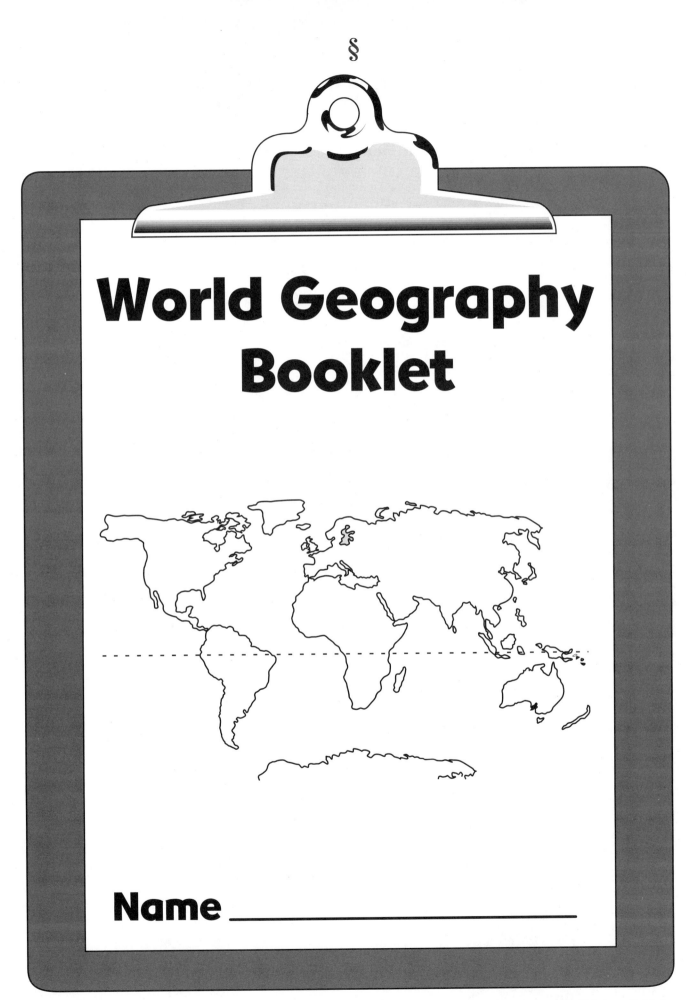

World Geography Booklet

Name _____

Map Activities

Directions: Use the *world map* on the following page to complete these activities.

1. Color North America red. Be sure to include Greenland, Central America, and the West Indies. Color EVERYTHING inside the dotted outline for North America.

2. Color South America green. Don't forget to color everything inside the dotted outline.

3. Color Europe yellow. Stay inside the outline.

4. Color Africa orange. Stay inside the outline.

5. Color Asia brown. Color the offshore islands that are *inside* the dotted outline, too.

6. Color Australia purple.

7. Color Antarctica light black.

8. Color Oceania pink. This will be all the Pacific Islands you haven't already colored.

9. Color all the oceans, seas, lakes, bays, and gulfs light blue. Then check to see that EVERYTHING on the map is colored.

Directions: For numbers 10 through 15, use a map of the world in your history book or encyclopedia for help, if you need it.

10. Write in black crayon "US" in the *three* spots on the map that are part of the United States.

11. Put a black dot where you live.

12. Put a black "C" on Canada.

13. Put a black "G" on Greenland.

14. Put a black "M" on Mexico.

Continents of the World

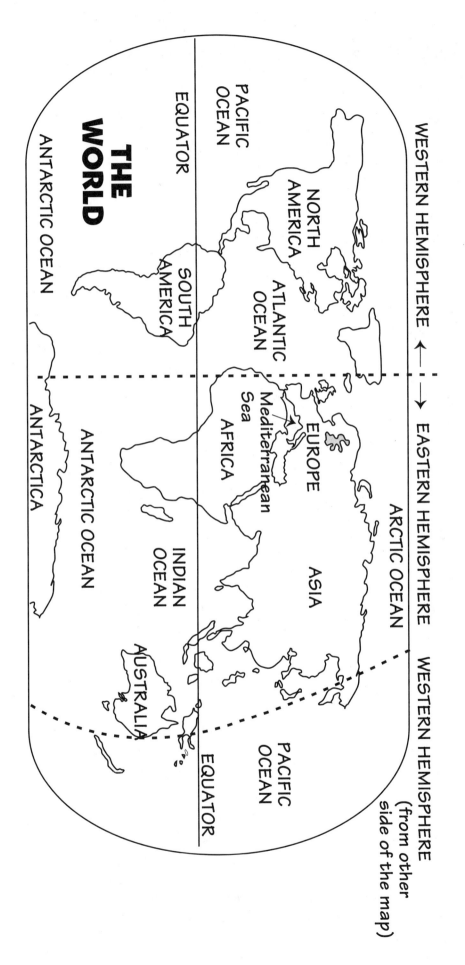

THE WORLD

EQUATOR

PACIFIC OCEAN

NORTH AMERICA

SOUTH AMERICA

ATLANTIC OCEAN

ANTARCTIC OCEAN

WESTERN HEMISPHERE

EASTERN HEMISPHERE

ARCTIC OCEAN

WESTERN HEMISPHERE

(from other side of the map)

Mediterranean Sea

EUROPE

AFRICA

ASIA

INDIAN OCEAN

ANTARCTIC OCEAN

ANTARCTICA

AUSTRALIA

PACIFIC OCEAN

EQUATOR

World Geography

In our world, there are seven large land masses called continents. These usually include some nearby, offshore islands. There is more and more evidence being discovered to support the idea that at one time all the continents were connected into one huge land mass, but all the volcano eruptions and earthquakes have caused the continents to drift apart.

In addition to the continents, there are some 30,000 islands in the Pacific Ocean that don't belong to any continent. These are called Oceania or the Pacific Islands. There are also five oceans. Land makes up about 30% of the earth's surface. Oceans, along with smaller bodies of water called seas, bays, and gulfs, cover 70% of the earth's surface.

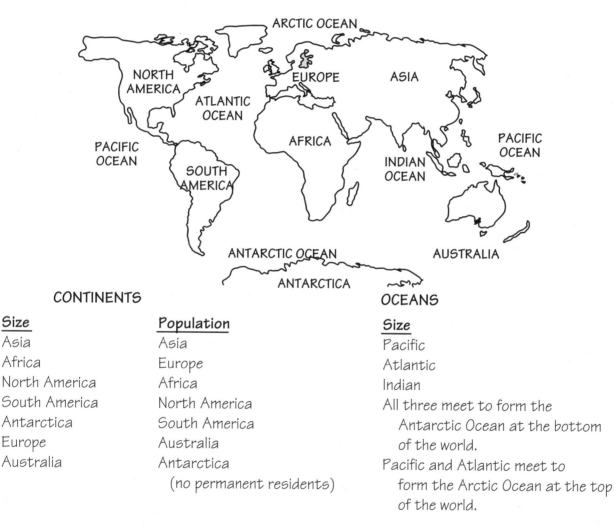

CONTINENTS

Size	Population
Asia	Asia
Africa	Europe
North America	Africa
South America	North America
Antarctica	South America
Europe	Australia
Australia	Antarctica
	(no permanent residents)

OCEANS

Size
Pacific
Atlantic
Indian
All three meet to form the Antarctic Ocean at the bottom of the world.
Pacific and Atlantic meet to form the Arctic Ocean at the top of the world.

The approximately 4.7 billion people in the world can live anywhere on the land of the earth, but people like to live on flat or hilly land in an area with a nice climate, good soil, and a source of fresh water. Only a few scientists are temporarily living on frozen Antarctica and no one lives in parts of some dry, hot, desolate deserts. Throughout the world, people have different looks, food, clothing, religions, customs, educational systems, homes, governments, and different levels of scientific and technological advancement. Yet EVERYONE shares the most popular forms of entertainment around the world—radio, TV, and motion pictures.

The following are the largest countries of the world in size and population:

Size	Population
Russia	China
Canada	India
China	U.S.
U.S.	Indonesia
Brazil	Brazil

There are many changes in political boundaries, usually due to war. New countries are formed and others are incorporated into stronger powers. In Africa alone, about 45 new nations have emerged since 1950 because of strong independence movements. The world is constantly changing. Even new islands appear as the result of volcanic eruptions.

You will hear the world spoken of in many different groupings. The Eastern Hemisphere is sometimes called the Old World. It is made up of Europe, Asia, Africa, Australia, part of Antarctica and part of Oceania. The Western Hemisphere, where the United States is, is sometimes called the New World. It is made up of North America, South America, part of Antarctica, and part of Oceania.

The location of a country, its natural resources or lack of them, its skilled labor, and its population size affect whether it is called a developed, industrial nation or a poor, developing nation, many of whose populations increase faster than the country's ability to produce or trade for food. These developing nations, often called third world countries, need training for their farmers, money for modern machinery and transportation, power sources for energy, and water supplies. Developed countries, on the other hand, need to attack the problem of how to reduce pollution. Many developed countries offer to host exchange students. Students of a developing nation will study in a developed nation and return to their own countries to help with their new knowledge. Areas such as the United States, Canada, Japan, and Western Europe are examples of developed, industrialized areas. Many of the countries of Latin America (Mexico, Central and South America, and the West Indies), Asia, and Africa are developing nations.

In our world, there are about 3,000 languages spoken. The top ten most-spoken languages, in order, are: Chinese, English, Hindustani, Spanish, Russian, German, Japanese, Arabic, Bengali, and French. At the United Nations, the largest international organization in the world, there are six official languages you can listen to translations in: Arabic, Chinese, English, French, Russian, and Spanish.

Some organizations have been formed to help certain countries work together. The largest is the United Nations, with its headquarters in New York City. It tries to work for world peace and a better world society. Many nations belong.

The Organization of Petroleum Exporting Countries (OPEC) establishes the same rules for the exporting of <u>oil</u> for all its member nations. The Organization of American States (OAS) is dedicated to the defense and economic progress of the United States and most Latin American countries. The International Olympic Committee (IOC) governs the modern Olympic games, which were established to promote amateur athletics and world friendship.

Introduction Activity

Directions: Use information from your pages, "World Geography," to answer the following. Write the answers on a separate piece of white lined paper.

1. What are the islands in the Pacific Ocean that don't belong to any continent called?

2. Name the largest continent.

3. Name the largest and deepest ocean.

4. Approximately what is the world's population?

5. Why do new countries form and other, older countries become larger?

6. Name the five largest countries in the world in order of size, largest first.

7. Name the five most populous countries of the world in order.

8. Name the continents belonging to the Western Hemisphere.

9. Which continents belong to the Eastern Hemisphere?

10. What is a "third world" country like?

11. What is the difference between a developed nation and a developing one?

12. Out of the 3,000 languages spoken in the world, which are the two most frequently spoken?

13. The OPEC countries have the same rules for exporting what natural resource?

14. What is the name of the organization that works for world peace?

Western Hemisphere

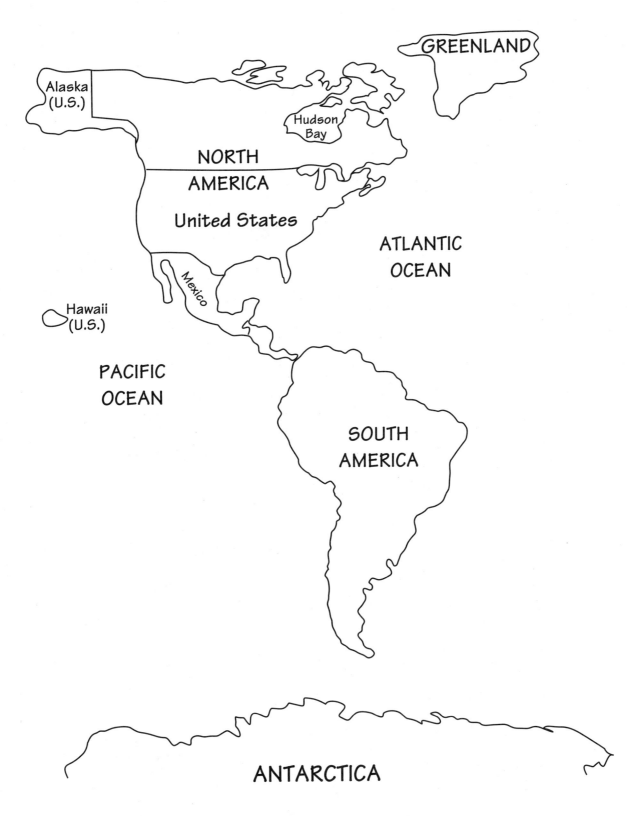

GREENLAND

Alaska (U.S.)

Hudson Bay

NORTH AMERICA

United States

ATLANTIC OCEAN

Mexico

Hawaii (U.S.)

PACIFIC OCEAN

SOUTH AMERICA

ANTARCTICA

Western Hemisphere

The Western Hemisphere includes the continent of North America. North America has Canada, most of Greenland, the United States, Mexico, and the nations of both the West Indies and Central America. The Western Hemisphere also includes the continent of South America, part of the continent of Antarctica, and most of Oceania. (Oceania is all the islands too far away from continent mainlands to be considered part of the actual continent.) The longitude lines usually used to separate the Western and Eastern Hemispheres are 20° W and 160° E. The Western Hemisphere is often referred to as the New World.

The International Date Line is in the Western Hemisphere. It mostly follows 180° longitude. Those living on the east side are one DAY ahead of those living on the west. The date line zigzags around somewhat so that no country will have two different days at the same time.

The Western Hemisphere also has three of the seven natural wonders of the world—the Grand Canyon, Paricutin, and the beautiful harbor at Rio de Janeiro. It also has three of the seven modern wonders of the world—the Golden Gate Bridge, the Empire State Building, and the Alaska Highway.

Map Activity

Directions: Use the Western Hemisphere map on the preceding page to complete these activities. When you color over labels of continents, oceans, countries, etc., color very lightly. Be sure to read carefully any coloring instructions given with a particular item number.

1. Color the Arctic Ocean DARK BLUE. Stay right up in that circular area. Do not color beneath Greenland.
2. Color the Pacific Ocean LIGHT BLUE. Stop coloring at Cape Horn and when you get to the Antarctic Circle. Color around islands, not over them.
3. Color the Antarctic Ocean DARK BLUE. That's the water inside the Antarctic Circle.
4. Color the Hudson Bay DARK GREEN.
5. Color the Great Lakes LIGHT PURPLE.
6. Color the Gulf of Mexico LIGHT PURPLE. Color above the western end of the West Indies. Stop coloring at the tip of Florida.
7. Color the Caribbean Sea YELLOW.
8. Color Greenland GREEN.
9. Color Canada ORANGE. Watch out that you don't color Alaska, which is part of the United States. Don't color south of the Great Lakes. Color all the islands between mainland Canada and Greenland, too.
10. Color the United States (U.S.) YELLOW. Be sure to include Alaska; the Aleutian Islands and St. Edward Island, which are part of Alaska and extend westward into the ocean; Hawaii; and the main part of the United States, which is called conterminous U.S.
11. Now color Mexico LIGHT GREEN. Stop coloring about two millimeters south of the Panama Canal.
12. Color Central America PURPLE. Color on both sides of the Panama Canal.
13. Color the West Indies ORANGE.
14. Color South America LIGHT BROWN.
15. Color Antarctica PURPLE. This is just a part of Antarctica, not the entire continent, because some of it is in the Eastern Hemisphere.
16. Color the Atlantic Ocean VERY LIGHT GREEN. Color all the way until you get to Greenland.
17. Color New Zealand RED.

Directions: Write the answers to the following questions on the back of this paper or on a separate piece of paper.

18. Name the two major continents of the Western Hemisphere.
19. What countries and groups of countries are included in the continent of North America?
20. If it were Wednesday on the eastern side of the International Date Line, what day would it be on the western side?
21. There are three of the seven *natural* wonders of the world in the Western Hemisphere. Have you ever been to any of them? If yes, write about it. If no, write about which one you'd like to go to first. Write on the back of this paper or on a separate piece of paper.
22. There are also three of the seven *modern* wonders of the world in the Western Hemisphere. Have you ever been to any of them? If yes, write about it. If no, write which one you'd like to go to first. Write on the back of this paper or on a separate piece of paper.

Continent Selection for the Western Hemisphere

North America

Highlights for Greenland, Canada, and the United States

North America, the third largest continent, looks somewhat like a giant "Y," with the Rockies on the left, the Appalachians on the right, the Canadian Shield and Interior Plains in the middle, and Mexico and Central America making up the stem. It extends from the Arctic region to the top of South America. It has a longer coastline than any other continent. About 387 million people live here.

In the center of the Arctic region in the ice-covered Arctic Ocean is the North Pole. Just as for the South Pole, a race was on to see who would reach the North Pole first. In 1909, U.S. Naval Commander Robert E. Peary reached the North Pole on a sled hauled by a dog team. Lt. Commander Richard E. Byrd and Floyd Bennett were the first to fly over the North Pole. (Byrd was the first to fly over the South Pole, too!) *Nautilus*, a nuclear submarine, crossed the North Pole *beneath the ice* in 1958. But in 1959, the nuclear sub, *Skate*, broke through the ice and surfaced at the North Pole.

The Arctic Circle marks the edge where the sun stays above the horizon for at least one full day a year. Areas of the Arctic Circle, like the northern part of Greenland and Canada, have midnight sun at least one day a year. But at the North Pole, if the sky is clear, you can see the sun for 90 days straight. Months of sunlight might be all right, but months of 24-hour darkness might be rather difficult!

Scientists use weather stations set up in the Arctic to predict weather all over North America.

There is very little rainfall here, but the Arctic lands are wet because the moisture evaporates so slowly. Herds of reindeer and caribou, bears, foxes, and squirrels are on the Arctic lands. Any land north of the tree line is called the tundra. Flowers, plants, and shrubs will grow here, but no trees. Even if you plant a willow tree, it will grow only as high as a shrub.

Included with the continent of North America is Greenland, a province of Denmark. Greenland is the largest island in the world (not including Australia or Antarctica, which are continents). Most of Greenland is buried under thick ice. The small population of about 56,000 lives mainly along the south-western coast where it is not quite so cold. The people speak Danish and Greenlandic. At home, they spend most of their time in *one room*, which is kept warmer than all the rest. The Greenlanders still hunt seals, fox, reindeer, and polar bears, but their main industry is commercial fishing.

Canada, the second largest country in the world, is made up of two territories and ten provinces. The two territories are the Northwest Territories, divided into the two districts of Mackenzie and Keewatin, and the Yukon Territory. Beginning with the westernmost province and proceeding east, the provinces are: British Columbia, Alberta, Saskatchewan, Manitoba, Ontario, Quebec, Newfoundland, and south of Quebec, New Brunswick, Nova Scotia, and Prince Edward Island.

Canada is an independent, self-governing nation of about 22 million. It recognizes the queen of England as queen of Canada. Its official languages are English and French. Many in Quebec speak only French.

About four-fifths of Canada is uninhabited because of the extreme cold. Indians and Eskimos live in this area with long, harsh, dark winters. Most Canadians live in the warmer southern region. Montreal, Quebec, is Canada's largest city and the largest French-speaking city in the world after Paris. Toronto, Ontario, is next largest in population. Ottawa, Ontario, is Canada's capital and a city of about 693,000. The University of Ottawa is the largest bilingual university in Canada. It offers courses in *both of Canada's lan-guages*—English and French. Quebec City, Canada's oldest, lies on the northern bank of the St. Lawrence River. Vancouver, in British Columbia, is the busiest port on the Pacific Coast of North America.

The Rocky Mountains extend along Canada's western coast. To the east of the Rockies are the Interior plains. To their east is the Canadian Shield, making up about half of Canada. This is land under which lies old, hard rock. Forests are on the southern part of this region. Because of these forests, Canada is a world leader in pulp and paper production. In the Atlantic provinces, which belong to the Appalachian Region, fishing is the main industry. Flowing out by these provinces into the Gulf of St. Lawrence and then into the Atlantic Ocean, is the St. Lawrence River. This river is a great sea transportation lane. It connects all the Great Lakes with the Atlantic Ocean.

Hudson Bay is huge—over three times the size of all five Great Lakes. It connects with the Atlantic and Arctic oceans. From mid-July to mid-October, the bay is usually free of ice and ships are able to use it. Hudson's Bay Company is one of Canada's largest corporations. If you like beautiful, warm blankets, you can buy a Hudson's Bay blanket. These are heavy woolen blankets with one or more broad stripes to indi-cate the blanket's weight. Usually there is a black stripe on a red blanket or multicolored stripes on white.

At Niagara Falls, Ontario, are the fabulous Horseshoe Falls. About 90 percent of the water from the Niagara River flows over them. At Toronto, Ontario, is the beautiful Canadian National Tower. This tower rises 1,815 feet into the air. You can ride in a glass elevator to Sky Pod, a seven-story restaurant. There is an observation center there, too. This communication and observation tower was complete in 1976. It is the world's highest free-standing structure.

At Montreal, Quebec, is The Underground City. This is a shopping area of over 200 shops and restau-rants under Montreal's downtown streets. You can take an escalator from most of the major hotels to get down there. It is the largest underground shopping center in the world. At Victoria, British Columbia, a city famous for its English look, you can visit the lovely Butchart Gardens and admire all the different kinds of flowers. At Ottawa, Ontario, if you visit in mid-February, you can go to Winterlude. This is a nine-day festival hosting such winter sports as broomball, which is a form of ice hockey usually played in Russia. Skates are not allowed and brooms are used in place of hockey sticks. People also participate in car and harness racing on ice and dog-sled racing.

Because of the heavy snow in the winter time in southern Canada, ice hockey is Canada's most popular sport, followed by snow skiing.

The United States is composed of fifty states and one federal district, the District of Columbia. Washington, D.C., the nation's capital, is located in this district.

The U. S. has many interesting geographical features. At the extreme west are Alaska's Aleutian Islands, a chain of volcanic islands. These extend into the Pacific over 900 miles. There are fourteen large islands and about fifty-five smaller ones. They separate the Bering Sea from the Pacific Ocean. About 8,000 Aleuts live on these islands. Aleuts are descendants of Eskimos but have their own Aleut language. Most Aleuts follow a modern way of life, but some still hunt for food and fish.

Hawaii, although *not* part of the continent of North America, is a state that is also on the tops of volcanoes. Hawaii is part of Oceania.

The forty-eight remaining states and the District of Columbia are called conterminous United States and are located just south of Canada and north of Mexico and the West Indies. The Coast Ranges and the Cascade-Sierra Nevadas extend along the western coast. The Rockies extend from Alaska to New Mexico. Their crest is the Great Continental Divide. On the west, all waters flow to the Pacific. On the east, all waters flow toward the Arctic, Atlantic, and Gulf of Mexico.

To the east of the Rockies is one of the world's largest plains called the Great Plains. These cover a great deal of the central United States. In the eastern part of the United States are the Appalachians. These mountains extend from Arkansas up through Maine and through Canada's Atlantic Provinces.

The United States has many unique places. In Alaska is the highest mountain in North America, Mt. McKinley. The lowest point in the Western Hemisphere is Death Valley, California. The world's largest river system, the Mississippi-Missouri, goes from the north-central United States down through Louisiana and empties into the Gulf of Mexico. It forms the longest river system on the continent.

The Great Salt Lake in Utah, the Great Lakes, the American Falls of Niagara Falls, and Yosemite Falls, California, the highest waterfall in North America, are all natural wonders of North America. But the United States has one of the seven natural wonders of the world—Arizona's Grand Canyon. It has three of the seven modern wonders of the world—Alaska Highway, about one-fourth of which is paved and the rest is gravel, the Golden Gate Bridge in San Francisco, and the Empire State Building in New York City.

The strongest winds on the earth's surface were recorded at Mt. Washington, New Hampshire. In 1934, the wind was 188 mph. One gust was 231 mph. The highest temperature ever recorded in North America was at Death Valley—134°F (57°C). The lowest temperature in North America was at Snag in the Yukon Territory of Canada. The temperature was −81°F (−63°C). The western slopes of the Olympic Mountains in the state of Washington are very rainy. They receive over 140 inches a year. Death Valley, on the other hand, gets about one and one-half inches a year!

Cape Canaveral is on the east coast of Florida, northeast of Lake Okeechobee. The John F. Kennedy Space Center is here. The first U.S. satellite, *Explorer I*, was launched from here in 1958. The first manned spacecraft, *Freedom 7*, was launched from the Cape in 1961 with Alan B. Shepard, Jr., aboard. It made a suborbital flight (not even one complete orbit) of fifteen minutes. In 1962, John Glenn, Jr., left here in *Friendship 7* to orbit the earth. In 1969, Edwin E. Aldrin, Jr., Neil Armstrong, and Michael Collins took off from the Cape in *Apollo 11*. Collins piloted the command module, *Columbia,* while Armstrong and Aldrin stepped out onto the moon from the lunar module (LM), *Eagle*. Armstrong, the first man out, then said his famous words, "That's one small step for man, one giant leap for mankind."

One of the largest cities in the United States is Chicago, Illinois. It is on the southwest shore of Lake Michigan. The Chicago River used to flow into Lake Michigan but engineers in 1900 reversed the flow so it wouldn't dump pollutants into the lake. Now it's famous as "the river that flows backward."

Charles A. Dana, a New York City newspaper editor, listened so long to the people of Chicago bragging and boasting about their city and its 1893 World Columbian Exposition that he nicknamed Chicago "the windy city." (People who brag a lot are humorously said to be blowing a lot of hot air and are often called wind bags.) The howling gusts of wind, which blow into Chicago from Lake Michigan, help keep this "windy city" nickname alive.

Chicago is a city of mass transit els, which are *elevated* trains running on tracks above city streets. This helps minimize traffic congestion. Els are the opposite of subways, which are underground. Chicago also has the busiest airport, O'Hare, and the world's tallest building, 110-story Sears Tower. Beautiful Buckingham Memorial Fountain in Grant Park in Chicago is the world's largest lighted fountain. Its main spout shoots water 135 feet into the air.

Western Hemisphere

Match and Fill In

Directions for Fill In: Use the information from the preceding pages on Greenland, Canada and the United States to fill in the correct answers.

1. People in the very northern part of Canada and Greenland have at least some.
   _ _ _ _ _ _ _ _ _ _ _ .

2. Land north of the tree line where no trees will grow is called the _ _ _ _ _ _ .

3. Not including any continents, Greenland is the largest _ _ _ _ _ _ in the world.

4. Canada has ten _ _ _ _ _ _ _ _ _ .

5. The largest French-speaking city in the world after Paris is _ _ _ _ _ _ _ _ , Quebec.

6. A great sea transportation lane in Canada is the
   _ _ _ _ _ _ _ _ _ _ _ _ _ _ _ _ .

Directions for Matching: Write the letter of the matching item from Column B on the correct line in Column A.

COLUMN A

_____ Cape Canaveral

_____ Alaska Highway

_____ Rockies

_____ Horseshoe Falls

_____ over three times the size of all five Great Lakes

_____ home of The Underground City

_____ Skate

_____ Aleutian Islands

_____ els

COLUMN B

a. trains that run on tracks above city streets

b. separate Bering Sea from Pacific Ocean

c. Montreal, Quebec

d. sub that surfaced at North Pole

e. Apollo 11 launch site

f. extend from Alaska to New Mexico

g. one of the seven modern wonders of the world

h. at Niagara Falls, in Ontario, Canada

i. Hudson Bay

Eastern Hemisphere

The Eastern Hemisphere is also known as the "Old World" because it is the area of the world where civilization began. It consists of the continents of Europe, Africa, Asia, Australia, part of the continent of Antarctica, and a part of Oceania.

The Eastern Hemisphere has four of the seven *natural* wonders of the world—the French and Spanish caves with prehistoric paintings in Europe, Victoria Falls in Africa, Mt. Everest in the Himalayan Mountains in Asia and the Great Barrier Reef of Australia. Four of the seven *modern* wonders of the world are in this hemisphere, too—the Ukraine's Dneproges Dam; Harwell, England's Atomic Energy Research Establishment; and the Eiffel Tower of Paris, France. All these are in Europe. The fourth wonder, the Suez Canal, is on the African-Asian border. The Pyramids of Egypt in Africa are one of the seven *ancient* wonders of the world, and the only one still standing today!

Map Activities

Directions: Use the Eastern Hemisphere map on the preceding page to complete these activities. When you color over *labels* of continents, oceans, etc., color *very lightly.* You will need information on this map at a later time. Be sure to read carefully any coloring instructions given with a particular item number.

1. Color the Arctic Ocean dark blue. Don't color below the Arctic Circle.
2. Color the Baltic Sea green. The North Sea is right under the "t" of "Baltic." You can color the North Sea brown.
3. Color the Atlantic Ocean light blue. Color on the western side only of Great Britain and Ireland. Color down south of the Cape of Good Hope to the Antarctic Circle.
4. Color the English Channel red.
5. Color the Strait of Gibraltar orange.
6. Color the Mediterranean Sea yellow.
7. Color the Black Sea black.
8. Color the Caspian Sea green.
9. Color the Red Sea and the Suez Canal red.
10. Color the Persian Gulf orange.
11. LIGHTLY color the Indian Ocean brown. There are some seas and gulfs in there too, but color the whole thing brown down to the Antarctic Ocean. Color brown right under the label "Indonesia" and color brown for the Indian Ocean all the way to Tasmania. Don't color the various seas between Indonesia and Australia.
12. Color the Pacific Ocean green. There are many gulfs, bays, and seas along the shore, but just color all the water green, beginning at the first water under the Arctic Circle and down to the Antarctic Circle.
13. Color the Antarctic Ocean purple.
14. Color the North Pole yellow.
15. Color the South Pole orange.
16. Color the Ural River blue.
17. Color the Ural Mountains brown.
18. Color both the Nile and the Congo River red.
19. Color the zigzag line of Victoria Falls red, too.
20. Color the Arabian Peninsula yellow. Don't color yellow above the label "Arabian."
21. Color Great Britain orange.
22. Color Ireland green. Watch out that you don't color the little section at the northern end of the island because that's Northern Ireland, which is part of Great Britain.
23. Color Iceland black.
24. Color Italy green.
25. Color the Sahara Desert orange. DO NOT color the very northern edge of Africa orange. Do color orange from just below the northern edge down to a little below the "Africa" label and all the way across to the Red Sea.
26. Color Madagascar, which is part of Africa, green.
27. NEATLY highlight the label for India yellow. (To highlight is to take your crayon, marker or colored pencil and color over a label or a group of words so they appear to be in a colored rectangle.)
28. Color Sri Lanka, the island off the coast of India, purple.
29. Neatly highlight the label for China orange.
30. Neatly highlight both labels for Russia red. This country is on two continents.
31. Color North Korea and South Korea yellow.

32. Color Japan orange.

33. Color Taiwan blue.

34. Color the Philippines brown.

35. Put a blue dot at the arrow for Vietnam. It is a narrow country right on the eastern coast of the Indochinese peninsula.

36. Color Malaysia red. Watch that you color both parts.

37. Carefully color Indonesia blue. Watch the arrows. (Japan, Taiwan, the Philippines, Malaysia, and most of Indonesia are all part of Asia.)

38. Neatly highlight the label for Australia light purple.

39. Color Tasmania, which is part of Australia, light red.

40. Color Antarctica light blue.

41. Highlight the labels for the Arctic Circle, Tropic of Cancer, Equator, Tropic of Capricorn and the Antarctic Circle all in yellow.

42. Circle Europe in a red dotted line. Be sure to include all the islands in the Mediterranean Sea except Cyprus, the most easterly island. Don't forget Great Britain, Ireland and Iceland. Make your line go on the northern side of the Black Sea, the western side of the Caspian Sea and then right up the Ural River and Ural Mountains, all of which are separators of Europe and Asia.

43. Circle Africa in a green dotted line. Make your line go right down the Suez Canal and Red Sea. Don't forget Madagascar.

44. Circle Asia in a blue dotted line. To do this, first draw a blue line just a little east of your red dotted line for Europe's east side. Go down the Ural Mountains and the Ural River to the Caspian Sea. Go over to the Black Sea. Go down the Suez Canal and the Red Sea. Cross the Indian Ocean. Stay right above Australia. Go a little to the east of Indonesia, then right up to the top of your map, including the Philippines, Taiwan and Japan along the way.

Directions: Write the correct answers on the lines.

45. Name the four major continents of the Eastern Hemisphere.

_____

46. In the Eastern Hemisphere, which one of the seven natural wonders of the world would you like to see?

_____

Why?_____

47. In the Eastern Hemisphere, which one of the seven modern wonders of the world would you like to see?

_____

Why?_____

48. Which is the only one of ancient wonders still standing today?

_____

Continent Selection
for the Eastern Hemisphere
Europe
Highlights for England, Russia and Italy

1 Denmark
2 Netherlands
3 Belgium
4 Liechtenstein

5 Slovenia
6 Croatia
7 Bosnia-Herzegovina
8 (The New) Yugoslavia
9 Macedonia

Europe is the second smallest continent, but has the second largest population. It is composed of about forty-five independent countries and four other political units, three under Great Britain and one under Denmark.

Since no body of water separates Europe from Asia, sometimes you'll hear both continents together called "Eurasia." Europe and Asia are only separated by the Ural Mountains, the Ural River, the Caspian Sea, and the Black Sea. Other times, you'll hear the term "Eurafrasia." This is Europe, Africa, and Asia combined because Africa was connected to Asia before the Suez Canal was built and Asia is connected to Europe.

Europe has a population of 692 million with about 140 million living in the part of Russia that is in Europe. Least populous is tiny Vatican City with only 1,000 residents. It is the smallest independent country in the world. It is the spiritual and governmental center of the Roman Catholic Church. One of its most famous structures is The Sistine Chapel, in which Michelangelo's paintings cover the ceiling and the rear wall behind the altar.

About 50 different languages are spoken throughout Europe and 100 dialects, which are local ways of speaking the languages. The Balto-Slavic languages of Bulgaria, Chech, Polish, and Russian are spoken in Eastern Europe. The Germanic languages of Danish, English, German, and Swedish are spoken in the northern part of Western Europe. The Romance languages of French, Italian, and Spanish are spoken in the southern part of Western Europe. Switzerland, for example, has three official languages—French, German, and Italian; therefore, Switzerland has *three* official names, one in each language.

Europe, a gigantic-looking peninsula itself, has the following five peninsulas on it: the Balkan Peninsula (Albania, Bulgaria, Greece, Turkey, and Yugoslavia); the Scandinavian Peninsula (Norway and Sweden); Jutland (Denmark, which is the other Scandinavian country); the Iberian Peninsula (Portugal and Spain); and the Apennine Peninsula (Italy).

The Great European Plain covers most of European Russia and extends over to France. This is an area of mostly flat land, some hills and good farming lands. Running across southern Europe from Spain to the Caspian Sea are several mountain chains, including the world-famous Alps, covering parts of France, Italy, Switzerland, Germany, Austria, and Yugoslavia. The Swiss Alps are popular for skiing vacations.

There are lots of rivers in Europe that provide good transportation. The longest, the Volga, goes through Russia to the Caspian Sea. Canals link the Volga to the Arctic Ocean, the Baltic Sea, and the Don River. The Don flows out to the Black Sea.

The world's largest saltwater lake, the Caspian Sea, is in Europe and Asia. This sea is really a lake because it is completely surrounded by land. The Black Sea is bigger, but it opens out to the Mediterranean Sea through two straits and a sea.

Up in northern Europe is Norway, "Land of the Midnight Sun." The sun doesn't set for two months here. Norway has long, narrow inlets of the sea extending into its coast. These are called fiords. Nearby Finland, "Land of Thousands of Lakes," has around 60,000 lakes.

There are many thousands of islands off the coast of Europe that are considered part of the continent of Europe. Chief among these are Great Britain, Ireland, and Iceland.

England is the largest of the four countries of the United Kingdom of Great Britain, also called Great Britain or the UK. The three other countries are Wales, Scotland, and Northern Ireland.

England has a population of about 47 million. Its capital city is London. A king or queen is the head of state; nonetheless, the real rulers of the country are the cabinet ministers and the prime minister. There are many royal ceremonies in this country.

England's official language is English, but there are a few different words from our English. A radio is a "wireless," trucks are "lorries," gasoline is "petrol," and elevators are "lifts."

The people in England enjoy going to the pub in the evening to meet their friends, discuss politics, play darts, talk about business and maybe drink a squash (a drink where water is mixed with a concentrate of crushed oranges or lemons). Around 4 P.M., many people also enjoy tea time and for dinner, they might eat fish and chips, or Yorkshire pudding (cake baked in meat fat) or bangers and mash (thick sausages and mashed potatoes with grilled tomatoes).

Many great writers have come out of England, including Dickens, Chaucer, and Shakespeare. Many great rock groups are from here too, including the Beatles and the Rolling Stones.

On England's southeast coast are the white cliffs of Dover. These cliffs are composed of chalk and really are white. Also, still standing in England is Hadrian's Wall, built by the Romans in A.D. 120, when England was a province of the Roman Empire. It was built to keep the Scottish raiders out and protect the English people. Stonehenge is one of the still-surviving circular stone monuments built by the European mainlanders who migrated to England.

The English Channel is the world's busiest sea passage. You can cross from England over the Strait of Dover, which is the narrowest point, to France. The seas here are rough with strong sea currents and winds. Travel is by ferry boat, air ferry, or hovercraft. A hovercraft, also known as an ACV, Air Cushion Vehicle, travels on a cushion of compressed air provided by two or more large fans blowing downward. They blow the air beneath the craft. The hovercraft, which travels just above water or land, can go backward, forward, or sideways. It can turn or hover.

On November 5, the British enjoy celebrating Guy Fawkes Day. In 1605, Guy Fawkes led a group that tried to blow up King James I and the House of Parliament. Today, during the celebration, guards "search" the cellars of Parliament looking for "guys" and kegs of gunpowder. Children make stuffed dummies, which are called "guys." They go around collecting "a penny for a guy." At night, there are huge fireworks displays and the "guys" are burned in a giant bonfire!

Russia is the largest country in area in the world. About 140 million people live there, making it sixth largest in population. Russia is on *two* continents. It covers a large part of Europe and about two-fifths of Asia. Most of the people live in European Russia, because Asian Russia is cold and desolate.

Schools teach in the local language or in Russian. If a student goes to a school where the main language is a local language, one other than Russian, that student begins taking Russian in first grade. Students go to school six days a week. In fifth through tenth grades, they study English, French, or German. In sixth grade, they take algebra, geometry, literature, physics, and zoology.

Russian schools stress science and technology. Students are graded on schoolwork, leadership, and behavior both at and *after* school. After-school activities are required. Those with the best grades go on to high-paying jobs. Those with low marks in behavior can place their educational careers in jeopardy.

Italy is a peninsula that extends into the Mediterranean Sea. The two nearby islands of Sicily and Sardinia are part of Italy. This country has 57 million people. Its capital is Rome. Inside Rome lies the independent state of Vatican City. Italy's official language is Italian.

The Italian Riviera is a popular resort area. The Riviera, which is a narrow strip of land on the Mediterranean Sea from southern France to northwestern Italy, has warm sunshine and balmy weather. The Alps provide a breathtaking background and keep out cold, harsh winds.

Snow-capped Mt. Etna is on the eastern coast of Sicily, one of Italy's two islands. The first known eruption of Mt. Etna was around 700 B.C. Since then, there have been over eighty more eruptions. In 1669, about 20,000 people were killed in an earthquake occurring with an eruption. A few towns were destroyed in eruptions in 1950–51.

The narrowest street in the world is in the Italian village of Ripatransone. It is 16.9 inches wide. Use your ruler to mark off 16.9 inches. You'll be surprised!

Map Study Sheet

When given an unlabeled map, be able to write the following names in the correct location:

North America

South America

Europe

Asia

Africa

Antarctica

Australia

Pacific Ocean

Atlantic Ocean

Indian Ocean

Arctic Ocean

Antarctic Ocean

Canada

United States (with Alaska and Hawaii)

Mexico

Great Britain

Mediterranean Sea

Equator

Greenland

Japan

Great Lakes

Italy

Russia

Eastern Hemisphere

Mystery Question

Directions: Use the pages on Europe to figure out these answers. Read each clue carefully. When you know each one-word answer, write it on the lines to the right of each clue. Write one letter on each line (—). Then unscramble the letters on the dark lines to form *two* words to answer the mystery question. Write the words on the lines at the bottom of the page.

1. Of all the continents, Europe's is second largest   — — — — — — — —
2. England's a country with many royal ones   — — — — — — — —
3. Longest river in Europe   — — — — —
4. "Land of the Midnight Sun"   — — — — —
5. Approximate number of languages spoken in Europe   — — — — —
6. Popular for skiiing vacations in Switzerland   — — — —
7. The largest country in Great Britain   — — — — — — —
8. The English word for gasoline   — — — — —
9. Kind of language spoken in southern parts of Western Europe   — — — — — —
10. A sea that's the world's largest saltwater lake   — — — — — — —
11. Name given to continents of Europe and Asia together — — — — — — —
12. One of many peninsulas in Europe   — — — — — —

MYSTERY QUESTION: What is another name for the UK? (Unscramble the letters on the dark lines for each word.)

— — — — —   — — — — — —

Hemisphere Project

WRITE one thing of interest to you in the Western Hemisphere. List all the things about it that you have learned. Using this list, write a rough draft in paragraph format covering what you've selected, what you know about it, and why it is of interest to you. Do the same for the Eastern Hemisphere. Revise your paper so it sounds good. Write your final copy and proofread it thoroughly. Give your paper a title.

DRAW something to illustrate your selection from the Western Hemisphere and something to illustrate your selection for the Eastern Hemisphere. Use unlined paper. Label each drawing so it's clear what they are. Color nicely. Give your paper a title.

MAKE a map of either the Western Hemisphere or the Eastern Hemisphere. Get a sturdy piece of chipboard or poster board. Paint it blue (for oceans and seas) using tempera or poster paints. Use papîer mâché or some similar building material for the continents. After they dry, paint them. Make a legend for your map listing your hemisphere's continents, oceans, major seas, Equator location, etcetera. Give your project a title. Proofread for correct spelling and correct use of capital letters. Make your map look neat, too!

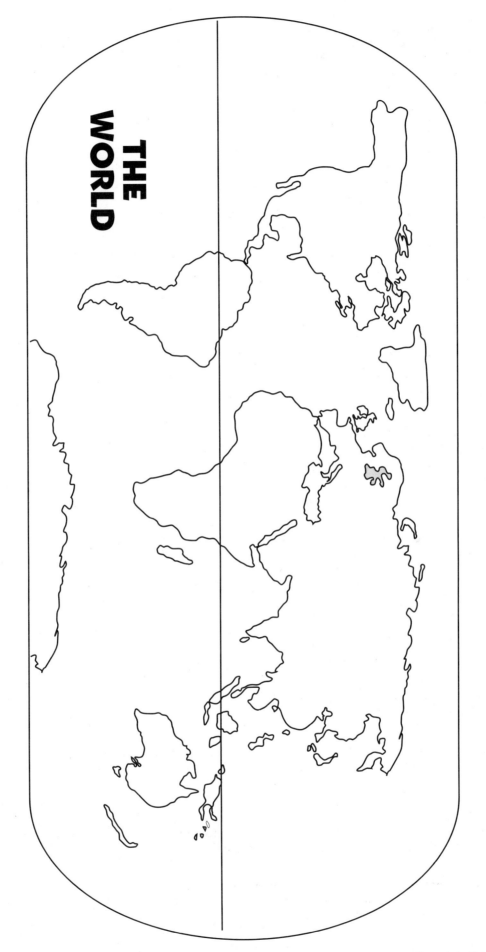

THE WORLD

World Geography

Study Sheet

1. What is the term given to the political divisions of Canada, such as British Columbia, Ontario, and Quebec?

_____

2. What is Oceania?

_____

3. In size, where does the United States rank?

_____

4. In population, where does the United States rank?

_____

5. What are the two most populous countries in the world?

_____

6. There are about 3,000 languages spoken in the world. Name the top four most-spoken languages.

_____

7. Name the largest continent and the largest ocean.

_____

8. What is the approximate population of the world?

_____

9. Name the continents belonging to the Western Hemisphere.

_____

10. Name the continents belonging to the Eastern Hemisphere.

_____

11. What is the International Date Line?

_____

12. Name the three natural wonders and the three modern wonders of the world located in the Western Hemisphere.

_____

13. What does the term "Land of the Midnight Sun" mean?

_____

14. To what country does Greenland belong?

_____

15. What are Canada's two official languages?

_____

16. What is The Underground City and where is it located?

_____

17. What is the term given to the forty-eight linked states and Washington, D.C.?

_____

18. What was and where was the highest temperature ever recorded in North America?

_____

19. What was and where was the lowest temperature ever recorded in North America?

_____

20. What are els and subways?

_____

21. Why is the Eastern Hemisphere called the "Old World"?

_____

22. The Eastern Hemisphere has the only one of the seven ancient wonders of the world still standing today. What is it?

_____

23. What does "Eurasia" mean?

_____

24. Name all the parts of the boundary line separating Europe and Asia.

_____

25. What is the name of the world's largest saltwater lake?

_____

26. Where is Big Ben?

_____

27. What is an ACV and how does it work?

_____

28. Where is the Leaning Tower of Pisa?

_____

World Geography Test

True or False

Print a "T" for true and an "F" for false on the line next to the number of the question.

_____ 1. The United States is the most populous country in the world.
_____ 2. The population of the entire world is approximately 5 billion people.
_____ 3. Big Ben is located in London, England.
_____ 4. The Great Salt Lake is the world's largest saltwater lake.
_____ 5. The Pacific Ocean is the largest ocean in the world.

Matching

Match the items in the left column with the correct ones in the right column.

6. Norway   largest continent
7. Denmark   Europe and Asia considered together as one continent
8. Asia   Land of the Midnight Sun
9. Ural Mountains   country to which Greenland belongs
10. Eurasia   partial border between Europe and Asia

Short Answer

Write the answers on the lines below the questions.

11. What is Oceania?

_____

_____

12. What is the International Date Line?

_____

_____

13. What is the Underground City and where is it located?

_____

_____

14. Where did the highest temperature ever recorded in North America occur?

_____

_____

15. What is an ACV?

_____

_____

§

List

List the answers on the lines below the questions.

16. What are the two most populous countries in the world?

_____

17. Name the continents belonging to only the Eastern Hemisphere.

_____

_____

18. Name two of the three modern wonders of the world located in the Western Hemisphere.

_____

_____

19. What are Canada's two official languages?

_____

20. Name the top four most-spoken languages in the world.

_____

_____

On the map on the next page, write in the following places in the correct locations:

North America
South America
Europe
Asia
Africa
Antarctica
Australia
Pacific Ocean
Atlantic Ocean
Indian Ocean
Arctic Ocean
Antarctic Ocean
Canada
United States (with Alaska and Hawaii)
Mexico
Great Britain
Mediterranean Sea
Equator
Greenland
Japan
Great Lakes
Italy
Russia

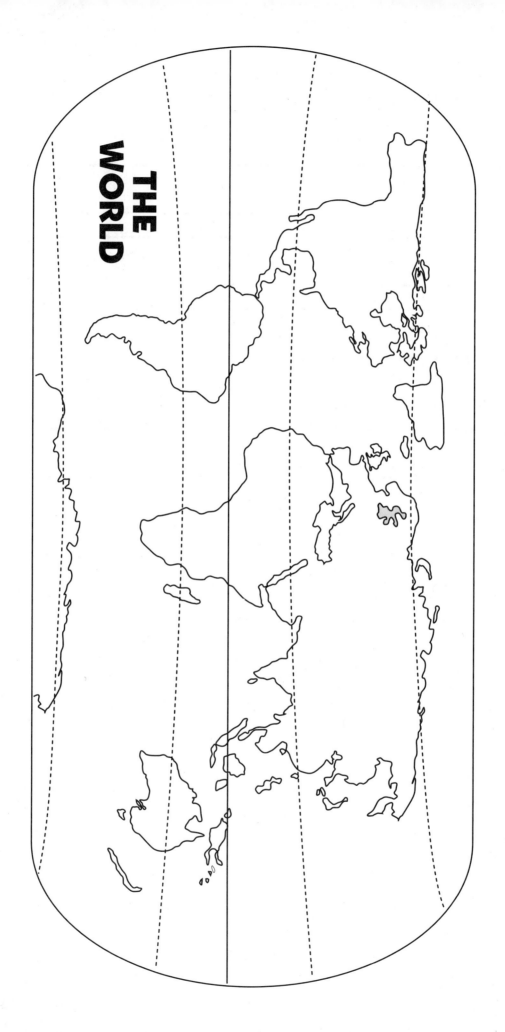

THE
WORLD

World Geography Winner

Student's Name

Teacher's Name

Date

§

FINE ARTS 2nd Quarter

O = Not Turned In
X = Excused, not able to make up

FIRST HALF

Assignment	Wesley	Manuel	Hieu	Maude	Adam	Lester
ART PROJ. — BUTTON ART	A	A+	C	A+	C+	A
MUSIC PERF. — PATRIOTIC	B	B	C	B	C	C
ART PROJ. — DOT ART	A	C	C	B	B	B-
SQUARE DANCE PRACTICE	A	A-	C	C-	X	B-
PUPPET SHOW	B	A+	C	B	C	A+
TEST/PROJECT AVERAGE (NO OTHER ASSIGN.)	A-	B	C+	B	C+	B
PROGRESS REPORT GRADE	A-	B	C+	B	C+	B

SECOND HALF

Assignment	Wesley	Manuel	Hieu	Maude	Adam	Lester
DISCO DANCE PERFORMANCE	A+	A+	C+	A-	C+	A-
ART PROJ. — SEWING	B	C	B	B-	B	A-
ART CONTEST — BUMPER ST.	B	B	C	O	C+	C
MUSIC — WE ARE THE WORLD	A-	C+	C	C	B	D
MUSIC — WINTER WONDERLAND	B-	C	C+	C+	B	C
GROUP PLAYS — HOLIDAYS IN OTHER COUNTRIES	B+	A+	C+	B	A+	A
TEST/PROJECT AVERAGE (NO OTHER ASSIGN.)	B+	B	C	D+	B	B
QUARTER AVERAGE	A-	B	C+	C+	B	B
REPORT CARD GRADE	A-	B	C+	C+	B	B

§

Grade Book Sample for Listening

FIRST HALF

LISTENING 2nd Quarter

Name	MARTIN L. KING, JR. STORY	CUCKOO AND HYENA STORIES	ISIAH THOMAS STORY	TEST AVERAGE	PROGRESS REPORT GRADE
Molly	85	79	81	82	B
Dominick	99	89	93	94	A
Isaac	98	89	93	93	A
Lindsey	81	75	68	75	C
Andrew	88	78	60	75	C
Alex	88	95	73	85	B

SECOND HALF

Name	DRACULA & BABE RUTH STORIES	COLONIAL SCHOOLS STORY	THE POLAR BEAR STORY	TEST AVERAGE	QUARTER AVERAGE	REPORT CARD GRADE
Molly	81	78	79	79	81	B
Dominick	99	89	95	94	94	A
Isaac	88	89	98	92	93	A
Lindsey	77	71	67	72	74	C
Andrew	60	55	65	60	68	C−
Alex	99	98	89	95	90	A−

O = Not Turned In
X = Excused, not able to make up

§

Grade Book Sample for Math

FIRST HALF

SECOND HALF

MATH 3rd Quarter

	Henry	Melissa	Adam	Bonnie	Truc	Alejandra
MULTIPLY BY 10, 100, 1000 WS	95	99	71	75	85	70
MULTIPLICATION FACTS TEST	P	P	F	F	P	F
1-DIGIT MULTIPLIERS TEST	88	95	65	70	88	62
GEOMETRY TEST — FIGURES	75	98	85	65	87	61
2 DIGIT X 2 DIGIT TEST	99	97	67	70	88	67
REVIEW TEST —, 1D X, 2D X	91	94	70	68	91	65
ONE-STEP WORD PROBLEMS TEST	88	98	65	71	55	61
AVERAGE	89	97	71	70	82	64
MISSING ASSIGN. OUT OF 12 OTHERS	3	0	0	7	0	9
	80			49		37
PROGRESS REPORT GRADE	B−	A	C	F	B+	F
PROGRESS REPORT EFFORT	S	O	O	N	O	U
TEST 3-DIGIT X 2-DIGIT	98	97	70	76	91	75
DIVISION FACTS TEST	P	P	F	P	P	F
TEST 78 ÷ 4	88	95	71	74	89	78
TEST 127 ÷ 3	89	97	68	78	92	75
TWO-STEP WORD PROBLEMS TEST	85	99	65	78	60	78
REVIEW TEST ON +, − X 1D ÷	95	98	71	78	92	79
AVERAGE	91	98	69	77	85	77
MISSING ASSIGN. OUT OF 12 OTHERS	0	0	0	0	0	0
QUARTER AVERAGE	86	98	70	63	84	57
REPORT CARD GRADE	B	A	C−	C−	B+	D
REPORT CARD EFFORT	S+	O	O	S+	O	S

Grade Book Sample for PE

PE — 2nd Quarter

	Lorenzo	Marilyn	Clark	Juanita	Gilberto	Nora
FIRST HALF						
DRIBBLING SKILLS	B	C	A	A+	B	A
PASSING SKILLS	C	C	A	A	B	A
BASKETBALL	B	C	A	A	C	A
BALL DISTANCE THROWING	A	C	A	A	C	A
NATIONBALL	A	C	A	A	B	A
AVERAGE	B	C	A	A	B	A
PROGRESS REPORT GRADE	B	C	A	A	B	A
SECOND HALF						
ENDURANCE PRACTICE	A	C+	A	A+	C+	A+
FITNESS SKILLS PRACTICE	A	C	A	A+	C	A
PHYSICAL FITNESS TESTING						
PULL-UPS	B	C	A	A	C	A
SIT-UPS	A	C	A	A	B	A
MILE JOG	A+	B	A+	A+	C+	A+
SIT AND STRETCH	C	C	A	A	C	A
SERVING, ROTATING SKILLS	B	A	A	A	C	A
VOLLEYBALL	B	A	A	A	C+	A+
AVERAGE	B+	B	A	A	C	A
QUARTER AVERAGE	B	C+	A	A	C+	A
REPORT CARD GRADE	B	C+	A	A	C+	A

Grade Book Sample for Reading

READING — 2nd Quarter

FIRST HALF

	Amanda	Frederico	Maria	Tuan	Chiyo	Andy
VOCABULARY TEST — ANNIE	97	98	72	60	68	81
COMPREHENSION TEST—EXPLORING	85	97	68	55	62	82
CHAPTER 7 QUESTIONS&ANSWERS	B	A-	C+	B	D-	C-
CHAPTER 8 PICTURES & CAPTION	B+	A+	C+	B-	D-	C
CHAPTER 9 NOTES & QUOTES	A-	A	C+	C+	C	C
BOOK REPORT — NONFICTION	C+	A	C+	B-	D	C
BOOK REPORT — FICTION	B-	B+	C-	B-	D	C
COMPREHENSION TEST—RED CYCLE	91	98	71	60	65	85
AVERAGE	87	95	74	72	67	77
MISSING ASSIGN. OUT OF 10 OTHERS	0	0	1	0	3	2
			71		58	71
PROGRESS REPT. GRADE	B	A	C	C	F	C
PROGRESS REPT. EFFORT	O	A	S	O	N	N

SECOND HALF

	Amanda	Frederico	Maria	Tuan	Chiyo	Andy
VOCABULARY TEST—TALL TALES	88	95	75	64	75	87
COMPREHENSION SHEET—POETRY	B	A+	B-	B	C+	B
COMPREHENSION TEST—THE HERO	79	89	75	65	78	88
BOOK REPORT — BIOGRAPHY	B-	A	B-	B-	B+	B-
BOOK REPORT — MYSTERY	A-	A-	C	B-	A	C+
AVERAGE	84	94	77	75	83	84
MISSING ASSIGN. OUT OF 10 OTHERS	0	0	2	0	0	0
			71			
QUARTER AVERAGE	86	95	71	74	71	78
REPORT CARD GRADE	B	A	C	C	C	C+
REPORT CARD EFFORT	O	O	S	O	S	S

§

Grade Book Sample for Research Skills

RESEARCH SKILLS 2nd Quarter

Assignment		Linda	Steven	Judy	Jim	Matthew	Donna
FIRST HALF							
MAP/KEY TEST		71	75	65	72	95	99
VERT. BAR GRAPH TEST		78	82	91	88	44	89
CREATE OWN BAR GRAPH		A–	B–	B	C+	D	A
ATLAS/ALMANAC ACTIVITY		B–	C	C	C–	A	A
ENCYCLOPEDIA ACTIVITY		C	C	C	C	A	A
REFERENCE MATERIALS TEST		77	74	78	88	92	94
AVERAGE (NO OTHER ASSIGNMENTS)		C+	C	C+	C+	B	A
PROGRESS REPORT GRADE		C+	C	C+	C+	B	A
SECOND HALF							
DICTIONARY SKILLS		C	C	B	C+	A–	A+
CREATE OWN LINE GRAPH		B	B–	B	C	A–	A+
MAP AND TABLE TEST		72	71	81	81	95	91
REPORT — COUNTRY		C	B	B+	C–	A+	A
AVERAGE (NO OTHER ASSIGNMENTS)		C	C	B	C	A	A
QUARTER AVERAGE		C+	C	B–	C+	B+	A
REPORT CARD GRADE		C+	C	B–	C+	B+	A

Grade Book Sample for Science

SCIENCE 2nd Quarter

FIRST HALF

Assignment	Gloria	Juan	Veronica	Junior	Jessica	Jonathan
OBSERVATION RECORDINGS	C+	A	A-	C	D	C
EXPERIMENT — WATER	C	B	C	C	D	B
TEST — WATER	85	88	65	66	62	61
VOCABULARY TEST CHAPTER 4	88	92	84	75	66	78
PENGUIN REPT. & PROJECT	B	A-	C+	C	D-	C
AVERAGE	82	90	79	73	64	75
MISSING ASSIGN. – 5 OTHERS	2	0	1	1	3	0
	76		76	70	55	
PROGRESS REPORT GRADE	C	A-	C	C-	F	C
PROGRESS REPORT EFFORT	N	O	S	S	U	O

SECOND HALF

Assignment	Gloria	Juan	Veronica	Junior	Jessica	Jonathan
SCI. DRAWING–LAYERS OF THE SKIN	A	A-	B+	C+	C-	A-
ESTIMATION EXP. — BEANS	A-	A+	C	C+	C+	A-
MICROSCOPE ACTIVITY	B	A	C	D	C+	A-
SCIENCE FAIR PROJECT	C	A	B	C	B+	B
SCI. DRAWING — BRAIN	C-	A+	B-	C+	B+	C+
AVERAGE	83	96	81	75	80	84
MISSING ASSIGN. – 6 OTHERS	2	0	1	2	0	0
	77		78	69		
QUARTER AVERAGE	77	97	77	70	68	80
REPORT CARD GRADE	C	A	C	C-	C-	B
REPORT CARD EFFORT	N	O	S	S	S	O

Grade Book Sample for Social Studies (History and Geography)

SOCIAL STUDIES — 1st Quarter

	Mike	Marita	Sylvester	Morgan	Lynn	Tracy
FIRST HALF						
CHRISTOPHER COLUMBUS	A	A	B+	A	C	B
GRP. SKIT — EXPLORERS	A-	A	C+	D	C	D
CHAPTER 2 TEST	95	97	88	77	72	66
MAP OF NORTH AMERICA	A	A	C	D	C	A
ESSAY CONTEST—WONDERS OF OUR STATE	A+	A+	C-	C	C+	C-
AVERAGE	95	96	80	75	75	75
MISSING ASSIGN. – 7 OTHERS	0	0	2	4	2	1
			74	63	69	72
PROGRESS REPORT GRADE	A	A	C	D	D	C
PROGRESS REPORT EFFORT	O	O	N	N	N	S
SECOND HALF						
PRESIDENT REPORT	A	B+	C	C	C	B-
CHAPTER 3 TEST	99	98	78	71	74	72
GEOGRAPHY BOOKLET — U.S.	A	A	C	C	C	D
GEOGRAPHY TEST — U.S.	99	97	78	75	72	71
AVERAGE	97	95	77	74	74	72
MISSING ASSIGN. – 7 OTHERS	0	0	1	1	2	2
			74	71	68	66
QUARTER AVERAGE	96	96	74	67	69	69
REPORT CARD GRADE	A	A	C	C-	D+	D+
REPORT CARD EFFORT	O	O	S	N	N	N

Grade Book Sample for Speaking

SPEAKING — 3rd Quarter

	Leslie	Heather	David	Jeremy	Samantha	Hilary
SCIENCE FAIR PROJ. REPORT	B	A	C	B	A+	D+
SURPRISE PACKAGE SPEECH	C	A	C–	B	A–	D
OPINION SPEECH	C–	A	C+	B	A–	D
SPEAKING AVERAGE	C	A	C	B	A	D
PROGRESS REPORT GRADE	C	A	C	B	A	D
DEMO SPEECH	A–	A	C+	B+	A–	C+
HISTORICAL CHARACTER DRESS-UP SPEECH	B–	A	A	B+	A	C+
GUESS WHO I'M DESCRIBING	C+	A	B	B	A	C+
SPEAKING AVERAGE	B	A	B	B	A	C+
QUARTER AVERAGE	C+	A	B–	B	A	C
REPORT GRADE AVERAGE	C+	A	B–	B	A	C

FIRST HALF — SECOND HALF

Grade Book Sample for Writing

WRITING 1st Quarter	Julianna	Hector	Lodley	Cynthia	Jose	An
FIRST HALF						
SPELLING TEST LESSON 1	65	95	88	62	85	98
ANSWERS 5 W'S IN COMP. SENTENCES	C	C+	A–	D	B	A
CLASS PARAGRAPH FOR FORMAT	C+	B	A	B	B	A+
PARAGRAPH — SECRET OF THE CAVE	B–	B	A+	D	B	A
SPELLING TEST LESSON 2	75	95	99	60	85	98
POETRY — YOUR NAME IN A POEM	B+	B+	A	B–	B+	A+
PARAGRAPH TEST	C+	B	A	D	B	A
AVERAGE	77	88	95	69	86	97
MISSING ASSIGN. – 9 OTHERS	2	3	0	0	0	0
	71	79				
PROGRESS REPORT GRADE	C	C+	A	C–	B	A
PROGRESS REPORT EFFORT	S	S	O	S+	O	O
SECOND HALF						
SPELLING TEST LESSON 3	68	95	95	71	88	98
FRIENDLY LETTER FORMAT&CURSIVE	B–	A–	A	C	B+	A
QUOTATIONS FOLLOWED BY SPEAKER	C	B	A–	D	B–	A+
SPELLING TEST LESSON 4	70	92	95	75	87	98
TEST ON PROPER NOUNS & CAPITALS	68	92	95	70	88	98
NARRATIVE — SPACE ROBOTS	C	B	A	D+	B	A+
AVERAGE	73	90	94	71	86	98
MISSING ASSIGN. – 11 OTHERS	2	4	0	0	0	0
	67	78				
QUARTER AVERAGE	69	79	95	70	86	98
REPORT CARD GRADE	C–	C+	A	C–	B	A
REPORT CARD EFFORT	S	N	O	O–	O	O

§ History

For the pages you have read and for the information you've acquired, do the following activities on a separate piece of paper:

1. List and tell all about ten things you have learned.

2. Write the letters (one below the other) of the title of what your social studies pages are about. Look through the pages and find a word related to social studies for each of the letters of the title.

Example: Suppose you are studying New York.

Niagara Falls
Empire State Building
World Trade Center

Yiddish
Overcrowding in some areas
Rapid transit
Know where Hudson River is

3. Write a short play that could be made to give the information you've learned to others. Give your play a title. Decide on a few characters for your play. They don't have to be people. They can be buildings, animals, cities, etc. Use play format.

Example of play format:

Official End to the Civil War
Setting — Courthouse at Appomattox
Characters — Gen. Robert E. Lee
Gen. Ulysses S. Grant
Narrator

Narrator: What person says
What person says
Grant: What person says
What person says
Lee: What person says
What person says

History

Christopher Columbus

You are Christopher Columbus. You have three ships, the Niña, the Pinta, and the Santa Maria. You are bound for the New World on your *first trip*. Read all about it in your social studies book, a library book, or an encyclopedia. Then answer the following questions.

1. What year is it?

   _____

2. From which country do you set sail?

   _____

3. Who is financing (paying for) your trip?

   _____

4. What are you expected to find and bring back from the New World?

   _____

5. Why were some people in those days afraid of ships sailing out of sight of land?

   _____

6. How do you feel while you're out sailing in the Atlantic Ocean?

   _____

   _____

7. What do you think about the idea of turning back?

   _____

   _____

8. Where exactly do you land?

_____

_____

9. Name three things you see now that you're off the ship.

a. _____

b. _____

c. _____

10. Name two things you take from the New World back to Europe.

a. _____

b. _____

11. How do you feel when you get back?

12. How do Ferdinand and Isabella feel about your trip?

_____

_____

13. List three reasons why you want to go back to the New World?

a. _____

b. _____

c. _____

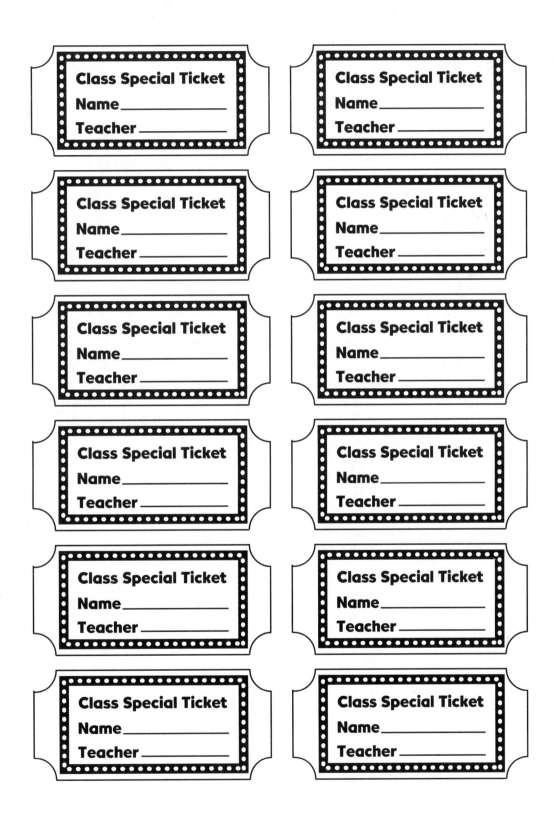

Job Interview

Introduce yourself. Shake hands. Sit up straight. Dress nicely. Act "up" and enthusiastic. Don't talk in a negative way about any student, teacher, principal, or school. Be positive!

The following are questions you might be asked by the interview team:

1. What grades are you interested in? Why? Is there any grade you wouldn't want to teach?
2. What are your policies and philosophies regarding discipline? (You might want to ask about theirs at this time. Be very careful not to be critical.)
3. What are your thoughts about teaching as part of a team?
4. How would you teach language arts?
5. What are your favorite subjects?
6. How would you keep the students motivated?
7. What do you think about year-round teaching? Would you be interested?
8. How would you meet the academic, social, and self-esteem needs of students in a combination class?
9. How would you meet the needs of ESL students?
10. Do you have any questions for us?

Plan answers *before* you go on an interview. Plan one or two questions about curriculum, team teaching, use of mentor teachers or something else along these lines to ask the interview team. At some interviews you may be given a "What if" scenario. This could be a difficult or touchy question. Answer it in a positive way. Show that you're flexible. If you don't know the exact answer, speak to what you *do* know about the topic.

Let the interview team know that you are *very* interested in their position and their district. If you are interviewing in an area where there's a great deal of competition for teaching jobs, be sure to follow up your interview with a thank-you letter and a minimum of one phone call. That way people will remember who you are.

Present your *best self* and you'll be great!

§

The Four Keys
to Academic Success

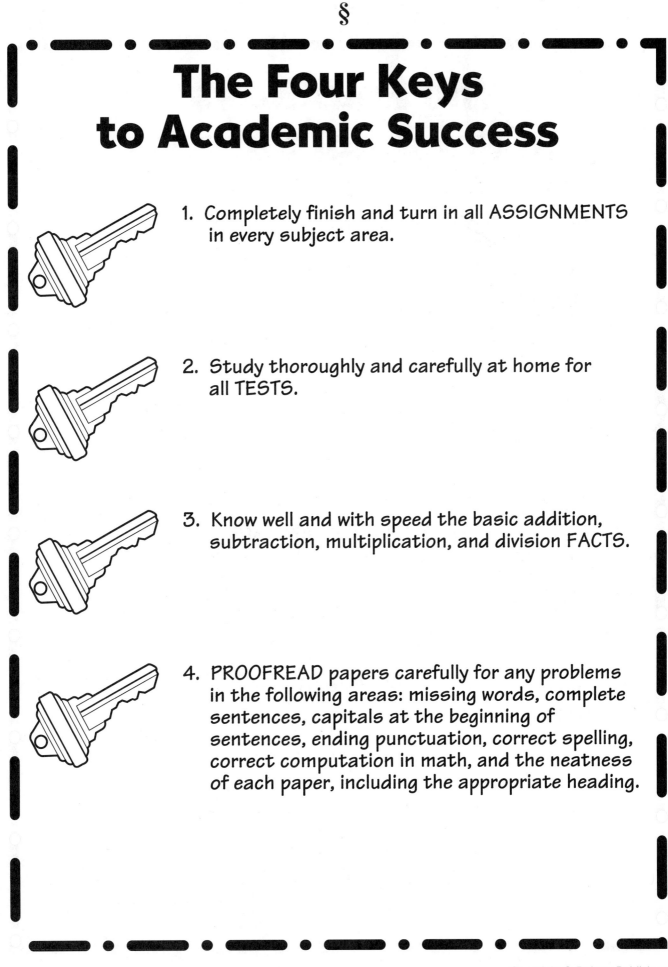

1. Completely finish and turn in all ASSIGNMENTS in every subject area.

2. Study thoroughly and carefully at home for all TESTS.

3. Know well and with speed the basic addition, subtraction, multiplication, and division FACTS.

4. PROOFREAD papers carefully for any problems in the following areas: missing words, complete sentences, capitals at the beginning of sentences, ending punctuation, correct spelling, correct computation in math, and the neatness of each paper, including the appropriate heading.

The Four Keys
to Personal Success

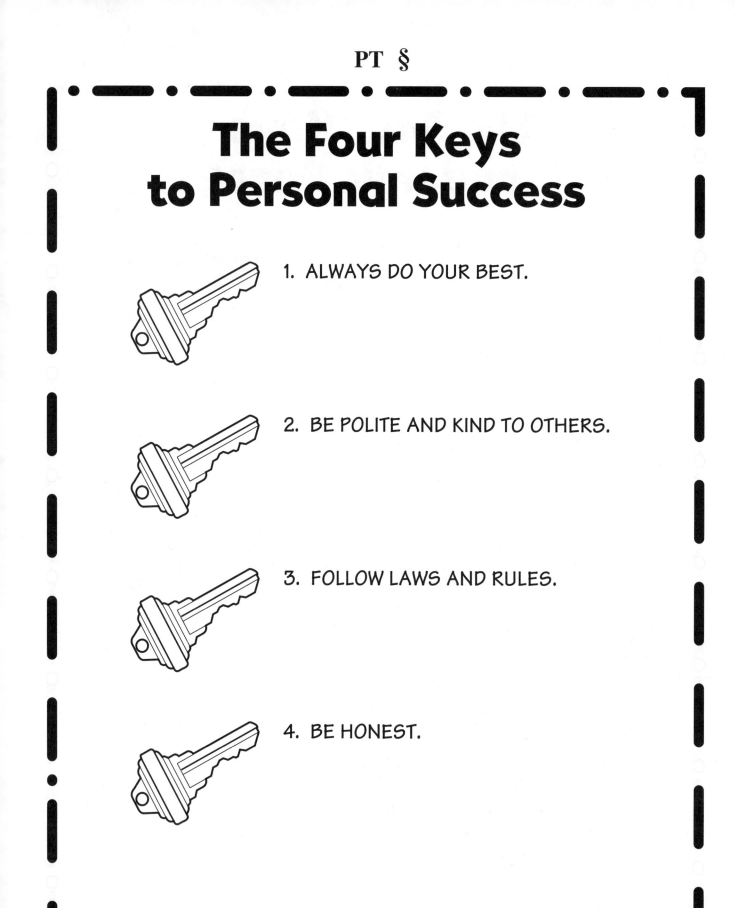

1. ALWAYS DO YOUR BEST.

2. BE POLITE AND KIND TO OTHERS.

3. FOLLOW LAWS AND RULES.

4. BE HONEST.

Directions for the Self-Image Q Sort

In this booklet you will be able to build a picture of yourself. Just follow these steps:

1. Take the cards from the card packet.
2. Read one card carefully and think about what it says. Decide whether the statement on the card is basically true or false for you.
3. Example: If the first card you picked said, "I don't like to do new things" and this is somewhat true for you, then you place this card in any box in the somewhat true row. If this card is very true or most true for you, place the card in any box in the very true row or the most true row. But if this card statement is basically false for you, place it in the false row that best describes you.
4. Continue placing all 26 cards in the rows that best fit you. Be sure to place one card in the most true box and one card in the most false box.
5. When you are finished with all 26 cards, there will be four boxes still empty. These boxes can be anywhere on the chart except in the most true and most false boxes. Be sure there is one card in each of these boxes.
6. Lower those cards that are true for you *now*, but you *wished* they were false for you, into the dotted line areas of the true boxes. Also lower those cards that are basically false for you *now*, but you *wished* they were true for you, into the dotted line areas of the false boxes.
7. There are no right or wrong answers. Just be honest and place the cards in the boxes that you feel best describe you.

§

I HAVE AN INTEREST OR HOBBY THAT MY FRIEND ENJOYS.

I THINK I AM AN INTERESTING PERSON.

I CAN TELL OTHER PEOPLE WHAT I FEEL.

I FEEL FUNNY OR STRANGE ABOUT THE WAY I ACT.

I DON'T DO REALLY WELL AT ANYTHING.

I AM OFTEN LATE GETTING MY WORK FINISHED.

I AM SCARED TO DO SOME THINGS I'D LIKE TO DO.

I CAN STAND UP FOR MYSELF.

I HAVE A POOR ATTITUDE ABOUT MANY THINGS.

I THINK PEOPLE EXPECT TOO MUCH OF ME.

I FEEL SAFE AND SECURE WITH MY TEACHERS.

I DO WELL IN MY SCHOOL WORK.

I KNOW I'M WANTED BY MY FAMILY.

I CAN USUALLY SOLVE MY OWN PROBLEMS.

I DON'T SEEM TO FIT IN WITH OTHERS.

I FEEL VERY IMPORTANT.

I DON'T KNOW HOW TO GET SOMEONE TO LIKE ME.

I DON'T LIKE THE WAY I LOOK.

I GET INTO TROUBLE QUITE A LOT.

I KEEP MY TEMPER IN CONTROL.

I DON'T LIKE TO DO NEW THINGS.

I DO NOT LIKE MYSELF VERY WELL.

I LIKE MY NAME.

I AM POPULAR WITH MEMBERS OF THE OPPOSITE SEX.

I ALWAYS TRY TO DO MY BEST.

I AM WELL-LIKED BY OTHER PEOPLE.

§

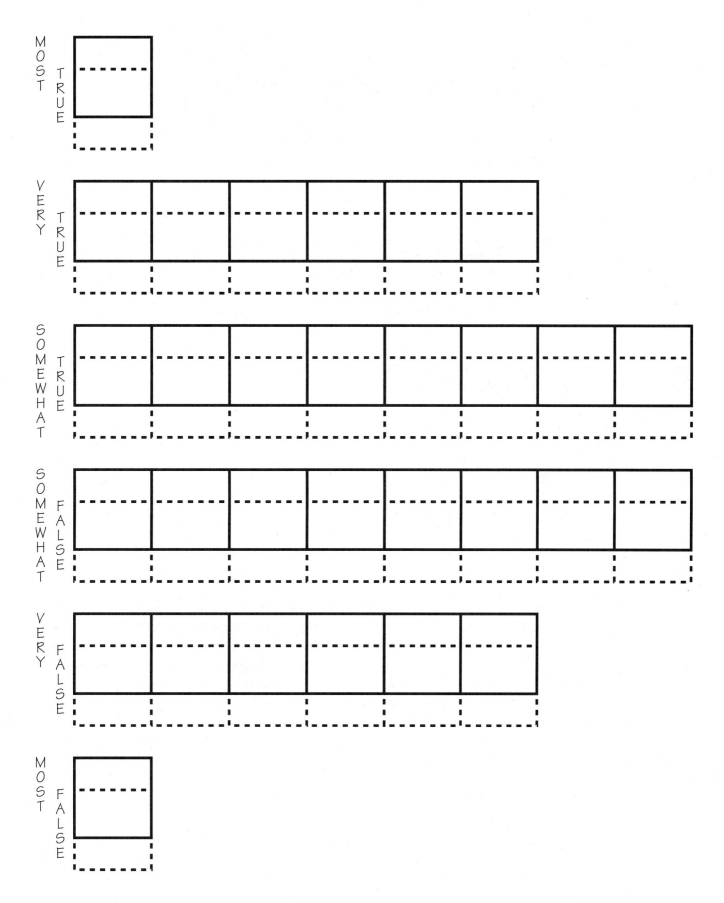

Listening Test

OBJECTIVE: After listening to a story, the student will describe the setting, state the problem, and tell the solution.

A MIND BOGGLER

It loomed behind the huge olive trees in the distance, set off from everything, like a world unto itself. It had been there for almost 61 years—that deserted old house—as long as most people could remember. But lately, something strange was happening on the first floor.

Jim and Peter decided to investigate one more time, hoping they wouldn't be scared away as they were during their other visits. There just had to be an explanation.

As they crept through the unlocked window, everything inside looked quite still and untouched. They moved across the creaky wooden floor carpeted by a flimsy oriental rug. They headed toward the object that had held their fascination. It didn't move. It just rested there defying their imagination. No . . . it's starting! The stately antique rocker, upholstered in beige and green needlepoint, was rocking by itself. How could this be?

In the midst of the racket of two pounding hearts, Jim and Peter picked up the chair and moved it to another spot on the rug. No movement. The indentations left in the rug by the heavy old rocker mystified them. They had learned in their previous visits that the rocker moved only when in its original place and even then it moved only sometimes. It was baffling.

Now Jim and Peter did not believe in ghosts and there were no wires or strings attached to the chair. But what? They began examining every inch of the chair. They even turned it upside down.

The runners looked quite normal except for a clean new strip of brown felt stretching the entire length of each of the runners. It caught their attention. Peter took a dime from his pocket and tried to peel off the felt, but to his amazement, his dime was so attracted to the felt—or what lay underneath it—that it was practically ripped out of his hand.

So that's it. Both boys had a smug grin on their faces. They found their way to the basement door and stealthily crept down the stairs. It wasn't difficult to locate the culprit. "Boo!" yelled Peter and Jim. The surprised town prankster tottered on his ladder, tumbled to the cement floor and along with him crashed the source of mystification—two large red magnets, which had been dragged many times across the ceiling in those two special places to rock the chair and tease the town's boys and girls.

Setting: The story takes place on the first floor and basement of an old deserted house.

Problem: Why did the rocking chair rock all by itself?

Solution: The discovery of the magnetized material under the brown felt led to the further discovery of the town prankster with his magnets. The solution was brought about through the courage and perseverance of Jim and Peter.

Plants Have Feelings, Too

Cleve Backster is a man who believes plants have feelings. He even thinks all living things send messages to each other. You probably think Backster is far out, but this is what he did.

First he hooked up a plant to a lie detector machine. A lie detector can tell how people feel. When a person is upset or afraid, the lie detector records it on a graph. But no one ever hooked one up to a plant before.

Next he put the plant in a room by itself. In another room far away, machines threw tiny shrimp into very hot water. When the shrimp died, Cleve looked at the graph. It was just like the graph of a person who is upset. It seemed to Cleve the shrimp sent a message through the walls when they died and the plant heard them.

So, the next time you pick a daisy and pull the petals to see if someone loves you or not, listen carefully. That daisy just might be saying "Ouch!"

1. The main idea of the story is
   a. shrimp die in very hot water.
   b. plants may have feelings.
   c. Cleve Backster is a nice man.

2. Cleve hooked up plants to
   a. a flower pot.
   b. a slow-moving train.
   c. a lie detector machine.

3. Cleve believes plants
   a. laugh at jokes.
   b. like animals.
   c. have feelings.

4. Cleve Backster is probably the kind of man who is
   a. upset.
   b. curious.
   c. a shrimp.

Nile Crocodile

Next time you're at the zoo, look closely at the crocodiles. Does one have big tears in its eyes? You don't have to feel sorry for him. He's not crying because he's sad. He's crying just to keep his eyes wet.

Crocodiles are most likely never sad about the things they do. And they do some pretty terrible things. Like eating people. Each year, about 1,000 people are killed by crocodiles. One big fellow in Central Africa was said to have killed 400 people in his lifetime.

Crocodiles are big. They can grow to be as big as a Cadillac car. And they are super strong. A Nile crocodile is not afraid to take on anything—even an elephant. One time, a crocodile grabbed the leg of a big elephant and tried to drag it into the river. But this time, the crocodile had met its match. The elephant dragged it off to where the other elephants were. They squashed it flat. Then they picked up the crocodile and sent it flying into the treetops.

1. The main idea of the story is
   a. Nile crocodiles shed tears.
   b. Nile crocodiles eat elephants.
   c. Nile crocodiles are mean and hungry.

2. Crocodiles cry because
   a. they're sad.
   b. they want to keep their eyes wet.
   c. they're hungry.

3. Each year, crocodiles kill
   a. 400 people.
   b. 1,000 people.
   c. 1,500 people.

4. That a crocodile would try to eat an elephant shows that
   a. crocodiles are smart.
   b. crocodiles are not very smart.
   c. crocodiles are sad.

Martin Luther King

His name was Martin Luther King and he is a legend. He had a dream . . . a dream that people of different colors and beliefs could live together in peace with equality. And he did not believe that violent action was necessary to make that dream come true for black Americans.

Martin Luther King lived his life believing in equality for blacks and he did some very important things to make it happen. One of them was eliminating discrimination on city buses. For many years black people were required to sit in the back of buses in many southern communities. He told his followers in Montgomery, Alabama, that if they were not allowed to sit in the front of the bus, they should refuse to ride the buses altogether. So many thousands of people quit using buses. This caused the United State Supreme Court to enact a law that said black citizens could sit anywhere they wanted to on a bus. King had won a major battle without violence. He also worked hard to get black people registered to vote. And getting black students admitted to segregated, all-white schools was another important thing Martin Luther King helped make happen.

Tragically, his great work was cut short in 1968 when he was shot by an assassin. But his dream had begun to come true and no assassin could stop it.

1. The main idea of the story is
   a. Martin Luther King dedicated his life to helping the black people gain their rights without using violence.
   b. Martin Luther King helped register black people to vote.
   c. Martin Luther King rode where he wanted on buses.

2. Martin Luther King worked hard to get people registered
   a. as aliens.
   b. for the army.
   c. to vote.

3. Martin Luther King believed
   a. that it was all right for black people to sit at the back of the bus.
   b. that people can live together in peace.
   c. that it is not important for people to vote.

4. If Martin Luther King did not lead the black people, there probably would have been
   a. more black people in Montgomery.
   b. more violence.
   c. more to talk about.

NAME _____

Tasmanian Devil

If ever an animal fit the name, devil, this small creature from the island of Tasmania near Australia does. Though not an enemy to humans, the Tasmanian devil is a danger to many other animals large and small.

The Tasmanian devil is a savage attacker who will feed on any flesh, dead or alive. Built something like a small bear, it makes good use of its 12 to 20 pounds. It is so strong that it can pull down a much larger animal like a sheep or a wallaby, the small kangaroo. Once caught by a Tasmanian devil, the end comes quickly.

Even when mating, these animals are a little devilish. For two weeks, the male holds the female in his den and will not let her escape. After mating, the tables are turned. The female snarls and bites the male whenever he comes near.

The next time you see Bugs Bunny being chased by a Tasmanian devil in the TV cartoon, you'll know one thing is true. The snarling, whirling animal chasing poor Bugs is just as mean as he looks.

1. The main idea of the story is
   a. the Tasmanian devil is only a cartoon animal.
   b. the Tasmanian devil is very dangerous.
   c. the Tasmanian devil weighs up to 20 pounds.

2. The Tasmanian devil looks something like a small
   a. sheep.
   b. kangaroo.
   c. bear.

3. When mating, these animals are
   a. very loving to each other.
   b. a little devilish with each other.
   c. are quiet and very seldom dangerous.

4. If you keep sheep on the island of Tasmania, you would probably
   a. guard your sheep against attacks.
   b. want to protect only the young sheep.
   c. not worry about any sheep being attacked.

The Polar Bear

The most dangerous hunter of the frozen North is the polar bear. Standing nine feet tall, it deserves the title, King of the **Arctic.** Not only is it larger than most bears, its bite is more powerful, too. In fact, the polar bear can crunch through skulls and backbones with ease. It must be a hungry hunter all the time. There is little vegetable food available in the frigid Arctic, so it must survive on what it hunts.

The polar bear is the furriest animal on earth; even the soles of its huge feet are hairy. The bristles growing between its toes and foot pads keep it from sticking to the ice or from slipping on it. They **muffle** the sound of its approach as it hunts, and they help it swim faster, too.

Many animals' fur becomes white in winter as protection, but polar bears stay white all year around. Their white coats help them sneak up on their prey. But not all parts of a polar bear's body are white. Its shiny black nose and eyes give it away, so sometimes, when a bear is **stalking** prey, it will half close its eyes to conceal them and cover its nose with its gray tongue or its big white paw.

Actually, the hairs of the polar bear's fur are not white at all. If you look at a hair in a **microscope,** you will see that the hair is **transparent** and hollow, full of air. This trapped air in millions of hairs keeps the warmth of the bear's body close to its skin and does not let it escape into the cold Arctic air. In fact, the polar bear's fur does such a good job that hunters who try to spot the bears from planes equipped with **devices** that sense body heat find that the bears do not register on these devices. This happens because no heat escapes from their coats. Eskimos prefer to wear polar bear fur, because it is warmer than the fur of any other animal.

Quiz

The Polar Bear

1. The main idea of the story is
   a. there is little vegetable food available in the Arctic.
   b. the polar bear covers it nose with its tongue.
   c. the polar bear is the most dangerous hunter of the North.

2. The hairs of the polar bear's fur
   a. are not white at all.
   b. are really light pink.
   c. let the warmth of its body escape into the cold air.

3. The bristles growing between the polar bear's foot pads
   a. become white in the winter as protection.
   b. keep the bear from slipping on the ice.
   c. register on devices that sense body heat.

4. True or false?
   a. Many animals' fur becomes white in winter.
   b. Eskimos like to wear polar bear fur.
   c. The polar bear is smaller than most bears.

5. The polar bear survives on what it hunts
   a. throughout its life.
   b. after it has eaten Arctic vegetables.
   c. while its coat is turning white.

6. Match the following words with their definitions by placing the number of the definition by the correct word from the story.
   a.__ transparent
   b.__ Arctic
   c.__ muffle
   d.__ microscope
   e.__ device

   1. the area around the North Pole.
   2. a device that magnifies small objects.
   3. to deaden a sound.
   4. a machine used to do one or more tasks.
   5. can be easily seen on the other side.

7. In this story, **stalk** means
   a. to track prey.
   b. the stem of a plant.
   c. to shy away from.

8. The polar bear tries to conceal its nose and eyes because
   a. it is playing hide and seek.
   b. it is easier to sneak up on an animal that way.
   c. it can't stand the sight of blood.

9. Do you think the polar bear deserves the title of King of the Arctic? Why or why not?

ENRICHMENT ACTIVITIES

1. Go to the library or your local museum and find out more about Eskimos and their way of life. What animals besides the polar bear do they hunt and use?

2. If you have access to a microscope, look at human, cat, and dog hair under it and note any differences you see.

Name _____

Lattices

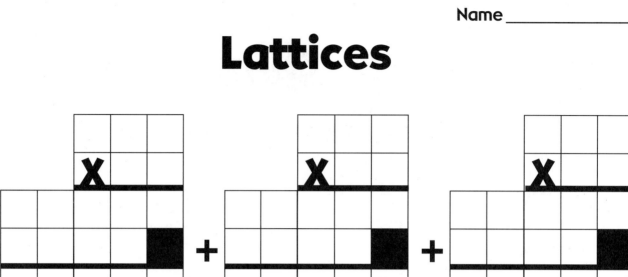

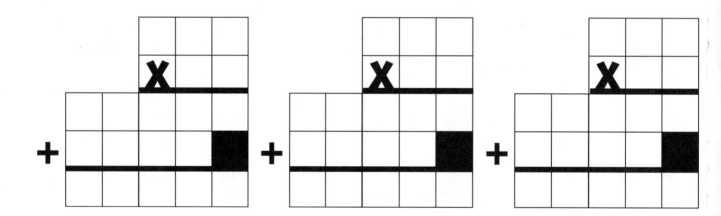

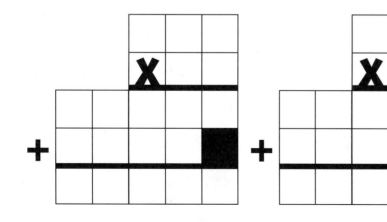 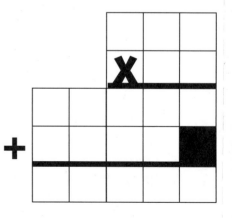

§

Name _____

(For 7⟌86)

Lattices

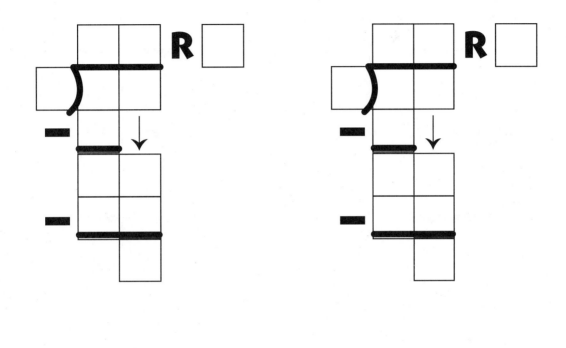

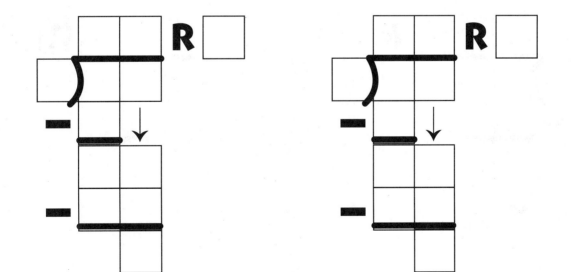

§

Lattices

(For 6)157)

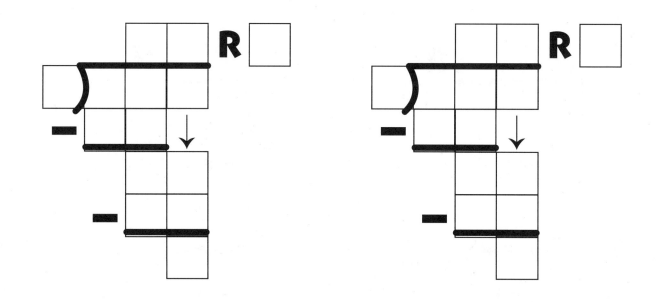

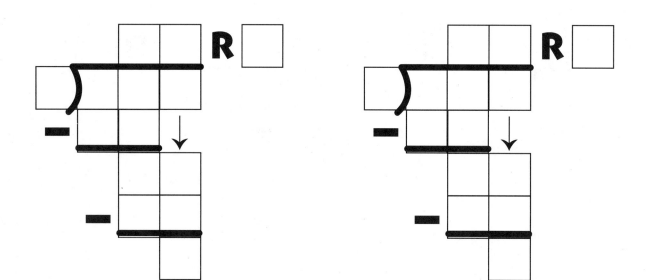

Subtraction with Borrowing

Study Sheet

* Always start with the bottom number.
* You MUST BORROW if the bottom number is bigger than the top.

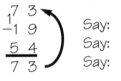

Say: 9 from 3 I cannot do, so borrow.
              Cross out my 7 and make it a 6.
              Put the 1 I borrowed by the 3.
              9 from 13 is 4.
Say: 1 from 6 is 5.

CHECK by adding the bottom sets of numbers. In the sample problem, you'll be adding 19 and 54.

$$\begin{array}{r} {}^1 7\ 3 \\ -1\ 9 \\ \hline 5\ 4 \\ \hline 7\ 3 \end{array}$$

Say: 4 plus 9 is 13. Put down my 3, carry my 1.
Say: 5 plus 1 is 6, plus the 1 I carried is 7.
Say: 73 matches 73. Draw my arrow to SHOW this.

* Make up at least ten other subtraction problems just like this one. Write your CHECK. Draw your arrow. Follow this procedure on the test, too!

Two-Digit Multipliers

Study Sheet

* Always start with the bottom number.
* Understand place value as it applies to multiplication. When you multiply by the ONES multiplier, your answer must start in the ONES place value column. When you multiply by the TENS multiplier, your answer must start in the TENS place value column.

$$
\begin{array}{r}
{}^{7}_{3}\,7\,9 \\
\times 8\ 4 \\
\hline
3\,1\,6 \\
+6\,3\,2 \\
\hline
6{,}6\,3\,6
\end{array}
$$

Say: This is for the ONES multiplier.
 4 times 9 is 36. Put down my 6, carry my 3.
Say: 4 times 7 is 28 plus the 3 I carried is 31. Write my 31.

Say: This is for the TENS multiplier.
 8 times 9 is 72. Put down my 2 in the TENS column and carry my 7.
Say: 8 times 7 is 56 plus the 7 I carried is 63. Write my 63.
Say: Draw my line to add and put in my plus sign.
Say: 6 plus nothing is 6.
 1 plus 2 is 3.
 3 plus 3 is 6.
 Nothing plus 6 is 6.
Say: My answer is 6,636.

***CHECK by reversing the numbers. Put the 84 on top and the 79 on the bottom and multiply again. Like this:

$$
\begin{array}{r}
8\ 4 \\
\times 7\ 9 \\
\hline
\end{array}
$$

**Make up at least seven other problems just like this one. Solve each problem. Then write out your check for each problem by reversing the number and multiplying again. You can check again with your calculator!

Two-Digit Divisors with Zeros

Study Sheet

* Use the division family.

  (Daddy)   D   ÷   < Use "DOES" to get MARKER. COVER to ESTIMATE

  (Mommy)   M   ×

  (Sister)   S   −

  (Brother)   B   ↓

               R   (Relatives)

* Always start with the divisor. You want to know how many times the divisor is contained in the dividend.

* Remember: A divisor does NOT go into a number smaller than itself.

* Use the word "Does" to get your marker.

         Problem   Check

                            20   (my divisor)

            7 R 18   × 7   (my quotient)

  20)158   140

    −140   +18 (my remainder)

        18   158 (my dividend)

Step 1: Daddy (divide)

       Say: DOES 20 go into 1? No! (1 is smaller than 20.)

                DOES 20 go into 15? No! (15 is smaller than 20.)

                DOES 20 go into 158? Yes! (This is the FIRST number not smaller than 20.)

Place my marker above the 8 of)158 . Like this:)15$\overline{\overline{8}}$

* COVER the number right in front of the)   and COVER the number right under the marker to ESTI-MATE.

       Say: COVER my 0 and COVER my 8.

                2 into 15 is 7.

                Put up my 7 right on my marker.

Step 2: Mommy (multiply)
    Say: 7 times 0 is 0. (Line up the 0 under my marker.)
            7 times 2 is 14. (Put my 14 right under the 15.)

Step 3: Sister (subtract)
    Say: 0 from 8 is 8.
            4 from 5 is 1.
            1 from 1 is nothing.

Step 4: Brother (bring down)
    Say: There is no number after the 158 to bring down.

Go to the Relatives.
    Say: Put up my remainder of 18.

Now, CHECK!!! The divisor times the quotient plus the remainder should equal the dividend. If it doesn't, see what's wrong and correct it.

**Make up at least seven problems just like this one. Solve each problem and write a check for each, too. Then check with your calculator.

Division of Decimals

Study Sheet

*   The divisor MUST BE or MUST BE MADE INTO a whole number.
    Examples where the divisor is already a whole number:
            7 stays 7   (There can be a decimal point after every whole number.)
            7=7.   15=15.   210=210.

    Examples where the divisor is not already a whole number:
                .6 becomes .6.   002 becomes .002.

                .32 becomes .32.   4.5 becomes 4.5.

*   Whatever you do to the divisor, you MUST also do to the dividend.
*   Put the decimal point DIRECTLY ABOVE the final resting place of the decimal point in the dividend.

    Examples: $7\overline{)1.4}$ stays $7\overline{)1.4}$

§

.6$\overline{)3.66}$ becomes .6$\overline{)3.6.6}$ (The decimal point is moved one place to the right in BOTH the divisor and the dividend.)

.32$\overline{)64}$ becomes .32.$\overline{)64.00.}$ (The decimal point is moved two places to the right in BOTH the divisor and the dividend.)

.002$\overline{)8}$ becomes .002.$\overline{)8.000.}$ (The decimal point is moved three places to the right in BOTH the divisor and the dividend.)

4.5$\overline{).9}$ becomes 4.5.$\overline{).9.0.}$ (The decimal point is moved one place to the right in BOTH the divisor and the dividend.)

16$\overline{)3.2}$ stays 16$\overline{)3.2}$. (The divisor is already a whole number. The decimal point is NOT moved at all in EITHER place!)

* After the decimal point is in its final resting point in the dividend, you may always add zeros. This would be done to make the answer come out even.

Example:	You can do this	instead of this.
Use short division whenever you can!	2.6 2.5.$\overline{)6.5.0}$	$2 \text{ R } 15$ 2.5.$\overline{)6.5.}$

* No decimal points are put in the "work" part of the problem.

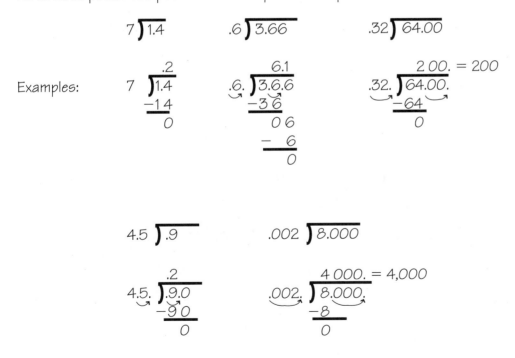

7$\overline{)1.4}$ .6$\overline{)3.66}$ .32$\overline{)64.00}$

Examples:

$$7\overline{)1.4} \quad \begin{array}{r} .2 \\ 7\overline{)1.4} \\ -1\,4 \\ \hline 0 \end{array}$$

$$\begin{array}{r} 6.1 \\ .6.\overline{)3.6.6} \\ -3\,6 \\ \hline 0\,6 \\ -\ 6 \\ \hline 0 \end{array}$$

$$\begin{array}{r} 2\,00. = 200 \\ .32.\overline{)64.00.} \\ -64 \\ \hline 0 \end{array}$$

4.5$\overline{).9}$ .002$\overline{)8.000}$

$$\begin{array}{r} .2 \\ 4.5.\overline{).9.0} \\ -9\,0 \\ \hline 0 \end{array}$$

$$\begin{array}{r} 4\,000. = 4,000 \\ .002.\overline{)8.000.} \\ -8 \\ \hline 0 \end{array}$$

* Be sure to use your division CHECK!

** Make up at least ten problems like the ones above. Solve and write a check for each. Then check again with your calculator.

Word Problems

Study Sheet

How to figure out one-step word problems:

1. There are TWO numbers in the problem. Watch out! One might be a number WORD like "three" instead of "3." Write the two numbers.

2. Decide on your mathematical operation. You have four choices: + (addition) and × (multiplication), which give higher answers; − (subtraction) and ÷ (division), which give lower answers. Do you want a higher number than the two numbers you wrote? If yes, try + or ×. If no, try − or ÷.

3. After you work the problem using +, × or −, ÷, ask yourself, "DOES THIS ANSWER MAKE SENSE?" If not, use the other operation until you get an answer that DOES!

Sample: Ron planted 25 tomato plants in each row on his farm. He had 38 rows altogether. How many tomato plants did he have?

Say: I want a higher number for his whole farm area for tomatoes.

I'll choose multiplication. 25 × 38 = 950. Does 950 plants for his farming area for tomatoes make sense? Yes!

Suppose I chose addition. 25 + 38 = 63. 63 is not nearly enough for his tomato area. In just TWO of his rows he'd have 50 plants.

Sample: Heather has 37 magazines. She gives 18 to Louis. How many magazines does Heather have now?

Say: I want a lower number. Heather will not have as many magazines now as she did before she gave some to Louis.

I'll choose subtraction. 37 − 18 = 19. Does 19 magazines for Heather make sense? Yes!

Suppose I chose division. 37 ÷ 18 = 2 R 1. Then your answer would mean there would be 2 (TWO!) magazines available for Heather. She certainly has more than two.

§

Sample: There were three hundred people at the fair on Saturday. On Sunday, there were 294. How many people were at the fair both days?

Say: I want a higher number. The answer is going to be more people than either number I have.

I'll choose addition. $300 + 294 = 594$. Does this answer make sense? Yes!

Suppose I chose multiplication. $300 \times 294 = 88{,}200$. Were there eighty-eight THOUSAND, 200 people at the fair over the weekend? No!

Sample: There were 36 students in Linda's room. She brought 110 cookies to school to be given to her classmates and to herself. Each student will get the same number of cookies. How many cookies will each student get?

Say: I want a lower number. No individual student is going to get 36 cookies and certainly not 110 cookies!

I'll choose division. $110 \div 36 = 3$ R2. Each student will be given three cookies and there will be two left over for Linda to take back home. Does THREE make sense for each student? Yes!

Suppose I chose subtraction. $110 - 36 = 74$. Each student would get 74 cookies. This is not possible because Linda only has 110 cookies with her. She'd run out of cookies on the SECOND student.

** Make up at least eight one-step word problems like these. Have at least two addition, two multiplication, two subtraction, and two division. Solve and check each problem. Be sure your answer makes sense.

Tangram Set

Trace each piece on to a piece of STURDY tag or railroad board. Do not use white. Choose red or blue or any other bold color. Cut and laminate. You'll probably want two sets.

There are lots of outlines of boats, animals, etc. that the students must fit all seven pieces into perfectly.

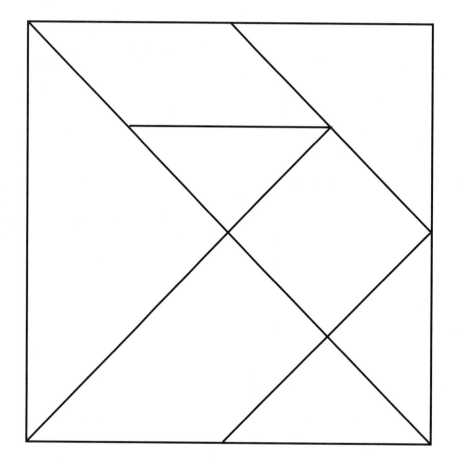

Name _____

Tangram Delight

Directions: Use all seven pieces —no more, no less —to fill in this design.

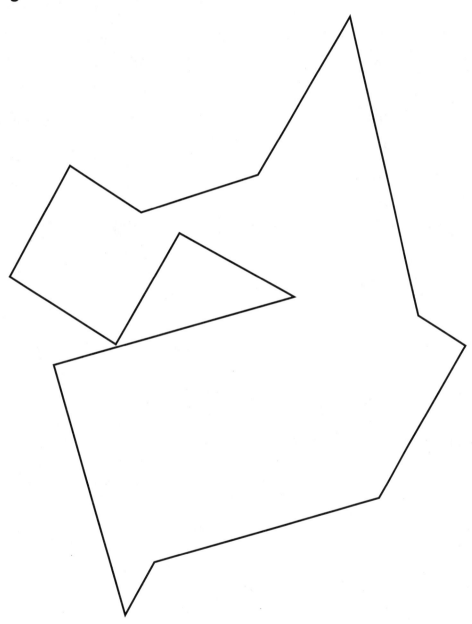

Name _____

Geoboard Problems
4 x 4's (4 by 4's)

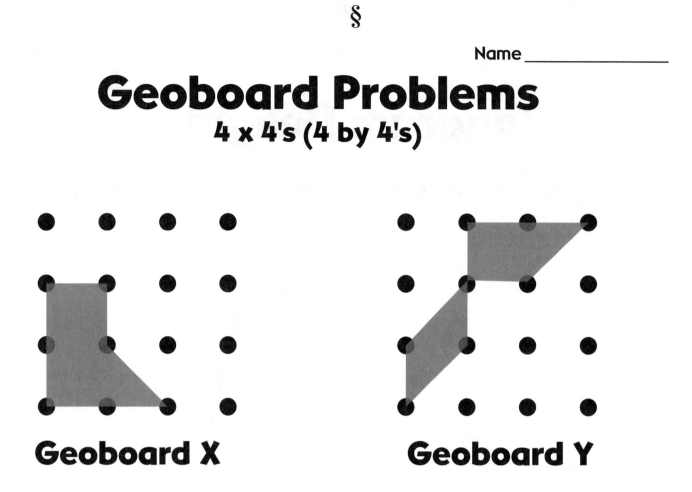

Geoboard X   **Geoboard Y**

1. Is the shaded area inside Geoboard X equal to the shaded area inside Geoboard Y?

_____

2. Write a thorough explanation of exactly how you got your answer to question 1.

_____

_____

_____

_____

_____

_____

_____

_____

_____

_____

_____

3. Now, draw two of your own 4x4 geoboards. In each one, shade in an area that is equal to the shaded area of Geoboard X, but make each shape LOOK different.

Name _____

Geoboard Problems
5 x 5's (5 by 5's)

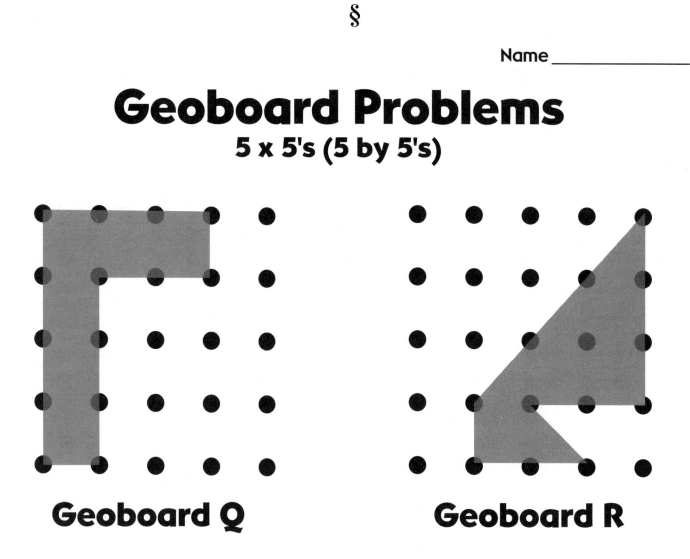

Geoboard Q   **Geoboard R**

1. Is the shaded area inside Geoboard Q equal to the shaded area inside Geoboard R?

_____

2. Write a thorough explanation of exactly how you got your answer to question 1.

_____

_____

_____

_____

_____

§

_____

_____

_____

_____

_____

_____

3. Now, draw two of your own 5x5 geoboards. In each one, shade in an area that is equal to the shaded area of Geoboard Q, but make each shape LOOK different.

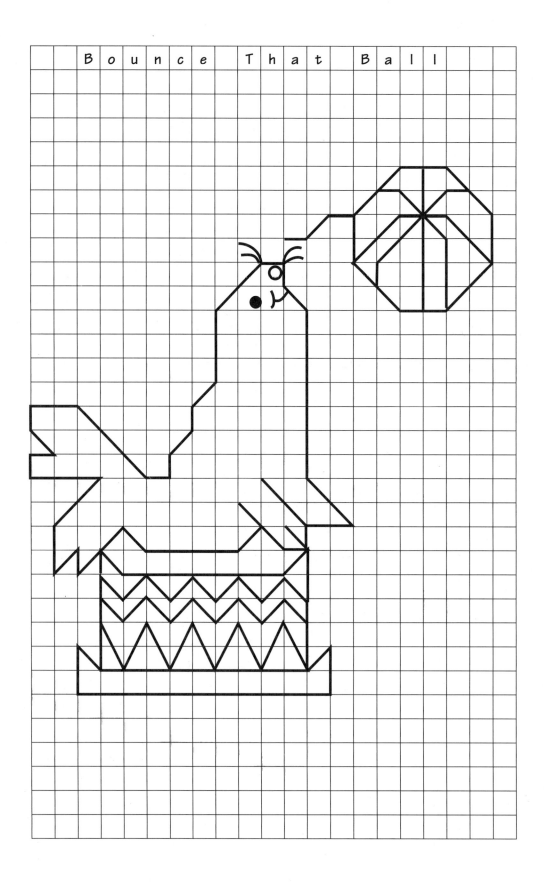

§

Math

NAME _____

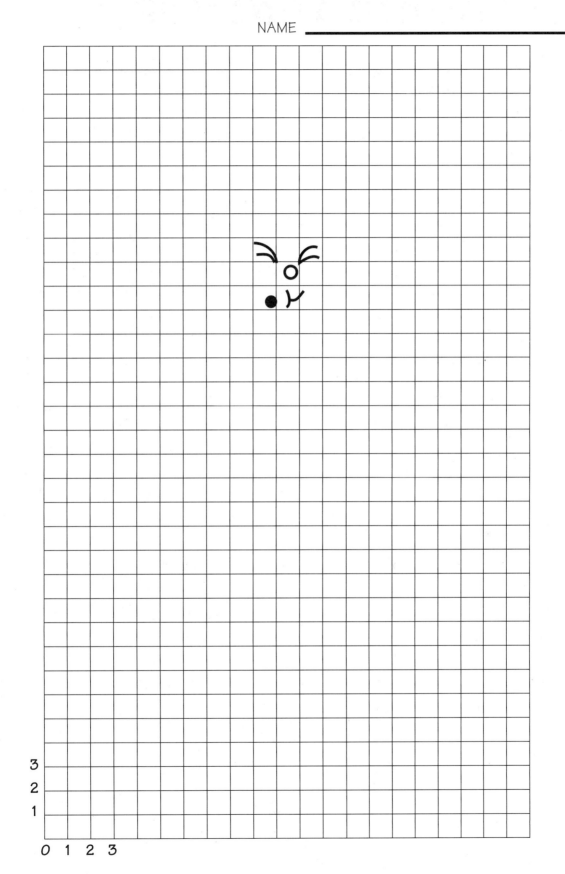

3
2
1

0 1 2 3

§

Bounce That Ball

Directions: On the piece of graph paper, number vertically on the left-hand side of the paper 0 to 30. Number horizontally across the bottom 0 to 20. The first few are done for you.

START	(12,15)	(11,9)	(14,26)
(10,24)	(12,22)	(12,7)	
(9,23)	(11,23)		STOP
(8,22)	(11,24)	STOP	(17,28)
(8,19)	(10,24)	(3,10)	(17,22)
(7,18)		(4,9)	
(7,17)	STOP	(5,10)	STOP
(6,16)	(12,13)	(6,9)	(17,26)
(6,15)	(10,15)	(7,10)	(16,27)
(5,15)		(8,9)	(15,27)
(4,16)	STOP	(9,10)	
(3,17)	(12,12)	(10,9)	STOP
(2,18)	(11,13)	(11,10)	(17,26)
(1,18)		(12,9)	(16,26)
(0,18)	STOP		(14,24)
(0,17)	(12,12)	STOP	
(1,16)	(11,12)	(3,11)	STOP
(0,16)	(10,13)	(4,10)	(17,26)
(0,15)	(9,14)	(5,11)	(15,24)
(3,15)		(6,10)	(15,23)
(2,14)	STOP	(7,11)	
(1,13)	(10,13)	(8,10)	STOP
(1,12)	(9,12)	(9,11)	(17,26)
(1,11)	(5,12)	(10,10)	(18,27)
(2,12)	(4,13)	(11,11)	(19,27)
(2,11)	(3,12)	(12,10)	
(3,12)	(4,11)		STOP
(3,7)	(11,11)	STOP	(17,26)
(2,8)	(12,12)	(11,25)	(18,26)
(2,6)		(12,25)	(20,24)
(13,6)	STOP	(13,26)	
(13,8)	(3,9)	(14,26)	STOP
(12,7)	(4,8)	(16,28)	(17,26)
(3,7)	(5,9)	(18,28)	(18,25)
	(6,7)	(20,26)	(18,22)
STOP	(7,9)	(20,24)	
(12,7)	(8,7)	(18,22)	FINISH
(12,13)	(9,9)	(16,22)	
(14,13)	(10,7)	(14,24)	

Math

Writing a One-Step Story Problem

1. Select two numbers.
2. Decide which ONE mathematical operation you'll use.

You could decide to:

(+)   ADD your two numbers together.
For example: 32   or $32.95
                  +68   +16.85

OR

(−)   SUBTRACT your smaller number from your larger one.
For example: 37   or $46.65
                  −21   − 9.91

OR

(×)   MULTIPLY your two numbers together.
For example: 13   or   23   or $3.95
                  × 3   ×24   × 2

OR

(÷)   DIVIDE your smaller number into your larger one.
For example: 2)‾14   or   30)‾150   or   5)‾$9.45

3. After you've selected your two numbers and your one mathematical operation, think about a story. It could be something about money, marbles, cookies, pizza, rows of chairs or crops, tile or carpet for a floor, pencils or candy for each student, etc.

4. Study these samples.

(+)   Cynthia deposited $12.50 in her savings account one week and $15.50 the following week. How much did she deposit altogether?

     $12.50
    +15.50
    $28.00

(−)   John had 22 marbles. He gave nine of them to Margo. How many marbles did John have left?

     22
    − 9
     13

(×)   There were 26 chairs in each row in the auditorium. Altogether there were fifteen rows. How many chairs in all?

$$\begin{array}{r} 26 \\ \times 15 \\ \hline 130 \\ 26 \\ \hline 390 \end{array}$$ chairs

(÷)   A box contained 36 pencils. They were to be divided evenly among nine students. How many pencils will each student get?

$$9\overline{)36}^{\displaystyle 4}$$

5.   End each story with a question.

(You can use larger numbers, fractions or decimals to make these problems more complex.)

Directions: Write a one-step story problem to go with the following numbers and mathematical operations. Make each of your story problems end in a question.

A.
$$\begin{array}{r} \$\ 1.48 \\ +19.36 \\ \hline \$20.84 \end{array}$$

_____

_____

_____

B.
$$\begin{array}{r} 736 \\ -\ 29 \\ \hline 707 \end{array}$$

_____

_____

_____

C.
$$\begin{array}{r} 13 \\ \times\ 21 \\ \hline 13 \\ 26 \\ \hline 273 \end{array}$$

_____

_____

_____

D. $3\overline{)636}$ 212

_____

_____

Directions: Write your very own story problems. Write one each for addition, subtraction, multiplication and division. After you write the story problem and end each in a question, solve the problems you wrote.

+   _____

_____

_____

−   _____

_____

_____

×   _____

_____

_____

÷   _____

_____

_____

§

Class Schedule

INTEGRATED LANGUAGE ARTS	8:15–10:15	M	T	W	TH	F

(Integrated Language Arts components are reading, writing with spelling and handwriting, speaking, and listening.)

MATH	10:30–11:30	M	T	W	TH	F
RESEARCH SKILLS	11:30–12:00	M				
PHYSICAL EDUCATION	11:30–12:00		T	W	TH	
FINE ARTS	11:30–12:00				F	
	and					
	1:00–2:30				F	

(Fine Arts components are music, dance, drama, and art.)

HOMEWORK—COMPOSITION BOOK	12:45–1:00	M	T	W	TH	F
COMPUTER LAB	1:00–2:30	M				

(Computer Lab involves all academic subjects as well as training in programming and word processing.)

HISTORY/SOCIAL SCIENCE	1:00–1:50		T	W	TH	
SCIENCE/HEALTH	1:50–2:30		T	W	TH	

§

Parent Information

The following information will help you understand two important areas related to grades: homework and grading periods.

Homework

Please expect your child to be doing HOMEWORK EVERY NIGHT. This will be in the form of math problems, reading assignments, book reports, history, science, research skills activities, reports, projects, studying for tests, etc. Your child should be spending plenty of time *studying for tests* at home. Test scores, as well as paragraph grades and project grades, are the ones that are averaged to determine the subject grade. Also, your child is expected to NEATLY AND TOTALLY COMPLETE all homework assignments and have them ready at school for recording on the classroom chart. If students are absent or are not completing assignments during class time, these assignments become homework for the weekend.

There is a LARGE CHART at the front of the classroom. Each assignment in every subject area is listed on the chart. If the assignment is completed and turned in, a check will be recorded after the student's name. If the student did not complete the assignment, a zero will be recorded. If the student was absent, a box will be recorded. All assignments with zeros or boxes need to be completed before the grading period closes.

Each student will be given a COMPOSITION BOOK. Each day, the student will be given class time to copy down that night's homework into the composition book. On Friday, *if* the student is up-to-date with all assignments, there is no assigned homework and the student will write this in his/her composition book and I'll sign it. Students who were absent or have overdue assignments need to copy them from the chart into their composition books. Again, I will be signing all books.

Grading Periods

Each grading period lasts approximately four weeks. A progress report will be sent home shortly after the end of half the quarter. A report card will be sent home shortly after the end of the entire quarter.

Grades will be averaged for each subject at each of these times. Your child will be receiving effort and achievement grades for the half-quarter on the progress report. When the half-quarter has arrived, no more make-up assignments for that half-quarter will be accepted, so it will help your child to stay up to date in all subject areas. Unfinished assignments can dramatically lower a course grade. Many paragraphs, projects, and papers are considered the same as a test score. If these are not turned in, zero points will be earned, dramatically lowering the grade average of that subject.

Grades will be averaged again for the second part of the quarter. These grades will be averaged with the progress report grades to determine the final report card grade for each quarter.

The student's effort grades are based on completing and turning in every assignment, as evidenced by a check on the classroom assignments chart, and studying thoroughly for tests, as evidenced by passing test scores.

§

Your child's good work habits are essential for his or her success and well-being.

I will be working hard to make this a productive year for your child.

You can help out by checking your child's composition book each night and by providing plenty of time to study for tests. Thanks!

Sincerely,

- -

Please return this bottom portion only.

I have discussed all of this information on homework and grading with my child. I understand that my child has homework each night and that he/she needs to spend plenty of time studying for tests and working on papers and projects.

_____

Parent Signature   Date

Parent Information Form on
Homework and Grading Periods

§

Areas Needing Attention

Homework   *Tests*   *Reports/Projects*

Date _____

Dear Parent of _____,

Your child is having difficulty in the following area(s), which will have an effect on his/her grades:

_____ NOT COMPLETING HOMEWORK

— Many homework assignments are corrected together as a class so students know right away if they're doing the work correctly. When students don't have their work finished, they miss out on this opportunity. Acquiring the habit of turning completed homework in on time helps develop responsibility in students.
— In addition, assignments provide the practice for the skills being learned in class. Again, students are being shortchanged if their work isn't completed.
— Furthermore, home study time is needed to be successful on tests. All students need to spend this time to do their best in all the subject areas.
— Projects and reports, paragraphs, scientific drawings, speeches, experiments, and various other activities are also a part of homework. It is important that students do their nicest, neatest, best work on these and be sure they are turned in for checking/recording.

How can you help? You can help out a lot in this area by checking your child's composition book every day and having your child complete any overdue assignments from this grading period. Thanks!

_____ NOT STUDYING HARD ENOUGH FOR TESTS

— Test scores and grades on projects, reports, compositions, paragraphs, etc. are the bulk of students' grades. If they turn in all their assignments but don't study hard to get good scores on tests, their report card grades won't be that good.

How can you help? You can help out in this area by encouraging your child to take good notes in class and to study hard for tests at home. Thanks!

§

_____ NOT SPENDING THE TIME AND EFFORT TO DO A GOOD JOB ON MAJOR REPORTS AND ACTIVITIES

— If students' reports, projects, paragraphs, compositions, scientific drawings, experiments, etc. are turned in, but *not done in an accurate way* or are not completely and thoroughly done or don't look nice and neat, it will hurt the students' grades.

How can you help? You can help in this area by having your child redo any poorly done reports, projects, compositions, drawings, etc. from this grading period. Thanks!

COMPOSITION BOOK

The children's composition books contain their daily homework assignments, information about tests, dates when projects are due, and the date grades will be closing down for each grading period. All overdue assignments are listed on Fridays. Please be checking this book regularly. Thanks!
I want your child to do the best work possible in school. Thanks for your help!

Sincerely,

- -

Please have your child return the bottom portion of this letter on the next school day.

_____   _____
Student Signature   Parent Signature

Date _____

Homework _____

Tests _____

Projects/Reports_____

PT

Midquarter Progress Report For _____ Quarter for _____

(Check means *needs improvement* in that area.)

☐ CITIZENSHIP/SOCIAL HABITS/BEHAVIOR

_____ is courteous	_____ doesn't touch others
_____ is responsible	_____ doesn't talk when not supposed to
_____ leaves work area neat	_____ follows school and playground rules
_____ demonstrates self-control	_____ follows classroom rules
_____ exhibits a positive attitude	_____ relates well to others
_____ stays at seat when required	

☐ WORK AND STUDY HABITS

_____ raises hand to speak in class	_____ pays good attention during all lessons
_____ participates well in group activities	_____ stays on-task
_____ always tries hard to do best work	_____ is showing progress
_____ works diligently to complete assignments/projects	_____ follows directions
	_____ works carefully and neatly
_____ completes homework on time	_____ is able to work well independently

☐ READING

_____ understands what is read aloud in a group	_____ understands what is read independently
_____ gets the facts	_____ reads well orally
_____ has a good vocabulary	_____ is able to draw appropriate conclusions
_____ has no letter reversals	_____ shows confidence with sight words
_____ chooses to read for enjoyment	_____ uses word attack skills
_____ completes all assignments	_____ is showing progress
_____ is able to retell a story	_____ gets the main idea

☐ WRITING (component of INTEGRATED LANGUAGE ARTS)

_____ uses appropriate spelling	_____ uses good grammar
_____ has satisfactory manuscript or cursive	_____ is able to write a sentence
_____ is able to write a story	_____ completes all assignments
_____ is showing progress	_____ uses capital letters correctly
_____ uses ending punctuation	_____ is able to write a dictated sentence

☐ SPEAKING (component of INTEGRATED LANGUAGE ARTS)

_____ speaks clearly and loudly	_____ has good eye contact
_____ uses proper grammar	_____ gives appropriate responses
_____ participates well in discussions	_____ is able to "share" or dictate a story
_____ is showing progress	

PT

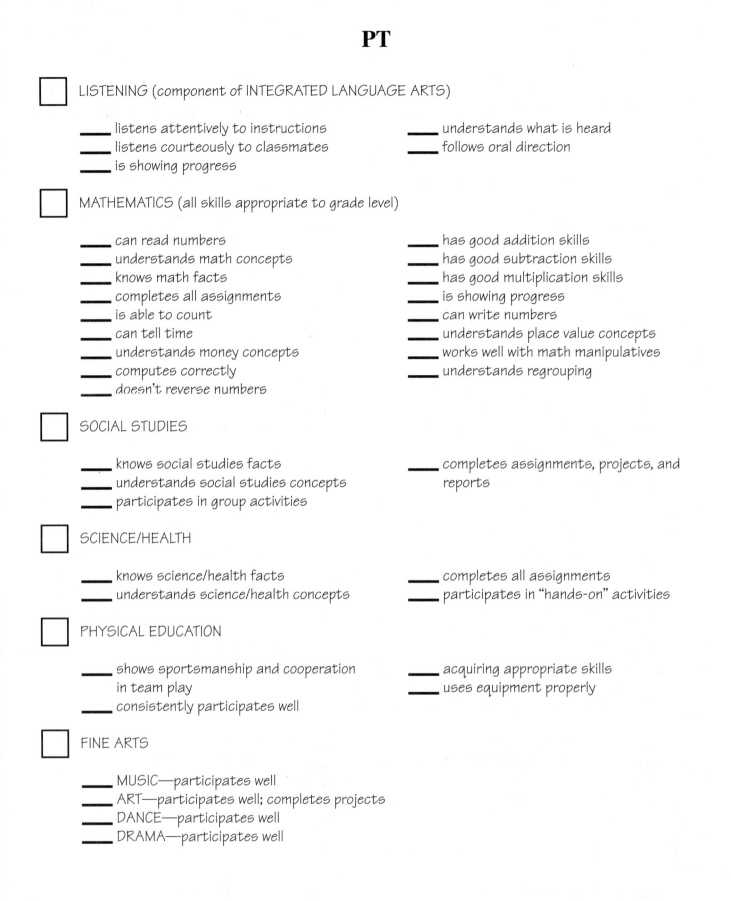

☐ LISTENING (component of INTEGRATED LANGUAGE ARTS)

_____ listens attentively to instructions _____ understands what is heard
_____ listens courteously to classmates _____ follows oral direction
_____ is showing progress

☐ MATHEMATICS (all skills appropriate to grade level)

_____ can read numbers _____ has good addition skills
_____ understands math concepts _____ has good subtraction skills
_____ knows math facts _____ has good multiplication skills
_____ completes all assignments _____ is showing progress
_____ is able to count _____ can write numbers
_____ can tell time _____ understands place value concepts
_____ understands money concepts _____ works well with math manipulatives
_____ computes correctly _____ understands regrouping
_____ doesn't reverse numbers

☐ SOCIAL STUDIES

_____ knows social studies facts _____ completes assignments, projects, and
_____ understands social studies concepts reports
_____ participates in group activities

☐ SCIENCE/HEALTH

_____ knows science/health facts _____ completes all assignments
_____ understands science/health concepts _____ participates in "hands-on" activities

☐ PHYSICAL EDUCATION

_____ shows sportsmanship and cooperation _____ acquiring appropriate skills
in team play _____ uses equipment properly
_____ consistently participates well

☐ FINE ARTS

_____ MUSIC—participates well
_____ ART—participates well; completes projects
_____ DANCE—participates well
_____ DRAMA—participates well

PT

Midquarter Progress Report For _____ Quarter for _____

Any check means NEEDS IMPROVEMENT in that area.

☐ CITIZENSHIP AND SOCIAL HABITS

_____ is courteous
_____ is responsible
_____ leaves work area neat
_____ demonstrates self control
_____ follows classroom rules
_____ exhibits a positive attitude
_____ relates well to others

_____ doesn't touch others
_____ doesn't talk when not supposed to
_____ has few/no marks on the behavior chart
_____ behaves well at assemblies
_____ does not throw anything in the classroom
_____ stays at seat as required

☐ WORK and STUDY HABITS

_____ raises hand to speak in class
_____ participates well in group activities
_____ always tries hard to do best work
_____ works diligently to complete assignments/projects
_____ consistently turns in completed homework on time
_____ is able to work well independently after regular assignments are completed
_____ studies thoroughly for tests

_____ pays good attention during all lessons
_____ doesn't waste time
_____ is showing progress
_____ doesn't have excessive absences
_____ arrives at school on time
_____ assignments are well prepared
_____ always has books and materials at class
_____ follows directions quickly
_____ works carefully and neatly

☐ RESEARCH SKILLS

_____ understands library organization
_____ understands use of dictionary and encyclopedia
_____ knows parts of a book and their uses
_____ earns passing test scores

_____ is able to gather information from graphs, tables, and charts
_____ completes all assignments

☐ READING (component of INTEGRATED LANGUAGE ARTS)

_____ understands what is read independently
_____ gets the main idea
_____ gets the facts
_____ reads well orally
_____ has a good vocabulary
_____ is able to draw appropriate conclusions
_____ has passing scores on comprehension tests

_____ has passing scores on vocabulary tests
_____ chooses to read for enjoyment
_____ uses word attack skills
_____ uses context clues for meaning
_____ completes all assignments
_____ is showing progress

§

☐ WRITING (component of INTEGRATED LANGUAGE ARTS)

____ uses correct spelling
____ uses good grammar
____ proofreads and corrects work
____ has letter writing skills
____ has good sentence writing—
(well developed, expressive)
____ earns passing scores on tests
____ has satisfactory handwriting

____ has neat final copy
____ good use of capitalization
____ good use of punctuation
____ writes satisfactory
paragraphs/compositions
____ uses writing process
____ completes all assignments
____ is showing progress

☐ SPEAKING (component of INTEGRATED LANGUAGE ARTS)

____ speaks clearly and loudly
____ uses proper grammar
____ participates well in discussions
____ is showing progress

____ has good eye contact
____ gives appropriate response
____ completes all assignments
____ has passing scores on oral reports

☐ LISTENING (component of INTEGRATED LANGUAGE ARTS)

____ listens attentively to instructions
____ listens courteously to classmates
____ is showing progress

____ understands and follows directions
____ earns passing scores on listening tests

☐ MATHEMATICS

____ has knowledge of and speed with basic
math facts
____ has good calculator skills
____ understands math concepts
____ uses computation checking skills for
accuracy
____ is able to solve word problems
____ completes all assignments

____ has good addition skills
____ good subtraction skills
____ good multiplication skills
____ good division skills
____ good fractions skills
____ good geometry skills
____ earns passing test scores
____ is showing progress

☐ HISTORY/SOCIAL SCIENCES

____ understands history facts and concepts
____ understands geography facts and concepts
____ earns passing test scores

____ reads and interprets maps
____ completes all assignments, projects, and
reports

§

☐ SCIENCE/HEALTH

___ understands science/health facts
and concepts
___ understands scientific method

___ completes all assignments
___ earns passing test scores

☐ PHYSICAL EDUCATION

___ shows sportsmanship and cooperation
in team play

___ is willing to practice appropriate skills
___ consistently participates well

☐ FINE ARTS

___ MUSIC—participates well and earns passing test scores
___ ART—participates well and turns in completed projects
___ DANCE—participates well and learns routines for performance
___ DRAMA—participates well and learns part for productions

§ Progress Report Confirmation Form

Please discuss this progress report with your child and return this page with your child's signature and your signature.

Please remember that your child should be doing homework every night. It is most important that your child keep up-to-date with all assignments. Each assignment not turned in results in three points deducted from the final subject grade; consequently, it is vitally important that each and every assignment is completed and turned in for recording.

The effort grade is based on completing and turning in every assignment, turning in completed work on time, studying thoroughly for tests (as evidenced by test grades), participation in class and small group discussions, and demonstrating the ability to work independently when class assignments are completed.

O	= Outstanding	N	= Needs improvement
S+	= Good	S−	= Poor
S	= Satisfactory; fair	U	= Unsatisfactory; very poor

The achievement grade is based on the average of tests, projects, paragraphs and compositions. The grade average will stand unless it is affected by the deduction of points due to incomplete assignments.

A+	= 100 average	C+	= 79
A	= 91–99	C	= 71–78
A−	= 90	C−	= 70
B+	= 89	D+	= 69
B	= 81–88	D	= 61–68
B−	= 80	D−	= 60
		F	= 59 and below

Your cooperation and support in matters of your child's work and behavior are always appreciated. Cooperative and supportive parents let children know that parents expect good work and good behavior.

I will be working hard to make this a happy, successful, and productive quarter for your child.

_____
Teacher's Signature

- -

This progress report was sent home on _____ .

_____   _____
Student Signature   Parent Signature

§

Classroom Management

Date _____

Dear Parent(s),

   It is with pleasure that I welcome your child to my class. We can all look forward to a very exciting and rewarding school year.

   In order to provide my students with the excellent educational climate they deserve, I have developed the following Classroom Management Plan that will be in effect at all times.

Rules:

1. Line up quickly and quietly at the bell and enter the room quietly.
2. Stay in your seat.
3. Stay quiet.
4. Stay busy at all times.
5. Follow directions quickly.
6. Act in a polite, respectful manner to all. (No touching, hitting, poking, shoving, name calling, making rude remarks/gestures, or using a sarcastic/hurtful tone of voice.)
7. Never throw anything in the classroom.
8. Leave work areas neat and tidy.
9. Do not get a school citation, referral, or suspension.

Positive Reinforcement:

1. At the end of each grading period, if your child has earned an excellent grade for Social Habits/Citizenship on his/her progress report or report card, he/she will receive an award certificate.

2. Each week that your child has no marks on the behavior chart, he/she will be able to participate in a classroom lottery.

Negative Consequences

1. If your child breaks a rule, the rule number is recorded in a box by his/her name under that day's date on a classroom behavior chart. Several numbers or repeats of the same number could appear in the same box for one day. A box with a mark in it will disqualify your child from participating in that week's classroom lottery.

2. If your child acquires fifteen poor behavior marks during a grading period (4–5 weeks), a behavior contract will be completed, identifying the exact areas in which this student is having difficulty. The behavior contract will be sent home for you to sign.

3. If your child continues to misbehave after the contract has been sent home, he/she will be issued a school citation.

4. The social habits grade on your child's report card will be based on the behavior chart. If there are a lot of marks, there will be a poor grade.

5. Severe Clause: In the face of any extremely poor or dangerous behavior, the student will be issued a school citation.

It will help if you let your child know that you expect excellent behavior at school. It will also help if you check with your child frequently about behavior in the classroom. Ask if your child has marks after his/her name, what the mark numbers are, and how many marks there are. This will be a big help. Thanks!

It is in your child's best interest that we work together with regard to his/her behavior. I will keep you informed about your child's behavior in my class by recording the week's total marks from the behavior chart into his/her composition book each Friday.

I have already discussed this plan with your child, but I'd appreciate it if you would review it with him/her before signing and returning the form below.

Thank you for your support.

Sincerely,

I've read your Classroom Management Plan and discussed it with my child.

_____

Parent(s)/Guardian Signature

_____

Child's Name   Date

§

Area Needing Attention Behavior

Date _____

Dear Parent of _____,

    Your child is experiencing difficulty with the appropriate behavior needed to follow the class rules, so that the school days will run smoothly for everyone. A check in front of any of the numbers means that's the area of difficulty. If any asterisk is circled, it means extra special attention needs to be given to that item.

_____ 1. LINING UP

      * not lining up quickly and quietly
      * talking in line
      * throwing/tossing/dribbling playground equipment in line
      * touching or hanging on other students
      * acting up in line to show off
      * calling out to other students
      * being rude or mean to other students lining up

_____ 2. STAYING IN SEAT

      * not staying in seat when supposed to
      * roaming around the classroom

_____ 3. NOT TALKING

      * talking in the classroom
      * making disruptive noises
      * calling another student's name
      * creating noise by acting up or trying to show off

_____ 4. STAYING BUSY

      * not willing to stay busy, but has plenty of work to get done
      * daydreaming, sitting doing nothing, but has plenty of work to get done

§

_____ 5. FOLLOWING DIRECTIONS

* not following directions QUICKLY; consequently, holding up and interrupting the class

_____ 6. BEING POLITE AND RESPECTFUL

* not being polite to an adult; speaking in a sarcastic way; showing a defiant, angry, or sullen attitude; talking back
* not being polite to other students
* not keeping hands and feet to self

_____ 7. NOT THROWING ANYTHING

* throwing pencils or pencil pieces, crayons or crayon pieces, paper or spit wads, etc.

_____ 8. CLEANING UP

* not willing to clean up when finished at desk, sink area, or table area
* at end of day, books, pencils or paper left out
* trash left on floor under desk

I would appreciate your having a talk with your child. When your child follows the rules, it helps him/her to feel better, more confident, and more successful. It also helps the other students learn better and be in a pleasant environment with minimal interruptions.

Please check with your child every day about his/her behavior in the classroom. Please ask how many times his/her name was down so you'll know the specifics. I will appreciate all your help in this matter. Thanks!

Sincerely,

- -

Please have your child return the bottom portion of this letter on the next school day. Thanks!

_____

Student Signature   Parent Signature

Date _____
Area Needing Attention
Behavior

Behavior Contract

Student's Name

I have earned _____ recordings of inappropriate behavior on the behavior chart in the past _____ days. I will improve my behavior by doing the following:

_____

_____

_____

I understand that this contract will be sent home to my parents. I also understand that if my behavior is not improved, then I will be issued a school citation.

_____   _____
Parent Signature   Student Signature

(PLEASE have your child return this contract to school. Thanks!)

Behavior Improvement Contract

STUDENT'S NAME

    I have been working hard to improve my behavior. My classroom behavior is now significantly better. As a result of my effort, I will now be able to do the following:

_____

_____

_____

_____

Student Signature   Parent Signature

Date _____

Citizenship

This Award Is Given to

_____

for Excellence in Citizenship

_____   _____

Teacher's Signature   Date

PT §
School Citation

Date _____

PARENTS:

Your child, _____ , has received this citation during

_____ for the following infraction(s):

___ Abusive or disrespectful language
___ Rude to other students
___ Improper use of playground equipment
___ Throwing food, dirt, sand, rocks, etc.
___ Not following the directions of adults
___ Not putting trash in the trash can

___ Writing or saying swear words
___ Playing or drinking after the bell
___ Disregarding bicycle rules
___ Tackling, fighting, roughhousing
___ Continued poor behavior in class
___ Other _____

Comments:

_____

_____

Citation given by: _____

Homeroom teacher: _____

- -

We request that you emphasize to your child the importance of good behavior. The following course of action was/will be taken at school:

___ Benched at recess on _____
___ Benched during lunch on _____
___ Benched recess and lunch on _____
___ 30 sentences to be written about correcting misbehavior

___ Benched for 3 days on _____
___ Sent to the principal
___ After school detention on _____
___ Other _____

Please sign and return this citation on the next school day.

_____
Parent's Signature

A copy of this citation will be given to the principal and the homeroom teacher.

A Special Note
About Someone Special

This note is to let you know that your child,

_____ , has done especially

fine work in_____

_____

Congratulations!

_____

Teacher's Signature

Substitute Teacher

Dear Substitute,

Welcome to this classroom!

Adult classroom helper: _____

Responsible student helpers: _____

The following ** RULES ** are those I use with this class:

1. Line up quickly and quietly at the bell and enter the room quietly.
2. Stay in your seat.
3. Stay quiet.
4. Stay busy at all times.
5. Follow directions quickly.
6. Act in a polite, respectful manner to all.
7. Never throw anything in the classroom.
8. Leave work areas neat and tidy.
9. Do not get a school citation, referral, or suspension.

These rules are also posted on the bulletin board by the flag.

If a student breaks a rule, please write his or her name down below with the rule number beside it. If that student breaks a rule again, just put the number down again after his or her name.

Example: Beatrice 3

Blake 2,4

Also, ** MATERIALS ** you might need can be found in the file cabinets in the back of the room labeled by subject, in the labeled boxes and binders stored in the cabinet, and in the files by the large classroom assignment chart.

If you have any trouble with lesson plans, you can use materials for ** SEAT WORK ** located in the cabinet in a box labeled "Substitute Teacher Seat Work." These materials are already reproduced and ready for use. Answer keys are included.

Have a good day! Thanks for your help!

Sincerely,

<u>DATE</u>   <u>NAME</u>   Comments

Lesson Plans

Teacher's Name _____

Grade _____

Room # _____

Recess Time(s) _____

Lunch Time _____

Special Event _____

Dismissal Time(s) _____

Language Arts—Read the first five pages of the next story in your reader.

1. Make up and write five questions for the part of the story you read. Write answers for your own questions.
2. Are there any words on the five pages you didn't know? If yes, write these words on your paper. If no, write No after #2.
3. Write about the part of the story you liked best. Tell all about it. Tell why you liked it.
4. Draw a picture to go with your favorite part of the story. Color it nicely.
5. List ten things that happened in this part of the story.
6. Tell about one of the characters.

Math

1. Make up twenty addition problems that are good and hard for you. Solve each problem.
2. Write three addition word problems and solve them. For example: Cindy has 15 baseball cards. Doug has 14. How many cards do Cindy and Doug have altogether.

$$\begin{array}{r} 15 \\ +14 \\ \hline 29 \end{array}$$

3. If you would like to, and you know how to subtract, you may make up ten good subtraction problems and find their answers.

PE—Play dodgeball.
   What to work on today:

1. Throw the ball low so that it doesn't hit a classmate in the head.
2. While you're playing, practice saying nice things to your classmates, like "Good try, Jimmy," "Good shot, Roberta," "Good throw, Luis," etc.

PT §

Printing—Today is practice printing only.

1. In your best printing, write each of these words five times:

home	school	playing	friend
because	breakfast	lunch	dinner
teacher	classroom	pencil	paper

2. Write your name five times in your best printing.

Social Studies

1. Pick one thing you've learned in social studies. Write all you can about it. Spell as best as you can.
2. Then draw a picture to go with your writing. Make your paper look nice and neat. Color it beautifully.
   If you can't think of something, you may write on one of these: school, neighborhood, firefighters, or police officers.

Science

1. Pick something you learned in science. Make a list of five things you know about it. Spell as best as you can.
2. Draw a picture to go with your list. Color it so it looks great.
   If you can't think of something, you may write on one of these: an animal, an ocean, a lake, a river, flowers, plants, trees, or weather (rain, snow, fog, hot days, and cold days).

Lesson Plans

§

Teacher's Name _____

Grade _____

Room # _____

Recess Time(s) _____

Lunch Time _____

Special Event _____

Dismissal Time(s) _____

Language Arts—Read the next story in your reader.

1. Make up and write ten *challenging* questions for the story. Have some *who* questions, some *what* questions, some *where* questions, some *when* questions, some *why* questions (the 5 W's), and some *how* questions. Write the answers to your questions.
2. Write five words from the story that you don't see a lot (or maybe have never seen before). Write the definition of each word.
3. Select the part of the story you liked best. Write one or two paragraphs telling about that part of the story and why you liked it.
4. On *unlined paper*, draw a picture to go with your paragraphs. Color the picture nicely.
5. Make up and write a totally different ending to the story.
6. On *unlined paper*, draw a picture that shows your new ending. Color it nicely.
7. Write a letter to a real or make-believe pen pal. Tell your pen pal all about some exciting thing that happened to you or some exciting thing that you did. You may make it up if you'd like. Be sure to brainstorm first. Write down all of your thoughts about this exciting thing on scratch paper. Select the most interesting parts to write about. Then write your rough draft. Next, proofread it and revise it so it's entertaining and fun to read. Finally, write your final copy. Be sure it's in friendly letter format: date, Dear Pen Pal, Your friend, and your name. Decorate the top, bottom, right-hand, and left-hand margins of your paper so it looks sharp.

Math

1. *Make up ten addition problems, ten subtraction problems, and ten multiplication problems that are challenging for you. Solve each problem. If you're good at division, you may make up four division problems and solve them.*
2. Write three addition *word* problems, three subtraction *word* problems, and three multiplication *word* problems that are challenging for you. Solve the problems.
3. *If you would like to, you may make a 4×4 magic number square. Each "across," each "down," and the upper left to lower right diagonal should equal 43.*

PE—Two teams for kickball. Two "strikes" and you're out. Two outs per team per inning.
  What to work on today:

1. When you're outfield, try to get the ball into the pitcher as fast as you can.
2. When your team is up, practice saying nice, encouraging things to your teammates, like "Good job!," "Good try!," "Great kick!," etc.

Handwriting

1. In your best handwriting, write each capital letter twice.
2. In your best handwriting, write each small letter twice.
3. In your best handwriting, write as many words as you can make from the following phrase:
    that cute little brown dog by school
    Your words can be one letter long, two letters long, three, and up. You may use names. Don't use any letters that aren't in the phrase.

Social Studies/Science
If it is a social studies day, use the social studies text.
If it is a science day, use the science text.

1. Read four to six consecutive pages of interest to you toward the back of your social studies book.
2. Use at least eight social studies words to make your own word search. Then find and circle your words.
3. Write the definition for each word in your word search.
4. On a separate piece of paper, write the page numbers you've read. then make up five hard questions and write the down. DO NOT write down the answers, but study the answers so you'll know them perfectly. At recess, lunch, or after school, give the paper to a friend and see if he or she can find and write down the answers to your questions. When your friend is finished, check his or her answers to be sure they're correct.
5. Write ten "Who am I?" or "What am I?" questions covering the material you've just read. Make them good questions. Write the answers on the back of your paper and then practice so you know the answers quickly.

Name _____

Reading

Reading

Name of the story _____

Story Map

Characters (Who's in the story?) _____

_____

_____

Setting (Where and when does the story take place? Example: on the farm in the summer)

_____

_____

Major events (big things that happen in the story)

1. _____

2. _____

3. _____

4. _____

5. _____

Ending _____

_____

_____

How did you like the story? Why? _____

_____

Name _____

Reading

Reading

Name of the story _____

Quote

Copy a small part of the story that you liked. Copy it into the box.

—————————————————
—————————————————
—————————————————
—————————————————

Now, write what's happening in that part of the story and why you liked it. Use the lines below.

_____

_____

_____

_____

Reading

Writing

Name of the story _____

Be sure you've already read the story.

Double Entry Journal

Pick something that happened in the story. Write three things about it.

1. _____

_____

_____

2. _____

_____

_____

3. _____

_____

_____

Pick something that happened in your life. Write three things about it.

1. _____

_____

_____

2. _____

_____

_____

3. _____

_____

_____

§ Reading

MARGINALIA

Reading

Name of the reading story: _____

As you begin to read your story:

Do *marginalia* for the first three pages of your story. Drawings, words, phrases, questions, and sentences are all fine.

When you've finished reading your story, do the following activities:

Story Map

Main characters: _____

Setting (where, when): _____

Problem of the story: _____

Major events of the story: _____

1. _____

2. _____

3. _____

4. _____

5. _____

Solution to the problem of the story: _____

_____

Personal Reaction (What do you think about the story? How did it make you feel? Does it remind you of something in your own life?)

_____

_____

_____

_____

§ Venn Diagram

Select from the story two things or persons or animals that are alike in some ways. Then fill in the Venn Diagram. Give each circle a title. Write each title on the line above the circle.

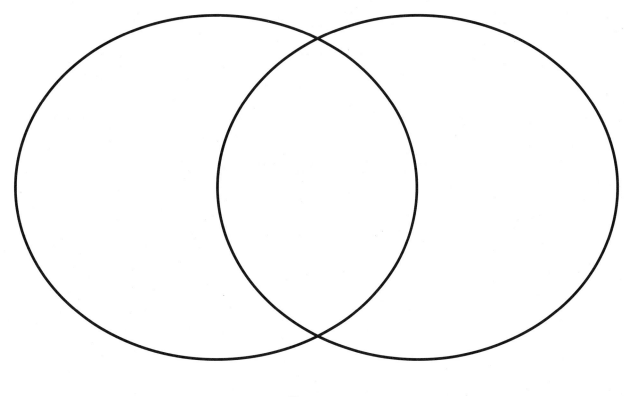

Quote

Copy from the story one or two lines that you find especially interesting. Copy them in the box below.

PT §

On the lines below, write what the quote means to you and why you chose it.

_____

_____

_____

_____

_____

Picture Explanation

Draw a picture about something that happened in the story or article.

WRITE an explanation of your picture.

Include:
- time and place of the picture
- character(s) and/or event(s)
- details of what's taking place
- why the picture is important in the story or article
- why you selected your picture

_____

_____

_____

_____

_____

§ Julius Caesar

Julius Caesar lived from *circa* 100 B.C. to 44 B.C. The word *circa* is used because that long ago, more than 2,000 years ago, accurate records were not always kept.

Julius Caesar was a famous military leader and helped make Rome the center of a huge empire. Today Rome is the capital of Italy, on the continent of Europe.

Caesar was also very skilled as an orator, a person who makes public speeches often on topics relating to government. His most famous speech to the Roman Senate to let it know he had just conquered another land (present day Turkey) was, in Latin: *Veni, vidi, vici.* Translated this means "I came, I saw, I conquered."

Caesar's power and military strength were unbelievable. He chased one of his opponents all the way to Egypt (on the continent of Africa). Once he arrived in Egypt, though, Caesar discovered his opponent, Pompey, had already been murdered.

While in Egypt, Caesar fell in love with Cleopatra and made her ruler of that land.

Unfortunately, some people within the Roman Empire were afraid of Caesar's power. On March 15 (the Ides of March), Brutus and Cassius stabbed Caesar to death.

Julius Caesar Worksheet

Vocabulary

Find the story and write the *one* word that means:

1. public speaker (paragraph 3) _____

2. well known (2) _____

3. restated in another language (3) _____

4. difficult to understand (4) _____

5. large land mass (2) _____

6. enemies (4) _____

7. practiced (3) _____

§

Locating details in the story

1. What does "Veni, vidi, vici" mean? _____

_____

2. Name a country in Africa. _____

3. Around when did Caesar live? _____

4. Name three of Caesar's enemies. _____

_____   _____

5. Who did Caesar make ruler of Egypt? _____

6. Name one country in Europe. _____

7. How was Caesar killed? _____

8. What happened to Pompey? _____

9. What is the capital of Italy? _____

Main ideas
1. Who was Julius Caesar?

2. Why was he killed?

3. Why did Caesar give a speech to the Senate?

4. What was Caesar's greatest accomplishment?

Drawing Conclusions
1. Do you think Caesar was romantic? Why or why not?

2. Do you think the word *circa* would be used to tell peoples' dates of birth who are living today? Why or why not?

NAME _____

Portfolio Evaluation for Reading

A. One thing I have improved on is _____

_____

_____

B. One thing I would like to do better is to be able to _____

_____

_____

_____

How will I do this? _____

1. _____

_____

2. _____

_____

3. _____

C. Overall, I think my work in this area is _____

_____

Comments: _____

_____

_____

Dear Parents,

The following items are information I would like for your child to include in an animal report. He/she may write on any wild animal—fish, amphibian, reptile, bird, or mammal. For references, he/she may use an encyclopedia or a library book. The report will be due by _____ (or may be brought in earlier).

Sincerely,

- -

Animal Report

1. What is the name of the animal?

2. What does the animal look like?

3. How big is the animal?

4. Where does the animal live? (in a tree, in a burrow, in the water, in a bush, in the desert)

5. In what country (or what continent) does the animal live?

6. What does the animal eat?

7. What does the animal do?

8. Is there something special about your animal?

9. What is the name of the book you used for your report?

10. Draw a picture of the animal.

Each child will share the report with the rest of the class.

Courtesy of Jan Bader

§

State Report

1. Get information about your state from at least TWO different sources. For example, use a library book and an encyclopedia. Magazines and travel brochures are great for pictures.

2. Take notes. Jot down ideas as you look at the encyclopedia and the library book or magazine. DO NOT COPY. Use your own words. Notes do not need to be in sentences. Organize your notes by paragraph topics.

3. When you've finished your notes, begin writing the report in your best handwriting. Write on ONE SIDE of each paper only. Use the following format:

COVER: Print the title of your report at the top of your cover. Have a drawing of your state. Have two or three pictures/drawings of interesting things about your state inside the drawing of your state. Or you can use the state report cover that comes with this geography unit. Color everything nicely. Use felt pens or colored pencils for a great look. Print your first and last name at the bottom right-hand corner. Your cover should be VERY NEAT.

Page 1: Page 1 is the title page.
Write the name of your report toward the top of the page and center the title.
At the bottom of the page, in the center, write your first and last name. Right below that, write STATE REPORT and right under STATE REPORT, write the date.
Your title page should be nice and neat.

Pages 2–4 : Write the name of your report at the top of page 2.
Skip a line.
Begin writing your report. INDENT for each paragraph.
Include the following in your paragraphs:
1st Par. —Write about the history of your state. Include when it was admitted to the Union. Include any important historical events that occurred in your state. Include any important battles, famous people born there, etc.
2nd Par.—Explain the government of your state. Write about the executive, legislative, and judicial branches of your state's government.
3rd Par.—Write what your state is like. Include information about the climate, population, location, lakes, mountains, national parks, and any other unusual geographic features.
4th Par.—Write about the big cities and the interesting cities. Include the state capital. Write a little about each of the cities you name.
5th Par. & 6th Par.—Write some interesting and fun things to do in your state and some fun places to visit.

§

Concluding Par.—Write two or three sentences about your state being important, being a nice place to live and being a place of interest and beauty. These are just suggestions. Use your imagination.

This section should take about three pages. DO NOT COPY from any book or magazine or brochure. Use your own words. PROOFREAD carefully for spelling, capitalization, indenting, punctuation, complete sentences, great handwriting and neatness.

Page 5:   The title of this page should be your state's name followed by a dash and its nickname. Draw pictures of your state's flag, seal, and flower. Label each. Color the pictures. Write the state motto and the name of the state song.

Pages 6 & 7:   Put a title at the top of page 6. (Examples: Interesting Places in Arizona or Exciting Times in New York). Neatly glue or paste pictures or draw some pictures about things or places in your state. Each picture should have a CAPTION.

Page 8:   Put the title of your state at the top of this page. Then draw a map of your state. Include the names of lakes, rivers, mountains, bays, capes, important cities, and the state capital. Color neatly.

Pages 9 & 10:   Make a *vertical bar graph* to show how many U.S. representatives your state has as compared with four other states. Next, make a *line graph* to show population in your state for five consecutive census years. Then, make a table to show average temperature and precipitation in your state for any three months of the year. (See examples.)

All graphs, tables, etc. should have a capitalized title and labels for both the horizontal and vertical axes.

§

Vertical Bar Graph

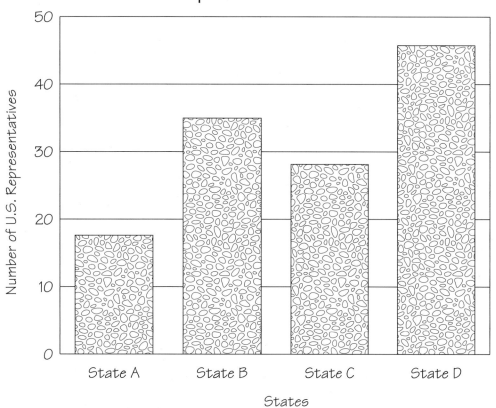

U.S. Representatives in Four States

Page 11: A bibliography is a list of the books, periodicals (magazines), and encyclopedias used for your report.

On lined paper, in the center of the first line, write the word *Bibliography*. Skip a line. Now begin your list. First, list your books, next your periodicals, and last your encyclopedia articles. You can use the sample format. Notice the indentation on the SECOND line of *each* entry (third line too if you need a third line). Notice the title of articles in magazines and encyclopedias are capitalized and in quotation marks. Notice the names of books, magazines, and encyclopedias are capitalized and underlined.

§

Bibliography

Smith, John B. <u>Norway, Land of the Midnight Sun,</u> New York: Macmillan, 1988.

   (The above is your library book entry, with the author's name, title of book, publishing city, publisher, and copyright date.)

Ward, Stuart. "The Excitement of Niagara Falls," <u>The Reader's Digest,</u> CLIV (September, 1993, 36–42).

   (The above is your periodical (magazine) entry with the author's name, the name of the article, the name of the magazine, the volume number, the month and year of the magazine, and the page numbers the article is on.)

"China," <u>The World Book Encyclopedia.</u> 1988 ed., Vol. 3.

   (The above entry is your encyclopedia article. The "ed." stands for "edition" or copyright date. "Vol." stands for the volume number, if there is one.)

margin

margin

PROOFREAD everything in the report for CORRECTNESS and NEATNESS. FASTEN your report together carefully and neatly.

Your report is due on: _____

§

Line Graph

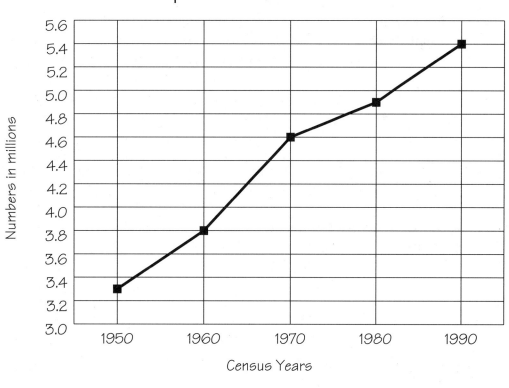

Population Information for State X

Hint: Use 2.4 for 2,406,018.
         Use 3.9 for 3,918,768.
         Use 22.8 for 22,806,395.

Table

Weather in State Z

Month	Low Temp.	High Temp.	Rain/Snow Days
April	35°F	59°F	2
August	51°F	78°F	0
December	−2°F	35°F	4

§ A Country Report

1. Select a country about which you're interested in learning a lot. You might select Germany, Canada, France, Brazil, or China. Maybe it will be a country where a relative or friend lives. It might be a country from which your parents, grandparents, or great-grandparents came.

2. Get information about your country from at least TWO different sources. For example, use a library book and an encyclopedia. Magazines and brochures are great for pictures. Almanacs are of interest, too.

3. Take notes. Jot down ideas as you look at the encyclopedia and the library book. DO NOT COPY. Use your own words. Notes do not need to be in sentences.

4. When you've finished your notes, begin writing the report. Write a rough draft first. Then, after you've proofread and made changes, write your final copy in your BEST handwriting. Write on ONE SIDE of each paper only. Use the following format:

    COVER: Print the title of your report at the top of your cover. Have a nice, well-done drawing, maybe an outline of your country or some interesting places or things in your country. Color the picture or drawing nicely in markers or colored pencils for a great look. Write your first and last name at the bottom right-hand corner. Look at your cover to be sure it's nice and neat.

    Page 1:   Page 1 is the title page. Write the name of your report toward the top of the page and center the title. At the bottom of the page, in the center, write your first and last name. Right below that, write the words, "Country Report." Right under that, write the date. Your title page should be nice and neat.

    Pages 2–5:   Write the name of your report at the top of page 2. Skip a line. Begin writing your report. Indent for a new paragraph when you change TOPICS. There will probably be at least seven paragraphs in this section. Include information about the following TOPICS: country's location; population and kind of people; history and government; climate; natural features, such as lakes, rivers, mountains, etc.; major cities, including the capital and interesting information about these cities; and special places to visit in your country. PROOFREAD CAREFULLY for writing on one side of the paper only; writing complete sentences; indenting for EACH new paragraph (maybe seven indentations); using correct spelling, capitalization, and punctuation; and using excellent, neat handwriting.

    Page 6:   On a piece of UNLINED paper, draw a map of your country. Label the natural features, like the rivers, lakes, mountains, capes, and bays. Label three or four of the major cities, including the capital. Label any unusual places to visit. Color everything neatly. Proofread your labels for correctness.

    Pages 7–8:   On unlined paper, NEATLY mount pictures or make drawings of interesting places in your country. Write a BRIEF caption under each picture to explain what it is. Color if you need to. PROOFREAD your captions. This section may be longer if you have lots of drawings or pictures.

    Pages 9–10:   Pick two areas (like lowlands and highlands) of your country, or two cities in your country. Then pick two areas or two cities in any other country. Make a combination vertical bar and line graph to show their average precipitation (rain, snow, etc.) and

§

low (or high) temperatures. Next, select four cities within your country, or one city in your country and three other cities, each in different countries. Make a table to compare their populations. Then, make a pie graph to represent the division of your country's population [percent (%) in urban (city) areas, percent in rural (country, farmland) areas]. All graphs and tables should have titles capitalized and labels clearly written. See examples.

Page 11:   A bibliography is a list of the books, periodicals (magazines), and encyclopedias used for your report.

On lined paper, in the center of the first line, write the word *Bibliography*. Skip a line. Now begin your list. First, list your books, next your periodicals, and last your encyclopedia articles. You can use the sample format below. Notice the indentation on the SECOND line of *each* entry (third line too if you need a third line). Notice the title of articles in magazines and encyclopedias are capitalized and in quotation marks. Notice the names of books, magazines, and encyclopedias are capitalized and underlined.

---

margin

Bibliography

Smith, John B. Norway, Land of the Midnight Sun, New York: Macmillan, 1988.

(The above is your library book entry, with the author's name, title of book, publishing city, publisher, and copyright date.)

Ward, Stuart. "The Excitement of Niagara Falls," The Reader's Digest, CLIV (September, 1993, 36–42).

(The above is your periodical (magazine) entry with the author's name, the name of the article, the name of the magazine, the volume number, the month and year of the magazine, and the page numbers the article is on.)

"China," The World Book Encyclopedia. 1988 ed., Vol. 3.

(The above entry is your encyclopedia article. The "ed." stands for "edition" or copyright date. "Vol." stands for the volume number, if there is one.)

margin

PROOFREAD everything in the report for CORRECTNESS and NEATNESS. FASTEN your report together carefully and neatly.

Your report is due on: _____

Combination Vertical Bar and Line Graph

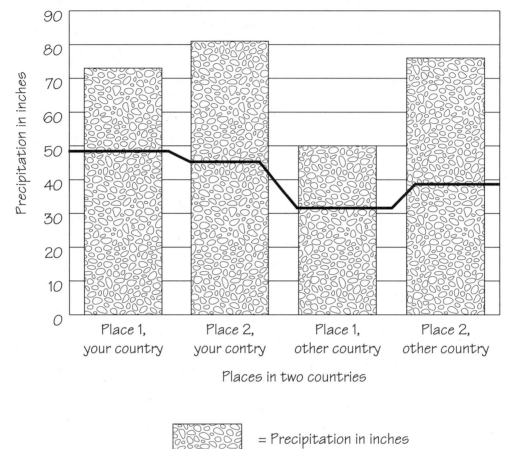

Climate for Places in Two Countries

Table

Comparing Populations of Four Cities

City	Population
City A	302,467
City B	28,138
City C	95,735
City D	211,411

Pie Graph

Population of Country X

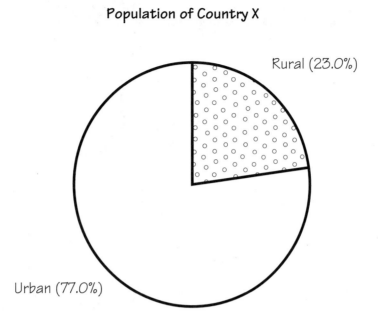

Rural (23.0%)

Urban (77.0%)

§

Name _____

Reading a Map

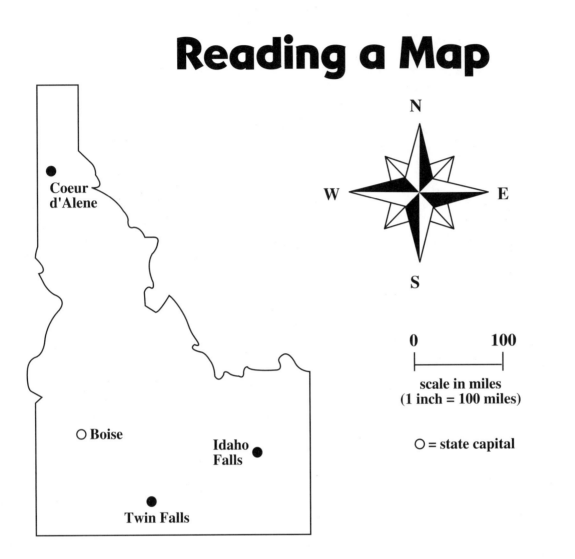

1. About how far is it from Boise to Idaho Falls?

_____

2. What city is the state capital?

_____

3. Which city is farthest north?

_____

4. Which city is farthest east?

_____

Name _____

Australia

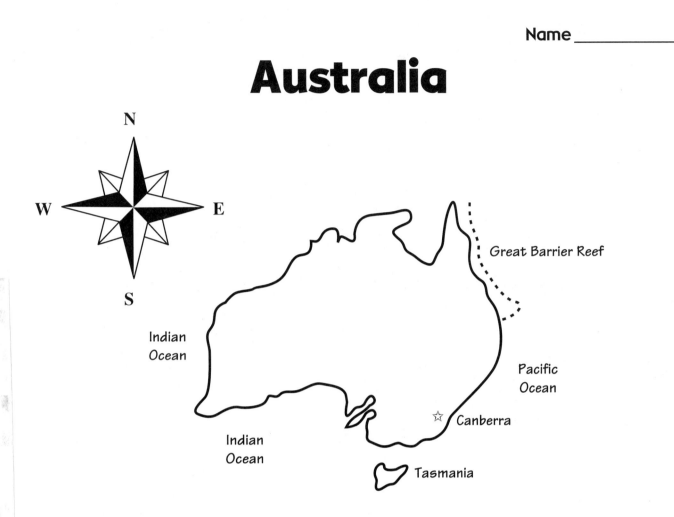

1. What does this map show?

_____

2. What is the name of the ocean directly east of Australia?

_____

3. What is the name of the ocean directly west of Australia?

_____

4. What is the name of the island directly south of Australia?

_____

Joe's Budget

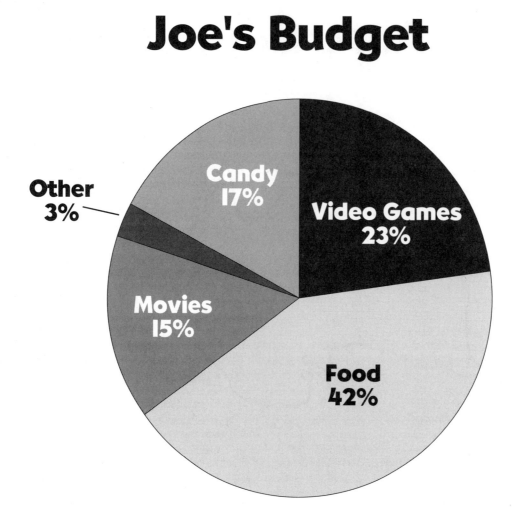

1. What does this pie graph show?

_____

2. What did Joe spend the largest part of his budget on?

_____

3. What percent (%) of Joe's budget was spent on video games?

_____

4. What might one of the things be in the "Other" category that Joe would spend his money on?

_____

Name _____

Daily High Temperatures During a Heat Wave

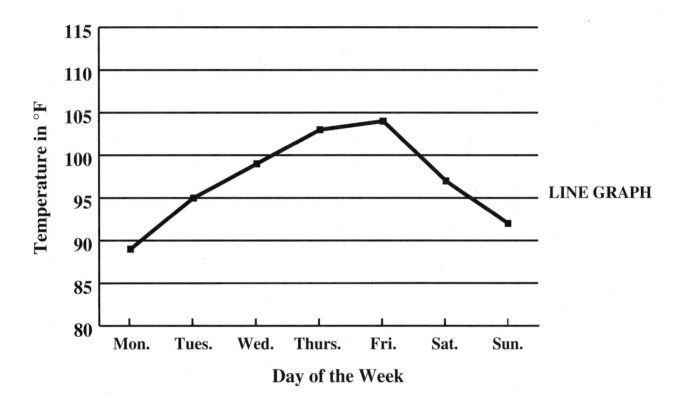

1. What does this line graph show?

_____

2. What day had the hottest temperature?

_____

3. What day had the coldest temperature?

_____

4. The temperature on Tuesday was _____ °F.

Molly and Her Jump Rope

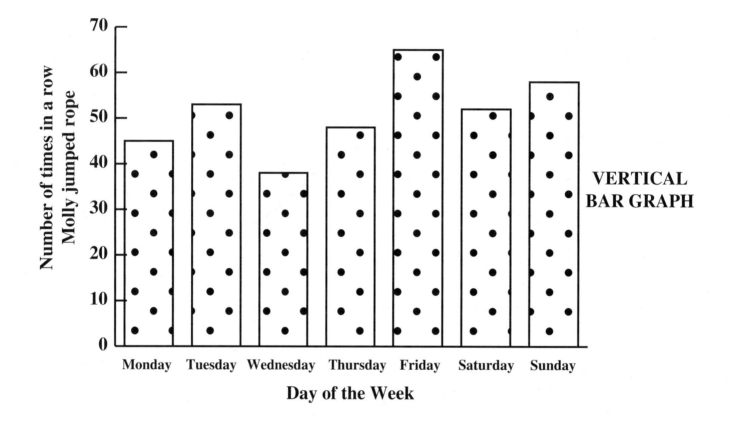

1. What does this vertical bar graph show?

   _____

2. On what day did Molly jump the fewest number of times in a row?

   _____

3. On what day did Molly jump the most number of times in a row?

   _____

4. Are there any two days on which Molly jumped exactly the same number of times in a row?

   _____

Name _____

Population of a Rural Area

City Names	Population
Ghost Town	98
Smallville	256
Trail Junction	174
Prairie View	219

TABLE

1. What does this table show?

   _____

2. What city has the highest population?

   _____

3. What city has the lowest population?

   _____

4. What does "rural" mean?

   _____

5. What are the names of the cities with populations of less than 200?

   _____

Name _____

The Family Car Trip

Distance Between Cities

| City A to City B |
| City B to City C |
| City C to City D |
| City D to City E |
| City E to City F |

= 100 miles

PICTOGRAPH

1. What does this pictograph show?

_____

2. Which two cities are farthest apart?

_____

3. How many miles is it between City E and City F?

_____

4. Approximately how many miles did the family travel over the entire trip?

_____

Name _____

Cookie Sale

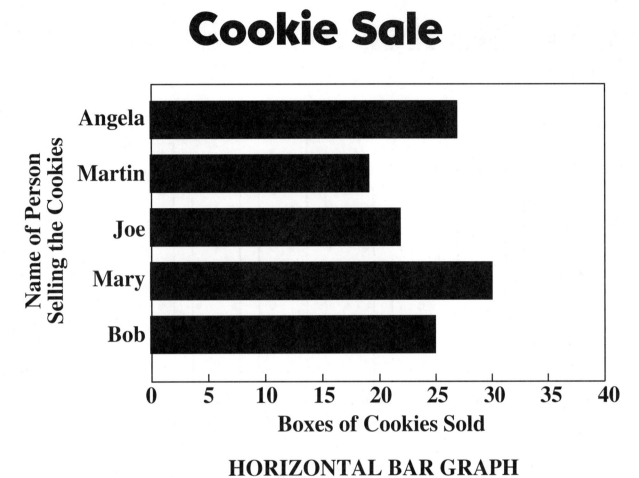

HORIZONTAL BAR GRAPH

1. What does this horizontal bar graph show?

_____

2. Who sold the fewest cookies?

_____

3. Who sold the most cookies?

_____

4. Who sold exactly 25 cookies?

_____

Name _____

Molly and Her Jump Rope

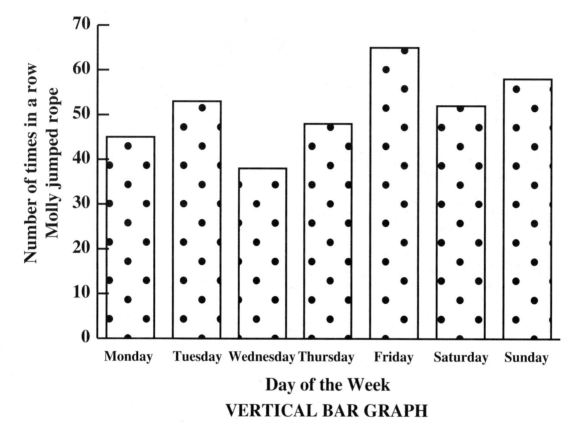

Day of the Week

VERTICAL BAR GRAPH

1. What does this vertical bar graph show?

_____

2. On what day did Molly jump the fewest number of times in a row?

_____

3. On what day did Molly jump the greatest number of times in a row?

_____

4. Approximately how many times in a row did Molly jump rope on that day?

_____

5. How many days did Molly jump rope more than 50 times in a row?

_____

Name _____

Daily High Temperatures During a Heat Wave

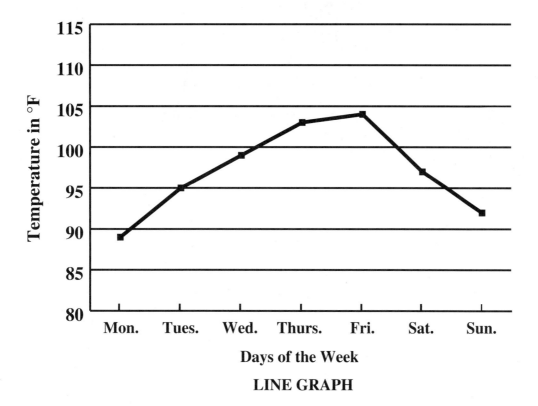

Days of the Week

LINE GRAPH

1. What does this line graph show?

_____

2. What was the temperature on Tuesday?

_____

3. On what day did the heat wave peak?

_____

4. For how many days was the temperature above 100°F?

_____

5. On what days was the temperature below 95° F?

_____

Name _____

Joe's Budget

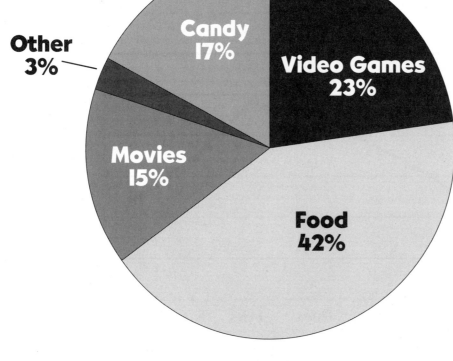

Pie Chart

1. What does this pie chart show?

_____

2. What category did Joe spend most of his money on?

_____

3. How much (what percent) did Joe spend on movies?

_____

4. If Joe's budget was $50, how much did he spend on movies?

_____

Name _____

How a Package Gets Delivered Across the Nation Overnight

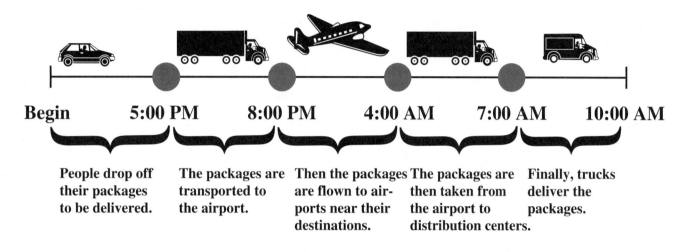

| Begin | 5:00 PM | 8:00 PM | 4:00 AM | 7:00 AM | 10:00 AM |

People drop off their packages to be delivered.

The packages are transported to the airport.

Then the packages are flown to airports near their destinations.

The packages are then taken from the airport to distribution centers.

Finally, trucks deliver the packages.

TIME LINE

1. What does this time line show?

_____

2. By what time are the packages delivered?

_____

3. During what time period do airplanes transport the packages?

_____

4. During what time periods are packages transported to and from the airport?

_____

5. How many hours does the entire process take, from pickup to delivery?

_____

Using Reference Materials

Directions: Use an atlas, history book, or encyclopedia for help. Use one letter per line (—). As a LAST RESORT, look for the answers at the bottom of this page.

1. I am our national bird. I look bald, but I'm not. What is my name? __ __ __ __ __ __ __ __ __

2. I am our national motto. Two of my words are "God" and "Trust." What are my words?
__ __ __ __ __ __ __ __ __ __ __ __

3. I was written by Francis Scott Key. Our country didn't have a national anthem, so they used me. What's my name? "__ __ __ __ __ __ __ __ __ __ __ __ __ __ __ __ __ __ __ __"

4. I am a famous bell in Independence Hall in Philadelphia, PA. I was rung after the Declaration of Independence was first read. What's my name? __ __ __ __ __ __ __ __ __ __ __

5. "US" was stamped on government goods in the War of 1812. The "US" stood for "Uncle Sam," a local title for Samuel Wilson, a government inspector. Today, Uncle Sam is a nickname for what country?
__ __ __ __ __ __ __ __ __ __ __ __

6. I'm a New England state. The first shot of the Revolutionary War was fired from me. Who am I?
__ __ __ __ __ __ __ __ __ __ __ __ __

7. I'm a state in the South. The first shot of the Civil War was fired at Fort Sumter in my state. Who am I? __ __ __ __ __ __ __ __ __ __ __ __ __

8. I'm another Southern state. The Wright Brothers made the first successful airplane flight at Kitty Hawk in my state. Who am I? __ __ __ __ __ __ __ __ __ __ __ __ __

9. I'm a Rocky Mountain state. I am the home of the first national park in the United States. Its name is Yellowstone. Who am I? __ __ __ __ __ __ __

10. I am a Southern state that looks like a shoe. The delta of the Mississippi is located by my toe. Who am I? __ __ __ __ __ __ __ __ __

11. I am a Midwestern state. The first night baseball game was played in me at Fort Wayne. Who am I?
__ __ __ __ __ __ __

§ Latitude and Climate

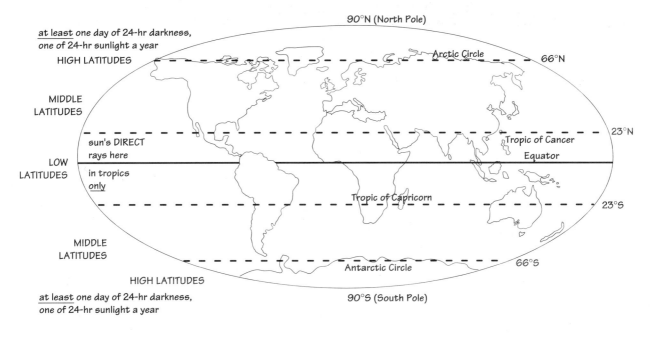

at least one day of 24-hr darkness, one of 24-hr sunlight a year

HIGH LATITUDES

MIDDLE LATITUDES

sun's DIRECT rays here

LOW LATITUDES

in tropics only

MIDDLE LATITUDES

HIGH LATITUDES

at least one day of 24-hr darkness, one of 24-hr sunlight a year

90°N (North Pole)

Arctic Circle — 66°N

23°N

Tropic of Cancer
Equator

Tropic of Capricorn — 23°S

Antarctic Circle — 66°S

90°S (South Pole)

Several things influence climate, including the elevation of the land and the presence of nearby bodies of water. But one big influencer of climate is latitude.

Generally speaking, the closer you get to the equator, where the sun's direct, straight rays are, the hotter it is. The closer you get to the poles, where the sun's slanted and very light rays are, the colder it is.

The equator is 0° latitude. Places near the equator, on either side of it, are in the low latitudes with low numbers like 15° South (of the equator) or 20° North (of the equator). Places here are in the tropical climate zone, where it's hot all year around with two seasons—wet and dry. Sometimes it's hot and wet, sometimes hot and dry.

The middle latitudes are between the Tropic of Cancer and the Arctic Circle, and the Tropic of Capricorn and the Antarctic Circle. These middle latitude areas have middle numbers like 35° North of the equator or 55° South of the equator. The middle latitudes have temperature (mild) climates with four seasons—winter, spring, summer, and fall. The middle latitude ABOVE the equator has seasons exactly the opposite of the middle latitude belt BELOW the equator. For example, if it's summer in the north, like at Los Angeles, it's winter in the south, like in southern Australia!

The high latitudes, with high numbers like 75° North or South and 85° North or South, are in the Arctic Circle in the north and the Antarctic Circle in the south. They are the polar climate zones and it's always cold there. Part of the Circles are in the icecap where temperatures never get above freezing. There are two seasons—light and dark. The North Pole, which is 90° North and at the top of the world, has six months of continuous darkness. At the same time, the South Pole, which is 90° South and at the bottom of the world, has six months of continuous sunlight. Then the North Pole has the sunlight while the South Pole has the darkness.

§

Name _____

Latitude and Climate Activity

1. On your Latitude and Climate map, color the Arctic and Antarctic Circles blue for ice cold.

2. Color the middle latitudes green.

3. Color the low latitudes red for red hot.

4. Name the one continent that would be cold all the time.

   _____

5. If you lived in the southeastern part of Australia, what kind of climate would you expect?

   _____

6. If you lived in the northern area of South America, what kind of climate would you expect?

   _____

7. If you lived in southern Europe, what kind of climate would you expect?

   _____

8. Which two continents are almost entirely in the middle latitudes?

   _____ and _____

9. If it were winter in southern Australia, what season would it be in California?

   _____

10. If the North Pole were in total darkness, what would you expect to find at the South Pole?

    _____

§

Volcanoes

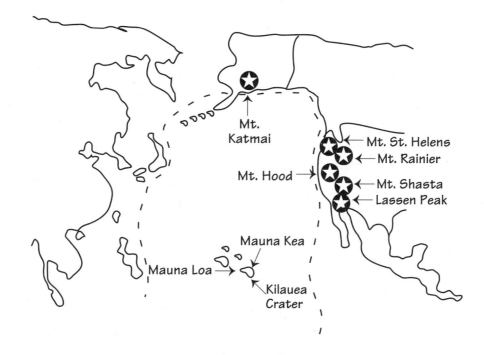

The Cascade Mountain Range, which extends from Southern California up through Washington, was formed by volcanoes. There are several interesting peaks in this range.

Mount Shasta, in California, was once an active peak in this range (called the Sierra Nevada in California) and Lassen Peak, also located in California, still is. Lassen Peak last erupted in 1921.

In Oregon, Crater Lake is located in an ancient volcano. Mt. Hood, also in the Cascades in Oregon, is an inactive volcano.

Mt. Rainier, in Washington, is an old volcanic cone. Probably the most famous volcano in the United States because of its recent activity is Mt. St. Helens, located in southwestern Washington. It's erupted several times since 1980. The eruptions caused forest fires and flooding. The volcanic ash destroyed crops and wildlife. Sixty people were killed in the 1980 eruptions. Mt. St. Helens was the first volcano to erupt in the conterminous United States since Lassen. Fourteen hundred feet of the top of the mountain were blown off.

The Aleutian Islands of Alaska are the tops of volcanoes. Some of these are still active. Mt. Katmai last erupted in 1912.

The Hawaiian Islands, part of the United States but not part of North America, are also the tops of volcanoes. Just like the Aleutian Islands, as the mountains erupted from the bottom of the sea, more and more lava built up on the sides and top. Finally, the mountains were built up so high, they stuck right out of the ocean. Active volcanoes on the Big Island are Mauna Loa, the world's largest volcano, Mauna Kea, and Kilauea. Two volcanoes on the "Big Island," Hawaii, erupt every few years. They are Mauna Kea and Mauna Loa. Kilauea is also on the Big Island. It last erupted in 1986.

Name _____

Notice that most of the volcanoes are on the coast of the Pacific Ocean or in the Pacific Ocean. This Pacific area, called the Pacific Plate, is one of the large, rigid plates of the Earth. Notice on the map that there are dashes outlining part of the Pacific Plate. There are about twenty plates on the Earth. They move very slowly while carrying the continents and ocean floor with them. The boundaries between one plate and another are usually the sites of volcanoes, mountains, and earthquakes. Among the world's major earthquakes are the San Francisco quake of 1906 and the Alaskan quake of 1964. Both of these sites are located in the area of the Pacific Plate.

But how do volcanoes erupt? Because the heat inside the Earth is so strong, it begins to melt rocks that are about 15 to 100 miles inside the Earth. When the melting begins, a lot of gas is produced. This mixes with the melted rock, also known as magma. This lighter-weight material starts rising toward the Earth's surface just because it IS lighter than the heavy rocks around it. All this pressure that's created causes the magma to keep pushing, pushing, pushing its way up to the surface of the Earth. The way out is through the top and sides of the volcano. Gas blasts out and magma flows down the sides of the volcano. This molten rock is now called lava.

Although volcanic eruptions can be very destructive, lava from the eruptions can also be useful. Lava rock is used in building roads. Pumice (pum'is), a volcanic glass, is used for polishing. Many people use a pumice stone to soften calluses on their feet. Volcanic ash can also be used as a fertilizer. Some areas of the United States use the underground steam of the volcanoes as a source of energy to produce electricity.

Wordsearch

V	C	R	A	T	E	R
E	O	E	T	A	L	P
L	O	L	A	V	A	B
H	I	N	C	E	S	T
M	A	G	M	A	H	S
L	A	S	S	E	N	A
E	C	I	M	U	P	O

In this wordsearch, there are seven words relating to volcanoes. Circle each word. Then write the definition of each word on the back of this paper.

Name _____

An Erupting Volcano

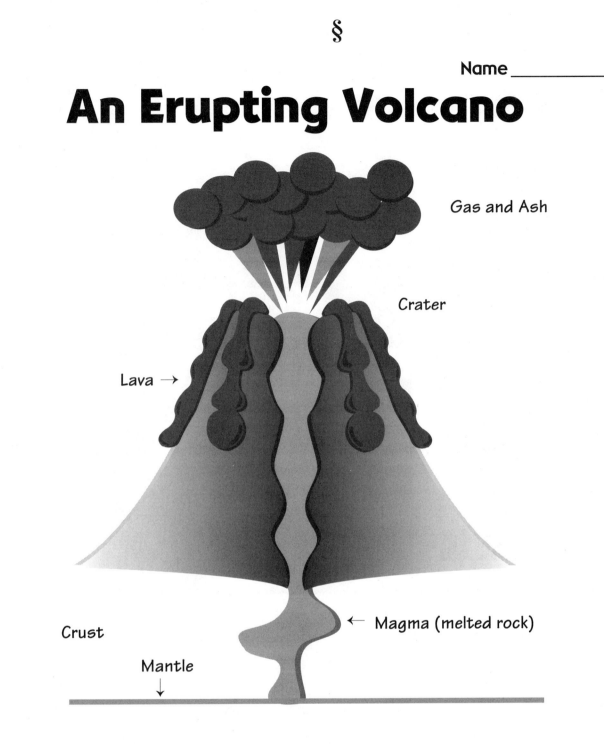

Gas and Ash

Crater

Lava →

← Magma (melted rock)

Crust

Mantle
↓

Looking just at the picture of the erupting volcano, write in your own words what happens when a volcano gets ready to erupt.

_____

_____

_____

_____

Volcano Crossword Puzzle

ACROSS

1. The Cascade Mountain Range was formed by _____ .

5. Most volcanoes are located around the _____ Plate.

6. Mt. St. Helens is a volcano in Washington that has recently _____ .

7. The Hawaiian and the Aleutian _____ are the tops of volcanoes.

8. Volcanic ash can destroy _____ .

9. An active volcano in California is _____   _____ .

DOWN

2. Crater Lake is located in _____ .

3. The name given to the forty-eight touching states is _____ .

4. The mountain range in the United States that was formed by volcanoes
   is the _____ .

10. An active volcano on the "Big Island" is Mauna _____ .

§

Science/Health

For the pages you have read and for the information you've acquired, do the following activities on separate pieces of paper:

1. Make a wordsearch using at least five scientific terms. Circle the words. Write what each word means.

2. Write ten things you learned. Explain each thoroughly. Do small illustrations or diagrams for three of the things.

3. Select one thing for a scientific drawing. Use one whole piece of unlined paper. Make your drawing nice and big. Be sure you have a title and be sure all the information is properly labeled and correctly spelled. Color your drawing nicely.

Science Experiment

Fingerprint Classification

1. Use an encyclopedia, a science book, or a library book to get information about fingerprints.

2. Although there are more than four types, use just the four basic ones of the arch, loop, whorl, and accidental. Study the pictures of these prints so you'll be able to identify them.

3. Get an ink pad. Be sure it has a good amount of ink in it. (Your teacher may have one or the school office will have one.)

4. Get a piece of white or yellow unlined paper.

5. Make a prediction. For example, out of ten students, 7 will have loop fingerprints. 7 out of 10 (7/10) = 70%. Use whatever prediction you think might work out based on EVIDENCE from your reading on fingerprints.

6. Now, select ten students who will allow you to fingerprint them. Take with you your piece of unlined paper, your ink pad, and some paper towels for the students to wipe the ink from their fingers.

   a. On your piece of paper, write the name of the student you're fingerprinting.
   b. Then have the student totally ink his/her thumb or index finger.
   c. Put your paper on a table top. Take this student's finger and roll the print on to the paper right by his/her name. Then give this student a towel. Do this for each of the students.
   d. Return the ink pad.

7. Examine each student's fingerprint. You might want to use a magnifying glass.

8. Classify each print. Next to each student's name and print, write what type it is (arch, loop, whorl, accidental).

9. Count up and write on the paper the number of students with each type of print. You might have a type of print that no one you fingerprinted had! You can easily change these into percentages. For example, 2 out of 10 had arch; therefore, 2 out of 10 (2/10) = 20% OR 4 out of 10 had loop; therefore, 4 out of 10 (4/10) = 40%; and so on.

10. WRITE a summary of the experiment. Look at your prediction. Were you close? What did you learn? What are your conclusions? How did you feel about this experiment?

Science/Math

Prediction/Estimation Experiment

1. Get a clear plastic jar. Put 78 beans in it.
2. Select ten students in your classroom to participate in the experiment. These ten students will estimate the number of beans in the jar.
3. Make a prediction. How many students out of the ten do you think will make a reasonable estimation? You can easily write this as a percentage. If you think 3 will make a reasonable estimation, then 3 out of 10 (3/10) is 30%. If you think 6, then 6 out of 10 (6/10) is 60%. If you think 8, then 8 out of 10 (8/10) is 80%, and so on.
4. Define "reasonable" as any number within plus or minus twelve (±12). A "reasonable" estimation, then, would be any number between 66 and 90.
5. Prepare a vertical bar graph to record the ten students' estimations. See the sample titled "How Many Beans in the Jar?"

How Many Beans in the Jar?

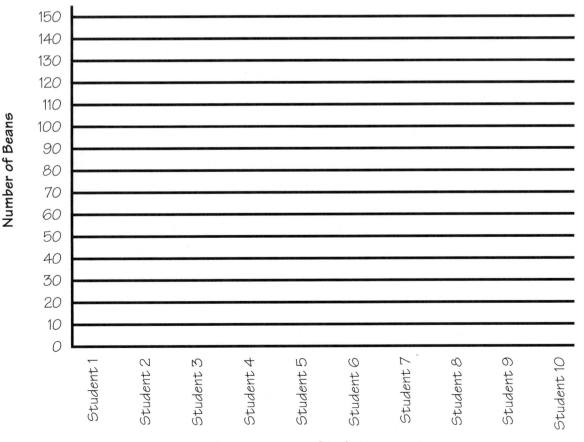

6. Tell each student to look at the size of the beans carefully. Then ask each of the ten students individually and privately how many beans are in the jar. Record their answers on the graph. If a student estimates a number over 150, just make the vertical bar go right off the top of the graph.

7. Count the number of students whose estimation was between 66 and 90. You can then change this answer to a percentage. If 5 students estimated in this range, then 5 out of 10 (5/10) is 50%; if 7 students, then 7 out of 10 (7/10) is 70%; etc.

8. What percentage of students' estimations were in a larger range, say between 50 and 110?

9. WRITE a summary of the experiment. How close was your prediction? What conclusions would you draw? What did you learn about the students' ability to make a reasonable estimation in an experiment like this? What effect might the size of the jar have? What effect might the size of the beans have? How did you feel about this experiment?

Scientific Method

Water Hardness

1. Make some general predictions.

    What might lead to water hardness? If you think there are any advantages or disadvantages to hard or soft water, what might they be?

2. Make a hypothesis. Example: Bottled water will be the softest.

3. Gather data.

    Wash and dry five glass or plastic containers with lids. Label each container using the following codes for labels: BW for bottled water, RHW for regular house water, SHW for soft house water from a house with a water softener, SW for school water, and PLR for pond, lake, river, ocean, etc., and SP for swimming pool water. Then collect a sample of each kind of water.

4. Write your predictions about the degree of the hardness of the water types on the lines below *before* you watch the experiment. "1" is extremely soft and "15" or more is very hard. Use any numbers in the range of 1 to 30.

5. Record your *observations* as you watch YOUR TEACHER perform the chemical test. AN ADULT MUST PERFORM THE CHEMICAL TEST.

Your Prediction	Type of Water	Test Results
_____	BW bottled water	_____
_____	RHW regular house water	_____
_____	SHW soft house water	_____
_____	SW school water	_____
_____	PLR pond, lake, river	_____
_____	SP swimming pool	_____

6. Was your hypothesis correct? _____ Were you surprised at the results? _____

7. Write your conclusions. What did you learn from the experiment? How did you feel about the experiment? Use the back of this paper or a piece of lined paper.

Speaking

SPEAKING

Name _____

Date _____

☐ Posture, poise

☐ Eye contact

☐ Voice—loud and clear

☐ Adequate time speaking

☐ Well prepared

TOTAL

☐ = Grade
1 = Very poor
2 = Poor
3 = Fair
4 = Good
5 = Excellent

A+ = 25
A = 24
A− = 23
B+ = 22
B = 20–21
B− = 19
C+ = 18
C = 14–17
C− = 11–13
D+ = 10
D = 9
D− = 8
F = 0–7

SPEAKING

Name _____

Date _____

☐ Posture, poise

☐ Eye contact

☐ Voice—loud and clear

☐ Adequate time speaking

☐ Well prepared

TOTAL

☐ = Grade
1 = Very poor
2 = Poor
3 = Fair
4 = Good
5 = Excellent

A+ = 25
A = 24
A− = 23
B+ = 22
B = 20–21
B− = 19
C+ = 18
C = 14–17
C− = 11–13
D+ = 10
D = 9
D− = 8
F = 0–7

Blueprint for Effective Teaching

READY the skill/concept/material you're going to teach in advance.
> How will you present it?
> What do you want your students to know?
> How will they be expected to demonstrate their knowledge?
> Ready the materials: books, reproducibles, pictures, audiotapes, videotapes, video discs, computers, overhead pens and transparencies, charts and markers, science equipment, math manipulatives, chalk, target vocabulary cards, etcetera.

SET the students for your lesson.
> Set the standards of behavior.
> Set a frame of reference from which the students can operate.
> Set the students' focus on why the learning is important and how they will be expected to demonstrate their understanding.

TEACH the students the skill/concept/material.
> Teach the students exactly what you want them to know, or use guided questioning to help them discover.
> Teach the material in a chronological or logical manner.
> Teach the most important aspects of the learning repeatedly.
> Teach using different styles to address the learning modalities: visual, auditory, and kinesthetic.
> Teach for transfer.

LISTEN AND WATCH the students as you teach.
> Can they answer your questions?
> Can they do what you're showing them?
> Can they tell you what they're learning?
> Can they write about the learning?

ASSIGN material, a project, a discussion session, etcetera that is directly related to the learning.

MONITOR the students' learning by walking around the classroom observing their work and asking them questions. Reteach as necessary to the whole class, to a small group, or to an individual student.

CHECK the assignment so that students know how they are doing. Make sure students are accountable for the assignment.

REVIEW the key elements of the learning during several different teaching periods.

EVALUATE periodically by means of projects, pencil-paper tests, student presentations, etcetera.

RECORD the evaluation mark for individual accountability and for tracking individual progress.

PT §

Test Study Note

_____ studied AT HOME for
Name of Student

_____ for the _____
How long   Name of Subject

test. _____ was the material
        Name of or list of material that was studied

that was studied.

_____
Parent Signature

Test Study Note

_____ studied AT HOME for
Name of Student

_____ for the _____
How long   Name of Subject

test. _____ was the material
        Name of or list of material that was studied

that was studied.

_____
Parent Signature

Test Study Note

_____ studied AT HOME for
Name of Student

_____ for the _____
How long   Name of Subject

test. _____ was the material
        Name of or list of material that was studied

that was studied.

_____
Parent Signature

There, Their, They're

* When spelling these words, notice each starts with the word the: there, their, and they're.

1. there = filler word
    There is (isn't) one girl.
    There are (aren't) three books.
    There was (wasn't) one boy.
    There were (weren't) three books.
    There will (won't) be one girl.
    There would (wouldn't) be three books.
    * All of these can also be in question sentences.
    Is there one girl?
    Isn't there one girl?
    Will there be any questions?
    there = place or location
    One book is over there.

2. their = ownership
    Their book is new.
    Are those their dogs?

3. They're = they are
    contraction with apostrophe replacing the letter *a* in *are*
    They're going to the store.
    They're late for the show.

To, Two, Too

to =   direction
        Give the book to him.
        Let's go to the movie.
        Why did the colonies go to war?
        Where is the key to the door?

two =   2
        There are two cute dogs in the house.
        She has two dollars.

too =   also, overly, excessively, besides
        Linda decided to go to the show, *too*. (also)
        He is *too* tired to go to the show. (overly, excessively)
        Sell the house and the furniture, *too*. (besides, also)

§

Practice sentences:

1. Go _____ the store now.

2. Give the girl _____ dollars.

3. The kids are _____ late for the game.

4. Let's go _____ dinner, _____ .

5. Get out your book and your paper, _____ .

6. Give _____ coins _____ that man, _____ .

Spelling Review List

its it's
are our
were where we're wear
you're your
friend
because
now know no
who how
first
use
then than
to too two
there their they're
which sandwich witch
they
that
through threw
write right
different
again
great grate
though thought through
although
another
until

new knew
much
does dose
why any
together
often
while
children
important
world
don't didn't weren't
hasn't haven't
brought bought bring
might mite
few
close clothes
looked
people
believe
wouldn't shouldn't
might have
could have
should have
isn't aren't
of off

§

Newscaster

Writing Project (five paragraphs)

Person: 1st

Setting: Channel 4 newsroom

Assignment: You are a newscaster on Channel 4's evening news. You are going to be reporting live on three newsworthy events of the day. (Remember the 5 W's.) Channel 4 reporters have already gathered and written up all the information for you to broadcast.

Events (Obstacles):

1. A big accident—freeway, plane, or train
2. Final sentencing of a drug king by an appellate court judge
3. Peace declared between two rival New York gangs.

Objective: Handle the stress of live TV and give a good report.

Use the writing process. Write one paragraph for each obstacle. You will each read your part to the class as if you were a newscaster giving your evening broadcast. The student who writes the introductory and concluding paragraphs will introduce the news.

Police Officer

Writing Project (five paragraphs)

Person: 3rd

Setting: Downtown Los Angeles at night

Assignment: A police officer on the night-shift patrol.

Obstacles	Tools
1. Store being burglarized by two heavy-set thugs dressed in black with black camouflage grease on hands and face.	Police gear: uniform, badge, gun, handcuffs, night stick, pencil, note pad.
2. Wino coming out of old, run-down, seedy residential hotel yelling about someone getting beat up in room 241.	Fully equipped patrol car. Highly trained police dog.
3. Druggie making a buy.	

To do:

- introductory paragraph including setting, assignment, and objective
- a paragraph for *each* obstacle
- a concluding paragraph
- a title
- proofreading—indenting, capitals, ending punctuation, spelling

To ask: Is my paper interesting and exciting?

Irish Setter

Writing Project (five paragraphs)

Person: 1st

Setting: neighborhood and nearby city

Assignment: You are someone's pet Irish Setter. Unfortunately, you accidentally get out of your house and yard. Then you get totally lost for two days.

The following are the three problems (obstacles) you face:

1. How to get food
2. How to avoid accidents, like car, bus, or train wrecks
3. How to handle yourself when you meet a pit bull or German shepherd

Objective: Get back to your master.

Write an introductory paragraph, three body paragraphs, and a short concluding paragraph.

Use the writing process.

Proofread your papers thoroughly.

Writing Cluster

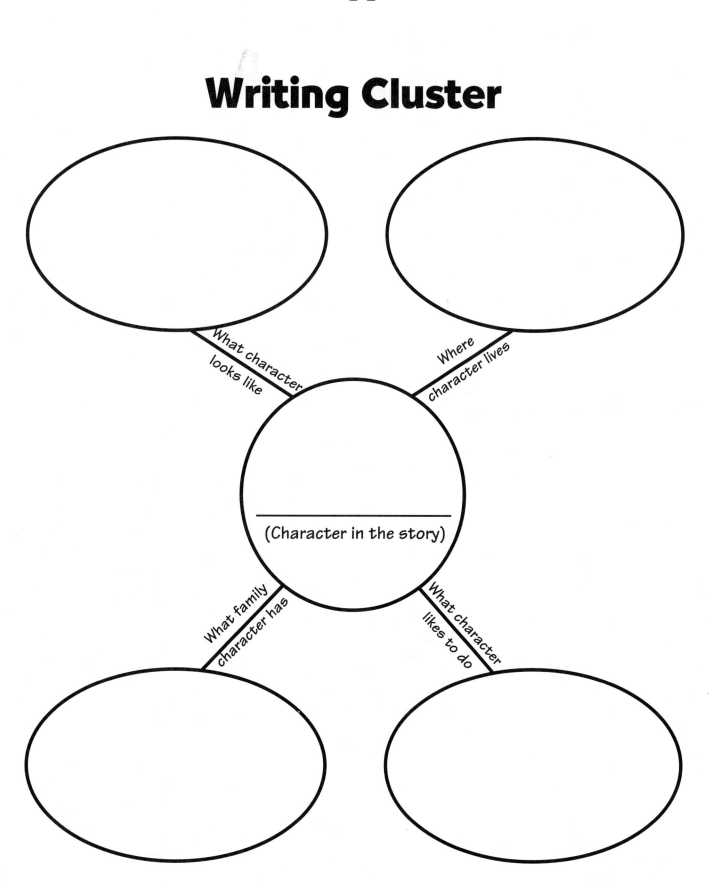

What character looks like

Where character lives

_____
(Character in the story)

What family character has

What character likes to do

Writing Cluster

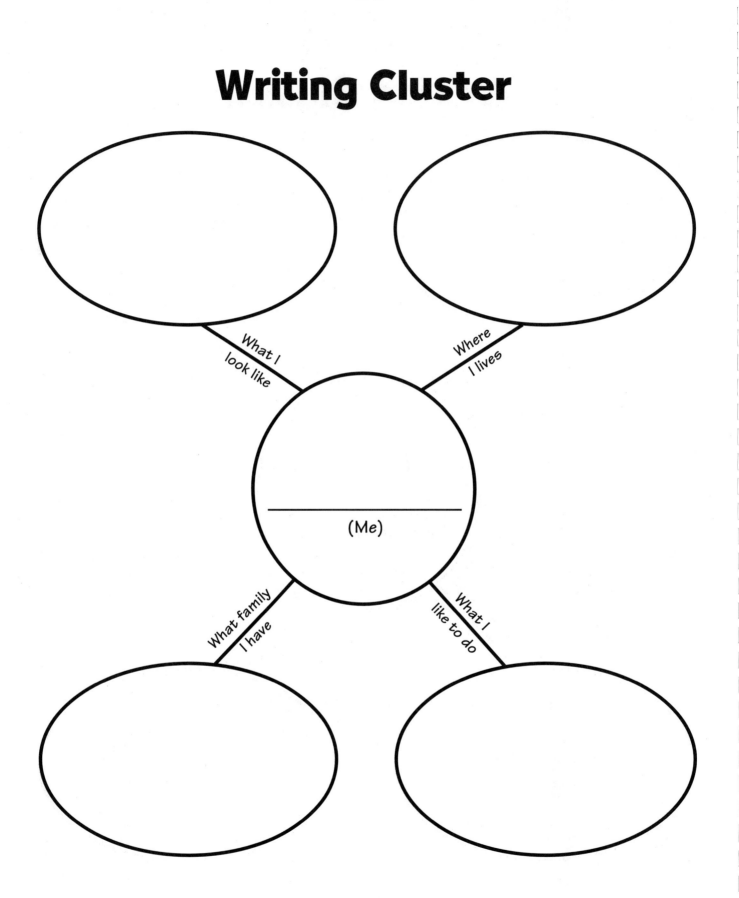

What I
look like

Where
I lives

(Me)

What family
I have

What I
like to do

Writing

ME

I am an interesting person. _____

_____

_____

_____

_____

_____

_____

_____

_____

§

Writing

Name of the reading story_____
The story needs to have been read and studied first.

  Use the double entry journal below to tell about *an event* from the story that reminds you about something that happened in your life. On the lines write *detailed notes* telling all about the event from the story. Then write *detailed notes* telling all about the event in your life. What happened? When did it happen? Where did it happen? Who was involved? What was the outcome? How did you feel?

Double Entry Journal

What happened in the story?   What happened in my life?

_____   _____

_____   _____

_____   _____

_____   _____

_____   _____

_____   _____

_____   _____

_____   _____

_____   _____

_____   _____

_____   _____

§

Cluster

Use the first cluster to describe a character in the story. Use the second cluster to describe yourself. A lot of information should be in EACH circle of the clusters.

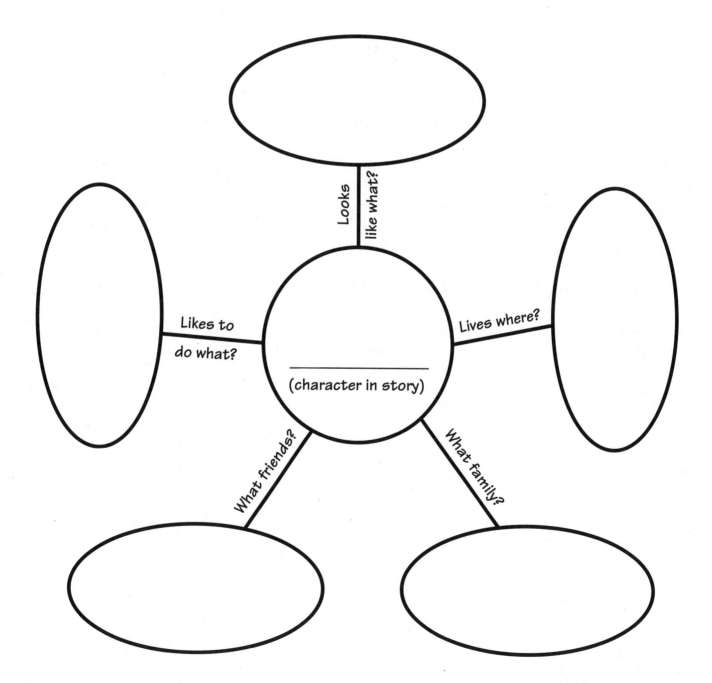

Looks like what?

Likes to do what?

Lives where?

_____
(character in story)

What friends?

What family?

§

Writing Activity

Select the topic from ONE of the activities you just completed.

Write about a time of your life using the information from the "What happened in my life?" side of the double entry journal.

OR

Write about yourself using the information from the "(you)" cluster.

Then do the following for whichever one you chose:

• Write a rough draft. Include all the interesting information.

• Revise it so it's fun and interesting to read.

• Write the final copy in your best and neatest handwriting.

• Proofread it carefully for title, correct margins, indentions, paragraphing, spelling, capital letters, punctuation, and understandability.

§
§

Name _____

Cluster

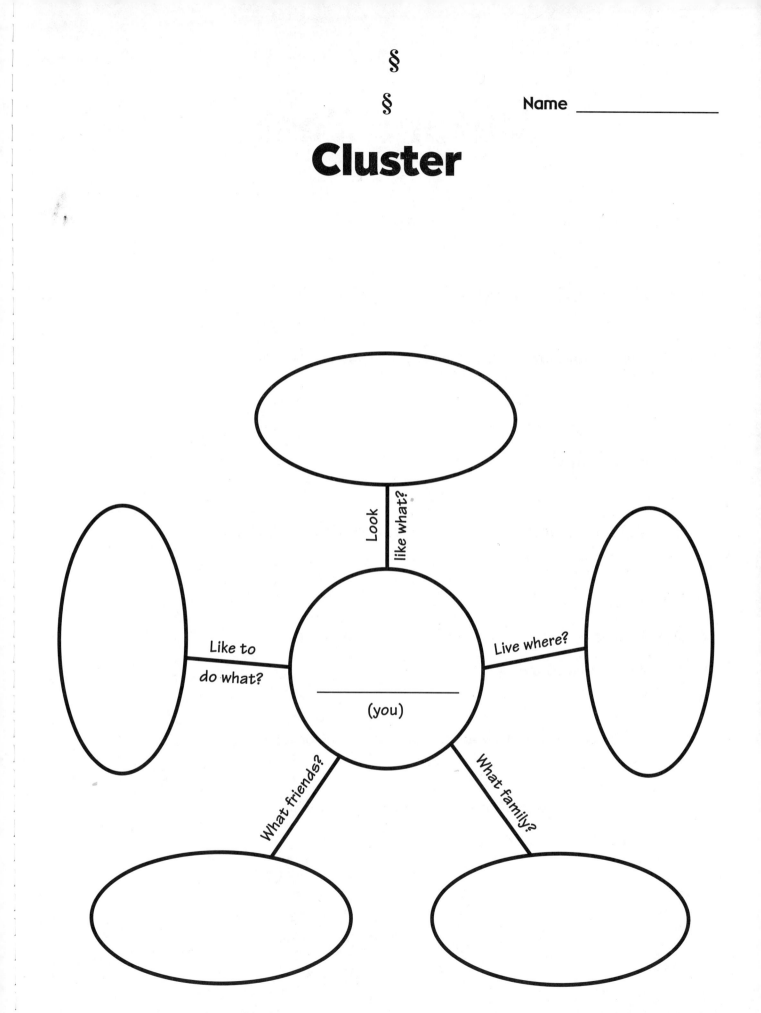

Look like what?

Like to do what?

Live where?

_____
(you)

What friends?

What family?

§

Writing Test

Directions: Work independently. Choose one activity.

1. Write a time-order paragraph on a trip to Disneyland.

2. Write a power paragraph on two pets you would like to have.

3. Write a five-paragraph composition.

    Write in the first person.

    You are a major movie star.

    You live in Southern California at the close of the twentieth century.

Obstacles:

1. You are going to Disneyland and you don't want to be
    recognized and mobbed.

2. You want to throw a party but you don't want any crashers.

3. You want to keep track of all your money so you don't
    get ripped off.

What Is It?

Direct students as they complete the picture by drawing lines between matching letters to connect the dots.

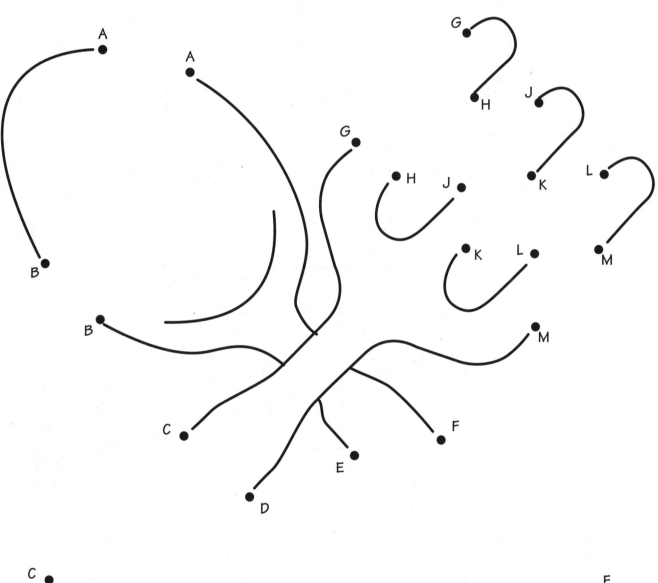

NAME _____

The Bouncing Ball

Direct students as they complete the maze, helping the ball reach the glove. The slide, seesaw, and swing will help them solve it.

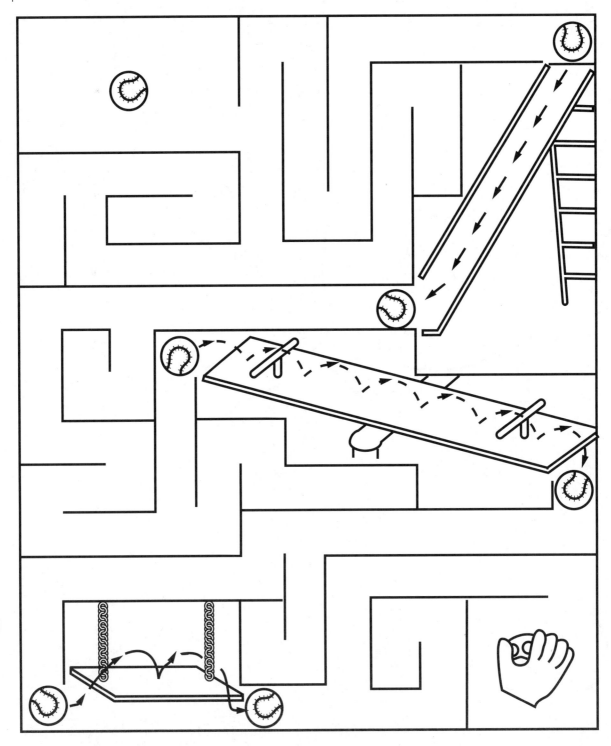

In the Swim

Direct students to reveal the hidden picture by coloring the spaces as follows: X, blue; O, orange; dots, yellow.

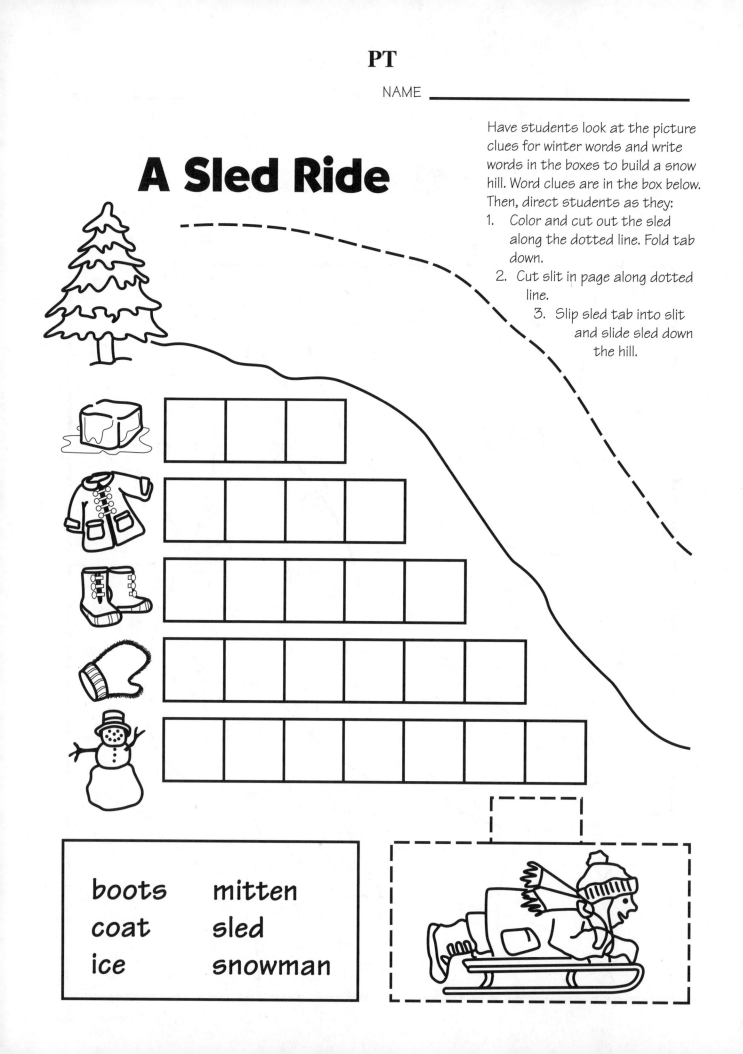

A Sled Ride

PT

NAME _____

Have students look at the picture clues for winter words and write words in the boxes to build a snow hill. Word clues are in the box below. Then, direct students as they:

1. Color and cut out the sled along the dotted line. Fold tab down.
2. Cut slit in page along dotted line.
3. Slip sled tab into slit and slide sled down the hill.

boots   mitten
coat   sled
ice   snowman

NAME _____

Direct students as they:
1. Color the picture.
2. Cut out along the dotted lines to create a puzzle.

Playground Fun

Thanksgiving

The Thanksgiving Game

April Fools' Day
We like for its pranks.
But why, you may wonder,
Have a day just for thanks?

To discover the answer,
Simply try to recall
What's good in your life,
List things big and things small.

If you spend a few minutes
On this game of thanksgiving,
You'll learn being thankful
Makes life more worth living.

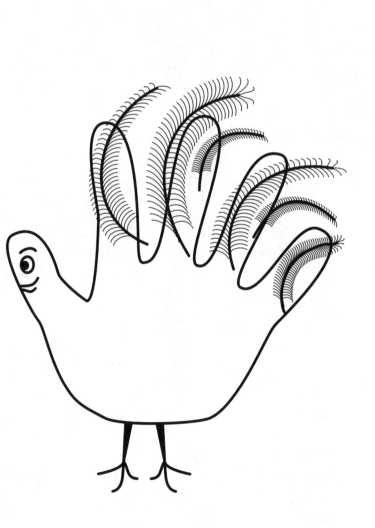

Thanksgiving Turkey Collage

You Will Need:
construction paper
nontoxic felt-tip pen or pencil
glue
different types of uncooked macaroni and beans

What You Do:
1. Place your hand with your fingers spread out on a piece of construction paper.
2. Trace around your hand with a felt-tip pen or pencil.
3. Use the pen or pencil to draw turkey feet at the bottom of the hand you drew. Draw an eye on the thumb.
4. Decorate the turkey by gluing on beans and macaroni.

Easter

The Easter Egg Surprise

When I sat down to paint an egg,
For Easter, first came blue.
Then I dipped my brush in pink,
and red and silver, too.

I painted birds and flowers,
Near a tiny wishing well.
Plus dogs and cats and children
All around that pretty shell.

But before I had a chance to let
My friends take one quick peek,
The egg went "crack" and then I saw
A pointed yellow beak.

"Stop!" I shouted. "Go back in.
You'll ruin my Easter egg."
The chick said only, "Peep, peep, peep,"
And pushed out one thin leg.

So now I have no painted egg,
Which makes me almost sad.
But when I hear that "Peep, peep, peep,"
I know the chick is glad.

"peep!
peep peep!"

Feel the Easter Bunny

You Will Need:
construction paper
cotton balls
glue
nontoxic felt-tip markers
glitter

What You Do:
1. Glue three cotton balls in the shape of a triangle to a piece of construction paper.
2. Draw two eyes on the top cotton ball and two bunny ears above it, on the construction paper, with a nontoxic felt-tip marker.
3. Surround the bunny with several Easter eggs using markers and glitter.
4. Show your friends your soft Easter bunny—they may want to pet it!

Name _____   Date _____

Portfolio Evaluation for Writing

A. One thing I have improved on is _____

_____

_____

B. One thing I would like to do better is to be able to _____

_____

_____

How will I do this?

1. _____

_____

2. _____

_____

3. _____

_____

Overall, I think my work in this area is

_____

Comments: _____

§

Portfolio Evaluation for Writing

Name _____   **Date** _____

Rubric for Individual Paper   Score _____

Friendly Letter Format _____
score

✓ = needs improvement
_____ three-line heading, including full address and date
_____ greeting
_____ body (indentions and margins)
_____ complementary close or closing
_____ signature
    * Except for "body," the rest must have correct *spelling, capitals, punctation,* and *location* on paper.

(F) 0 = 4 or more errors
(D) 1 = 3 errors
(C) 2 = 2 errors
(B) 3 = 1 error
(A) 4 = no errors

Body Content/Paragraph(s) Content _____
weighted score

* Initial score x weight factor of 2 = weighted score (minimum of 0, maximum of 8). The weight factor allows the content portion of the paper to carry the weight or importance it deserves.

✓ = needs improvement
+ = unusual strength
_____ content responsive, related, appropriate
_____ adequate length for the assignment
_____ interesting, commanding
_____ easy to understand
_____ enriched vocabulary
_____ good sentence structure
_____ sentence variation
_____ good transitions
_____ demonstrates growth in written language

	initial score	weighted score
(F)	0 = failing, extremely poor	x2 = 0
(D)	1 = poor	x2 = 2
(C)	2 = average	x2 = 4
(B)	3 = good	x2 = 6
(A)	4 = excellent	x2 = 8

§

Writing Formalities in Body/Paragraph(s) _____
                                                    score
✓ = needs improvement
_____ capitals: first word of sentence
                  titles of books, shows, etc.
                  word I
                  proper nouns
                  first word of a quote
_____ punctuation: use of . , ? ! ; : '
_____ grammar: verb tense
                 subject-verb agreement
                 personal pronoun usage
                 double negative
                 slang

(F) 0 = failing, extremely poor
(D) 1 = poor
(C) 2 = average   (errors proportionate to length and sophistication
(B) 3 = good   of student's writing)
(A) 4 = excellent

Spelling _____
              score
(for common words in body of letter only)

*Students may use dictionary, thesaurus, or speller

(F) 0 = failing, extremely poor
(D) 1 = poor
(C) 2 = average
(B) 3 = good   (errors proportionate to length and sophistication
(A) 4 = excellent   of student's writing)

Handwriting _____
                 score
✓ = needs improvement
_____ lowercase letter formation
_____ uppercase letter formation
_____ letter connections in words
_____ neatness

(F) 0 = failing, extremely poor
(D) 1 = poor
(C) 2 = average
(B) 3 = good
(A) 4 = excellent

§

Grade Conversions

An overall grade *could* be given for the paper (total of points divided by 5) or any two or three areas could be evaluated on a particular assignment (total ÷2, total ÷3, etc.).

0	0.0	F		10	2.0	C–		20	4.0	A–
1	0.2	F		11	2.2	C		21	4.2	A
2	0.4	F		12	2.4	C		22	4.4	A
3	0.6	F		13	2.6	C		23	4.6	A
4	0.8	F		14	2.8	C+		24	4.8	A+
5	1.0	D–		15	3.0	B–				
6	1.2	D		16	3.2	B				
7	1.4	D		17	3.4	B				
8	1.6	D		18	3.6	B				
9	1.8	D+		19	3.8	B+				

Or to evaluate more generally or for fewer areas, consider

0 to 4 (or 5)		The 0's	= F
5 to 9		The 1's	= D
10 to 14		The 2's	= C
15 to 19		The 3's	= B
20 to 24		The 4's	= A

- -

Student Assessment

Use the back of this paper for your answers.

1. What do *you* think is your best piece in your portfolio? What is it about? When did you write it? Write *at least* three things you like about it.

2. Write all you can about what you've learned in writing since your last "Student Assessment."

3. Write everything about how you feel (your attitude) about writing. Do you feel you have creative and original ideas? Do you like the topics about which you write? Are you good at writing? Do you think it's difficult? How do you feel you do in writing a story or an explanation of something or trying to persuade your friend to believe what you write about? How do you feel about writing poetry? Is writing something you enjoy?

4. What would you like to learn next?

5. On what would you like to improve?

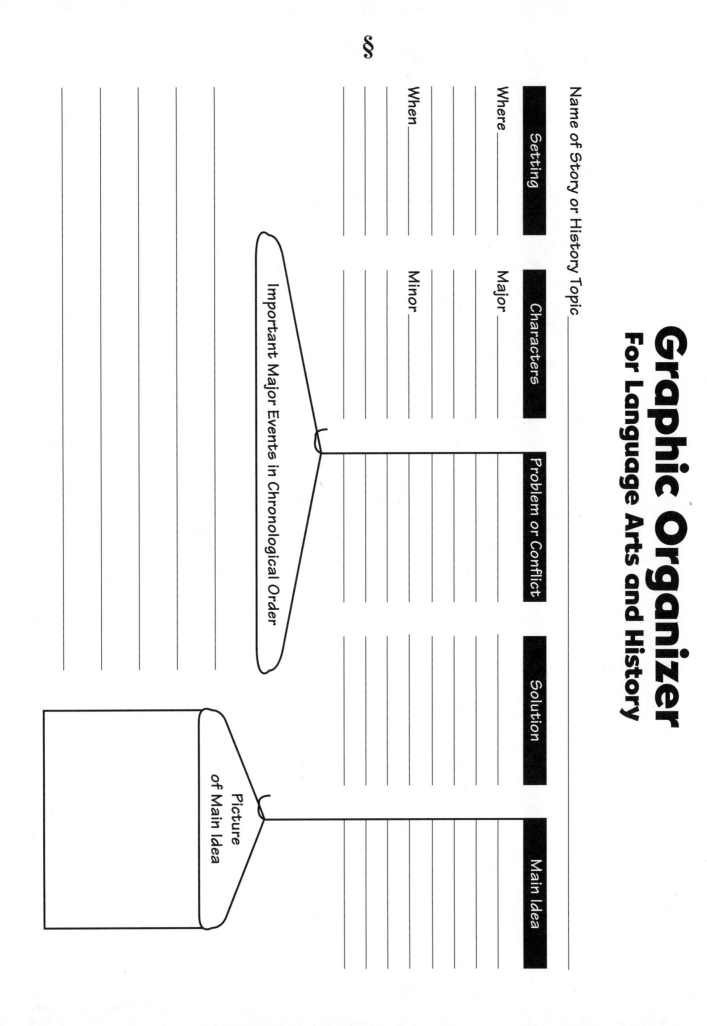

Graphic Organizer
For Language Arts and History

Name of Story or History Topic

Setting

Where

When

Characters

Major

Minor

Problem or Conflict

Solution

Main Idea

Important Major Events in Chronological Order

Picture
of Main Idea

§

§

Umbrella

§

Experiment/Activity Synopsis

Background/Introductory Material: _____

_____

_____

_____

Hypothesis H: _____

_____

_____

_____

Data Construction Chart

§

(P. 2 of Experiment/Activity Synopsis)

Results: _____

_____

_____

_____

Summary of Activity

• what you did
• what you learned
• personal response

_____

_____

_____

_____

_____

_____

INDEX